ECONOMIC DEVELOPMENT AND COOPERATION IN THE PACIFIC BASIN

Trade, Investment, and Environmental Issues

This volume brings together contributions from leading economic analysts around the Pacific Basin, reporting on their research into three of the most important issues facing the region: trade, investment flows, and the environmental effects of economic growth. Each of these issues has important domestic and multilateral ramifications, and the Pacific Basin's status as the world's most dynamic economic region makes this analysis relevant to policymakers and researchers in all countries. The collection offers up-to-date appraisals available from economists representing the principal economies of the region. Among other contributions in the book are new insights into the forces animating regional trade and investment; detailed assessment of leading East Asian economies, such as those of China, Indonesia, Japan, Korea, and Singapore; and innovative research on economy–environment linkages.

Hiro Lee is Associate Professor in the Graduate School of International Development at Nagoya University. He was previously Assistant Professor of Economics at the University of California–Irvine and worked on a global environment project at the OECD. Professor Lee has worked extensively in quantitative analysis of international trade and development, particularly on Pacific Basin economies, and is currently working on policy assessments of APEC trade and investment liberalization and structural adjustment. In 1992 he was awarded an Abe Fellowship to undertake a research project on Cooperative Trade Strategies for the United States and Japan. His studies have been published in a variety of journals, including the *Journal of Development Economics*, the *World Economy*, and the *Journal of Asian Economics*.

David W. Roland-Holst is Associate Professor of Economics at Mills College and Research Associate at the Centre for Economic Policy Research (London). An authority on policy modeling, with extensive research experience in international trade and development, he has held academic positions in the United States, Switzerland, and the Netherlands and worked for a variety of U.S. domestic and international agencies, including the U.S. International Trade Commission, OECD, and the World Bank. In addition to seminal research on methodology, Professor Roland-Holst has done applied research on and in more than twenty developing countries. In addition to providing expert consultation to domestic and international agencies, he has published extensively in the academic literature, including such professional journals as the *Review of Economics and Statistics*, the *Canadian Journal of Economics*, the *Journal of Development Economics*, and the *Review of Income and Wealth*.

ECONOMIC DEVELOPMENT
AND COOPERATION
IN THE PACIFIC BASIN

Trade, Investment, and Environmental Issues

Edited by

HIRO LEE

DAVID W. ROLAND-HOLST

 **CAMBRIDGE**
UNIVERSITY PRESS

H F 4030.7
A 4 6 E 3 7

PUBLISHED BY THE PRESS SYNDICATE OF THE UNIVERSITY OF CAMBRIDGE
The Pitt Building, Trumpington Street, Cambridge CB2 1RP, United Kingdom

CAMBRIDGE UNIVERSITY PRESS
The Edinburgh Building, Cambridge CB2 2RU, UK   http://www.cam.ac.uk
40 West 20th Street, New York, NY 10011–4211, USA   http://www.cup.org
10 Stamford Road, Oakleigh, Melbourne 3166, Australia

First published 1998

Printed in the United States of America

Typeset in Baskerville 11/12.5, in Quark XPress™ [BTS]

*A catalog record for this book is available from
the British Library.*

Library of Congress Cataloging-in-Publication Data
Economic development and cooperation in the Pacific Basin : trade,
investment, and environmental issues / edited by Hiro Lee and David
W. Roland-Holst.
p.   cm.
Revised versions of papers originally presented at an
international conference held at the University of California–
Berkeley on June 30–July 1, 1995.
Includes index.
ISBN 0-521-58366-7 (hardcover)
1. Pacific Area – Commerce – Congresses.   2. Investments – Pacific
Area – Congresses.   3. Pacific Area cooperation – Congresses.
4. Environmental policy – Pacific Area – Congresses.   I. Lee, Hiro.
II. Roland-Holst, David W.
HF4030.7.A46E27   1998
338.99 – dc21   97-40982
                                                          CIP

ISBN 0 521 58366 7 hardback

Contents

v

Acknowledgments

On June 30–July 1, 1995, we held an international conference on "Economic Development and Cooperation in the Pacific Basin" at the University of California, Berkeley. Earlier versions of most of the chapters contained in this volume were first presented at this conference and have been substantially revised since then. We thank the conference participants, three anonymous referees for the volume, and Scott Parris for their helpful comments on earlier drafts. Thanks also to Rosalie Herion Freese of Cambridge University Press for the final copy edit.

We gratefully acknowledge the Japan Foundation's Center for Global Partnership (CGP) for its financial support on our project, making possible the conference and the editors' collaboration. The conference not only disseminated research findings by experts on and from the region but also created an international network of interested researchers and policymakers who will contribute to a more cooperative policy agenda across the Asian Pacific region in this decade and the coming century.

Contributors

Iwan J. Azis
Faculty of Economics
University of Indonesia
Jakarta
Indonesia

John Beghin
Department of Agricultural and
　Resource Economics
North Carolina State University
Raleigh, NC 27695
USA

Jeffrey H. Bergstrand
Department of Finance and
　Business Economics
University of Notre Dame
Notre Dame, IN 46556
USA

Alain de Janvry
Department of Agricultural and
　Resource Economics
University of California
Berkeley, CA 94720
USA

Barry Eichengreen
Department of Economics
University of California
Berkeley, CA 94720
USA

Linda Fernandez
Department of Agricultural and
　Resource Economics
University of California
Berkeley, CA 94720
USA

Albert Fishlow
Council on Foreign Relations
New York, NY 10021
USA

K. C. Fung
Department of Economics
University of California
Santa Cruz, CA 95064
USA

Pearl Imada Iboshi
Department of Business,
　Economic Development and
　Tourism
State of Hawaii
Honolulu, HI 96804
USA

William E. James
International Centre for the Study
　of East Asian Development
Kitakyushu 803-0814
Japan

Masahiro Kawai
Institute of Social Science
University of Tokyo
Tokyo 113-0033
Japan

Chung H. Lee
Director, Center for Korean
    Studies
University of Hawaii at Manoa
Honolulu, HI 96822
USA

Hiro Lee
Graduate School of International
    Development
Nagoya University
Nagoya 464-8601
Japan

Li Shantong
Deputy Director, Department of
    Development and Forecasting
Development Research Center
State Council of the PRC
Beijing 100017
China

Julia Lowell
International Policy Department
RAND Corporation
Santa Monica, CA 90406
USA

Marcus Noland
Institute for International
    Economics
Washington, DC 20036
USA

Arvind Panagariya
Department of Economics
University of Maryland
College Park, MD 20742
USA

Peter A. Petri
Dean, Graduate School of
    International Economics and
    Finance
Brandeis University
Waltham, MA 02254
USA

Michael G. Plummer
Graduate School of International
    Economics and Finance
Brandeis University
Waltham, MA 02254
USA

Mark Poffenberger
Center for Southeast Asian
    Studies
University of California
Berkeley, CA 94720
USA

David W. Roland-Holst
Department of Economics
Mills College
Oakland, CA 94613
USA

Jai-Won Ryou
Department of Economics
Konkuk University
Seoul 133-701
Korea

Tan Kong Yam
Head, Department of Business
   Policy
Faculty of Business
   Administration
National University of Singapore
Singapore

Shujiro Urata
School of Social Sciences
Waseda University
Tokyo 169-8050
Japan

Dominique van der Mensbrugghe
OECD Development Centre
75016 Paris
France

Wang Huijiong
Vice President, Academic
   Committee
Development Research Center
State Council of the PRC
Beijing 100017
China

Shang-Jin Wei
Kennedy School of Government
Harvard University
Cambridge, MA 02138
USA

Brian Woodall
School of International Affairs
Georgia Institute of Technology
Atlanta, Georgia 30332
USA

David Zilberman
Department of Agricultural and
   Resource Economics
University of California
Berkeley, CA 94720
USA

PART I

Introduction and Overview

CHAPTER 1

Prelude to the Pacific Century: Overview of the Region, Leading Issues, and Methodology

Hiro Lee and David Roland-Holst

1. INTRODUCTION

The Pacific Basin is the most robust economic region of the world. More than half the world's population resides in countries bordering on it, and this region's average economic growth rate has been double that of the rest of the world since 1970. The volume of trade on the Pacific is three times that on the Atlantic and has been growing twice as fast. In less than a generation, this region has become the global pacesetter for market-based economic development and a model of efficient international specialization. This volume examines a number of leading issues facing the Pacific Basin and collects the research and opinions of experts from around the region on its economic prospects into the next generation. In particular, some authors examine the received history of trade rivalry and the new initiatives for regional cooperation in trade. Other authors examine Pacific multilateralism from the capital account perspective, detailing a complex web of foreign direct investment linkages that now pervade the region. Finally, two chapters examine an important emergent issue in the region and the world – links between trade, sustainable resource use, and the environment. Taken together, these studies cover issues of the highest priority for policy dialogue and research, in this region and in the context of multilateralism generally, now and for the foreseeable future.

As we enter the Pacific Century, an unprecedented set of promises and challenges lies ahead. Can a new global paradigm of market-based, open multilateralism provide the economic momentum to lift over one-quarter of humankind out of poverty at last? Can such a complex mosaic of trading economies also provide a basis for sustained cooperation, peace, and political stability?

There are no definitive answers to these questions, but recent history and current trends appear to justify an optimistic perspective. At the same time, however, the promise of sustained economic prosperity must be tempered with real concern about how the diverse and partially conflicting aims of so vast an area can be reconciled.

Table 1.1 provides GNP per capita and other economic indicators for fifteen major Asia Pacific Economic Cooperation (APEC) countries.[1] An extremely large variance in GNP per capita among these countries indicates that the APEC members are at very different stages of development. In 1995, China's per capita income of $620 was only about 1.6 percent of Japan's per capita income of $39,640. If GNP is measured at purchasing power parity (PPP) dollars – i.e., using a common set of prices for goods and services – instead of using nominal exchange rates, then the ratio of the lowest to highest per capita income countries in the region would increase to 10.8 percent.

The economic dynamism we see in the region today has arisen from two trends that are inextricably linked – rapid domestic growth and expanding trade.[2] Japan led the postwar expansion, growing at an average rate of 8.2 percent from 1955 to 1980, and was followed by "Four Tigers" – Korea, Taiwan, Hong Kong, and Singapore – which together grew by 8.8 percent from 1965 to 1990. More recently, China and the Association of Southeast Asian Nations (ASEAN) members have experienced unprecedented growth rates. China's real GDP grew by an annual average of 9.5 percent over the period 1980–95. Other high-performing Asian economies (HPAEs) – Malaysia, Thailand, and Indonesia – grew by 7.2 percent per annum from 1970 to 1995.[3] Indeed, it is remarkable to see how, across this immense region, a few decades of market forces have delivered higher living standards than did several generations of traditional development policy.

In all these cases, trade with much larger external markets lever-

---

[1] Three APEC members – Brunei, Papua New Guinea, and Chile – are not included in the table because of their small economic size relative to the other fifteen members.

[2] Growth rates across the region are summarized in Table 1.1.

[3] While the Philippines was an exception in that it experienced an extremely turbulent period with the debt crisis, the subsequent application of a stringent IMF adjustment program, and severe recessions over the period 1982–92, its economy has achieved a steady growth in recent years.

Table 1.1. *Economic Indicators for Major APEC Countries*

	GNP per capita in 1995		Population (millions)	Real GDP Growth Rates			Exports/GDP (%)		Imports/GDP (%)	
	US$	PPP$	mid–1995	1970–80	1980–90	1990–95	1970	1995	1970	1995
Japan	39,640	22,110	125.2	5.0	4.1	1.2	9.5	12.3	9.3	11.1
China	620	2,920	1200.2	5.7	8.6	11.2	2.9	21.5	3.0	19.1
Korea	9,700	11,450	44.9	9.5	9.7	7.8	9.5	27.5	22.6	29.7
Taiwan	12,490	⋯	21.2	10.2	8.0	6.3	26.2	42.2	26.9	39.1
Hong Kong	22,990	22,950	6.2	9.3	7.1	5.3	66.5	120.9	76.5	134.2
Singapore	26,730	22,770	3.0	8.5	6.4	8.5	82.0	141.2	129.8	148.6
Malaysia	3,890	9,020	20.1	7.8	5.2	8.9	42.5	83.1	35.3	84.0
Thailand	2,740	7,540	58.2	7.2	7.6	8.9	10.0	31.6	18.4	38.0
Indonesia	980	3,800	193.3	7.6	5.5	7.1	12.0	22.9	10.9	18.3
Philippines	1,050	2,850	68.6	6.3	0.9	2.3	14.6	23.4	17.2	35.7
United States	26,980	26,980	263.1	3.0	3.4	2.5	5.7	8.1	5.5	10.3
Canada	19,380	21,130	29.6	3.9	3.4	1.6	23.3	32.5	20.6	28.9
Mexico	3,320	6,400	91.8	5.2	1.0	0.8	7.7	23.9	9.7	21.6
Australia	18,720	18,940	18.1	3.0	3.4	2.6	12.5	14.8	11.8	16.4
New Zealand	14,340	16,360	3.6	2.3	1.9	3.2	19.7	25.1	20.2	25.5

Sources:
World Bank, *World Development Report*, 1982, 1992, 1997.
International Monetary Fund, *International Financial Statistics*, various issues.
OECD, *Main Economic Indicators*, June 1996.
United Nations, *National Accounts Statistics*, various issues.
Republic of China, Executive Yuan, *Statistical Yearbook of the Republic of China*, various issues.

aged the expansion of domestic GDP. The exports to GDP ratios increased sharply in most East Asian countries between 1970 and 1995 (Table 1.1), indicating sharply rising participation in the global economy. The increases were particularly dramatic in China (2.9 percent in 1970 to 21.5 percent in 1995), Korea (9.5 to 27.5 percent), Hong Kong (66.5 to 120.9 percent), Malaysia (42.5 to 83.1 percent), and Thailand (10.0 to 31.6 percent).

The success of these trading economies had no precedent since the times of Western colonialism. Unlike their predecessors, however, the early Asian exporters (Japan and Four Tigers) did not rely on political power to project their economic interests abroad. Instead, they used a combination of disciplined domestic industrial policies and aggressive international competition to penetrate established Western markets. Although there were significant reciprocal trade flows from these trading partners, the approach was essentially neo-mercantilist. National industry groups sought ever-increasing exports to stimulate domestic capacity, meeting foreign competitors on their own terrain and opening market share against domestic import substitutes. At the same time, domestic growth in these countries was financed by a combination of retained profits from domestic and foreign operations. Sustained trade surpluses made an essential contribution, accelerating the growth of domestic savings and investment in these export-dependent countries. Among the results of this approach were rapid capital accumulation, meteorically rising incomes, and often problematic bilateral trade relationships. Because of its bias toward national industry, internal finance, and asymmetric trade, the traditional model of export orientation has led to chronic dissonance of trade policies and impeded the progress of multilateralism. Voluntary export restraints (VERs) on Japanese autos, the Multifibre agreement (MFA), and a long litany of actual and threatened retaliatory trade measures are all evidence of this.

In addition to export-led industrialization, there are other note-worthy similarities between earlier and more recent Asian Pacific growth. As was the case for the more mature economies, income growth in the new Asian exporters is relatively egalitarian. We identify this with an enterprise and investor emphasis on human resource development that fosters steadily rising labor productivity, real wages, and labor market flexibility. These attributes, in turn, lead ultimately to greater economic diversification and more balanced and sustainable growth. Such an approach can be contrasted with some Latin American economies, for example, whose colonial experience with resource boom export activities has fostered an apparent bias against investment in human capital.

Despite their similarities, however, early and modern Asian Pacific exporters differ in very important ways. First, the latter countries are exporting not only to Europe and North America but to the world's most rapidly growing regional market, the Asian Pacific itself. Since 1980, intraregional trade has expanded twice as fast as trade with the rest of the world.[4] At the same time, developing Asian countries are rapidly diversifying beyond the traditional primary products that were the mainstay of regional exports to the North. More than just an alternative to Northern markets, Asian Pacific regional trade is qualitatively different. Export opportunities have been created largely through new domestic growth in importing countries rather than by market penetration. This increases the net gains from trade for both parties, supercedes important obstacles to market openness, and facilitates cooperation.

A second important difference in the outward orientation of today's Asian Pacific growth economies is microeconomic in nature – a pervasive trend toward joint ventures that might be termed "private multilateralism." Long before the Uruguay Round was successfully negotiated or the terms APEC, AFTA, and even NAFTA were coined, private business interests have been forging alliances for trade and domestic market development that transcend national boundaries.[5] Nowhere has this trend been more rapid and diversified than in the Asian Pacific, where nearly every permutation of nationalities has joined together to work across markets and jurisdictions, pooling expertise, market access, and capital to take fuller advantage of economies of scale and informational and other externalities. The result contrasts sharply with the narrower national economic interests of the older export economies and represents a spontaneous and more intrinsic form of the liberal trading spirit so laboriously enunciated in regional and global trade agreements.

---

[4] During 1980–95, intra-APEC trade grew 10.7 percent per annum while APEC countries' trade with the rest of the world grew 5.5 percent per annum.

[5] For reference, the acronyms refer to the ASEAN Free Trade Area (AFTA) and the North American Free Trade Area (NAFTA).

Evidence of the advantages of private multilateralism can also be found in the capital accounts. Instead of relying on investment resources to accrue from perennial trade surpluses, newly emergent economies in the region are benefiting from vast infusions of foreign direct investment. Sometimes referred to as "Tiger's Milk," much of this growth of capital originates within the region itself and from joint ventures that represent complex marketing alliances. This more elaborate process of capitalization is an essential attribute of the new model of export-led, investment-driven growth, including significant new advantages like technology transfer and a more collaborative basis of market linkages. The historic, one-country approach to rapid Asian growth, typified by Japan and the Four Tigers, has given way to extensive private networks of investment syndication arising with joint commercial and financial ventures. Taken together, the collective forces of this "Invisible Handshake" give rise to myriad commercial linkages for market participants and pervasive growth externalities for their domestic economies.

Thus it is reasonable to argue that there exists in the Asian Pacific a new paradigm for the outward-oriented economy. Such an economy draws a significant growth impetus from the global economy, but not by developing a national commercial export platform from which to penetrate foreign markets, maximize net exports, and relentlessly accumulate savings at home and from abroad. The modern outward-oriented economy opens itself to fuller participation in a complex web of self-interested but mutually advantageous trade and investment linkages. Many of these take the form of explicit joint ventures, but most arise as spontaneous market interactions. The private sector across the Pacific Basin has already developed this multilateralism to a relatively high degree (by comparison to other regions), and a number of regional initiatives (e.g., APEC) are being crafted to formalize the institutional context for this. If the promise of these agreements is fulfilled, we may see a new and more collaborative basis for prosperity that could significantly improve long-term prospects for stability and security in this region and throughout the world.

2. OVERVIEW OF REGIONAL TRADE PATTERNS

Trade is the animating force behind domestic economic growth and multilateral relations across the Pacific region, and the chapters in this volume examine many specific aspects of this phenomenon. To introduce this work, however, we begin with a broad overview of historical trade patterns. These trends clearly reveal a transition from more focused, bilateral trade ties, from traditional, neo-mercantilist and even neo-colonial trade to a new, more diversified regime. Today's Pacific Basin is a complex universe of multilateralism, arising not from negotiating tables but from the myriad initiatives of market forces. Indeed, it is striking how rapidly regional trade has advanced ahead of regional conventions such as APEC. Although stubborn details about trade barriers and distortions still need to be resolved, the spontaneous potential of this market is remarkable.[6]

The four panels of Table 1.2 lay out detailed patterns of bilateral and multilateral trade for the region over the last fifteen years. These will provide a useful reference for reading other parts of the book, but it is also worth digressing here to examine the evolution of trade relations from the Pacific perspective. Panel A of Table 1.2 details trade shares for leading East Asian economies for the years 1980, 1990, and 1995.[7] The trade destinations included in this table are the same East Asian economies and, in the first trading partner column, an aggregate of these. The most notable feature of these results is the steady growth of the "internal" East Asian market. Many of these countries now trade more than half their goods within the region, and this share has increased substantially in the last fifteen years for all but one.[8] Apart from this, only China saw its East Asian trade share decline from 1990 to 1995, because of booming trade with the United States, but still targeted over half its trade to neighboring Pacific countries.

Most countries actually reduced or held steady their share of trade with Japan, still the dominant regional importer. The most rapid growth in trade opportunities came instead from the Four Tigers and other emerging regional partners. Such diversification

---

[6] Indeed, the relative caution of Asian parties to APEC may be a partial concession to market forces as the leading agent of regional growth and change. Markets are, after all, designed to take risks, and politicians are notoriously reluctant to do so.

[7] In all the entries of these tables, trade is defined as the sum of exports and imports with respect to the two trading partners under consideration.

[8] Only Indonesia's regional share has fallen, but this country's trade statistics are misleading for two reasons, both related to its primary export good. Oil prices have dropped significantly during the period considered, and their revenues are denominated in a currency (the U.S. dollar) that has depreciated significantly against the dominant East Asian currency (the Japanese yen).

within the region represents both vertical and horizontal market expansions. In the first case, the emerging traders are fitting into the lower tiers of more complex trade hierarchies, including economies at the early, intermediate, and advanced stages of industrialization. This tendency has been particularly evident in association with the avalanche of FDI (foreign direct investment) into China and Southeast Asia. Over the past ten years, Japan, Korea, and Taiwan have sharply increased their commitments in these markets, building links to subsidiaries or partners in the host countries who then export intermediate goods to the investor's home country or its subsidiaries elsewhere. In the latter case, horizontal expansion, they are participating in widening regional distribution systems. This growth is usually mediated by complex commercial alliances in which the new partners enjoy more equal status and many growth externalities.

This trend can be contrasted with older, bilateral spoke links to hubs in Japan and the industrialized West. Most of these situations entailed projection of domestic marketing and production operations abroad, and the growth externalities for destination countries were more limited.

Apart from general trends, there are several specific aspects of internal East Asian trade worth highlighting. Despite its decline as a regional trade partner, Japan has steadily expanded its own sales in the region, increasing trade share in all East Asian economies except in Indonesia.[9] For most of the countries considered, Japan's trade share rose more than one-third in five years from 1990 to 1995.

As one might expect, the implications of historical trade patterns between China, Hong Kong, and Taiwan are complex. Chinese trade dependence on Hong Kong dropped precipitously from 1990 to 1995, largely as a result of developing its direct trade capacity in the southeast and elsewhere. China still has the largest trade share to Hong Kong (15.9 percent) but is closely followed by Taiwan, with whom it has negligible bilateral shares.[10] One might

[9] While the decline in the oil price reduced Japan's imports from Indonesia during 1980–95, its exports to Indonesia also declined as a result of the sharp appreciation of the yen during the period.

[10] There is an inconsistency in reporting trade data by China and Taiwan. A large fraction of Taiwan's trade with China is still reported as trade with Hong Kong, which jumped from 8.2 percent of Taiwan's trade in 1990 to 13.0 percent in 1995 (Table 1.2, panel A).

expect the events of 1997 to exert some adjustment pressure on these trade flows. For its part, Hong Kong has the biggest relative commitment to intra–East Asian trade, but 34.8 percent of its 63 percent regional trade share is directed to China. Thus the accord of 1997 will internalize over half of Hong Kong's East Asian trade.

Panel B of Table 1.2 summarizes the composition of total trade flows from the same East Asian countries. In addition to East Asia itself, trade with other destinations in the Pacific Basin and elsewhere are given. Among the most arresting features of this table is the predominance of APEC trade. For all the East Asian economies represented here, APEC accounts for two-thirds to three-quarters of their total trade by 1995. Of particular interest is how Japan has diversified toward APEC since 1980, moving from 51.6 to 70.4 percent of total trade. These figures make plain the stakes for APEC members.

Among individual countries, the United States is the largest non–East Asian destination. Whereas this is hardly surprising given the size of its economy, it still exceeds large regional groupings such as Europe, Latin America, and the rest of the world aggregate. In most cases, the United States represents one-quarter to one-half of APEC trade for each East Asian country (1995). Although one might reasonably expect these shares to diminish over time (as indeed they have done in many cases), they help explain the special status accorded to this country in trade negotiations.

East Asian trade links to the rest of NAFTA are still negligible and have fallen somewhat since that agreement was signed, but this may have more to do with the decline of the Mexican economy than with trade diversion. Despite the initiative of some countries (Japan, China, Korea, and Taiwan), Latin America remains a marginal trade partner for East Asia. Most interesting perhaps is Europe, whose relative importance to East Asian trade has declined monotonically and nearly uniformly (except in Indonesia) over the last fifteen years. The same diversion of market share is occurring with respect to the residual, rest-of-the-world (ROW) region, including South Asia, Africa, and the former Soviet Union. Together, these areas have steadily declined in relative importance as markets for East Asian goods.

Panels C and D of Table 1.2 tell a story analogous to that of

Table 1.2. *Gross Trade Shares of Major APEC Countries (Percentages)*

Panel A. East Asian countries' bilateral trade

Country	Year	East Asia	JPN	CHN	KOR	TWN	HKG	SGP	MYS	THA	IDN	PHL
Japan	1980	24.0	...	3.4	3.0	3.6	1.9	1.9	2.0	1.1	5.9	1.3
(JPN)	1990	28.2	...	3.5	5.6	4.6	2.9	2.7	2.1	2.5	3.4	0.9
	1995	38.8	...	7.4	6.2	5.6	3.9	3.8	3.5	3.8	3.1	1.4
China	1980	42.5	24.4	...	0.1	0.0	13.1	1.6	1.1	1.2	0.1	0.9
(CHN)	1990	58.5	14.4	...	0.6	2.2	35.7	2.3	1.0	0.9	1.1	0.3
	1995	54.5	20.5	...	6.0	6.4	15.9	2.0	1.2	0.8	1.2	0.5
Korea	1980	33.0	22.6	0.1	...	1.6	2.3	1.1	1.6	0.6	2.1	1.1
(KOR)	1990	36.2	23.1	0.5	...	2.0	3.3	2.0	1.7	1.1	2.0	0.6
	1995	42.3	19.1	6.4	...	2.5	4.4	3.4	2.1	1.3	2.4	0.8
Taiwan	1980	32.3	19.0	0.0	1.2	...	4.6	1.9	1.5	0.7	2.6	0.8
(TWN)	1990	39.3	19.9	0.3	2.1	...	8.2	3.0	1.7	1.5	1.8	0.9
	1995	49.2	20.2	1.6	3.2	...	13.0	3.4	2.7	2.1	1.9	1.1
Hong Kong	1980	44.1	13.6	12.7	2.3	5.4	...	5.3	0.9	1.2	1.7	1.2
(HKG)	1990	59.1	10.9	30.8	3.4	6.6	...	3.6	1.0	1.3	0.8	0.7
	1995	63.0	10.7	34.8	3.4	5.8	...	4.1	1.4	1.2	0.7	0.8
Singapore	1980	48.9	13.2	2.1	1.3	2.3	4.5	...	14.0	3.0	7.7	0.8
(SGP)	1990	48.7	14.4	2.5	2.5	3.8	4.5	...	12.9	4.4	2.7	0.8
	1995	55.9	14.3	2.7	3.5	4.0	5.7	...	16.9	5.3	2.1	1.2
Malaysia	1980	49.7	22.1	1.9	1.9	3.2	1.6	15.2	...	2.1	0.5	1.3
(MYS)	1990	55.6	19.7	2.0	3.6	3.9	2.5	18.9	...	3.0	1.1	0.9
	1995	55.6	20.2	2.4	3.5	4.1	3.7	16.2	...	3.3	1.4	0.7
Thailand	1980	40.0	18.3	3.4	1.5	2.2	2.6	6.9	2.9	...	1.8	0.6
(THA)	1990	47.7	25.0	2.4	2.5	3.7	2.6	7.4	3.0	...	0.6	0.5
	1995	50.5	23.8	2.9	2.5	3.7	2.8	9.2	3.7	...	1.1	0.8
Indonesia	1980	60.7	41.7	0.6	1.5	4.0	0.9	10.0	0.3	0.9	...	0.8
(IDN)	1990	58.0	34.3	3.1	4.9	4.6	1.9	6.7	1.1	0.8	...	0.5
	1995	56.3	27.3	3.9	7.2	4.6	3.0	5.4	2.5	1.7	...	0.7
Philippines	1980	37.9	22.0	1.8	2.4	2.9	2.7	1.7	1.8	0.6	2.1	...
(PHL)	1990	40.9	19.0	1.2	3.4	4.9	4.3	3.5	2.0	1.4	1.2	...
	1995	46.8	20.0	2.1	4.1	4.7	5.0	4.4	2.2	2.6	1.6	...

Sources:
International Monetary Fund, *Direction of Trade Statistics*, various issues.
Monthly Statistics of Exports and Imports, Taiwan Area, Republic of China, various issues.

Table 1.2 *(continued)*

Panel B. East Asia's trade with NAFTA, Australasia, and non-APEC countries

Country	Year	East Asia	USA	CAN	MEX	AUS	NZ	APEC	Latin Amer	EUR[a]	ROW
Japan	1980	24.0	20.0	2.6	0.8	3.7	0.5	51.6	4.4	11.3	32.7
	1990	28.2	27.5	2.9	0.8	3.7	0.6	63.8	2.8	20.1	13.3
	1995	38.8	25.4	2.1	0.6	2.9	0.5	70.4	3.2	16.4	9.9
China	1980	42.5	12.8	2.5	0.3	3.4	0.5	62.0	3.0	16.1	19.0
	1990	58.5	10.2	1.6	0.2	1.6	0.2	72.2	1.5	13.9	12.4
	1995	54.5	14.6	1.3	0.1	1.5	0.2	72.2	1.9	15.0	10.9
Korea	1980	33.0	23.5	1.8	0.3	2.2	0.3	61.1	1.9	11.5	25.5
	1990	36.2	27.0	2.4	0.6	2.6	0.4	69.2	2.2	15.0	13.6
	1995	42.3	20.9	1.7	0.5	2.5	0.4	68.3	3.0	13.8	14.9
Taiwan	1980	32.3	28.9	1.8	0.3	2.7	0.2	66.1	2.4	12.6	18.9
	1990	39.3	28.1	2.0	0.4	2.4	0.3	72.5	1.8	17.3	8.4
	1995	49.2	21.9	1.4	0.3	2.0	0.3	75.1	2.1	14.6	8.2
Hong Kong	1980	44.1	17.5	1.2	0.1	1.8	0.3	65.2	1.5	19.7	13.7
	1990	59.1	16.1	1.1	0.2	1.2	0.2	77.9	1.1	16.0	5.0
	1995	63.0	14.4	1.1	0.2	1.1	0.2	79.9	1.5	13.8	4.8
Singapore	1980	48.9	13.1	0.6	0.1	3.0	1.0	66.6	1.5	13.4	18.5
	1990	48.7	18.0	0.7	0.1	2.1	0.3	70.0	1.1	15.1	13.8
	1995	55.9	16.3	0.4	0.1	1.8	0.2	74.8	1.0	14.0	10.2
Malaysia	1980	49.7	15.3	0.7	0.0	3.2	0.7	69.6	0.5	17.5	12.3
	1990	55.6	16.9	0.9	0.1	2.6	0.5	76.6	1.1	16.5	5.8
	1995	55.6	18.5	0.7	0.2	2.1	0.3	77.5	1.1	15.8	5.6
Thailand	1980	40.0	13.4	1.0	0.1	1.5	0.3	56.3	0.7	21.1	22.0
	1990	47.7	15.7	1.2	0.3	1.7	0.3	66.7	1.4	20.7	11.1
	1995	50.5	14.2	0.8	0.2	1.6	0.2	67.5	1.1	16.5	14.9
Indonesia	1980	60.7	16.7	0.4	0.1	2.1	0.5	80.5	3.0	9.1	7.5
	1990	58.0	12.3	1.1	0.2	3.4	0.4	75.5	1.1	16.6	6.9
	1995	56.3	12.5	1.0	0.2	3.3	0.4	73.9	1.4	18.6	6.1
Philippines	1980	37.9	24.5	1.0	0.2	2.4	0.6	66.6	1.5	14.3	17.6
	1990	40.9	26.6	1.5	0.1	2.4	0.5	72.0	1.9	14.9	11.3
	1995	46.8	25.0	1.1	0.2	2.1	0.4	75.5	1.2	13.8	9.5

[a] Europe includes Austria, Belgium, Denmark, Finland, France, Germany, Greece, Iceland, Ireland, Italy, Luxembourg, Netherlands, Norway, Portugal, Spain, Sweden, United Kingdom.

Table 1.2 *(continued)*

Panel C. APEC countries' trade with East Asian countries

Country	Year	East Asia	JPN	CHN	KOR	TWN	HKG	SGP	MYS	THA	IDN	PHL
							Trading Partner					
10 East Asian	1980	33.9	11.0	3.0	2.1	2.9	2.9	3.1	2.5	1.2	4.1	1.1
Countries	1990	41.3	11.3	5.7	3.5	3.8	6.0	3.6	2.6	2.0	2.2	0.7
	1995	49.2	12.5	8.7	4.3	4.5	5.6	4.3	3.8	2.5	2.0	1.0
United States	1980	22.9	10.9	1.0	1.8	3.1	1.6	1.0	0.8	0.4	1.4	0.8
(USA)	1990	32.3	15.6	2.3	3.7	3.7	1.8	2.0	1.0	0.9	0.6	0.7
	1995	35.2	14.1	4.5	3.7	3.4	1.8	2.5	2.0	1.3	0.8	0.9
Canada	1980	7.9	4.7	0.7	0.5	0.7	0.5	0.2	0.1	0.1	0.1	0.1
(CAN)	1990	11.6	6.2	1.0	1.4	1.1	0.7	0.3	0.2	0.3	0.2	0.1
	1995	11.0	4.9	1.6	1.3	1.0	0.6	0.4	0.5	0.3	0.3	0.2
Mexico	1980	5.7	4.7	0.5	0.1	0.0	0.1	0.1	0.0	0.0	0.1	0.0
(MEX)	1990	6.8	4.9	0.5	0.5	0.2	0.5	0.1	0.0	0.1	0.0	0.0
	1995	5.9	3.0	0.4	0.7	0.5	0.4	0.3	0.3	0.1	0.1	0.0
Australia	1980	37.9	22.0	2.5	1.6	2.5	1.8	2.7	1.7	0.5	1.9	0.7
(AUS)	1990	43.8	22.5	2.6	4.1	3.7	2.1	3.6	1.6	1.1	1.9	0.6
	1995	48.4	19.1	4.7	5.7	4.1	2.6	4.2	2.6	1.9	2.6	0.8
New Zealand	1980	25.1	13.5	1.9	0.8	NA	1.3	3.9	1.1	0.4	1.6	0.7
(NZ)	1990	27.9	15.6	1.1	2.9	2.1	1.3	1.3	1.3	0.7	0.9	0.5
	1995	32.9	15.0	3.0	3.4	2.8	2.1	1.7	1.9	1.0	1.3	0.6
15 APEC	1980	26.4	10.6	1.9	1.8	NA	2.0	1.9	1.5	0.7	2.5	0.8
Countries	1990	34.8	12.5	3.9	3.3	3.4	3.8	2.6	1.8	1.4	1.4	0.6
	1995	40.5	12.2	6.5	3.8	3.8	3.8	3.3	2.8	1.9	1.4	0.9

Panels A and B, but this time from the perspective of all the fifteen APEC economies considered here. The East Asian ten are aggregated in the first row for comparison; the remaining rows detail trade shares for the NAFTA countries, Australia, New Zealand (referred to subregionally as ANZ), and a representative APEC-15 aggregate.

Note first that the NAFTA and ANZ countries generally had significant and steadily increasing trade shares to East Asia. Although Mexico apparently has not committed itself beyond 6 percent of total trade, the rest of these countries now maintain over 10 percent, and in some cases almost half, of their trade with East Asia. Japan appears to be the primary partner. The real growth in

Table 1.2 *(continued)*

Panel D. APEC countries' trade with NAFTA, Australasia, and non-APEC countries

Country	Year	East Asia	USA	CAN	MEX	AUS	NZ	APEC	Latin Amer	EUR^a	ROW
10 East Asian	1980	33.9	19.2	1.9	0.5	3.1	0.5	59.1	3.1	13.0	24.8
Countries	1990	41.3	22.3	2.0	0.5	2.7	0.4	69.3	2.0	17.6	11.2
	1995	49.2	19.6	1.4	0.4	2.2	0.4	73.1	2.2	15.2	9.6
United States	1980	22.9	...	15.7	5.7	1.4	0.3	46.0	13.7	23.3	17.1
	1990	32.3	...	19.4	6.5	1.5	0.3	60.0	6.8	24.3	8.9
	1995	35.2	...	20.3	8.0	1.1	0.2	64.7	7.0	20.7	7.6
Canada	1980	7.9	63.4	...	0.6	0.8	0.2	72.9	2.8	11.9	12.5
	1990	11.6	69.3	...	0.9	0.6	0.1	82.5	1.7	11.6	4.2
	1995	11.0	74.1	...	1.4	0.5	0.1	87.1	1.7	8.8	2.5
Mexico	1980	5.7	63.0	1.3	...	0.1	0.1	70.3	5.4	16.4	7.9
	1990	6.8	67.6	1.1	...	0.1	0.3	76.0	5.6	16.6	1.8
	1995	5.9	79.2	2.2	...	0.1	0.1	87.4	4.4	7.3	0.9
Australia	1980	37.9	16.5	2.4	0.1	...	4.1	61.1	1.1	20.4	18.7
	1990	43.8	17.6	1.9	0.2	...	4.7	68.2	1.0	21.4	9.4
	1995	48.4	14.4	1.8	0.2	...	5.9	70.7	1.0	19.6	8.7
New Zealand	1980	25.1	13.7	2.3	0.3	15.8	...	57.3	1.2	23.3	18.1
	1990	27.9	15.5	1.8	0.7	19.3	...	65.2	1.4	20.7	12.7
	1995	32.9	14.3	1.7	0.3	21.0	...	70.2	1.7	18.6	9.5
15 APEC	1980	26.4	17.3	7.0	2.4	2.1	0.5	55.8	7.1	17.2	19.8
Countries	1990	34.8	19.8	7.7	2.5	2.1	0.5	67.4	3.7	19.4	9.5
	1995	40.5	19.8	6.9	2.7	1.7	0.4	72.1	3.6	16.2	8.1

^{a} Europe includes Austria, Belgium, Denmark, Finland, France, Germany, Greece, Iceland, Ireland, Italy, Luxembourg, Netherlands, Norway, Portugal, Spain, Sweden, United Kingdom.

trade has been to other East Asian countries, particularly China, with respect to which most trade shares have at least doubled.

Such imbalances also reveal an important difference between the East Asian (EA) and the NAFTA members of APEC. Trade by the latter group is more diversified outside the Pacific, and this has advantages and disadvantages for all members. The NAFTA countries are less regionally dependent on EA markets and thus can expect to see slower trade growth than their EA partners as long as this region is the most rapidly growing in the world. EA countries have the good fortune to be concentrated in trade growth markets but have relatively less bargaining power in a global trading context.

Panel D of Table 1.2 summarizes the trade links among the EA-10, NAFTA countries, and ANZ, as well as for the APEC-15 as a whole. The first group has already been discussed in the context of Panel B, but comparison with the others indicates the real trade diversification that the non-EA members bring to APEC. This diversification mainly takes the form of increased European, Latin American, and intra-NAFTA market access. Given the scale of these three, if not their growth rates, this is a very attractive component of the APEC regional accord from the East Asian (and ANZ) perspective. Canada and Mexico's trade dependence on the United States limits the diversity they contribute to APEC, but it is worth noting that the U.S. trade share to EA is larger than its combined NAFTA share. This fact, combined with the relative growth rates of the two regions, helps explain the impetus coming from Washington for this agreement. Indeed, the APEC-15 accounted for 64.7 percent of U.S. trade in 1995, and almost 90 percent for its other NAFTA partners.

The receding markets during this period are Europe and ROW, which have lost significant trade share from EA-10, AFTA, and APEC-15 since 1990. In 1995, Europe absorbed only 16.2 percent of APEC-15 trade, and the residual ROW only 8.1 percent. Although the relative merits of regionalism and globalization are still being intensively discussed, the APEC regional initiative certainly covers the vast majority of the member countries' current trade. For this reason, APEC's success is essential to realizing the trade potential of the regional economies, and it will be a forceful precedent for global liberalization.

3. TRADE POLICY ISSUES

The dynamism of the Pacific regional economy is apparent not only in the volume of trade but in the rapid evolution of trade relations. Beginning from a postcolonial setting, the early Asian growth economies built prosperity on neo-mercantilist strategies of intensive export promotion, protected internal markets, and accelerating capital accumulation. This approach was feasible as long as these countries were relatively few in number, and their market shares in other countries remained small, but it is incompatible with the broadly based multilateral trade and growth that we see in the region today. Pacific trade has expanded in recent years largely because of qualitative changes in policy that take account of commonality of interests. Increased recognition of the importance of reciprocity, joint venture activity, and even explicit regional agreements have all contributed to an expanding universe of economic opportunity for the regional economies. The chapters in Part II of this book evaluate some of the leading issues in this area, with particular emphasis on the challenges facing policymakers.

In Chapter 2, Hiro Lee and David Roland-Holst examine the state of the trade relationship between the two largest economies in the region, the United States and Japan. In the half-century since its modern inception, trade between these two industrial powers has matured, but now it faces one of its greatest challenges, shifting comparative advantage. Indeed, recent friction in this relationship is perhaps an inevitable result of its failure to adapt to changing circumstances. Improved U.S. export competitiveness in agriculture and services has coincided with Japanese intensification of industrial exports, yet trade policies in the two countries have not fully accommodated this reality. Lee and Roland-Holst use a two-country calibrated general equilibrium (CGE) model to estimate the opportunity cost of this policy dissonance in terms of forgone economic opportunity, efficiency, and incomes. In addition to detailing the complex adjustments that would ensue, the authors conclude that both countries would gain substantially if they removed the significant residual protection against each other's imports. Furthermore, they show that free movements of direct investment flows provide greater welfare for the two countries than fully liberalized bilateral trade without such investment flows.

A broader lesson may be drawn from this work, one that resonates with the later contributions. Traditional neo-mercantilist policies are an artifact of a fading era, when trading partners were at vastly different levels of development. They are incompatible with an economic future that promises increasing parity between industrialized, diversified economies. The adjustment costs of outgrowing these bad habits may be nonnegligible, but the economic potential thereby liberated is far greater.

In Chapter 3, Marcus Noland takes a closer look at the special characteristics of Asian exporting economies. In doing so, he reveals much about the transition alluded to previously. In a thorough review of export-based growth experience in East Asia, Noland compares output and trade composition in the high-performing Asian economies with countries in Europe, Latin America, and elsewhere. His empirical results suggest that while the Asian countries as a whole may exhibit greater export orientation, this is matched on the import side and should instead be interpreted as greater *trade* orientation. In addition, given the diversity of the Asian economies, it is difficult to characterize an "Asian export model" as such. Concerning the sectoral composition of exports, Asian economies have specialized more rapidly in some manufacturing industries than would be predicted by factor endowment changes. Interestingly, Noland does detect high degrees of specialization, apparently more associated with targeted industrial policies than with relative factor endowments, yet there is little evidence that these specializations are innately Asian or even likely to be persistent sources of comparative advantage.

The three chapters in Section III deal with the dominant trade policy issue in the Pacific, regionalism. Just as Europe did when its economies modernized and diversified after World War II, today's East Asian economies are looking to increased economic interdependence as a source of new growth and mutual advantage. Unlike Europe in the 1950s and 1960s, however, Asian regional consciousness is embedded in an era of globalization, where both official and market institutions are promoting open multilateralism on a worldwide scale. Thus the choice for Asia is less obvious, and regionalism, even as a piecemeal approach to globalization, is a more uncertain prospect.

Arvind Panagariya presents a detailed analysis of this complex issue in Chapter 4, weighing the apparent merits of incremental cooperation against the more subtle pitfalls of global market segmentation. After thoroughly scrutinizing the options open to East Asian economies, Panagariya expresses deep skepticism about the wisdom of systems of trade preferences within or across the region. He argues that there is little rationale for such an approach on theoretical grounds, and it seems quite unrealistic on practical grounds. Instead, he argues, these economies would be better off upholding more universal principles of economic openness, using the APEC forum, if necessary, to leverage a faster transition to World Trade Organization (WTO)–sponsored global liberalization.

In Chapter 5, Hiro Lee and Brian Woodall use empirical methods to evaluate regional trade policy in the context of domestic political agendas. Because trade policy is often formulated from the bottom up, it is reasonable to expect that a more modern view of national interest, such as that based on trade reciprocity, might encounter conflicts with established domestic interests. Lee and Woodall compare the prospects of Pacific regionalism from two perspectives, a heuristic indicator analysis designed to measure domestic political feasibility and a multicountry CGE model. Their findings indicate that one can expect significant contention between vested domestic economic interests and those who rightly anticipate significant economic gains from more liberal trade. This conclusion may help explain the unusual degree of policy independence that APEC members have negotiated into their agreements.

A special challenge facing East Asia is reconciling new regional and global trade initiatives with older multilateral agreements. ASEAN is one such arrangement, forged in a different time and with somewhat different objectives including security, but it has evolved in response to new economic forces. In Chapter 6, Tan Kong Yam clearly enunciates an East Asian perspective on both APEC and globalization. Among other things, he emphasizes the pivotal but somewhat ambiguous role of the United States in most of the world's major regional initiatives, arguing that East Asia generally and Southeast Asia in particular should hedge itself to avoid being played off against the EU or NAFTA. Tan also observes that complexities in U.S.–Japan and U.S.–China bilateral relations should not obscure Southeast Asia's fundamental interest in more open trade with both sides. In concluding, Tan sustains Panagariya's case that APEC should be implemented only as a complement to, rather than a substitute for, more open global trade. He further amplifies by arguing that ASEAN should leverage its position in APEC to push the latter organization closer to WTO standards. This argument is based on the belief that the WTO holds the promise "to sustain economic dynamism in the Pacific Basin."

4. FOREIGN DIRECT INVESTMENT
AND PRIVATE MULTILATERALISM

In concert with, and sometimes well ahead of, official efforts at multilateralism, market forces and private enterprise have moved rapidly to expand the collaborative basis for trade across the Pacific region. This market-directed interaction has few direct counterparts in national trade policy, yet strongly influences and is influenced by the latter. Although it is not a sufficient condition for policy coherence between trading partners, it is certainly necessary for such policies to succeed. The process arises from the myriad small and large business initiatives referred to earlier as the "Invisible Handshake." Although it is difficult to observe the countless communications, meetings, and contracts that make up this web of market interdependence, we can observe it indirectly in the flows of foreign direct investment (FDI) that facilitate it. The chapters in Part IV all examine FDI in the Pacific region, and from these comes a better understanding of one of the most dynamic determinants of regional trade and economic growth, private multilateralism.

In Chapter 7, Peter Petri and Michael Plummer give an extensive survey of FDI. After a brief theoretical overview of the determinants of FDI, the key empirical characteristics of FDI flows, and related research, the authors provide their own empirical results in the Pacific context. Among other things, their findings emphasize the importance of FDI as a mediator of intraindustry and intrafirm trade. By extensifying and intensifying commercial linkages, FDI has accelerated the growth of regional trade and strengthened the basis for multilateralism.

Given its senior status among modern Asian export economies, Japan has undergone more extensive adaptation to the changing regional economy. For example, it was the first traditional Asian exporter to diversify itself from commodities to capital services, shifting production capacity abroad and becoming a private-sector partner in regional development. Initiating these financial links to neighboring economies has had complex implications for the private sectors in both Japan and its partner countries, and this experience has amplified the debate over whether trade and investment are substitutes or complements. In Chapter 8, Masahiro Kawai and Shujiro Urata appraise this question in the context of

Japanese manufacturing. These authors find strong and positive two-way interactions, complementarity, between trade and FDI. Their results for a variety of Japanese industries demonstrate that FDI not only expands external capacity, but facilitates domestic capacity use. In short, FDI is an essential factor in deepening regional interdependence.

In the same context, Korea's experience with outward FDI has many similarities and some important differences. In Chapter 9, Jai-Won Ryou examines patterns of Korean overseas investment from the perspective of labor utilization. Of particular interest in this article is the emphasis on outward FDI as a potential threat to domestic employment, a concern more often raised in Europe and North America. In the Korean context, Ryou finds that the domestic effects of outward FDI differ across sectors but that the overall effect on trade and the economy reaffirms strong complementarity. Although some labor-intensive sectors, like textiles, have experienced "deindustrialization" symptoms in concert with FDI outflows, these are natural attributes of shifting comparative advantage in the global economy, and it would be risky to jeopardize emergent trade opportunities by trying to obstruct this market-driven adjustment process with protectionist measures. The lessons drawn from Chapter 9 certainly have significance for other mature industrial countries.

The next two chapters reverse perspective on foreign capital flows, looking this time at inbound investment in two of the world's largest and dynamic developing countries. In Chapter 10, Shang-Jin Wei examines the provocative question of whether or not China is an underachiever as a foreign investment destination. Despite the meteoric rise of foreign capital inflows into China and an equally expeditious proliferation of joint ventures, Wei infers that China is still behind its absorptive capacity and could probably utilize significantly more FDI in mutually profitable ventures. Using the same model, one that combines standard economic variables and indicators of the receptiveness of the investment environment, Wei shows that Hong Kong is a dramatic overachiever as an FDI destination. In summary, post-1997 China will be more average in all these respects, but given China's size, it is still reasonable to expect dramatic future growth in its inbound FDI.

In Chapter 11, Iwan Azis examines FDI into Indonesia in a

broader historical and institutional context. Azis begins with an authoritative review of the country's experience with foreign investment, a lengthy transition from colonialism to inward orientation to outward orientation. One important insight from this long view of economic development is how well established many "modern" economic phenomena were across three centuries of colonialism, including FDI, intraindustry trade, export orientation, import substitution, and regionalism. The author then goes on to appraise the domestic effects of FDI on the modern economy, with particular emphasis on income distribution. He points out that historical FDI has not fostered very uniform income growth, particularly in the regional sense. This may contribute to political uncertainty unless future investment trends help diversify the economy and broaden its basis of income generation.

5. TRADE, RESOURCES, AND THE ENVIRONMENT

Most of the contributions to this book focus on the positive aspects of Pacific multilateralism – public and private initiatives to improve individual and collective living standards through expanded regional trade and economic growth. While reference has been made to institutional or structural impediments to this trend, most of the previous material focuses on the positive side of the policy agenda. There have been and will certainly be many serious challenges to expanding multilateralism, however, and this book would be incomplete without some substantive discussion of them.

Challenges to multilateralism that arise from past norms and traditional institutions are treated in the earlier chapters. The future holds many new challenges, most of which cannot be anticipated. An important one that is clearly discernible, however, is the environment, and we examine it in this book as a case study in the risks of policy discord. The status of the environment raises very intrinsic questions of national interest (e.g., local public health and resource degradation), yet these are increasingly linked to multilateral relations and global events. Although the maturity of domestic environmental policies varies widely, a multilateral perspective on environment is relatively new. Indeed, this issue has in many ways grown up with the new regionalism and globalization debates, and trade and environment linkages have been intensively discussed and researched in recent years.[11]

The final two chapters of this book examine trade and environment issues from two perspectives, that of a regional trade agreement and that of a single, large country whose environmental policies have implications for transboundary pollution and other multilateral externalities. In the first case, John Beghin, David Roland-Holst, and Dominique van der Mensbrugghe use a CGE model of Mexico to assess the environmental effects of its accession to the NAFTA regional trade pact. Although this issue has been intensively debated before, during, and after the negotiation of the NAFTA, very little evidence has been presented about the economywide impact on the Mexican environment until now. The authors conclude that, contrary to some thinking that NAFTA would induce the country to specialize in pollution-intensive products, Mexico actually shifts the composition of its economic activities toward lower than average pollution intensity. Despite this, however, aggregate growth impelled by trade liberalization leads to higher total pollution levels for the country. The authors then go on to examine a number of mitigation policies and conclude that targeted emission taxes can achieve significant abatement for Mexico, while it still realizes most of the growth benefits accruing from the NAFTA agreement.

When the issue of pollution growth is raised in the Pacific region, attention is usually drawn to China. Because of this country's combination of rapid economic growth, low current pollution per capita, and vast population, it is reasonable to expect dramatic changes in this country's contribution to regional emission levels. In Chapter 12, two distinguished Chinese policy economists appraise this issue, beginning with an overview of environmental conditions and concluding with a discussion of trade linkages and multilateral externality issues. The authors concede that many challenges lie ahead for China in regulating its effect on the domestic and regional environment, but they argue that multilateral cooperation in general and trade in particular can facilitate their efforts at pollution mitigation, greater energy efficiency, and more sustainable development policies. The threats that might be posed by acid rain, global warming, and soil and other renewable

---

[11] See Beghin, Roland-Holst, and van der Mensbrugghe (1994) for a survey.

resource depletion are very serious indeed. If more liberal trade contributed to faster technology transfer, stricter environmental standards induced by rising incomes, and more efficient and sustainable resource utilization, this would indeed be a triumph for multilateralism.

6. METHODOLOGICAL NOTES

The contributions in this book come from a group of experts with quite diverse backgrounds and professional emphasis. In order to achieve the greatest coherence and policy relevance in this collection, we have asked them to focus their analysis and methodology on a specific region and set of issues. While representing many different perspectives and insights, the empirical work represented here emphasizes two main approaches: general equilibrium simulation models and the so-called gravity equation approach to econometric modeling. In this section, we provide a synopsis of each of these methods, with references to guide the interested reader to more complete introductions.

6.1. Calibrated General Equilibrium Models

A confluence of neoclassical economic theory, dramatically improved computing and data resources, and renewed interest in reform-growth linkages has led to the advent of a new generation of policy simulation models. These calibrated general equilibrium (CGE) models are economywide in scope and simulate price-directed resource allocation in product and factor markets.[12] Although their veracity rests as much on assumptions and data quality as any empirical economics, these models have especially desirable properties:

1. closed-form accounting for economic activity that helps ensure consistency;
2. emphasis on linkages, which captures myriad indirect effects beyond the ken of partial equilibrium analysis or conventional intuition;
3. a simulation structure permitting extensive counterfactual analysis in support of economic policymaking.

[12] For more thorough background on this methodology, the reader is referred to Dervis, de Melo, and Robinson (1982), Shoven and Whalley (1984), Borges (1986), Francois and Reinert (1997), and Devarajan, Lewis, and Robinson (1997).

Because of these structural features, CGE models are particularly useful for detailed incidence analysis, where movements in relative prices of goods and factors can have pervasive effects on incomes. This approach has been widely applied for evaluating the economywide effects of trade and fiscal reforms, as well as other policies that entail removal or imposition of distortions to commodity or factor prices. By combining market simulation with detailed information on income and expenditure linkages, complex patterns of structural adjustment can be elucidated.

In recent years, the number of studies that employ CGE models has proliferated. Such models have now been constructed for over fifty countries, and they are in active use supporting government policy in countries as diverse as China, Morocco, and the United States. A CGE model is particularly useful in assessing sectoral adjustments and income distribution and is ideally suited to evaluation of new trading arrangements because it can detail the impacts on both member and nonmember countries. Studies evaluating the effects of alternative trade liberalization scenarios among Pacific Basin countries include Brown, Deardorff, and Stern (1996), Lee and Roland-Holst (1995), Lee, Roland-Holst, and van der Mensbrugghe (1997), Lewis, Robinson, and Wang (1995), and Young and Chye (1997). These studies generally find that, in percentage terms, both discriminatory and nondiscriminatory liberalization by East Asian or APEC countries would lead to welfare gains to developing countries (such as China and ASEAN) that are significantly greater than those to developed countries. Recent studies assessing the impact of the Uruguay Round (e.g., Francois, McDonald, and Nordström, 1996; Goldin, Knudsen, and van der Mensbrugghe, 1993; Harrison, Rutherford, and Tarr, 1996; Hertel et al., 1996; Yang, Martin, and Yanagishima, 1997) also show substantial variations in the distribution of world welfare gains across regions.

6.2. Gravity Models

The gravity model has been one of the most successful empirical tools in explaining cross-sectional trade patterns.[13] In a simple form, it relates volume of trade between two countries positively

---

[13] See Baldwin (1994) and Oguledo and MacPhee (1994) for surveys. Bayoumi and Eichengreen (1995) stated that "the gravity model has long been the work-horse for empirical studies of the pattern of trade."

to their incomes and negatively to geographical distance, analogous to gravitational attraction between two masses in physics. The standard gravity equation may be specified as:

$$T_{ij} = \beta_0 Y_i^{\beta_1} Y_j^{\beta_2} d_{ij}^{\beta_3} A_{ij}^{\beta_4} e^{\beta_5 D_{ij}} u_{ij}, \qquad (1.1)$$

where T_{ij} is the bilateral trade flow from country i to country j, Y_i and Y_j are the exporting and importing countries' gross domestic products, and d_{ij} is the geographical or economic distance between the two countries. D_{ij} is an array of dummy variables such as those for preferential trading arrangements, A_{ij} is an array of other factors that could either facilitate or impede trade between i and j, and u_{ij} is a log-normally distributed error term with E $(\log u_{ij}) = 0$.[14]

Earlier empirical papers employing the gravity model to estimate trade flows (e.g., Tinbergen, 1962; Linnenmann, 1966; Leamer and Stern, 1970; Aitken, 1973; Leamer, 1974) consistently provided a good fit, yet they were often criticized because of the absence of strong theoretical foundations. Anderson (1979) was the first to provide a rigorous economic justification, deriving a reduced-form gravity equation from a general equilibrium model incorporating the properties of expenditure systems.[15] Subsequently, Helpman and Krugman (1985, ch. 8) derived a version of the gravity equation from a model that consisted of sectors producing homogeneous products with constant returns to scale and those producing differentiated products with increasing returns to scale.

A series of papers by Bergstrand further developed microeconomic foundations of the gravity equation under alternative assumptions. In Bergstrand (1985), he assumed that goods are differentiated by country of origin and derived a generalized gravity equation consisting of price variables. He suggested that the assumption of perfect product substitutability would result in the omission of price variables and could lead to misspecification of the equation.[16] In Bergstrand (1989), he assumed non-

---

[14] The per capita income variable is generally included in A_{ij} because rich countries are expected to trade more than poor ones.

[15] Linnenmann (1966), Leamer and Stern (1970), and Leamer (1974) attempted to provide theoretical foundations for the gravity model, but they lacked a compelling economic justification.

[16] Anderson (1979) and Helpman and Krugman (1985) also shared this view.

homothetic tastes for a representative consumer and relative factor-endowment differences between two monopolistically competitive sectors in a two-factor, two-sector, N-country model. His reduced-form equation consisted of the exporter's national output and capital-labor ratio and the importer's income and per capita income, as well as distance and price-related variables. Using this theoretical framework, Bergstrand (1990) evaluated the determinants of cross-country bilateral intraindustry trade and presented some testable propositions.

Derivations of alternative versions of the gravity equation by Anderson (1979), Helpman and Krugman (1985), and Bergstrand (1985, 1989) did not directly rely on the Heckscher-Ohlin (H-O) model but instead on product differentiation models. A recent paper by Deardorff (1998) showed that the gravity equation can also be derived from two extreme cases of the H-O model – one with identical, homothetic preferences and frictionless trade, and the other with impeded trade where every country produces and exports different goods. Given that the gravity equation may be derived from a large class of models, Deardorff points out that its empirical success does not imply support of any particular trade model.[17]

The main purpose of most of the empirical papers employing the gravity model has not been testing of an imperfect competition trade model, the H-O model, or any other trade models, however. Instead, a number of recent papers (e.g., Frankel, 1993; Frankel and Wei, 1993a,b; Frankel, Stein, and Wei, 1995; Baldwin, 1994; Oguledo and MacPhee, 1994; Bayoumi and Eichengreen, 1995) have attempted to capture a special regional effect on bilateral trade flows. This is accomplished by including a dummy variable for a common membership in a regional trade grouping. A major objective of these papers is to determine whether or not the high level of trade within a given region has been beyond what could be explained by economic characteristics common to bilateral trade throughout the world and thus could be attributable to the regional effect.

Although the gravity model might be able to describe factor movements as well as commodity movements between countries,

---

[17] For example, Deardorff cites Helpman's (1987) study, which interpreted the good fit of the gravity equation with bilateral trade of the OECD countries as evidence for the monopolistic competition model.

that for foreign direct investment has not been formally derived. To date, Eaton and Tamura (1996) have made a good attempt to link together a theoretical model of trade and investment and gravity equations for trade and FDI. Specifically, they develop a model that can predict the extent to which innovators will alter exports and FDI to changes in the destination country's characteristics. Inevitably, more theoretical work is needed to provide satisfactory explanations of the activities of multinational corporations and how they affect trade and direct investment decisions.

The gravity equation has increasingly been used to explain FDI flows (e.g., Eaton and Tamura, 1994, 1996; Kawai, 1994; Wei, 1996) with a relatively good fit. The determinants of bilateral FDI flows could differ from those of bilateral trade flows. For example, in addition to the standard variables such as GDP, per capita GDP, and distance between two countries, Wei's FDI equation in this volume (Chapter 10) includes the host country's wage rate (labor cost), a measure of corruption and red tape, and a dummy variable for source and host countries that speak a common language.

Kawai and Urata's and Ryou's chapters (8 and 9) explore interactions between bilateral FDI outflows and trade for Japanese and Korean industries. Specifically, they examine whether outward FDI would lead to an increase in the source country's trade and vice versa using gravity equations. They are aware of the FDI-trade simultaneity problem and use lagged values of trade and FDI in their FDI and trade equations, respectively. As long as the error terms in each equation are not serially correlated, lagged endogenous variables would be predetermined. This is likely to be the case when one uses only cross-country data but is less likely to be the case when one uses pooled cross-country, time-series data.

Despite these limitations, the chapters that employ gravity equations provide us with new insights on FDI in the Asian Pacific region. Discussion by Kawai and Urata on Japanese FDI and patterns of trade by foreign affiliates of Japanese firms is important because Japan is the world's largest FDI source country. Korea has emerged as a major supplier of capital to China and the ASEAN countries, and Ryou's chapter provides an excellent case study for Korea. Furthermore, these authors estimate trade and FDI flows for selected manufacturing industries, enabling the readers to examine the differences in behavior across sectors.

7. CONCLUDING REMARKS

The contributions to this volume were assembled to shed light on the most dynamic economic region of the world. We hope that the lessons learned thereby will help to sustain and propagate the successes of the Pacific Basin economies, making a lasting contribution to improved living standards around the world. For decades after World War II, many international trade and development economists were haunted by one question: Why, two hundred years after the Industrial Revolution, does more than one-quarter of humankind still live in poverty? Despite the best intentions of donors and social reformers, a generation of development assistance and political experimentation produced no general prototype for rapid and sustainable growth in developing countries. Only in recent years, with the fuller articulation of economies in the Asian Pacific, and the advent of rapid growth in China and ASEAN countries, has a new paradigm for economic modernization begun to manifest itself.

The early positive examples of this period, such as Japan, Taiwan, and Korea, gave some indications about how to industrialize in a modern, postwar era. These economies revealed the importance of leveraging domestic capacity growth with exports, dedicated public and private investment in infrastructure and especially in human capital, and rigorous attention to market forces. Despite such important features, however, the example of early Asian export economies is of limited relevance to poor countries today. This is largely because the former based their industrialization and export strategies on neo-mercantilist principles, domestic protection and single-minded projection of national business interests into foreign export markets. Such an approach cannot be readily generalized across the developing world and in any case is inconsistent with the norms of multilateral trade prevailing today.

What we see emerging now in the Pacific Basin is a new paradigm of market-directed economic coordination and the kind of synergistic multilateral growth envisioned by classical trade theorists, significantly improved upon by modern private enterprise. Although elements of comparative advantage exert a strong influence on resource allocation in individual countries, specialization is much less extreme than that which resulted from historic trade patterns. Multinational business exerts a pervasive influence on growth patterns in these economies, replicating abroad to exploit not only natural resources but also internal markets in each country. By infusing each FDI destination with new capital, technology, and expertise, thousands of foreign private interests contribute simultaneously to greater economic diversity within each economy and greater uniformity across economies. For the poorer countries, the result is a broader basis for employment and opportunity in their own economy, leading to greater diversification, stability, and generally higher rates of growth in productivity and wages.

Two of the most compelling aspects of this new, private multilateralism are its spontaneity and collaborative nature. Historically, economic policy in general and trade policy in particular were closely circumscribed by official institutions representing abstraction notions of national interest. Like many forms of regulation, the relatively simplistic agendas of national trade policy do not mesh well with complex and often conflicting incentives/signals that permeate today's international commerce. But the risks of commerce always carry the prospect of reward and, for every reticent trade negotiator, there may be hundreds of firms eager to establish a lucrative foreign partnership or open a new market. The resulting "Invisible Handshakes" ultimately serve national interest by transcending it, reaching beyond the short-term perspective of, for example, domestic protection, to broaden the basis for economic activity globally and take a (national) material interest in the resulting economic growth.

The spontaneous and collaborative aspects of this process are intuitively appealing, but they also have one very profound historical implication. By transcending national policy control and relying instead on voluntary private cooperation, a multilateral basis for security may be emerging that is unprecedented in history. Private multilateralism is not simply a new source of global prosperity; it may be the new foundation for sustained global peace. If open multilateralism and market forces can supercede destructive national rivalry, it will be neither the End of History nor the Clash of Civilizations that prevails in the Pacific Century, but individual aspiration and enterprise, freeing most of us at last from the millennial scourges of war and deprivation.

REFERENCES

Aitken, Norman D. (1973), "The Effect of the EEC and EFTA on European Trade: A Temporal Cross-Section Analysis," *American Economic Review*, 63: 881–892.

Anderson, James E. (1979), "A Theoretical Foundation for the Gravity Equation," *American Economic Review*, 69: 106–116.

Baldwin, Richard E. (1994), *Toward an Integrated Europe*, London: Centre for Economic Policy Research.

Bayoumi, Tamim, and Barry Eichengreen (1995), "Is Regionalism Simply a Diversion? Evidence from the Evolution of the EC and EFTA," NBER Working Paper No. 5283, October.

Beghin, John, David Roland-Holst, and Dominique van der Mensbrugghe (1994), "A Survey of the Trade and Environment Nexus: Global Dimensions," *OECD Economic Studies*, 23: 167–192.

(1997), "Trade and Pollution Linkages: Piecemeal Reform and Optimal Intervention," *Canadian Journal of Economics*, 30: 442–455.

Bergsten, C. Fred, and Marcus Noland, eds. (1993), *Pacific Dynamism and the International Economic System*, Washington, DC: Institute for International Economics.

Bergstrand, Jeffrey H. (1985), "The Gravity Equation in International Trade: Some Microeconomic Foundations and Empirical Evidence," *Review of Economics and Statistics*, 67: 474–481.

(1989), "The Generalized Gravity Equation, Monopolistic Competition, and the Factor-Proportions Theory in International Trade," *Review of Economics and Statistics*, 71: 143–153.

(1990), "The Heckscher-Ohlin-Samuelson Model, the Linder Hypothesis, and the Determinants of Bilateral Intra-Industry International Trade," *Economic Journal*, 100: 1216–1229.

Borges, A. M. (1986), "Applied General Equilibrium Models: An Assessment of Their Usefulness for Policy Analysis," *OECD Economic Studies*, 7: 8–43.

Brainard, S. Lael (1993a), "A Simple Theory of Multinational Corporations and Trade with a Trade-Off between Proximity and Concentration," NBER Working Paper No. 4269, February.

(1993b), "An Empirical Assessment of the Factor Proportions Explanation of Multinational Sales," NBER Working Paper No. 4583, December.

(1997), "An Empirical Assessment of the Proximity-Concentration Tradeoff between Multinational Sales and Trade," *American Economic Review*, 87: 520–544.

Brown, Drusilla K., Alan V. Deardorff, and Robert M. Stern (1996), "Computational Analysis of the Economic Effects of an East Asian Preferential Trading Bloc," *Journal of the Japanese and International Economies*, 10: 37–70.

Deardorff, Alan V. (1984), "Testing Trade Theories and Predicting Trade Flows," in R. W. Jones and P. B. Kenen, eds., *Handbook of International Economics*, Vol. 1, Amsterdam: North-Holland.

(1998), "Determinants of Bilateral Trade: Does Gravity Work in a Neoclassical World?" in Jeffrey A. Frankel, ed., *The Regionalization of the World Economy*, Chicago: University of Chicago Press.

Dervis, Kermal, Jaime de Melo, and Sherman Robinson (1982), *General Equilibrium Models for Development Policy*, Cambridge: Cambridge University Press.

Devarajan, Shantayanan, Jeffrey D. Lewis, and Sherman Robinson (1998), *Getting the Model Right: The General Equilibrium Approach to Adjustment Policy*, Cambridge: Cambridge University Press.

Eaton, Jonathan, and Akiko Tamura (1994), "Bilateralism and Regionalism in Japanese and U.S. Trade and Direct Foreign Investment Patterns," *Journal of the Japanese and International Economies*, 8: 478–510.

(1996), "Japanese and U.S. Exports and Investment as Conduits of Growth," in T. Ito and A. O. Krueger, eds., *Financial Deregulation and Integration in East Asia*, Chicago: University of Chicago Press and NBER.

Francois, Joseph F., Bradley McDonald, and Håkan Nordström (1996), "The Uruguay Round: A Numerically Based Qualitative Assessment," in W. Martin and L. A. Winters, eds., *The Uruguay Round and the Developing Countries*, Cambridge: Cambridge University Press.

Francois, Joseph F., and Kenneth A. Reinert, eds. (1997), *Applied Methods for Trade Policy Analysis: A Handbook*, Cambridge: Cambridge University Press.

Francois, Joseph F., and Clinton R. Shiells, eds. (1994), *Modeling Trade Policy: Applied General Equilibrium Assessments of North American Free Trade*, Cambridge: Cambridge University Press.

Frankel, Jeffrey A. (1993), "Is Japan Creating a Yen Bloc in East Asia and the Pacific?" in J. A. Frankel and M. Kahler, eds., *Regionalism and Rivalry: Japan and the United States in Pacific Asia*, Chicago: University of Chicago Press and NBER.

Frankel, Jeffrey, Ernesto Stein, and Shang-Jin Wei (1995), "Trading Blocs and the Americas: The Natural, the Unnatural, and the Super-natural, *Journal of Development Economics*, 47: 61–95.

Frankel, Jeffrey A., and Shang-Jin Wei (1993a), "Trade Blocs and Currency Blocs," NBER Working Paper No. 4335, April.

(1993b), "Is There a Currency Bloc in the Pacific?" in A. Blundell-Wignall, ed., *Exchange Rates, International Trade and the Balance of Payments*, Sydney: Reserve Bank of Australia.

Goldin, Ian, Odin Knudsen, and Dominique van der Mensbrugghe (1993), *Trade Liberalization: Global Economic Implications*, Paris and Washington, DC: OECD and World Bank.

Hamilton, Carl and L. Alan Winters (1992), "Opening Up International Trade in Eastern Europe," *Economic Policy* 7: 78–116.

Harrison, Glenn W., Thomas F. Rutherford, and David G. Tarr (1996), "Quantifying the Uruguay Round," in W. Martin and L. A. Winters, eds., *The Uruguay Round and the Developing Countries*, Cambridge: Cambridge University Press.

Helpman, Elhanan (1987), "Imperfect Competition and International Trade: Evidence from Fourteen Industrial Countries," *Journal of the Japanese and International Economies*, 1: 62–81.

Helpman, Elhanan, and Paul R. Krugman (1985), *Market Structure and Foreign Trade*, Cambridge, MA: MIT Press.

Hertel, Thomas W., ed. (1997), *Global Trade Analysis: Modeling and Applications*, Cambridge: Cambridge University Press.

Hertel, Thomas W., Will Martin, Koji Yamagishima, and Betina Dimaranan (1996), "Liberalizing Manufactures Trade in a Changing World Economy," in W. Martin and L. A. Winters, eds., *The Uruguay Round and the Developing Countries*, Cambridge: Cambridge University Press.

Hufbauer, Gary, Darius Lakdawalla, and Anup Malani (1994), "Determinants of Direct Foreign Investment and Its Connection to Trade," United Nations Conference on Trade and Development (UNCTAD), *UNCTAD Review*, New York: United Nations.

Kawai, Masahiro (1994), "Interactions of Japan's Trade and Investment: A Special Emphasis on East Asia," Discussion Paper Series No. F-39, Institute of Social Science, University of Tokyo, October.

Leamer, Edward E. (1974), "The Commodity Composition of International Trade in Manufactures: An Empirical Analysis," *Oxford Economic Papers*, 26: 350–374.

Leamer, Edward E., and Robert M. Stern (1970), *Quantitative International Economics*, Boston: Allyn and Bacon.

Lee, Hiro, and David Roland-Holst (1995), "Trade Liberalization and Employment Linkages in the Pacific Basin," *Developing Economies*, 33: 155–184.

Lee, Hiro, David Roland-Holst, and Dominique van der Mensbrugghe (1997), "APEC Trade Liberalization and Structural Adjustments: Policy Assessments," Discussion Paper No. 11, APEC Study Center, Nagoya University and Institute of Developing Economies.

Lewis, Jeffrey D., Sherman Robinson, and Zhi Wang (1995), "Beyond the Uruguay Round: The Implications of an Asian Free Trade Area," *China Economic Review*, 6: 35–90.

Linnenmann, Hans (1966), *An Econometric Study of International Trade Flows*, Amsterdam: North-Holland.

Markusen, James R., and Anthony J. Venables (1995), "Multinational Firms and the New Trade Theory," NBER Working Paper No. 5036, February.

Martin, Will, and L. Alan Winters, eds. (1996), *The Uruguay Round and the Developing Countries*, Cambridge: Cambridge University Press.

Melo, Jaime de, and Arvind Panagariya, eds. (1993), *New Dimensions in Regional Integration*, Cambridge: Cambridge University Press and CEPR.

Mercenier, Jean, and T. N. Srinivasan, eds. (1994), *Applied General Equilibrium and Economic Development*, Ann Arbor: University of Michigan Press.

Oguledo, Victor I., and Craig R. MacPhee (1994), "Gravity Models: A Reformulation and an Application to Discriminatory Trade Arrangements," *Applied Economics*, 26: 107–120.

Shoven, John B., and John Whalley (1984), "Applied General-Equilibrium Models of Taxation and International Trade: An Introduction and Survey," *Journal of Economic Literature*, 22: 1007–1051.

Srinivasan, T. N., and John Whalley, eds. (1986), *Genereal Equilibrium Trade Policy Modeling*, Cambridge: MIT Press.

Tinbergen, Jan (1962), *Shaping the World Economy: Suggestions for an International Economic Policy*, New York: The Twentieth Century Fund.

Wei, Shang-Jin (1996), "Foreign Direct Investment in China: Source and Consequences," in T. Ito and A. O. Krueger, eds., *Financial Deregulation and Integration in East Asia*, Chicago: University of Chicago Press and NBER.

Wong, Kar-Yiu (1995), *International Trade in Goods and Factor Mobility*, Cambridge: MIT Press.

Yamazawa, Ippei (1996), "APEC's New Development and Its Implications for Nonmember Developing Countries, *Developing Economies*, 34: 113–137.

Yang, Y., W. Martin, and K. Yanagishima (1997), "Evaluating the Benefits of Abolishing the MFA in the Uruguay Round Package," in T. W. Hertel, ed., *Global Trade Analysis: Modeling and Applications*, Cambridge: Cambridge University Press.

Young, Linda M., and Karen M. Chye (1997), "Free Trade in the Pacific Rim: On What Basis?" in T. W. Hertel, ed., *Global Trade Analysis: Modeling and Applications*, Cambridge: Cambridge University Press.

PART II

U.S.–Japan and Asian Trade Patterns

CHAPTER 2

Cooperative Approaches to Shifting Comparative Advantage: The Case of Bilateral Trade between the United States and Japan

Hiro Lee and David Roland-Holst

1. INTRODUCTION

The primary strategic challenge for trade policymakers is managing a continuously shifting pattern of trading opportunities. Apart from notable exceptions such as GATT (General Agreement on Tariffs and Trade) and an increasing number of regional trade accords, most of this policy is formulated and implemented unilaterally and with narrowly defined national interests. In this chapter, we argue that there exist cooperative trade strategies that can serve the domestic political agendas of national policymakers and can facilitate, rather than impede, the evolution of a trading system based on efficient international resource allocation. A larger set of cooperative solutions for policymakers would do much to foster the continued growth of the world economy and world incomes.

Trade between the United States and Japan has evolved dramatically over the last three decades, growing from a trickle to one of the world's largest bilateral trade flows.[1] During the same period, the roles of the two countries in the world economy have also

We thank Akihiro Amano, Taeho Bark, Masahiro Kuroda, Will Martin, Masahiko Shimizu, John Ying, and Kanji Yoshioka for helpful comments and Li Gan for research assistance. This research was assisted by a grant from the Abe Fellowship Program of the Social Science Research Council and the American Council of Learned Societies with funds provided by the Japan Foundation's Center for Global Partnership.

[1] In 1995, the world's largest bilateral trade flow took place between the United States and Canada, totaling $274 billion. U.S.–Japan trade was the second largest, amounting to $198 billion.

changed as new patterns of comparative advantage have developed between them and their trading partners. The United States has maintained prominence as an agricultural exporter and expanded service exports as a share of its total trade, but its leadership in a variety of manufacturing exports has been lost or seriously challenged as East Asian economies have aggressively developed new market niches in textiles, metal products, and consumer electronics.

Meanwhile, the Japanese economy experienced an unprecedented period of economic growth during 1955–73 and strong sustained growth during 1976–90, followed by a recession and slow recovery during 1992–97. The robust expansion of Japanese exports during 1955–90 was accompanied by extensive shifts in its underlying composition. Japan began this period with labor-intensive exports of light manufactures, shifting to capital-intensive goods (e.g., steel, shipbuilding, and heavy machinery) in the late 1960s and 1970s, and moving toward more technology-intensive goods (e.g., automobiles, consumer electronics, semiconductors, and precision instruments) since the late 1970s.[2] During the 1982–91 period, for example, the Japanese share of world semiconductor production rose from 33 to 47 percent, while the U.S. share fell from 57 to 39 percent (Howell et al., 1992).[3]

Despite extensive changes in the composition of commodity trade that have largely been caused by shifts in comparative advantage, there are still areas where policy intervention has limited each country's adjustment. While agricultural protection is common among industrialized countries, in Japan it appears to be a more determined effort to resist the natural evolution of trade patterns. The decline in real terms of trade for Japanese agriculture has been long and monotonic, and contraction in this sector has been forestalled only with extensive subsidies and prohibitive import restrictions. In the United States, this kind of intervention is more apparent in manufacturing sectors, where significant

---

[2] Johnson, Tyson, and Zysman (1989) argue that Japan's activist approach to trade and industrial policy has been tailored to the evolution of comparative advantages and has even manipulated that evolution in several instances. Lee (1993) shows that Japan's industrial policy significantly contributed to the expansion of production levels and promotion of exports for several capital-intensive industries in the 1960s.

[3] The world semiconductor market share of Japanese firms, however, has declined since 1992. In 1995, the U.S. and Japanese makers each captured about 40 percent of world semiconductor sales.

import barriers have been erected in a number of sectors to compensate for declining competitiveness of domestic producers.

In both countries, such policies have three things in common. First of all, they are essentially nonconstructive because they impede any adjustments to changes in underlying competitive conditions. Second, they distort prices and impose inefficiency and rent transfers on domestic and international markets. Third, these policies usually represent noncooperative solutions to the problems posed by changing patterns of competitiveness or comparative advantage.[4]

Corresponding to the large Japanese current account surpluses was a sharp increase in capital outflows from Japan in the 1980s. Japanese exports of capital services grew from $9 billion in 1981 to $68 billion in 1989. By far the largest recipient of these services has been the United States, receiving an average 40 percent of all Japanese foreign direct investment over the same period.[5] If viewed from an accounting perspective, these capital outflows might be interpreted as transitory residuals. It has become increasingly apparent, however, that Japan's international financial activity is a relatively autonomous response to surplus domestic savings and saturated domestic capital markets. Although Japanese direct investment declined during 1989–92, the significant appreciation of the yen during 1993–95 has raised the expected rate of return on overseas investment and sharply increased Japan's capital exports in the past few years.

In a fully liberalized trading regime, shifting comparative advantage would generally occasion shifts in trade patterns for both commodities and factor services. Changes in commodity trade adapt the international composition of production to changing patterns of factor productivity. Direct trade in factor services, however, can adapt the international composition of factor productivity to the existing pattern of production, essentially countering the shifts in comparative advantage by transferring productivity between countries. The purpose of this study is to evaluate the potential gains to the United States and Japan in this new diversified trade regime.

---

[4] Voluntary export restraints (VERs) and voluntary import expansions (VIEs) might appear to be an exception, but these negotiated trade policies are Pareto inferior to free trade.

[5] See Glick (1991) for a survey of Japanese capital outflows. Data on Japanese foreign direct investment have been collected from the Ministry of Finance's *Zaisei Kinyu Tōkei Geppo: Tai-naigai Minkan Tōshi Tokushu*.

Our results indicate that sector-specific direct investment between the two countries can provide greater welfare than either the prevailing regime of protection or fully liberalized bilateral trade without such investment flows.

In the sense that factor mobility amplifies the national gains of import liberalization, commodity and factor trades appear to exhibit aggregate complementarity. However, results from theoretical models (e.g., Mundell, 1957; Markusen, 1983; Markusen and Svensson, 1985; Wong, 1986, 1995; Neary and Ruane, 1988) find that they may be substitutes or complements depending upon the assumptions.[6] Thus it is desirable to examine empirically whether commodity and factor trades are substitutes or complements. Our results support complementarity not only at the aggregate level; we find that bilateral commodity and capital flows exhibit complementarity in many manufacturing sectors.[7]

To evaluate the policies of bilateral liberalization and foreign direct investment, we use an applied general equilibrium model calibrated to a U.S.–Japan social accounting matrix (SAM) for the year 1985. The next section discusses the two-country SAM and gives an overview of the composition of production, demand, and bilateral trade for the two countries. Section 3 contains a brief description of the two-country computable general equilibrium (CGE) model used for the policy experiments. In section 4, we present the results of U.S.–Japan trade liberalization experiments, and the final section offers conclusions.

2. AN OVERVIEW OF BILATERAL ECONOMIC STRUCTURE

In this section, we provide an overview of U.S. and Japanese economic structure represented in a two-country SAM for the year 1985. The SAM details the composition of production, value-added, demand, and trade at the sectoral level for each economy and the rest of the world. It fully captures the circular flow of income between trading partners and from firms to factors, from factors

---

[6] Wong (1995) asserts that capital mobility augments commodity trade if and only if the volume of trade under free commodity trade and capital mobility is greater than the volume of trade under free trade but no capital mobility.

[7] Kawai and Urata's results in Chapter 8 of this volume also suggest that trade and foreign direct investment are complements in a number of Japanese manufacturing sectors.

to households, and from households back to firms as final demand. This table has been estimated from the *1985 Japan–U.S. Input– Output Table* published by MITI and national income and product account (NIPA) data.[8] The sectoring scheme for the SAM is chosen to disaggregate seventeen sectors of special policy interest.[9]

The SAM provides highly detailed information on the structure of the two countries and their trade patterns, but its extensive form makes interpretation difficult. Table 2.1 provides the main sectoral features of the two countries in the base year. Service-oriented sectors 15–17 together account for a very large proportion of total output, but significantly more so in the United States (64.9 percent) than Japan (57.9 percent). Although both countries have about equal total agricultural shares, their composition differs noticeably (meat and poultry dominate in the United States). U.S. mining in total domestic output is almost double that in Japan, while combined nondurables (sectors 5–7) are slightly higher in Japan. The share difference in services and mining is thus largely made up in durable manufacturing sectors 8–14, where Japanese share (20.4 percent) outweighs the U.S. share (14.1 percent) by 45 percent.

As one would expect for two diversified economies with high levels of self-sufficiency, the composition of domestic demand in column 2 largely mirrors that of domestic supply. Notable exceptions are apparent in import-dependent and export-oriented sectors such as mining and automobiles. Differences in the sectoral composition of value-added (column 3) are generally greater than output comparisons would imply, suggesting that factor prices differ markedly between the two countries on an average as well as a sector-by-sector basis. This observation is reinforced by the data in column 6, which lists labor/capital value-added ratios by sector. Interindustry factor price differentials are the subject of a large and rather controversial literature, and no effort is made in this study to interpret these international comparisons. We have calibrated them into our CGE model, however, and this feature is discussed in section 3.

The composition of trade for each country differs in ways that have received enough scrutiny elsewhere to seem intuitive now.

---

[8] The U.S.–Japan SAM is available from the authors upon request.
[9] See Table 2.1 for sectoral classifications.

Table 2.1. *Sectoral Composition of Output, Demand, Income, and Trade, 1985*

	(1) X	(2) Q	(3) VA	(4) E	(5) M	(6) V^L/V^K	(7) E/X	(8) M/Q	(9) M^F/M	(10) E^b/E	(11) M^b/M
United States											
1 Cereals	1.1	0.9	0.6	3.1	0.1	0.2	11.9	0.4	19.6	15.0	0.8
2 MeatPoult	2.3	2.3	0.7	1.5	1.1	1.2	2.6	2.9	46.2	16.9	0.2
3 AgForFsh	1.1	1.2	1.0	2.9	3.4	0.6	10.4	17.0	31.3	26.4	2.1
4 PetMining	5.2	5.7	3.7	4.2	12.2	0.4	3.2	12.8	13.0	11.5	0.2
5 FoodProc	2.6	2.6	1.6	2.9	2.8	1.0	4.6	6.5	62.6	13.6	2.5
6 Chemicals	2.6	2.5	1.6	7.3	3.1	1.9	11.1	7.4	14.5	13.1	9.5
7 NonDrMfg	6.3	6.8	4.8	5.1	13.2	2.7	3.2	11.7	53.9	9.1	4.6
8 MchPreIns	3.1	3.2	3.0	10.5	9.5	2.9	13.5	17.6	65.2	6.0	27.2
9 ElecAppl	0.3	0.5	0.2	0.7	3.3	1.6	9.2	42.1	83.9	2.3	61.3
10 CompTelcm	1.5	1.3	1.2	6.9	2.4	6.7	19.1	10.8	74.1	5.9	54.9
11 SemiElec	0.6	0.6	0.5	2.7	3.0	5.0	19.3	28.6	9.0	9.4	22.5
12 Autos	2.2	2.7	1.3	6.8	14.0	4.6	12.6	31.1	79.2	0.6	35.6
13 Aircraft	0.9	0.7	0.9	7.0	1.2	8.6	30.6	10.1	74.4	9.7	2.5
14 OthDurMfg	5.5	5.9	4.5	8.7	13.9	3.0	6.3	14.0	34.6	9.9	17.4
15 TrComUt	9.5	9.0	10.4	11.9	2.4	1.4	5.0	1.6	44.4	3.8	4.9
16 Trade	11.1	10.6	11.5	8.0	1.2	2.9	2.9	0.7	73.9	12.8	11.6
17 Services	44.3	43.9	52.4	10.1	13.5	1.9	0.9	1.8	66.2	3.6	11.6
Total	100.0	100.0	100.0	100.0	100.0						
Weighted Avg						1.9	4.0	5.9	51.0	8.5	17.9

Japan

	(1)	(2)	(3)	(4)	(5)	(6)	(7)	(8)	(9)	(10)	(11)
1 Cereals	1.7	1.9	1.1	0.0	1.9	0.1	0.1	6.3	2.4	3.5	45.6
2 MeatPoult	1.3	1.5	0.5	0.1	2.3	0.5	0.6	9.6	20.5	4.5	20.1
3 AgForFsh	1.6	2.1	1.8	0.2	7.4	0.3	0.8	22.1	11.9	86.2	19.0
4 PetMining	2.7	5.2	0.6	0.8	41.8	0.6	2.4	49.3	1.8	4.9	2.1
5 FoodProc	4.1	4.3	2.1	0.5	3.0	1.4	0.9	4.3	38.1	28.8	25.0
6 Chemicals	3.0	3.1	1.9	3.8	5.0	0.8	9.8	10.0	8.4	15.3	35.4
7 NonDrMfg	7.3	7.5	5.2	4.7	6.1	1.9	5.0	5.1	33.7	25.8	13.8
8 MchPrclns	4.1	3.1	3.6	15.4	2.7	1.4	29.6	5.3	66.9	32.8	43.3
9 ElecAppl	1.4	0.8	0.8	8.2	0.1	1.1	47.0	1.1	83.5	48.4	21.9
10 CompTelcm	1.3	1.1	1.0	4.2	1.1	1.3	25.4	6.4	56.7	60.3	69.3
11 SemiElec	1.4	1.2	1.1	4.4	0.9	1.1	24.0	4.7	6.5	30.2	51.7
12 Autos	2.8	1.3	2.0	19.7	0.5	1.4	55.9	2.6	72.2	49.9	13.3
13 Aircraft	0.1	0.2	0.1	0.1	1.3	1.0	5.0	43.7	56.7	85.6	95.9
14 OthDurMfg	9.3	8.4	6.8	19.6	9.1	1.3	16.6	6.6	29.4	24.5	17.4
15 TrComUt	8.9	8.8	10.3	8.3	5.6	1.7	7.3	3.9	22.4	2.8	15.0
16 Trade	10.1	10.1	12.8	6.3	3.9	3.0	4.8	2.4	9.9	38.0	49.0
17 Services	38.9	39.8	48.3	3.8	7.2	1.3	0.8	1.1	22.9	82.4	9.4
Total	100.0	100.0	100.0	100.0	100.0						
Weighted Avg						1.4	7.8	6.2	15.6	35.4	15.7

Definition of sectors: (1) cereals, (2) meat, poultry, and dairy products, (3) other agricultural products, forestry, and fisheries, (4) petroleum and mining, (5) food processing, (6) chemicals, (7) other nondurable manufacturing, (8) nonelectric machinery and precision instruments, (9) electric appliances, (10) computers and telecommunication equipment, (11) semiconductors and other electronic parts, (12) automobiles, (13) aircraft, (14) other durable manufacturing, (15) transport, communication, and utilities, (16) wholesale and retail trade, and (17) services.

Definition of variables: (1) real gross output shares, (2) real composite demand shares, (3) nominal value-added shares, (4) export shares, (5) import shares, (6) ratios of labor value-added to capital value-added, (7) shares of exports in total output, (8) shares of imports in total demand, (9) final goods import shares in total imports, (10) bilateral export shares in total exports, and (11) bilateral import shares in total imports. All variables other than (6) are expressed in percentages.

Agricultural products (rows 1–3) constitute 7.5 percent of U.S. exports and only 4.6 percent of imports, while the corresponding figures for Japan are 0.3 and 11.6 percent, respectively. Petroleum and mining goods dominate Japan's imports, while the United States has more balanced trade shares in this sector. Durable manufactures (rows 9–14) represent 71.6 percent of all Japanese exports, indicating the strong trade orientation underlying that country's industrial policy. The exports to output ratios in column 7 further emphasize this manufacturing export orientation. The export share of durable manufactures for the United States is 43.3 percent, reflecting its greater degree of diversification. The opportunity cost of U.S. export diversity is apparent in the import figures, however. The imports to total domestic demand shares in column 8 clearly reveal its manufacturing import dependence.

Another perspective on imports is provided in column 9, which lists the shares of final good imports in all sectoral imports. With weighted averages of 51.0 and 15.6 percent for the United States and Japan, respectively, it is apparent that Japan has achieved significantly higher levels of value-added capture for those goods that it does import. The last two columns list shares of bilateral trade in overall imports and exports for each country. Both countries have about equal trade dependence on their import accounts, but the composition of this dependence differs markedly. In terms of exports, Japan is much more dependent on the U.S. market, and its bilateral export links (totaling 35.4 percent of all Japanese exports in 1985) are much more diversified. The United States sends only 8.5 percent of all exports to Japan, however, and these goods fall into relatively narrow product categories.

What emerges from this structural information is a portrait of two economies that are highly diversified but nonetheless interdependent in important ways. Japan has aggressively developed its manufacturing potential by exploiting international market opportunities. Its resulting prosperity comes at the price of considerable dependence on stable and growing trade relations, particularly for exports of manufactured products and imports of primary products. The United States has been less activist toward international competitiveness, relying increasingly on imported substitutes in sectors that used to represent its industrial mainstream. The result is more diversified trade but greater reliance on imports.

3. TWO-COUNTRY CALIBRATED GENERAL EQUILIBRIUM MODEL

Our two-country CGE model is a seventeen-sector economywide model that simulates price-directed resource allocation in commodity and factor markets (see Appendix A at chapter end for model equations). It maintains detailed information on sectoral prices, output, trade, consumption, and factor use in a consistent framework that also accounts for national aggregates such as income, expenditures, and savings. The extent of price adjustments, as well as the volume and pattern of trade creation and trade diversion, all are important factors in determining the ultimate aggregate and sectoral effects of bilateral trade policy.

Trade is modeled according to differentiated products by country of origin and destination (e.g., Armington, 1969; de Melo and Tarr, 1992). This implies a two-level nested CES (constant elasticity of substitution) structure for domestic demand and nested CET (constant elasticity of transformation) structure for domestic production. On the demand side, each agent in the economy first divides an aggregate demand between a domestic component and an aggregate import component. The aggregate import demand is then distributed between imports from the trading partner and imports from ROW. On the supply side, domestically produced goods supplied to the domestic market differ from those exported. Exports to the bilateral partner and exports to ROW are also differentiated. In both countries, import and export demand and supply are fully endogenous. In other words, the United States and Japan are large enough to affect prices in the bilateral and the rest-of-the-world (ROW) markets. The resulting six sets of sectoral trade flows are thus governed by six endogenous price systems (U.S.–Japan, U.S.–ROW, and Japan–ROW import and export prices).

Production is modeled as a nested structure of CES functions. At the first level, a Leontief structure governs intermediate inputs and an aggregate capital-labor bundle (i.e., no substitutability between intermediate inputs and the capital-labor bundle). At the second level, a CES function is used to disaggregate labor and composite capital. The composite capital is further split between domestic capital and foreign capital, as described later. Supply of labor is specified as an increasing function of the wage rate and a decreasing function of the marginal budget share for leisure.[10] In each domestic product market, prices are normalized to a fixed numéraire given by the GDP price deflator.

Perhaps the most important feature of this model is its endogenous treatment of international capital mobility. Although labor movement between the United States and Japan is negligible, foreign direct investment (FDI) by both countries has increased dramatically since 1980. For this reason, we have endogenized trade in capital services (FDI) or sector-specific capital flows between the United States, Japan, and the rest of the world. Capital is specified as a tradeable factor service whose demand is determined by domestic production functions and whose supply is determined by rental rate arbitrage conditions. A number of attempts have been made to model financial markets explicitly in CGE models, but these usually entail ad hoc specifications of monetary phenomena that are difficult to motivate from neoclassical principles. We have chosen instead to model capital flows in response to real rates of return that arise from production technologies.

In our model, sectoral demands for composite capital, domestic capital, and imports of foreign capital are denoted by KD_i, KD_{D_i}, and KM_i. Let KM_i^b and KM_i^r be the accumulated stock of inward FDI from the bilateral partner and ROW, respectively. Then, the CES aggregate demands for KD_i and KM_i are given by

$$KD_i = A_i \left[\alpha_i KM_i^{(\eta_i-1)/\eta_i} + \left(1 - \alpha_i\right) KD_{D_i}^{(\eta_i-1)/\eta_i} \right]^{\eta_i/(\eta_i-1)} \qquad (2.1)$$

and

$$KM_i = B_i \left[\beta_i KM_i^{b^{(\zeta_i-1)/\zeta_i}} + \left(1 - \beta_i\right) KM_i^{r^{(\zeta_i-1)/\zeta_i}} \right]^{\zeta_i/(\zeta_i-1)}, \qquad (2.2)$$

where η_i and ζ_i are the elasticities of substitution between domestic and imported capital and between bilateral and ROW capital,

---

[10] Although the total supply of labor is assumed to be fixed in most of the static CGE models, we have chosen instead to specify it endogenously to capture the positive income effects of liberalization on aggregate employment. It is assumed that labor supply is relatively inelastic in Japan because of certain institutional factors (e.g., lifetime employment and flexible bonus payments) while it is more elastic in the United States. The wage elasticities of 0.1 and 0.5 are used for Japan and the United States, respectively.

respectively. A_i, B_i, α_i ($0 \le \alpha_i \le 1$), and β_i ($0 \le \beta_i \le 1$) are constants.

Similarly, let KS_i, KD_{S_i}, KE_i, KE_i^b, and KE_i^r denote sectoral supplies of composite capital and domestic capital, total outward FDI stock, FDI stock in the bilateral partner, and FDI stock in ROW, respectively. Then the CET aggregate supplies for KS_i and KE_i are given by

$$KS_i = \Gamma_i \left[\gamma_i KE_i^{\left(\varkappa_i + 1\right)/\varkappa_i} + \left(1 - \gamma_i\right) KD_{S_i}^{\left(\varkappa_i + 1\right)/\varkappa_i} \right]^{\varkappa_i/\left(\varkappa_i + 1\right)} \quad (2.3)$$

and

$$KE_i = Z_i \left[\delta_i KE_i^{b\left(\lambda_i + 1\right)/\lambda_i} + \left(1 - \delta_i\right) KM_i^{r\left(\lambda_i + 1\right)/\lambda_i} \right]^{\lambda_i/\left(\lambda_i + 1\right)}, \quad (2.4)$$

where $\varkappa_i$ and λ_i are the elasticities of transformation between domestic and exported capital and between exported capital to the bilateral partner and ROW. The parameters Γ_i, Z_i, γ_i ($0 \le \gamma_i \le 1$), and δ_i ($0 \le \delta_i \le 1$) are exogenous estimates. Since FDI flows are intraindustry, they are specified as differentiated capital services.

As shown by Harris (1984), Brown and Stern (1989), and de Melo and Roland-Holst (1994), market structure and scale economies can exert an important effect on the nature and magnitude of the gains from trade liberalization. To account for this possible effect, we allow for increasing returns in manufacturing and transport sectors in one experiment. Following de Melo and Tarr (1992), we define a cost disadvantage ratio

$$CDR_i = \left(AC_i - MC_i\right)\Big/ AC_i = FC_i\big/ TC_i \quad (2.5)$$

where AC_i, MC_i, FC_i, and TC_i are average, marginal, fixed, and total costs, respectively. In the presence of scale economies, fixed costs become positive and are calibrated from

$$FC_i = CDR_i \left[INTC_i + PVC_i \right], \quad (2.6)$$

where $INTC_i$ and PVC_i are intermediate input and primary variable costs. We assume contestable market pricing where a threat of entry forces identical firms to set their price (P_{X_i}) net of indirect taxes (t_{D_i}) to the average cost[11]

$$\left(1 - t_{D_i}\right)P_{X_i} = AC_i. \qquad (2.7)$$

The U.S.–Japan CGE model is calibrated to the 1985 SAM. Structural parameters have been determined by calibration, direct estimation, or imputation from other sources. Calibrated values are available for most share parameters, input–output coefficients, nominal ad valorem taxes, and tariffs from the SAM itself. Employment, capital stock, and foreign direct investment data are taken from official publications. Elasticity parameters have been obtained from a variety of published and unpublished sources and are listed in Appendix B (at chapter end).

Sectoral rates of nominal import protection for Japan and the United States required for trade liberalization experiments are summarized in Table 2.2. Since a significant component of protection consists of nontariff barriers (NTBs), particularly in Japan, some ad valorem equivalent estimates of their distortionary effects have been collected from a variety of sources. Japanese NTBs based on estimates of the difference between the domestic producer price and CIF import price are available in Sazanami, Urata, and Kawai (1995).[12] Approximate estimates of intangible barriers in the Japanese automobile and service sectors have been inferred from the literature.[13] U.S. NTBs are imputed from estimates in Hufbauer and Elliot (1994), USITC (1990), and de Melo and Tarr (1992).

The present version of the U.S.–Japan model does have some limitations. First, the model is static that does not account for capital accumulation through domestic investment and FDI inflows or augmentation of human capital. In models that incorporate accumulation effects (e.g., Goldin et al., 1993; Francois et al., 1995; Harrison et al., 1995), the static effects of trade liberalization are generally magnified over the medium run. Thus it is likely that our results underestimate the amplitude of some adjustments, particularly those where long-term investment and innovation are impor-

---

[11] Since modeling imperfect competition is not a primary focus of this chapter, a simple pricing rule is used. Alternative models of imperfect competition are evaluated in Lee and Roland-Holst (1993).

[12] Anderson and Tyers (1987) provide ad valorem NTB rates for agricultural products.

[13] See Christelow (1985/86) and U.S. Congress (1991).

Table 2.2. *Bilateral and ROW Import Tariff Rates and ad valorem Equivalents of Nontariff Barriers, United States and Japan, 1985 (percentages)*

		United States		Japan	
		tm	NTB	tm	NTB
1	Cereals	3.7		0.8	439.8
2	MeatPoult	2.7	5.3	8.2	68.5
3	AgForFsh	1.3	9.3	5.8	10.9
4	PetMining	0.5		0.9	11.9
5	FoodProc	5.7		8.8	59.1
6	Chemicals	4.6		3.8	39.5
7	NonDrMfg	11.2	16.5	5.8	24.9
8	MchPrcIns	4.4	4.7	2.9	
9	ElecAppl	6.4		0.6	15.8
10	CompTelcm	6.0		4.2	69.4
11	Semicond	5.4		0.8	45.3
12	Autos	2.4	12.0	2.8	10.0
13	Aircraft	0.0		0.0	
14	OthDurMfg	3.8		1.8	
15	TrComUt	0.0		0.0	
16	Trade	0.0		0.0	
17	Services	0.0		0.0	10.0
	All Sectors	3.7		3.2	

Note: tm = nominal tariff rates; NTB = ad valorem equivalents of nontariff barriers.
Sources:
(1) tm: MITI (1989). Commodity taxes imposed on imported products are excluded.
(2) NTB
    (a) U.S. sectors 2–3: Hufbauer and Elliott (1994) and USITC (1990).
    (b) U.S. sectors 7, 8, 12: de Melo and Tarr (1992) and Hufbauer and Elliott (1994).
    (c) U.S. NTB on automobiles are applied to Japanese imports only.
    (d) Japanese sectors 1–11, 13–14: Sazanami, Urata, and Kawai (1995).
    (e) Japanese sectors 12, 17: Approximate estimates are inferred from Christelow
       (1985/86) and U.S. Congress (1991).
Ad valorem equivalents of nontariff barriers are weighted averages, where shares of total demand (sum of imports and domestic demand) are used as weights.

tant.[14] Second, since 1985 was the year in which the U.S. dollar was overvalued, updating of the SAM database would be desirable. Because *The 1985 Japan–U.S. Input–Output Table* (MITI, 1989) pro-

---

[14] If discount rates are relatively high, the cost of forgone consumption could outweigh long-run benefits of capital accumulation it allows. See Harrison et al. (1995, pp. 27–28).

vided detailed sectoral classification (162 sectors), which disaggregated all important sectors for this study, it was used as the principal data source to estimate the two-country SAM.[15] Third, Japanese NTB estimates taken from Sazanami et al. (1995) do not include some of the important barriers, such as *keiretsu* ties, government procurement practices, regulations and other restrictions embedded in the distribution system, and collusive bidding practices in the construction industry. Thus the NTB estimates provided in Table 2.2 are closer to the lower bound.

4. EMPIRICAL RESULTS

In this section, we discuss the results of trade policy experiments that entail bilateral and nondiscriminatory import liberalization by the United States and Japan. Using the CGE model described in the previous section, we give particular attention to the response of sectoral trade flows of both commodities and capital services. Aggregate economywide results are discussed in section 4.1, followed by a more detailed assessment at the sectoral level in section 4.2.

The first of four experiments reported in Table 2.3 provides aggregate results of bilateral import liberalization between the two countries, assuming constant returns to scale in all sectors and no international capital mobility. This case provides a quasi-lower bound for the adjustment process in both economies, because no sector has unrealized efficiency gains to bid away resources and the aggregate capital supply available to each country is fixed. In experiment 2, we allow for the possibility of sectoral trade in capital services (FDI) as discussed in section 3. To assess the potential significance of scale economies, the third experiment calibrates declining average costs into the manufacturing and transport sectors (5–15) of both economies. For illustrative purposes, we have assumed that each of these sectors has a cost disadvantage ratio (as defined in equation 5) of 10 percent.[16] In experiment 4, con-

---

[15] Although the Global Trade Analysis Project (GTAP) database (Hertel, 1997) provides 1992 data, many of the important sectors for U.S.–Japanese trade, including automobiles, computers and telecommunication equipment, and semiconductors, are aggregated into more broadly defined sectors (i.e., transport equipment and machinery).

[16] Econometric estimates of CDR vary substantially across studies (e.g., Harris, 1984; Pratten, 1988; Neven, 1990). The CDR values used in CGE models also vary consider-

stant returns are again assumed across the board, but both the United States and Japan liberalize their imports from all sources. As discussed in section 3, capital can be treated as a tradeable factor in this model. In the absence of FDI, capital is immobile between the same sectors in the two countries and mobile across sectors in each country. In this case, the economywide average rental rate adjusts to equate aggregate capital demand to the fixed aggregate capital supply. In the presence of FDI, however, the composite capital stock adjusts through international capital flows to meet the composite capital demand. Under this assumption, an individual industry can reallocate its capital to a foreign operation in the same activity. Capital would thus move between the same sectors across countries, as well as across sectors within each country, to maintain equality of base relative productivities.

4.1. Aggregate Results

Table 2.3 summarizes the aggregate results for the five experiments. As is apparent from the first row of the table, all the liberalization experiments yield benefits to both economies in terms of percentage of real income growth. The relative gains between experiments and between countries differ significantly, however. The first three experiments all entail bilateral liberalization, and the United States gains more than Japan in percentage terms under constant returns. This occurs for two reasons. First, because of the higher prior protection, Japan experiences a decline in its terms of trade, offsetting some of the efficiency gains. Second, the assumption of a more elastic U.S. labor supply schedule implies greater output response to increased export and domestic demand. Japan would need larger real productivity growth to expand output because of relatively low labor supply response. A low wage elasticity induces the relatively greater increases in Japanese wage and rental rates (rows 2–3).

In the presence of FDI (experiment 2), both countries experience real output gains that are larger than under liberalization without FDI. The economywide capital stock increases in both countries (row 5), but the United States benefits relatively more

ably. For example, for the food processing sector, Francois et al. (1995, Appendix Table 1) use 15 percent while Harrison et al. (1995, p. 33) use 3 percent.

Table 2.3. Aggregate effects of U.S.–Japan trade liberalization (percentage changes)

| | Experiments[a] | | | | | | | |
| | 1 | | 2 | | 3 | | 4 | |
	U.S.	Japan	U.S.	Japan	U.S.	Japan	U.S.	Japan
1 Real GDP	0.09	0.08	0.18	0.11	0.19	0.33	0.54	0.30
2 Wage Rate	0.03	0.75	0.05	0.76	0.06	0.96	0.53	2.53
3 Avg Rental Rate on Capital	0.32	0.91	0.27	0.86	0.29	1.04	1.29	3.36
4 Employment	0.24	0.15	0.29	0.17	0.29	0.16	0.89	0.56
5 Agg Capital Stock			0.16	0.08	0.16	0.13	0.03	-0.04
6 Agg Bilat Inward FDI[b]			-0.44	0.37	-0.88	0.78	0.34	1.22
7 Agg ROW Inward FDI[c]			1.52	2.49	1.55	3.40	0.43	1.87
8 Agg Bilat Outward FDI[d]			0.37	-0.44	0.78	-0.88	1.22	0.34
9 Agg ROW Outward FDI[e]			-1.77	-1.65	-1.85	-2.53	-0.19	1.56

10 Total Imports	2.23	3.10	1.91	2.85	2.03	3.27	6.57	16.09
11 Bilateral Imports	11.34	31.46	11.43	31.46	12.33	32.01	17.71	24.76
12 ROW Imports	0.38	-1.06	-0.03	-1.35	-0.07	-0.92	4.38	15.16
13 Total Exports	2.42	5.29	2.93	5.65	3.03	6.39	8.24	18.56
14 Bilateral Exports	31.46	11.34	31.46	11.43	32.01	12.33	24.76	17.71
15 ROW Exports	-0.86	1.90	-0.30	2.41	-0.29	3.09	6.24	18.96
16 Import Diversion	2.55	6.42	2.67	6.50	2.89	6.46	2.74	1.58
17 Export Diversion	4.11	3.94	4.02	3.76	4.13	3.80	2.31	0.45
18 Structural Adjustment	0.39	0.97	0.40	1.01	0.42	1.12	0.75	2.72
19 Employment Adjustment	0.30	0.87	0.27	0.90	0.29	0.99	0.49	2.63

[a] Definition of experiments: (1) U.S.–Japan bilateral trade liberalization in the absence of foreign direct investment (FDI) under constant returns to scale. (2) Same as experiment 1 except that FDI is permitted. (3) Same as experiment 2 except that sectors 5–15 are characterized by increasing returns. (4) U.S. and Japanese liberalization on a nondiscriminatory basis in the presence of FDI under constant returns.

[b] Aggregate stock of inward FDI from the bilateral partner.

[c] Aggregate stock of inward FDI from ROW.

[d] Aggregate stock of outward FDI to the bilateral partner.

[e] Aggregate stock of outward FDI to ROW.

because the percentage increase in its capital stock resulting from inward FDI is larger. Overall, these results are consistent with a theoretical finding that trade in capital services can amplify the gains from liberalization.

As demonstrated by previous studies, the existence of unrealized scale economies increases the scope for gains from trade liberalization. As compared with experiment 2, the relatively modest scale economies in experiment 3 triple Japan's gains from bilateral liberalization, while they increase U.S. gains only slightly. Intra-industry trade expands under increasing returns, extending the gains from liberalization to both countries. Although not reported in the table, the incorporation of scale economies increases bilateral exports and imports in every manufacturing sector. At the same time, equal percent scale economies magnify Japan's comparative advantage in manufacturing and induce a greater percentage change in its real income.

For the first three experiments, the effects on trade volumes and trade diversion are quite similar. Bilateral imports and exports expand dramatically (rows 11 and 14) as barriers on imports from the bilateral partner are removed. Trade diversion occurs as Japanese imports from ROW and U.S. exports to ROW fall in each case. Import and export diversion indices, defined as the normalized changes in the composition of trade between the bilateral partner and ROW, are given in rows 16 and 17.[17] Largely because of the higher protection levels against ROW imports, Japan experiences more diversion from bilateral liberalization than the United States.

The last two rows of Table 2.3 contain indices of sectoral reallocation of resources and production activities induced by liberalization. The index in row 18 measures the normalized change in the composition of domestic production, generally indicating the extent of real structural adjustment in each economy. Employment adjustment (row 19) is an index of sectoral labor reallocation,

---

[17] In the case of imports, for example, the diversion measure is given by

$$\delta\left(M_0, M_1\right) = 100 \frac{\left\|M_1 \left|M_0\right| / \left|M_1\right| - M_0\right\|}{\left\|M_0\right\|},$$

where $M_0 = (M_0^b, M_0^r)$ and $M_1 = (M_1^b, M_1^r)$ are the 2-tuple of partner and ROW imports in the base and after the experiment, respectively, and $\|\cdot\|$ and $|\cdot|$ denote Euclidean and simplex norms.

showing the extent of sectoral shifts in employment.[18] Both types of adjustment are two to three times larger for Japan under bilateral liberalization because of its greater specialization, more variable prior protection across sectors, and higher dependence on bilateral trade.

In the fourth and final experiment, the United States and Japan remove tariff and nontariff barriers on a nondiscriminatory basis. Removal of all import barriers would result in real income gains for both countries that are about triple the gains from bilateral liberalization. Relatively large increases in aggregate income and output lead to substantial growth in employment: 0.89 percent for the United States and 0.56 percent for Japan (row 4). Furthermore, because no trade diversion occurs under nondiscriminatory liberalization, both countries' trade with ROW, as well as with the bilateral partner, increase substantially.[19] As discussed in the sectoral results, however, Japanese liberalization on all import sources would lead to drastic contractions of the agricultural sectors, casting doubt on the feasibility of such a policy.

4.2. Sectoral Results

While the aggregate results generally mirror neoclassical intuition about the efficiency gains of removing price distortions, the most useful results are at the industry level, where structural adjustments and resource reallocations occur in response to policy changes. The sectoral effects on trade flows, output, and employment are of greater relevance than the economywide impact on aggregate welfare. In this section, we discuss three representative experiments (2 and 4) at the sectoral level.

4.2.1. Bilateral Liberalization
Table 2.4 presents the results of bilateral liberalization with constant returns and FDI (experiment 2). A small outward shift in the aggregate production frontier of each country is effected by more dramatic expansions and contractions of individual sectors. The percentage changes in output (column 1) are congruent with each country's prior comparative advantage and protection with the exception of the U.S. aircraft industry. The United States gains

---

[18] These are defined analogously to the trade diversion indices.
[19] The import (export) diversion index would become zero only when bilateral imports (exports) and ROW imports (exports) increase by the same percentages.

Table 2.4. Sectoral results for U.S.–Japan Bilateral Liberalization (percentage changes unless indicated)

	1 X	2 VA	3 ΔVA ($billion)	4 C	5 LD	6 KD	7 KM^b	8 KM^r	9 KE^b	10 KE^r	11 M^b	12 M^r	13 E^b	14 E^r
United States														
1 Cereals	12.0	12.2	2.7	2.0	12.2	12.0					1.9	-4.4	310.6	13.3
2 MeatPoult	1.8	2.0	0.5	0.6	1.9	1.7					11.2	-1.4	81.8	7.2
3 AgForFsh	0.9	1.1	0.4	0.1	1.1	0.9					12.1	1.1	10.1	0.8
4 PetMining	0.3	0.5	0.7	0.1	0.5	0.2	0.6	1.8	0.0	-2.4	1.1	0.6	9.4	-0.7
5 FoodProc	0.7	0.8	0.5	0.4	0.8	0.6	0.1	2.0	0.0	-1.4	5.4	0.6	40.9	-3.1
6 Chemicals	1.1	1.2	0.7	0.5	1.1	0.9	0.0	2.4	0.0	-1.0	4.5	0.8	29.8	-1.9
7 NonDrMfg	0.0	0.1	0.2	0.2	0.1	-0.2	0.1	1.3	0.1	-1.9	28.1	0.2	21.4	-1.7
8 MchPrcIns	-0.2	-0.1	-0.1	0.3	-0.1	-0.4	0.4	1.2	0.4	-2.2	9.2	-0.6	0.1	-0.5
9 ElectAppl	-0.2	-0.1	0.0	2.6	-0.1	-0.5	1.6	1.2	1.7	-2.2	9.1	-0.3	14.4	-0.6
10 CompTelcm	1.5	1.6	0.7	1.5	1.5	1.1	1.4	2.7	1.5	-0.6	6.4	0.0	62.5	-1.1
11 Semicond	0.9	1.0	0.2	1.3	1.0	0.5	1.2	2.1	1.1	-1.5	6.3	0.1	40.1	-2.2
12 Autos	-0.7	-0.6	-0.3	1.5	-0.7	-0.9	4.2	0.8	4.4	-2.3	23.0	-3.0	7.5	-1.0
13 Aircraft	-0.3	-0.2	-0.1	0.0	-0.2	-0.6	-1.0	0.9	-0.7	-2.0	0.9	0.7	-2.3	-0.5
14 OthDurMfg	-0.1	0.0	0.0	0.2	0.0	-0.3	0.4	1.1	0.5	-1.9	5.2	0.3	0.0	-0.3
15 TrComUt	0.2	0.3	1.0	0.0	0.3	0.0	0.0	1.4	0.1	-1.5	1.2	0.7	-0.8	-0.3
16 Trade	0.1	0.2	1.0	0.0	0.2	-0.1	-0.6	1.0	0.0	-1.6	1.6		-1.4	-0.8
17 Services	0.1	0.2	4.7	0.1	0.2	0.0	-0.5	1.3	-0.1	-1.5	1.1	0.6	6.2	-0.4

Japan

	1	2	3	4	5	6	7	8	9	10	11	12	13	14
1 Cereals	-7.2	-6.3	-0.8	2.5	-7.0	-7.2	0.0				310.6	0.0	1.9	1.1
2 MeatPoult	-1.2	-0.3	0.0	0.6	-1.0	-1.2	0.0				81.8	-7.2	11.2	7.5
3 AgForFsh	-0.5	0.4	0.1	-0.3	-0.3	-0.5	0.0				10.1	-1.8	12.1	4.9
4 PetMining	1.1	1.9	0.2	-1.5	1.2	1.0	0.1	2.4	0.6	-0.5	9.4	-0.6	1.1	2.0
5 FoodProc	-0.4	0.4	0.1	0.0	-0.3	-0.5	0.0	1.3	0.1	-1.8	40.9	-2.1	5.4	0.4
6 Chemicals	-0.7	0.2	0.0	0.2	-0.5	-0.8	0.0	1.0	0.0	-2.2	29.8	0.1	4.5	0.1
7 NonDrMfg	0.7	1.5	1.0	-0.2	0.8	0.5	0.1	2.1	0.1	-1.1	21.4	-1.6	28.1	-5.9
8 MchPrcIns	1.6	2.5	1.1	0.5	1.7	1.5	0.4	3.0	0.4	-0.4	0.1	-2.9	9.2	0.7
9 ElectAppl	4.6	5.5	0.5	2.5	4.8	4.4	1.7	5.8	1.6	2.1	14.4	-3.7	9.1	4.8
10 CompTelcm	2.2	3.1	0.4	3.6	2.4	2.0	1.5	3.6	1.4	0.2	62.5	-13.1	6.4	1.3
11 Semicond	2.4	3.3	0.5	0.8	2.6	2.2	1.1	3.7	1.2	0.3	40.1	-7.1	6.3	2.8
12 Autos	11.3	12.2	3.0	6.5	11.5	11.0	4.4	11.6	4.2	7.8	7.5	-4.5	23.0	8.4
13 Aircraft	-0.8	0.0	0.0	-1.8	-0.6	-1.0	-0.7	0.5	-1.0	-2.9	-2.3	-3.3	0.9	1.1
14 OthDurMfg	1.6	2.5	2.1	-0.9	1.8	1.5	0.5	2.9	0.4	-0.4	0.0	-2.2	5.2	1.7
15 TrComUt	0.2	1.1	1.3	-0.8	0.3	0.1	0.1	1.6	0.0	-1.4	-0.8	-1.1	1.2	1.7
16 Trade	-0.1	0.7	1.1	-0.9	0.0	-0.4	0.0	1.6	-0.6	-2.2	-1.4	-1.8	1.6	3.0
17 Services	-0.3	0.5	3.0	-0.7	-0.2	-0.5	-0.1	1.3	-0.5	-2.3	6.2	-1.8	1.1	1.5

Definition of variables: (1) real output, (2) nominal value-added, (3) changes in nominal value-added in billions of US dollars, (4) real consumption, (5) labor demand, (6) composite capital demand, (7) stock of inward FDI from the bilateral partner, (8) stock of inward FDI from ROW, (9) stock of outward FDI to the bilateral market, (10) stock of outward FDI to ROW, (11) bilateral imports, (12) ROW imports, (13) bilateral exports, and (14) ROW exports.

most in agriculture, followed by computers and telecommunications equipment, chemicals, semiconductors, and food processing. Real output contracts slightly in automobiles, aircraft, machinery and precision instruments, electric appliances, and other durable manufactures. The output growth of the expanding sectors is largely driven by new export demand induced by the removal of Japanese trade barriers, which would eventually lead to real income and consumption gains for the U.S. economy. As industries compete for scarce resources, the sectors with small export expansion could experience a decline in demand for labor and capital, however. Because Japan has no trade barriers on aircraft, the relative demand for U.S. aircraft declines, inducing a movement of labor and capital out of the aircraft industry. Thus changing trade regimes might put industries with comparative advantage on the defensive as other sectors contend for limited labor and capital to meet new export opportunities.

In Japan, agriculture contracts as expected, but the extent of contraction is small relative to the magnitude of prior protection. The removal of import barriers on rice and wheat reduces domestic cereal output by only 7.2 percent.[20] Nevertheless, the effect on the output composition for Japanese sectors is more distinct. The big winner in Japan is the automobile sector, which experiences an 11.3 percent gain in real output, followed by the high-technology (sectors 9–11) and durable manufacturing sectors (8 and 14), while the food processing, chemical, aircraft, and service sectors contract, like agriculture.

The changes in value-added (columns 2 and 3) indicate "effective liberalization" effects. In every sector, value-added effects exceed output effects because the overall increase in output bids up factor prices. The absolute change figures in column 3 show that the gains from expanding sectors far outweigh the income losses of those which contract.

The differential impact on real consumption (column 4) stems from the bilateral disparity in trade barriers and the distinctive effects of liberalization on relative prices. Because U.S. protection is more uniform, relative prices change much less and real consumption changes more uniformly, rising in every sector. In con-

---

[20] This is largely a consequence of limited substitutability of rice varieties in the Japanese diet, low import dependence on cereals, and positive Japanese income effects resulting from liberalization.

trast, the composition of real consumption in Japan shifts substantially in favor of tradeables in general, and agricultural products in particular.

Adjustments in sectoral employment of labor and capital services (columns 5 and 6) are consistent with output changes, but trade in capital services exhibits a more complex adjustment pattern. Intraindustry FDI is pervasive between the United States and Japan, particularly in the automobile and high-technology sectors (columns 7 and 9). Although foreigners increase direct investment in the United States and Japan (column 8), both countries reduce their direct investment in ROW (column 10), with the exception of the Japanese automobile, electric appliance, computers and telecommunications equipment, and semiconductor industries. These trends represent investment diversion away from the status quo ROW to more productive operations in the United States and Japan.

Why do inward and outward FDIs occur at the same time in some sectors? In the automobile industry, for example, U.S. and ROW firms increase their direct investment in Japan while Japanese firms increase their direct investment in the U.S. and ROW (row 12, columns 7–10 in the bottom panel). The removal of voluntary export restraints increases Japanese exports of automobiles, raising the sectoral rate of return on investment and capital stock sharply. An increase in the rate of return in the Japanese auto sector attracts foreign capital, from both the United States (KM^b) and ROW (KM^r). An increase in the rate of return on domestic investment relative to direct investment abroad increases the ratio of domestic capital stock (KD) to the stock of outward FDI (KE). When the composite capital increases substantially, as in the Japanese auto sector, KE may increase although by less proportionally than the increase in KD.[21]

The last four columns of Table 2.4 detail trade flow adjustments, which have important effects on other sectoral adjustments. Bilateral trade (columns 11 and 13) changes much more in magnitude and often differs in direction from its ROW counterpart (12 and 14). When both bilateral and ROW trade flows expand from liber-

---

[21] In the model, the elasticity of transformation between domestic capital and exported capital is set equal to 5.0. Bilateral liberalization leads to a 0.8 percent increase in r_D/r_E for the Japanese automobile sector, which causes a 4.0 percent increase in the KD/KE ratio.

alization, trade creation dominates trade diversion. Because of the higher base-year protection levels in Japan for many products, Japanese imports from the United States and U.S. exports to Japan increase substantially after bilateral liberalization. Large changes in the bilateral to ROW import and export price ratios cause Japanese imports from ROW and U.S. exports to ROW to decline in many product categories, leading to large import diversion for Japan and large export diversion for the United States.

Comparisons of columns 7 and 11 and columns 9 and 13 show that bilateral commodity and capital trade are complements in all U.S. and Japanese manufacturing sectors except aircraft. Although complementarity with ROW is much less pervasive, bilateral liberalization without restrictions on FDI increases sector-specific bilateral capital flows in both directions. The increase in sectoral capital stock resulting from inward FDI raises labor productivity, generating a greater welfare gain than under restricted international capital mobility. This result suggests that if both governments could agree upon a cooperative investment policy, both could attain a higher level of welfare.

4.2.2. Nondiscriminatory Liberalization
Table 2.5 presents the results of removing U.S. and Japanese protection on imports from all sources (nondiscriminatory liberalization). The Japanese cereal sector would contract by 22.6 percent and the meat and poultry sector by 11.6 percent (column 1).[22] At the same time, however, the opportunity cost of protecting these sectors is quite high as Japanese manufacturing sectors would expand at a considerably greater rate than realized under bilateral liberalization. Large expansions in the automobile, electric appliance, and semiconductor sectors would also induce a substantial increase in demands for intermediate goods. Lower import prices of intermediate goods strengthen international competitiveness of many Japanese sectors and promote exports to both the United States and ROW.

---

[22] The percentage increase in Japan's agricultural imports from ROW (row 11) is considerably larger than those from the United States (row 12) because ROW's import supply function is more elastic than that of the United States. When lower values of ROW import supply elasticities are calibrated, the percentage increase in Japanese imports from ROW and those from the United States become comparable.

Production sectors in the United States enjoy more uniform gains, and free trade might thus appear easier to implement, but these results are of course predicated on Japanese liberalization. Under nondiscriminatory liberalization, the U.S. cereal sector would expand 12.6 percent. Output and value-added would decrease only in nondurable manufactures (which includes textiles and apparel), but the contraction is dwarfed by the expansion of output and value-added elsewhere in the economy. In service-oriented sectors (15–17), the increase in value-added is particularly large, amounting to 36.3 billion 1985 dollars. In addition, the sectors expected to contract under bilateral liberalization (machinery and precision instrument, electric appliances, automobiles, aircraft, and other durable manufactures) expand in this experiment, driven by the increase in domestic income and consumption. An increase in output of automobiles is also facilitated by a sharp increase in Japanese FDI (column 7).

These results also exhibit complementarity between trade in goods and capital services in several sectors. For high-technology sectors (9–11), both types of flows increase with both the bilateral partner and ROW (i.e., KM^b, KM^r, KE^b, KE^r, M^b, M^r, E^b, and E^r all increase). Only in Japanese food processing, chemicals, and nondurable manufactures, commodity trade and FDI are substitutes. In many sectors, both inward FDI and outward FDI increase in both countries, contributing to additional employment opportunities for domestic workers and providing income opportunities for domestic investors.

5. CONCLUSIONS

Noncooperative trade practices, such as import protection, most often arise to serve specific interests. The impediments they exert on economic efficiency, resource allocation, and the course of growth can be much more pervasive, however. In this chapter, we have used a general equilibrium framework to evaluate bilateral import protection between the two largest industrialized economies, the United States and Japan. Our results confirm that the opportunity costs of sector-specific protection are not trivial and exceed the benefits conferred by trade restraints.

For its part, the United States apparently has an interest in more, not less, liberal trade relations with Japan. Individual cries

Table 2.5. Sectoral results for U.S. and Japanese Liberalization on a Nondiscriminatory Basis (percentage changes unless indicated)

	1 X	2 VA	3 ΔVA ($billion)	4 C	5 LD	6 KD	7 KM^b	8 KM^r	9 KE^b	10 KE^r	11 M^b	12 M^r	13 E^b	14 E^r
United States														
1 Cereals	12.6	13.9	3.1	2.1	13.4	12.5					5.2	-6.3	297.7	21.0
2 MeatPoult	2.1	2.9	0.8	0.8	2.4	1.6					20.7	4.4	59.8	19.4
3 AgForFsh	0.2	1.2	0.4	0.8	0.7	-0.1					15.6	8.5	6.3	11.9
4 PetMining	1.1	2.2	2.9	-0.4	1.9	0.8	1.2	1.0	0.9	0.6	2.1	-1.2	3.5	5.5
5 FoodProc	1.4	2.3	1.3	1.0	1.9	1.0	0.2	1.1	-0.2	0.9	5.8	1.7	34.1	3.3
6 Chemicals	1.2	2.0	1.2	1.4	1.6	0.6	-0.2	0.7	-0.6	0.4	3.6	-0.1	24.9	2.9
7 NonDrMfg	-3.7	-3.0	-5.2	2.9	-3.4	-4.6	-2.4	-4.2	-2.6	-4.7	17.3	36.8	16.6	-1.6
8 MchPrcIns	0.7	1.4	1.5	1.5	0.9	0.1	3.1	0.3	3.0	0.0	10.2	4.5	-7.5	4.3
9 ElectAppl	1.6	2.4	0.2	6.6	2.2	0.7	7.8	1.4	7.2	0.6	18.7	1.6	5.7	6.4
10 CompTelcm	3.4	4.0	1.8	3.2	3.6	2.1	4.0	2.3	3.7	2.0	10.6	1.5	48.5	3.6
11 Semicond	3.6	4.2	0.7	3.5	3.8	2.4	5.9	2.7	5.5	2.2	10.0	0.7	28.3	5.6
12 Autos	1.9	2.6	1.2	3.0	2.1	0.8	11.5	1.7	10.8	1.0	37.0	-7.9	1.4	8.3
13 Aircraft	3.2	3.8	1.2	0.6	3.3	1.8	-0.1	1.9	-0.3	1.4	2.6	-7.2	-6.6	8.2
14 OthDurMfg	1.0	1.8	2.9	0.5	1.3	0.3	3.3	0.7	2.8	0.2	8.3	-1.0	-8.8	4.5
15 TrComUt	0.8	1.6	6.0	0.1	1.2	0.2	1.0	0.4	0.7	0.1	4.6	-4.8	-3.5	5.8
16 Trade	0.6	1.3	5.6	0.2	0.9	-0.1	0.1	0.0	-0.3	-0.3	6.6		-4.0	10.8
17 Services	0.5	1.3	24.7	0.3	0.9	-0.1	-0.5	-0.1	-0.8	-0.3	4.8	-5.3	1.0	5.9

Japan

	1	2	3	4	5	6	7	8	9	10	11	12	13	14
1 Cereals	-22.6	-20.2	-2.7	9.0	-22.1	-22.7					297.7	501.0	5.2	18.2
2 MeatPoult	-11.6	-9.0	-0.5	4.2	-11.2	-11.8					59.8	113.8	20.7	39.8
3 AgForFsh	-2.7	0.3	0.1	-0.5	-2.1	-2.8					6.3	3.6	15.6	25.7
4 PetMining	1.5	4.5	0.4	-1.1	2.1	1.2	0.9	0.6	1.2	1.6	3.5	1.9	2.1	14.7
5 FoodProc	-1.0	1.8	0.5	1.5	-0.7	-1.4	-0.2	-1.7	0.2	-0.5	34.1	53.0	5.8	11.6
6 Chemicals	-1.4	1.5	0.3	2.8	-0.9	-1.8	-0.6	-2.1	-0.2	-0.9	24.9	39.4	3.6	8.7
7 NonDrMfg	0.6	3.4	2.2	0.2	1.0	-0.1	-2.6	-1.1	-2.4	-0.4	16.6	29.2	17.3	2.8
8 MchPrcIns	7.1	10.1	4.5	2.5	7.5	6.6	3.0	5.5	3.1	6.2	-7.5	-13.8	10.2	16.5
9 ElectAppl	16.6	19.9	1.9	9.7	17.4	15.8	7.2	13.6	7.8	14.9	5.7	4.9	18.7	29.3
10 CompTelcm	6.6	9.6	1.2	8.0	7.3	5.8	3.7	4.9	4.0	5.9	48.5	105.2	10.6	16.9
11 Semicond	10.5	13.7	1.9	5.2	11.2	9.7	5.5	8.4	5.9	9.5	28.3	56.4	10.0	22.0
12 Autos	25.0	28.6	7.0	13.6	25.8	24.0	10.8	20.8	11.5	22.5	1.4	-3.4	37.0	33.3
13 Aircraft	-2.0	0.7	0.0	-5.4	-1.4	-2.7	-0.3	-2.5	-0.1	-1.9	-6.6	-17.6	2.6	17.2
14 OthDurMfg	7.0	10.0	8.3	-0.9	7.4	6.4	2.8	5.0	3.3	6.1	-8.8	-17.3	8.3	13.8
15 TrComUt	2.1	4.9	6.3	-1.8	2.5	1.5	0.7	0.8	1.0	1.8	-3.5	-8.9	4.6	15.8
16 Trade	0.4	3.1	5.0	-2.5	0.6	-0.3	-0.3	-0.9	0.1	0.4	-4.0	-12.3	6.6	26.9
17 Services	-0.8	1.9	11.6	-2.1	-0.4	-1.4	-0.8	-1.8	-0.5	-0.7	1.0	-2.0	4.8	16.7

See Table 2.4 for the definition of variables.

for protection from rising Japanese import shares ignore the general welfare and expansionary opportunities that would follow from more cooperative policies. The main opportunity cost of U.S. and Japanese protection is not a lower volume of imports and higher import prices for a few products but rather a trade-driven expansion of domestic demand, which would increase real output in a wide range of activities. The gains from this commodity liberalization would be even greater if another dissonant voice, that crying out against foreign investment, went unheeded. Freer trade in capital services in both directions benefits the United States and Japan by increasing the flexibility of their adjustment to the evolving opportunities of the international economy.

The results obtained in this study support theoretical findings on the complementarity between commodity and factor service trade. In the aggregate, capital mobility increases the welfare gains that accrue from liberalization. At the sectoral level, the interplay between FDI and trade pattern adjustments is more complex. However, our experiments show that an increase in intraindustry trade in both commodities and factor services would enlarge the scope for gains from trade. Both countries are more likely to share in balanced expansion because the required degree of international specialization to achieve relative cost parities is reduced.

The trading relationship between the United States and Japan has been one of the world's largest and most dynamic in the last half century. Despite its uneven political history, the economic partnership still confers immense prosperity on both countries and their neighbors in the Pacific Basin. This vast region has been dubbed the economy of the twenty-first century, but it is unlikely to realize its full potential unless its two largest economies achieve more harmonious and efficient trade relations.

REFERENCES

Anderson, Kym, and Rod Tyers (1987), "Japan's Agricultural Policy in International Perspective," *Journal of the Japanese and International Economies*, 1: 131–146.

Brown, Drusilla K., and Robert M. Stern (1989), "U.S.–Canada Bilateral Tariff Elimination: The Role of Product Differentiation and Market Structure," in F. C. Feenstra, ed., *Trade Policies for International Competitiveness*, Chicago: University of Chicago Press and National Bureau of Economic Research.

Christelow, Dorothy (1985/86), "Japan's Intangible Barriers to Trade in Manufactures," Federal Reserve Bank of New York *Quarterly Review* (Winter), 11–18.

Francois, Joseph F., Bradley McDonald, and Håkan Nordström (1995), "Assessing the Uruguay Round," paper presented at the Conference on The Uruguay Round and the Developing Countries, World Bank, Washington, DC, January 26–27.

Glick, Reuven (1991), "Japanese Capital Flows in the 1980s," Federal Reserve Bank of San Francisco *Economic Review* (Spring), 18–31.

Goldin, Ian, Odin Knudsen, and Dominique van der Mensbrugghe (1993), *Trade Liberalization: Global Economic Implications*, Paris and Washington, DC: OECD and World Bank.

Harris, Richard G. (1984), "Applied General Equilibrium Analysis of Small Open Economies with Scale Economies and Imperfect Competition," *American Economic Review*, 74: 1017–1032.

Harrison, Glenn W., Thomas F. Rutherford, and David G. Tar (1995), "Quantifying the Uruguay Round," paper presented at the Conference on The Uruguay Round and the Developing Countries, World Bank, Washington, DC, January 26–27.

Hertel, Thomas W., ed. (1997), *Global Trade Analysis: Modeling and Applications*, Cambridge: Cambridge University Press.

Howell, Thomas R., Brent L. Bartlett, and Warren Davis (1992), *Creating Advantage: Semiconductors and Government Industrial Policy in the 1990s*, San Jose: Semiconductor Industry Association.

Hufbauer, Gary C., and Kimberly A. Elliot (1994), *Measuring the Costs of Protection in the United States*, Washington, DC: Institute for International Economics.

Johnson, Chalmers, Laura D'Andrea Tyson, and John Zysman, eds. (1989), *Politics and Productivity: The Real Story of Why Japan Works*, Cambridge: Ballinger.

Lee, Hiro (1993), "General Equilibrium Evaluation of Industrial Policy in Japan," *Journal of Asian Economics*, 4: 25–40.

Lee, Hiro, and David Roland-Holst (1993), "Cooperation or Confrontation in U.S.–Japan Trade? Some General Equilibrium Estimates," Irvine Economics Paper No. 92–93-08, University of California, Irvine, March.

Markusen, James R. (1983), "Factor Movements and Commodity Trade as Complements," *Journal of International Economics*, 14: 341–356.

Markusen, James R., and Lars E. O. Svensson (1985), "Trade in Goods and Factors with International Differences in Technology," *International Economic Review*, 26: 175–192.

Melo, Jaime de, and David Roland-Holst (1994), "Tariffs and Export Subsidies when Domestic Markets Are Oligopolistic: Korea," in J. Mercenier and T. N. Srinivasan, eds., *Applied General Equilibrium and Economic Development*, Ann Arbor: University of Michigan Press.

Melo, Jaime de, and David Tarr (1992), *A General Equilibrium Analysis of U.S. Foreign Trade Policy*, Cambridge: MIT Press.

MITI (1989), *The 1985 Japan–U.S. Input–Output Table*, Tokyo: Ministry of International Trade and Industry.

Mundell, Robert A. (1957), "International Trade and Factor Mobility," *American Economic Review*, 47: 321–335.

Neary, J. Peter, and Frances Ruane (1988), "International Capital Mobility, Shadow Prices, and the Cost of Protection," *International Economic Review*, 29: 571–585.

Neven, Damien J. (1990), "Gains and Losses from 1992," *Economic Policy*, April, 13–61.

Nogues, Julio J., Andrzej Olechowski, and L. Alan Winters (1986), "The Extent of Nontariff Barriers to Industrial Countries' Imports," World Bank Staff Working Paper No. 789, Washington, DC: World Bank.

Petri, Peter A. (1984), *Modeling Japanese–American Trade: A Study of Asymmetric Interdependence*, Cambridge: Harvard University Press.

Pratten, C. (1988), "A Survey of the Economies of Scale," in *Research on the Cost of Non-Europe*, Vol. 2, Brussels: Commission of the European Communities.

Reinert, Kenneth A., and David Roland-Holst (1991), "Parameter Estimates for U.S. Trade-Policy Analysis," Washington, DC: U.S. International Trade Commission, April.

Sazanami, Yoko, Shujiro Urata, and Hiroki Kawai (1995), *Measuring the Costs of Protection in Japan*, Washington, DC: Institute for International Economics.

Stone, J. A. (1979), "Price Elasticities of Demand for Imports and Exports: Industry Estimates for the U.S., E.E.C. and Japan," *Review of Economics and Statistics*, 61: 306–312.

Tsujimura, K., and M. Kuroda (1974), *Nihon Keizai no Ippan Kinko Bunseki* [General Equilibrium Analysis of the Japanese Economy], Tokyo: Tsukuma Shobo.

U.S. Congress (1991), *Reviewing Structural Impediments Initiative (SII)*, Hearing before the Subcommittee on International Trade of the Committee on Finance, United States Senate, One Hundred Second Congress, first session, April 15.

USITC (1990), "Estimated Tariff Equivalents of U.S. Quotas on Agricultural Imports and Analysis of Competitive Conditions in U.S. and Foreign Markets for Sugar, Meat, Peanuts, Cotton, and Dairy Products," USITC Publication 2276, Washington, DC: U.S. International Trade Commission.

Wong, Kar-Yiu (1986), "Are International Trade and Factor Mobility Substitutes?" *Journal of International Economics*, 21: 25–43.

(1995), *International Trade in Goods and Factor Mobility*, Cambridge: MIT Press.

APPENDIX A: EQUATIONS OF THE U.S.–JAPAN CGE MODEL

I. COUNTRY-SPECIFIC EQUATIONS

Consumer Behavior

$$C_i = LES_C\left(P_Q, Y\right) \tag{A2.1}$$

Production Technology

$$X_i = \min\left[CES_X\left(LD_i, KD_i; \phi_i\right), V_{l_i}/a_{l_i}, \ldots, V_{n_i}/a_{n_i}\right] \tag{A2.2}$$

Commodity Demands, Supplies, and Allocation of Traded Goods

$$Q_i = CES_Q\left(D_{D_i}, M_i; \sigma_i\right) \tag{A2.3}$$

$$D_{D_i}/M_i = f^1\left(P_{D_i}/P_{M_i}; \sigma_i\right) \tag{A2.4}$$

$$M_i = CES_M\left(M_i^b, M_i^r; \mu_i\right) \tag{A2.5}$$

$$M_i^b/M_i^r = f^2\left(P_{M_i}^b/P_{M_i}^r; \mu_i\right) \tag{A2.6}$$

$$X_i = CET_X\left(D_{S_i}, E_i; \tau_i\right) \tag{A2.7}$$

$$D_{S_i}/E_i = g^1\left(P_{D_i}/P_{E_i}; \tau_i\right) \tag{A2.8}$$

$$E_i = CET_E\left(E_i^b, E_i^r; \upsilon_i\right) \tag{A2.9}$$

$$E_i^b/E_i^r = g^2\left(P_{E_i}^b/P_{E_i}^r; \upsilon_i\right) \tag{A2.10}$$

Commodity Prices

$$P_{Q_i}Q_i = P_{D_i}D_{D_i} + P_{M_i}M_i \tag{A2.11}$$

$$P_{X_i}X_i = P_{D_i}D_{S_i} + P_{E_i}E_i \tag{A2.12}$$

Factor Demands

$$LD_i/KD_i = \psi\left(w/r_{Q_i};\ \phi_i\right) \tag{A2.13}$$

$$KD_i = CES_{KD}\left(KD_{D_i},\ KM_i;\ \eta_i\right) \tag{A2.14}$$

$$KD_{D_i}/KM_i = h^1\left(r_{D_i}/r_{M_i};\ \eta_i\right) \tag{A2.15}$$

$$KM_i = CES_{KM}\left(KM_i^b,\ KM_i^r;\ \zeta_i\right) \tag{A2.16}$$

$$KM_i^b/KM_i^r = h^2\left(r_{M_i}^b/r_{M_i}^r;\ \zeta_i\right) \tag{A2.17}$$

Factor Supplies

$$LS = LES_L\left(w,\ Y\right) \tag{A2.18}$$

$$KS_i = CET_{KS}\left(KD_{S_i},\ KE_i;\ \varkappa_i\right) \tag{A2.19}$$

$$KD_{S_i}/KE_i = k^1\left(r_{D_i}/r_{E_i};\ \varkappa_i\right) \tag{A2.20}$$

$$KE_i = CET_{KE}\left(KE_i^b,\ KE_i^r;\ \lambda_i\right) \tag{A2.21}$$

$$KE_i^b/KE_i^r = k^2\left(r_{E_i}^b/r_{E_i}^r;\ \lambda_i\right) \tag{A2.22}$$

Rental Rate on Capital

$$r_{Q_i}KD_i = r_{D_i}KD_{D_i} + r_{M_i}KM_i \tag{A2.23}$$

$$r_{X_i}KS_i = r_{D_i}KD_{S_i} + r_{E_i}KE_i \tag{A2.24}$$

Domestic Market Equilibrium

$$Q_i = C_i + \Sigma_j a_{ij}X_j \tag{A2.25}$$

$$D_{S_i} = D_{D_i} \tag{A2.26}$$

$$LS = \Sigma_i LD_i \tag{A2.27}$$

$$KD_{S_i} = KD_{D_i} \tag{A2.28}$$

Income and Government Revenue

$$Y = \left(1 - t_L\right)\sum_i wLD_i + \left(1 - t_K\right)\sum_i r_{Q_i} KD_i + Y_G$$
$$+ \sum_i \left[\left(1 - \theta_i^b\right)PREM_i^b + \left(1 - \theta_i^r\right)PREM_i^r\right] \tag{A2.29}$$

$$Y_G = t_L \sum_i wLD_i + t_K \sum_i r_{Q_i} KD_i + \sum_i t_{D_i} P_{X_i} X_i$$
$$+ e^b \sum_i \left(t_{M_i}^b \pi_{M_i}^b M_i^b - t_{E_i}^b \pi_{E_i}^b E_i^b\right) + e^r \sum_i \left(t_{M_i}^r \pi_{M_i}^r M_i^r - t_{E_i}^r \pi_{E_i}^r E_i^r\right) \tag{A2.30}$$

$$PREM_i^b = e^b \varrho_i^b \left(1 + t_{M_i}^b\right)\pi_{M_i}^b M_i^b \tag{A2.31}$$

$$PREM_i^r = e^r \varrho_i^r \left(1 + t_{M_i}^r\right)\pi_{M_i}^r M_i^r \tag{A2.32}$$

Balance of Payments

$$\sum_i \left[\left(e^b \pi_{E_i}^b E_i^b + e^r \pi_{E_i}^r E_i^r\right) - \left(e^b \pi_{M_i}^b M_i^b + e^r \pi_{M_i}^r M_i^r\right)\right]$$
$$+ \sum_i \left[\left(r_{E_i}^b KE_i^b + r_{E_i}^r KE_i^r\right) - \left(r_{M_i}^b KM_i^b + r_{M_i}^r KM_i^r\right)\right]$$
$$+ B - \sum_i \left(\theta_i^b PREM_i^b + \theta_i^r PREM_i^r\right) = 0 \tag{A2.33}$$

Foreign Commodity Prices

$$P_{M_i} M_i = P_{M_i}^b M_i^b + P_{M_i}^r M_i^r \tag{A2.34}$$

$$P_{E_i} E_i = P_{E_i}^b E_i^b + P_{E_i}^r E_i^r \tag{A2.35}$$

$$P_{M_i}^b = \left(1 + t_{M_i}^b\right)\left(1 + \varrho_i^b\right)e^b \pi_{M_i}^b \tag{A2.36}$$

$$P_{M_i}^r = \left(1 + t_{M_i}^r\right)\left(1 + \varrho_i^r\right)e^r \pi_{M_i}^r \tag{A2.37}$$

$$P_{E_i}^b = \left(1 + t_{E_i}^b\right)e^b \pi_{E_i}^b \tag{A2.38}$$

$$P^r_{E_i} = \left(1 + t^r_{E_i}\right)e^r \pi^r_{E_i} \tag{A2.39}$$

$$P^r_{M_i} = \left[M^r_i / M0^r_i\right]^{1/\zeta_i} \tag{A2.40}$$

$$P^r_{E_i} = \left[E^r_i / E0^r_i\right]^{-1/\omega_i} \tag{A2.41}$$

Numéraire

$$P_{GDP} = 1 \tag{A2.42}$$

II. BILATERAL EQUATIONS

Trade Flow Equivalence

$$E^b_i\left(\text{U.S.}\right) = M^b_i\left(\text{Japan}\right) \tag{A2.43}$$

$$E^b_i\left(\text{Japan}\right) = M^b_i\left(\text{United States}\right) \tag{A2.44}$$

FDI Stock Equivalence

$$KE^b_i\left(\text{U.S.}\right) = KM^b_i\left(\text{Japan}\right) \tag{A2.45}$$

$$KE^b_i\left(\text{Japan}\right) = KM^b_i\left(\text{United States}\right) \tag{A2.46}$$

Trade Price Equivalence

$$\pi^b_{E_i}\left(\text{U.S.}\right) = \pi^b_{M_i}\left(\text{Japan}\right) \tag{A2.47}$$

$$\pi^b_{E_i}\left(\text{Japan}\right) = \pi^b_{M_i}\left(\text{United States}\right) \tag{A2.48}$$

$$r^b_{E_i}\left(\text{U.S.}\right) = e^b\left(\text{United States}\right)r^b_{M_i}\left(\text{Japan}\right) \tag{A2.49}$$

$$r^b_{E_i}\left(\text{Japan}\right) = e^b\left(\text{Japan}\right)r^b_{M_i}\left(\text{United States}\right) \tag{A2.50}$$

Exchange Rate Arbitrage

$$e^r\left(\text{U.S.}\right) = e^b\left(\text{United States}\right)e^r\left(\text{Japan}\right) \tag{A2.51}$$

III. DEFINITION OF VARIABLES AND PARAMETERS

Price Variables

e^b	Real bilateral exchange rate (domestic/foreign currency)
e^r	Real ROW exchange rate (domestic/foreign currency)
P_{D_i}	Domestic purchaser prices of domestic goods
P_{E_i}	Domestic prices of exports
$P^b_{E_i}$	Domestic prices of bilateral exports
$P^r_{E_i}$	Domestic prices of ROW exports
P_{M_i}	Domestic prices of imports
$P^b_{M_i}$	Domestic prices of bilateral imports
$P^r_{M_i}$	Domestic prices of ROW imports
P_{Q_i}	Purchaser prices of composite domestic demand
P_{X_i}	Producer prices of domestic output
P_{GDP}	GDP price deflator (fixed)
$\pi^b_{M_i}$	World prices of bilateral imports
$\pi^r_{M_i}$	World prices of ROW imports
$\pi^b_{E_i}$	World prices of bilateral exports
$\pi^r_{E_i}$	World prices of ROW exports
r_{D_i}	Rental rates on domestic capital
r_{E_i}	Rental rates on capital outflow
$r^b_{E_i}$	Rental rates on bilateral capital outflow
$r^r_{E_i}$	Rental rates on ROW capital outflow
r_{M_i}	Rental rates on capital inflow
$r^b_{M_i}$	Rental rates on bilateral capital inflow
$r^r_{M_i}$	Rental rates on ROW capital inflow
r_{Q_i}	Rental rates on composite capital demand
r_{X_i}	Rental rates on composite capital supply
w	Average wage rate

Quantity Variables

C_i	Personal consumption
D_{D_i}	Domestic demand for domestic goods
D_{S_i}	Domestic production for domestic use
E_i	Total sectoral exports
E^b_i	Commodity exports to bilateral partner
E^r_i	Commodity exports to ROW
$E0^r_i$	Commodity exports to ROW in base year (fixed)
KD_i	Composite capital for domestic service (domestic capital and inward FDI stock)

KS_i	Supply of composite capital (domestic capital and outward FDI stock)
KD_{D_i}	Demand for domestic capital
KD_{S_i}	Supply of domestic capital
KE_i	Stock of composite outward FDI
KE_i^b	Stock of outward FDI to bilateral market
KE_i^r	Stock of outward FDI to ROW
KM_i	Demand for foreign capital
KM_i^b	Stock of inward FDI from bilateral partner
KM_i^r	Stock of inward FDI from ROW
LD_i	Demand for labor
LS	Aggregate labor supply
M_i	Total sectoral imports
M_i^b	Commodity imports from the bilateral partner
M_i^r	Commodity imports from ROW
$M0_i^r$	Commodity imports from ROW in base year (fixed)
Q_i	Composite goods for domestic consumption
V_{ji}	Demand for intermediate good j in sector i
X_i	Gross domestic output

Nominal Variables

B	Net foreign remittances and savings (exogenous)
$PREM_i^b$	Premium income on constrained bilateral imports
$PREM_i^r$	Premium income on constrained ROW imports
Y	Nominal domestic income
Y_G	Government income

Structural and Policy Parameters

a_{ij}	Intermediate use coefficients (Leontief technology)
ϕ_i	Elasticities of substitution between labor and capital in domestic production
η_i	Elasticities of substitution between domestic and imported capital
ξ_i	Elasticities of substitution between bilateral and ROW imported capital
$\varkappa_i$	Elasticities of transformation between domestic and exported capital
λ_i	Elasticities of transformation between bilateral and ROW exported capital
σ_i	Elasticities of substitution between domestic and imported products
μ_i	Elasticities of substitution between bilateral and ROW imported products
τ_i	Elasticities of transformation between domestic and exported products
υ_i	Elasticities of transformation between bilateral and ROW exported products
ϱ_i^b	Ad valorem equivalents of constrained bilateral imports
ϱ_i^r	Ad valorem equivalents of constrained ROW imports
θ_i^b	Premium repatriation rates on constrained bilateral imports
θ_i^r	Premium repatriation rates on constrained ROW imports
ξ_i	ROW import supply elasticities
ω_i	ROW export demand elasticities

t_{D_i}	Indirect tax rates on domestic sector production
t_K	Tax rate on capital income
t_L	Tax rate on labor income
$t_{M_i}^b$	Bilateral import tariff rates
$t_{M_i}^r$	ROW import tariff rates
$t_{E_i}^b$	Bilateral export subsidy rates
$t_{E_i}^r$	ROW export subsidy rates

Functional Forms

LES	linear expenditure system
	e.g., $LES_C(\cdot) = a_i + (b_i/P_{Q_i})(Y - \Sigma_i a_i P_{Q_i})$. a_i, b_i: constants
CES	constant elasticity of substitution
	e.g., $CES_Q(\cdot) = A_Q[\alpha M^{(\sigma-1)/\sigma} + (1 - \alpha)D_D^{(\sigma-1)/\sigma}]^{\sigma/(\sigma-1)}$. A_Q, a: constants
CET	constant elasticity of transformation
	e.g., $CET_X(\cdot) = A_X[\beta E^{(\tau+1)/\tau} + (1 - \beta)D_S^{(\tau+1)/\tau}]^{\tau/(\tau+1)}$. A_X, b: constants
$\psi(\cdot)$	the first-order condition for CES_X
$f^1(\cdot)$	the first-order condition for CES_Q
$f^2(\cdot)$	the first-order condition for CES_M
$g^1(\cdot)$	the first-order condition for CET_X
$g^2(\cdot)$	the first-order condition for CET_E
$h^1(\cdot)$	the first-order condition for CES_{KD}
$h^2(\cdot)$	the first-order condition for CES_{KM}
$k^1(\cdot)$	the first-order condition for CET_{KS}
$k^2(\cdot)$	the first-order condition for CET_{KE}

APPENDIX B: KEY MODEL PARAMETER VALUES

	σ	τ	μ	υ	ξ	ω	ϕ
United States							
1 Cereals	2.00	2.00	1.99	2.00	100.00	3.00	1.19
2 MeatPoult	2.00	2.00	1.96	2.00	17.79	100.00	1.19
3 AgForFsh	1.70	2.20	1.50	2.00	99.97	21.89	1.19
4 PetMining	0.65	0.91	0.58	2.00	16.20	43.65	1.48
5 FoodProc	1.55	0.73	1.49	2.00	66.30	66.90	1.19
6 Chemicals	0.94	0.64	1.56	2.00	91.48	22.58	1.47
7 NonDrMfg	1.70	0.56	2.34	2.00	53.92	43.58	1.75
8 MchPrcIns	1.23	0.58	1.92	2.00	33.98	15.41	1.28
9 ElecAppl	1.65	0.77	1.82	2.00	13.49	48.78	2.15
10 CompTelcm	1.49	0.58	1.77	2.00	5.53	2.04	2.15
11 Semicond	1.56	0.58	1.64	2.00	3.85	23.86	2.15
12 Autos	2.12	1.03	2.84	2.00	5.00	10.00	2.15
13 Aircraft	1.62	1.22	1.50	2.00	63.35	5.56	2.15
14 OthDurMfg	1.58	0.46	2.12	2.00	45.09	15.45	1.43

	σ	τ	μ	υ	ξ	ω	φ
15 TrComUt	1.25	1.00	1.85	2.00	100.00	100.00	1.49
16 Trade	1.90	2.00	2.41	2.00	100.00	100.00	1.49
17 Services	1.30	1.00	1.90	2.00	100.00	100.00	1.49
Japan							
1 Cereals	1.59	2.00	1.28	2.00	5.00	100.00	1.19
2 MeatPoult	2.19	2.00	2.00	2.00	45.92	100.00	1.19
3 AgForFsh	1.22	2.14	0.99	2.00	100.00	100.00	1.19
4 PetMining	2.24	0.88	1.32	2.00	8.85	100.00	1.48
5 FoodProc	1.04	0.73	1.00	2.00	100.00	100.00	1.19
6 Chemicals	1.55	0.66	1.13	2.00	97.76	62.15	1.47
7 NonDrMfg	1.67	0.36	1.21	2.00	68.05	38.85	1.75
8 MchPrcIns	1.49	0.54	1.17	2.00	89.82	11.87	1.28
9 ElecAppl	1.46	0.89	2.10	2.00	75.99	6.08	2.15
10 CompTelcm	1.49	0.58	1.99	2.00	56.40	8.77	2.15
11 Semicond	1.48	0.58	2.03	2.00	20.69	13.66	2.15
12 Autos	1.68	1.03	1.45	2.00	100.00	5.07	2.15
13 Aircraft	2.39	1.22	1.43	2.00	100.00	100.00	2.15
14 OthDurMfg	2.28	0.48	1.43	2.00	29.46	7.32	1.43
15 TrComUt	0.89	1.00	1.25	2.00	100.00	100.00	1.49
16 Trade	2.03	2.00	1.69	2.00	100.00	100.00	1.49
17 Services	0.84	1.00	1.23	2.00	100.00	100.00	1.49

Definition of parameters:
σ = elasticities of substitution (EOS) between domestic and imported products;
τ = elasticities of transformation (EOT) between domestic and exported products; μ = EOS between bilateral and ROW imported products; υ = EOT between bilateral and ROW exported products; ξ = ROW import supply elasticities; ω = ROW export demand elasticities; φ = EOS between labor and composite capital.

Sources:
(1) U.S. parameters:
    (a) Base values of σ, τ, ξ, and ω for the 17 sectors are import-, export-, ROW import-, and ROW export-weighted averages, respectively, of σ, τ, ξ, and ω estimated at the 6-digit U.S. Bureau of Economic Analysis (BEA) sectors by Reinert and Roland-Holst (1991). The export and import weights are obtained from MITI (1989). ξ for the automobile sector is taken from de Melo and Tarr (1992).
    (b) μ are computed using equation

$$\mu = -\left(\varepsilon^b_M - \theta^b_M \varepsilon_M\right)\Big/\left(1 - \theta^b_M\right),$$

while ε_M (import demand elasticities) are calculated by

$$\varepsilon_M = -\left[\sigma - \theta_M\left(\sigma + \varepsilon\right)\right].$$

Both equations are derived from CES trade aggregation equations (A2.3) and (A2.5). θ_M (import shares in total sectoral demand) and θ_M^b (bilateral import shares in total sectoral imports) are gathered from MITI (1989). ε (composite demand elasticities) and ε_M^b (bilateral import demand elasticities) are taken from Petri (1984).
  (c) The base value of υ is set equal to 2.0 in every sector.
  (d) ϕ for Japanese sectors are obtained from Tsujimura and Kuroda (1974). The same sectoral values of ϕ are used in U.S. sectors.
(2) Japanese parameters:
  (a) σ are computed using equation

$$\sigma = -\left(\varepsilon_M - \theta_M \varepsilon\right)\Big/\left(1 - \theta_M\right),$$

ε_M are averages of those estimated by Petri (1984) and Stone (1979). θ_M and ε are obtained from MITI (1989) and Petri (1984), respectively.
  (b) At the 6-digit level of disaggregation, τ for Japanese and U.S. sectors are assumed to be equal. Japanese export shares are used to estimate τ for the 17 sectors.
  (c) ξ and ω are approximated by taking the U.S. estimates and multiplying them by $M^r(\text{U.S.})/M^r(\text{Japan})$ and $E^r(\text{U.S.})/E^r(\text{Japan})$, respectively. Since Japan could potentially absorb a significant share of world cereal production, we used a lower value of ξ (5.0) for the cereal sector. Those estimates of ξ and ω larger than 100 are set equal to 100.
  (d) μ: see (1b).
  (e) υ: see (1c).
  (f) ϕ: see (1d).

Comment

Peter A. Petri

This chapter by Hiro Lee and David Roland-Holst provides an overview and CGE simulation of U.S.–Japan–ROW trade and trade liberalization. The analysis is based on good data, is carefully done, and incorporates appropriate modeling features. The policy scenarios include elimination of bilateral and multilateral trade barriers – reasonable benchmarks, even if not likely to happen soon. The results are generally reasonable, but as is often the case with detailed CGE models, there are so many results that a typical reader is not likely to be able to absorb (much less really understand the underlying causes of) them all. In any case, the simulations are favorable for liberalization in the case of both countries, suggesting U.S. and Japanese gains that are reasonably large for CGE models, ranging from 0.08 to 0.54 percent of real GDP. The fact that the largest gains are obtained from Most-Favored Nation (MFN) liberalization is also plausible and good to see confirmed with the CGE model.

The sectoral results are interesting and plausible, and not unlike those found in other CGE exercises on related liberalization experiments. The United States switches to agriculture, while Japan intensifies its manufacturing exports. I think it is worth emphasizing this result (which incidentally parallels closely those I found in modeling U.S.–Japan trade liberalization in Petri [1984]) because it is not at all what U.S. negotiators have in mind when they argue for more open Japanese markets. The fact that, all else equal, large grain imports tend to depress the real yen and thus result in manufactured exports, is probably an important constant in Japan's trade structure. This will not happen if liberalization is accompanied by more imports in general (i.e., a diminished national savings rate, which is in fact likely to happen due to Japan's aging population and the further liberalization of Japanese financial markets). The chapter does not consider experiments that would shift the model's macroeconomic balances.

The methodological twists incorporated in the model include price-elastic labor supply, economies of scale, and international capital mobility. Each of these is relevant to the U.S.–Japan trade relationship, so it would be interesting to isolate the effects of these mechanisms. The assumption of the price-elastic labor supplies appears to be doing a lot of the work, because employment increases are usually on the same scale as (and sometimes larger than) GDP increases. This mechanism may explain also why one finds a larger percentage increase for the United States than for Japan, which one does not usually see in CGE experiments. Indeed, some of the related results are puzzling: The components of GDP seem to go up more than GDP itself. For example, in experiment 2 in the United States, employment goes up by 0.29 percent and wages by 0.05 percent (for a 0.34 percent increase in labor income) and capital stock goes up by 0.16 percent and the rental rate by 0.27 percent (for a 0.43 percent increase in capital income), yet real GDP, which ought to be close to a weighted average, increases by only 0.18 percent. Something like this is true in experiment 1, where capital flows are not allowed (capital flows were my first candidate for resolving the puzzle). My guess is that there is an explanation (perhaps having to do with how wages and rates of return are defined), but in this area, some more intuition on where the income increases come from would help. Terms-of-trade effects appear to be important also – perhaps they should appear in the aggregate result table.

The introduction of capital mobility is perhaps the most unusual feature of the model, and having worked on endogenizing FDI recently myself (Petri, 1997), I find this effort especially interesting. The results that FDI reinforces liberalization benefits are encouraging and in line with other research, including my own results. The way capital is introduced by Lee and Roland-Holst differs from my approach, however. Here, foreign capital becomes a part of a capital bundle used in each country's production activities, rather than "running its own show," that is, being used in activities that are specific to the foreign investing firm. This chapter is not the right place to do it, but at some point, those of us working in the area should sort out what the options are and which best represent how the "real world" works.

In sum, this is a well-crafted chapter on an important set of issues. It has detailed and useful results, which generally confirm the benefits of greater openness in the United States and Japan, while highlighting the adjustments that are likely to be implied.

REFERENCES

Petri, Peter A. (1984), *Modeling Japanese-American Trade: A Study of Asymmetric Interdependence*, Cambridge: Harvard University Press.
(1997), "Foreign Direct Investment in a Computable General Equilibrium Framework," paper presented at the Brandeis-Keio Conference on "Making APEC Work: Economic Challenges and Policy Alternatives," Keio University, Tokyo, March 13–14.

CHAPTER 3

Is There an Asian Export Model?

Marcus Noland

1. INTRODUCTION

Over the past quarter century, the high-performing Asian econo-mies (Japan, Hong Kong, Singapore, Taiwan, Korea, Malaysia, Thailand, and Indonesia) have nearly tripled their shares of world trade and income. Many observers have identified openness or pos-itive trade orientation as a primary explanation for this enviable performance, though controversy remains as to the nature of the causality between trade and growth.

There is a large and venerable literature that attempts to use cross-national data to model the relationship between trade and growth. These studies typically find a positive relationship between some measure of trade openness or export orientation and income growth, which is interpreted in a causal manner.[1] For example, Levine and Renelt (1992) nested a variety of trade orientation variables in a general model and subjected the estimated regres-sions to sensitivity tests. They found that there was a positive and robust correlation between investment share and income growth, and between investment and trade shares. They inter-preted this as indicating that trade (not exports per se) affects growth through investment, not through improved resource allo-cation or spillover externalities as previous studies have posited. They did not obtain any robust relationships between a variety of trade policy indicators and growth.

I would like to thank Chongshan Liu for research assistance, and Howard Pack, Susan Collins, and the conference participants for insightful comments on an earlier draft.

[1] See Jung and Marshall (1985) for a summary of studies through the early 1980s, and Brad-ford (1994) for a survey of the more recent literature. See also Ram (1985, 1987), Dollar (1992), Helliwell (1992), and Fukuda and Toya (1993).

A concern with these studies is possible simultaneity bias problems arising between national income (or growth) on the left-hand side of the regression and its components (exports, investment, or their growth rates) on the right-hand side. Frankel, Romer, and Cyrus (1995) attempt to address this issue by constructing instruments for trade based on the fitted values of a "gravity equation." They find that trade explains a large amount of growth for Hong Kong and Singapore, and a lesser though positive amount for Korea, Malaysia, and Taiwan; a lack of trade contributes to the relatively poor growth performance of the Philippines. Moreover, by controlling for trade naturally arising from location, common languages, and so on, they are able to identify residual openness (or lack thereof) possibly associated with policy. So, for example, they find that in the case of Korea, although it is relatively trade dependent, this is due to location and other factors – residual openness is actually negative. In contrast, for Malaysia and Singapore, unexplained openness was more important than naturally arising trade dependence due to location.

These studies examine trade and growth linkages, and possible Asian distinctiveness, at the level of macroeconomic aggregates.[2] The purpose of this study is to extend the analysis another level of specificity by examining the commodity composition of trade. This is of interest because it is often argued that technological spillovers or other externalities associated with exports or trade are sector specific, as in the case of most of the recent endogenous growth theorizing and, at a more prosaic level, as in the World Bank's "East Asian Miracle" study (World Bank, 1993).[3]

---

[2] In addition to the cross-national approach, other studies have applied Granger-Sims causality tests to time series data for individual countries to analyze the trade and growth relationship. Jung and Marshall (1985) performed bivariate Granger-Sims tests on export and income growth for five of the Asian countries. They found that for Indonesia export growth caused income growth; that for Korea export growth reduced income growth; that for Thailand income growth caused export growth; and that no causality relationship could be uncovered for the Philippines and Taiwan.

Hutchison and Singh (1992) criticized the theoretical underpinning of the Jung and Marshall study and modeled the causal relationships among exports, non-export output, and investment growth. They found that exports cause non-export sector growth for Taiwan; in the cases of Indonesia, Korea, Singapore, and Thailand, no causality relationships could be identified. Both studies are based on very short sample periods (a maximum of thirty-one observations), and this, together with questions about specification and the well-known fragility of Granger-Sims tests, suggests that the conclusions of these studies should be greeted with a considerable degree of skepticism.

[3] One could question (as Albert Fishlow does in his comments) whether this is a meaningful definition of Asia, or if the very diversity of these economies obviates the analytical

This chapter attempts to answer three interrelated sets of questions. First, have the aggregate exports of the Asian economies been unusually high? Are the Asian economies unusually open or trade dependent? For the Newly Industrialized Economies (NIEs), to ask the question is to answer it, but in the cases of the other countries, particularly Japan, the answer is not so obvious.

A second and more subtle view involves the sectoral composition of exports. Have the Asian countries exhibited unusually high (or low) exports in particular industries? Have the export profiles of the Asian countries been unusually concentrated in a few sectors?

The analysis of sectoral composition leads naturally to a third set of questions: Has trade specialization in particular sectors emerged relatively early (or late) in the development of the Asian countries? Is there an "Asian development path"?

The chapter begins by developing some simple descriptive statistics and then formal econometric models of trade. To preview the results, the analysis in this chapter suggests that the Asian countries are too diverse for a simple "Asian model" to be identified. Nonetheless, certain results stand out. First, neither the static nor the dynamic pattern of Japanese export specialization can be adequately explained by the factor endowment model. A similar, though far less clear-cut, conclusion could be deduced for Korea and Taiwan. As a group, the Asian economies appear to be unusually *trade* (as opposed to *export*) dependent.

Second, because of the diversity of the Asian economies, no industries of unusual specialization could be identified when each country is considered individually. However, there are a group of manufacturing industries (radio, television, and telecommunications equipment, apparel, plastic products, and office and computing equipment) in which Asian economies have specialized more rapidly and to a greater extent than would be predicted on the basis of their factor endowments alone.

2. ARE ASIAN COUNTRIES DIFFERENT?

Data on the distribution of exports across product categories of the eight high-performing Asian (the Asian-8) economies are reported

usefulness of this grouping. This is certainly a valid question. Yet at the same time it must be recognized that for better or for worse, East Asia has become a definitive unit of analysis in policy debates, a point made most obviously with reference to the widely circulated World Bank report cited in the main text.

in the first eight columns of Table 3.1.[4] The figures reveal considerable differences in the pattern of specialization across the group: Japan's exports of motor vehicles, Thailand's exports of food crops, and Indonesia, Malaysia, and Singapore's exports of petroleum all stand out relative to the group. Averaged together, the single biggest sector of export concentration is radio, television, and telecommunications equipment (13 percent), followed by petroleum and petroleum products (9 percent) and apparel (8 percent).

For purposes of comparison, the averaged figures for Argentina, Brazil, Mexico, and Pakistan (A-B-M-P) are also reported, along with a test for differences in the means across the two groups. The Asian group means are higher than the A-B-M-P means at the 1 percent level of significance in three sectors: the aforementioned radio, television, and telecommunications equipment sector, other electrical machinery (mostly household appliances), and office and computing equipment. There are no product categories in which the Asian group mean is lower than the A-B-M-P mean at the 1 percent level, though the Asian group mean is lower and significant at the 5 percent level in food crops, and lower and significant at the 10 percent level in basic chemicals.

Figures on the Asian-8's shares of world exports are reported in Table 3.2. Interestingly, each Asian-8 economy accounts for a double-digit share of world exports in at least one product category, with Japan's shares of motorcycles and bicycles (34 percent), radio, television, and telecommunications equipment (30 percent), and motor vehicles (23 percent) being the largest entries. Taken together, the Asian-8 account for more than half of world exports in natural and synthetic rubber and gums (60 percent), motorcycles and bicycles (59 percent), and radio, television, and telecommunications equipment (52 percent).

The predominance of the Asian-8 in certain export categories points toward the question perennially on the minds of policymakers – namely, whether their export performance could be emulated, or whether there is an adding-up problem (e.g., Cline, 1982, 1984, 1985; Ranis, 1985). The elasticities of their real exports with respect to world exports for the period 1968–88 are reported

---

[4] The forty-six commodity categories encompassing the whole of the traded goods sector. (Primary product sectors are arranged by SITC category; manufactured products by ISIC category.)

Table 3.1. *Export Shares, 1988*

	HKG	IDN	JPN	KOR	MYS	SGP	TWN	THA	Simple mean of Asian-8	Simple mean of A-B-M-P	Null test of mean
Animals & animal products	0.11	0.73	0.09	0.14	2.66	1.27	1.35	1.62	1.00	3.07	-1.2809
Fish and preparations	0.42	3.38	0.30	2.95	0.86	0.92	2.39	10.25	2.68	2.17	0.4029
Food crops	0.21	6.32	0.15	0.77	2.84	2.63	1.18	21.45	4.44	11.98	-2.5097\b
Tobacco	0.82	0.34	0.02	0.15	0.03	0.33	0.03	0.34	0.26	0.63	-1.1207
Agricultural commodities	0.30	3.44	0.19	0.52	8.82	1.46	0.37	1.76	2.11	10.99	-1.1852
Beverages	0.15	0.02	0.03	0.07	0.11	0.40	0.02	0.10	0.11	0.37	-0.8463
Natural fibres	0.05	0.10	0.32	0.36	0.40	0.10	0.82	0.17	0.29	5.51	-1.3370
Natural rubber & gums	0.00	6.46	0.18	0.04	9.16	3.02	0.11	6.85	3.23	0.15	2.3234\b
Wood & wood pulp	0.22	3.07	0.01	0.10	11.01	0.85	0.24	0.42	1.99	0.87	0.7808
Crude minerals	0.69	3.47	0.11	0.19	0.87	0.59	0.19	1.05	0.90	2.44	-1.0617
Coal, coke, & briquettes	0.00	0.22	0.09	0.00	0.00	0.01	0.01	0.00	0.04	0.01	0.9935
Petroleum & products	0.24	38.51	0.16	0.92	15.19	12.97	0.59	0.77	8.67	9.07	-0.0449
Nonferrous metals	0.29	2.82	0.82	0.68	2.02	2.21	0.67	0.74	1.28	2.71	-1.3166
Spinning & weaving	5.34	3.22	1.85	6.61	1.25	1.44	5.41	3.95	3.63	8.75	-0.7407
Other textile products	7.00	1.13	0.38	3.55	0.71	1.14	3.96	2.51	2.55	3.51	-0.3079
Wearing apparel	26.25	3.57	0.21	12.60	3.26	2.56	6.22	10.72	8.17	3.65	1.0803
Leather & products	0.93	0.38	0.14	2.05	0.03	0.20	2.06	1.81	0.95	2.89	-1.3989
Footwear	0.63	0.34	0.02	5.06	0.20	0.12	5.12	1.96	1.68	1.01	0.6680
Wood products	0.16	14.97	0.06	0.39	5.56	1.69	2.07	1.22	3.27	0.61	1.4692
Furniture & fixtures	0.24	0.25	0.15	0.31	0.21	0.34	1.82	1.05	0.54	0.08	2.2092\b
Pulp & paper	0.09	0.69	0.48	0.45	0.26	0.52	0.41	0.30	0.40	1.37	-1.3136
Paper products	0.80	0.02	0.16	0.09	0.11	0.23	0.16	0.10	0.21	0.20	0.1054
Printing & publishing	1.83	0.05	0.28	0.41	0.17	0.67	0.53	0.19	0.52	0.18	1.6184

Industry											
Basic chemicals	0.13	0.45	2.77	1.20	0.92	2.63	0.99	0.46	1.19	3.92	-1.8857[c]
Synthetic resins	1.22	0.26	1.81	1.44	0.31	2.47	2.38	0.54	1.31	1.63	-0.5471
Other industrial chemicals	0.02	0.73	0.15	0.41	0.34	0.23	0.07	0.04	0.25	0.15	0.9865
Drugs & medicine	0.12	0.10	0.27	0.11	0.09	0.49	0.06	0.12	0.17	0.23	-0.7284
Other chemical products	0.45	0.30	1.22	0.26	0.44	1.26	0.38	0.38	0.59	0.51	0.3819
Rubber products	0.08	0.27	1.15	1.67	0.41	0.32	0.90	0.67	0.68	0.44	0.9731
Plastic products	4.03	0.17	0.44	2.28	0.48	0.72	5.58	1.57	1.91	0.33	2.2528[b]
Pottery, china, etc.	0.08	0.06	0.38	0.24	0.15	0.05	1.05	0.30	0.29	0.12	1.3119
Glass & glass products	0.51	0.49	0.43	0.29	0.18	0.21	0.84	0.32	0.41	0.39	0.0900
Other mineral products	0.13	0.47	0.39	0.78	0.34	0.15	0.50	0.44	0.40	0.48	-0.3609
Iron & steel	0.11	1.42	5.97	5.62	0.88	0.99	1.60	1.08	2.21	5.45	-1.2864
Fabricated metal products	3.40	0.24	2.21	2.97	0.60	1.58	5.55	1.13	2.21	0.88	1.9994
Office & computing equipment	5.88	0.01	7.10	4.19	0.30	14.34	8.87	3.28	5.50	1.00	2.6082[a]
Other machinery	3.64	0.16	12.46	3.81	2.00	5.92	6.03	2.33	4.54	2.40	1.3585
Radio, television	10.40	0.23	16.92	17.41	21.63	20.99	10.95	6.02	13.07	0.60	4.6463[a]
Other electrical machinery	5.76	0.17	5.57	3.20	1.92	5.01	5.14	3.03	3.72	0.81	3.6532[a]
Shipbuilding & repairing	0.10	0.08	2.47	2.96	0.40	1.75	0.47	0.08	1.04	1.16	-0.1487
Railroad equipment	0.00	0.00	0.20	0.85	0.00	0.01	0.23	0.06	0.17	0.05	1.1358
Motor vehicles	0.06	0.04	23.17	6.52	0.13	0.81	1.48	0.79	4.12	5.38	-0.3158
Aircraft	0.00	0.05	0.16	0.55	0.76	0.81	0.05	0.01	0.30	0.31	-0.0396
Motorcycles & bicycles	0.94	0.08	1.21	0.56	0.09	0.29	2.46	0.30	0.74	0.08	2.3159[b]
Professional goods	9.95	0.18	5.95	1.39	1.03	2.26	2.48	1.15	3.05	0.74	1.9331[c]
Other industries	6.20	0.56	1.39	2.92	0.87	1.08	6.18	6.57	3.22	0.75	2.3957[b]

Note: The null hypothesis is that the simple means are the same. The letters a, b, and c indicate that the null hypothesis can be rejected at the significance levels of 1, 5, and 10 percent, respectively. A-B-M-P refers to Argentina, Brazil, Mexico, and Pakistan. HKG = Hong Kong; IDN = Indonesia; JPN = Japan; KOR = Korea; MYS = Malaysia; SGP = Singapore; TWN= Taiwan; THA = Thailand. See the chapter-end Appendix for data sources and definitions.

Table 3.2. Asian-8's Share of World Exports in Each Sector, 1988

	Hong Kong	Indonesia	Japan	Korea	Malaysia	Singapore	Taiwan	Thailand	Asian-8
Animals & animal products	0.05	0.21	0.36	0.13	0.88	0.72	1.23	0.38	3.95
Fish and preparations	0.43	2.46	2.95	6.72	0.72	1.31	5.47	6.11	26.18
Food crops	0.06	1.20	0.37	0.46	0.61	0.97	0.70	3.33	7.71
Tobacco	2.18	0.63	0.60	0.87	0.07	1.20	0.18	0.52	6.23
Agricultural commodities	0.17	1.36	1.00	0.64	3.96	1.12	0.46	0.57	9.28
Beverages	0.26	0.02	0.42	0.26	0.16	0.95	0.09	0.10	2.27
Natural fibres	0.06	0.09	3.75	0.98	0.40	0.17	2.29	0.13	7.87
Natural rubber & gums	0.00	12.40	4.69	0.25	20.01	11.33	0.68	10.77	60.12
Wood & wood pulp	0.17	1.60	0.09	0.16	6.54	0.86	0.40	0.18	10.00
Crude minerals	0.54	1.89	0.80	0.32	0.54	0.63	0.33	0.47	5.52
Coal, coke, & briquettes	0.00	0.29	1.64	0.01	0.00	0.02	0.03	0.00	1.98
Petroleum & products	0.05	5.73	0.31	0.43	2.57	3.77	0.28	0.09	13.23
Nonferrous metals	0.14	0.98	3.86	0.74	0.80	1.50	0.73	0.21	8.95
Spinning & weaving	2.25	0.95	7.41	6.13	0.42	0.83	5.05	0.96	24.01
Other textile products	5.44	0.61	2.82	6.06	0.44	1.22	6.79	1.12	24.51
Wearing apparel	11.07	1.06	0.82	11.68	1.10	1.48	5.80	2.60	35.62
Leather & products	1.76	0.50	2.51	8.54	0.05	0.52	8.63	1.97	24.47
Footwear	0.91	0.35	0.22	16.25	0.24	0.24	16.51	1.64	36.35
Wood products	0.15	9.60	0.53	0.78	4.06	2.12	4.19	0.64	22.07
Furniture & fixtures	0.43	0.32	2.66	1.24	0.30	0.84	7.32	1.09	14.20
Pulp & paper	0.04	0.23	2.22	0.47	0.10	0.35	0.44	0.08	3.94
Paper products	2.03	0.04	3.88	0.51	0.23	0.81	0.93	0.14	8.58
Printing & publishing	2.92	0.06	4.32	1.43	0.21	1.46	1.86	0.17	12.44

Basic chemicals	0.04	0.09	7.06	0.70	0.20	0.97	0.59	0.07	9.70
Synthetic resins	0.53	0.08	7.49	1.38	0.11	1.48	2.29	0.14	13.49
Other industrial chemicals	0.04	1.05	2.83	1.83	0.55	0.64	0.31	0.05	7.29
Drugs & medicine	0.12	0.07	2.69	0.25	0.08	0.71	0.14	0.07	4.14
Other chemical products	0.36	0.17	9.35	0.46	0.28	1.39	0.68	0.17	12.86
Rubber products	0.11	0.25	14.84	4.98	0.44	0.59	2.70	0.53	24.45
Plastic products	3.94	0.12	4.12	4.90	0.37	0.96	12.09	0.88	27.39
Pottery, china, etc.	0.37	0.20	17.08	2.51	0.59	0.34	11.14	0.82	33.05
Glass & glass products	1.01	0.68	8.12	1.25	0.28	0.55	3.65	0.36	15.91
Other mineral products	0.21	0.53	5.91	2.75	0.44	0.32	1.76	0.41	12.32
Iron & steel	0.03	0.30	17.14	3.73	0.21	0.41	1.07	0.19	23.09
Fabricated metal products	1.38	0.07	8.51	2.65	0.19	0.88	4.97	0.26	18.91
Office & computing equipment	1.65	0.00	18.96	2.59	0.07	5.53	5.52	0.53	34.85
Other machinery	0.45	0.01	14.53	1.03	0.20	1.00	1.64	0.16	19.01
Radio, television	1.93	0.03	29.85	7.11	3.21	5.35	4.50	0.64	52.62
Other electrical machinery	1.93	0.04	17.67	2.35	0.51	2.30	3.80	0.58	29.18
Shipbuilding & repairing	0.09	0.05	20.27	5.62	0.28	2.07	0.90	0.04	29.31
Railroad equipment	0.00	0.01	15.30	15.01	0.02	0.06	4.11	0.28	34.78
Motor vehicles	0.01	0.00	23.28	1.52	0.01	0.12	0.35	0.05	25.33
Aircraft	0.00	0.02	0.82	0.65	0.33	0.59	0.06	0.00	2.46
Motorcycles & bicycles	2.78	0.16	34.04	3.61	0.21	1.18	16.09	0.51	58.59
Professional goods	3.44	0.04	19.51	1.06	0.28	1.07	1.90	0.23	27.53
Other industries	3.56	0.23	7.55	3.68	0.40	0.85	7.85	2.17	26.28

See the chapter-end Appendix for data sources and definitions.

in Table 3.3.[5] The key result is that the exports of the Asian-8 grew more rapidly than those of the world as a whole during the period 1968–1988 in every manufacturing sector save one, shipbuilding.[6] The material presented thus lends support to the notion that as a group, the Asian-8's exports have an unusual commodity composition, relative to both a group of comparator countries and to the world as a whole. Moreover, their exports have grown far more rapidly than world exports in virtually every manufactured product category. Less clear is to what extent these results reflect a common tendency among the Asian-8 and to what extent the results are driven by the performance of individual countries.

3. IS THERE AN ASIAN EXPORT PATTERN?

To investigate whether there is a distinctively Asian export pattern, export similarity indices have been calculated for nine Asian economies and a sample of twenty-one other countries.[7] The index varies between 0 and 100, with 0 indicating complete dissimilarity, and 100 indicating identical export composition.[8] Summary results

[5] The data have been expressed in constant price terms with 1980 as the base year. Primary products price deflators were calculated as world trade weighted averages of individual primary commodity price series found in the International Monetary Fund (IMF), *International Financial Statistics*.

For manufactures, the task is more problematic as international price series do not exist. The U.S. producer price series found in the Commerce Department, *Producer Prices*, have been used as an admittedly second-best solution.

[6] These figures should be treated with some care. The Asian countries exhibit high elasticities for some primary products in which their exports are trivial. (The case of petroleum, in which all of the elasticities are negative, stands out. The reason is that the nominal price of oil increased so dramatically between 1968 and 1988 that world real export volumes fell. With the numerator of the elasticity positive in all cases and the denominator negative, the apparent elasticity is negative.) Moreover, the elasticities vary considerably among the Asian-8 in many product categories. Confining the discussion to manufactures, the highest elasticities for the group as a whole are in the other machinery category (1.60), leather and leather goods (1.46), and pulp and paper products (1.46). The lowest elasticities were in shipbuilding (0.96), pottery (1.03), and apparel (1.03). In the categories where Asian-8 exports made up the largest share of world exports – motorcycles and bicycles, and radio, television, and telecommunications equipment – the elasticities were 1.08 and 1.09, respectively.

[7] The countries are Argentina, Austria, Brazil, Canada, Denmark, Finland, France, Federal Republic of Germany, Greece, Hong Kong, Indonesia, Israel, Italy, Japan, Republic of Korea, Malaysia, Mexico, Norway, Pakistan, Peru, the Philippines, Singapore, Spain, Sweden, Taiwan, Thailand, Tunisia, Turkey, United Kingdom, and the United States. This was the largest set of countries for which a complete set of the factor endowment variables used in the following section could be constructed for the years 1968 and 1988.

[8] The index is defined as:

for 1968 and 1988 are presented in the first two panels of Table 3.4; reported in the third panel are the export similarity indices computed for the Asian countries in 1988 against the entire sample of countries for 1968.

As can be seen in the first panel of Table 3.4, Japan's export pattern in 1968 was already more like those of Western European countries than those of any other countries, including Asian countries, for which the situation is somewhat different.

Hong Kong, Taiwan, and Korea are consistently among each other's highest export similarity values, with some of the lower-income Western European countries turning up in the high rankings. Moreover, the export patterns of these three countries appear to be growing more similar: The indices in 1988 are higher than in 1968. There is some support for the result found earlier by Pearson (1994) and Noland (1990) that Korea is "following" Japan's export pattern. When Korea's export pattern for 1988 is compared to the sample countries' export patterns in 1968, the Japanese pattern has the highest similarity value (64), though this is lower than the contemporaneous value for Taiwan (70). It is possible, however, that if other noncontemporaneous pairings for Japan were calculated, higher values might be obtained.

The results for Singapore are different from the other NIEs, perhaps reflecting its extensive investment relations both with other Southeast Asian countries and with the developed countries. In 1968, its highest export similarity pairings were with Indonesia (75), Malaysia (52), and Spain (50); in 1988, the highest values were with Malaysia (66), the United Kingdom (61), and Taiwan (58). When the noncontemporaneous pairings are calculated, Singapore's export similarity is the highest with Western European countries [Italy (60), Spain (54), Austria (51), and France (51)], suggesting that, if anything, Singapore is following a Western European path.[9]

$$S(a, b) = \sum_i \min\left(X_{ia}, X_{ib}\right) \cdot 100,$$

where X_{ia} (X_{ib}) is the industry i export share in country a's (b's) exports. This measure was originally proposed by Finger and Kreinin (1979). See also Kellman and Schroeder (1983) and Pearson (1994).

[9] Again, it should be noted that these results simply compare two points in time. If a different lag degree were examined (ten instead of twenty years, for instance), different similarity rankings might be obtained.

Table 3.3. *Elasticities of Real Exports, 1968–1988*

	Hong Kong	Indonesia	Japan	Korea	Malaysia	Singapore	Taiwan	Thailand	Asian-8
Animals & animal products	1.16	1.17	1.02	1.66	1.79	1.54	1.80	1.58	1.59
Fish and preparations	0.61	1.79	-0.46	1.60	0.60	1.57	1.76	1.68	1.11
Food crops	0.55	1.94	0.50	2.39	1.96	1.38	0.16	1.72	1.47
Tobacco	1.81	0.73	1.10	1.36	0.47	1.47	1.19	0.88	1.35
Agricultural commodities	1.11	0.99	1.06	1.57	1.50	0.84	1.64	1.27	1.26
Beverages	1.68	1.63	1.14	1.59	1.26	1.37	1.62	1.62	1.39
Natural fibres	1.93	3.96	3.46	2.65	4.10	2.78	4.20	-2.57	3.13
Natural rubber & gums	3.08	1.49	3.08	3.07	0.92	0.73	3.08	2.06	1.31
Wood & wood pulp	7.46	6.11	2.55	7.49	3.09	7.38	5.52	3.54	3.99
Crude minerals	3.79	4.56	4.55	-0.18	-0.01	3.53	4.53	2.97	3.15
Coal, coke, & briquettes	NA	2.26	2.10	-1.88	1.73	1.91	1.40	2.28	1.99
Petroleum & products	-1.45	-6.20	-2.77	-12.90	-6.78	-2.94	-9.61	11.61	-5.36
Nonferrous metals	2.60	3.08	2.11	3.49	-1.25	3.36	3.31	-1.18	1.67
Spinning & weaving	1.07	1.42	0.60	1.35	1.37	1.15	1.32	1.39	1.04
Other textile products	1.09	1.44	0.44	1.34	1.40	1.33	1.41	1.37	1.16
Wearing apparel	0.96	1.21	-0.17	1.15	1.19	1.11	1.13	1.21	1.03
Leather & products	0.84	1.78	0.42	1.77	1.71	1.41	1.72	1.77	1.46
Footwear	0.36	1.32	-1.00	1.32	1.13	0.99	1.31	1.34	1.17
Wood products	-0.20	1.88	-0.99	0.18	1.39	1.32	1.31	1.52	1.27
Furniture & fixtures	0.66	1.21	0.95	1.22	1.18	1.16	1.23	1.24	1.14
Pulp & paper	1.62	1.92	1.25	1.91	1.84	1.69	1.61	1.90	1.46
Paper products	1.32	1.40	1.05	1.34	1.18	1.17	1.33	1.37	1.18
Printing & publishing	1.35	1.89	0.95	1.87	1.31	1.52	1.68	1.88	1.31

Industry									
Basic chemicals	1.06	1.49	1.01	1.50	1.43	1.42	1.42	1.47	1.11
Synthetic resins	1.54	1.63	0.92	1.63	1.59	1.58	1.58	1.63	1.18
Other industrial chemicals	1.37	2.27	0.33	2.16	1.99	1.25	1.18	2.25	1.12
Drugs & medicine	0.65	1.18	1.10	1.53	0.83	1.29	1.42	1.35	1.15
Other chemical products	1.12	1.30	1.25	1.39	1.00	1.27	1.29	1.39	1.25
Rubber products	0.87	1.40	1.09	1.38	1.20	1.11	1.33	1.38	1.18
Plastic products	0.87	1.24	0.61	1.23	1.21	1.19	1.18	1.25	1.04
Pottery, china, etc.	1.21	1.72	0.62	1.71	1.65	1.03	1.71	1.71	1.03
Glass & glass products	0.97	1.90	1.13	1.86	1.85	1.15	1.66	1.79	1.33
Other mineral products	1.35	1.73	0.77	1.72	1.28	1.27	1.19	1.55	1.10
Iron & steel	-0.01	2.42	0.98	2.42	2.23	1.64	2.21	2.18	1.24
Fabricated metal products	1.07	1.70	0.96	1.65	1.53	1.36	1.69	1.70	1.26
Office & computing equipment	1.08	0.71	1.06	1.08	1.07	1.08	1.08	1.08	1.07
Other machinery	1.62	1.91	1.54	1.87	1.65	1.74	1.86	1.90	1.60
Radio, television	1.01	1.03	1.04	1.17	1.18	1.18	1.13	1.18	1.09
Other electrical machinery	1.27	0.64	1.18	1.38	1.35	1.35	1.37	1.40	1.24
Shipbuilding & repairing	0.22	1.86	0.67	2.02	1.59	1.95	1.96	2.02	0.96
Railroad equipment	2.21	2.21	0.86	2.20	0.94	1.51	2.21	2.21	1.49
Motor vehicles	1.38	0.50	1.29	1.39	0.19	0.83	1.39	1.39	1.29
Aircraft	2.06	1.08	0.59	2.04	2.00	2.03	2.05	1.72	1.40
Motorcycles & bicycles	0.91	1.31	0.97	1.32	1.26	1.22	1.31	1.32	1.08
Professional goods	1.25	1.30	1.12	1.30	1.27	1.24	1.29	1.30	1.16
Other industries	0.84	1.51	0.86	1.42	1.48	1.35	1.50	1.47	1.17

See the chapter-end Appendix for data sources and definitions.

Table 3.4. *Export Similarity Indices*

1968				
Japan	1) Austria (67)	2) Italy (64)	3) Germany (63)	
Hong Kong	1) Korea (60)	2) Taiwan (52)	3) Japan (46)	
Singapore	1) Indonesia (75)	2) Malaysia (52)	3) Spain (50)	
Taiwan	1) Spain (58)	2) Korea (53)	3) Hong Kong (52)	3) Israel (52)
Korea	1) Hong Kong (60)	2) Taiwan (53)	3) Austria (41)	
Malaysia	1) Singapore (52)	2) Indonesia (51)	3) Thailand (40)	
Thailand	1) Brazil (70)	2) Mexico (59)	3) Turkey (50)	
Philippines	1) Peru (53)	3) Tunisia (46)	3) Brazil (42)	
Indonesia	1) Singapore (75)	2) Malaysia (51)	3) Tunisia (49)	

1988				
Japan	1) Germany (69)	2) UK (62)	3) Sweden (61)	
Hong Kong	1) Taiwan (65)	2) Korea (60)	3) Thailand (50)	
Singapore	1) Malaysia (66)	2) UK (61)	3) Taiwan (58)	
Taiwan	1) Korea (70)	2) Italy (66)	3) Hong Kong (65)	
Korea	1) Taiwan (70)	2) Italy (64)	3) Hong Kong (60)	3) Japan (60)
Malaysia	1) Singapore (66)	2) Philippine (53)	3) Indonesia (52)	
Thailand	1) Taiwan (57)	1) Philippine (57)	3) Korea (56)	
Philippines	1) Thailand (57)	2) Brazil (55)	3) Malaysia (53)	
Indonesia	1) Mexico (59)	2) Norway (56)	3) Malaysia (52)	

1968–88				
Japan	1) Germany (58)	2) Japan (57)	3) UK (55)	
Hong Kong	1) Hong Kong (72)	2) Korea (48)	3) Taiwan (42)	
Singapore	1) Italy (60)	2) Spain (54)	3) Austria (51)	3) France (51)
Taiwan	1) Hong Kong (63)	2) Japan (60)	3) Taiwan (52)	
Korea	1) Japan (64)	2) Hong Kong (58)	3) Taiwan (49)	3) Italy (49)
Malaysia	1) Malaysia (62)	2) Singapore (54)	3) Italy (49)	
Thailand	1) Taiwan (62)	2) Korea (53)	3) Hong Kong (51)	
Philippines	1) Taiwan (56)	2) Korea (54)	3) Mexico (50)	
Indonesia	1) Singapore (77)	2) Indonesia (73)	3) Tunisia (70)	

See text for definition.

Malaysia consistently exhibits the highest degree of export similarity with its Southeast Asian neighbors Singapore, Indonesia, Thailand, and the Philippines. In contrast, the export similarity of Thailand has shifted from non-Asian [Brazil (70), Mexico (59), and Turkey (50) in 1968] to Asian economies [Taiwan (57), the Philippines (57), and Korea (56) in 1988]. Interestingly, Thailand's export pattern in 1988 was more similar to that of Taiwan in 1968 (62) than any contemporaneous pairing, with the next highest noncontemporaneous pairings being Korea (53) and Hong Kong (51). In this sense, Thailand might be said to be "following" the export path of the Hong Kong–Taiwan–Korea trio.

Somewhat similar results were obtained for the Philippines. In 1968, the highest export similarity pairings were with non-Asian countries [Peru (53), Tunisia (46), and Brazil (42)], but by 1988, the highest pairings were with Thailand (57), Brazil (55), and Malaysia (53). The highest noncontemporaneous pairings were with Taiwan (56), Korea (54), and Mexico (50), suggesting that the Philippines too might be following in the Asian NIEs export path.

The export similarity indices for Indonesia perhaps exhibit the greatest amount of change. In 1968, the export similarity pairings were highest with Singapore (75), Malaysia (51), and Tunisia (49). In 1988, presumably due to its oil exports, its export similarity pairings were the highest with Mexico (59), Norway (56), and Malaysia (52). Surprisingly, the export patterns of four countries in 1968 were more similar than any of the contemporaneous pairings for 1988: Singapore (77), Indonesia (73), Tunisia (70), and Spain (60). On this basis, it could be argued that Indonesia is following the Singapore path, as distinct from the Hong Kong–Taiwan–Korea path.

To recapitulate, there does not appear to be a unique Asian export path. The export pattern of Japan is more like that of some Western European countries, both contemporaneously and noncontemporaneously, than it is with any other Asian countries, and there is little evidence that other Asian countries (with the possible exception of Korea) are "following" the Japanese export path. There is some evidence of other clusters (Hong Kong, Taiwan, and Korea; Malaysia, Thailand, and the Philippines), and these clusters may have grown more similar over time.

4. MODELING EXPORT PATTERNS

The analysis thus far has involved a descriptive examination of export patterns, and some of the evidence appears to support the idea that the export performance of the Asian-8 has been unique. The obvious question is whether these observed outcomes are themselves explained by the distinctive economic characteristics of the Asian-8. Answering this question requires a model of the determinants of export specialization. A conventional starting point for

econometric analysis of international trade flows is the Heckscher-
Ohlin-Vanek model. This approach employs the standard assumptions of microeconomic trade models (factor price equalization or
endowment similarity, identical homothetic preferences, etc.) to
generate a reduced-form representation of a country's trade
pattern based on available technology and its relative factor endowments.[10] A country's output (Q), is produced from a factor use
matrix (A), and a set of endowments (V):

$$Q = A^{-1}V. \tag{3.1}$$

World output can be described similarly:

$$Q_w = A^{-1}V_w \tag{3.2}$$

Under the assumption of identical homothetic utility functions and
factor price equalization, each country consumes each variety of
the commodities in the same proportion:

$$C = sQ_w, \tag{3.3}$$

where s is the country's share of world output defined as

$$s = \left(Y_i - B_i\right)\Big/Y_w \tag{3.4}$$

where Y is income and B is the trade balance evaluated at the
vector of common goods prices, p.[11]

Net exports (T) are simply the difference between production
and consumption

$$T = Q - C, \tag{3.5}$$

or, by back substituting,

$$T = A^{-1}V - A^{-1}sV_w$$
$$= A^{-1}\left(V - sV_w\right).$$

Unfortunately, as Leamer (1984) notes, it is "wildly optimistic" to
expect to be able to estimate this model directly. The excess factor
supplies are correlated, and a regression of trade on a subset of

---

[10] See Leamer (1984) for a discussion of these assumptions and how they can be relaxed
while preserving the linear (or at least monotonic) relationship between trade and factor
endowments.
[11] The assumption of homotheticity can be replaced with that of a linear expenditure system
without changing the ultimate reduced form of the regressions, though the interpretation of the coefficient on the labor endowment is different.

them is bound to lead to biased and inconsistent estimates, a problem compounded by any errors in measurement of the endowments. Instead, researchers have estimated reduced forms where data on industry net exports are regressed on national factor endowment data:

$$T_{ij} = \Sigma_k \beta_{ik} V_{kj} + u_{ij} \qquad (3.6)$$

where T_{ij} = net exports of commodity i by country j, V_{kj} = endowments of resource k of country j, β_{ik} = coefficients indicating the impact on net exports of commodity i of an increase in the kth endowment, and u_{ij} = a disturbance term.

For some purposes, it may be desirable to examine gross rather than net exports. The natural theoretical starting point for such an investigation would be through the specification of a differentiated products model, in which product varieties are differentiated by country of origin. Under the prior assumption of identical homothetic preferences, each country will consume identical proportions of each variety of each good; hence each country will export $(1 - s)$ of its production:

$$X = \left(1 - s\right)Q \qquad (3.7)$$

or, by back substituting,

$$X = \left(1 - s\right)A^{-1}V.$$

Again, it is effectively impossible to estimate equation (3.7) directly; instead, a reduced form analogous to (3.6) is estimated:

$$X_{ij} = \Sigma_k \beta_{ik} V_{kj} + u_{ij}. \qquad (3.8)$$

The explanatory variables consisted of nine factor endowments (labor, physical capital, human capital, arable land, pasture land, forest land, coal, oil, and minerals), and the c.i.f./f.o.b. ratio, which was used as a proxy for transport costs.[12] A dummy variable for membership in the European Community was also included to account for any trade-creating effects of that organization. Documentation of data sources is contained in the chapter-end Appendix.

---

[12] Alternatively, one could think of locational proximity as an endowment. The regressions were also estimated with the length of coast included as an endowment; the coast variable was significant in neither the fish and preparations regressions nor any other regression in the sample.

All regressions were initially estimated using ordinary least squares (OLS).[13] Lagrange multiplier tests (Breusch and Pagan, 1979) revealed evidence of cross-sectional heteroscedasticity in around half of the estimates; in these cases, White's heteroscedastic-consistent covariance matrix estimator was used (White, 1980). In the case of gross exports, the regressions have been estimated with the dependent and explanatory variables in both log and level form.

These regressions are quite tedious to report and are available from the author on request. In general, the regressions appear to explain a high degree of cross-sectional variation. The coefficients of determination in the net export regressions range from 0.068 to 0.977 with a median value of 0.804. For the export regressions, the coefficients of variation range from 0.139 to 0.987 with a median of 0.826; for the log export specifications, the minimum coefficient of determination is 0.539, and the maximum is 0.930, with a median of 0.794. In only 13 of 138 cases can we not reject the hypothesis that all of the explanatory variables are jointly equal to zero at the 10 percent level.

Of more interest than the details of the coefficient estimates are the residuals derived from these equations. Studentized residuals were calculated for each observation. (The studentized residual is a residual that has been adjusted for the standard error of the regression.) It has an interesting interpretation because it can be shown that it is the t-statistic that one would obtain for a dummy variable taking the value 1 for that observation and 0 otherwise in the original regression (Belsley, Kuh, and Welsch, 1980).[14] The

---

[13] In principle, since gross exports are truncated at zero, these regressions should be estimated using limited dependent variable techniques. In reality, there were very, very few zero-valued observations: 1988 rubber for Pakistan, Peru, and Tunisia; 1988 coal for Hong Kong, Israel, the Philippines, and Tunisia; 1988 nonferrous metals for Pakistan; and 1988 railroad equipment for Peru. Indeed, with so few (and apparently random) zero-valued observations, the Tobit estimates were virtually identical to those obtained from OLS.

[14] The studentized residual of observation j, e_j^*, is defined as

$$e_j^* = e_j \bigg/ \left[s(j)(1 - h_j)^{1/2} \right],$$

where e_j is the residual from the original regression, $s(j)$ is the estimated standard error of the residual from a regression where the jth row of the matrix of explanatory variables, X, and the vector of dependent variables, Y, has been deleted, and

$$h_j = x_j \left(X, X \right)^{-1} x_j,$$

where x_j is the jth row vector from the X matrix.

sums of squares and means of these residuals by country are reported in Table 3.5. A significant value for the sum of squares statistic would indicate that there is something unusual about a country's trade pattern not predicted by the model. This could occur if, for example, a country's exports were unusually concentrated in a few sectors.

As can be seen in Table 3.5, Taiwan and Japan have statistically unusual export patterns, regardless of which specification is used. For the other economies, the results are more ambiguous. Significant values for the sum of squares statistic are relatively common, with more than 40 percent of the observations significant at the 10 percent level. For the net export regressions, the sum of squares statistic is significant for Japan, Indonesia, Hong Kong, Taiwan, and Korea at the 1 percent level, and for Malaysia at the 5 percent level. For gross exports, Indonesia, Japan, Taiwan, and Thailand are significant at the 1 percent level, while Malaysia and Korea are significant at the 10 percent level. Lastly, for the log export specification, the Philippines, Taiwan, Hong Kong, and Thailand are significant at the 1 percent level, while Singapore and Japan are significant at the 5 percent level.

These statistics refer to the pattern of trade. To examine whether the regressions provided any information on the relative degree of openness or trade dependency, the means of the studentized t's were computed. A significant positive (negative) value of this statistic would imply that a country maintained higher (lower) level of exports than the regression model would predict. In ninety observations (thirty countries for three specifications), there were only two statistically significant values: Germany for exports (higher than expected), and Pakistan for log exports (lower than expected). In none of the cases was the level of net exports higher than expected. This, together with the scarcity of significant studentized means for the export specifications, is reassuring in that it suggests that these regressions are not unduly influenced by country size or by aggregate trade balances. This simply means that whereas the pattern *across* sectors may be unusual, the aggregate level of exports, or the balance on net exports, is not.

The studentized residuals can also be analyzed by sector. Industries of unusual Asian exports do not appear prevalent in the data, however. There are no sectors in which four or more of the Asian countries have studentized residuals in absolute value of 2.0 or

Table 3.5. *Sum of Squared Studentized Residuals (SSSR) and Mean of Studentized Residuals (MSR)*

Country	Net Exports – 1988		Exports – 1988		Log Exports – 1988	
	SSSR	MSR	SSSR	MSR	SSSR	MSR
Argentina	45.14	0.26	38.69	0.23	81.49\a	0.56
Austria	9.87	-0.08	8.70	-0.30	53.28	0.46
Brazil	43.65	-0.06	75.08\a	0.45	47.39	0.73
Canada	58.80\c	0.00	49.51	0.57	22.89	-0.05
Denmark	38.65	0.08	46.71	-0.62	22.78	-0.20
Finland	22.93	0.08	37.11	-0.46	19.11	-0.29
France	278.11\a	0.16	181.68\a	0.93	11.01	-0.01
Germany	514.75\a	1.46	672.61\a	2.36\b	11.30	-0.02
Greece	32.97	0.07	54.06	-0.78	46.73	-0.24
Hong Kong	96.23\a	-0.85	22.64	0.18	135.91\a	-0.78
Indonesia	111.35\a	-0.01	199.00\a	-1.43	45.81	-0.15
Israel	11.78	-0.02	13.95	-0.37	29.84	-0.20
Italy	278.00\a	0.25	169.00\a	0.39	22.86	0.16
Japan	181.91\a	-0.02	166.45\a	-1.04	63.74\b	-0.41
Korea	76.59\a	0.01	59.90\c	0.19	33.33	0.11

Malaysia	65.69\b	0.36	62.71\c	0.41	36.40	0.58
Mexico	99.17\a	0.22	78.44\a	0.52	24.13	-0.31
Norway	50.30	0.03	26.07	-0.05	75.43\a	-1.08
Pakistan	33.72	0.06	40.86	0.47	740.93\a	-1.84\c
Peru	31.85	0.07	36.67	0.34	94.90\a	-0.90
Philippines	29.51	-0.07	37.37	-0.29	151.87\a	-1.17
Singapore	22.06	-0.11	28.58	-0.14	70.49\b	0.40
Spain	29.64	-0.09	35.56	-0.61	17.21	0.05
Sweden	24.61	-0.06	34.02	-0.40	17.84	0.05
Taiwan	83.67\a	0.39	149.52\a	0.86	139.43\a	1.34
Thailand	30.52	0.08	72.51\a	1.06	130.76\a	1.36
Tunisia	5.70	0.04	5.13	-0.19	78.75\a	0.60
Turkey	60.12\c	0.17	27.42	-0.04	58.25	-0.42
United Kingdom	145.45\a	-0.98	126.00\a	-0.12	12.74	0.17
United States	247.26\a	-0.48	251.78\a	-1.44	33.01	-0.10

Note: Letters a, b, and c denote significance levels of 1, 5, and 10 percent, respectively.

more (roughly the 10 percent level). Indeed, out of 138 possible cases (46 industries and three specifications), in only eight cases did three of the Asian countries have significant studentized residuals, and in none of these cases were the three significant residuals of the same sign.[15]

The analysis thus far has focused on the residuals for individual countries, and not much evidence has been found to support the existence of a distinctly "Asian export pattern." Perhaps this should not be surprising given the diversity of economies under consideration. Nonetheless, it might be possible that while every country might not exhibit the same peculiarities, there might be certain group tendencies that might be uncovered. To investigate this possibility, the regressions were reestimated with a dummy variable of the Asian countries included. Since there is some reason to believe that the Philippines performance has been unlike that of the rest of the group, the regressions were estimated with the Philippines both included (A9) and excluded (A8) from the group. For comparative purposes, a dummy variable for Latin America was also included.

These results are summarized in Table 3.6. The results for the net export specification are reported in the first panel. The A9 dummy was negative and significant at the 5 percent level or higher in four of forty-six cases, and positive and significant in one case at the 10 percent level. When the Philippines was excluded from the group (A8), the dummy was negative and significant at the 5 percent or higher level in three cases, and positive and significant at the 10 percent or higher level in three cases. Indeed, the dummies for the European Community (EC) and Latin America (LA) were statistically significant in more cases. In all cases, the sums of the squared t-statistics were significant at the 1 percent level, while all the means were statistically insignificant.

The results for the gross export specification are reported in the second panel. Both the A9 and A8 dummies were positive and significant at the 10 percent or higher level in eleven of forty-six cases; they were not negative and significant in any cases. Interestingly,

---

[15] There were some extremely high values, individual residuals, however. The studentized residual for Taiwan's exports of motorcycles and bicycles was 7.92; the value for Japan's net exports of shipbuilding and repairing was 5.21; the Philippines' value for log exports of the same industry was −5.10; and Malaysia's studentized residual of rubber exports was 5.02.

Table 3.6. *Summary Statistics for Group Dummies*

Net exports 1988		≤1% (−)	≤1% (+)	≤5% (−)	≤5% (+)	≤10% (−)	≤10% (+)	SUMST	MEANT
Case A	DUMMYA9	1	0	4	0	4	1	92.43a	−0.09
	DUMMYEC	0	1	3	1	7	2	75.74a	−0.15
	DUMMYLA	1	1	2	5	2	7	107.60a	0.38
Case B	DUMMYA8	1	0	3	2	3	3	86.02a	−0.02
	DUMMYEC	0	1	5	2	8	2	77.23a	−0.13
	DUMMYLA	1	1	2	4	3	7	109.24a	0.42

Exports 1988		≤1% (−)	≤1% (+)	≤5% (−)	≤5% (+)	≤10% (−)	≤10% (+)	SUMST	MEANT
Case A	DUMMYA9	0	1	0	4	0	11	85.78a	1.08
	DUMMYEC	0	1	0	5	3	9	92.56a	0.85
	DUMMYLA	0	8	0	15	0	18	176.72a	1.44
Case B	DUMMYA8	0	1	0	5	0	11	98.52a	1.20
	DUMMYEC	0	1	0	6	2	7	98.75a	0.96
	DUMMYLA	0	8	0	14	0	17	183.59a	1.49

Exports of 1988 in logs		≤1% (−)	≤1% (+)	≤5% (−)	≤5% (+)	≤10% (−)	≤10% (+)	SUMST	MEANT
Case A	DUMMYA9	0	9	0	18	0	22	240.08a	1.66
	DUMMYEC	0	6	0	13	0	18	196.43a	1.72c
	DUMMYLA	0	2	0	6	1	10	92.04a	0.74
Case B	DUMMYA8	0	13	0	26	0	31	395.41a	2.45b
	DUMMYEC	0	11	0	22	0	28	291.37a	2.14b
	DUMMYLA	0	2	1	6	2	9	109.32a	0.84

Note: Letters a, b, and c denote significance levels of 1, 5, and 10 percent, respectively.
See text for definitions.

the Latin America dummy was positive and significant in eighteen and seventeen cases, respectively, and not negative and significant in any cases in the two specifications. As with the net export models, the sums of the squared t-statistics were significant at the 1 percent level in all cases, and the means were not significant in any cases.

Lastly, the log export specification is reported in the third panel. The A9 and A8 dummies were positive and significant in twenty-two and thirty-one cases, respectively, while in no case were they negative and significant. Once again, the sums of the squared t-statistics are significant at the 1 percent level in all cases. In three cases (A8, and EC in both specifications), the means of the dummies are significant (in all three cases positive). In other words, in the log specification, membership in the EC is associated with higher than expected exports, as is membership in the Asian-8.

These results can be summarized as follows. Overall, each of the regional dummies is a significant explanatory variable for the regressions as a whole, as indicated by the significance of their sum of squares statistics. For the Asian countries, the dummy variable is always associated with higher than expected exports. The exclusion of the Philippines from the group makes this effect more pronounced. There are fewer cases in the net export specification where the Asian dummy is significant, and in these cases, the dummy may take either sign. This suggests that while the Asian countries as a whole may exhibit greater export orientation, this is matched on the import side and should really be interpreted as greater *trade* orientation, not *export* orientation per se.[16]

Table 3.7 summarizes the results for the A8 dummy by industry. There are three cases out of forty-six in which the A8 dummy is significant at the 10 percent or greater level in all three specifications: fish and preparations; radio, television, and telecommunications equipment; and other electrical machinery (which includes household appliances). In each of these cases, the dummies are all positive, meaning that the group exhibits both gross and net exports higher than expected on the basis of their factor endow-

---

[16] This could be interpreted as being consistent with the results obtained from aggregate models by Levine and Renelt (1992) and Frankel, Romer, and Cyrus (1995).

ments alone. There are five more cases in which both of the gross export, but not the net export, dummies are positive and significant: rubber, apparel, rubber products, plastic products, and office and computing equipment.

5. MODELING CHANGES IN EXPORTS

Changes in the export pattern can be modeled quite straight-forwardly by observing the variables during two time periods and taking first differences.[17] This has been done for the longest period for which a complete data set could be assembled, 1968–88.[18] In basic outline, the results are similar to those obtained in the previous section, and as in the previous section, studentized residuals were calculated for each observation.[19]

The sum of squares and means of these residuals by country are reported in Table 3.8. Among the Asian countries, only in the case of Malaysia is the change in export specialization unambiguously not different from that predicted by the model. As indicated by the sum of squares statistics, the change in export specialization is unambiguously different from that predicted by the model for Japan and Korea. Strikingly, in the case of Japan, the results indi-

---

[17] Alternatively, these regressions could be interpreted as regressions on the pattern of exports in which the possibility of additive errors in the measurement of the explanatory variable are taken into account. This could arise if, for example, the services of very long-lived assets (physical infrastructure, for instance) are undercounted in capital stock estimates.

A second type of measurement error, multiplicative measurement error, could arise if there were international differences in factor quality or differences in the intensity of employment of factors. In theory, the multiplicative error terms can be estimated through instrumental variables techniques. However in practice, previous attempts to estimate multiplicative factor quality differences have generated implausible, indeed bizarre, estimates of these parameters (cf. Bowen, Leamer, and Sveikauskas, 1987; Saxonhouse, 1989; Noland, 1997).

[18] Most of the factor endowments are expressed in quantity terms and did not require any adjustment. The two exceptions are the capital stock data, which are expressed in constant terms using the price series supplied by the original source, and the minerals endowment data, which were put into constant terms using the IMF price data cited earlier.

[19] For the net export regressions, the coefficients of determination range from 0.149 to 0.948 with a median of 0.704; for the export regressions, the equivalent values are 0.152, 0.956, and 0.777; for the log exports specifications, the minimum was 0.210, the maximum was 0.828, and the median was 0.548. There were 17 cases out of 138 in which all of the estimated coefficients were insignificant, and the hypothesis that they were jointly equal to zero could not be rejected at the 10 percent level.

MARCUS   NOLAND

Table 3.7. *A8 Dummy Variable Significance by Industry*

Industry	RNEX 88 in level		REX 88 in level		REX 88 in log	
	(+)	(−)	(+)	(−)	(+)	(−)
1 Animals & animal products			c			
2 Fish and preparations	b		a		c	
3 Food crops			c			
4 Tobacco						
5 Agricultural commodities						
6 Beverages					b	
7 Textile fibres						
8 Rubber crude, synthetic			b		b	
9 Wood & wood pulp						
10 Crude minerals						
11 Coal, coke, briquettes						
12 Petroleum & products					c	
13 Nonferrous metals						
14 Spinning, weaving, etc.					c	
15 Other textile products				c		
16 Wearing apparel				b	c	
17 Leather and products					c	
18 Footwear					b	
19 Wood products						
20 Furniture & fixtures					b	
21 Pulp, paper and products					b	
22 Paper products					b	
23 Printing, publishing					a	

cate that the growth of exports was *less* than expected on the basis of Japan's factor endowments.[20]

There is little evidence of a distinctive Asian export pattern at the industry level. There are no industries for which the studentized residuals are 2.0 or more in absolute value for four or more Asian countries. Indeed, there are only two cases in which three of the studentized residuals are significant, and in neither case are they of common sign.[21]

---

[20] A possible explanation that receives support from econometric results presented in Noland (1997) is that trade barriers imposed by Japan's partners reduced Japanese exports over this period.

[21] Once again, there were some extremely large individual studentized residuals: Japan, professional goods net exports, 8.16; Taiwan, pottery, china, etc., exports, 6.85, and motor-

Table 3.7 *(continued)*

Industry	RNEX 88 in level (+)	RNEX 88 in level (−)	REX 88 in level (+)	REX 88 in level (−)	REX 88 in log (+)	REX 88 in log (−)
24 Basic chemicals					b	
25 Synthetic resins					b	
26 Other industrial chemicals						
27 Drugs and medicine						
28 Other chemical products					a	
29 Rubber products				b	a	
30 Plastic products				c	a	
31 Pottery, china, etc.					a	
32 Glass & glass products					a	
33 Other mineral prods					a	
34 Iron & steel					a	
35 Fabricated metal prods					a	
36 Office computing equip				c	a	
37 Other machinery					b	
38 Radio & television	b		b		b	
39 Other elec. machinery	c		c		b	
40 Shipbuilding & repairing					b	
41 Railroad equipment		b			a	
42 Motor vehicles					a	
43 Aircraft					b	
44 Motorcycles & bicycles					a	
45 Professional goods		b				
46 Other industries		a				

Note: Letters a, b, and c denote significance levels of 1, 5, and 10 percent, respectively.

As in the previous section, the regressions were reestimated with dummy variables for the Asian countries, the EC, and the Latin American countries included. These results are summarized in Table 3.9. The net export results indicate that in some industries the Asian dummy is associated with larger than expected positive-change net exports and in some cases larger than expected negative-change net exports. The likelihood of the dummy being positive increases (decreases) when the Philippines is excluded

cycles and bicycles exports, 6.54; Japan, shipbuilding and repairing net exports, 6.33, aircraft exports, −5.72, chemical products exports, −5.18, and beverages exports, −5.11.

Table 3.8. *Sum of Squared Studentized Residuals (SSSR) and Mean of Studentized Residuals (MSR)*

Country	Net Exports 1968–88		Exports 1968–88		Log Exports 1968–88	
	SSSR	MSR	SSSR	MSR	SSSR	MSR
Argentina	24.18	0.13	17.53	−0.17	25.40	0.23
Austria	13.64	−0.11	11.89	−0.21	19.91	−0.29
Brazil	88.33\a	0.11	90.52\a	0.31	114.91\a	−0.45
Canada	141.49\a	−0.06	137.68\a	0.39	25.91	−0.50
Denmark	5.60	0.05	10.15	−0.11	27.84	0.20
Finland	23.54	0.21	22.09	0.21	21.51	0.20
France	407.39\a	0.48	251.36\a	1.25	11.86	−0.37
Germany	177.89\a	0.70	276.09\a	1.37	15.53	−0.20
Greece	17.52	0.13	15.00	0.08	56.55	−0.09
Hong Kong	93.54\a	−0.78	28.36	0.16	116.34\a	0.93
Indonesia	46.66	0.20	49.91	0.46	202.78\a	0.06
Israel	7.65	−0.02	6.90	−0.17	124.15\a	0.16
Italy	232.64\a	0.23	256.81\a	1.01	8.09	0.05
Japan	370.21\a	0.38	451.84\a	−2.19b	95.57\a	−1.19
Korea	135.64\a	0.02	106.48\a	−0.28	81.18\a	0.28

Malaysia	16.22	0.19	20.68	-0.28	23.00	-0.16
Mexico	46.26	0.28	120.14\a	1.18	73.07\a	-0.55
Norway	33.68	-0.07	90.13\a	-1.11	41.08	-0.46
Pakistan	35.93	0.01	32.64	-0.53	83.41\a	0.05
Peru	14.00	-0.04	8.53	0.02	143.47\a	0.04
Philippines	21.66	-0.23	53.80	-0.96	69.96\b	0.60
Singapore	16.58	-0.04	23.27	0.31	80.47\a	-0.57
Spain	18.85	0.08	38.38	0.55	18.39	0.25
Sweden	46.33	0.31	45.39	0.15	19.46	0.16
Taiwan	106.89\a	0.38	162.15\a	0.68	53.83	0.08
Thailand	25.70	-0.08	31.32	-0.10	65.75\b	0.32
Tunisia	4.52	-0.02	8.67	-0.39	154.94\a	0.49
Turkey	109.28a	-0.00	74.15\a	-0.45	471.97\a	1.67
United Kingdom	376.63\a	-0.70	193.51\a	0.27	19.98	0.23
United States	331.55\a	-0.56	168.08\a	0.30	14.77	-0.38

Note: Letters a, b, and c denote significance levels of 1, 5, and 10 percent, respectively.
See text for definitions.

(included). The Asian and EC dummies on the whole are significant explanatory variables as indicated by the sum of squares variable, though in this case, the Latin American dummy is not. On average, the dummies are not associated with a greater or less than expected change in net exports in any case.

The change in exports results are presented in the second panel. In four cases, the Asian dummy is negative and significant at the 10 percent or greater level if the Philippines is included; these cases disappear when the Philippines is excluded. In this case, the A8 dummy is positive and significant in eleven of forty-six cases. Once again, the sum of squares statistic is significant at the 1 percent level for the Asian economies and the EC and insignificant for the Latin American countries.

Finally, the log export specification results are reported in the third panel. These results are somewhat different from those presented thus far. The EC dummy is an insignificant explanatory variable for the regressions as a whole. The Asian dummy is positive in some cases and negative in others; including the Philippines in the group *reduces* the likelihood of the dummy being negative. The Latin American dummy sum of squared t-values is significant in both specifications. Both the A9 sum of squares statistic and the A8 sum of squares statistic are significant at the 1 percent level. For none of the group dummies is the mean t-statistic significantly different from zero.

Taken together, these results are slightly puzzling. There is little evidence in Table 3.9 that the Latin American dummy has anything to do with the *change* in exports, as contrasted to the *level* of exports evidence presented in Table 3.5. The EC dummy appears not to be strongly associated with the level of exports in Table 3.5, but there is some evidence that it is associated with an increase in exports in Table 3.9. If the regression is expressed in logs, however, these relationships are reversed: The EC dummy is unambiguously associated with higher than expected log exports (Table 3.5) but not with their growth (Table 3.9).

To a certain extent, the results for the Asian dummies are similarly nonrobust. The A8 dummy is associated with higher than expected log exports in Table 3.5 but not with their growth in Table 3.9. Even the pattern of exclusion of the Philippines observation in the Asian group increasing (decreasing) the likelihood of a positive (negative) dummy breaks down in the third panel of Table 3.9.

Table 3.9. *Summary Statistics for Group Dummies*

		≤1% (−)	≤1% (+)	≤5% (−)	≤5% (+)	≤10% (−)	≤10% (+)	SUMST	MEANT
Net exports 1968–88									
Case A	DUMMYA9	0	0	3	2	6	5	85.90a	−0.17
	DUMMYEC	0	0	3	0	6	4	68.45b	−0.06
	DUMMYLA	0	0	0	1	0	1	26.25	0.02
Case B	DUMMYA8	0	1	4	3	6	6	96.38a	−0.07
	DUMMYEC	0	0	5	2	6	4	75.41a	−0.01
	DUMMYLA	0	0	0	1	0	1	22.96	0.08
Exports 1968–88									
Case A	DUMMYA9	0	1	0	3	4	4	73.64a	0.10
	DUMMYEC	0	5	0	16	0	21	163.89a	1.42
	DUMMYLA	0	1	0	1	0	1	35.09	0.42
Case B	DUMMYA8	0	1	0	4	0	11	89.90a	0.56
	DUMMYEC	0	7	0	20	1	23	196.73a	1.62
	DUMMYLA	0	1	0	1	0	1	36.57	0.51
Exports of 1968–88 in logs									
Case A	DUMMYA9	0	2	0	4	3	6	76.64a	0.14
	DUMMYEC	0	1	1	1	1	1	55.43	0.11
	DUMMYLA	0	0	3	1	4	2	64.53b	−0.34
Case B	DUMMYA8	0	2	3	3	8	4	82.78a	−0.29
	DUMMYEC	0	1	1	2	1	3	54.96	0.07
	DUMMYLA	2	0	3	1	6	2	74.11a	−0.42

Note: Letters a, b, and c denote significance levels of 1, 5, and 10 percent, respectively. See text for definitions.

Table 3.10. *A8 Dummy Variable Significance by Industry*

Industry	RNEX 88 in level		REX 88 in level		REX 88 in log	
	(+)	(−)	(+)	(−)	(+)	(−)
1 Animals & animal products					a	
2 Fish and preparations			b			
3 Food crops						
4 Tobacco						
5 Agricultural commodities					a	
6 Beverages						
7 Textile fibres		b				
8 Rubber crude, synthetic						
9 Wood & wood pulp						
10 Crude minerals		c				
11 Coal, coke, briquettes		c			b	
12 Petroleum & products						
13 Nonferrous metals		b				b
14 Spinning, weaving, etc.				c		
15 Other textile products	b		b			
16 Wearing apparel	b		b			
17 Leather and products						
18 Footwear	c		c			
19 Wood products						
20 Furniture & fixtures						
21 Pulp, paper and products						c
22 Paper products						c
23 Printing, publishing						

The industry results are similarly less robust in the export change models than for the export pattern models discussed in the previous section.[22] As indicated in Table 3.10, there are no cases in which the A8 dummy was significant in all three specifications; indeed, there are no cases in which the A8 dummy is significant in both of the gross export specifications. There are six cases, however, in which the A8 dummy was positive and significant in the net export and in the change in gross exports in levels regressions:

[22] One possibility is that the dummies are picking up differences in technology or home demand biases. Results obtained by Trefler (1995) suggest that these effects may be empirically important. Changes in technology *over time* might be particularly important if technologically lagging countries were "catching up."

Table 3.10 *(continued)*

Industry	RNEX 88 in level		REX 88 in level		REX 88 in log	
	(+)	(−)	(+)	(−)	(+)	(−)
24 Basic chemicals		b				
25 Synthetic resins						
26 Other industrial chemicals						c
27 Drugs and medicine						b
28 Other chemical products						
29 Rubber products				c		
30 Plastic products	c			c		
31 Pottery, china, etc.						
32 Glass & glass products						
33 Other mineral prods						b
34 Iron & steel						
35 Fabricated metal prods						
36 Office computing equip	c			c		
37 Other machinery						
38 Radio & television	a			a		
39 Other elec. machinery				c		c
40 Shipbuilding & repairing						
41 Railroad equipment						
42 Motor vehicles						c
43 Aircraft		b				
44 Motorcycles & bicycles				c		
45 Professional goods						
46 Other industries					c	

Note: Letters a, b, and c denote significance levels of 1, 5, and 10 percent, respectively.

apparel, textile products, footwear, plastic products, office and computing equipment, and radio, television, and telecommunications equipment. In these six cases, net exports and (in one specification) gross exports grew more rapidly than expected solely on the basis of the Asian-8's changes in factor endowments.

6. CONCLUSIONS

As a group, the eight high-performing Asian economies examined in this chapter (Japan, Hong Kong, Singapore, Taiwan, Korea, Malaysia, Thailand, and Indonesia) appear to have some distinctive characteristics with regard to export performance. The commodity composition of their exports differs from those of comparator countries as well as the world as a whole. The rate of growth in their real exports was faster than that of the world as a whole in every manufactured export category except one.

The diversity of the Asian economies mitigates against much deeper generalities, however. The evidence points away from an "Asian export path," for example. The export pattern of Japan (and to a certain extent Singapore) was found to be more similar to those of some Western European countries, both contemporaneously and noncontemporaneously, than with other Asian countries. The export patterns of Hong Kong, Taiwan, and Korea tend to cluster, as do Malaysia, Thailand, and the Philippines, and there is evidence that these patterns have grown more similar over time, while Indonesia, perhaps because of its oil exports, remains somewhat different from the others. Only in the case of Korea was any support uncovered for the proposition that a country was "following" the Japanese export path.

Next, the determinants of these patterns were examined by estimating cross-national regressions of factor endowments on trade flows and generating a variety of descriptive statistics from these regressions. The regressions were estimated in two forms: on the levels of exports in 1988, and on the change in exports from 1968 to 1988. Three export specifications were used: net exports, gross exports, and log gross exports.

The main result of these regressions is that the trade pattern of Japan, and to a lesser extent of Taiwan and Korea, cannot be adequately explained by the factor endowment models. In the case of Japan, the growth in Japanese exports was *less* than what would be explained on the basis of its factor accumulation.

When regional dummy variables were introduced to capture group effects, there was a tendency for the Asian dummies to be positive with respect to gross exports and insignificant with respect to net exports, supporting the idea that these economies are unusually *trade* oriented, as distinct from *export* oriented. However, the European and Latin American dummies were significant about as frequently as the Asian dummies, suggesting that Asian peculiarities in the data, while present, were not particularly unique.

These results refer to exports as a whole. The models in this chapter have also been used to analyze results for industries considered individually. Examination of the residuals industry by industry for each of the Asian economies identified no industries of unusual Asian specialization. However, when dummy variables were introduced to capture group effects, some industries repeatedly revealed positive and statistically significant dummies, indicating greater than predicted levels of specialization: radio, television, and telecommunications equipment (in five of six possible cases), and apparel, plastic products, and office and computing equipment (in four out of six specifications).

The question naturally arises as to what explains this deviance from the norm. One obvious possibility is that industrial policies successfully facilitated the development of these industries. Noland (1991, 1993) shows that Japanese industrial targeting had a demonstrable impact on Japanese exports and net exports, beyond what could be explained on the basis of comparative advantage alone. The World Bank reports mixed evidence on the impact of government interventions on the composition of output for several additional Asian countries. Overall, although there is evidence that such interventions had effects, their quantitative importance is much less clear, and after reviewing this evidence, it is hard to believe that industrial policies alone could have given rise to deviations from the norm of the magnitude reported here. Indeed, the opposite may be the case. It is important to remember that the norm derived from the regression model embodies the average interventions of the sample countries – not laissez faire or free trade. If a country had significantly less than average intervention, it would appear to be overspecialized in its areas of comparative advantage and overly trade dependent (since the interventions, either forward- or backward-looking, promote not currently competitive sectors at the expense of contemporaneously competitive sectors). This is precisely the pattern observed for the Asian economies as a whole. And at least in the case of the Asian developing countries, there is evidence reported by the World Bank that the degree of relative price distortion in these economies, although nontrivial (with the exception of the city-states where it was trivial), was considerably less than for other developing countries on average. Whether this is in fact the explanation for the results presented here requires further substantiation.

REFERENCES

Belsley, David A., Edwin Kuh, and Roy E. Welsch (1980), *Regression Diagnostics*, New York: Wiley.

Bowen, Harry P., Edward E. Leamer, and Leo Sveikauskas (1987), "Multicountry, Multifactor Tests of the Factor Abundance Theory," *American Economic Review*, 77: 791–809.

Bradford, Colin (1994), *From Trade-Driven Growth to Growth-Driven Trade: Reappraising the East Asian Development Experience*, Paris: OECD.

Breusch, T. S., and A. R. Pagan (1979), "A Simple Test for Heteroskedasticity and Random Coefficient Variation," *Econometrica*, 47: 1287–1294.

Cline, William R. (1982), "Can the East Asian Model of Development Be Generalized?" *World Development*, 10: 81–90.

——— (1984), *Exports of Manufactures from Developing Countries*, Washington, DC: Brookings Institution.

——— (1985), "Reply," *World Development*, 13: 547–548.

Dollar, David (1992), "Outward Oriented Developing Countries Really Do Grow More Rapidly," *Economic Development and Cultural Change*, 40: 523–544.

Finger, J. M., and M. E. Kreinin (1979), "A Measure of 'Export Similarity' and Its Possible Uses," *Economic Journal*, 89: 905–912.

Frankel, Jeffrey A., David Romer, and Teresa Cyrus (1995), "Trade and Growth in East Asian Countries: Cause and Effect?" Paper presented at the American Economic Association meetings, Washington, DC, January.

Fukuda, Shin-ichi, and Hideki Toya (1993), "The Conditional Convergence in East Asian Countries: The Role of Exports for Economic Growth," Discussion Paper No. 57, Economic Research Institute, Economic Planning Agency, Tokyo.

Helliwell, John (1992), "International Growth Linkages: Evidence from Asia and the OECD," NBER Working Paper No. 4245, December.

Hutchison, Michael, and Nirvikar Singh (1992), "Exports, Non-Exports, and Externalities: A Granger Causality Approach," *International Economic Journal*, 6: 79–94.

Jung, Woo S., and Peyton J. Marshall (1985), "Exports, Growth, and Causality in Developing Countries," *Journal of Development Economics*, 18: 1–12.

Kellman, Mitchell, and Tim Schroeder (1983), "The Export Similarity Index: Some Structural Tests," *Economic Journal*, 93: 193–198.

Leamer, Edward E. (1984), *Sources of International Comparative Advantage*, Cambridge: MIT Press.

Levine, Ross, and David Renelt (1992), "A Sensitivity Analysis of Cross-Country Growth Regressions," *American Economic Review*, 82: 942–963.

Noland, Marcus (1990), *Pacific Basin Developing Countries: Prospects for the Future*. Washington, DC: Institute for International Economics.

(1991), "Export Targeting and Japanese Industrial Policy," in Jaime de Melo and Andre Sapir, eds., *Trade Theory and Economic Reform*, Cambridge: Basil Blackwell.

(1993), "The Impact of Industrial Policy on Japan's Trade Specialization," *Review of Economics and Statistics*, 75: 241–247.

(1997), "Public Policies, Private Preferences, and the Japanese Trade Pattern," *Review of Economics and Statistics*, 79: 259–266.

Pearson, Charles S. (1994), "The Asian Export Ladder," in Shu-Chin Yang, ed., *Manufactured Exports of East Asian Industrializing Economies*, Armonk: M. E. Sharpe.

Ram, Rati (1985), "Exports and Growth: Some Additional Evidence," *Economic Development and Cultural Change*, 33: 415–425.

(1987), "Exports and Economic Growth in Developing Countries," *Economic Development and Cultural Change*, 35: 51–72.

Ranis, Gustav (1985), "Can the East Asian Model of Development Be Generalized? A Comment," *World Development*, 13: 543–546.

Saxonhouse, Gary R. (1989), "Differentiated Products, Economies of Scale, and Access to the Japanese Market," in Robert C. Feenstra, ed., *Trade Policies and International Competitiveness*, Chicago: University of Chicago Press and NBER.

Trefler, Daniel (1995), "The Case of the Missing Trade and Other Mysteries," *American Economic Review*, 85: 1029–1046.

White, Halbert (1980), "A Heteroscedastic-Consistent Covariance Matrix Estimator and a Direct Test for Heteroscedasticity," *Econometrica*, 44: 817–838.

World Bank (1993), *The East Asian Miracle*, Oxford: Oxford University Press.

APPENDIX: DATA SOURCES

The trade data originate from the GATT tapes. The labor endowment was defined as the economically active population; the data come from International Labour Organisation (ILO), *Yearbook of Labour Statistics*, various issues. The capital stock was calculated by summing and depreciating the purchasing power adjusted gross fixed investment series in the diskette accompanying Robert Summers and Alan Heston, "The Penn World Table (Mark 5)" *Quarterly Review of Economics*, May 1991. The asset life of capital was assumed to be eighteen years, and the depreciation rate 13 percent.

Human capital was calculated by multiplying the economically active labor force by the Psacharopoulos index of per-capita educational capital. The Psacharopoulos index is defined as the average per-capita expenditure on education embodied in the labor force calculated from data on the highest level of educational achievement, years duration of schooling at each level, and expenditures per year at each level normalized by the amount of expenditure for one year of primary school education. Data on educational achievement and schooling duration are found in the United Nations Educational Social and Cultural Organisation (UNESCO), *Statistical Yearbook*. Expenditure weights come from George Psacharopoulos, 1973, *Returns to Education*, Jossey-Bass, San Francisco.

Data on land endowments come from the Food and Agricultural Organisation (FAO), *Production Yearbook*. The coal endowment was measured by domestic production in thousands of metric tons and comes from U.S. Bureau of Mines, *Minerals Yearbook*. (Data on coal mining capacity or reserves were unavailable for most countries.) The minerals index is the value of domestic production of thirteen minerals; the production data are from the *Minerals Yearbook*, the price data are from the *International Financial Statistics*. (The composition of this index was determined by taking the top twenty minerals [excluding oil, natural gas, and coal] by value of world output in 1984 and then dropping those for which price data could not be found.) The oil endowment in proven reserves was taken from the *Oil and Gas Yearbook*, published by the American Petroleum Institute. Lastly, the c.i.f./f.o.b. data come from the IMF, *International Financial Statistics: Trade Supplement*.

In some cases, data for Taiwan were unavailable from these sources and instead come from *Taiwan Statistical Data Book*, Council for Economic Planning and Development, Executive Yuan, Republic of China.

Comment

Albert Fishlow

I address the three major points in Marcus Noland's paper – the points that he selected in his presentation as the critical ones to establish. Let me also note that the written version is not only comprehensive but also rich and relevant, reflecting his knowledge of the Asian economies.

I begin with the first, and admittably, minor one – that it makes sense to focus exclusively upon East Asia as a coherent group to establish the hypothesis that Asian export performance as a whole is qualitatively different from that of other regions. Such a position is not only logically inadmissible, but it misses the important point that there are significant and systematic differences among East Asian countries that are worth exploiting in a comparative sense. We see this in the tables. Thus Indonesia appears as a lagged country at the beginning of its industrialization experience with considerable exports of petroleum and lumber products. Japan is at a much higher level of income, with a full range of manufactured exports. Korea and Taiwan have still a third pattern of emerging specialization, with a pattern that differs from countries such as Indonesia, Malaysia, and Thailand.

Thus, while I am willing to accept the conclusion that East Asia has a significantly different pattern of export growth than other regions, I feel that the additional effort to separate the Asian countries makes sense. After all, that is the very logic of the flying geese theorem: Countries can imitate their predecessors to their advantage. It is central to the *regional* success obtained in East Asia relative to other geographic areas.

A second emphasis was the small size of the residual sectoral composition of trade after correcting for variation in factor composition. Noland argues that factor composition is crucial in explaining the patterns of trade. Owing to the absence of the disaggregated data available in the Appendix, one of the things readers may not fully appreciate is the considerable difference in goodness of fit attained. The coefficients of determination turned out to have a significant variation. While the median value is 0.8, the lowest result is a much more reduced 0.06.

A central issue, however, is the failure to allow for systematic differences in technology among the countries included. There are measures of human capital as well as estimates of physical capital, but despite important difference in income level, technology is assumed to be the same in all countries. Given the difference in income between Indonesia and Japan, for example, this seems dubious. Moreover, I would stress the consequences of looking at matters from the perspective of the Asian-8. There are frequent cases where there are four countries with significant coefficients, others with three. In short, one is not dealing with a uniform class of observations here but rather a different set. It would be interesting to see, and catalogue, the cases in which classification of the countries by relevant characteristics might help to sort out patterns with common features.

I turn last to the fundamental conclusion – that there is in fact no common East Asian style to successful development. One should emphasize that this conclusion holds only in the sense of trade. But equally, there *is* an East Asian style of development that is apparent in the similarity of the style of capital accumulation. Simply put, East Asia saves more than other countries at comparable levels of income. This is what differentiates this group of countries from those of other developing countries in Latin America, the Middle East, Africa, or elsewhere. Given this common characteristic, one would want to factor it into the process of changing trade specialization that occurs as income rises. In other work, Noland is factoring in the importance of foreign investment; it plays an obvious role in the case of Singapore and, more recently, Thailand, which has greatly expanded its trade in recent years. But the key relationship I would stress, which we do not fully comprehend, is the interaction of export growth and saving rate increases. To consider only the former important, as the World Bank's East Asian 'Miracle' story frequently seems to do, is to reach a conclusion that is not fully justified. And finally, even on the trade side, one would want to look at more than period averages: Temporal ordering may be quite relevant. There may be particular sequences or patterns of imports and exports that are significant. They would not be captured by the form in which the data and the regressions were cast in this study.

Thus, while I praise the author plenteously for what he has accomplished in the chapter presented here, there are still interesting questions to be pursued. Particularly, when the issues are so central to the development strategies that follower countries might choose, it is important to broaden the initial inquiry. Marcus Noland has made a fine beginning.

## PART III

Regional Trading Arrangements in the Pacific Basin

CHAPTER 4

Should East Asia Go Regional?

Arvind Panagariya

1. INTRODUCTION

By June 1, 1995, the World Trade Organization (WTO) – the successor institution to General Agreement on Tariffs and Trade (GATT) – had been notified of more than 130 regional arrangements (Bhagwati and Panagariya, 1996b). Today, with the exception of Hong Kong and Japan, every WTO member boasts of a membership in at least one regional arrangement.[1] Neither the successful completion of the Uruguay Round nor the recent peso crisis in Mexico has been able to reverse the rising tide of regionalism. Having already concluded Free Trade Area (FTA) agreements with its neighbors in Central and Eastern Europe, the European Union (EU) is now beginning to bring the countries in North Africa into its fold. The United States, on the other hand, has set a target date of 2005 for the creation of the Free Trade Area of the Americas (FTAA), consisting of the entire Western Hemisphere. Germany has even made overtures for a Trans-Atlantic Free Trade Area (TAFTA) between the United States and the EU.

Historically, East Asia has not been enthusiastic toward preferential trading. Until recently, the only functioning preferential

An earlier version of this chapter was circulated as the World Bank's Policy Research Working Paper #1209. A shorter paper based on that version appeared in the November 1994 issue of the *World Economy* under the title "East Asia and the New Regionalism." I thank Hiro Lee and David Roland-Holst for comments and Sumana Dhar for excellent research assistance. The original version of the chapter was written as a part of the Regional Integration Initiative Study of the East Asia Region of the World Bank and of RPO 677-86. Findings, interpretations, and conclusions in this chapter are entirely those of the author and should not be attributed in any manner to the World Bank, its affiliated organizations, or to members of its Board of Executive Directors or the countries they represent.

[1] Not all of these countries belong to regional arrangements under Article XXIV of GATT. Many developing countries belong exclusively to south-south arrangements under the Enabling Clause of GATT.

119

trading scheme in the region was the Association of Southeast Asian Nations (ASEAN) Preferential Trading Area (APTA), which was very limited in scope. Starting in 1989, the rise of regionalism in North America and Europe led to some rethinking in the region. In 1989, the forum for Asia Pacific Economic Cooperation (APEC) was created to bring the Uruguay Round to a speedy conclusion and to promote liberalization of trade and investment policies at the regional level. APEC, which has eighteen members currently, includes countries from not only East Asia but also the Americas.[2] In 1990, Prime Minister Mahathir of Malaysia announced the formation of the exclusively Asian East Asian Economic Group (EAEG), which, under U.S. pressure, was later recast as the East Asian Economic Caucus (EAEC).[3] In January 1992, members of ASEAN signed an agreement to turn the APTA into the ASEAN Free Trade Area (AFTA) by the year 2008.[4] In 1994, at its Bogor meeting, APEC members agreed to establish free trade by the year 2010 in the developed member countries and by 2020 in the developing member countries.

In the light of these developments, it is timely to ask whether regionalism should assume a more central role in East Asia. If yes, in what form and, if not, why not? And what are the implications of the APEC process in general and Bogor agreement in particular? In this chapter, I subject these important issues to a systematic analysis. In section 2, I subject the literature on regional integration to a critical examination. I argue that, from the viewpoint of small countries willing to liberalize trade unilaterally, a clear economic justification for regional arrangements is difficult to find. In section 3, I consider the case for exclusively East Asian regional integration schemes. Cases for three possible forms of integration are evaluated: subregional groupings such as ASEAN, a regionwide trading bloc, and regionwide nondiscriminatory liberalization. I argue that the first of these is undesirable, the second is infeasible, and the third holds some promise though the case for it is far from clear-cut. In section 4, I discuss the implications of

---

[2] APEC membership includes the six original members of ASEAN, Korea, China, Hong Kong, Taiwan, Mexico, Chile, Papua New Guinea, Japan, Canada, Australia, New Zealand, and the United States.

[3] The proposed membership of the EAEG included ASEAN, NIEs, China, and Japan. But the United States opposed the idea and "persuaded" Japan to stay out of the group. When the EAEG was recast as EAEC, Vietnam also became a member.

[4] This timetable was moved forward to 2003 two years later. See Tan (Chapter 6, this volume) for more details.

the APEC process for the region. Because APEC includes the United States, its implications are more complicated than for the exclusively Asian arrangements discussed in section 3. In section 5, brief concluding remarks are offered.

2. THE ECONOMICS OF DISCRIMINATORY LIBERALIZATION

The term "regional integration" has been used traditionally to refer to discriminatory trade liberalization,[5] whereby two or more countries lower trade barriers against one another relative to the rest of the world. Because such liberalization makes the participating countries more open to each other but possibly less open to outside countries, its effects on economic efficiency are ambiguous in general. This fact has made regional integration a highly contentious issue.

In this section, I summarize the broad implications of discriminatory liberalization by a pair of countries. The analysis is essentially applicable to more than two countries. The discussion begins with an exposition of the influential concepts of trade creation and trade diversion introduced by Viner (1950) in his classic work, *The Customs Union Issue.* This is followed by a comparison between a free trade area and nondiscriminatory, unilateral trade liberalization. The section is concluded with a discussion of why countries find regional integration an attractive option today.

2.1. Trade Creation and Trade Diversion

Let us begin with the standard, static analysis of a discriminatory liberalization by a pair of countries. Imagine that starting from a nondiscriminatory tariff, Japan and Indonesia form an FTA. For simplicity, focus on the market for VCRs. Assume that VCRs are a homogeneous good and that Indonesia is a net importer of them. At $200 per VCR, Korea is the cheapest supplier of the product in the world.[6] Japan supplies the product at a per-unit price of $220.

---

[5] Some of the points made in this section can be found in Melo and Panagariya (1992), which in turn is based on Melo and Panagariya (1993). For a summary of theoretical developments, see Bhagwati and Panagariya (1996a).

[6] Note that we deliberately assume that Japan is not the cheapest source of VCRs. If it were, a free trade area in VCRs would be vacuous in that, given constant costs, the outcome would be unaffected by whether liberalization is preferential or nondiscriminatory.

Unit costs and, hence, the selling prices of Korea and Japan are constant.

Assume that Indonesia initially imposes a 50 percent tariff on all imported VCRs. This makes the tariff-inclusive price of VCRs from Korea $300 and those from Japan $330. All imports come from Korea, and the price of VCRs in Indonesia settles at $300. At this price, suppose that Indonesians buy a total of 150,000 VCRs. Of these, 100,000 are supplied by Indonesian sellers, who produce VCRs at increasing marginal costs. The remaining 50,000 units come from Korea. Indonesia collects $5,000,000 in import duties.

Now suppose that Indonesia forms a free trade area with Japan. The two countries drop tariffs on each other but retain them on outside countries including Korea. Because there is no longer any tariff on VCRs from Japan, these latter can be sold in Indonesia at $220, while Korean VCRs are priced at $300. All imported VCRs now come from Japan, and the price of VCRs in Indonesia declines to $220. From an efficiency standpoint, assuming for now a fixed total demand of 150,000 VCRs in Indonesia, two effects can be identified.

First, the original imports of 50,000 VCRs, which came from the lowest-cost supplier, Korea, now come from the higher-cost partner, Japan. In Vinerian terms, this is "trade diversion" and is associated with a loss for Indonesia. The loss is manifest in the disappearance of tariff revenue, which is recaptured only partially by consumers in the form of a lower price of VCRs. The remainder of tariff revenue goes to pay for less efficiently produced VCRs of the partner country. Second, because VCRs are produced under increasing marginal costs in Indonesia, the output there declines with the decline in price. VCRs produced at a marginal cost higher than $220 in Indonesia are replaced by cheaper imports. This "trade creation" improves efficiency by replacing higher-cost Indonesian production by lower-cost imports from Japan.[7]

Trade diversion reduces efficiency while trade creation improves it. Therefore, the net effect of an FTA is ambiguous in general.

---

[7] Observe that as noted before, resources released from the VCR industry in Indonesia are assumed to be reallocated to other sectors that are more productive. In the transition, there is likely to be unemployment. Moreover, reallocation of resources may involve training and other adjustment costs. These costs are not incorporated into the analysis in the text. If we could measure these costs satisfactorily, however, the analysis could be modified to take them into consideration without harm to the basic conclusions.

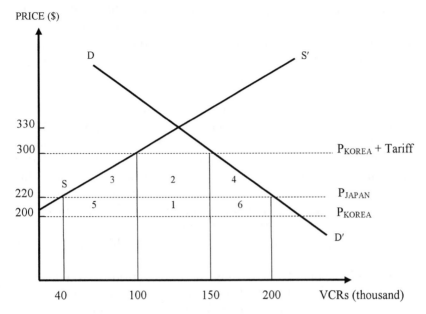

Figure 4.1 Welfare effects of free trade area.

Ceteris paribus, the higher the initial tariff, the lower the difference between the prices of the two suppliers of imports; and the larger the economic size of the union, the more likely that the FTA will improve efficiency. A high initial tariff means that the potential gains from deprotecting the domestic industry even on a discriminatory basis are large, or, equivalently, the trade creation effect is likely to dominate. A small difference between the prices of the partner and the outside source means that the terms-of-trade deterioration from switching to the partner is small, or, equivalently, the trade diversion effect is small. Finally, the larger the union, the more likely that the lowest-cost source of supply would be within the union. For instance, in our example, if Korea was also included in the union, there would be no trade diversion in the VCR market, and welfare would rise unambiguously.

As an anchor for future discussion, it is useful to summarize this analysis graphically. In Figure 4.1, *DD'* and *SS'*, respectively, represent Indonesia's demand for and supply of VCRs of a given quality. The vertical axis shows the price of a VCR in U.S. dollars, and the horizontal axis shows the quantity of VCRs in thousands. Under a nondiscriminatory tariff of 50 percent, the price in Indonesia is $300 and quantities consumed, produced, and imported are 150,000, 100,000, and 50,000, respectively. All imports come from Korea at a border price of $200. Import duties sum to areas 1 plus 2.

An FTA between Indonesia and Japan lowers the price in Indonesia to $220 per VCR, and all imports now come from Japan. Of the original 150,000 VCRs bought earlier, 40,000 are now produced domestically, and 110,000 are imported from Japan. The 60,000 additional imported units replace higher-cost domestic units. This is trade creation and yields a gain of area 3 for Indonesia. The other 50,000 units replace cheaper Korean units. This is trade diversion and leads to a loss of area 1 for Indonesia.[8]

There is one more source of efficiency effect which, in the spirit of Viner, we have not identified so far.[9] The reduction in price from $300 to $220 per VCR expands the consumption of VCRs and brings the marginal benefit from consumption closer to the marginal cost of it. This generates a further welfare gain represented by area 4. The net effect of the FTA is positive or negative as the sum of areas 3 and 4 is larger or smaller than area 1.

2.2. A Puzzle: Why Form an FTA When Nondiscriminatory, Unilateral Liberalization Is Superior?

In the small-country context chosen in the previous subsection, it is easy to see that Indonesia can improve its welfare unambiguously relative to the initial as well as the post-FTA equilibrium by liberalizing trade unilaterally on a nondiscriminatory basis. For example, if Indonesia lowers its tariff on both Japan and Korea to 10 percent, Korea continues to outcompete Japan. The tariff-inclusive price of Korean VCRs is now $220; we obtain the same equilibrium as under FTA but without any trade diversion. Indonesia is able to collect import duties represented by areas 1, 5, and 6 in addition to the efficiency gains represented by areas 3 and 4 in

---

[8] Observe that all of tariff revenue represented by areas 1 and 2 disappears. But area 1 is recaptured by consumers via a lower price of VCRs.

[9] Viner implicitly assumed a completely inelastic demand. This practice is surprisingly common in policy analyses, which often ignore changes in demand.

Figure 4.1; the country gains relative to the initial as well as FTA equilibrium.

The proposition that unilateral, nondiscriminatory liberalization is superior to an FTA is robust to a variety of modifications provided we continue to make the "small-union" assumption (i.e., the countries forming the union are too small to influence the terms-of-trade in the outside world). Three such modifications may be mentioned. First, in the Indonesia–Japan example, suppose we introduce increasing marginal costs of production in Japan. In this case, Indonesia is likely to import VCRs from both Japan and Korea before as well as after the FTA. This will not change our conclusion, however. Indonesia's welfare under a nondiscriminatory liberalization will remain unambiguously higher than under an FTA. Moreover, the gains from Indonesia's preferential liberalization will accrue largely to Japan.

Second, suppose we now recognize the fact that as a part of the FTA, Japan also lowers its tariffs on Indonesian goods. This will surely create benefits for Indonesia that are not available through unilateral liberalization. Although this is true, we also know from our earlier analysis that the gains to Japan from lowering its tariff are higher if it does so on a nondiscriminatory basis. Indeed, it can be shown that the extra gains to Indonesia from preferential liberalization by Japan are less than the extra benefits to Japan from a nondiscriminatory liberalization. Put differently, although one country can enjoy a higher real income under an FTA than under a nondiscriminatory liberalization, the *combined* income of the partners will be lower under the former scenario. The country benefiting more from an FTA than from nondiscriminatory liberalization cannot afford to bribe the other country into forming an FTA.

Third, suppose there are scale economies. Here again, as long as we maintain the small-union assumption, nondiscriminatory liberalization dominates. The simple point is that with declining costs, if it is at all profitable for the country to produce the good subject to economies of scale, it should expand production all the way to the minimum cost point, consume what it can consume domestically, and export the residual to the outside world. To exploit scale economies, one does not need a "partner country's" market when the world market is there.

2.3. The Attraction of Regionalism: Some Answers?

In spite of this dominance of unilateral, nondiscriminatory liberalization, how do we explain the attraction of regionalism today? The literature offers a number of explanations, but, as I will argue later, none of them is persuasive.[10]

(i) The small-union assumption may not be valid. Thus, in our Japan–Indonesia example, the price at which Korea sells VCRs to Indonesia may depend on the number of VCRs sold. In response to a switch in demand from Korea to Japan due to preferential liberalization, Korea may lower its price to remain competitive in the Indonesian market. The terms-of-trade for Indonesia improve. Likewise, the price paid by Japan to extra-union suppliers may decline in response to the preferential access offered by it to Indonesia. This improvement in the terms-of-trade yields benefits not available through nondiscriminatory, unilateral liberalization.[11]

(ii) There is the closely related issue of access to the world markets. In a world infested with voluntary export restraints, administered protection, and a strong tendency for the formation of trading blocs, the difference between discriminatory and nondiscriminatory liberalization may be blurred. In the limit, we can imagine an outside world that does not trade externally at all. Then trade restrictions on the outside world are vacuous, and it does not matter whether liberalization is discriminatory or nondiscriminatory. What is important is that liberalization be undertaken on a regionwide basis, and for this, regional integration may be a powerful instrument. By bringing countries together to liberalize *simultaneously*, the regional approach can help solve the same prisoners' dilemma at the regional level that the GATT helps solve at the multilateral level.

(iii) Once we admit the limits on access to the world market,

---

[10] For a detailed critique of discriminatory liberalization, see Bhagwati (1995), Bhagwati and Panagariya (1996b), and Panagariya (1996a).

[11] In the same vein, if the union is not small, it can benefit by exploiting the economies of scale more effectively. In a three-country model, if each country restricts imports from the other, each may produce the good subject to scale economies and fail to take full advantage of declining costs. If two of the countries form a regional arrangement with one country becoming the exporter and the other the importer of the product, the union as a whole can benefit. The difficulty with this argument, however, is that with relatively open U.S., European, and Japanese markets, for most countries, market size is not a major constraint.

large gains from regional integration are possible if scale economies are present. Mutual liberalization by countries in the region will then provide room for expanded scale of operation, specialization, and plant rationalization. Regional opening may also offer gains from increased product variety.

(iv) Even when the rest of the world is open, there may be goods that are tradeable only regionally. For these goods, a simultaneous liberalization through a regional approach can bestow gains for the same reasons as multilateral trade liberalization. Trade in electricity between neighboring countries is one such example. Under a broad interpretation, we can include cooperation on projects of regional interest – development of roads, dams, and water resources – in this category. A concrete example is the recent agreement, signed in 1991, under which Singapore will cooperate with Indonesia to develop water resources in the latter's province of Riau in return for guaranteed water supply for fifty years.

(v) For smaller economies of the region, a regional arrangement with Japan can guarantee future access to a large, developed-country market. Under normal circumstances, this may not be important, but in the event that the EU and Americas continue to travel down the road leading to inward-looking blocs, such access may be crucial. From the viewpoint of entire East Asia, the threat of a regional arrangement may also serve to deter the EU and Americas from turning more inward.

(vi) Unilateral liberalization, even if superior to the regional route in principle, may be politically infeasible. At political levels, there is a strong mercantilist bias in trade-policy thinking. Any reduction in trade barriers is viewed as a concession given to foreigners. Under this mind set, unilateral import liberalization is a free gift to the world, and liberalization via the regional route brings concessions from partners. In practice, this factor seems to become particularly important when the level of protection is not wildly high. Mexico and Chile have been able to liberalize imports unilaterally to a considerable degree, but further liberalization seems to require a regional context. In East Asia, countries such as Malaysia, Thailand, Korea, and the Philippines have also been successful in unilateral liberalization up to a degree, but they may require a regional context for further import liberalization.

(vii) Regional integration can go far beyond trade liberalization. In East Asia, intraregional labor mobility, foreign direct invest-

ment, and financial-capital flows will play an increasingly important role in forthcoming years. To the extent that harmonization
of policies across countries can help facilitate such movements,
regional integration can offer gains not available through either
unilateral or global actions.[12]

(viii) For a small developing country, a regional arrangement
with a large, developed country may be an effective instrument of
making its trade reform credible. Even if future governments
happen to be more protectionist, they cannot reverse liberalization
undertaken via an international treaty with a large developed
country. Credibility will, in turn, induce investment from both
domestic and foreign sources and stimulate growth.

(ix) Finally, regional integration may be an instrument of promoting peace and harmony among participating countries. The
most dramatic example of this is the EC, which has united two
former enemies – France and Germany – in such a tight economic
union that another war between them is unthinkable. In East Asia
also, a regional arrangement can help reduce political tensions and
promote political harmony among former enemies (e.g., China and
Japan; China and Taiwan; Republic of Korea and Japan; and North
Korea and the Republic of Korea).

Let us examine each of these arguments critically. The first
relies on the member countries' ability to exploit monopoly power
over outside countries. If the outside countries do not retaliate, and
if initial structure of tariffs in member countries is such that it
permits each member to obtain approximately as much preferential access to other member countries' markets as it gives them to
its own, a discriminatory arrangement may benefit all members.[13]
But this is the traditional optimum-tariff argument, which economists generally do not recommend.

Arguments (ii)–(iv) are all correct, but they do not require *discriminatory* liberalization. It is important to guard against these
arguments because they often get used to promote discriminatory

---

[12] Melo, Rodrik, and Panagariya (1993) develop a formal model in which regional integration leads to "trade" in institutions between partner countries. Among other things, they
show that this type of integration may serve to dilute the power of lobbies and help create
superior institutions.

[13] The second condition is not fulfilled by the North American Free Trade Agreement
(NAFTA) because the initial protection in Mexico is much higher than in the United
States and Canada. As a result, Mexico receives a much lower margin of preference than
it gives. This means a deterioration of Mexico's intraunion terms-of-trade.

liberalization. Argument (v) is examined in detail later. I conclude that it cannot serve as the basis of a discriminatory bloc in Asia. Argument (vi) has at least two flaws. First, it assumes that when tariffs are very low, discriminatory liberalization is a welfare-improving proposition. We saw even within the restrictive case depicted in Figure 4.1 that the possibility of a gain from discriminatory liberalization declines sharply if the level of initial tariffs is low. In general, ruling out the optimum-tariff argument and assuming that the union is small, discriminatory liberalization is welfare worsening. Second, due to lobbying pressures, removal of tariffs on the union partner can lead to an increase in tariffs on nonmembers. This was illustrated recently by the Mexican experience. In the wake of the macroeconomic crisis, because Mexico was unable to raise tariffs against the United States, she raised tariffs on 502 products on outside countries from 20 percent or less to as much as 35 percent. If Mexico's hands had not been tied against the United States, the required tariff increase would have been much smaller. Argument (vii) assumes once again that harmonization of domestic policies is desirable. A strong case can be made that optimum domestic policies for countries with different per-capita income levels are likely to be quite different and that harmonization under such circumstances is likely to be harmful, not beneficial.[14] Argument (viii) was used widely to support NAFTA from Mexico's viewpoint. A critique of this argument requires more space than is available here, and the reader is referred to Bhagwati (1995), Panagariya (1996a), and Bhagwati and Panagariya (1996b) for a detailed discussion. Here it suffices to note that if the country is serious about its trade reform, it can do so credibly by binding its tariff with the WTO.

The last argument (ix) has some validity, but its significance is greatly exaggerated. There are innumerable examples of former enemies living in peace in the absence of a regional arrangement. During the last fifty years, Japan has lived in peace with China, Korea, and other Asian neighbors without a regional arrangement. We give much credit to the EC for keeping peace between Germany and France. But in World War II, Germany also fought against Austria, Czechoslovakia, Hungary, and Poland yet has lived in

---

[14] For example, it is easy to show in a reasonable model that the optimal pollution abatement policy for Japan is more stringent than for China.

peace with them since 1945. With U.S. troops stationed in both Japan and Germany, it is inconceivable that these countries could have gone to a war against their former enemies even if there had been no EC. And we cannot rule out the possibility that the GATT process would have led to the (nondiscriminatory) integration of the EC countries independently of the EC. Recall that until the beginning of the Tokyo Round, there were only six countries in the EC/EU. But this did not hamper the integration of the non-EC countries into the world economy and with each other.

In the end, unless regional arrangements are designed to enhance and exploit the member countries' monopoly power, one must seek the explanation for their existence in their underlying political economy. Attraction to regionalism today is not unlike the attraction to import-substitution policies in developing countries in the 1950s through 1970s. Like import-substitution policies in those days, regionalism is being embraced today despite its inferiority to alternative policies.

3. SHOULD EAST ASIA GO REGIONAL?

Having discussed different aspects of regionalism, we are now in a position to confront directly the central question of this chapter: Should East Asia go regional? Not surprisingly, I argue in this section that both economics and politics are against a discriminatory bloc in East Asia. Historically, as summarized in section 1, East Asia has benefited greatly from an open world trading system. The region's future interests will continue to be served best by a strategy that ensures an open world trading system.

In the following, I evaluate the role of regionalism at three levels. First, I examine closely the only serious attempts at preferential trading – the ASEAN – which has recently announced plans to form the ASEAN Free Trade Area (AFTA). I suggest that the costs of such subregional schemes far outweigh their expected benefits. Second, I evaluate the case for a formal East Asian bloc along the lines of the EC or North America and conclude that though the *threat* of such a bloc may serve some purpose, its actual execution is a highly risky proposition. Finally, I evaluate the case for *simultaneous*, MFN-style, nondiscriminatory liberalization on a *regionwide* basis. I argue that a case for such a regional approach is at best weak.[15]

3.1. Subregional Groupings? No

I divide the discussion in this subsection into three parts. Sections 3.1.1 and 3.1.2 *describe* the evolution of ASEAN in trade area and plans for the AFTA, respectively. Section 3.1.3 evaluates the case for discriminatory liberalization in the subregion.

3.1.1. ASEAN: The Disappointing Past

Major developments in ASEAN[16] are associated with four summit meetings attended by the heads of states of the member nations. The First Summit, held in August 1967, created the association through the ASEAN Declaration. The Second Summit produced the ASEAN Concord of February 24, 1976, which paved the way for economic cooperation among member nations. The Third Summit attempted to strengthen cooperation through the Manila Declaration of December 15, 1987. Finally, the Fourth Summit concluded with the Singapore Declaration of January 28, 1992, which announced plans for an ASEAN Free Trade Area (AFTA). In-between, numerous ministerial meetings have taken place to give shape to the broad intentions in the declarations signed at the summits.

Areas of economic cooperation in ASEAN are wide ranging. They include trade, industry, energy, tourism, forestry, minerals, food and agriculture, and finance. In the following, I focus primarily on three programs that fall in areas of trade and industry and are designed to promote preferential trade and investment within the region: (i) Preferential Trading Arrangements (PTA) introduced in 1977; (ii) ASEAN Industrial Joint Ventures (AIJVs); and (iii) ASEAN Industrial Complementation (AIC) schemes.

(i) Preferential Trading Arrangements (PTA). The PTA provides for tariff preferences, referred to as the "margin of prefer-

---

[15] Chapter 5, by Lee and Woodall, this volume, offers an analysis of static welfare effects of some of these possibilities using a computable general equilibrium model.

[16] For details on ASEAN until 1987, see Sopiee, See, and Jin (1987). For more recent developments, see Pangestu, Soesastro, and Ahmed (1992) and Ariff and Tan (1992). In the following, I draw freely on Pangestu et al.

ence," for intra-ASEAN trade.[17] Until the announcement of AFTA, the rules of origin required that the ASEAN content of a product be 50 percent or more to qualify for tariff preference. On a case-by-case basis, this limit could be reduced to 35 percent. Initially, items for tariff preferences were negotiated on a product-by-product basis. In 1980, an across-the-board minimum margin of preference was introduced for imports above a certain value, but because countries were allowed to have exclusion lists, the provision had little effect.

In 1987, preferences actually granted under the PTA were minimal. Based on the 50 percent (or 35 percent if agreeable) ASEAN content requirement, there were 12,783 items on the PTA list. Out of these eligible items, only 337, or 2.6 percent of the items, were actually granted tariff preferences. Furthermore, only 19 percent of the total value of imports of these items enjoyed the preferential tariff.

At the Manila Summit in 1987, the member countries adopted changes aimed at strengthening tariff preferences. The countries agreed to shorten the exclusion list to 10 percent of the eligible items on the PTA list by 1992 (1994 in the case of Indonesia and the Philippines). They agreed to reduce the value of imports on the exclusion list to 50 percent or less of intra-ASEAN trade by the same date. There was also an agreement to freeze the level of non-tariff barriers and to negotiate reductions in them.

Systematic data on the progress toward achieving these goals is not available. But from what is available, progress appears to have been less than sparkling. Thus the share of Indonesia's exports to ASEAN, which benefited from tariff preferences, rose from 1.4 percent in 1987 to 3.5 percent in 1989. Similarly, Indonesia's imports entering under preferential tariffs as a proportion of its total imports from other ASEAN countries rose from 1.2 percent in 1987 to 1.6 percent in 1989.

(ii) ASEAN Industrial Joint Ventures (AIJVs). Introduced in 1983, the AIJV program is aimed at promoting intra-ASEAN investment among private investors. The main incentive is a tariff

---

[17] The PTA was introduced initially through the Agreement on ASEAN Preferential Trading Arrangements (APTA) signed in Manila on February 24, 1977, and was strengthened later in the Protocol on Improvements on Extension of Tariff Preferences under the ASEAN Preferential Trading Arrangements, signed in Manila on December 15, 1987.

preference. The countries participating in an AIJV project charge only 10 percent of their prevailing tariff (i.e., give a 90 percent margin of preference) on goods produced by and imported from the latter. There have to be at least two ASEAN countries participating in the project. Foreign participation in equity is allowed but ASEAN participants must own at least 40 percent of the equity.

To receive the tariff preference, the product must be first included in the list of AIJV products. The process of getting a new product included in the list is cumbersome. To date, only twenty-six products have been granted the AIJV status. These include automotive components and parts, mechanical power rack and steering systems, chemicals, enamel, food products, and so forth.

It is not clear how much *extra* investment has been generated by this scheme. There is only one AIJV having equity participation by all ASEAN countries. Most AIJVs have foreign equity participation. Projects under the scheme are concentrated largely in Malaysia and Thailand. In some cases, AIJVs have experienced difficulties in getting tariff preferences from participating countries. Sometimes, participating countries want a quid pro quo under which they ask the project to import goods from them.

(iii) ASEAN Industrial Complementation (AIC) schemes. The AIC scheme was introduced in 1981 with the objective of dividing different production stages of an industry among ASEAN countries. The idea was to avoid duplication and take advantage of scale economies. The first AIC scheme, involving automotive parts and components, was a failure due to differences in brands and types of vehicles among the ASEAN countries. Intra-ASEAN trade under the scheme remained minimal.

Recognizing the brand-incompatibility problem in the first scheme, the second AIC scheme was based on Brand to Brand Complementation (BBC) in the automotive sector. The scheme lets the private sector determine the division of production across member countries. Products of the BBC firms automatically receive a 50 percent tariff preference provided they satisfy the PTA's rules of origin. In 1991, the BBC was extended to nonautomotive products.

Brunei, Indonesia, and Singapore chose to stay out of the BBC scheme. Brunei and Singapore do not have an automotive industry, and Indonesia wanted to protect its own automotive industry. Progress to date under the BBC scheme has consisted of approval of eight packages involving Mitsubishi, Volvo, Mercedes Benz, Nissan, Toyota, DAF group from Belgium, and Renault.

3.1.2. AFTA: Time for Serious Business?
Negotiations for the NAFTA and for a Single European Market in the early 1990s swung the ASEAN members into action. At the Fourth ASEAN Summit in Singapore, on January 28, 1992, the member nations signed a framework agreement to establish and participate in the ASEAN Free Trade Area by the year 2008. Although the "framework" agreement is less binding than a treaty, member nations expect it to serve as an instrument of speeding up the integration process in the region.

The key vehicle for implementation of the AFTA is the Common Effective Preferential Tariff (CEPT), which will be applied to goods originating from ASEAN member states. The difference between the CEPT and PTA is that the former is slightly more encompassing. The margin of preference under the PTA is granted only by the nominating country, whereas that under the CEPT is granted by all members. The ASEAN content for qualifying for the CEPT is 40 percent lower than the PTA's 50 percent.

The AFTA covers all manufactured products, including capital goods, processed agricultural products, and those products falling outside the definition of agricultural products in the CEPT scheme. Products for the CEPT scheme are identified on an HS 6-digit sectoral level. Exceptions at the HS 8/9-digit level are permitted. The Third AFTA Council, held on December 11, 1992, identified a total of 38,680 items for inclusion in the CEPT. These items represent an average of 88 percent of the total tariff lines of the ASEAN member states. The coverage ranges from 80 percent to 98 percent among the six member countries. A total of 3,321 items have been identified for exclusion on a temporary basis. These items are to be reviewed at the end of eight years.

The Third AFTA Council also drew detailed schedules of reductions in CEPTs for all member countries. The Framework Agreement had identified fifteen products as *Fast Track* products for a more speedy liberalization.[18] For these products, tariffs above

---

[18] These products include vegetable oils, cement, chemicals, pharmaceutical, fertilizer, plastics, rubber products, leather products, pulp, textiles, ceramic and glass products, gems and jewelry, copper cathodes, electronics, and wooden and rattan furniture.

20 percent are to be reduced to 0 to 5 percent by January 1, 2003, while those at or below 20 percent are to be reduced to 0 to 5 percent by January 1, 2000. The remaining products are on the *Normal Track*. Products in this category with tariff rates 20 percent or less are to be reduced to 0 to 5 percent by January 2003, while those with tariff rates above 20 percent are to be first reduced to 20 percent by 2003 and then to 0 to 5 percent by 2008. According to the schedules drawn by the Third AFTA Council, except Malaysia, no member plans any tariff reductions in the first two years of AFTA, and even reductions planned by Malaysia are very small.

The AFTA agreement also calls for a removal of quantitative restrictions on products as soon as they are subject to the CEPT. It also provides for the elimination of other nontariff barriers over a period of five years after the product is brought under the CEPT. This provision is stronger than the PTA, which allowed members to maintain their quantitative restrictions.

3.1.3. Evaluating AFTA: A Wrong Turn

The sudden upsurge in FTAs around the world notwithstanding, on balance, the AFTA is likely to contribute only marginally to prosperity in the region. Indeed, the net effect of it may well be negative. As a forum for promoting political and cultural harmony and as an instrument of encouraging cooperation on projects of regional interest, the ASEAN has served the member countries well. But the preferential trading and investment promoted by the ASEAN and planned by the AFTA are likely to be counterproductive. Several points may be noted.

(i) Small Internal Markets. The case against the AFTA lies primarily in the small size of the regional market. Because Singapore already has complete, nondiscriminatory free trade, the AFTA can, by definition, involve no greater access to its market than what exists currently. Therefore, the gains from AFTA, if any, must come from integration of the remaining five countries' markets. But markets in these countries are quite small in relation to the world. The share of ASEAN-4 (the ASEAN exclusive of Singapore and Brunei) in the world GDP has declined from a low 1.5 percent in 1980 to 1.3 percent in 1990. The share in the world exports is bigger – 2.4 percent in 1990 – but not big by any stretch of imagination. If we include Singapore in our calculations, the 1990 shares of the ASEAN in the world GDP and exports, respectively, rise to 1.43 percent and 3.87 percent. These ratios are still quite small so that the possibility that the most efficient producers are located outside the region is high.

(ii) Low Levels of Intraregional Trade. An analysis of intraregional trade flows tells a similar story.[19] Tables 4.1 and 4.2, respectively, show destinations of exports and origins of imports of the ASEAN countries. Because Singapore is already a free-trading country, exports to that country are shown separately from the remaining ASEAN countries. Though intra-ASEAN trade has gone up between 1990 and 1995, it nevertheless remains small in relation to extra-ASEAN-4 trade. Given the low share of ASEAN-4 countries in the world GDP, this should be hardly surprising.

The ASEAN-4 countries, taken as a whole, sent 4.2 percent of their exports to each other in 1990 and 5.6 percent in 1995. On the import side, these figures are 3.9 percent in 1990 and 5.4 percent in 1995. The rise in the share is largely due to the higher growth in income in these countries relative to the rest of the world. The redirection of trade has taken place for all ASEAN members. Remarkably, exports by ASEAN-4 countries to Singapore were more than twice of those to each other in both 1990 and 1995.

(iii) Higher levels of Protection in Bigger Countries. Within the ASEAN-4, Indonesia and Thailand together accounted for approximately 70 percent of the region's GDP and 56 percent of its imports from anywhere in 1990. These are also the countries that are most protected within the region. Gains from discriminatory liberalization, if any, must come primarily from liberalization in these countries. But they did not plan to offer any preference in the first two years of the AFTA. Therefore, the impact of the AFTA – positive or negative – in the first two years will be minimal. Indeed, in the case of Indonesia, nondiscriminatory liberalization through unilateral reforms – a superior strategy from its viewpoint – has outpaced preferential liberalization by a long shot.

Closely related to this point is the issue of distribution of gains from preferential liberalization when such liberalization is under-

---

[19] As Bhagwati and Panagariya (1996b) have shown, the extent of trade creation and trade diversion cannot be inferred from intraregional trade. The argument here is twofold. First, with a very large number of potential suppliers left outside the union, the probability of trade diversion is large. Second, a focus on a relatively small market detracts sellers from aiming the much larger world market.

Table 4.1. *Direction of Exports: ASEAN-5 (as percentage of total exports to the world)*

Exporting Country		ASEAN -4	SGP[a]	NIEs excl. SGP[b]	Japan	East Asia	EC-12	NA	Other
ASEAN-4	1980	3.2	11.8	5.3	34.6	55.6	13.6	19.2	11.5
	1985	4.5	11.9	8.1	30.8	56.7	12.0	20.6	10.7
	1990[c]	4.1	12.2	9.7	24.7	52.8	16.0	20.1	11.1
	1990[d]	4.2	12.3	9.6	24.3	52.5	16.1	20.3	11.2
	1995[d]	5.6	13.5	11.2	17.9	51.1	14.7	21.0	13.1
Indonesia	1980	1.3	11.3	3.7	49.3	65.5	6.5	19.8	8.1
	1985	1.9	8.7	7.3	46.2	64.7	6.2	22.0	7.1
	1990	2.4	7.1	10.9	42.7	66.4	11.9	13.9	7.9
	1990[d]	2.3	7.4	11.0	42.5	66.6	11.8	13.6	8.0
	1995[d]	5.0	4.9	14.2	28.4	56.6	15.7	16.8	10.9
Malaysia	1980	3.2	19.1	5.7	22.8	52.5	17.6	16.9	13.0
	1985	6.3	19.5	9.6	23.8	60.2	14.6	13.7	11.5
	1990	6.0	22.8	10.0	15.8	56.6	14.9	17.9	10.5
	1990[d]	6.0	23.0	10.0	15.3	56.4	15.0	17.7	11.0
	1995[d]	6.2	20.3	11.3	12.7	53.1	13.8	21.5	11.6
Thailand	1980	8.5	7.4	7.1	15.3	40.1	26.4	13.2	20.2
	1985	6.4	7.7	7.5	13.4	38.8	19.2	21.1	20.9
	1990	3.9	7.3	7.8	17.2	37.3	21.6	24.5	16.6
	1990[d]	3.9	7.4	7.7	17.2	37.3	21.6	24.0	17.1
	1995[d]	4.9	14.0	9.0	16.7	47.5	14.5	18.9	19.2
Singapore	1980	20.8	(15.0)	10.9	8.1	41.3	12.8	13.6	32.3
	1985	20.6	(15.5)	9.3	9.4	40.7	10.6	22.0	26.7
	1990	20.9	(13.0)	13.6	8.7	44.8	14.4	22.3	18.5
	1990[d]	22.8	(12.7)	12.0	8.5	44.8	14.1	21.6	19.5
	1995[d]	27.7	(18.9)	15.2	7.7	52.8	12.8	18.5	15.9
Philippines	1980	4.6	1.9	8.5	26.5	42.2	17.6	29.1	11.2
	1985	6.0	5.3	7.5	19.0	39.5	15.8	37.5	7.2
	1988	3.7	2.9	9.9	20.3	37.7	17.7	37.4	7.1
	1990[d]	4.2	2.9	9.4	19.8	37.1	18.0	39.4	5.5
	1995[d]	7.3	5.2	10.7	16.0	40.4	17.1	37.1	5.5

SGP = Singapore; NIEs = Asia's newly industrialized economies; NA = North America.
[a] Figures in parenthesis are imports of Singapore from Malaysia.
[b] NIEs excluding Singapore.
[c] Figures for Philippines used to calculate 1990 ASEAN-4 shares correspond to 1988.
[d] International Monetary Fund's *Direction of Trade Statistics* data are used.
Source: United Nations, COMTRADE data, unless otherwise indicated.

ARVIND PANAGARIYA

Table 4.2. *Direction of Imports: ASEAN-5 (as percentage of total imports from the world)*

Importing Country		ASEAN -4	SGP[a]	NIEs excl. SGP[b]	Japan	East Asia	EC-12	NA	Other
						Trading Partner			
ASEAN-4	1980	6.0	7.4	6.1	24.1	44.5	13.4	17.8	24.3
	1985	3.0	9.7	6.8	23.4	48.7	14.4	17.6	19.3
	1990[c]	3.9	8.9	10.9	26.2	52.7	14.9	15.4	16.9
	1990[d]	3.9	8.8	10.9	25.7	51.8	15.2	15.2	17.8
	1995[d]	5.4	7.8	11.9	27.1	55.0	14.1	14.3	16.6
Indonesia	1980	3.8	8.6	7.4	31.5	53.2	13.6	14.0	19.2
	1985	1.2	8.2	5.3	25.8	42.9	17.6	18.8	20.7
	1990	2.6	5.8	11.9	24.3	47.6	18.6	13.7	20.1
	1990[d]	2.5	5.8	11.9	24.8	48.0	18.8	13.3	21.8
	1995[d]	4.8	5.9	15.5	26.2	56.1	17.7	10.1	16.1
Malaysia	1980	4.7	11.7	5.5	23.0	47.2	15.7	16.1	21.0
	1985	6.6	15.8	6.6	23.2	54.2	14.1	16.4	15.2
	1990	4.2	14.6	10.4	25.3	56.5	13.2	18.5	11.7
	1990[d]	4.0	14.8	10.0	24.2	54.9	14.7	17.9	12.4
	1995[d]	4.8	12.4	11.3	27.3	58.1	13.9	16.9	11.2
Philippines	1980	4.5	1.6	6.5	19.9	35.1	10.7	24.7	29.5
	1985	11.5	2.6	11.1	14.4	45.0	8.5	26.0	20.5
	1988	4.7	4.0	14.5	17.4	43.7	12.6	22.3	21.3
	1990[d]	4.9	3.9	14.7	18.4	43.4	11.2	21.0	24.5
	1995[d]	6.0	4.0	15.7	22.4	50.6	10.2	19.3	19.8
Thailand	1980	3.1	6.3	5.1	20.7	39.5	13.0	18.2	29.3
	1985	7.2	7.5	6.3	26.5	49.9	14.8	12.9	22.4
	1990	4.3	7.5	9.6	30.6	55.3	14.5	12.2	18.0
	1990[d]	4.3	7.4	9.5	30.4	54.9	14.8	11.9	18.4
	1995[d]	6.1	5.6	9.0	29.2	52.7	13.7	12.1	21.4
Singapore	1980	16.2	(13.9)	5.6	17.8	42.2	11.0	14.7	32.1
	1985	17.2	(14.4)	6.8	17.0	49.6	11.3	15.6	23.5
	1990	16.9	(13.7)	10.7	20.1	51.2	12.9	16.7	19.3
	1990[d]	19.3	(13.1)	9.9	19.5	52.1	12.4	16.2	19.3
	1995[d]	23.6	(15.1)	11.4	20.6	58.8	11.9	15.1	14.3

SGP = Singapore; NIEs = Asia's newly industrialized economies; NA = North America.
[a] Figures in parenthesis are imports of Singapore from Malaysia.
[b] NIEs excluding Singapore.
[c] Figures for Philippines used to calculate 1990 ASEAN-4 shares correspond to 1988.
[d] International Monetary Fund's *Direction of Trade Statistics* data are used.
Source: United Nations, COMTRADE data, unless otherwise indicated.

taken. It stands to reason that the arrangement will benefit Malaysia and Singapore at the expense of other countries. This is because Malaysia and Singapore have either no or low tariffs to begin with. Therefore, the potential for discriminatory liberalization by them is minimal. Much of the liberalization will have to come from the more protected Indonesia, Philippines, and Thailand. This means that the terms-of-trade for Malaysia and Singapore will improve. The tariff revenue collected on goods exported by these countries to Indonesia, Philippines, and Thailand will disappear to the extent of liberalization and become a part of the former's profits on export. There will not be a corresponding gain for Indonesia, Philippines, and Thailand on goods exported to Singapore and Malaysia because the latter have relatively few high tariffs to liberalize.

These lopsided distributional effects may well explain why the progress on *preferential* liberalization in the region has been outstripped by unilateral, nondiscriminatory liberalization. For example, while Indonesia and Philippines have lowered trade barriers substantially during the 1980s as a part of their trade reform policies, they have been generally reluctant to offer tariff preferences under the PTA. In July 1992, Indonesia announced a list of 250 tariff cuts, but 90 percent of these were on different types of batik cloth produced in Indonesia only. The distributional conflict is illustrated well by a remark made by the former foreign minister of Indonesia, Dr. M. Kusumaatmadja, at a meeting in 1992 to celebrate the twenty-fifth anniversary of the ASEAN:[20]

Singapore and Malaysia are always telling us to lower tariffs and duties and let their goods into the country. But in return, how about the free movement of labor? We will take your goods if you will take our surplus labor supply. When they hear this and think about all those Indonesians coming to work in their countries, then they say, "wait a minute, maybe it's not such a good idea."

In the past, to lengthen their lists, member countries have gone so far as to include snow ploughs among items to receive preferential tariffs! There are also instances of tariff preferences on zero-tariff goods. Most recently, the liberalization package announced by Indonesia lowers trade barriers on an MFN basis and does not offer any significant preferences to AFTA members.

[20] *Financial Times*, January 26, 1993.

Assuming net benefits from preferential liberalization, in principle, gainers could compensate the losers. But in practice, compensation schemes tend to be distortionary, and AFTA has been wise to stay away from them. Compensation schemes adopted by regional arrangements in Africa proved highly distortionary.[21] In NAFTA, no compensation has been offered by the United States to Mexico, which, on conventional criteria, is likely to lose from the arrangement.[22] Only the EC has been successful in affecting large transfers to its poorer partners as a part of the Southern Enlargement. This has been largely due to a very strong commitment on the part of the original members to unify Europe into a single market.

3.2. An East Asian Trading Bloc? No

Two main issues must be addressed when considering the case for a bloc consisting of all major players in East Asia: (i) Is the bloc economically desirable; and (ii) Is the bloc feasible? I argue that the answer to the first question is at best uncertain, while that to the second is negative.

3.2.1. Is a Trading Bloc Economically Desirable?

The economic desirability of an East Asian bloc is difficult to assess. This is because the effects of such a bloc go well beyond the simple efficiency effects discussed in section 2. The region accounts for approximately one-fifth of the world's GDP and exports. Any major actions in the area of international trade at the regionwide level that discriminate against the rest of the world will lead to repercussions in and perhaps retaliation from the rest of the world. Without being able to predict those reactions, it is difficult to estimate the costs and benefits of forming a regionwide bloc.

The paramount objective of East Asia's regional trade policy has to be to ensure an open world trading system. Despite some redirection of trade toward itself in recent years, East Asia ships

---

[21] See, for example, Foroutan (1993).

[22] To the extent that Mexico's tariffs are far higher than those in the United States, the NAFTA is likely to worsen its terms-of-trade. On top of that, Mexico must effectively raise its environmental and labor standards.

Table 4.3. *Direction of Exports: NIEs, China, and Japan (as percentage of total exports to the world)*

Exporting Country		NIEs	ASEAN -4	China[a]	Japan	East Asia	EC-12	NA	Other
NIEs	1980	9.0	8.9	0.9	10.3	29.1	17.2	28.3	25.3
	1985	8.5	7.0	2.3	10.7	28.5	11.4	40.7	19.5
	1990	13.0	9.3	3.2	12.7	38.2	15.5	31.1	15.2
	1990[b]	12.4	8.7	8.0	11.3	40.4	14.5	29.3	15.8
	1995[b]	16.0	11.1	13.2	9.4	49.7	12.8	22.3	15.1
Hong Kong	1980	4.2	2.8	2.4	3.4	12.8	29.5	36.0	21.7
	1985	3.0	2.0	11.7	3.4	20.1	18.4	47.9	13.5
	1990	6.8	3.2	24.0	5.3	36.3	20.4	32.1	11.2
	1990[b]	9.7	4.0	24.8	5.7	44.2	14.3	26.3	15.2
	1995[b]	7.1	3.6	33.3	6.1	50.2	13.9	23.6	12.4
Korea	1980	7.4	4.9	0.0 (4.7)	17.3	29.6	15.6	28.6	26.2
	1985	7.4	3.4	0.0 (5.2)	15.0	25.8	10.7	39.8	23.7
	1990	10.4	5.0	0.0 (5.8)	19.4	34.8	13.7	33.5	18.1
	1990[b]	10.5	5.0	0.4 (5.8)	19.4	35.3	13.6	33.4	17.6
	1995[b]	16.9	7.8	7.3 (8.5)	13.6	45.7	11.6	21.5	21.1
Singapore	1980	10.9	20.8	1.6	8.1	41.3	12.8	13.6	32.3
	1985	9.3	20.6	1.5	9.4	40.7	10.6	22.0	26.7
	1990	13.6	20.9	1.5	8.7	44.8	14.4	22.3	18.5
	1990[b]	12.0	22.8	1.5	8.5	44.8	14.1	21.7	19.3
	1995[b]	15.2	27.7	2.3	7.7	52.8	12.8	18.6	15.8
Taiwan	1980	12.0	5.1	0.0 (7.9)	11.0	28.1	14.6	37.0	20.3
	1985	12.0	3.1	0.0 (8.3)	11.3	26.4	8.8	51.6	13.1
	1990	17.8	6.8	0.0 (12.8)	12.4	37.1	16.0	35.3	11.7
	1990[b]	17.8	6.8	0.1 (12.7)	12.4	37.1	16.1	35.1	11.7
	1995[b]	29.6	8.5	0.3 (23.4)	11.8	50.3	12.6	25.3	11.9
China	1980	N.A.	N.A.	N.A.	N.A.	N.A.	N.A.	N.A.	N.A.
	1984	31.5	3.0	(26.5)	20.6	55.1	9.0	10.3	25.6
	1990	48.6	2.8	(42.9)	14.5	65.9	9.1	9.2	15.8
	1990[b]	47.3	2.6	(43.2)	14.6	64.5	9.5	9.3	16.6
	1995[b]	32.3	3.0	(24.2)	19.1	54.4	12.4	17.7	15.5
Japan	1980	14.8	7.0	3.9	. . .	25.7	13.9	27.3	33.1
	1985	12.8	4.2	7.1	. . .	24.1	12.0	40.7	23.3
	1990	19.7	7.7	2.1	. . .	29.6	18.8	34.8	16.8
	1990[b]	19.7	7.7	2.1	. . .	29.6	18.8	34.8	16.8
	1995[b]	25.1	12.1	5.0	. . .	42.1	14.9	28.9	14.1

[a] Figures in parenthesis are exports to Hong Kong.
[b] International Monetary Fund's *Direction of Trade Statistics* data are used.
Source: United Nations, COMTRADE data, unless otherwise indicated.

Table 4.4. *Direction of Imports: NIEs, China, and Japan (as percentage of total imports from the world)*

Importing Country		NIEs	ASEAN -4	China[a]	Japan	East Asia	EC-12	NA	Other
NIEs	1980	6.9	8.2	5.7	23.4	44.2	9.8	18.9	27.1
	1985	8.3	8.1	9.2	22.7	48.3	10.7	18.2	22.8
	1990	10.6	7.4	12.2	22.6	52.8	11.7	18.6	16.9
	1990[b]	10.3	8.0	12.3	22.2	52.8	12.2	18.3	16.6
	1995[b]	11.7	9.6	15.1	21.1	57.5	11.9	16.4	14.3
Hong Kong	1980	15.8	3.9	20.0	23.3	63.0	12.5	12.8	11.7
	1985	17.5	2.8	25.5	23.1	68.8	11.6	9.9	9.7
	1990	17.5	3.6	36.8	16.1	74.0	9.8	8.6	7.7
	1990[b]	17.5	3.6	36.8	16.1	74.0	10.1	8.6	7.4
	1995[b]	18.8	4.6	36.2	14.8	74.5	10.1	8.5	6.9
Korea	1980	2.6	5.9	0.0 (0.4)	26.2	34.7	7.3	23.9	34.1
	1985	3.5	7.1	0.0 (1.6)	24.2	34.8	9.8	23.3	32.1
	1990	4.3	5.6	0.0 (0.9)	26.7	36.6	12.1	26.8	24.5
	1990[b]	4.2	5.6	0.6 (0.9)	26.6	37.1	12.0	26.7	24.2
	1995[b]	4.1	5.5	5.5 (0.6)	24.1	39.2	12.1	24.6	24.1
Singapore	1980	5.6	16.2	2.6	17.8	42.2	11.0	14.7	32.1
	1985	6.8	17.2	8.6	17.0	49.6	11.3	15.6	23.5
	1990	10.7	16.9	3.4	20.1	51.2	12.9	16.7	19.3
	1990[b]	9.9	19.3	3.3	19.5	52.1	12.4	16.2	19.2
	1995[b]	11.4	23.6	3.2	20.6	58.8	11.9	15.2	14.1
Taiwan	1980	3.4	5.9	0.0 (1.3)	27.2	36.5	8.2	25.2	30.2
	1985	3.9	5.7	0.0 (1.6)	27.5	37.2	10.2	25.9	26.4
	1990	8.1	4.9	0.0 (2.3)	30.0	42.9	13.0	25.4	18.6
	1990[b]	7.6	4.7	0.6 (2.6)	29.1	42.0	15.4	24.7	17.9
	1995[b]	8.8	7.0	3.0 (1.8)	29.2	48.0	14.9	21.9	15.3
China	1980	N.A.	N.A.	N.A.	N.A.	N.A.	N.A.	N.A.	N.A.
	1984	11.5	2.6	(10.9)	31.3	45.4	12.7	19.1	22.8
	1990	33.6	3.9	(26.5)	14.2	51.8	15.0	15.2	18.0
	1990[b]	33.2	4.0	(27.0)	14.2	51.4	11.2	15.2	22.2
	1995[b]	28.1	4.5	(6.5)	22.0	54.6	14.4	14.1	16.9
Japan	1980	5.3	14.1	3.1	...	22.4	5.8	21.5	50.3
	1985	7.7	13.1	5.1	...	25.9	6.9	25.5	41.7
	1990	11.2	10.5	5.2	...	26.9	15.0	27.1	31.1
	1990[b]	11.1	10.4	5.1	...	26.6	15.0	26.9	31.5
	1995[b]	12.3	11.4	10.7	...	34.4	13.2	26.3	26.2

[a] Figures in parenthesis are imports from Hong Kong.
[b] International Monetary Fund's *Direction of Trade Statistics* data are used.
Source: United Nations, COMTRADE data, unless otherwise indicated.

two-thirds of its exports to the rest of the world.[23] There is little doubt that the phenomenal growth of East Asia during the past three decades has been facilitated greatly by relatively open world markets. Almost without exception, studies of the NIEs draw a direct connection between growth in exports and that in the GDP. More recently, Indonesia, Malaysia, Thailand, and China have been repeating the experience of the NIEs.

This suggests that the case for an East Asian bloc should be evaluated primarily not on the basis of static gains, including those arising from an improvement in the terms-of-trade, but in terms of its impact on the world trading system. If a regional approach is to be pursued, it should help keep the world markets open. There are two arguments in favor of a discriminatory regional bloc that deserve a close scrutiny.

First, an East Asian bloc may serve as a deterrent to the formation of closed trading blocs around the world. According to this argument, the world is already dividing into blocs. To ensure that the blocs do not become overly protective of their own markets and limit East Asia's access to them, East Asia should be united and be in a position to retaliate. Unilateral actions such as those taken by the United States under its Super 301 provisions will also be harder to take if East Asia is united.

Second, frustration with slow progress of the Uruguay Round led some proponents of the regional approach to argue that the free-rider problem associated with the multilateral process makes the multilateral approach unworkable. In the multilateral setting, trade concessions negotiated by large, developed countries become automatically available to smaller countries through the MFN clause of the GATT. Negotiations with the latter are difficult because their numbers are large, and each of them is individually too small to make such negotiations worthwhile. Therefore, if the world can be first divided into a small number of blocs, it will be easier to organize future GATT/WTO negotiations.[24] Regional

---

[23] Data on the extent of intraregional trade vary according to the source and definition of the region. My tables rely primarily on the United Nations' Commodity Trade data, which do not report data for China for the early part of the 1980s. Therefore, in Table 4.3, East Asia does not include China. According to Lee and Woodall (Chapter 5, this volume), the proportion of total trade of East Asia, where East Asia includes China, was 29.8 percent in 1970 and had grown to 49.2 percent in 1995. Based on these data, the redirection of trade has been considerably more than suggested by the data in the text.

[24] The argument can be found in Summers (1991) and Krugman (1993).

blocs could free up trade internally while the GATT process, once freed from the free-rider problem, could serve to bring down the barriers between blocs rapidly and with greater certainty. Proponents of the argument suggest that one reason why the past GATT rounds were so successful is that the United States could deal with the EC as a single unit. According to this view, if East Asia is turned into a bloc and the Americas into another, they together with the EU can move the world faster toward free trade.

Both of these arguments have some merit but are highly contentious. Regarding the first argument, critics note that countries organized into a bloc enjoy more market power than they do individually. Therefore, in principle, there is nothing to prevent blocs from *raising* rather than lowering trade barriers. The deterrence role of blocs is good only as long as the threat is not carried out. Once a threat is carried out and trade war breaks out, retaliatory actions are likely to be larger with than without blocs.

As for the second argument, critics note that the Uruguay Round has been successfully concluded, and the small and developing countries have given major concessions through accepting the Trade-Related Intellectual Property Rights (TRIPs) Agreement of the Uruguay Round Agreement. Equally important, small numbers do not necessarily mean faster progress.[25] The EC process began in 1957 and is still working toward a "Single Market." In the meantime, the EC's nontariff barriers have proliferated: According to Winters (1993), the coverage of these trade restrictions has expanded fivefold from 1966 to 1986. More importantly, this argument had some force at a time when the Uruguay Round negotiations were faltering. But that has changed with a successful completion of the Round and creation of the WTO.

3.2.2. Is a Trading Bloc Feasible?
Although the economic desirability of a trading bloc in East Asia is difficult to assess, its feasibility – or lack thereof – is more predictable. Both internal circumstances of the region and possible retaliatory actions from outside – particularly from the United States – make the formation of an East Asian free trade area an unlikely event.

---

[25] For example see Bhagwati (1993) and Winters (1993). A summary of the debate can be found in Melo and Panagariya (1992).

Internally, there are at least three interrelated factors at work against a regionwide FTA. First, historically, the major players in the region have been political rivals. Although time, trade, and intraregional investments have gone a long way toward bringing the former enemies closer, they still do not appear ready to form a free trade area with one another. In this respect, the situation in East Asia is fundamentally different than in Western Europe after World War II. Then, backed by the United States, for economic as well as geopolitical reasons, Europeans were able to move into treaties establishing first the European Coal and Steel Community and later the European Community. Today, there are no similar pressures on Japan. Nor are countries such as Korea and China expressing eagerness to form an FTA with Japan.

Second, the countries in East Asia have very different levels of protection and are at very different stages of development. This makes the distribution of gains from an FTA rather uneven. With discriminatory liberalization under an FTA, poorer countries, which are also more highly protected, are likely to lose or gain less than their relatively open and richer counterparts. This raises the specter of compensation, which, as noted in the context of the ASEAN, is a barrier not easily overcome.

Third, the number of countries in the region is large, which makes the task of far-reaching negotiations required for an FTA a daunting task. We saw earlier how difficult it has been for even six ASEAN countries to make progress toward the AFTA. It has taken the countries twenty-five years to reach the "framework agreement," and progress on serious preferential liberalization is still out of sight. With this background, it is not clear how disparate countries such as China, Japan, Korea, and the members of ASEAN can be engaged in a dialogue that will lead to a free trade area among them.

The external factors at work against an East Asian FTA are even more formidable. Because of perceptions that its markets are de facto closed to outsiders, Japan has been a persistent target of aggressive unilateralism by the United States during the last two decades. These actions have included voluntary export restraints, structural impediments initiative, and Super 301 threats. Developing countries in the region, such as Korea and China, have also been subject to Super 301 threats. Initiatives by these countries for a free trade area, which can potentially divert trade from the

United States, are almost certain to be met with retaliation by the latter.

From the viewpoint of smaller nations, this external environment is quite different from that faced by Mexico in negotiating the NAFTA. Apart from the fact that, with the United States as the other negotiating party, the threat of overt retaliation did not exist, Mexico was simply not very vulnerable to such actions. In 1990, Mexico exported 71 percent of its goods to North America, only 13 percent to Western Europe, and 6 percent to East Asia. For the latter regions, imports from Mexico amounted to approximately a half percent of their total imports.

The situation is dramatically different for countries such as China and Korea. They not only face an environment that is hostile to an FTA in East Asia but also are *individually* very vulnerable to actions against them by the United States. In 1990, Korea sold a quarter of its exports to the United States. China's direct exports were not as large, but once reexports through Hong Kong are taken into account, it too sent a quarter of its goods to the United States. With such large concentration of exports to the United States, risks for Korea and China of an FTA that the United States opposes are immense. This in turn suggests that an East Asian FTA is not a feasible proposition in the near future.

3.3. Regionwide Nondiscriminatory Liberalization? Maybe

Having argued that subregional grouping and trading blocs that promote discriminatory liberalization are not worth the effort required to create and sustain them, I now turn to the discussion of the so-called "open" regional approach centered around a GATT-style, MFN-based nondiscriminatory liberalization.[26] I argue that although this regionalism has certain advantages over discriminatory approaches, it, too, has serious limitations.

The key element distinguishing this approach from a regional bloc will be the nondiscriminatory nature of liberalization. The

---

[26] To my knowledge, a proposal to this effect has been made for the first time in a recent World Bank (1993) report. Petri (1992) offers a similar proposal but makes the United States, Australia, and New Zealand a part of the overall scheme. Because intraregional trade among these countries and East Asia is so intense, the economic case for this proposal can be hardly disputed. But the same factors that make an open trading bloc á la Bhagwati and Cooper politically infeasible also cast a serious doubt on the workability of this proposal.

countries in the region will come together at a common forum and, very much in the spirit of the various GATT rounds, negotiate reductions in trade barriers. Any concessions made by a country to another will be extended automatically to all WTO members. In the following, I offer a detailed discussion of the positive as well as negative side of this approach.

3.3.1. The Positive Case

(i) No Trade Diversion. Because tariff reductions are nondiscriminatory under this approach, by definition, there can be no trade diversion. In terms of our VCR example, if Indonesia lowers its tariffs on Japanese VCRs in return for a tariff concession from Japan, the same reduction is extended to Korea and all other suppliers of VCRs. The reduction in tariff then benefits Indonesia's consumers rather than Japanese VCR producers.

A lack of trade diversion takes away one major obstacle in the way of a discriminatory bloc: Countries with high initial tariffs need not feel that they will lose as a result of liberalization. Any gains from liberalization will accrue to consumers inside the country rather than the partner country. Problems mentioned earlier regarding compensation will simply not arise.

(ii) External Constraints. This regionalism will certainly face a much less serious challenge from the United States. Because the liberalization is nondiscriminatory, it will improve the U.S. access to East Asia's markets as well. Indeed, the negotiations could go a long way toward answering U.S. complaints about a lack of openness of markets in East Asia in general, and Japan and China in particular.

More importantly, liberalization at the regional level may help alleviate two major problems that provide fuel for aggressive unilateralism in the United States against Japan and other trading partners. First, to the extent that such liberalization is likely to shift the region's exports away from the United States and toward East Asia, some of the current competitive pressure on U.S. industry may be relieved. At the least, a decline in Japan's share in the U.S. market and possibly a rise in the share of domestic producers there will weaken the lobbies' case for trade-policy actions against the former. Second, the possible shift in exports toward East Asia may alleviate trade deficits of the United States with Japan and China. Because the overall trade deficit is a macroeconomic phenomenon governed by investment-savings gap, this redirection may not help the *total* U.S. trade deficit. But it may help lower *bilateral* trade deficit. If so, nondiscriminatory liberalization will weaken considerably the case for unilateral actions by the United States.

(iii) Low Adjustment Costs. Because liberalization will take place simultaneously in all the major countries of the region, this approach will help minimize the costs of adjustment. In the GATT style, liberalization will be in areas of mutual interest. Therefore, countries will improve export prospects at the same time that they subject their import competing industries to competition from abroad. In contrast, if liberalization is unilateral or, worse still, in response to Super 301 types of threats from the United States, adjustment costs will be higher. In the spirit of the GATT rounds, it may also be possible to allow the liberalization process to be spread over a period of, say, ten years. This will further smoothen the path of adjustment.

(iv) East Asia's Role in World Economic Affairs. In recent decades, the United States has become what Jagdish Bhagwati calls a "Diminished Giant." Simultaneously, East Asia, particularly Japan, has emerged as the major economic power in the world. Gradually, commensurate with their current economic weight and future potential, Japan and the Greater China region (including China, Hong Kong, and Taiwan) must assume the leadership role in world economic affairs. Japan has already emerged as a major donor country in the world. Within East Asia, it now enjoys the same central role as the United States in the Americas and Germany in the EC. It provided more than half of the official development assistance commitments to East Asia in 1992 against only 6 percent from the United States. More than 30 percent of the region's net foreign direct investment in 1990 came from Japan compared with 10 percent from the United States. Parallel with these developments in Japan, China is rapidly becoming a major engine of growth in Asia. According to a recent World Bank report, Greater China has become the world's "fourth growth pole" after Europe, North America, and Japan. The report notes that imports into the Greater China region are already two-thirds as much as Japan and will surpass the latter by the year 2002 if growth continues at the present rate.[27] Import liberalization by China in the

---

[27] See the article by Laurence Zuckerman in the *Wall Street Journal*, May 17, 1993.

years to come will further enhance that country's role in global economic affairs. Regionwide liberalization could then serve as a steppingstone to the eventual leadership role for East Asia in general, and Japan and China in particular.

3.3.2. The Negative Case

The discussion up to this point makes nondiscriminatory liberalization almost too good to be true. And it is. Although there is much to be gained from this type of liberalization in the long run, the short- to medium-run economic effects are not favorable. This means that it will be difficult to mobilize support for implementation of the scheme. Let me elaborate.

The existing levels of tariffs, at least in Japan, are relatively low. This means that potential gains from lowering this most transparent barrier to trade in Japan are limited. Indeed, matters are worse than the official tariff rates may reveal. Japan gives very extensive trade preferences under the GSP (Generalized System of Preferences) to its East Asian trading partners. For example, in the case of Korea, 88 percent of the Japanese tariff lines facing it are either zero or below the MFN level. For approximately two-thirds of the tariff lines, the GSP gives Korea a duty-free access. A similar pattern applies to other countries.[28] This means that if Japan lowers its tariffs in a nondiscriminatory fashion, developing East Asian countries will lose the tariff preferences they currently enjoy. This is most likely to be a losing proposition for them.

There does not appear to be a substantial scope for gains from a reduction in tariffs in other countries either. Because tariff levels across countries are highly variable, the scope for quid pro quo is limited. Thailand, Indonesia, and arguably China have the highest levels of tariffs. At the other extreme, Singapore and Hong Kong have virtually no tariffs, while Japan imposes very low tariffs on its East Asian partners. In between we have Korea and the Philippines with tariffs generally below 20 percent. Given this cross-country structure of tariffs, it will be rather difficult to engineer an MFN-style liberalization.

---

[28] Singapore pays a positive MFN tariff in only 8 percent of the cases. At 15 percent, among the ASEAN countries, Indonesia has the largest share of tariff lines with positive MFN rates.

The picture with respect to nontariff barriers is similar. Identifiable nontariff barriers are limited. We do not have information on all countries, but in the cases where it is available, these barriers are not extensive. Japan employs few formal nontariff barriers. Among the major developing East Asian countries, the coverage of such barriers is currently less than 10 percent. In terms of formal barriers, perhaps China is most protective. But in reality, China's imports have risen sharply in recent years, suggesting that its import regime is freer than may be suggested by formal restrictions.

This discussion leads to the conclusion that the only significant trade liberalization in the region may come from lowering the so-called "informal" barriers to trade that Japan is often alleged to have. In order to bring to the negotiating table the countries with high formal trade barriers, only Japan can make attractive concessions. But the problem with "informal" barriers is that either they may not exist or they are invisible. It is simply not clear how countries can negotiate around these barriers.

It is possible that purely on the basis of intertemporal balance of trade, Japan's imports in the coming years will rise faster than its exports.[29] Then it may be argued that Japan can use this opportunity aggressively to lead other East Asian countries toward liberalization. But once again, it is difficult to imagine other countries participating in a negotiation when import expansion in Japan is expected to happen through market forces in any case, and there are no formal offers on the table for a reduction in trade barriers.

A final and perhaps the most important point is that in Japan and other countries even if we can somehow identify substantial trade barriers that can be negotiated away on a nondiscriminatory basis, the likely decline in the terms-of-trade of the region could be substantial. This is because more than 50 percent of the region's imports come from outside countries. In the case of Japan, this number is as large as 70 percent. Unilateral liberalization by the region as a whole must worsen the terms-of-trade. Moreover, because the current level of protection is low, it is likely that such a reduction in the terms-of-trade would worsen welfare.

---

[29] The argument here is that Japan will not keep accumulating dollars forever. It must spend them some time.

The major negotiating parties at the GATT rounds have faced this same problem, referred to as a "free-rider problem." The United States, EC, and Japan feared that the benefits of liberalization by them on the MFN basis would spill over to nonparticipating – mostly developing – countries. But as Finger (1979) has shown, they were able to avoid this problem by limiting liberalization to those goods in which they themselves traded intensively. Goods in which developing countries had a comparative advantage – agricultural products, textiles, shoes, and other labor-intensive products – were not liberalized. Given that Japan imports 65 percent of its goods from countries outside East Asia, a major expansion of its imports cannot occur without liberalization of products coming from outside the region.

4. APEC AND REGIONALISM IN ASIA

By the end of 1993, APEC, which came into existence in 1989 as a low-key consultative body, began to emerge as the central institution for promoting liberalization of trade and investment at the regional level.[30] Because APEC consists of not only East Asian countries as members but also the United States, its evolution into a regional trading bloc is not ruled out by the arguments made in this chapter.

I have discussed the role of APEC in promoting regional integration in detail elsewhere (Panagariya, 1996b) recently. Here it suffices to note a fundamental conflict between Asian members of APEC and the United States. The former are keen to undertake trade liberalization only on the Most-Favored Nation (MFN) basis while the latter insists on reciprocity. In particular, the United States is unwilling to extend its liberalization commitments within the APEC context to the rest of the world, especially the European Union, without reciprocal liberalization by the latter. Thus, while the Asian members advocate liberalization along the lines of section 3.3, the United States prefers to follow the discriminatory route.

---

[30] It was not until its 1992 meeting in Singapore that APEC decided to establish a permanent secretariat. In 1993, in order to pressure the European Union into bringing the Uruguay Round to its logical conclusion, the United States upgraded the November 1993 meeting of APEC into a high-profile Leaders' Meeting. The subsequent APEC annual meetings have been accompanied by summits of heads of states of member nations.

A key development in APEC's history took place at its 1994 annual meeting in Bogor, Indonesia. At that meeting, APEC members signed a (nonbinding) agreement to achieve free trade in developed-member countries by the year 2010 and in developing-member countries by 2020. Because of the conflict between Asian and American approaches to liberalization, the future of this agreement remains in doubt, however. At the 1995 Osaka meeting, the United States stood firm and offered no import liberalization to make progress toward the 2010 goal. Some developing-country members from Asia, particularly China and Indonesia, offered limited tariff reductions but even these did not go beyond what was planned by the countries as a part of their own trade reform policies or promised under the Uruguay Round agreement.

At the 1996 meeting in the Philippines, the United States did not make any significant offers other than the proposal for the elimination of tariffs for information technology products by 2000. Japan made very few offers, and excluded agricultural products from its individual action plans. Therefore, once again, the momentum for liberalization would have to come from Asian developing-country members, Australia, and New Zealand. For signs of more substantive progress, which inevitably requires active participation from the United States, we must await 1998 and beyond.

5. CONCLUSIONS

On the whole, this chapter takes a pessimistic view of regionalism in East Asia. The pessimism follows, inter alia, from low or negative gains in the case of subregional groupings such as the AFTA, insurmountable external and internal barriers to effective integration in the case of an Asia-wide discriminatory bloc, and adverse terms-of-trade effects in the case of concerted nondiscriminatory liberalization by the region.

This leaves the possibility of pursuing a regional approach to liberalization on an APEC-wide basis. In 1993, in order to pressure the European Union into bringing the Uruguay Round to a speedy conclusion, the United States upgraded the November 1993 meeting of APEC into a high-profile Leaders' Meeting. That and the subsequent APEC summit in Bogor, Indonesia, has led to a great deal of optimism toward the regional approach in some quarters. Indeed, at the end of the Bogor summit in 1994, an agreement was signed by APEC members to establish free trade by the year 2010 in developed-country members and 2020 in developing-country members.

Will this approach succeed? My answer is in the negative. The Bogor agreement is nonbinding, and some members have already gone on to declare that free trade does not mean zero tariffs. More importantly, there is a fundamental conflict between the interpretations of the Bogor agreement by the Asian members and the United States. While the former expect liberalization to be on the MFN basis, the latter insists on reciprocity. Given that countries outside APEC, especially those in Europe, will not liberalize in response to liberalization by APEC members, reciprocity necessarily amounts to taking a discriminatory approach and turning APEC into an FTA.

Given this conflict, the future of the 2010/2020 goal is in some doubt. Therefore, as suggested by Bhagwati (1995), the best strategy for East Asian members of APEC will be to use this forum to push for further multilateral liberalization. On the one hand, they should develop a consensus among themselves that APEC will not be turned into another preferential trading arrangement, and on the other, they should persuade the American members that multilateral free trade, not a spaghetti bowl of preferential free trade areas, should be the centerpiece of the emerging world trading system. Recently, many economists have noted that a weakness in the WTO system is the absence of a deadline for achieving worldwide free trade. APEC could remedy this weakness by persuading WTO to adopt the 2010/2020 deadline for free trade on a worldwide basis.

REFERENCES

Ariff, Mohamed, and Eu Chye Tan (1992), "ASEAN-Pacific Trade Relation Relations," *ASEAN Economic Bulletin*, 8: 258–283.

Bhagwati, Jagdish (1993), "Regionalism and Multilateralism: An Overview," in Melo and Panagariya.

——— (1995), "U.S. Trade Policy: The Infatuation with Free Trade Areas," in J. Bhagwati and A. O. Krueger, eds., *The Dangerous Drift to Preferential Trade Agreements*, Washington, DC: American Enterprise Institute for Public Policy Research.

Bhagwati, Jagdish, and Arvind Panagariya (1996a), "The Theory of Preferential Trade Agreements: Historical Evolution and Current

Trends," *American Economic Review, Papers and Proceedings*, 86 (May): 82–87.

(1996b), "Preferential Trading Areas and Multilateralism: Strangers, Friends and Foes," in J. Bhagwati and A. Panagariya, eds., *The Economics of Preferential Trade Agreements*, Washington, DC: AEI Press.

Finger, J. M. (1979), "Trade Liberalization: A Public Choice Perspective," in R. C. Amachen, G. Haberler, and T. Willett, eds., *Challenges to a Liberal International Economic Order*, Washington, DC: American Enterprise Institute.

Foroutan, Faezeh (1993), "Regional Integration in Sub-Saharan Africa: Past Experience and Future Prospects," in Melo and Panagariya.

Krugman, Paul R. (1993), "Regionalism versus Multilateralism: Analytical Notes," in Melo and Panagariya.

Melo, Jaime de, and Arvind Panagariya (1992), *The New Regionalism in Trade Policy*, Washington, DC: World Bank.

eds. (1993), *New Dimensions in Regional Integration*, Cambridge: Cambridge University Press.

Melo, Jaime de, Dani Rodrik, and Arvind Panagariya (1993), "The New Regionalism: A Country Perspective" in Melo and Panagariya.

Panagariya, Arvind (1996a), "Free Trade Area of the Americas: Good for Latin America?" *World Economy*, 19: 485–515.

(1996b), "APEC and the United States," paper presented at the Conference on International Trade Policy and the Pacific Rim, University of Sydney, Australia.

Pangestu, Mari, Hadi Soesastro, and Mubariq Ahmed (1992), "A New Look at Intra-ASEAN Economic Cooperation," *ASEAN Economic Bulletin*, 8: 333–352.

Petri, Peter (1992), "One Bloc, Two Blocs or None? Political-Economic Factors in Pacific Trade policy," in K. Okuizumi, K. E. Calder, and G. W. Gong, eds., *The U.S.–Japan Economic Relationship in East and Southeast Asia: A Policy Framework for Asia–Pacific Economic Cooperation*, Significant Issues Series, 14(1). Washington, DC: Center for Strategic and International Studies.

Sopiee, Noordin, C. L. See, and L. S. Jin, eds. (1987), *ASEAN at the Crossroads: Obstacles, Options, and Opportunities*, Kuala Lumpur: ISIS.

Summers, Lawrence (1991), "Regionalism and the World Trading System," in *Policy Implications of Trade and Currency Zones*, the proceedings of a symposium sponsored by the Federal Reserve Bank of Kansas City, Jackson Hole, WY.

Viner, Jacob (1950), *The Customs Union Issue*, New York: Carnegie Endowment for International Peace.

Winters, Alan (1993), "The European Community: A Case of Successful Integration?" in Melo and Panagariya.

World Bank (1993), *East Asia and the Pacific Regional Development Review: Sustaining Rapid Development*, Washington, DC: World Bank.

Comment

Barry Eichengreen

In previous writings, Arvind Panagariya has been uniformly criti-cal of arguments for regional rather than multilateral trade liber-alization. In this chapter, he brings this critical perspective to bear on proposals for regional liberalization in East Asia.

Panagariya starts with the textbook model of a customs union, the focus of which is the balance of trade creation and trade diver-sion. He shows, given the small country assumption – which is not too unrealistic for much of East Asia, Japan and China notwith-standing – that unilateral free trade dominates a regional FTA, because the former delivers all the benefits of trade creation while the latter not only limits those gains but also is a source of trade diversion. According to the standard model, then, it is never in the interest of small, price-taking economies to form a regional trade bloc.

Panagariya then asks whether the case for regional FTAs can be salvaged by relaxing the restrictive assumptions of the textbook model. For example, one can imagine that an exporting country that negotiates a free trade agreement with a foreign market can secure better access for its goods than if it liberalizes unilaterally. But even if the exporters' welfare is improved as a result of this bilateral negotiation, the combined welfare of the two countries concerned is still lower than if they had both liberalized unilater-ally, as Panagariya shows.

The basic model assumes away economies of scale in production. One can imagine that regional liberalization will be efficiency enhancing if it enables the participating countries to exploit scale economies and reduce production costs. But as long as foreign markets do not have to be pried open through the exchange of tariff concessions, scale economies can also be reaped through unilateral liberalization, as countries like South Korea have shown. Because unilateral liberalization is every bit as effective at encouraging domestic producers to shift resources out of import-competing industries and into export-oriented sectors (where, for present pur-poses, we can assume the increasing-returns technologies reside), a regional FTA is not needed for a country to capitalize on the exis-tence of scale economies.

By limiting the negotiating costs arising from the large number of participants in a global liberalization round, regional initiatives may be a more practical way of freeing trade. But negotiation costs depend on more than the number of governments seated at the table. Institutionalized rules, procedures, and precedents can be even more important for resolving conflicts and facilitating the exchange of concessions. The GATT and the WTO, which have been around in one form or another for fully half a century, have developed the institutional expertise needed to offset the costs associated with a large and growing membership, as evidenced in the successful outcome of the recently concluded Uruguay Round.

Invoking the regional option may deter the rest of the world from traveling down the trade-bloc route. The threat of an East Asian trade bloc could deter the United States from forming an exclusionary Western Hemispheric FTA and the European Union from constructing a Fortress Europe. If Asian producers are shut out of North American and European markets, and North American and European producers are in turn shut out of Asian markets, this knowledge should discourage U.S. and EU leaders from erecting exclusionary FTAs of their own. The fact that the Single European Act and North American Free Trade Agreement encouraged the ASEAN countries in 1992 to sign a framework agreement to create an ASEAN Free Trade Area within fifteen years is at least consistent with this view. But as a matter of empirical fact, there is no evidence that either the EU or the United States is intent on forming an exclusionary trade bloc. And the countries of East Asia depend on U.S. export markets as heavily as on their own. It is not clear that threatening to cut off their collective nose to spite their face would be regarded as credible.

Finally there is the fact that political rivalry remains intense in East Asia and continues to pose a barrier to regional integration. The question is whether the region could transform its political landscape as dramatically as did Western Europe after World War II by negotiating an Asian Treaty of Rome. Could economic integration provide the impetus for political reconciliation, in other words? Panagariya's response is negative; he notes that U.S. support for the European Coal and Steel Community and the European Economic Community provided critical external impetus for Europe's postwar regional initiative. Without the Marshall Plan, which made steps toward European integration a prerequisite for the disbursement of funds, and the European Payments Union, which was supported with Marshall Plan money, the reconciliation and integration of Germany and France would have hardly proceeded at the same pace.

While I agree completely with this analysis, I believe that it places too much weight on immediate post–World War II events. There are even more fundamental reasons why the political prospects for regional integration are not equally bright in East Asia. (Here I draw on the analysis of Eichengreen and Bayoumi, 1996.) Proponents of European integration trace their antecedents back to Pierre Dubois, a jurist and diplomat in the French and English courts, who in 1306 proposed a permanent assemblage of European princes working to secure a lasting peace. The English Quaker William Penn proposed a European parliament and a supranational European government in 1693. Jeremy Bentham advocated a European assembly, Jean-Jacques Rousseau a European federation, and Henri Saint-Simon a European monarch and parliament. By the middle of the nineteenth century, intellectuals like Victor Hugo spoke of a United States of Europe. The point is that the ideal of European integration is intimately connected with the liberal and democratic principles of the Enlightenment and has roots in centuries of European history.

Interwar developments further suggest that post–World War II events were hardly a break with the past. Belgium and Luxembourg established an economic union in 1922. The Low Countries and Scandinavia agreed to harmonize their tariffs as part of the 1930 Oslo Convention. The Pan-European Union, founded by the Austrian Count Richard Coudenhove-Kalergi in 1923, lobbied for a European federation and attracted the support of Aristide Briand and Edouard Herriot, future premiers of France. In 1924, Herriot, by then French prime minister, spoke out for the creation of a United States of Europe. In 1929, Briand proposed to the League of Nations the creation of a European confederation. Konrad Adenauer and Georges Pompidou were also members of the Pan-European Union. One can thus say that by 1945 the intellectual preconditions for European integration were in place.

East Asia, in contrast, lacks the political solidarity and cohesion to support the equivalent of Europe's Single Market. It lacks a Jean Monet or Paul-Henri Spaak to speak out for regional integration. Before World War I, many countries were under the dominance of colonial powers that provided little scope for self-determination. The military governments that emerged after the war discouraged cross-border bridges for fear that this would undermine their domestic political control. Then there is the fact that ideological distance between China's communist government and market-oriented regimes elsewhere in East Asia is so great (in contrast to Western Europe, where after World War II variants of the social market economy were embraced by virtually all the members of the present-day European Union).

At a deeper level, East Asia lacks a tradition of self-governance through the creation of political institutions. It lacks a Benthamite/Rousseauian/Saint-Simonian heritage of collective democratic governance through integration. As Katzenstein (1996, p. 147) puts it, "the notion of unified sovereignty . . . central to the conception of continental European states, does not capture Asian political realities." Not only in China do the regions resist the attempts of the center to exercise its political power through the operation of political and legal institutions. The idea of a central-ized state with a monopoly of force that regiments its citizens through the superimposition of a common set of institutions is a European conception, not an Asian one. Asian civil society is struc-tured by ritual, ceremony, and economic networks more than by military force or the rule of law. Because the notion of strong, cohe-sive nation-states in the Western mold are foreign to Asia, it is unrealistic to speak of pooling national sovereignties that don't exist.

Consequently, integrationist initiatives in Asia have proceeded not through the creation of strong supranational institutions but by establishing loose networks of cooperation. It is revealing that APEC, which is essentially just a consultative forum, has succeeded where initiatives to create smaller, more cohesive Asian analogues to the EEC or EFTA have repeatedly failed.

Thus, my own analysis, like Panagariya's, comes to relatively negative conclusions about the prospects for a serious regional inte-gration initiative in East Asia.

REFERENCES

Eichengreen, Barry, and Tamim Bayoumi (1996), "Is Asia an Optimum Currency Area? Regional, Global and Historical Perspectives on Asian Monetary Relations," unpublished manuscript, University of California, Berkeley, and International Monetary Fund.

Katzenstein, Peter J. (1996), "Regionalism in Comparative Perspective," *Cooperation and Conflict*, 31: 123–160.

CHAPTER 5

Political Feasibility
and Empirical Assessments
of a Pacific Free Trade Area

Hiro Lee and Brian Woodall

1. TOWARD A FREE TRADE AGREEMENT IN
EAST ASIA OR THE PACIFIC BASIN?

During the past quarter-century, intraregional trade has expanded
dramatically in East Asia and the Pacific Basin. In 1970, 29.8
percent of gross trade (the sum of exports and imports) was
intraregional among ten selected countries in East Asia – Japan,
China, the newly industrialized economies (NIes: South Korea,
Taiwan, Hong Kong, and Singapore), and the ASEAN-4 (Malaysia,
Thailand, Indonesia, and the Philippines). By 1995, intra–East
Asian trade accounted for 49.2 percent of gross trade flows. Similarly, intraregional trade among the countries of Pacific Basin – the
ten East Asian countries, along with the United States, Canada,
Mexico, Australia, and New Zealand – climbed from 58.4 percent
in 1970 to 72.1 percent in 1995.[1] Emerging in tandem with the formation of the European Union (EU) in 1992, this expansion in
intraregional trade led many analysts to ponder the possibility of
an East Asian or a Pacific free trade agreement.[2]

We thank Alain de Janvry and Ippei Yamazawa for helpful comments and Laura Xia for
research assistance. The financial support from the Japan Foundation's Center for Global
Partnership and the University of California's Pacific Rim Research Program is gratefully
acknowledged.

[1] The calculation is based upon the International Monetary Fund's *Direction of Trade
Statistics* data.
[2] An FTA can be defined as a "group of two or more customs territories in which duties and
other restrictive regulations of commerce . . . are eliminated on substantially all trade
between constituent territories in products originating in such territories" (GATT, 1947,
Article XXIV: 8b). An FTA differs from a customs union in that the latter is "the substitution of a single customs territory for two or more customs territories" and "substantially

While much has been written about the significance of expanded intraregional trade flows in East Asia and the Pacific Basin (e.g., Drysdale and Garnaut, 1993; Frankel, 1993; Krugman, 1991; Petri, 1993; Saxonhouse, 1993; Yamazawa, 1992, 1994), considerably less attention has been paid to the political feasibility and the economic benefits and costs of such. Is an East Asian free trade area (EAFTA) agreement politically feasible? What about a Pacific free trade area (PAFTA)? How likely is it that the governments of the various countries of the region can successfully negotiate an agreement establishing a free trade area? Which countries would stand to benefit economically, and which will lose in the event that trade barriers are removed in conjunction with the creation of one or the other of the proposed free trade agreements? What about the effects of possible retaliation by the United States against EAFTA member countries? In this chapter, we seek to provide answers to these and other related questions.

A brief word about our analytic itinerary is in order. Section 2 is devoted to consideration of the factors that bear upon the political feasibility of the creation of an FTA in East Asia or the Pacific Basin.[3] We seek to illuminate the relevant issues by looking at the salient transnational and national-level considerations through the eyes of a negotiator charged with representing the interests of a hypothetical country in the region. We begin by identifying three sets of regional-level conditions that must be solved in order to enable the creation of a regional free trade agreement. Specifically, the transnational feasibility of a free trade agreement is facilitated by the existence of mechanisms to delineate and facilitate cooperation among candidate countries, similar or compatible political regimes and regime-objectives among the governments of the candidate countries, and relatively similar levels of economic development. The remainder of section 2 is devoted to consideration of the sort of domestic political objective function confronting a negotiator as he or she explores the pros and cons of possible participation in an FTA from the perspective of his or her country.

the same duties and other regulations of commerce are applied by each of the members of the union to trade of territories not included in the union" (GATT, 1947, Article XXIV: 8a).

[3] The focus in this chapter is on the conditions conducive to the creation of a formal free trade agreement, in contrast to less elaborate or informal arrangements such as export processing zones, "growth triangles," and ethnic business networks. These other arrangements are discussed in Lloyd (1996) and Peng (1996).

This political objective function considers aggregate national welfare in the absence of nonmember retaliation, the interests of important industry lobbies, and the aggregate welfare in the event of nonmember retaliation.

Section 3 summarizes the results of empirical assessments using a computable general equilibrium model for four separate scenarios. Scenario 1 considers the effects that would accompany the removal of tariff and nontariff barriers by the EAFTA countries among themselves in the event that these countries maintain existing trade barriers against nonmember countries. We find that, under this scenario, all four East Asian regions (Japan, China, the NIEs, and the ASEAN-4) would experience gains in welfare (measured in Hicksian equivalent variations) and real gross domestic product (GDP), while welfare and real GDP of nonmember countries are affected very little. Scenario 2, which considers the consequences of American retaliation in response to East Asian FTA followed by a U.S.–East Asian trade war, unfolds in six steps. We find that the United States experiences welfare increases if it seeks to maximize its welfare by imposing optimal tariffs on imports from the four East Asian regions. However, U.S. gains would be more than offset by welfare losses in East Asia. In step 2 of this scenario, East Asia would retaliate by imposing optimal tariffs on imports from the United States. This would result in smaller welfare losses for the East Asian countries (although they would not be able to recover losses incurred in step 1), in addition to losses for American as well as global welfare. The United States and East Asia take turns in imposing optimal tariffs in the final four steps. By the sixth iteration, equilibrium is attained (i.e., no change in solution values beyond the sixth iteration). As expected, all four East Asian regions and the United States would become worse off compared with the initial situation, and global welfare losses are substantial. However, owing to the increased demand for their exports, Canada, Mexico, and the EU would actually experience some welfare gains.

Scenario 3 focuses on the effects of the formation of an FTA among the countries of the Asia Pacific Economic Cooperation (APEC) group. We find that trade liberalization among the APEC members will produce benefits for each country, while global welfare gains will also be realized. Finally, scenario 4 assesses the effects of nondiscriminatory liberalization by the APEC members.

In this scenario, the Asian NIEs, Australia, New Zealand, and the North American countries realize greater welfare gains than under the third scenario, whereas smaller gains are realized by Japan, China, and the ASEAN-4. Nevertheless, the APEC region as a whole will benefit by expending liberalization to all imports. In addition to the fact that this scenario is more in keeping with the spirit of the multilateral trade liberalization process envisioned under the World Trade Organization (WTO), it also creates substantial global welfare increases.

2. IS A FREE TRADE AGREEMENT POLITICALLY FEASIBLE?

Two sets of concerns confront a chief negotiator in weighing the pros and cons of a free trade agreement. First, it is necessary to solve for the conditions under which the country represented would enter into an FTA with a specific group of other countries. At the same time, and perhaps more importantly, the negotiator must consider the situation "back home." From the negotiator's perspective, therefore, the political feasibility of an FTA is a "two-level game" (Putnam, 1988, and Evans et al., 1993; Grossman and Helpman, 1995, employ a variation of this framework). In other words, that negotiator must assess political and economic conditions at the regional level, while being attentive to what will fly with the political elite and the key demand claimants on the home front.

2.1. Conditions at the Regional Level

At the regional level, the fulfillment of three sets of conditions increases the likelihood of successful negotiations leading to the creation of a free trade agreement. First, it is necessary to determine the member states. In this regard, it is reasonable to assume that the likelihood of the achievement of such an accord is greater when the candidate countries are located in relatively close geographic proximity to one another, beset by few if any significant disputes, and bound together by some existing organizations or institutions at the regional level. Second, the establishment of an FTA is more likely among countries with compatible political regimes and regime objectives. And, third, the realization of an

FTA is facilitated when candidate countries are at similar levels of economic development. The dismantling of barriers alters trade flows, resulting in a redistribution of income and employment among member countries. As Schott (1991, p. 2) explains, trading blocs "with wide disparities in national incomes face difficulties because producers in the richer countries are invariably seen as swamping those in the poorer countries (while the reverse is seen to occur with regard to labor)."

To what extent would the negotiator representing a hypothetical candidate country find these regional-level conditions fulfilled among the prospective member countries of an East Asian or Pacific free trade agreement? Regarding the matter of delineating member countries, the first condition, it is instructive to compare the state of affairs in East Asia with that in the European Union. As for the presumably lower intraregional transportation costs derived from close geographic proximity to one another, the candidate countries of East Asia are markedly more dispersed than the EU countries.[4] In contrast to the EU, where country capitals lie, on average, 575 miles from Brussels, the average distance from the East Asian capitals to Singapore (home to the Secretariat of the Asia Pacific Economic Cooperation, the closest equivalent to the EU) is 1,900 miles. And the EU is even more geographically compact than would be the case with a Pacific free trade area, where an average of more than 4,000 miles separates country capitals from APEC's headquarters. Nevertheless, it bears stressing that in this day and age lower transportation costs are not as important as comparative advantage in determining trading patterns (Lloyd, 1996).

Moreover, relations among the East Asian countries are not entirely rosy, as reflected in the relatively large number of intraregional territorial disputes. The only conflicting territorial claims among EU countries involve the Rockall continental shelf (claimed by Denmark, Ireland, and the United Kingdom), Northern Ireland (claimed by Ireland and the UK), and Gibraltar (claimed by Spain and the UK). On this score, the average EU country is involved in 0.67 territorial disputes with other countries in the region. In con-

---

[4] It is also well to recognize the number of prospective member states as a variable in facilitating or hindering the creation of a trading bloc. Indeed, more prospective members means more coordination problems and greater difficulties (i.e., higher transaction costs) in achieving consensus.

trast, the average East Asian state is embroiled in 2.2 territorial disputes with its neighbors in the region. Indeed, only Singapore has no territorial conflicts, while Malaysia is at odds with no less than five other East Asian countries. However, once we bring the North American countries, Australia, and New Zealand into the picture, the only additional controversy involves the disputed maritime boundary between the United States and Canada. This does not imply that, in and of itself, the existence of a comparatively large number of conflicting territorial claims forecloses the possibility of a free trade agreement in East Asia or on the Pacific Rim. Rather, the point to be made is that such disputes represent an additional barrier that must be surmounted in negotiations aiming to fashion such an agreement.

Perhaps more importantly, East Asia is beset with enduring historical animosities, the most visceral of which involve lingering tensions concerning Japan's imperialist legacy. In Europe, the German government has taken visible steps to atone for past aggression, and in North America, resentment of U.S. economic and cultural "imperialism" tends to be a relatively minor irritant in intraregional relations. In contrast, the Japanese political leadership has refused to offer an unambiguous apology for actions taken during the country's period of imperialist expansion. Generally speaking, the image of Japan as a "restive marauder" is more pronounced in Northeast Asia (Calder, 1991), although Singapore's Lee Kuan Yew has stated that no leader in the East favors a yen bloc. As long as Japan's political leaders denounce foreign criticism of historical interpretations found in Japanese high school history textbooks, the visits of cabinet ministers to Yasukuni Shrine, and the enslavement of Asian "comfort women" during World War II, suspicions will persist concerning Tokyo's capability to assume de facto regional leadership (Woodall, 1993). Indeed, most East Asian leaders find comfort in an American security presence to counterbalance Japan's "legitimacy deficit," although recent downsizing of the U.S. armed forces and scandals involving American forces in Okinawa raise doubts about the future of the country's role as regional constable. This, coupled with the heavy dependence on American markets for East Asian exports, points to a widespread preference for a Pacific free trade area, in the event that a formal regional trading bloc becomes reality.

In terms of its regional institutional infrastructure, East Asia lags far behind the European Union. The idea of a European "community" dates back at least to the interwar period, and the creation of a "single market" in 1992 was predated by the establishment of the European Community in 1958 and the European Free Trade Agreement (EFTA) in 1960.[5] The passage of time has witnessed the creation of a European Parliament and an impressive array of formal institutions intended to facilitate increased regional integration. Although numerous problems remain to be solved, it is clear that regional economic and political integration in Western Europe has progressed much further than in any other region of the world.

In contrast, the existing institutional infrastructure in East Asia and on the Pacific Rim is markedly primitive. It is fair to say that present-day East Asia is the least "regionalized" of the world's regions (e.g., Lloyd, 1996). Although the idea of an East Asian "community" also dates back to the interwar period, it is embodied in the Greater East Asian Co-Prosperity Sphere, the geopolitical masterplan to replace Western imperialism with an Asian empire ruled by Japan. Indeed, all other pre–World War II institutional antecedents aimed to foster intraregional social and cultural exchange (e.g., the Pan-Pacific Union), rather than economic integration (Yamaoka, 1996). In fact, the oldest existing regional organization, the Association of Southeast Asian Nations (ASEAN), was formed in 1967 to address security concerns. Yet ASEAN did not produce a free trade agreement until 1992, and a common preferential tariff scheme among the seven member states will not be fully implemented until 2003 (Tan, Chapter 6, this volume). APEC, the broadest and most ambitious regional institution on the Pacific Rim, was founded in 1989 and established a modest secretariat three years later. Even if APEC is able to keep to its current goal, the day of "free and open trade and investment" among the eighteen member countries will not dawn until the year 2020.[6]

A second regional-level condition assumes that the creation of a free trade agreement is less complicated in a setting in which the candidate countries have similar political structures and compati-

---

[5] The original member countries included Belgium, France, West Germany, Italy, Luxembourg, and the Netherlands. The EFTA member countries included Austria, Denmark, Finland, Norway, Portugal, Sweden, Switzerland, and the United Kingdom.
[6] The developed members have committed to trade and investment liberalization by 2010.

ble regime objectives. Empirical fodder for this reasoning is found in an extensive literature in which it is demonstrated that democracies are unlikely to conflict with one another (Bueno de Mesquita and Lalman, 1992; Russett, 1993; Ray, 1995). For instance, a recent study argues that while not necessarily more peace-loving than nondemocratic polities, democracies tend not to fight one another (Rousseau et al., 1996). Employing similar logic, it is reasonable to assume that it would be easier for a set of advanced industrialized democracies to negotiate a formal free trade agreement than would be the case if the candidate countries included a mixture of authoritarian as well as democratic polities. In the case of the latter, for example, one might anticipate conflicts arising from differing conceptions of human rights and environmental protection policies.

Although regime categorization is far from an exact science, it can be said that all fifteen member states of the European Union are parliamentary democracies in which political leaders are chosen through relatively upright elections. Such is not the case with the East Asian countries. According to the thoughtful categorization proposed by Ichimura and Morley (1993, p. 27), it is possible to identify no less than four separate regime types: eroding Leninist (China), authoritarian (Indonesia and Singapore), quasi-democratic (Malaysia, Taiwan, and Thailand), and democratic (Japan, South Korea, and the Philippines).

In a related vein, it is logical to assume that the likelihood of achieving a free trade agreement is enhanced when candidate countries have similar or compatible trading regimes. Whereas the existence of trading regimes with similar trade laws and regulations contributes to the durability of an FTA, it is also likely to demand the forfeiture of some degree of national sovereignty to a regional body. Subordinating national sovereignty in favor of broader regional interests generally, but not always, requires tenacious commitment at the highest political level and among the country's political elite (Schott, 1991, p. 3). At any rate, the latitude of a negotiator is greater in the event that his or her top political "boss" is unequivocally committed to the empowerment of a regional organization to serve as traffic cop in regulating trade flows and to referee in mediating disputes. In this regard, it is well to note the proposals for regional institutions advocated, respectively, by Malaysian Prime Minister Mahathir Mohamad and former Australian Prime Minister Bob Hawke.[7] On this score, it is difficult to say whether or not the political commitment in East Asia and the Pacific Rim is more or less lukewarm and occasionally wavering than the political resolve that led to the creation of the EU and NAFTA.

More importantly, the candidate countries for an East Asian FTA embody a far broader range of economic development levels than is the case in Western Europe. In 1994, the unweighted average of purchasing power parity (PPP) estimates of per capita GNP for the ten East Asian countries was $11,321, as compared with $17,627 for the EU-12 countries.[8] The standard deviation in per capita GNP was perceptibly wider among the East Asian states ($7,836) than was the case with the EU states ($4,425). More to the point, the ratio of the country with the highest per capita GNP to that with the lowest per capita GNP in PPP was 8.7 among the East Asian countries and 2.5 among the EU countries.[9] According to the World Bank categorization scheme based on per capita GNP in U.S. dollars, all of the EU member states are high-income economies with the exception of Greece, which is an upper-middle-income economy. In contrast, the East Asian states run the gamut from a low-income economy (China) to lower-middle-income economies (Indonesia, Philippines, Thailand) to upper-middle-income economies (Malaysia, Korea, Taiwan) to high-income economies (Hong Kong, Singapore, Japan).[10] Although this diversity represents a potentially salubrious division of labor à la the "flying geese" pattern of East Asian economic development (Akamatsu, 1962), it also contains the seeds of discontent, especially among the region's developing countries, which might harbor suspicions of perpetual subservience to the advanced countries.

---

[7] Mahathir originally proposed an East Asian Economic Group that included ASEAN, China, Japan, and the newly industrialized economies. The proposal was later recast as the East Asia Economic Caucus, which also included Vietnam and an apparent commitment to "open regionalism." The Hawke proposal called for the creation of a regional body whose membership includes Australia, New Zealand, ASEAN, Japan, China, South Korea, Canada, and the United States.

[8] The three new members of the EU – Austria, Finland, and Sweden – are excluded from the computation because they became members in 1995.

[9] The calculation is largely based on the data from the *World Development Report*, 1996. If per-capita GNP measured in U.S. dollars was used instead, then this ratio would become 65.3 for East Asia and 4.6 for the EU-12.

[10] If per-capita GNP in PPP is used instead, China will be included in lower-middle-income economies.

The experience of the EU highlights the transnational difficulties that must be surmounted to achieve regional integration. Nevertheless, a single European market has been realized, and the process of economic and political integration proceeds apace. Despite numerous obstacles, the trend toward economic regionalization has revealed itself in the Western hemisphere in the form of NAFTA and a series of less ambitious accords. In this regard, the European and North American achievements convey a demonstration effect to would-be emulators in other regions of the world. Moreover, the realization of significant degrees of integration in two extremely important regions of the world economy significantly alters the terms of competition in international trade. Hence, an already partially regionalized world economy creates a more compelling incentive for regionalism elsewhere. Indeed, the major proposals for an East Asian free trade area emerged from suspicions concerning the ultimate intentions of the Europeans and North Americans. In the final analysis, therefore, while the EU benchmark is suggestive, it is well to bear in mind the implications of the demonstration effect and the changed incentive structure in the world economy in assessing the political feasibility of an East Asian and/or a Pacific free trade area.

2.2. Conditions at the National Level

Assuming that the regional conditions are solved for, the chief negotiator must define a political objective function to determine the domestic feasibility of entering into such an accord. This involves a painstaking assessment of the pros and cons of regional free trade for the country's political economy as well as the particular interests of key industrial lobbies. In addition, it is essential to consider the possible consequences of participation in an FTA (i.e., the possibility of retaliation by an important nonmember trading partner or competing regional trading bloc).

In simple terms, a negotiator's domestic political objective function, Y, might take the following form:

$$Y = f\left(W, \Sigma_i C_i, R, p\right) \quad (5.1)$$

where W is aggregate national welfare in the event that no nonmember country retaliates, C_i is the contribution of the lobby

representing industry i, R is the aggregate welfare in the event of
retaliation on the part of a nonmember country or union, and p is
the probability of retaliation. Of course, quantifying the specific
variables and assessing the effects of their interaction in this kind
of political objective function is extremely difficult.

What specific domestic concerns demand to be weighed? First,
in order to get a tentative sense for the aggregate welfare gains or
losses in the absence of any nonmember retaliation (about which
more attention is given in section 3), it is well to take a longitu-
dinal look at changes in intraregional trade shares for each of the
East Asian states. For every East Asian country except Indonesia,
the share of intraregional trade increased between 1980 and 1995.
For example, Japan's trade with other East Asian countries
increased from 24 percent of its total trade in 1980 to 39 percent
in 1995, while China's intraregional trade grew from 43 to 55
percent during the same period. Although the most dramatic rise
is seen in the figures for Hong Kong, whose intraregional trade
share jumped from 44 to 63 percent between 1980 and 1995, it is
well to bear in mind that those figures may be biased upward owing
to the fact that a large share of Chinese exports to Hong Kong are
reexported to other East Asian countries (and vice versa). Overall,
intra–East Asian trade shares increased an average of 7.4 percentage points between 1980 and 1990 and an additional 7.9
percentage points between 1990 and 1995.[11]

At the same time, intraregional trade shares increased among
nearly all of the Asian Pacific countries. For example, the share of
America's overall trade with other Pacific Basin countries grew dramatically from 46 percent in 1980 to 65 percent in 1995, while the
figures for Japan rose from 52 to 70 percent during the same
period. The average increase in intraregional trade for fifteen
Asian Pacific countries was 17 percentage points during the
1980–95 period. Only Indonesia witnessed a drop in its intraregional trade share during the period. To the extent that the
removal of barriers to intraregional trade contributes to an
increase in aggregate national welfare in a country whose share
of trade with other countries in the region is rising, there is an

[11] See Table 1.2 of the introductory chapter. The increase in the intra–East Asian trade share
during the 1980–90 period is partly induced by the reduction in the region's trade share
with OPEC countries caused by sharp declines in oil prices.

incentive for participation in a regional free trade agreement. Still, it remains an open question as to whether preferential liberalization (i.e., removal of trade barriers among members of an exclusive trading bloc) or nondiscriminatory liberalization is preferable. The negotiator must also weigh the pros and cons of participation in a regional trading bloc for each of the key domestic demand claimants. Special consideration must be paid to the interests of lobbies representing producer interests, which tend to be better organized and more politically potent than is the case with consumer lobbies. Ultimately, this is a complex and highly "political" matter, whose resolution is shaped by the character of authority relations in the political regime (e.g., legal-rational authority relations in a democratic regime versus authoritarian coercion in a Leninist regime). Regime objectives (e.g., industrial targeting and import substitution versus unilateral liberalization and/or policies to attract foreign direct investment), as well as labor force and industrial structure considerations, also must be given due heed.

A survey of the East Asian scene reveals the complexity posed by regional trade liberalization vis-à-vis the domestic politics of each candidate country. For example, notwithstanding its relatively insignificant contribution to aggregate welfare, the agricultural sector (including agriculture, forestry, fisheries, and food processing) in Japan (which contributed a mere 2.2 percent of GDP in 1992), South Korea (7.1 percent), and Taiwan (3.6 percent) are highly subsidized and shielded against foreign imports by a variety of tariffs, import quotas, and nontariff barriers (NTBs).[12] Among the EAFTA countries in 1992, Japan (73.3 percent) had far and away the highest ad valorem equivalents of tariff and nontariff barriers, while the prominent barriers also applied in the Asian NIEs (56.6 percent) and the ASEAN-4 (28.6 percent) (Table 5.1).[13] The protection afforded agriculture – and the concomitant tax burden and higher food prices for consumers – attests to the political clout wielded by the agricultural lobbies in these countries (Anderson and Hayami, 1986). At the same time, agricultural producers are

[12] By way of comparison, in 1992, agriculture contributed 28 percent of GDP in China, 22 percent in the Philippines, 21 percent in Indonesia, 16 percent in Malaysia, and 12 percent in Thailand.

[13] These countries impose import quotas on a number of agricultural products, and ad valorem equivalents of nontariff barriers are significantly higher than the tariff rates. For estimates of Japan's NTBs by commodities, see Sazanami, Urata, and Kawai (1995).

Table 5.1. *Ad Valorem Equivalents of Tariff and Nontariff Barriers, 1992 (percent)*

	Japan	China	Asian NIEs	ASEAN -4	Australia -NZ	US	Canada	Mexico	Latin America	EU
1 AgricFood	73.3	20.2	56.6	28.6	7.3	9.9	16.0	7.7	16.8	36.6
2 EnergRes	0.7	10.7	3.6	10.5	0.9	0.8	0.4	9.9	5.2	0.9
3 TextApLea	12.7	62.4	2.2	36.7	17.9	15.1	20.7	16.8	21.5	11.1
4 ChemRbPls	5.5	18.3	5.2	19.2	17.1	10.8	10.6	8.3	16.2	13.6
5 Metals	2.6	17.4	5.0	12.1	17.5	7.4	9.1	7.9	17.0	4.5
6 Machinery	3.4	29.9	5.5	20.5	20.4	16.7	8.8	12.2	20.1	9.6
7 TranspEq	3.0	37.5	7.4	26.7	20.9	3.8	7.8	13.8	16.7	8.1
8 OtherMfg	4.2	47.8	3.1	24.6	16.8	5.2	9.0	10.7	19.0	5.4
9 TradeTrnsp	0.0	0.0	0.0	0.0	0.0	0.0	0.0	0.0	0.0	0.0
10 Services	0.0	2.9	0.0	0.0	0.0	0.0	0.0	3.7	0.0	0.0
Weighted Avg	13.0	30.4	8.1	19.6	13.8	8.7	8.8	9.8	13.9	8.3

Notes:
1. These rates are the sum of tariff rates and ad valorem equivalents of nontariff barriers.
2. AgFood = agriculture, forestry, fishery, and food processing. EnergRes = energy and resources. TextApLea = textiles, apparel, and leather. ChemRbPls = chemicals, rubber, and plastics. Metals = primary metals and metal products. Machinery = non-electrical and electrical machinery. TranspEq = transport equipment. OtherMfg = other manufacturing. TradeTrnsp = trade and transport. Services = construction, finance, and other services.
Source: GTAP database, Version 2.

taxed – while tariffs and government policies protect certain manufacturing industries – in China, Indonesia, the Philippines, and Thailand.

The effects of liberalization also pose problems for certain protected manufacturing industries. Through the acquisition of capital and technology, the East Asian countries – led by Japan, followed by the NIEs, with China and the developing countries of Southeast Asia taking up the rear – have shifted from primary products to simple and then more sophisticated manufactures. Many countries in the region have employed infant-industry arguments to justify the protection of a number of manufacturing products, such as petrochemicals, steel, passenger cars, and electronics products. Yet for obvious reasons, even well-established industries that have been shielded from foreign imports by tariffs, quotas, and other devices are loath to leave the warm embrace provided by government protection.

Such has been the case in many of the East Asian countries. Although Hong Kong and Singapore have led the way in a general trend toward free trade, significant barriers remain in other East Asian countries. In the case of simple manufactures in the more industrialized countries, such barriers are imposed to protect unskilled workers. This is illustrated in the case of Japan, where protection for particular footwear and leather products (with tariffs as high as 60 percent) is rationalized as an affirmative action policy to assist a discriminated minority. Nevertheless, the ad valorem equivalents of tariff and nontariff barriers in 1992 for Japan's textile industry (including textiles, apparel, and leather) were relatively low (12.7 percent) compared to those figures for China (62.4 percent) and the ASEAN-4 (36.7 percent) (Table 5.1).

As for more advanced manufactures, infant-industry arguments continue to sustain trade barriers in many East Asian countries. Perhaps the paradigmatic illustration is the case of Malaysia, which maintains a short list of prohibited manufactures in the country's "pioneer industries" (e.g., semiconductors) in spite of relatively low import duties on most manufactured goods. Other countries, such as Thailand, employ a policy of import licensing in industries designated for domestic development (e.g., some textiles and machinery, chemicals, paper products, and motor vehicles [World Bank, 1994]). Even after China reduced or abolished tariffs and import surcharges on a host of items and product groups in 1992, the unweighted average tariff rate (43 percent) was higher than the 1986 figure. Moreover, numerous tariffs continued to apply to a widely dispersed range of items (Dean et al., 1994). In 1992, China's ad valorem equivalents of tariff and nontariff barriers for transportation equipment and machinery were high (37.5 and 29.9 percent, respectively), while the ASEAN-4 also erected steep barriers to protect those sectors (26.7 and 20.5 percent).

Although liberalization is opposed by protected industries, it is viewed with suspicion by governments and nationalistic leaders intent upon "ramping-up" their countries' economies to the next level of industrial sophistication. On the surface, the experience of Japan and Korea, and to a lesser extent that of Taiwan, appear to demonstrate government's ability to reshape a country's comparative advantage through the development of strategic technologies and export promotion. The debate rages as to whether these governments have been more effective at picking winners or losers, but it cannot be denied that economic intervention by the majority of East Asian states has been "strong," if not always "smart" (Amsden, 1989; Beason and Weinstein, 1996; Inoue et al., 1993; Katzenstein, 1985; Wade, 1990). Moreover, as late as the mid-1980s, import duties constituted a significant share of total tax revenue for the governments of certain East Asian countries, specifically, the Philippines (29 percent), Thailand (22 percent), and South Korea (17 percent) (Dean et al., 1994). It would be expected that governments that stand to face diminished tax revenues would oppose liberalization and the creation of a free trade agreement.

In other words, the domestic political feasibility of a free trade area is a function of a complex calculus of conflicting sector-level interests. The agricultural sector in Japan and the Asian NIEs will contract substantially in the event of the creation of an East Asian or Pacific Basin FTA or the achievement of open regionalism. Even though these welfare losses will be more than offset by expansion in most of the manufacturing sectors, the agricultural lobby is a vocal opponent of trade liberalization in each of these countries. Whereas liberalization would level the playing field for the heavily taxed farmers of China and the ASEAN-4, it would mean a loss of tax revenue for their governments and painful adjustment for protected sectors. As for the United States, the creation of PAFTA or open regionalism would produce lower output levels in the textile and machinery sectors (see Table 5.6).[14] Although liberalization will lead to increased aggregate welfare through expanded trade and enhanced economywide efficiency in the more industrialized countries, individual protected sectors – particularly primary-product sectors or highly cartelized manufacturing or service sectors with well-organized producer lobbies – will seek to retain import protection. From the perspective of the less industrialized countries, liberalization threatens to eliminate sources of government revenue and to undermine state-sponsored efforts to develop industries deemed strategic to the national interest.

Finally, a negotiator must soberly assess the risk of potential welfare losses in the event of nonmember retaliation. Given their dependence on American markets as a destination for their exports, the East Asian countries might stand to suffer were the United States to retaliate. In 1995, for example, 35.8 percent of the Philippines' exports went to the United States, while Japan (27.5 percent), Taiwan (23.6 percent), Hong Kong (21.8 percent), and Malaysia (20.7 percent) all sent in excess of one-fifth of their exports to American markets. On average, the United States was the destination for 22.5 percent of the exports of EAFTA countries in 1995. In the next section, we employ a general equilibrium model to provide empirical assessments of the various scenarios involving the removal of trade barriers among the East Asian countries (i.e., the formation of EAFTA) and the Pacific Basin countries (i.e., the formation of PAFTA).

3. EMPIRICAL ASSESSMENTS OF A FREE TRADE AGREEMENT IN THE ASIAN PACIFIC

3.1. The Model

There are advantages in using a computable general equilibrium (CGE) model. Most importantly, a CGE model represents an excellent empirical tool with which to assess the impact of alternative trade policy scenarios. An important advantage of a CGE model is that it can capture significant indirect effects between countries

---

[14] We estimate and discuss the sector-level effects of liberalization in section 3.3.

and regions, such as interindustry linkages between sectors and trade linkages.[15] Inasmuch as it enables assessment of these effects in both member and nonmember countries, a CGE model is particularly well suited for estimating the impact of a new trading arrangement, which, of course, is our central focus in this study.

We have developed a CGE model to assess the aggregate and sectoral effects of various trade policy scenarios on the Pacific Basin economies (the PAC model). The model employed in the present study is a ten-region, ten-sector model that contains four East Asian regions (Japan, China, Asian NIEs, and ASEAN-4), Australasia (Australia and New Zealand), three North American countries (the United States, Canada, and Mexico), Latin America, and the European Union (EU).[16] The model is calibrated to the social accounting matrices (SAMs) of the ten regions, which have been constructed from the Global Trade Analysis Project (GTAP) database (Hertel, 1997). The original database provides 1992 data concerning bilateral trade, transport, and protection data, as well as individual country data on input–output, value-added, and final demand for twenty-four regions and thirty-seven sectors. In constructing the PAC model, we have aggregated this into a ten-region, ten-sector data set.[17]

Before elaborating the assumptions that undergird our analysis, it is well to point out two fundamental limitations of the PAC model. First, a comparative static model cannot account for capital accumulation, technological change, and other dynamic processes that might result from liberalization. For this reason, our findings may underestimate the magnitude of gains and adjustments resulting from liberalization, particularly in countries and sectors in which long-term investment and innovation are important. Second, a comparative static model does not allow for a process of gradual liberalization or the sort of liberalization timetable between developed and developing countries such as the one agreed upon by leaders of the APEC countries. At the same time, however, our model has the advantage of capturing medium-term structural adjustments to the removal of trade barriers with greater clarity than a dynamic model.

---

[15] See the introductory chapter by Lee and Roland-Holst in this volume for advantages and limitations of CGE models.
[16] See notes on Table 5.1 for sectoral classifications.
[17] A SAM for the rest of the world was not constructed for the present analysis.

The PAC model is premised upon three important assumptions.[18] First, the model assumes that bilateral trade between all ten regions is fully endogenous, while each region's trade flows with the rest of the world (ROW) are governed by export supply and import demand functions whose elasticities depend upon the size of each country in the ROW market. The resulting 110 sets of sectoral trade flows are then governed by an equal number of endogenous price systems.[19]

Second, as with other CGE constructs (e.g., de Melo and Tarr, 1992), the PAC model employs differentiated product specification for the demand and supply for tradeable commodities. Domestic demand is a constant elasticity of substitution (CES) composite of goods differentiated by origin. For each product category,

$$D_i = \overline{A}_{D_i} \left[\sum_k \beta_i^k \left(D_i^k \right)^{(\sigma_i - 1)/\sigma_i} \right]^{\sigma_i/(\sigma_i - 1)} \tag{5.2}$$

where k includes the ten regions and ROW. D_i^k's consist of domestic goods, imports from each region including ROW. σ_i are elasticities of substitution between D_i^k's, and $\overline{A}_{D_i}$ and β_i^k are intercept and share parameters. Similarly, domestic production is supplied to differentiated destinations (domestic market and exports to each region including ROW), which is specified as a constant elasticity of transformation (CET) composite:

$$S_i = \overline{A}_{S_i} \left[\sum_k \delta_i^k \left(S_i^k \right)^{(\tau_i + 1)/\tau_i} \right]^{\tau_i/(\tau_i + 1)} \tag{5.3}$$

where τ_i are elasticities of transformation between S_i^k's, and $\overline{A}_{S_i}$ and δ_i^k are intercept and share parameters.

Third, the PAC model specifies labor supply endogenously in order to capture the positive income effects of liberalization on aggregate employment. While most static CGE models assume fixed aggregate employment, a positively sloped labor supply curve is better suited for the present study. This is particularly evident in the cases of China and the ASEAN countries, both of which

---

[18] For a complete set of equations describing the model, see Lee and Roland-Holst (1995).
[19] There are $\Sigma_{i=1}^{r-1} i = 55$ sets of sectoral import and export flows, where r denotes the number of regions including the ROW.

have relatively large reservoirs of surplus labor. We assume that a representative consumer maximizes a Stone-Geary utility function over leisure and ten composite product categories. Labor supply then becomes an increasing function of the wage rate and a decreasing function of the marginal budget share for leisure.[20]

3.2. Aggregate Results

We conducted four trade policy experiments using the PAC model. Scenario 1 assumes that an East Asian free trade agreement is formed by the removal of tariffs and NTBs governing trade among four East Asian regions (Japan, China, Asian NIEs, and ASEAN-4) (Table 5.2). Under this scenario, member countries maintain trade barriers on imports from nonmember countries at the base year (1992) levels. In scenario 2, the United States retaliates against this discriminatory trading bloc by imposing optimal tariffs on its imports from the East Asian regions. The result is a trans-Pacific trade war. We assume that, in step 1, the United States chooses a vector of tariff rates to maximize its equivalent variations, a broadly used measure of domestic welfare, subject to tariff rates of the Asian regions.[21] In step 2, the East Asian trading bloc retaliates by choosing a vector of tariff rates to maximize the joint welfare of the bloc, subject to American tariff rates. The respective combatants seek to maximize their welfare functions sequentially until a noncooperative (Nash) equilibrium is attained. No changes in endogenous variables result after the sixth iteration, at which point convergence is reached.

---

[20] The labor supply function that is consistent with our consumption specification is given by

$$LS = \overline{LS}^{\max} - \left(\frac{\beta_0}{w}\right)\left[\frac{Y - \Sigma_{i=1}^{n} p_i \lambda_i}{1 - \beta_0}\right], \ \overline{LS}^{\max} = LS + C_0 - \lambda_0, \ 0 \le \beta_0 < 1,$$

where β_0 is the marginal budget share for leisure, w is the wage rate, Y is disposable income, p_i are prices of composite goods, λ_i are subsistence minimum consumption levels (λ_0 is the corresponding level for leisure), and C_0 is the amount of leisure consumed. The elasticity of labor supply with respect to wage is

$$\varepsilon_{LW} = \left[\left(1 - \beta_0\right)\overline{LS}^{\max}\Big/LS\right] - 1.$$

[21] Although a common sectoral tariff rate is imposed regardless of the origin country of East Asia, different optimal tariff rates are chosen across commodities.

Table 5.2. *Aggregate Results of Regional Tariff and NTB Liberalization among East Asian Countries*

	(1) Japan	(2) China	(3) Asian NIEs	(4) ASEAN -4	(5) Australia -NZ	(6) US	(7) Canada	(8) Mexico	(9) Latin America	(10) EU	(11) Subtotal (1)–(4)	(12) Subtotal (5)–(10)
1 Welfare ($ billion)	6.48	3.41	5.72	1.91	0.08	0.23	0.17	0.02	−0.04	0.97	17.52	1.34
2 Welfare (%)	0.18	0.78	0.93	0.55	0.02	0.00	0.03	0.01	−0.01	0.01		
3 Real GDP ($ billion)	2.68	7.99	3.91	4.51	−0.03	−0.35	0.06	0.02	0.01	0.57	19.07	0.31
4 Real GDP (%)	0.07	1.63	0.68	1.28	−0.01	−0.01	0.01	0.01	0.00	0.01		
5 Terms of trade	0.74	−4.74	0.67	−2.09	0.15	0.12	0.07	−0.01	−0.05	0.04		
6 Total imports	4.14	14.34	5.57	6.25	0.13	0.25	0.14	0.01	−0.05	0.04		
7 Total exports	2.40	11.81	5.65	7.57	−0.05	−0.01	0.05	0.02	−0.01	−0.01		
8 Intra-East Asian imp.	11.97	28.18	9.39	14.84								
9 Intra-East Asian exp.	10.10	16.82	16.84	10.66								

Note: All figures are percentage changes except welfare (row 1) and real GDP (row 3).

Scenario 3 assumes that the APEC regions (four East Asian regions, the United States, Canada, Mexico, and Australasia) form a Pacific free trade agreement by removing tariff and nontariff protection. Tariffs and NTBs on imports from the European Union, Latin America, and the rest of the world are maintained at base year levels. Finally, in scenario 4, all the APEC regions remove trade barriers in a nondiscriminatory manner on imports from all countries and regions. If APEC's largely nondiscriminatory trade liberalization plan is realized, this fourth scenario might more closely approximate the process leading to free trade.[22]

3.2.1. Scenario 1: The Formation of an East Asian Trading Bloc

Aggregate results of scenario 1 are summarized in Table 5.2. The welfare measure in the first row represents changes in Hicksian equivalent variations (EVs), or changes in real consumer purchasing power, measured in 1992 billions of U.S. dollars.[23] This can be contrasted with the real GDP measure given in the third row, which does not include the terms-of-trade effect. An improvement in the terms-of-trade raises welfare because it allows an increase in real consumption of imported products for a given quantity of exports.

All four East Asian regions would realize gains in both welfare and real GDP from the formation of an East Asian trading bloc although the gains are unevenly distributed across regions. In percentage terms, China would experience a 1.63 percent increase in real GDP. Because of relatively high rates of initial protection, however, its terms-of-trade deteriorates 4.74 percent, resulting in smaller welfare gains (0.78 percent) compared with real GDP. The NIEs experience the largest welfare gains among the four East Asian regions (0.93 percent) while the gains to Japan are substantially smaller (0.18 percent). In absolute terms, the East Asian bloc gains $17.5 billion in EVs, while the welfare levels of nonmember countries, with the exception of Mexico and Latin America, increase modestly ($1.3 billion) largely as the result of improved terms-of-trade for nonmembers. The welfare and real GDP of the United States are virtually unaffected.

---

[22] We also conducted a multilateral liberalization experiment even though we did not report the results. Not surprisingly, the global welfare gains were largest under this scenario.
[23] EV is the amount of real income that would have to be taken away from the representative consumer at pre-policy consumer prices to make the individual as well off as he/she would be at post-policy consumer prices.

Total imports and exports (rows 6–7 of Table 5.2) of East Asian regions increase substantially, particularly for China. As one might expect, intra–East Asian imports and exports (rows 8–9) would rise by significantly larger percentages than total imports and exports. As East Asian imports of products previously imported from other member countries increase considerably, the extent of trade creation may be substantial. At the same time, however, trade diversion would also occur as some imports from nonmember countries are replaced by higher-cost imports from the member countries.

The proposition that a more protected developing member is likely to lose or gain less than a more liberalized developed member (e.g., Panagariya, Chapter 4, this volume) does not necessarily hold under a general equilibrium framework. While more protected economies have to undergo greater structural adjustments, the removal of trade barriers leads to economywide efficiency gains and enhancement of competition. The major beneficiaries are consumers, whose purchasing power increases because of lower import prices. This income effect serves as a tonic for many domestic industries. In addition, if developing members import large quantities of parts, materials, and other intermediate inputs from developed members, trade liberalization could lead to a significant reduction in the average production cost. Our results suggest that, when both direct and indirect effects are taken into account, the benefits accrued to the more protected members are greater than the gains realized by more liberalized members.

3.2.2. Scenario 2: U.S.–East Asian Trade War

Given heightened trade tensions in recent years between the United States and the East Asian countries, particularly Japan and China, it is not unlikely that America would at least threaten to retaliate in response to the formation of a discriminatory East Asian bloc. Although the possibility of actual U.S. retaliation may be remote, it is nonetheless useful to examine the consequence of a hypothetical U.S.–East Asian trade war.

Table 5.3 reports the economywide results of trade war simulation experiments. In the first iteration, the terms-of-trade improve for the country initiating trade hostilities. When the United States imposes optimal tariffs on East Asian products, its terms-of-trade increase by more than 10 percent (row 5, column 6). Moreover, the gains in terms-of-trade more than offset a reduction in real GDP, resulting in $32.4 billion gains (0.55 percent) in American EVs. On

Table 5.3. *Aggregate Results of US–East Asian Trade War Experiments*

	(1) Japan	(2) China	(3) Asian NIEs-4	(4) ASEAN-4	(5) Australia-NZ	(6) US	(7) Canada	(8) Mexico	(9) Latin America	(10) EU	(11) Subtotal (1)–(4)	(12) Total (1)–(10)
Iteration 1: US imposes optimal tariffs on imports from East Asian regions (1-4).												
1 Welfare ($ billion)	-46.39	-13.82	-6.28	-7.45	-1.49	32.39	4.23	0.27	0.15	8.83	-73.94	-29.57
2 Welfare (%)	-1.31	-3.07	-1.02	-2.08	-0.45	0.55	0.75	0.08	0.02	0.13		
3 Real GDP ($ billion)	-8.01	-1.25	-7.52	-2.25	-0.28	-9.07	1.22	-0.13	-0.08	-1.59	-19.04	-28.95
4 Real GDP (%)	-0.22	-0.26	-1.28	-0.63	-0.08	-0.15	0.21	-0.04	-0.01	-0.02		
5 Terms of trade (%)	-9.31	-7.03	-2.32	-4.74	-1.79	10.16	0.52	1.20	-0.35	1.05		
Iteration 2: East Asian regions (1-4) impose optimal tariffs on imports from the US.												
1 Welfare ($ billion)	-29.52	-11.42	-3.71	-6.67	-0.41	-15.24	2.45	0.72	0.07	7.91	-51.32	-55.82
2 Welfare (%)	-0.83	-2.54	-0.60	-1.86	-0.12	-0.26	0.43	0.21	0.01	0.12		
3 Real GDP ($ billion)	-14.85	-2.34	-13.39	-3.60	-0.14	-19.75	0.94	0.04	0.14	-1.36	-34.19	-54.31
4 Real GDP (%)	-0.41	-0.48	-2.28	-1.01	-0.04	-0.34	0.16	0.01	0.02	-0.02		
5 Terms of trade (%)	-2.30	-5.00	1.99	-2.37	-0.29	1.66	0.72	1.26	-0.13	1.19		
Iteration 6: Equilibrium												
1 Welfare ($ billion)	-30.71	-11.66	-4.00	-6.85	-0.45	-15.25	2.61	0.73	0.08	7.96	-53.22	-57.55
2 Welfare (%)	-0.86	-2.59	-0.65	-1.91	-0.14	-0.26	0.46	0.21	0.01	0.12		
3 Real GDP ($ billion)	-15.34	-2.42	-13.66	-3.72	-0.14	-20.49	0.99	0.04	0.15	-1.39	-35.13	-55.99
4 Real GDP (%)	-0.42	-0.50	-2.33	-1.04	-0.04	-0.35	0.17	0.01	0.02	-0.02		
5 Terms of trade (%)	-2.55	-5.10	1.88	-2.46	-0.35	1.95	0.76	1.30	-0.13	1.20		

the other hand, American retaliation would prove devastating to the East Asian countries, which would suffer $73.9 billion losses in total EVs (row 1, column 11) owing to the loss of American export markets. The newly imposed tariffs sharply alter the relative prices of American imports by country of origin. These tariffs would cause a significant shift in U.S. imports away from East Asia and to the Western Hemisphere and Europe, providing some welfare gains to Canada, Mexico, and the EU. However, this scenario results in a significant trade diversion and a $29.6 billion decrease in global welfare.[24]

Were the United States to initiate a trade war, the East Asian countries would be likely to retaliate. In iteration 2, we assume that the East Asian bloc chooses a set of sectoral tariff rates on U.S. products to maximize jointly its EVs, subject to the U.S. tariff rates imposed in the first step. The middle panel of Table 5.3 indicates that the East Asian countries would recover only about 30 percent of the losses incurred in iteration 1 (losses of $51.3 billion as compared with $73.9 billion), whereas the United States would incur $15.2 billion in losses. Meanwhile, global welfare would be reduced by $55.8 billion relative to the benchmark equilibrium value.

Under these conditions, the United States and the East Asian bloc would likely take turns retaliating until a noncooperative equilibrium were attained. Our results indicate that such an equilibrium is attained in iteration 6, after which no change would occur in the endogenous variables. The bottom panel of Table 5.3 shows that the United States and all four East Asian regions would suffer substantial losses in a trade war. In particular, China and ASEAN-4 would suffer relatively large losses in EVs (2.59 and 1.91 percent). Although some countries would gain – including Canada, Mexico, and the European Union – the price tag for global welfare would be $57.6 billion.

Although the possibility of American retaliation must be considered, there are conditions under which the United States is unlikely to resort to such action. In a simple two-period game, the United States would not be expected to initiate a trade war if

$$U\left[\left(1 - p\right)EV_1 + pEV_2\right] \leq EV_0 \qquad (5.4)$$

---

[24] The figure for global welfare is only approximate because the rest-of-the-world's welfare is not calculated by the PAC model.

where U is the U.S. social welfare function ($U' > 0$, $U'' < 0$), and p is the probability of East Asian retaliation in period 2 if the United States initiates a trade war (i.e., U.S. retaliation in response to EAFTA) in period 1. EV_0, EV_1, and EV_2 are U.S. equivalent variations when it takes no action in period 1, when it imposes optimal tariffs on East Asian imports in period 1, and if East Asia retaliates in period 2, respectively. If either the Unites States is infinitely risk averse or $p = 1$, equation (5.4) always holds. East Asian negotiators must consider this in evaluating the potential benefits and costs of an East Asian free trade agreement.

3.2.3. Scenario 3: The Formation of a Pacific Free Trade Area
As demonstrated in scenario 2, the formation of an East Asian FTA may be politically tricky, especially if strong U.S. retaliation is anticipated. But what about the possibility of a free trade agreement that bridges the Pacific (PAFTA)? Scenario 3 considers a situation wherein the eight APEC regions (the four East Asian regions, America, Canada, Mexico, and Australasia) remove all barriers to intraregional trade. In order to quantify the welfare effects of PAFTA net of NAFTA, we have created a post-NAFTA data set whose base solution values are calculated from the results of the NAFTA experiment and the removal of tariffs and NTBs. The aggregate results of this scenario are presented in Table 5.4.

In the event that a PAFTA were to be created, every member country with the exception of Mexico (which would experience a mere 0.02 percent reduction in its EVs) would stand to benefit. Because America is the largest trading partner for many of the East Asian countries (Table 1.2) and trade diversion would be considerably smaller by including the United States in the trading bloc, the gains to the East Asians are substantially larger under this scenario than under the EAFTA scenario. In percentage terms, the welfare of China, the Asian NIEs, and Australasia each increases by over 1 percent, Japan and the ASEAN-4 by about 0.6 percent, and the United States and Canada by about 0.5 percent. Thus, the United States would benefit significantly by extending the free-trade agreement from North America across the Pacific Basin. The Pacific region as a whole would gain $68.0 billion in EVs, while welfare of nonmember countries (Latin America and the EU) would be little affected.

Table 5.4. *Aggregate Results of Regional Tariff and NTB Liberalization among APEC Countries*

	(1) Japan	(2) China	(3) Asian NIEs	(4) ASEAN 4	(5) Australia-NZ	(6) US	(7) Canada	(8) Mexico	(9) Latin America	(10) EU	(11) Subtotal (1)–(4)	(12) Subtotal (5)–(10)
1 Welfare ($ billion)	20.26	4.53	6.42	2.08	3.58	28.61	2.60	-0.06	-0.17	1.28	68.02	1.11
2 Welfare (%)	0.57	1.04	1.05	0.60	1.07	0.48	0.46	-0.02	-0.02	0.02		
3 Real GDP ($ billion)	21.40	9.79	11.35	6.76	1.29	17.36	-1.31	0.37	0.05	1.28	66.99	1.33
4 Real GDP (%)	0.59	2.00	1.96	1.92	0.38	0.29	-0.22	0.11	0.01	0.02		
5 Terms of trade	0.24	-4.91	-0.65	-3.22	1.89	0.93	1.55	-0.61	-0.23	-0.03		
6 Total imports	10.85	17.90	8.69	8.57	10.56	6.11	2.93	0.23	-0.22	-0.04		
7 Total exports	8.95	14.40	11.28	11.09	6.19	4.59	0.03	0.96	-0.03	-0.04		
8 Intra-APEC imp.	16.98	24.87	11.24	13.56	15.01	8.93	3.03	0.36				
9 Intra-APEC exp.	14.16	16.11	15.98	11.63	11.41	9.95	0.81	1.16				

Note: All figures are percentage changes except welfare (row 1) and real GDP (row 3).

*3.2.4. Scenario 4: Pursuit of Open Regionalism
by APEC Countries*
It has been suggested that trade liberalization by APEC members
should be based on Most-Favored Nation (MFN) principles and that
regional integration in the Asian Pacific should be nondiscriminatory toward the rest of the world (Drysdale and Garnaut, 1993;
Elek, 1992; Yamazawa, 1994; Yoo, 1995). Hence, it is necessary that
a fourth and final scenario consider the case of "open regionalism,"
wherein the APEC regions remove all trade barriers.[25] Table 5.5
summarizes the aggregate results for this scenario.

When the APEC regions abolish all import tariffs and nontariff
barriers, the result is welfare gains for all the regions – members
and nonmembers alike. Open regionalism produces larger real
GDP gains for all eight APEC regions than is the case under the
discriminatory liberalization (PAFTA) scenario. However, while
nondiscriminatory liberalization produces larger welfare gains for
the Asian NIEs ($8.5 billion versus $6.4 billion), the gains are
smaller for Japan ($18.2 billion versus $20.3 billion), China ($3.3
billion versus $4.5 billion), and the ASEAN-4 ($1.8 billion versus
$2.1 billion). The reason for this is that reductions in these coun-
tries' terms-of-trade would more than offset additional gains in real
GDP relative to the PAFTA scenario. In the meantime, the United
States, Canada, and Mexico would all realize additional welfare
gains net of NAFTA.

At the same time, global welfare would be enhanced since there
would be no trade diversion under open regionalism. Both intra-
APEC and inter-APEC trade would expand considerably (rows
6–9). Thus, even though some individual APEC countries might be
better off under the discriminatory liberalization of the PAFTA
scheme, open regionalism produces greater benefits for the Asia–
Pacific region as a whole ($75.5 billion in EVs as opposed to $68.0
billion in EVs under the PAFTA scenario).

One potential sticking point involves the U.S. position concerning Most-Favored Nation treatment for non-APEC members.
Indeed, the American side has argued that APEC liberalization
be extended only to those nonmember countries that implement matching liberalization on an MFN basis (e.g., Panagariya,

---

[25] Whereas we use "open regionalism" and "nondiscriminatory liberalization"
interchangeably, the former may include liberalization on a reciprocal basis.

Table 5.5. *Aggregate Results of Nondiscriminatory Tariff and NTB Liberalization by APEC Countries*

	(1) Japan	(2) China	(3) Asian NIEs 4	(4) ASEAN 4	(5) Australia-NZ	(6) US	(7) Canada	(8) Mexico	(9) Latin America	(10) EU	(11) Subtotal (1)-(4)	(12) Subtotal (5)-(10)
1 Welfare ($ billion)	18.20	3.28	8.53	1.75	3.98	36.96	2.68	0.11	3.31	14.79	75.48	18.10
2 Welfare (%)	0.51	0.75	1.39	0.50	1.19	0.63	0.48	0.03	0.37	0.22		
3 Real GDP ($ billion)	24.84	13.77	12.82	10.05	2.75	29.37	0.61	0.86	-1.11	-1.14	95.08	-2.25
4 Real GDP (%)	0.68	2.82	2.22	2.85	0.81	0.50	0.10	0.26	-0.13	-0.02		
5 Terms of trade	-0.63	-7.14	-0.73	-5.16	0.59	0.34	0.82	-1.46	3.31	1.90		
6 Total imports	11.73	20.19	10.33	11.23	12.07	7.46	3.37	0.98	4.17	2.51		
7 Total exports	10.98	19.29	12.89	15.99	9.21	6.62	1.54	2.36	0.51	0.49		
8 Intra-APEC imp.	17.05	22.07	12.29	11.40	13.49	9.61	2.71	-0.29				
9 Intra-APEC exp.	13.79	18.74	14.79	13.85	12.18	9.09	1.43	1.54				

Note: All figures are percentage changes except welfare (row 1) and real GDP (row 3).

Chapter 4, this volume; Yamazawa, 1996). The U.S. government is concerned that the European Union would reap free-rider benefits in the event that the APEC countries were to opt for blanket liberalization. In fact, we estimate that the EU would reap $14.8 billion in EVs under this scenario. Nevertheless, our results indicate that the United States would gain more from nondiscriminatory liberalization than from discriminatory liberalization ($37.0 billion versus $28.6 billion in EVs). In the event that the EU were to apply reciprocal liberalization, even greater welfare gains would be realized for every APEC member, including the United States. Thus APEC members have an incentive to bargain with the EU to accelerate implementation of multilateral liberalization as agreed upon in the Uruguay Round.[26]

3.3. Sectoral Results

While these scenarios demonstrate that greater liberalization produces greater overall welfare gains, it is essential to recognize that economywide efficiency gains are rarely distributed uniformly across sectors. For this reason, adversely affected sectors are likely to raise challenges to the establishment of free trade agreements. In this section, we discuss the sectoral adjustments in output, demand, and trade flows under the three alternative EAFTA, PAFTA, and open regionalism scenarios.

As shown in Table 5.6, output and trade adjustments vary significantly across sectors. For instance, under the EAFTA scenario, the Asian NIEs would experience a contraction in their agriculture and food, energy and resources, trade and transport, and service sectors; meanwhile, the textile and apparel sector would expand substantially. The removal of tariff and nontariff barriers leads to an increase in imports of almost every product category in the four East Asian regions. Those sectors with high protection rates (e.g., agriculture in Japan and NIEs, textiles and apparel in China) would experience a sharp increase in imports. Although consumers would shun domestic products for lower-priced imports, the removal of import barriers also serves to reduce the cost of

---

[26] During the first Asia–Europe Summit Meeting (ASEM) in Bangkok in March 1996, Asian leaders in fact advocated the EU counterparts to match APEC's accelerated timetable for multilateral liberalization.

imported intermediate inputs for domestic producers. This would result in a decrease in output in many of the highly protected sectors. In some cases, however, the expansionary effect resulting from input cost reductions outweighs the contractionary effect resulting from a substitution from domestic to imported products (e.g., textiles and apparel in China and the ASEAN-4).

Sectoral adjustments are far more dramatic under a Pacific free trade agreement than under an exclusionary East Asian free trade scenario. For example, Japan's agriculture and food sector would contract by 9.4 percent under the PAFTA scheme, while the textile and apparel sector in the Asian NIEs and the ASEAN-4 would expand by 24.8 and 16.5 percent, respectively. Because Japan imports a relatively large share of its food from the United States, Canada, and Australia, the removal of high barriers on agricultural and food products among APEC countries would cause an extremely large increase in Japanese imports (58.9 percent), leading to a large contraction in domestic output. Similarly, since the Asian NIEs as well as the ASEAN-4 export large quantities of textiles and apparel to the United States, export expansion in the wake of the formation of PAFTA would sharply raise domestic output.

The liberalization of agricultural trade among APEC countries would have especially strong resource-pull effects in Australasia and Canada. As the agricultural sector expands substantially in these countries, factors of production would be diverted from other sectors, causing an output contraction in almost all other sectors. However, this assumes that labor is homogeneous and perfectly mobile across sectors. When labor is disaggregated by type and skill, however, limited labor mobility may have prevented contraction in many of nonagricultural sectors.

Liberalization of APEC agricultural trade would serve to expand U.S. agricultural exports, although the resource-pull effects would not be as dramatic as those in Australasia or Canada. This is because the number of workers is smaller in agriculture and food processing as a percentage of economywide employment in the United States (4.2 percent) than in Australasia (7.4 percent) or Canada (5.6 percent). Moreover, some American manufacturing sectors, particularly the aircraft industry (aggregated into transport equipment) and high-technology industries, have a high level of revealed comparative advantage (Balassa and Noland, 1988,

Table 5.6. Sectoral Results of Discriminatory and Nondiscriminatory Liberalization Experiments (percentage changes)

Region	Sector	EAFTA				PAFTA				Open Regionalism			
		Output	Cons.	Imp.	Exp.	Output	Cons.	Imp.	Exp.	Output	Cons.	Imp.	Exp.
Japan	AgricFood	-1.7	0.5	13.8	14.1	-9.4	2.6	58.9	10.2	-10.6	2.9	68.6	10.5
	EnergRes	-0.2	0.2	1.2	4.7	0.6	0.4	1.1	6.0	1.4	0.1	-0.1	7.5
	TextApLea	-0.8	1.1	14.6	10.9	-0.7	1.6	17.7	13.5	-1.1	1.8	21.3	15.0
	ChemRbPls	0.4	0.2	1.9	5.6	1.1	0.6	3.0	13.2	1.1	0.5	4.2	14.4
	Metals	0.6	0.2	2.5	4.4	2.1	0.4	3.4	8.1	2.4	0.3	2.5	9.6
	Machinery	0.8	0.3	2.8	2.7	4.3	0.9	4.0	13.6	4.6	0.8	4.4	14.8
	TranspEq	0.4	0.3	2.0	0.9	1.9	0.6	3.7	4.2	3.3	0.6	3.0	7.3
	OtherMfg	0.2	0.2	3.1	3.3	0.8	0.6	3.5	8.0	0.9	0.6	3.9	9.9
	TradeTrnsp	-0.1	0.1	0.8	-1.1	0.2	0.3	-0.1	-0.1	0.5	0.2	-2.0	4.0
	Services	0.1	0.1	1.0	0.2	0.3	0.2	-0.4	0.5	0.2	0.1	-1.5	2.3
China	AgricFood	3.7	-0.4	8.6	51.9	2.9	-0.4	16.6	42.0	3.0	-0.8	22.1	45.5
	EnergRes	0.0	-0.1	1.7	2.6	-0.1	0.1	5.7	3.1	1.3	-0.5	5.2	6.8
	TextApLea	2.9	6.8	42.4	13.2	6.4	8.0	50.0	19.4	9.9	7.9	52.7	24.8
	ChemRbPls	0.2	0.8	5.9	4.8	0.7	1.3	9.3	9.6	1.3	1.0	11.9	13.7
	Metals	-1.2	0.9	7.2	6.0	-0.8	1.2	9.7	9.6	0.2	0.9	11.3	14.6
	Machinery	-1.2	4.0	11.5	3.7	-0.9	5.0	13.8	5.0	-0.2	5.9	16.9	9.2
	TranspEq	0.7	10.1	10.9	9.8	-0.3	11.6	12.6	9.0	3.5	13.5	14.5	16.6
	OtherMfg	-2.4	3.0	33.6	3.5	-0.8	3.5	36.1	7.8	0.8	3.2	36.4	12.1
	TradeTrnsp	0.6	-0.4	-2.4	1.9	1.0	-0.3	-1.9	2.6	2.1	-0.8	-4.8	9.8
	Services	-0.2	-0.4	-0.8	1.3	0.0	-0.2	0.1	2.2	-0.1	-0.8	-2.4	12.6

Asian NIEs	AgricFood	-2.0	1.8	20.1	20.3	-9.0	4.0	41.3	18.0	-10.8	4.6	48.5	17.4
	EnergRes	-1.9	0.7	2.4	-1.4	-0.8	0.2	3.2	-0.2	-0.9	0.5	3.8	0.2
	TextApLea	12.7	2.9	8.8	17.9	24.8	3.4	12.7	33.8	26.9	4.3	15.3	37.2
	ChemRbPls	2.3	1.0	5.5	5.1	5.2	0.7	7.9	8.8	4.9	1.1	9.1	8.4
	Metals	0.3	0.7	4.9	2.8	3.1	0.4	6.7	8.4	2.8	0.8	8.2	8.5
	Machinery	2.7	2.7	3.7	4.5	6.0	2.8	5.4	9.4	6.4	3.8	6.6	10.3
	TranspEq	4.7	2.8	3.9	9.4	6.0	3.6	6.0	13.2	7.1	4.6	7.7	15.8
	OtherMfg	1.6	1.3	3.7	5.0	4.2	1.1	4.5	10.2	4.5	1.6	5.7	11.3
	TradeTrnsp	-1.3	-0.1	3.2	-4.5	-0.6	-0.5	2.7	-3.3	0.0	-0.5	2.4	-1.5
	Services	-0.1	0.0	2.9	-5.7	0.0	-0.5	1.7	-4.7	0.3	-0.4	2.3	0.0
ASEAN -4	AgricFood	3.0	-0.2	9.0	16.0	1.5	-0.3	19.4	12.9	1.3	-0.3	32.0	16.1
	EnergRes	0.5	-0.6	1.5	1.7	1.3	-0.9	2.1	3.0	1.3	-0.7	6.6	4.9
	TextApLea	6.9	5.0	24.7	15.4	16.5	6.0	32.6	29.7	25.4	6.5	38.3	42.5
	ChemRbPls	-0.3	1.7	5.6	5.0	1.3	1.9	7.6	8.9	1.8	2.7	10.6	12.6
	Metals	-1.6	1.3	3.7	4.7	-0.4	1.2	4.7	7.9	0.9	1.0	5.7	12.0
	Machinery	5.4	5.3	5.0	6.6	9.0	6.5	6.6	10.7	13.1	7.2	7.8	15.4
	TranspEq	0.7	5.6	9.2	17.5	0.8	6.6	11.2	21.3	0.5	7.7	13.0	25.1
	OtherMfg	0.4	1.4	10.3	4.2	2.7	1.7	12.1	9.0	4.7	1.9	14.2	13.4
	TradeTrnsp	-0.2	-1.0	0.3	-0.7	0.2	-1.3	-0.4	0.5	0.9	-1.9	-2.6	4.1
	Services	-0.3	-0.5	-1.0	1.2	-0.2	-0.7	-2.9	2.3	-0.2	-1.1	-5.4	7.7
Australia -NZ	AgricFood	-0.3	0.0	0.0	-0.8	10.2	1.2	8.6	27.2	11.3	1.2	10.1	30.4
	EnergRes	0.3	0.0	-0.4	0.5	-1.0	0.5	5.1	-1.9	0.5	0.5	2.4	1.0
	TextApLea	-1.6	0.5	3.7	-3.4	-5.6	3.0	19.9	1.0	-6.3	3.5	23.1	3.1
	ChemRbPls	-0.1	0.0	0.0	-0.2	-3.0	2.4	8.9	1.7	-4.4	3.5	13.6	3.4
	Metals	0.1	0.0	-0.5	0.1	-2.7	1.4	15.1	0.3	-2.7	1.7	20.2	2.4
	Machinery	-0.3	0.0	0.1	-1.1	-6.1	6.7	11.1	-1.9	-6.5	8.1	13.3	0.9
	TranspEq	-0.2	0.0	0.0	-1.9	-5.6	6.3	16.1	3.6	-5.7	7.1	17.6	6.1
	OtherMfg	0.0	0.0	0.0	0.0	-2.5	1.7	13.4	-1.0	-2.7	2.0	16.7	1.1
	TradeTrnsp	0.1	0.0	-0.4	0.9	-0.5	0.3	4.2	-4.7	0.0	0.2	2.1	-1.8
	Services	0.0	0.0	-0.3	0.1	0.1	0.3	3.6	-5.6	0.3	0.3	1.4	-0.1

Table 5.6 (continued)

Region	Sector	EAFTA				PAFTA				Open Regionalism			
		Output	Cons.	Imp.	Exp.	Output	Cons.	Imp.	Exp.	Output	Cons.	Imp.	Exp.
United States	AgricFood	0.0	0.0	-0.1	-0.3	6.7	0.9	3.4	45.1	6.6	1.0	7.0	46.0
	EnergRes	-0.1	0.0	0.1	0.0	0.1	0.2	1.8	-0.3	0.5	0.1	-0.1	2.2
	TextApLea	-1.4	0.6	3.5	-1.1	-4.5	2.3	14.8	0.5	-5.6	3.1	19.1	2.3
	ChemRbPls	0.0	0.0	-0.1	0.3	-0.1	0.7	5.5	1.8	-0.1	1.0	8.6	3.1
	Metals	0.1	-0.1	-0.3	0.2	0.1	0.3	3.6	1.4	0.1	0.4	6.4	2.5
	Machinery	-0.1	0.0	0.2	-0.2	-2.0	3.0	11.1	0.3	-1.7	3.7	13.6	2.0
	TranspEq	0.2	0.2	-0.2	-0.1	1.4	1.4	2.0	2.4	2.4	1.9	2.4	5.1
	OtherMfg	0.0	0.0	-0.1	0.0	-0.1	0.4	4.7	0.2	0.1	0.6	5.8	1.7
	TradeTrnsp	0.0	0.0	-0.7	0.6	0.2	0.2	1.2	-1.4	0.5	0.2	-0.3	1.2
	Services	0.0	0.0	-0.1	0.0	0.2	0.1	1.2	-1.9	0.4	0.2	-1.0	2.0
Canada	AgricFood	0.1	0.1	-0.1	0.1	6.1	0.9	5.0	21.3	6.5	1.0	7.2	23.8
	EnergRes	0.1	0.0	0.0	0.2	-1.2	0.3	2.7	-2.1	0.0	0.0	0.1	-0.3
	TextApLea	-1.1	0.4	2.2	-1.8	-5.1	2.0	12.8	-4.9	-6.2	2.5	16.3	-4.7
	ChemRbPls	-0.2	-0.1	0.1	-0.3	-1.0	0.5	2.2	-1.2	-0.9	0.7	3.0	-0.4
	Metals	0.0	-0.1	0.1	-0.1	-2.2	0.3	2.4	-2.6	-1.5	0.4	3.7	-0.9
	Machinery	-0.4	-0.1	0.0	-0.5	-3.6	1.6	1.8	-4.3	-2.9	1.7	2.1	-3.3
	TranspEq	0.5	0.2	0.1	0.5	-1.6	2.1	1.9	-1.5	-0.6	2.2	2.3	-0.3
	OtherMfg	-0.1	-0.1	0.1	-0.1	-1.1	0.4	3.9	-1.8	-0.6	0.5	4.4	-0.4
	TradeTrnsp	0.0	0.0	-0.2	0.4	-0.1	0.1	2.2	-2.6	0.1	0.1	1.0	-0.4
	Services	0.0	0.0	-0.1	0.1	0.0	0.2	1.6	-1.7	0.2	0.2	0.9	-0.1

Mexico	AgricFood	0.0	0.0	-0.1	0.0	0.2	0.0	1.4	4.6	0.0	0.0	2.3	5.2
	EnergRes	0.0	-0.1	0.0	0.1	1.0	-0.2	-1.1	1.6	2.2	-0.1	-0.8	4.1
	TextApLea	-0.4	0.1	1.2	-1.4	-1.2	0.3	5.1	-2.5	-1.8	0.5	8.1	-2.8
	ChemRbPls	-0.1	-0.1	0.0	-0.2	0.4	-0.2	-0.5	2.4	0.4	0.0	0.4	4.9
	Metals	0.0	-0.1	0.0	0.1	0.4	-0.1	0.1	2.4	0.4	0.1	1.6	4.2
	Machinery	0.1	-0.1	0.0	0.1	-0.9	0.2	0.1	-1.0	-0.4	1.1	0.8	-0.3
	TranspEq	0.2	0.1	0.1	0.2	0.7	0.4	0.7	1.5	0.8	1.2	2.2	2.5
	OtherMfg	0.0	-0.1	-0.1	0.0	0.2	-0.1	0.2	1.9	0.2	0.0	1.1	2.6
	TradeTrnsp	0.0	0.0	-0.2	0.2	0.1	-0.1	-1.4	1.6	0.3	-0.2	-2.6	3.4
	Services	0.0	0.0	-0.8	0.1	0.0	0.0	-1.9	0.8	0.1	-0.1	-2.3	4.7
Latin America	AgricFood	0.0	0.0	0.0	-0.1	-0.2	0.0	0.5	-0.8	0.8	0.3	5.9	5.3
	EnergRes	0.1	0.0	-0.2	0.3	0.4	0.0	-0.4	1.4	-1.1	0.3	3.8	-2.9
	TextApLea	-0.4	0.1	2.3	-1.4	-0.7	0.1	3.3	-3.2	-0.2	0.5	9.6	2.6
	ChemRbPls	0.0	0.0	-0.1	0.1	0.1	-0.1	-0.6	0.7	-0.4	0.5	3.2	1.5
	Metals	0.1	0.0	-0.2	0.2	0.2	0.0	-0.6	0.6	-0.6	0.4	3.7	0.2
	Machinery	0.0	0.0	-0.1	-0.1	0.0	-0.1	-0.4	-0.8	-1.0	1.2	3.1	-1.9
	TranspEq	0.0	0.0	-0.1	-0.2	-0.1	0.0	0.1	-0.7	-1.4	1.4	4.6	-1.1
	OtherMfg	0.0	0.0	-0.2	0.1	0.1	0.0	-0.7	0.5	-0.4	0.4	3.8	-1.5
	TradeTrnsp	0.1	0.0	-0.3	0.5	0.1	0.0	-0.8	1.0	-0.5	0.3	4.0	-4.3
	Services	0.0	0.0	-1.0	0.1	0.0	0.0	-1.6	0.5	0.0	0.2	4.3	-3.0
EU	AgricFood	0.0	0.0	-0.1	-0.1	-0.1	-0.1	0.1	-1.3	0.2	0.2	2.0	4.4
	EnergRes	0.0	0.0	0.0	0.1	0.1	0.0	-0.1	0.7	-0.2	0.2	1.1	-1.6
	TextApLea	-0.5	0.2	2.5	-0.3	-0.8	0.4	3.9	-0.5	-1.0	0.8	7.2	1.3
	ChemRbPls	0.0	0.0	-0.1	0.2	0.1	0.0	-0.4	0.6	0.4	0.4	1.7	2.8
	Metals	0.0	0.0	-0.2	0.1	0.1	0.0	-0.4	0.5	0.0	0.2	1.7	0.8
	Machinery	-0.1	0.0	0.0	-0.4	-0.3	0.0	0.0	-0.9	0.5	0.9	2.7	2.5
	TranspEq	0.0	0.0	-0.2	-0.4	0.0	0.0	-0.1	-0.4	-0.4	0.5	3.7	-0.7
	OtherMfg	0.0	0.0	-0.1	0.1	0.1	0.0	-0.2	0.5	-0.2	0.3	2.5	0.4
	TradeTrnsp	0.1	0.0	-0.5	0.4	0.1	0.0	-0.9	0.6	-0.4	0.1	1.8	-2.8
	Services	0.0	0.0	-0.4	0.1	0.0	0.0	-1.5	0.8	0.1	0.1	1.7	-2.4

p. 34). Nevertheless, output contraction is predicted in four American manufacturing sectors – textiles and apparel, chemicals and rubber, machinery, and other manufacturing.

An open regionalism scenario would demand reinforced comparative advantage and greater sectoral adjustments for each region. This would bring both gain and pain for particular countries and particular sectors. Overall, open regionalism would produce trade expansion in most product categories, especially inexpensive imports at the expense of high-priced domestic products. At the same time, it is well to observe that in the case of some domestic products with comparative disadvantage – such as agriculture in Japan and the NIEs, and textiles and apparel in the United States and Canada – the shares of intra-APEC imports are already extremely high. Thus, even though these sectors would suffer output losses, open regionalism would produce relatively small additional contractions.

Two caveats should be borne in mind in light of the foregoing analysis. First, liberalization of the service trade has been excluded from our experiments. In this regard, the welter of regulations in various categories of services in the APEC countries suggests that barriers to trade in services may be extremely high (APEC and PECC, 1995). However, there is no appropriate method for converting frequency measures into ad valorem equivalents; hence, no attempt to do so has been made in the present study. Service trade accounted for 16.2 percent of APEC's total exports and imports in 1992 (the GTAP database), and its share in gross trade would have been much greater in the absence of regulations. For this reason, service liberalization is expected to result in substantial economy-wide and sectoral effects.

Second, the PAFTA and open regionalism scenarios assume a one-time, across-the-board removal of trade barriers among the APEC member. In fact, however, liberalization programs for the developed members are to be implemented over the 1997–2010 period, while the developing members will remove barriers during the 1997–2020 period. A flexible timetable for liberalization recognizes the wide gulf in the level of economic development as well as a diversity of domestic situations among the APEC countries. If there is to be a flexible liberalization schedule, it is likely that adversely affected domestic interests may attempt to block or postpone liberalization. Although it is beyond the scope of the present model to consider these possibilities fully, the aggregate results from sections 3.2.3 and 3.2.4 suggest that the benefits to consumers, as well as to the expanding sectors, significantly outweigh the costs to the contracting sectors.

4. CONCLUSIONS

Despite the economic incentives for establishing an East Asian or a Pacific free trade agreement, the realization of such an arrangement demands the resolution of transnational as well as domestic political difficulties. The removal of trade barriers will lead to expanded economywide and global efficiency, leading to increased aggregate welfare. Yet considerations of aggregate welfare seldom play a decisive role in the formation of a country's trade policy. Instead, individual sectors seek to elicit or retain government protection in order to avoid the potentially painful and destabilizing adjustments and tradeoffs that accompany liberalization. In sum, economic rationality and political feasibility are not necessarily coterminous. Nevertheless, the trend toward greater interdependence in trade and investment among the Asian Pacific countries may eventually dismantle regional and domestic political barriers and pave the way for deeper formal integration.

Even though every country in the East Asian region would stand to benefit, our empirical results suggest that the formation of an East Asian trading bloc may be difficult to realize. A major consideration is the possibility of American retaliation, which, if it led to a trans-Pacific trade war, would impose substantial welfare losses on the East Asian countries. In the event that a Pacific free trade area were to be created, every member country, with the exception of Mexico, would realize aggregate welfare gains. In fact, creation of a Pacific free trade area promises to produce global welfare gains almost four times greater than would be the case with an East Asian trading bloc. However, even greater welfare gains would be realized in the event that the APEC countries were to opt for total, nondiscriminatory liberalization. The message to policymakers is straightforward: Despite large disparities in per capita income, open regionalism promises to benefit the welfare of every country and people on the Pacific Basin.

The wider the scope of liberalization, the stronger and more widespread the anticipated opposition by adversely affected industry lobbies. Resistance to proposals for open regionalism or a Pacific free trade agreement would be expected to elicit broader and more intense industry opposition than would be the case with a proposal for an East Asian trading bloc. However, APEC trade liberalization under the flexible program is based on "individual action plans" and predicated upon a gradual process of nondiscriminatory liberalization. If each government implements an adjustment program, including the training of workers in depressed sectors, the pains of economic transition could be ameliorated.

The potential benefits of open regionalism far outweigh the potential costs of structural adjustment. Thus free trade in the Asian Pacific region would contribute to regional growth, prosperity, and cooperation.

REFERENCES

Akamatsu, K. (1962), "A Historical Pattern of Economic Growth in Developing Countries," *Developing Economies*, 1: 3–25.

Amsden, Alice (1989), *Asia's Next Giant: South Korea and Late Industrialization*, New York: Oxford University Press.

Anderson, Kym, and Yujiro Hayami, eds. (1986), *Agricultural Protection: East Asia in Comparative Perspective*, London: Allen and Unwin.

Asia-Pacific Economic Cooperation (APEC) and Pacific Economic Cooperation Council (PECC) (1995), *Surveys of Impediments to Trade and Investment in the APEC Region*, Singapore: Pacific Economic Cooperation Council for Asia–Pacific Economic Cooperation Secretariat.

Balassa, Bela, and Marcus Noland (1988), *Japan in the World Economy*, Washington, DC: Institute for International Economics.

Beason, Richard, and David E. Weinstein (1996), "Growth, Economies of Scale, and Targeting in Japan," *Review of Economics and Statistics* 78: 286–295.

Bueno de Mesquita, Bruce, and David Lalman (1992), *War and Reason*, Ann Arbor: University of Michigan Press.

Calder, Kent E. (1991), *Japan's Changing Role in Asia: Emerging Co-Prosperity?* New York: The Japan Society.

Dean, Judith M., Seema Desai, and James Riedel (1994), "Trade Policy Reform in Developing Countries Since 1985: A Review of the Evidence," Washington, DC: World Bank.

Drysdale, Peter, and Ross Garnaut (1993), "The Pacific: An Application of a General Theory of Economic Integration," in C. F. Bergsten and M. Noland, eds., *Pacific Dynamism and the International Economic System*, Washington, DC: Institute for International Economics.

Elek, Andrew (1992), "Trade Policy Options for the Asia-Pacific Region in the 1990's: The Potential of Open Regionalism," *American Economic Review, Papers and Proceedings*, 82: 74–78.

Evans, Peter, Harold Jacobson, and Robert D. Putnam, eds. (1993), *Double-Edged Diplomacy: International Bargaining and Domestic Politics*, Berkeley: University of California Press.

Frankel, Jeffrey A. (1993), "Is Japan Creating a Yen Block in East Asia and the Pacific?" in J. A. Frankel and M. Kahler, eds., *Regionalism and Rivalry: Japan and the United States in Pacific Asia*, Chicago: University of Chicago Press and NBER.

GATT (1947), *General Agreement on Tariffs and Trade*, Geneva: GATT Secretariat. Reprinted in GATT (1994), *The Results of the Uruguay Round of Multilateral Trade Negotiations: The Legal Text*, Geneva: GATT Secretariat.

Grossman, Gene M., and Elhanan Helpman (1995), "The Politics of Free-Trade Agreements," *American Economic Review*, 85: 667–690.

Hertel, Thomas W., ed. (1997), *Global Trade Analysis: Modeling and Applications*, Cambridge: Cambridge University Press.

Ichimura, Shinichi, and James W. Morley (1993), "Introduction: The Varieties of Asia–Pacific Experience," in J. W. Morley, ed., *Driven by Growth: Political Change in the Asia-Pacific Region*, New York: M. E. Sharpe.

Inoue, Ryuichiro, Hirohisa Kohama, and Shujiro Urata, eds. (1993), *Industrial Policy in East Asia*, Tokyo: Japan External Trade Organization.

Katzenstein, Peter J. (1985), *Small States in World Markets: Industrial Policy in Europe*, Ithaca, NY: Cornell University Press.

Krugman, Paul (1991), "The Move toward Free Trade Zones," in *Policy Implications of Trade and Currency Zones*, the proceedings of a symposium sponsored by the Federal Reserve Bank of Kansas City, Jackson Hole, WY.

Lee, Hiro, and David Roland-Holst (1995), "Trade Liberalization and Employment Linkages in the Pacific Basin," *Developing Economies*, 33: 155–184.

Lloyd, P. J. (1996), "Regional Trading Arrangements and Regional Integration," *Asian Economic Journal*, 10: 1–28.

Melo, Jaime de, and David Tarr (1992), *A General Equilibrium Analysis of US Foreign Trade Policy*, Cambridge: MIT Press.

Peng, Dajin (1996), "Can Japan Build a New East Asian Cooperation," paper presented at the Southern Japan Seminar, Atlanta, May 4.

Petri, Peter A. (1993), "The East Asian Trading Bloc: An Analytical History" in J. A. Frankel and M. Kahler, eds., *Regionalism and Rivalry: Japan and the United States in Pacific Asia*, Chicago: University of Chicago Press and NBER.

Putnam, Robert D. (1988), "Diplomacy and Domestic Politics: The Logic of Two-Level Games," *International Organization*, 42: 427–460.

Ray, James L. (1995), *Democracy and International Politics*, Columbia, SC: University of South Carolina Press.

Rousseau, David L., Christopher Gelpi, Dan Reiter, and Paul K. Huth (1996), "Assessing the Dyadic Nature of the Democratic Peace, 1918–88," *American Political Science Review*, 90: 512–533.

Russett, Bruce (1993), *Grasping the Democratic Peace: Principles for a Post–Cold War World*, Princeton, NJ: Princeton University Press.

Sazanami, Yoko, Shujiro Urata, and Hiroki Kawai (1995), *Measuring the Costs of Protection in Japan*, Washington, DC: Institute for International Economics.

Saxonhouse, Gary R. (1993), "Trading Blocs and East Asia," in J. de Melo and A. Panagariya, eds., *New Dimensions in Regional Integration*, Cambridge: Cambridge University Press and Centre for Economic Policy Research.

Schott, Jeffrey J. (1991), "Trading Blocs and the World Trading System." *World Economy*, 14: 1–18.

Wade, Robert (1990), *Governing the Market: Economic Theory and the Role of Government in East Asian Industrialization*, Princeton: Princeton University Press.

Woodall, Brian (1993), *Japan's Changing World Role: Emerging Leader or Perpetual Follower?* New York: The Japan Society.

World Bank (1994), *East Asia's Trade and Investment: Regional and Global Gains from Liberalization*, Washington, DC: World Bank.

Yamaoka, Michio (1996), "PBEC, PECC, and APEC," paper presented at the Southern Japan Seminar, Atlanta, May 4.

Yamazawa, Ippei (1992), "On Pacific Economic Integration," *Economic Journal*, 102: 1519–1529.

(1994), "Asia Pacific Economic Community: New Paradigm and Challenges," *Journal of Asian Economics*, 5: 301–312.

(1996), "APEC's New Development and Its Implications for Nonmember Developing Countries, *Developing Economies*, 34: 113–137.

Yoo, Jang-Hee (1995), "A Future Perspective of APEC," *Asian Economic Journal*, 9: 1–12.

Comment

Alain de Janvry

This chapter provides assessments of the likelihood that a free trade area would emerge either among ten countries of East Asia (EAFTA) including Japan or among an expanded set of fifteen Pacific Rim countries that would include the United States, Canada, and Mexico (PAFTA).

To explore this question, the authors proceed in two steps. They first develop a set of indicators to assess the political feasibility of a free trade agreement. At the regional level, these indicators include the following variables:

- Close geographical proximity
- Few regional and territorial disputes
- A sophisticated regional institutional infrastructure
- Similarity of political regimes
- Similarity of regime objectives
- Similarity of trade regimes
- A narrow range of levels of economic development.

At the national level:

- Past increases in intraregional trade shares
- Homogenous pre-liberalization levels of protectionism
- High potential welfare losses in case of retaliation by a large nonmember country.

Use of these indicators is suggestive. Although no systematic standard is used, reference is most frequently made to the experience of the European Union (EU). This is, however, an excessively demanding benchmark. Since the American continent has recently been successful in promoting regional integration (NAFTA, extension of NAFTA to include Chile a practically certain achievement, Mercosur, the Agreement on Economic Complementarity between Mexico and Chile, the Group of Three including Mexico, Venezuela, and Colombia; and Caricom among the Caribbean countries), a more adequate standard would have been to use the structural conditions of these countries. Had these been used, the likelihood that free trade areas may emerge in the Pacific Rim would have appeared much more positive. If applied to Latin America, virtually none of the European standards for successful integration would have been met: Like Asia, much of Latin America is plagued by lack of proximity (Mexico–Chile), territorial disputes (Central America), weak regional institutions (the whole continent), differences in political regimes (ranging from democratic Chile to unstable regimes in Bolivia and to token democracies in Mexico and Colombia), and a wide range of levels of economic development (the United States versus Mexico). In any case, we do not have systematic probit-type relations between

successful regional integration and the determinants of integration, so it is difficult to attribute any predictive power to these analytical categories. Before using them to cast doom on the likelihood
of Asian integration, we need to develop predictive models where
these variables are used. This is a research agenda that I would
urge the authors to pursue.

The second instrument that the authors use to explore the likelihood of a Pacific Free Trade Area is a CGE model for the three
levels of integration: EAFTA, PAFTA, and open multilateralism.
Here again, the results are suggestive, but they do not have many
elements of surprise and could derive directly from trade theory
without the need for CGE modeling: The broader the trade area,
the greater the net social gains; trade wars and the escalation of
retaliatory tariffs are devastating for all; even the observed loss of
welfare for post-NAFTA Mexico as a consequence of PAFTA is predicted by theory (it has been used by Bhagwati to warn of the
dangers of seeking convergence toward multilateralism through
the stepwise extension of regional trade agreements, since privi-
leged beneficiaries like Mexico may oppose such extension). Differential gains across countries and sectors are more useful to
analyze the forces at play in the political economy of integration.
In general, CGE models are more useful to analyze distributional
effects than aggregate effects. What would be needed to conduct a
political economy analysis is a mapping of the income effects of
integration by country and sector on the distribution of political
power in negotiating trade agreements.

In addition, as we have seen during the debate on NAFTA with
the work of Sherman Robinson and Santiago Levy, among others,
static CGE models, which capture only the reallocative gains from
trade, both identify only minuscule efficiency gains and miss the
main objectives of integration. Insignificance of the quantitative
gains from trade liberalization is seen in the percentage gains in
real GDP predicted by the model that never come close to 2 percent
in any country. It is hard to believe that countries would incur the
costs of negotiating trade agreements for a one-shot GDP growth
effect of less than 2 percent. Similarly, why would the United States
enter a trade war over EAFTA when the measured effect of
regional integration (Table 5.2) is 0.00 percent? The main gains
from trade liberalization clearly have to be others: They result from
capital movements, technological change, institutional change,

human capital formation, credibility in trade policy achieved by wresting trade policy instruments from control by politicians of the moment, and political bargaining power. It is consequently hard to be sanguine about the results obtained. They are fairly well known from theory, are quantitatively insignificant, and do not include the important purposes of regional integration. This again opens an important research agenda: to include into CGE models the dynamic features of regional integration that really matter.

The conclusions, however, open a number of very important issues about the future of regional integration that merit further discussion. First, there is the contrast in the paths followed by Latin American and Asian integration: It has been formal in Latin America and largely informal in Asia, even if these two paths have the shared stated purpose of converging toward multilateralism.

The Asian informal process of integration has given rise to a set of ideas recognized as the doctrine of open regionalism. These ideas have been promoted by multinational institutions such as the Pacific Economic Cooperation Council (PECC) and the Asia Pacific Economic Cooperation (APEC) Forum. The doctrine of open regionalism promotes principles of nondiscrimination and economic opening, which are very much in the spirit of GATT. It opposes any form of discriminatory regionalism and explicitly rejects the formation of large trading blocs eventually centered around Washington, Tokyo, and Berlin. In 1992, however, a regional integration scheme emerged, in part created as a response to the bargaining power of the European Union and NAFTA: the ASEAN Free Trade Area (AFTA), which regroups Malaysia, Thailand, Indonesia, Brunei, the Philippines, and Singapore. This suggests that there are other inducements to regional integration that are not explored in this chapter.

By analogy with NAFTA and its ongoing Latin American extension, regional integration in Asia would likely come about as a formalization of the de facto yen area, centered on the geopolitical interests of Japan. If this is the case, integration could occur by stages, just as it is happening as a dollar area around the United States, allowing to resolve piecemeal the observed impediments to integration. And it will fundamentally depend on other purposes that Japan may want to pursue in the future: increase its bargaining power in front of the European Union and NAFTA, play a more explicit geopolitical role than it has done since World War II, and formalize policy instruments that achieve credibility in the political sustainability of free trade policies in the weaker member countries.

If this is the case, the motivations to shift from open regionalism to formal regional integration may in fact be a setback in the evolution toward multilateralism. They may well be symptomatic of the emergence of relatively closed trading blocs constructed for geopolitical purposes.

The second observation is that, in recent years, developments in trade theory and the very practice of trade relations have been increasingly distanced from the pure neo-liberal doctrines of free trade and laissez-faire that underpin the vision of multilateralism. Strategic trade has demonstrated the logic for government intervention in technological development and export promotion to change a country's comparative advantages, particularly when potential gains from economies of scale and learning-by-doing are involved. Managed trade argues for the benefits of cross-boundary agreements among multinational corporations, backed by governments, which result in nontariff forms of protectionism. And the resilience of unemployment in the more developed countries, with part of the blame placed on cheap imports from less developed countries, is adding pressure to shelter the unemployed and the poor through trade restrictions. In this case, again, the emergence of regional integration schemes can be seen as mechanisms to create exclusive trading blocs that would play against the forces of bloc-by-bloc expansion of free trade in Latin America, open regionalism in Asia, and ultimately multilateralism as advocated by GATT. From a free trade standpoint, regional integration may thus well have the wrong purpose. These are some of the forces currently at play behind the logic of regional integration. Although analysis of these forces provides a start in the right direction, it transcends the use of indicators of regional heterogeneity and the lessons derived from static trade models. I am not saying that Asian regional integration is likely to occur but that the arguments that need to be taken into account to assess the likelihood of this move go beyond the analysis of this chapter. I thus conclude by urging the authors to extend their analysis beyond the use of indicators, formalize the use of the selected indicators as a predictive tool of regional integration, and go beyond static CGE modeling to answer the question posed.

## CHAPTER 6

Regionalism in the Pacific Basin: Strategic Interest of ASEAN in APEC

Tan Kong Yam

1. INTRODUCTION

The unprecedented expansion of world output and trade in the post–World War II era provided the East Asian economy of Japan and the four newly industrialized economies (NIEs) of South Korea, Taiwan, Hong Kong, and Singapore with a favorable international environment for export-led growth. These countries were able to embark on the path of industrial catch-up when the gust of wind was strongest. While Japan's growth rate has slowed down considerably after the first oil crisis of 1973–74, the four East Asian NIEs have become the most dynamic economies in the world during the past three decades. Their annual growth rates of per capita GNP during the 1965–95 period averaged 6 to 8 percent, triple the average rate of 2.3 percent for middle-income economies and almost double the 4.0 percent average for countries in the Association of Southeast Asian Nations (ASEAN) excluding Singapore.

Thus, with the benefits of latecomers in the process of industrialization and taking full advantage of the conducive world trading system, as well as the ideological imperatives of the free world, the NIEs have been able to telescope an industrialization process that took the OECD countries 100 to 150 years to complete in the nineteenth and early twentieth centuries into 25 to 30 years in the postwar era. However, unlike Japan, they have industrialized with a greater degree of dependence on foreign direct investment (FDI), particularly for Singapore. Throughout the 1980s and the first half of the 1990s, foreign firm exports accounted for about 80 percent of total exports for Singapore, 25 percent for Korea, 15 percent for Taiwan, and 20 percent for Hong Kong.

The author is grateful to financial support from the National University of Singapore (RP 3940008) and to Pearl Imada Iboshi and Hiro Lee for their helpful comments.

By the beginning of the 1980s, the successes of the NIEs have begun to have significant demonstration effect on policymakers in ASEAN and China. A liberal trade and investment regime has increasingly been looked upon as an effective way to embark on the process of industrialization.

The steady progress in multilateral trade liberalization also witnessed counter-currents in the form of regional trading arrangements. The first postwar wave came in the early 1960s. Spurred by the European Common Market, regional trading arrangements proliferated in Latin America, Africa, and other developing countries. This wave of regionalism did not succeed as they tended to be inward looking. More significantly, the hegemonic United States, confident of its dominance under the imperatives of the Cold War, had a strong vested interest in multilateralism.

The revival of regionalism since the mid-1980s saw the United States becoming a major player, however. Partly frustrated by the slow progress under the General Agreement on Tariffs and Trade (GATT), the United States negotiated bilateral free trade areas with Israel and Canada, initiated the agreement for the North American Free Trade Area (NAFTA), and proposed the Free Trade Area in the Americas (FTAA). Meanwhile, the European Union (EU) continued to deepen and widen its integration. In 1995, it extended the membership to Austria, Finland, and Sweden, and it envisions expansion to include some Central and Eastern European countries such as the Czech Republic, Hungary, Poland, and Slovakia.

While the rapid pace of regionalism has spread in Europe and the Americas, Pacific Asia has had a history of weak regionwide economic and security institutions. This was partly a reflection of the fact that the United States was the preponderant power in the region and preferred to have a hub-spoke bilateral relationship with its major Asian allies. The cut-off of trade and investment linkages between China and other East Asian countries until the early 1980s have also made the other East Asian countries like Japan, Korea, Taiwan, and Hong Kong look across the Pacific for trade and market. However, the postwar success of the United States in fostering prosperity and democracy in Europe and East Asia have resulted in the onset of full economic tripolarity. The earlier economic basis for U.S. hegemony has been undermined.

Together with the collapse of the Soviet Union, the security imperatives for U.S. hegemony have also evaporated.

Since the early 1990s, the debate over the advantages and disadvantages of regionalism has intensified. On the one hand, those who view the trend in somewhat favorable light suggest that (1) these blocs are formed along "natural" geographical boundaries, thereby limiting trade diversion effect and producing substantial trade creation effect; (2) they can politically lock in pro-liberalization policies in individual countries; and (3) they can be a promising alternative to cumbersome, protracted multilateral negotiation for promoting free trade (Krugman, 1991b; Summers, 1991; Lawrence, 1991). On the other hand, those who view the trend as, on balance, negative suggest that (1) regionalism could potentially lead to protectionism; (2) it would be particularly detrimental to the world economy if it is regarded as an alternative to globalism; and (3) regionalism should occur only under an effective and credible global trading system so that it would be a supplement rather than an alternative to globalism (Bhagwati, 1991; Bergsten, 1991; Krugman, 1991a).

This chapter examines the rise of regionalism in the Pacific Basin and the strategic interest of the ASEAN countries within APEC. In section 2, regional institutions such as ASEAN and an East Asian economic grouping are discussed. Data suggest that trade and investment linkages with extra-ASEAN economies are far more significant than intra-ASEAN linkages. Section 3 then examines the patterns of trade and the extent of trade barriers in ASEAN countries, followed by a summary of the effects of liberalization within ASEAN and APEC in section 4. It is suggested that ASEAN could best achieve its long-term strategic economic interests through liberalization under the larger regional framework of APEC. In section 5, some specific strategies are proposed for ASEAN, including the extension of its preferential trading arrangement to other APEC members to spur more extensive and rapid liberalization in the Asia–Pacific region. Section 6 provides concluding remarks.

2. REGIONAL INSTITUTIONS IN THE ASIA–PACIFIC

Since the mid-1980s, competitive unilateral liberalization among the ASEAN countries and China in attracting FDI has intensified.

In addition, the steadily increased pressure of appreciating exchange rates and rising wage costs in Japan and the NIEs have resulted in substantial investment flowing out from the more developed NIEs and Japan into the developing economies of ASEAN and China. These significant expansions in intraregional trade and investment linkages have fostered an increasing trend of market-driven economic regionalism within East Asia.

Currently, regional institutions within Asia–Pacific could be conceived as concentric rings of regional grouping. At the first level is the grouping of ASEAN countries, currently encompassing Brunei, Indonesia, Malaysia, the Philippines, Singapore, Thailand, Vietnam, and recently inducted Laos and Myanmar. Although its inclusion has been delayed by domestic political uncertainties, Cambodia is likely eventually to complete this ten-country regional core group. At the next level within East Asia is the controversial proposal by Malaysia's Prime Minister Mahathir for an East Asian Economic Caucus (EAEC), including largely ASEAN and Northeast Asian countries such as Japan, China, Korea, and Taiwan, but excluding the Anglo-Saxon countries of North America and Australasia. At the most extensive level is the established institution of APEC, encompassing the eighteen countries in East Asia, North America, and Australasia.

2.1. ASEAN

It was common political fear that brought the nonsocialist countries of Southeast Asia, ASEAN, together in 1967. By and large, it was also an external threat that had held ASEAN together right through the years. But while peace and stability within ASEAN provided a conducive environment for economic growth and development during the past thirty years, each member in ASEAN had developed largely out of its own independent achievement. They owed relatively little to joint ASEAN economic cooperation despite the efforts. Economic cooperation programs, such as the ASEAN industrial projects (AIP), the ASEAN industrial complementation scheme (AIC), and the ASEAN industrial joint venture scheme (AIJV), were based on inward-looking, bureaucratic, protracted negotiations and were largely unsuccessful in fostering growth and intraregional trade expansion. Since the mid-1980s, the competitive unilateral liberalization in the ASEAN countries, substantial

FDI inflows from Japan and the NIEs, as well as the competitive challenge posed by China's extensive liberalization, have been far more important in fostering ASEAN trade liberalization, boosting growth, and promoting intra-ASEAN trade than any of the officially initiated joint ASEAN schemes.

With the revival of regionalism, particularly the then-impending formation of NAFTA, the idea of an ASEAN Free Trade Area (AFTA) was revived by Thailand in early 1991. It was first endorsed by Singapore. It was more enthusiastically received at the ASEAN Foreign Ministers' meeting in Kuala Lumpur in July 1991, and an agreement was reached at the ASEAN Economic Ministers' meeting in October 1991. It gained an official endorsement in January 1992 at the Singapore Summit, which set a timetable for trade liberalization by the year 2008.

A number of new economic and political stimuli from within and outside ASEAN have accounted for this renewed interest in the AFTA proposal. The most significant internal factor is the successive waves of unilateral tariff reductions and economic liberalization in the ASEAN countries, particularly Indonesia, Thailand, and Malaysia, during the past eight to ten years. Second, there has been an external pressure for ASEAN to come together as prodded by other trade blocs or groups in rapid formation. These include the Single European Market and NAFTA. The then-protracted Uruguay Round under the GATT, in the face of rising protectionism and nontariff barriers (NTBs), also raised some doubts in multilateral negotiations. In the increasingly fierce competition for foreign direct investment in a rapidly capital-scarce global market, at a time when the strategic bargaining power of an extensive market is becoming more critical, ASEAN countries perceive that a market pooling among them is a necessary defensive response.

The Singapore Summit endorsed the Thai proposal of establishing an AFTA within fifteen years from January 1, 1993, using the Common Effective Preferential Tariff (CEPT) scheme. Under the CEPT, tariff rates currently above 20 percent are to be reduced to 20 percent within five to eight years. Subsequent tariff reductions to 0–5 percent are to be spread over a maximum of seven years. In other words, the goal is to lower all tariff rates to below 5 percent in fifteen years for manufactured goods, processed agricultural products, and capital goods (see Table 6.1).

Table 6.1. *Accelerated Tariff Reduction Schedule for ASEAN Free Trade Area*

	Old Timetable	Accelerated Timetable
Normal Track		
Tariffs > 20%	20% by 2001	20% by 1998
	15% by 2003	0–5% by 2003
	10% by 2005	
	0–5% by 2008	
Tariffs < 20%	15% by 2003	0–5% by 2000
	10% by 2005	
	0–5% by 2008	
Fast Track		
Tariffs > 20%	0–5% by 2003	0–5% by 2000
Tariffs < 20%	0–5% by 2000	0–5% by 1998

Source: ASEAN Secretariat.

Under greater external pressure, the ASEAN Economic Ministers' (AEM) meeting in Manila in October 1992 not only managed
to resolve the sticky issue of the reporting line for the AFTA
council, but it also succeeded in reaching agreement on a more
rapid rate of tariff reduction. It was decided that the tariff rates
on products above 20 percent would be lowered to a maximum of
5 percent within ten years while products with tariff rates of 20
percent or less would be reduced to below 5 percent within seven
years.

Spurred by external forces, such as the first APEC summit in
Seattle in November 1993, the successful completion of the
Uruguay Round and the ratification of WTO, the ASEAN members
again accelerated the original AFTA agreement and expanded its
scope. Specifically, at the AEM meeting in Chiangmai in September 1994, the timetable for all CEPT products to lower tariff rates
to 0–5 percent was accelerated from fifteen to ten years (i.e., by
2003 instead of 2008), bringing forward the target date for AFTA
(Table 6.1). The product coverage of CEPT was broadened to
include unprocessed agricultural products. More significantly, dis-

Table 6.2. *Cumulative Inward Foreign Direct Investment in ASEAN,*
1986–92 (percentage shares)

	Indonesia	Malaysia	Thailand	Singapore
United States	8.0	6.0	10.5	40.0
Europe	21.0	20.8	16.8	34.5
Japan	22.5	27.0	41.5	23.6
NIEs[a]	24.5	28.6	20.4	. . .
ASEAN	4.2	12.5	6.0	. . .
Other Regions	19.8	5.1	4.8	1.9
Total (%)	100.0	100.0	100.0	100.0
Total (US$ million)	38,876	25,505	46,680	7,218

[a] NIEs refer to Korea, Taiwan, and Hong Kong and exclude Singapore.
Sources:
   Indonesia: Capital Investment Coordinating Board (BKPM).
   Malaysia: Malaysian Industrial Development Authority.
   Thailand: Board of Investment.
   Singapore: Economic Development Board.

cipline was introduced in the use of temporary exclusion lists by requiring that products in the "temporary exclusion list" be transferred to the "inclusion list" in five equal installments of 20 percent beginning January 1, 1996.

As Table 6.2 suggests, ASEAN countries are heavily dependent on FDI from outside their region to drive their industrialization process. For Indonesia, out of the cumulative total inward FDI of US$38,876 million during 1986–92, only 4.2 percent came from other ASEAN countries (primarily from Singapore), whereas Northeast Asian countries like Japan and the NIEs (excluding Singapore) accounted for 47.0 percent. Similarly for Malaysia, out of the total FDI inflow of US$25,505 million during the same period, 55.6 percent came from Japan and the NIEs.[1] The corresponding share for Thailand was even higher at 61.9 percent. Only Singapore, with its higher income and average skill level, was much more dependent on the United States and Europe and derived an insignificant amount from the other NIEs.

---

[1] The 12.5 percent share from other ASEAN countries largely came from Singapore.

As pointed out by Panagariya (Chapter 4, this volume), the ASEAN countries have very limited trade links with one another. The only extensive trading relationships are between Singapore and other ASEAN countries, arising largely from Singapore's role as a port for entrepôt and reexport trade, as well as from a large number of multinational corporations (MNCs) using Singapore as their regional headquarters in managing their production bases in other ASEAN countries. All the ASEAN countries traded heavily with the United States, Japan, the Asian NIEs, and the EU while their trade with other ASEAN countries comprised only between 10.3 percent (Indonesia) and 25.6 percent (Singapore) of their total trade in 1995 (see Table 1.2 of the introductory chapter by Lee and Roland-Holst). Consequently, extra-ASEAN investment inflows and trade are far more important than intra-ASEAN economic linkages. The integrative forces among ASEAN economies are investments from industrialized countries and the NIEs and not autonomous trade and investment among the ASEAN members.

2.2. East Asian Economic Grouping

The idea of the East Asian Economic Grouping (EAEG) came from the Prime Minister of Malaysia, Dr. Mahathir, in late 1990 when he suggested that Malaysia would take the lead to set up an East Asian trading group to counter the single-market concept of the European Community and the North American Free Trade Area. The EAEG concept was to embrace countries including ASEAN, Hong Kong, China, South Korea, Taiwan, Japan, and other countries in the Indochina region, though no firm list of countries was made. The United States, Canada, Australia, and New Zealand were to be excluded. The rationale was that economic cooperation and speaking in one voice were necessary among the Asia–Pacific countries, especially in the face of the deadlock in multilateral liberalization talks in Brussels at that time. In particular, Mahathir desired to anchor Japan to East Asia, arguing that East Asia should be Japan's natural constituency. He also chose the occasion of the visit of the Chinese premier to launch his idea in the hope that China would play an important role in the face of trade blocs springing up in Europe. It is worth quoting Mahathir's first comprehensive speech articulating the idea in Bali on March 4, 1991, to get a flavor of the sentiment behind the proposal:

It is paradoxical that even as the centrally planned Eastern block economies espouse the free market systems as a solution to their economic problem, the erstwhile free traders of the west are opting for a controlled international marketing system. But the fact is that with the formation of the European Union and the American free trading zone, that is what is happening.

The question is what do we in this region do to rescue the free trading system of the world? Do we refuse to acknowledge the gloomy facts? Do we hush up things? Do we look the other way? Do we accept them without a whimper? Or do we confront them: the reality of those trade blocs, that is, not the nations.

Two wrongs do not make one right. We in East Asia must not form a trading bloc of our own. But we know that alone and singly we cannot stop the slide towards controlled and regulated international commerce; which in fact is no different from the command economies of the socialist Soviets, only the scale is international; which is obviously going to replace free trade if the EC and the American Union are allowed to rewrite the rules. To stop the slide and to preserve free trade the countries of East Asia, which contain some of the most dynamic economies in the world today, must at least speak with one voice.

It will be impossible to do this unless we can consult each other, unless we can have some form of grouping which is recognisable. A free trade arrangement between us is impossible at this point in time. There is too much disparity in our development. An Economic Community after the EC pattern is far too structured and is well nigh impossible to achieve. But a formal grouping intended to facilitate consultation and consensus prior to negotiating with Europe or America or in multilateral fora such as the GATT is not too far-fetched an idea. It is also not against the GATT principle, nor will it run contrary to membership in such organizations as the APEC, in which the United States and Canada are members while having an economic union with each other.[2]

When ASEAN trade ministers met in Kuala Lumpur in October 1991, the EAEG was supported as an ASEAN initiative after Indonesia was successful in getting the name changed to East Asian Economic Caucus (EAEC). This was to defuse allegations that it was intended as a trading bloc.

The EAEG concept, in excluding North America and Australasia, faced significant opposition from them. Their opposition further resulted in the cautious attitude of Japan and some ASEAN countries toward the idea, though it is noteworthy that China has

---

[2] Speech delivered by Dr. Mahathir Mohamed, Prime Minister of Malaysia, at the International Conference on ASEAN, March 4, 1991, Bali, Indonesia.

been a staunch supporter all along. In addition, the insufficient consultation among the ASEAN countries before floating the concept has made it more difficult for Malaysia to sell the EAEG as an ASEAN idea. Moreover, a very high dependence of East Asian countries on the U.S. market – averaging 22 percent for the ASEAN, the NIEs, China, and Japan in 1995 – would make it very costly for an East Asian grouping to exclude the United States.

3. ASEAN'S TRADE PATTERNS AND BARRIERS

In this section, we examine the patterns of trade and the extent of trade barriers in each of the five major ASEAN countries. Because of the extensive work already done by the Global Trade Analysis Project (GTAP) on assembling data on trade flows and protection rates by commodity and country, we have relied primarily on its trade and protection data (see Hertel, 1997). We have aggregated the GTAP database with the base year 1992 into twelve countries/regions and thirteen sectors for the present discussion. The countries/regions are (1) Australia and New Zealand, (2) Japan, (3) Indonesia, (4) Malaysia, (5) Thailand, (6) the Philippines, (7) Singapore, (8) China, (9) South Korea, Taiwan, and Hong Kong (NIEs), (10) Canada and the United States (North America), (11) the EU-12, and (12) the rest of the world (ROW).[3]

3.1. Trade Patterns

Tables 6.3a–6.3e provide exports and imports by commodity and country for the five ASEAN countries in 1992. For Indonesia, the largest export market is Japan, accounting for 31 percent of total exports. The key export products are crude oil (aggregated into mining), wearing apparel (aggregated into textiles), lumber and wood, and agricultural and fishery products. The EU (17 percent) and North America (14 percent) constitute other large export markets where main export products are garments, leather products, and lumber and wood. Exports to the NIEs (Korea, Taiwan, and Hong Kong) account for 11 percent of the total exports, comprising largely crude oil and lumber and wood. Among the ASEAN

---

[3] For present discussion, the EU includes the twelve member states of the European Community in 1992 but excludes the three new member states (Austria, Finland, and Sweden).

Table 6.3a. *Indonesia's Exports and Imports by Commodity and Country, 1992 (percent, total figures in millions of US dollars)*

Exports	MYS	PHL	THA	SGP	JPN	NIEs	CHN	ANZ	NA	EU-12	ROW	Total
				Exports to Destination Country/Region as a % of Total Exports								
Agriculture	2.5	0.2	2.8	14.0	24.4	4.9	2.0	1.0	24.6	15.2	8.2	3,351
Mining	0.4	0.6	0.3	1.5	62.7	17.8	6.3	2.8	5.5	1.3	0.8	11,029
Processed food	5.2	0.4	0.2	8.5	6.7	6.2	2.1	1.9	12.5	46.0	10.3	1,585
Textiles	1.3	0.4	0.5	17.2	6.3	3.2	1.5	1.8	23.3	28.2	16.4	7,559
Wood	0.3	0.0	0.3	3.4	26.6	17.7	13.4	1.1	12.4	17.6	7.2	4,749
Paper	11.5	0.6	2.0	8.3	1.6	19.3	12.8	4.4	2.5	7.2	29.7	457
Petroleum prod.	1.1	0.0	1.0	13.9	37.0	14.6	2.3	1.7	7.5	18.2	2.9	370
Chemicals	1.7	1.9	1.4	7.6	31.5	13.0	2.9	10.1	5.2	11.0	13.7	2,101
Steel	15.6	0.4	20.4	13.2	11.1	13.2	3.3	0.1	0.3	15.7	6.6	289
Nonferrous metal	0.5	1.2	1.4	29.7	37.2	6.3	3.9	0.1	5.8	12.2	1.7	550
Metal products	4.9	1.5	1.1	13.9	18.6	5.9	1.5	2.4	26.1	12.1	12.0	234
Machinery	1.2	0.4	2.6	24.5	9.1	3.8	1.0	8.2	25.3	15.9	8.1	1,357
Transport equip.	5.9	0.1	10.4	17.5	7.2	7.7	3.8	0.2	6.4	21.3	19.6	234
Other manufac.	2.1	2.8	1.2	12.4	6.3	4.4	0.6	2.6	36.8	12.7	18.1	936
Trade and trans.	0.0	0.1	0.3	0.4	31.8	4.2	0.0	1.1	4.7	44.5	12.9	1,543
Services	0.1	0.0	0.2	1.7	10.2	4.2	0.2	0.9	18.8	51.1	12.5	942
All sectors	1.4	0.5	1.0	8.6	30.7	10.8	4.7	2.6	13.9	17.1	8.7	37,286

Imports	MYS	PHL	THA	SGP	JPN	NIEs	CHN	ANZ	NA	EU-12	ROW	Total
				Imports from Origin Country/Region as % of Total Imports								
Agriculture	0.6	0.1	0.8	0.5	0.4	2.1	10.5	24.0	33.4	2.0	25.5	1,472
Mining	11.0	0.0	0.6	0.5	0.6	0.6	0.9	14.5	3.1	1.7	66.5	1,503
Processed food	14.8	1.1	18.6	4.5	2.0	2.8	4.3	12.0	8.8	12.9	18.1	975
Textiles	1.3	0.1	0.8	0.8	12.9	65.4	3.8	0.7	6.0	5.1	3.2	1,932
Wood	1.3	0.1	0.3	6.4	39.5	4.8	1.6	6.7	18.5	17.6	3.2	79
Paper	0.6	0.0	0.2	7.0	5.4	14.4	0.5	8.4	32.8	12.0	18.5	700
Petroleum prod.	0.1	0.0	0.2	64.1	3.6	3.1	1.0	1.6	3.4	5.9	17.1	1,105
Chemicals	1.1	0.5	1.1	6.6	18.5	16.1	2.8	4.6	14.1	20.9	13.6	3,882
Steel	2.1	0.2	0.1	3.7	41.7	15.5	3.0	6.4	3.6	12.1	11.5	1,516
Nonferrous metal	1.2	0.7	0.1	4.3	11.5	7.3	1.3	41.1	5.9	8.9	17.7	459
Metal products	0.9	0.0	0.7	4.8	20.4	19.3	5.5	13.1	4.6	23.1	7.8	821
Machinery	1.3	0.0	0.4	3.7	33.9	9.3	1.7	1.4	15.3	28.4	4.5	10,143
Transport equip.	0.7	0.0	0.1	3.5	25.0	2.3	0.4	0.9	25.1	38.3	3.7	2,287
Other manufac.	1.2	0.2	2.2	4.7	34.2	17.3	8.2	1.7	5.4	20.5	4.4	652
Trade and trans.	0.2	0.1	0.3	1.2	5.2	1.7	0.0	0.3	17.0	55.4	18.6	2,353
Services	0.0	0.1	0.1	1.7	3.4	6.0	0.4	1.1	15.4	61.5	10.4	3,179
All sectors	1.8	0.2	1.0	5.4	19.5	11.7	2.3	4.8	14.3	26.7	12.5	33,058

Definition of countries/regions: IDN = Indonesia, MYS = Malaysia, PHL = Philippines, THA = Thailand, SGP = Singapore, JPN = Japan, NIEs = Korea, Taiwan and Hong Kong, CHN = China, ANZ = Australia and Zealand, NA = Canada and the United States, EU-12 = European Union 12, ROW = rest of the world.
Source: GTAP database, Version 3.

Table 6.3b. *Malaysia's Exports and Imports by Commodity and Country, 1992 (percent, total figures in millions of US dollars)*

	IDN	PHL	THA	SGP	JPN	NIes	CHN	ANZ	NA	EU-12	ROW	Total
Exports				Exports to Destination Country/Region as a % of Total Exports								
Agriculture	0.2	1.0	2.4	12.9	35.0	18.4	6.2	0.8	4.4	9.1	9.6	3,965
Mining	3.0	3.9	10.3	18.0	36.4	13.2	1.6	2.7	1.9	1.5	7.3	5,050
Processed food	3.6	1.4	0.6	22.2	6.0	5.5	5.2	2.5	5.8	14.1	33.1	3,658
Textiles	1.0	1.7	0.9	15.1	5.2	4.3	3.1	1.7	33.1	26.9	7.1	2,291
Wood	0.0	0.2	8.3	11.9	14.2	13.4	6.2	4.2	10.7	23.3	7.5	2,859
Paper	1.3	0.1	2.4	52.3	3.8	9.5	4.1	4.8	4.5	3.1	14.1	301
Petroleum prod.	0.3	0.0	0.3	68.2	18.1	5.8	0.0	0.4	0.3	0.0	6.6	503
Chemicals	1.7	1.6	4.3	20.8	11.7	7.3	3.9	3.3	19.4	17.9	8.2	2,370
Steel	8.2	1.1	8.8	33.6	3.0	21.3	3.0	3.7	3.7	3.2	10.4	346
Nonferrous metal	1.1	0.5	2.8	23.1	14.4	13.7	2.6	3.7	4.1	26.2	7.8	468
Metal products	1.9	1.1	1.4	37.7	9.3	7.1	2.3	2.7	13.7	13.2	9.5	380
Machinery	0.7	0.4	2.2	23.6	8.4	6.5	1.6	1.0	32.6	18.5	4.4	17,728
Transport equip.	2.1	0.2	2.8	23.6	1.2	4.2	0.2	21.0	6.8	33.8	3.9	738
Other manufac.	0.3	0.9	0.6	41.5	4.3	1.5	0.3	1.7	33.0	9.7	6.3	2,729
Trade and trans.	0.2	0.1	0.2	0.4	31.9	4.2	0.0	1.1	4.7	44.6	12.7	3,284
Services	0.1	0.1	0.2	1.7	10.1	4.4	0.2	1.0	18.6	50.6	12.9	551
All sectors	1.2	1.0	3.2	20.7	15.2	8.2	2.6	2.1	19.2	17.8	8.9	47,221
Imports				Imports from Origin Country/Region as a % of Total Imports								
Agriculture	7.0	0.5	7.7	10.4	1.2	2.4	18.8	21.0	11.6	1.3	18.1	1,379
Mining	6.2	0.8	2.7	12.7	2.5	0.5	3.0	11.0	4.8	18.5	37.4	759
Processed food	5.4	1.1	11.7	7.4	1.8	2.9	3.1	29.0	7.1	13.4	17.1	1,651
Textiles	6.4	0.1	2.5	21.2	10.4	37.2	6.8	0.9	1.7	5.2	7.8	1,661
Wood	13.3	3.1	1.9	17.1	20.6	6.0	2.6	3.3	17.1	11.0	3.9	122
Paper	7.0	0.0	1.2	14.4	13.9	8.9	1.4	5.6	21.2	18.3	8.2	848
Petroleum prod.	0.3	0.0	0.0	93.6	1.8	1.2	0.3	0.8	0.5	1.0	0.6	1,462
Chemicals	1.1	0.2	2.6	23.3	19.8	11.1	2.4	2.3	11.4	17.2	8.6	3,346
Steel	2.8	0.1	0.3	6.7	40.7	12.7	2.1	5.7	2.8	9.8	16.2	1,763
Nonferrous metal	0.4	1.4	0.4	21.9	20.5	7.4	0.9	19.5	3.0	5.9	18.6	801
Metal products	1.4	0.2	1.7	20.0	33.1	16.9	3.6	2.9	3.9	10.3	5.9	853
Machinery	0.1	1.1	2.3	19.8	30.5	11.3	1.1	0.6	16.8	13.5	2.9	16,202
Transport equip.	0.5	0.1	0.2	9.7	27.5	7.2	0.7	0.3	34.3	12.7	6.9	2,863
Other manufac.	1.3	0.1	2.7	21.5	42.1	9.7	3.5	0.8	6.5	8.1	3.6	1,652
Trade and trans.	2.7	2.8	2.8	4.6	7.0	13.0	3.1	5.7	11.0	3.5	43.9	14
Services	0.0	0.0	0.0	1.5	2.4	5.3	0.3	1.4	13.2	64.9	10.8	6,222
All sectors	1.4	0.6	2.2	17.8	21.2	9.9	2.2	3.6	13.6	19.9	7.7	41,598

Source: GTAP database, Version 3.

Table 6.3c. *Philippines' Exports and Imports by Commodity and Country, 1992 (percent, total figures in millions of US dollars)*

Exports	IDN	MYS	THA	SGP	JPN	NIEs	CHN	ANZ	NA	EU-12	ROW	Total
			Exports to Destination Country/Region as a % of Total Exports									
Agriculture	0.1	0.6	0.2	1.0	56.7	9.7	1.3	1.4	14.1	9.9	4.9	1,000
Mining	0.1	0.9	0.1	1.2	73.3	10.2	7.2	0.0	2.5	1.1	3.3	641
Processed food	0.9	1.4	0.1	1.3	7.1	5.9	1.3	0.8	47.7	26.5	7.1	1,190
Textiles	0.1	0.1	0.1	0.5	4.7	1.4	0.7	1.0	62.6	21.1	7.7	2,400
Wood	0.0	0.8	0.1	1.7	13.9	2.5	0.7	3.4	34.8	37.1	4.8	408
Paper	0.3	0.5	0.1	7.1	24.1	3.3	2.1	5.2	19.2	35.7	2.2	67
Petroleum prod.	0.1	0.1	0.4	5.2	82.0	8.3	3.9			9.1	0.0	124
Chemicals	4.5	1.4	8.2	4.6	25.1	8.9	13.9	3.0	12.3	6.9	11.0	418
Steel	7.8	4.7	5.3	5.6	15.9	9.3	21.4	3.6	11.7	1.1	13.8	38
Nonferrous metal	1.2	4.0	4.2	3.5	31.5	39.6	13.8	0.1	0.2	1.7	0.3	262
Metal products	0.4	1.7	7.3	3.4	24.1	5.0	3.5	1.8	25.7	22.7	4.5	76
Machinery	0.1	4.7	0.7	5.4	11.7	6.3	1.5	1.0	47.9	18.5	2.2	3,661
Transport equip.	0.1	3.4	32.8	5.2	18.7	1.8	0.3	0.7	18.7	4.2	14.2	57
Other manufac.	0.1	0.3	0.3	2.1	20.1	3.1	0.8	2.8	38.9	26.8	4.6	588
Trade and trans.	0.2	0.0	0.2	0.4	31.8	4.2	0.0	1.1	4.7	44.6	12.8	2,118
Services	0.1	0.1	0.1	1.5	9.2	4.9	0.2	1.0	16.8	54.8	11.4	2,009
All sectors	0.3	1.5	0.8	2.3	20.2	5.8	1.8	1.2	32.5	26.8	6.9	15,057

Imports	IDN	MYS	THA	SGP	JPN	NIEs	CHN	ANZ	NA	EU-12	ROW	Total
			Imports from Origin Country/Region as % of Total Imports									
Agriculture	1.2	7.2	0.8	2.6	3.9	3.0	2.5	8.9	54.7	3.1	12.2	691
Mining	3.3	9.7	0.2	0.3	0.9	0.2	0.9	1.4	3.8	0.4	78.8	2,200
Processed food	0.6	5.1	1.0	4.0	0.9	2.1	4.0	20.4	24.2	25.6	12.1	1,088
Textiles	2.4	3.0	2.5	0.9	13.3	50.5	8.5	0.5	8.6	6.1	3.9	1,479
Wood	1.9	12.0	0.9	2.9	30.2	10.2	3.8	3.5	21.0	13.0	0.8	65
Paper	0.9	0.1	0.4	5.4	11.6	13.8	1.0	2.7	36.9	11.5	15.7	326
Petroleum prod.	0.0	0.0	0.3	18.4	11.5	19.9	10.9	0.3	29.9	1.8	7.1	229
Chemicals	2.1	2.0	0.9	8.7	16.4	18.2	2.4	2.4	17.8	17.0	12.1	2,012
Steel	0.1	0.5	0.4	0.8	28.1	13.8	0.8	6.0	3.6	6.3	39.6	857
Nonferrous metal	3.2	1.2	0.1	4.3	19.1	14.9	0.9	29.3	12.6	7.9	6.5	228
Metal products	1.3	1.6	1.7	7.1	24.4	15.3	9.2	2.5	19.4	14.6	3.0	291
Machinery	0.1	1.4	1.5	6.4	33.5	9.5	1.9	0.6	23.8	17.2	4.2	5,647
Transport equip.	0.0	0.2	0.2	2.1	68.5	3.6	0.5	0.5	10.5	12.8	0.9	954
Other manufac.	5.8	5.1	1.9	5.4	28.1	13.0	13.2	1.4	9.1	12.0	5.0	507
Trade and trans.	0.1	0.2	0.3	1.2	5.2	1.7	0.0	0.3	17.0	55.1	18.7	1,417
Services	0.1	0.1	0.1	1.9	4.3	7.9	0.5	0.9	17.0	57.1	10.2	619
All sectors	1.2	2.9	1.0	4.3	20.5	11.6	2.7	3.0	18.1	17.2	17.6	18,610

Source: GTAP database, Version 3.

Table 6.3d. *Thailand's Exports and Imports by Commodity and Country, 1992*
(percent, total figures in millions of US dollars)

Exports	\multicolumn{11}{c}{Exports to Destination Country/Region as a % of Total Exports}

Exports	IDN	MYS	PHL	SGP	JPN	NIEs	CHN	ANZ	NA	EU-12	ROW	Total
Agriculture	0.2	2.0	0.1	4.5	32.3	8.3	4.0	1.1	15.7	26.6	5.1	4,657
Mining	0.7	1.6	0.3	5.8	18.4	10.7	0.7	11.2	19.6	19.5	11.5	1,172
Processed food	3.2	3.3	0.2	3.2	19.4	8.2	1.7	2.4	19.4	13.7	25.2	5,356
Textiles	0.2	0.6	0.5	2.6	8.1	2.4	2.3	1.7	25.9	26.9	28.8	6,520
Wood	0.0	0.3	0.1	1.3	35.1	3.4	1.1	1.5	29.2	20.6	7.3	725
Paper	1.1	7.3	1.0	6.9	4.8	26.8	8.7	4.2	12.2	12.2	14.9	124
Petroleum prod.	1.8	0.6	0.5	57.9	0.3	1.6	1.3	0.0	0.2	0.8	34.9	109
Chemicals	2.6	5.2	1.0	6.7	15.8	10.6	5.7	4.0	15.4	15.6	17.5	1,581
Steel	0.9	2.6	2.0	7.5	21.2	10.1	5.3	3.5	19.4	6.6	20.9	172
Nonferrous metal	0.5	3.1	0.2	11.6	23.3	11.5	8.2	0.3	8.4	23.3	9.6	97
Metal products	1.3	3.5	1.2	5.6	32.7	3.2	1.4	3.1	20.8	15.9	11.2	399
Machinery	0.5	4.1	0.9	19.6	15.5	6.7	1.8	0.9	29.9	15.0	5.1	8,600
Transport equip.	0.9	1.6	0.8	4.8	6.6	6.4	1.2	3.0	12.4	36.7	25.6	282
Other manufac.	0.5	1.5	0.3	4.9	13.5	1.9	0.4	2.3	43.0	24.6	7.0	2,812
Trade and trans.	0.2	0.0	0.1	0.4	32.0	4.2	0.0	1.1	4.7	44.8	12.7	4,486
Services	0.1	0.2	0.0	1.6	9.8	4.7	0.2	1.3	18.0	51.2	12.8	1,471
All sectors	0.8	2.2	0.5	7.1	18.9	5.9	1.9	1.9	22.2	24.2	14.4	38,563

Imports	\multicolumn{11}{c}{Imports from Origin Country/Region as a % of Total Imports}

Imports	IDN	MYS	PHL	SGP	JPN	NIEs	CHN	ANZ	NA	EU-12	ROW	Total
Agriculture	5.4	5.9	0.1	1.7	3.7	14.7	6.6	5.1	12.7	5.2	38.8	2,025
Mining	2.1	32.6	0.1	1.2	1.7	0.9	1.9	8.1	8.8	19.9	22.8	1,727
Processed food	0.3	2.4	0.1	3.1	6.4	2.1	8.3	11.3	14.0	32.9	19.2	1,071
Textiles	2.7	1.4	0.2	2.2	17.0	46.6	9.1	1.0	5.9	8.5	5.5	1,642
Wood	3.4	53.3	0.1	3.3	4.4	2.0	0.5	0.3	4.2	4.7	24.0	517
Paper	1.4	1.1	0.0	8.1	17.2	8.4	1.0	5.3	19.7	15.5	22.3	721
Petroleum prod.	0.3	0.1	0.0	78.2	4.0	6.9	3.9	1.7	2.1	1.4	1.4	1,330
Chemicals	0.7	2.2	0.8	8.5	23.1	17.1	2.9	1.4	11.1	18.5	13.8	4,754
Steel	2.0	1.0	0.1	2.2	39.0	9.9	6.5	1.1	2.0	6.0	30.3	3,341
Nonferrous metal	1.0	1.6	1.4	8.7	16.8	7.4	1.3	19.8	8.7	6.2	27.1	864
Metal products	0.3	0.7	0.7	5.7	43.5	17.0	3.2	1.5	7.1	15.5	4.7	826
Machinery	0.3	3.0	0.2	10.7	38.1	10.9	1.5	0.8	13.7	14.9	6.0	13,807
Transport equip.	0.6	0.5	0.4	1.9	47.2	1.8	1.4	0.2	24.8	18.6	2.7	4,362
Other manufac.	0.9	1.3	0.2	11.3	40.3	11.7	4.0	0.9	9.7	11.7	8.0	1,287
Trade and trans.	0.1	0.2	0.1	1.2	5.2	1.6	0.0	0.3	17.1	55.6	18.6	3,830
Services	0.0	0.0	0.1	2.0	4.4	6.6	0.5	0.9	17.6	58.0	10.0	3,584
All sectors	0.9	3.6	0.3	8.0	25.7	10.2	2.6	2.0	13.1	21.0	12.8	45,688

Source: GTAP database, Version 3.

Table 6.3e. *Singapore's Exports and Imports by Commodity and Country, 1992 (percent, total figures in millions of US dollars)*

| Exports | Exports to Destination Country/Region as a % of Total Exports | | | | | | | | | | | |
	IDN	MYS	PHL	THA	JPN	NIEs	CHN	ANZ	NA	EU-12	ROW	Total
Agriculture	0.5	9.7	1.2	2.3	6.2	16.1	3.4	1.3	8.7	16.6	34.2	1,283
Mining	1.2	16.0	1.1	3.2	1.6	4.1	4.6	5.4	4.5	7.5	50.9	570
Processed food	1.7	4.7	1.6	1.3	29.6	22.7	4.0	3.3	2.4	4.4	24.5	2,416
Textiles	0.6	14.4	0.5	1.5	1.9	6.3	1.7	0.5	31.2	19.3	22.1	2,206
Wood	0.6	2.6	0.2	2.1	11.6	10.3	4.1	3.6	10.1	28.6	26.2	700
Paper	5.7	14.1	2.0	6.7	3.3	11.9	3.1	8.9	14.5	14.1	15.8	776
Petroleum prod.	8.0	15.5	0.5	8.6	19.7	9.6	2.9	0.6	2.6	20.2	8,485	
Chemicals	4.9	14.9	3.3	7.7	6.7	15.3	9.4	2.8	13.5	9.2	12.4	4,994
Steel	10.1	21.1	1.2	12.9	2.5	7.7	3.9	1.3	1.8	1.0	36.7	506
Nonferrous metal	3.4	30.2	1.7	12.9	3.3	20.8	6.0	0.8	0.9	5.9	14.2	534
Metal products	4.5	19.9	2.4	5.5	8.9	9.5	3.5	2.3	5.6	14.4	23.4	816
Machinery	1.1	9.8	1.1	4.5	5.1	11.1	2.3	2.8	30.9	19.9	11.5	31,332
Transport equip.	4.9	17.1	1.3	5.0	0.9	16.5	2.1	0.4	6.4	22.9	22.6	1,564
Other manufac.	0.9	11.1	0.8	4.5	6.3	6.9	1.8	1.6	15.0	30.9	20.1	3,017
Trade and trans.	0.3	0.0	0.2	0.4	35.5	15.9	0.0	4.5	8.3	22.3	12.7	10,494
Services	2.1	3.6	0.5	2.7	11.4	15.1	4.5	2.9	12.7	8.6	35.9	2,589
All sectors	2.3	9.7	1.0	4.8	11.0	13.5	3.5	2.9	18.4	16.6	16.2	72,282

| Imports | Imports from Origin Country/Region as % of Total Imports | | | | | | | | | | | |
	IDN	MYS	PHL	THA	JPN	NIEs	CHN	ANZ	NA	EU-12	ROW	Total
Agriculture	20.7	22.0	0.5	9.3	1.2	11.9	8.3	6.3	3.9	1.2	14.7	2,611
Mining	2.4	13.5	0.1	1.0	0.3	2.1	3.9	1.4	0.8	1.6	72.8	7,242
Processed food	4.8	29.3	0.6	6.1	3.6	3.3	8.5	8.5	9.9	18.8	6.5	3,021
Textiles	29.8	7.8	0.3	3.9	6.5	21.4	11.3	0.4	3.3	8.2	7.1	4,796
Wood	22.3	46.3	1.0	1.3	2.4	4.0	2.5	1.4	5.6	7.3	5.9	849
Paper	4.0	16.6	0.5	0.9	17.2	6.2	3.7	3.4	17.7	15.3	14.5	1,060
Petroleum prod.	1.8	11.9	0.2	2.2	2.6	8.4	13.2	5.0	8.7	4.0	41.9	3,007
Chemicals	2.8	8.7	0.3	1.9	15.7	10.7	2.7	3.1	18.4	25.0	10.6	5,950
Steel	2.1	6.3	0.1	0.7	38.0	7.2	3.0	3.6	3.2	12.8	23.1	2,051
Nonferrous metal	11.9	7.8	0.7	0.8	16.8	10.0	5.8	5.6	8.0	11.1	21.6	1,497
Metal products	2.5	10.9	0.2	1.7	21.6	12.9	6.4	2.3	12.4	19.5	9.5	1,377
Machinery	1.2	14.8	0.7	5.9	28.3	13.1	1.4	0.9	18.1	11.8	3.8	29,721
Transport equip.	1.0	4.1	0.1	0.3	30.5	6.0	1.5	0.5	26.4	22.2	7.5	4,412
Other manufac.	2.5	24.5	0.3	3.0	25.3	7.0	4.7	1.0	16.5	11.9	3.3	4,921
Trade and trans.	0.7	1.4	0.9	2.0	26.5	10.3	0.0	3.3	16.8	15.6	22.5	817
Services	0.2	0.1	0.4	0.3	15.5	12.7	2.7	2.7	27.0	26.9	11.5	7,618
All sectors	4.4	12.9	0.5	3.6	19.1	10.6	3.8	2.1	15.0	13.4	14.7	80,950

Source: GTAP database, Version 3.

countries, only Singapore (9 percent) is a major export market, with textiles, nongrain crops, and machinery as major export products. On the import side, Indonesia highly depends upon products from the EU (27 percent), Japan (20 percent), and North America (14 percent), particularly machinery, transport equipment, and chemicals. Imports from the NIEs account for 12 percent, consisting largely of textiles, machinery, and chemicals. Both exports to and imports from other ASEAN countries apart from Singapore are quite small (Table 6.3a).

Malaysia's exports are largely destined to Singapore (21 percent), North America (19 percent), the EU (18 percent), and Japan (15 percent), and its imports primarily come from Japan (21 percent), the EU (20 percent), Singapore (18 percent), and North America (14 percent). Similar to Indonesia, trade with other ASEAN countries other than Singapore is small. Malaysia's major export products are machinery and equipment (particularly electronics equipment), crude oil and minerals, food products, and lumber and wood, whereas its major import products include machinery, electronics parts and components, chemicals, and transport equipment (Table 6.3b).

The most important export market for the Philippines is North America (33 percent), followed by the EU (27 percent) and Japan (20 percent). The principal export products are machinery and equipment, wearing apparel, and food (e.g., coconuts). The Philippines is highly dependent on imports from Japan (21 percent), North America (18 percent), the EU (17 percent), and the NIEs (12 percent). The major import products are machinery, crude oil, and chemicals, as well as textiles from the NIEs. None of the ASEAN countries is a significant trading partner (Table 6.3c).

For Thailand, the key export markets are the EU (24 percent), North America (22 percent), Japan (19 percent), and Singapore (7 percent), and its imports largely come from Japan (26 percent), the EU (21 percent), North America (13 percent), the NIEs (10 percent), and Singapore (8 percent). Indonesia, Malaysia, and the Philippines are relatively minor trading partners. The major export products are machinery and equipment (especially electronics equipment), agricultural products and processed food, wearing apparel and leather products, and other light manufactured products. The key import products are machinery, electronics parts and components, chemicals, steel, and transport equipment (Table 6.3d).

Finally, for Singapore, the important export markets are North America (18 percent), the EU (17 percent), the NIEs (14 percent), Japan (11 percent), and Malaysia (10 percent). Its imports largely originate from Japan (19 percent), North America (15 percent), Malaysia (13 percent), the EU (13 percent), and the NIEs (11 percent). The principal export products are machinery and equipment (particularly electronics equipment), petroleum products, and chemicals, and the major import products are machinery, electronics parts and components, oil, chemicals, and primary metals. Compared with the ASEAN countries already discussed, Singapore's trade with the AFTA members is relatively large, with the exception of the Philippines (Table 6.3e).

3.2. Protection Rates

Although the five ASEAN countries exhibit considerable similarity in the trade patterns in that they highly depend on trade with North America (particularly the United States), the EU, Japan, and the NIEs, protection rates differ significantly across the member countries. The protection rates provided in the GTAP database are the sum of tariff rates and tariff equivalents of nontariff barriers (NTBs). Those for the five ASEAN countries in 1992 are summarized in Table 6.4.

Both Indonesia and Malaysia have liberalized substantially since the mid-1980s. As a result of successive phases of recent liberalization, Indonesia's average protection rate was lowered to 12.3 percent by 1992 and has continued to fall in the past five years. Agricultural products, textiles and wearing apparel, lumber and wood, metal products, and transport equipment have above-average protection rates, while petroleum, minerals, chemicals, and primary metals have below-average protection rates. For Malaysia, substantial reductions in tariffs and NTBs over the past decade reduced the overall protection rate to 13.7 percent. However, high protection rates are still found in agricultural products (such as wheat, grains, meat, and dairy products), textiles and wearing apparel, leather products, and lumber and wood. Protection rates on many manufactured products including petroleum

Table 6.4. *Sectoral Protection Rates in ASEAN Countries, 1992 (percent)*

	Indonesia	Malaysia	Philippines	Thailand	Singapore
Agriculture	37.6	117.7	143.7	65.6	14.0
Mining	1.0	2.8	10.7	16.7	0.0
Processed food	11.9	52.9	57.1	66.5	23.3
Textiles	27.0	24.4	38.5	58.6	1.0
Wood	34.5	34.6	31.8	26.5	1.0
Paper	7.7	5.9	30.1	24.5	0.0
Petroleum prod.	4.8	4.3	20.5	29.7	8.1
Chemicals	6.3	8.1	18.7	34.8	1.4
Steel	7.8	6.0	13.7	17.0	0.0
Nonferrous metal	8.8	5.1	18.4	15.7	0.0
Metal products	23.0	14.2	31.6	33.1	0.0
Machinery	14.5	8.8	21.3	35.1	0.0
Transport equip.	22.6	14.5	19.6	55.4	3.0
Other manufac.	23.6	15.5	33.9	43.4	0.1
Trade and trans.	0.0	0.0	0.0	0.0	0.0
Services	0.0	0.0	0.0	0.0	0.0
All sectors	12.3	13.7	25.7	31.6	2.0

These rates are the sum of tariff rates and ad valorem equivalents of nontariff barriers.
Source: GTAP database, Version 3.

products, chemicals, steel, and machinery are now under 10 percent.

Thailand and the Philippines have maintained high protection rates, and unlike Indonesia and Malaysia, neither country has gone through successive phases of liberalization. The average protection rate on imports was 25.7 percent in the Philippines and 31.6 percent in Thailand. In both countries, trade barriers remain high for agricultural and food products, labor-intensive manufactured products such as textiles, wearing apparel, and leather products, as well as metal products, machinery, and transport equipment.

In contrast, Singapore has one of the most liberal trade and investment regimes in the world. It is a leading world port and a major crossroads of international trade and transport, and it has played an entrepôt role in Southeast Asia. As such, Singapore has very low protection rates, averaging 2.0 percent. Tariff and non-tariff barriers exist for some agricultural and food products, but they are either zero or minimal for most of the mining and manu-factured products.

4. THE EFFECTS OF REGIONAL INTEGRATION
ON ASEAN COUNTRIES

A number of studies have attempted to assess the impact of region-alization in Pacific Asia using a computable general equilibrium model (e.g., Lee and Roland-Holst, 1995; Lee and Woodall, Chapter 5, this volume; Lewis, Robinson, and Wang, 1995; Wang, 1994; Young and Chye, 1997). These studies show that although all APEC members stand to gain from regional liberalization, the extent of gains in welfare or real GDP may be relatively small. In addition, domestic firms in infant industries may not be able to compete with firms from developed members once protection is removed. As pointed out by Alain de Janvry in his comments on Lee and Woodall (Chapter 5, this volume), countries may be reluc-tant to agree on a regional trade accord unless expected gains are large.

Apart from the standard static gains from trade, there are significant trade-productivity linkages that arise from openness (Baldwin and Seghezza, 1996; Barro, 1991; Levine and Renelt, 1992). These dynamic effects of productivity gain through trade lib-eralization include positive externalities through export expansion and the importation of intermediate and capital goods. In their APEC CGE model, Lewis, Robinson, and Wang (1995) allow for the incorporation of three different kinds of trade-productivity links: (1) an increase in sectoral productivity resulting from sectoral imports of intermediate and capital goods, (2) an externality asso-ciated with sectoral export growth, and (3) an externality associ-ated with aggregate exports (i.e., increased exports make physical capital more productive). They find that the addition of trade-productivity linkages could more than double the benefits accruing to FTA member countries.

To what extent APEC trade liberalization can generate benefits to ASEAN countries beyond AFTA is of considerable importance to ASEAN policymakers. If additional gains are relatively small, then the costs of negotiation and structural adjustments may outweigh the expected benefits. We now summarize some of the main results presented in Tan (1996), which makes a comparison between the effects of AFTA and those of APEC.

The gains of AFTA will be unevenly distributed among the five major ASEAN countries. Assuming the existence of trade-productivity linkages as modeled by Lewis, Robinson, and Wang (1995), Singapore gains the most from AFTA with a 1.5 percent increase in real GDP, followed by Malaysia (0.7 percent), Thailand (0.6 percent), the Philippines (0.3 percent), and Indonesia (0.2 percent). Low existing tariff and nontariff barriers are the principal reason why Singapore becomes the chief beneficiary of AFTA. The increase in exports to the ASEAN members (export creation) is estimated to be about three times the reduction in exports to nonmembers (export diversion).

Every ASEAN country will be able to attain significantly greater gains in real GDP from regional trade liberalization encompassing the whole of APEC compared with AFTA. The percentage gains to Malaysia (6.5 percent), the Philippines (6.4 percent), and Thailand (4.4 percent) are particularly noteworthy.[4] Indonesia's gains (2.3 percent) are 2.1 percentage points greater than those realized from AFTA, while Singapore's gains (2.1 percent) are only 0.6 percentage point larger.[5] When the APEC countries remove trade barriers among themselves, Singapore faces a greater competitive pressure from Japan and the NIEs for its exports of electric and electronics products to North America. However, because it is already close to being a free-trade country, the additional costs of negotiation and structural adjustments are also expected to be quite low.

Tan (1996) also evaluates the effects of regional liberalization undertaken at the East Asian level that excludes North America and Australasia. Not surprisingly, every ASEAN country will suffer reductions in real GDP and welfare gains compared with the APEC trade liberalization case. The extent of loss in real GDP ranges from 0.4 percentage point (Indonesia) to 3.2 percentage points (Philippines). The Philippines would suffer the most because of its large share of exports to the United States (31 percent).

---

[4] As noted earlier, the inclusion of trade-productivity linkages magnifies gains from trade liberalization.

[5] DeRosa (1995) gets qualitatively similar results for Singapore in comparing the ASEAN free trade area on a preferential basis against MFN basis.

5. ASEAN'S STRATEGIC INTEREST IN THE ASIA–PACIFIC REGION

Given its great dependence on extra-ASEAN trade and foreign direct investment for industrialization, ASEAN has a strong vested interest in the global free trade regime. ASEAN by itself is too small, too competitive in economic structure, and too dependent on extraregional trade and FDI to be a regional grouping of any significance. An economic grouping at the East Asian level is also inappropriate because it could potentially cause too many conflicts across the Pacific and lead to a loss in market shares in the United States for East Asian exporters. How should ASEAN then pursue its strategy among the choice of various regional groupings in fostering global free trade?

At the outset of APEC's formation in 1989, ASEAN has insisted that APEC should evolve as a relatively loose form of cooperation, a voluntary association with decisions made through consensus rather than through formal negotiations. Fearful of being overwhelmed and subsumed by the United States and other more powerful economies in APEC, ASEAN ministers adopted the Kuching Consensus in early 1990 (see ASEAN, 1990), which emphasized that:

i. ASEAN's identity and cohesion should be preserved and should not be diluted in any enhanced APEC.

ii. An enhanced APEC should be based on the principles of equality, equity, and mutual benefit, taking fully into account the differences in the stages of economic development and sociopolitical systems among countries of the region.

iii. APEC should provide a consultative forum on economic issues and should not lead to the adoption of mandatory directives for any participant to undertake or implement.

iv. APEC should not be directed toward the formation of an inward-looking economic or trading bloc; instead, it should strengthen the open multilateral economic and trading systems in the world.

This focus on a loose consultative forum and the fear of institutionalization has been expounded strongly by Malaysia, which was concerned about U.S. dominance and the tendency in using its leverage in APEC to pry open the East Asian markets, particularly in agricultural and service sectors. However, as the host country of the November 1994 APEC Summit, Indonesia changed its position significantly. President Suharto coordinated the positions of the ASEAN countries, persuaded Malaysian Prime Minister Mahathir to attend the Summit, and successfully accommodated the APEC leaders to the Bogor Declaration (i.e., the declaration by the APEC heads to commit trade and investment liberalization by 2010 for the developed members and 2020 for the developing members).

Despite the Bogor Declaration, Malaysia, Thailand, and to a lesser extent the Philippines, as well as a significant number of Indonesian officials, remain lukewarm to APEC in comparison with AFTA. However, the general equilibrium results reported in Tan (1996) suggest that for Pacific regionalism the appropriate line for the ASEAN countries should be drawn at the APEC level. With the trend toward increasing regionalization of the world economy, APEC could facilitate the open and free global trading system envisioned by the WTO to sustain economic dynamism in the Pacific Basin. It appears that APEC played a contributory role in the successful conclusion of the Uruguay Round.

More significantly for the ASEAN countries, the present diverse composition of countries in APEC has a certain inherent stability. The presence of the United States, Japan, and emerging China prevents dominance by any one large country. Compared with the EAEC, this is a situation more advantageous for small ASEAN countries by preventing an extremely high dependence on Japan for capital goods and technology. In addition, a significant complementarity in the economic structure and factor endowments exists between North America and Australasia on the one hand and East Asian countries such as China and ASEAN on the other, ensuring that the web of economic and trade linkages across the Pacific would be mutually beneficial. The presence of the United States in the grouping would also allow the NIEs, who are somewhat dissatisfied with the extent of technology transfer from Japanese firms, to pursue a greater collaboration with U.S. firms on technology transfer.

APEC dovetails well with the U.S. strategy of increasing access to the dynamic East Asian markets as well as preventing the rise of a hegemonic power or coalition threatening its interests in East Asia. The United States is not interested in confining itself to a Western Hemisphere trading bloc. Because East Asian countries are expected to achieve significantly higher growth rates than the world average in the next decade or two, the United States has vested interests in penetrating into East Asian markets. Thus it has a strategic interest in sustaining a major economic presence and preventing large Japanese conglomerates from "*keiretsu*ing" the whole region, as well as discouraging the rapidly emerging Greater China from dominating East Asia.

The reductions in trade barriers, the rapid growth in international trade, and the U.S. provision of security (i.e., an international public good) in the region have fostered the rapid growth of East Asian economies in the postwar era. To sustain the high growth rates, East Asian countries should continuously liberalize unilaterally to facilitate global free trade. It is their interest to liberalize and allow the U.S. economy to benefit from the expanding East Asian markets. As the U.S. share in world GDP declines, its incentives as a hegemonic power to sustain the global free trading system and to supply the international public good might diminish. With the greatest interest and stake in such a system, East Asia should cooperate with the United States to help strengthen the multilateral system and internalize the gains from the security and political stability in the region.

6. CONCLUDING REMARKS

Despite its grand vision for trade and investment liberalization, APEC members' "individual action plans" unveiled at the Subic Summit in November 1996 was somewhat modest. This was because the APEC members had agreed upon unilateral announcement and implementation of individual liberalization programs, rather than binding agreements. The lack of concessions on agricultural products by Japan and Korea, the absence of service trade liberalization in the great majority of action plans, and no acceleration by the developed members in their timetable to remove trade barriers on labor-intensive products have somewhat slowed down the momentum of APEC liberalization. Because ASEAN economies are relatively small, with a much heavier dependence on foreign trade, investment, and external markets for economic prosperity than the large APEC economies such as the United States and Japan, the stake for ASEAN countries is high.

ASEAN could take a leading role in giving APEC an impetus by extending its list of Common Effective Preferential Tariff offers to all APEC countries and challenging all the other APEC members to follow suit. This would be a significant step because the tariff reductions cover a wide range of commodities including food products, textiles and garments, wood products, chemicals, plastics, primary metals, machinery, electrical appliances, and precision instruments. This would lead to additional gains for both ASEAN and non-ASEAN countries of APEC beyond those expected to be realized from the individual action plans announced at the Subic Summit.

Aside from the proposed extension of ASEAN preferential trading arrangement to the other APEC members, the evolution toward free trade and investment should involve a concrete program for APEC that would move beyond the achievements of the Uruguay Round. This could start out by including a foreign investment code to facilitate trade and investment in the region and by strengthening dispute-settlement processes. APEC could also discuss issues ranging from competition policies to environmental and labor standards and promote regional agreements that might serve as a model at the global level. In addition, the development of an independent and authoritative mechanism that can monitor the extent of protection of each member country is needed. It is in the interest of ASEAN countries to take a more proactive role to nudge APEC economies toward these objectives.

REFERENCES

ASEAN (1990), Joint Statement of ASEAN Foreign and Economic Ministers, Kuching, Malaysia, February.

Baldwin, R. E., and Seghezza, E. (1996), "Trade-Induced Investment-Led Growth," National Bureau of Economic Research Working Paper No. 5582, May.

Barro, Robert (1991), "Economic Growth in a Cross-Section of Countries," *Quarterly Journal of Economics*, 106: 407–443.

Bergsten, C. Fred (1991), "Commentary: The Move Toward Free Trade Zones," in *Policy Implications of Trade and Currency Zones*, the proceedings of a symposium sponsored by the Federal Reserve Bank of Kansas City, Jackson Hole, WY.

Bhagwati, Jagdish N. (1991), *The World Trading System at Risk*, Princeton, NJ: Princeton University Press.

DeRosa, Dean A. (1995), *Regional Trading Arrangements Among Developing Countries: The ASEAN Example*, Research Paper Report 103, Washington, DC: International Food Policy Research Institute.

Hertel, Thomas W., ed. (1997), *Global Trade Analysis: Modeling and Applications*, Cambridge: Cambridge University Press.

Krugman, Paul (1991a), "Is Bilateralism Bad?" in E. Helpman and A. Razin, eds., *International Trade and Trade Policy*, Cambridge, MA: MIT Press.

——— (1991b), "The Move toward Free Trade Zones," in *Policy Implications of Trade and Currency Zones*, the proceedings of a symposium sponsored by the Federal Reserve Bank of Kansas City, Jackson Hole, WY.

Lawrence, Robert (1991), "Emerging Regional Arrangement: Building Blocks or Stumbling Blocks?" in R. O'Brien, ed., *Finance and International Economy*, Oxford: Oxford University.

Lee, Hiro, and David Roland-Holst (1995), "Trade Liberalization and Employment Linkages in the Pacific Basin," *Developing Economies*, 33: 155–184.

Levine, R., and Renelt, D. (1992), "A Sensitivity Analysis of Cross-Country Growth Regressions," *American Economic Review*, 82: 942–963.

Lewis, J. D., Robinson, S., and Wang, Z. (1995), "Beyond the Uruguay Round: The Implications of an Asian Free Trade Area," *China Economic Review*, 6: 35–90.

Summers, Lawrence (1991), "Regionalism and the World Trading System," in *Policy Implications of Trade and Currency Zones*, the proceedings of a symposium sponsored by the Federal Reserve Bank of Kansas City, Jackson Hole, WY.

Tan, Kong Yam (1996), "Regionalism in the Pacific Basin: Implications for the ASEAN Countries," Research Paper Series No. 96-49, Faculty of Business Administration, National University of Singapore, December.

Wang, Zhi (1994), "The Impact of Economic Integration Among Taiwan, Hong Kong and China: A Computable General Equilibrium Analysis," Ph.D. Dissertation, Department of Agricultural and Applied Economics, University of Minnesota.

Young, Linda, M., and Karen, M. Chye (1997), "Free Trade in the Pacific Rim: On What Basis?" in T. W. Hertel, ed., *Global Trade Analysis: Modeling and Applications*, Cambridge: Cambridge University Press.

Comment

Pearl Imada Iboshi

Regionwide economic arrangements in Asia have not taken root as they have in the Americas and Europe. Dr. Tan suggests that this is partly a reflection of the preference of the United States, the main power in the region, to have a hub-spoke bilateral relationship with its major Asian allies. Additionally, the severance of trade and investment linkages to China until the early 1980s made the other East Asian countries look across the Pacific for trade and markets.

I believe that Dr. Tan gives the United States far more credit than it deserves. A regionwide East Asia grouping would not have been possible in the postwar period. Even with the increased potential trade of China, a cooperative agreement would have been difficult to achieve both politically and economically. All of the countries would have been attempting to sell similar goods, and the low per-capita incomes would have limited sales. The reasons for the large trade with developed countries are based more on practical economic and market realities. This is clearly shown in the performance of ASEAN, the only formal regional trading institution that has been established in Asia.

ASEAN began with political rather than economic goals. It was nearly a decade after its initial formation that a real attempt was made to establish economic mechanisms for cooperation. Over the next years, ASEAN moved cautiously to expand coverage of its preferential trading arrangements until 1992 when the ASEAN Free Trade Area was officially endorsed. As with its earlier preferential trading arrangements, the member countries have continuously improved upon the initial agreement, expanding coverage and accelerating schedules. With these moves, trade among ASEAN countries has risen to 19.5 percent of their total trade as compared to 17.0 percent in 1990 (International Monetary Fund, *Direction of Trade Statistics Yearbook*). But this share compares to 46 percent for intra-NAFTA trade and 62 percent for intra-EU trade. The chapter points out that the only extensive trading relationship arises largely from Singapore's role as a port for entrepôt and reexports, trade and the large numbers of multinational corporations based in Singapore.

The main trade and investment partners of the ASEAN countries have been and continue to be developed countries despite the progress made toward freer trade among member countries. In fact, Dr. Tan indicates that the forces that encourage greater integration of the ASEAN economies are investments from industrialized countries and the NIEs. This shows that despite the encouragement of the United States and other countries, and the progress made toward freer trade among the countries under AFTA, economic and market conditions are not conducive to large increases in trade between member countries.

Using a CGE model developed in a previous paper, Dr. Tan's chapter indicates that the economic benefits of eliminating tariff and nontariff barriers in AFTA will be small and that most of the benefit will go to Singapore. This finding corresponds with those of earlier findings (e.g., Imada, 1993). He also indicates that the economic benefits will increase and shift to the other ASEAN countries as larger groupings, the EAEC and APEC, are considered.

Given this finding that the potential economic impact of AFTA is negligible to all except the richest country in the group, and that the member countries would benefit more from a wider trading arrangement, it seems reasonable to ask why so much effort is being spent on AFTA by the member countries. The chapter does not attempt to answer this question nor does it recommend that ASEAN countries refocus their efforts on the two larger groups.

Regarding the EAEG, Dr. Tan recommends that since "two wrongs do not make a right," East Asia should not follow North America and Europe and form a trading bloc of its own. He also points out that the disparity in the levels of development among the East Asian countries would make a free trade agreement an impossible task, and the high level of dependence on the U.S. market will make it costly to exclude the United States. These economic realities would have made the EAEG less than attractive to potential members even without opposition from North America and Australia.

But he argues that a formal grouping to facilitate consultation and consensus prior to negotiating with Europe, America, or the WTO would be useful. The common interest in East Asia to maintain access to the American and European markets would provide a good basis for such a group.

Dr. Tan's findings that ASEAN countries could gain substantially from freer trade among APEC members does not lead to a recommendation that ASEAN refocus its efforts away from AFTA toward APEC. ASEAN countries have been historically reluctant participants to the APEC process. Dr. Tan points out that the Kuching Consensus in early 1990 made it clear that members wanted to ensure that ASEAN's identity and cohesion would be preserved and not diluted in any enhanced APEC.

To take advantage of the benefits of free trade in the larger APEC region, and at the same time being sensitive to the concerns of dilution of the importance of ASEAN, Dr. Tan suggests that the

AFTA agreements can serve a purpose within the APEC context. ASEAN countries could thus take a leading role and extend their list of Common Effective Preferential Tariff offers to all APEC countries. By taking such an initiative, ASEAN can motivate other countries to increase their offers in the slow APEC voluntary process. This approach would have an additional benefit, not mentioned in the chapter, of allowing the ASEAN countries to determine the pace and breadth of the reductions in tariff and nontariff barriers.

This proposition makes eminent sense. It allows ASEAN countries to maintain a strong identity and yet extends free trade in a manner that increases the economic benefits to members. The problem with the voluntary approach taken by APEC is that unless one country or group of countries is willing to take the plunge and be the first one in the pool, no one will swim. ASEAN countries would be able to use the capital that they have invested in AFTA to realize the APEC vision of free trade in the region.

If ASEAN countries do not take such an initiative, it is likely that the interest in APEC will wane. Unfortunately, because of the focus on trade liberalization, the success of APEC will be judged by the concessions made by members to eliminate trade barriers. The diversity in the EAEG pointed out by Dr. Tan still exists in APEC, making the negotiations for free trade a difficult prospect.

Yet the potential benefit of APEC goes beyond trade liberalization. Trade and investment facilitation measures, including standardization of customs codes and procedures, and adoption of similar product standards and investment guidelines, can increase regional trade substantially (Imada Iboshi, Plummer, and Naya, 1996). In fact, as trade barriers are reduced under the WTO process, these facilitation measures become even more important. It is hoped that ASEAN countries will take the lead not only in trade liberalization but in trade facilitation as well.

REFERENCES

Imada, Pearl (1993), "Production and Trade Effects of an ASEAN Free Trade Area," *Developing Economies*, 31: 3–23.

Imada Iboshi, Pearl, Michael G. Plummer, and Seiji F. Naya (1996), "Evolutionary Integration: Building Blocks of Economic Cooperation in the Asia-Pacific Region," *Research in Asian Economic Studies*, Volume 7, Part A, Greenwich, CT: JAI Press.

PART IV

Foreign Direct Investment:
Determinants and Consequences

CHAPTER 7

The Determinants of Foreign
Direct Investment: A Survey
with Applications to the United States

Peter A. Petri and Michael G. Plummer

1. INTRODUCTION

As several contributions in this volume affirm, foreign direct investment (FDI) is emerging as an essential element in the economic
strategies of virtually all East Asian countries.[1] This is a relatively
new development. The earlier policy regimes of Japan and Korea
actively discouraged FDI. Many other countries heavily regulated
FDI flows, and often banned investments in key sectors. These
restrictions were typically aimed at U.S. FDI, which accounted for
nearly two-thirds of developed-country FDI outflows in the 1960s
and about one-half in the 1970s (Lipsey, 1993). But the positive
experiences of countries that welcomed FDI, including especially
Singapore and Malaysia, have shown that FDI can augment
national savings and foreign exchange without creating debt, and
can also provide access to technology and management know-how.
Today FDI is typically seen as a facilitator of development and technological catch-up, and even as a source of "leapfrogging technologies" that allow developing countries to bypass intermediate
stages of development in some industries.[2]

In line with these changing perspectives, many of the developing countries of the Asia–Pacific region have recently liberalized

We are grateful to Theresa Greaney and Shang-Jin Wei for suggestions on an earlier draft;
to Guangzhou Hu, Sulochana Musyayu, and Mauricio Jenkins for excellent research assistance; and to the Center for Global Partnership of the Japan Foundation for research
support.

[1] For a review of the literature pertaining to FDI in the development process, see James,
Naya, and Meier (1989).
[2] Using a model that builds on endogenous growth theory in the presence of sunk technological costs in developed economies, Brezis, Krugman, and Tsiddon (1993) show how
"leapfrogging" could be expected in certain industries.

restrictions on FDI and introduced promotional incentives. These policy measures have interacted with the region's attractive growth prospects, efficient production environment, and stable macroeconomic performance to produce impressive results. The region's FDI inflows have sharply expanded and now flow not only from traditional developed partners such as the United States and Japan but also from the region's own newly industrialized economies (NIEs) (Ramstetter and Plummer, 1991).

Commensurate with the boom in worldwide and Asia–Pacific FDI flows has been the extraordinary rise in international trade. The correlation is not spurious; intrafirm trade has grown to constitute over one-third of global trade, and trade and investment links are being increasingly recognized as inseparable. Yet econometric models that seek to gain insight into the determinants of either trade or investment usually ignore this link.[3]

This context helps to explain why several of the volume's chapters address FDI and its relationship with trade. As a starting point for these empirical analyses, this chapter offers a brief theoretical survey of the determinants of FDI and the key empirical characteristics of FDI flows. Section 2 begins with an analytical review of the FDI literature, with special attention to the relationship between FDI and trade. Section 3 describes recent patterns of U.S. multinational investment. Section 4 then summarizes some empirical results on the determinants of FDI, with special attention to trade-investment linkages. Section 5 offers concluding remarks.

2. OVERVIEW OF FDI THEORY

A key point of departure in the theory of foreign investment is the distinction between portfolio investment and FDI. The former includes private and public transactions in securities (e.g., stocks and bonds, sovereign debt, concessional loans from foreign donors). Portfolio flows can play a constructive role in economic development by providing investible funds and foreign exchange, and by sharing the risks of productive activity.[4] Foreign direct investment differs from portfolio investment because, by definition,

---

[3] Exceptions include Petri (1992) and Kawai and Urata (Chapter 8, this volume).

[4] It is not the purpose of this chapter to review at length the role of FDI in the development process. One source for such a review is Ramstetter (1991). In addition, this theoretical review borrows from Plummer and Montes (1994).

it involves substantial ownership control. Since control is typically associated with organizational and managerial participation by the investor, FDI produces a more complex matrix of economic interactions between source and host countries. The minimum stock ownership used to define "control" varies from country to country, but an investment is generally considered FDI if it involves at least 11 to 14 percent of the voting shares.

2.1. Theories of FDI

The economic literature on foreign investment is extensive.[5] Lizondo (1991) distinguishes between models that assume perfect markets for capital flows and those that depend on incomplete or imperfect markets. He identifies three approaches based on the assumption of perfect markets: (1) differential rates of return, (2) portfolio diversification, and (3) output and market size. In the first, foreign capital flows from regions with lower rates of return to those with higher rates. In the second, foreign capital flows are induced by opportunities to reduce the risk. In the third, foreign investment simply varies proportionally with activity, and hence with output and market size. The general problem with perfect-markets approaches, however, is that they fail to provide a special reason for FDI in contrast to portfolio investment. If the control of foreign activities involves some cost, then the foregoing objectives will be satisfied via arm's-length portfolio transactions rather than FDI.

The first complete theory of FDI based on imperfect markets is usually attributed to Hymer (1976). His approach built on Coase's (1937) view of the firm as an organization that overcomes market imperfections by replacing costly market transactions with internal transactions. Central to this approach is the idea of a "firm-specific asset" (FSA) – some capability unique to the firm that generates a lower return when transferred to another firm. Examples include technical knowledge, managerial expertise, distribution networks, product complementarities, credit advantages, brand recognition, and internalized economies of scale.

Firm-specific assets – for example, in technology and manufacturing know-how – can sometimes be exploited through licensing

---

[5] This review draws in part from Plummer and Montes (1994). See also Ramstetter (1993).

rather than FDI. A theory of FDI, therefore, needs to be based on FSAs that are not easily commercialized through markets – such as knowledge of the final markets for the manufactured goods. Buckley and Casson (1976) argue that advanced, large-scale multinationals rely on FSAs extensively by producing complex products requiring coordination of labor procurement and training, marketing, research and development, and so on.

In addition to firm-specific assets, a firm choosing to invest abroad needs to have a reason for producing abroad rather than exporting from home. Several theories focus on the factor endowment characteristics of the host country – for example, cheap labor or plentiful resources of a particular type. A novel endowment-based argument (Helpman, 1984) attributes multinational activity to the relative scarcity of managerial endowments in the host country. Helpman's model assumes differentiated products, economies of scale, and monopolistic competition, as well as a well-defined FSA (which includes, for example, management, marketing, and R&D). Helpman uses this model to describe endowment conditions under which firms decide to become multinationals and to explain trade patterns in which FDI is an important determinant.

The importance of endowment explanations, however, has been recently challenged on empirical grounds. Brainard (1993b) notes that while the factor proportions explanation of FDI may be theoretically valid, a close analysis of multinational investment patterns suggests that endowments do not play a major empirical role. Brainard uses tests involving the sales and export propensities of parent and affiliate production to find that only a minor element of U.S. FDI inflows in the late 1980s can be accounted for by factor endowment differences.

As an alternative to endowment-based explanations of FDI, Brainard (1993a), Horstman and Markusen (1992), and others have proposed theories based on market structure, involving new developments in microeconomic theory. Brainard (1993a) examines industries characterized by firm-level economies of scale, multistage production, differentiated products, and transport barriers, and she argues that firms will engage in two-way trade in the common "intangible" intermediate product instead of trade in the final product (i.e., FDI instead of trade) even in the absence of endowment differences. Horstman and Markusen (1992) note that the trade, trade policy, and multinational-activity literature works within a predetermined market structure. They endogenize market structure as a plant-location decision by firms, using FSAs as fixed-cost inputs and Cournot-Nash behavior by firms, and run simulations regarding the effects of changing commercial policies.[6]

All of these theories of FDI are encompassed in Dunning's (1985) "eclectic" approach. Dunning highlights three key requirements for direct investment: (1) the firm must possess "ownership advantages" over other firms (FSAs); (2) the firm must find it beneficial to utilize these advantages directly instead of selling or leasing them ("internalization" advantages); and (3) the firm must find it profitable to combine these advantages with at least one factor input abroad so that local production dominates exporting ("locational" advantages). Locational advantages include proximity to markets, specialized suppliers, evasion of protective barriers, and factor endowment advantages (Ramstetter, 1992).

2.2. FDI and Trade

Within the general context of FDI theory, the relationship between trade and investment has received special attention in a literature that begins with the seminal contributions of Kojima (1973) and Vernon (1966). Kojima distinguished between "trade-oriented" and "anti–trade-oriented" FDI. Trade-oriented investment occurs when the source country has a comparative *dis*advantage in the industry of the investment, and so capital flows toward countries with a comparative advantage in the activity. This kind of investment leads to greater trade and greater worldwide efficiency. Anti–trade-oriented investments occur in industries in which the source country has a comparative advantage, but investment nevertheless occurs, perhaps because of protection or oligopolistic competition. This kind of investment leads to diminished trade, market segmentation, and possibly reduced global welfare.

Vernon's "product life-cycle" hypothesis argues that FDI takes place as the production process of a new product in the innovating country (the United States) becomes standardized, making it more

[6] See also related work by Brainard (1997).

profitable to move production off-shore, first to other developed countries and eventually to developing countries. In this model, the investment flow initially tends to diminish trade by replacing exports, but as the industry shifts entirely abroad, it tends to increase trade again.

By the 1970s, the accumulated investment experience of U.S. multinationals abroad had considerably foreshortened the linear progression suggested by the product life-cycle hypothesis. As Vernon (1993, p. 62) argues:

The role played by experience during these early postwar decades could be seen even more directly by trends in the reaction times of U.S.-based firms in setting up foreign production facilities. Where new products were involved, U.S.-based firms characteristically set up their first production sites within the United States. Eventually, however, they set up production sites abroad as well; as these firms gained experience with producing in a given country, the time interval involved in setting up production facilities in the country for new products showed a marked decline. Moreover, as the number of foreign production sites in any product increased, the time interval in setting up another facility in a foreign country also declined. By the 1970s, therefore, U.S.-based firms were beginning to show less hesitation in setting up production subsidiaries abroad for their new productions and were scanning a rapidly widening circle of countries for their production sites. . . . The pattern toward which U.S.-owned multinational networks seem to be moving, therefore, is one in which the parent firm in the United States is prepared to survey different geographic locations on their respective merits, with a much reduced presumption in favor of a U.S. location.

In other words, experience gained in the investment process reduced the costs of producing abroad so much that even relatively new products could now be located in the country with the optimal factor endowments. In this context, provided that location makes a difference, foreign investment is likely to lead to the concentration of production and increased international trade.

The quotation just cited also calls attention to the powerful role of international experience in the investment process. The relatively limited role of FDI in most national economies suggests that foreign investment is costly, presumably because of the investing firm's inadequate knowledge of and experience in the foreign business environment. A history of successful investments and/or close contacts through trade and other economic linkages can substantially reduce this cost.

3. CHARACTERISTICS OF U.S. FDI

Perhaps because of abundant managerial and technological endowments, the lion's share of U.S. capital flows abroad is in the form of FDI instead of portfolio flows. The share of FDI in outward U.S. foreign investment was in the 59–75 percent range in the 1914–60 period, or nearly three times the corresponding share of FDI in foreign investment in the United States (Lipsey, 1993). In the decades after World War II, the United States became a major supplier of FDI to the world, accounting for nearly two-thirds of FDI outflows. This changed rapidly in the 1980s, as other countries became important investors, while U.S. outward FDI stagnated and the U.S. became a net importer of capital. By the late 1980s, the United States accounted for only one-sixth of world FDI outflows.

There are significant variations in the industry pattern of U.S. FDI into different host countries. As Table 7.1 shows, while the share of manufacturing is around one-half for all FDI destinations taken together, the range varied in 1994 from only 4 percent in Indonesia to 63 percent in Taiwan. In Indonesia, the most resource-rich ASEAN country (excluding Brunei), U.S. investment is dominated by petroleum.[7] In Hong Kong, over two-thirds of the $12 billion invested by the United States is in trade, banking, and finance; in Singapore and Taiwan, it is concentrated in manufacturing. Similar differences are evident in the subsectoral composition of investment within manufacturing. These differences are significant, because econometric analyses of FDI often lump all sectors together and then take observations from different countries as data points representing the same underlying relationship.

Table 7.2 provides additional data on the income that U.S. firms earned from FDI in selected countries over the 1984–94 period. In 1994, total income on U.S. FDI abroad came to $65 billion, the best (nominal) performance over the period. Income in Japan was highest at $3 billion, exceeding even the average for EC countries. After several years of losses, U.S. FDI in China became profitable in 1992 and came to $79 million in 1994, after reaching a peak of $130 million in 1993.

---

[7] Because the Indonesian government requires that most investment in the petroleum sector be undertaken as "product-sharing" arrangements that are not included in FDI calculations, the figures reflect a large downward bias, perhaps even being one-third of the true figure (see, for example, Naya et al., 1990).

Table 7.1. *US Direct Investment Position Abroad: Industry Cross-Sections, Selected Years (millions of US$)*

Sector	Japan			Taiwan			Korea			Hong Kong			Singapore		
	1982	1986	1994	1982	1986	1994	1982	1986	1994	1982	1986	1994	1982	1986	1994
All sectors	6,407	11,839	37,027	544	1,003	3,882	690	897	3,612	2,854	4,227	11,986	1,720	2,481	10,972
Petroleum	1,650	2,712	6,124	(D)	−11	(D)	(D)	8	88	330	235	552	553	455	2,127
All manufac.	3,058	5,560	15,844	340	745	2,459	167	341	1,391	333	553	1,902	615	1,456	5,316
Food products	166	159	1,121	25	40	96	(D)	47	261	3	(D)	(D)	4	15	112
Chemicals	778	1,588	3,634	87	235	894	58	116	291	66	188	99	32	146	122
Metals	67	125	298	(D)	(D)	(D)	7	(D)	66	18	−1	(D)	8	2	176
Machinery	1,103	1,828	4,425	(D)	122	280	0	(D)	40	80	(D)	435	119	308	2,556
Electronics	243	515	1,665	107	243	959	48	83	195	12	60	492	313	863	2,099
Transport equip.	380	703	1,842	(D)	26	(D)	−6	(D)	78	0	4	(D)	130	76	(D)
Other manufac.	322	642	2,860	43	(D)	97	(D)	45	460	153	117	652	9	46	(D)
Trade	1,093	2,303	6,844	62	166	528	(D)	(D)	422	778	1,649	4,209	191	302	1,638
Banking	166	209	420	115	47	435	132	282	1,426	512	340	1,094	288	153	489
Finance	312	782	6,400	7	22	168	(D)	160	204	459	1,246	3,013	36	58	690
Services	42	144	496	1	16	160	8	(D)	29	182	52	698	14	30	514
Others	85	131	900	(D)	19	(D)	34	22	51	260	152	517	25	27	197

Table 7.1 (continued)

Sector	Indonesia			Thailand			Malaysia			Philippines			China		
	1982	1986	1994	1982	1986	1994	1982	1986	1994	1982	1986	1994	1982	1986	1994
All sectors	2,295	3,369	5,015	780	1,152	3,762	1,221	1,019	2,382	1,315	1,274	2,374	49	183	1,699
Petroleum	1,958	3,044	4,341	484	726	1,185	(D)	613	396	410	123	(D)	39	(D)	675
All manufac.	134	98	181	161	274	1,341	245	301	1,582	366	558	1,167	11	43	765
Food products	(D)	6	(D)	8	6	50	6	9	5	23	190	350	0	(D)	128
Chemicals	38	54	83	23	49	290	20	19	66	153	186	417	2	4	188
Metals	(D)	4	7	5	10	(D)	5	1	(D)	8	10	31	0	0	10
Machinery	3	2	(D)	0	20	(D)	(D)	(D)	(D)	(*)	(*)	-2	0	8	29
Electronics	(D)	(D)	(D)	105	161	358	161	219	1,209	123	98	247	6	4	(D)
Transport equip.	0	0	(D)	0	0	(*)	0	0	0	(D)	-1	0	0	(D)	(D)
Other manufac.	49	(D)	(D)	20	28	105	(D)	(D)	208	(D)	75	124	3	(*)	89
Trade	30	(D)	58	(D)	48	344	45	63	142	81	60	177	0	(D)	131
Banking	7	(D)	111	36	75	365	13	1	57	149	239	321	0	(*)	(D)
Finance	17	19	(D)	5	9	63	(D)	24	153	(D)	106	(D)	0	0	(D)
Services	15	2	(D)	8	12	70	(D)	(*)	(*)	48	23	60	0	1	(D)
Others	133	(D)	259	(D)	9	394	(D)	18	53	(D)	165	67	0	7	38

(*): Value between −$500,000 and $500,000.
(D): Suppressed to avoid disclosure of data of individual companies.
Source: U.S. Department of Commerce, Bureau of Economic Analysis (BEA), International Investment Division.

Table 7.2. *Income from US Direct Investment Abroad, 1984–94 (millions of US$)*

Year	All countries	Japan	Hong Kong	Indonesia	Malaysia	Philip.	Singap.	Korea	Taiwan	Thailand	China	EC average[a]
1984	30,746	870	637	1,985	377	129	524	174	193	95	-91	501
1985	28,778	823	543	1,434	324	103	402	181	107	154	-87	1,646
1986	31,040	1,788	682	667	125	168	519	109	107	154	-61	1,561
1987	40,028	2,026	1,087	944	227	146	729	132	318	179	-72	2,257
1988	52,057	2,621	1,058	859	380	206	825	196	344	296	-36	1,931
1989	53,929	2,070	1,282	1,057	231	270	727	245	443	471	-56	1,863
1990	58,004	1,722	1,200	1,886	469	227	1,127	269	341	358	-20	2,210
1991	52,087	2,293	1,540	1,785	505	232	1,138	70	414	408	-12	1,930
1992	50,565	1,979	1,855	1,509	666	369	1,539	143	411	435	2	1,470
1993	59,175	1,723	2,100	1,251	701	409	1,835	218	423	438	130	1,644
1994	64,789	2,894	1,664	1,308	583	440	1,593	339	583	720	79	1,946
Total	521,198	20,809	13,648	14,685	4,588	2,699	10,958	2,076	3,684	3,708	-224	18,959

[a] EC average based on ten countries (1984–85) and twelve countries (1986–94).
Source: Department of Commerce, *Survey of Current Business*, various issues.

In general, U.S. affiliates abroad had an important impact: They employed 6.7 million laborers worldwide in 17,724 ventures.[8] They also had a major impact on world trade: Their worldwide intrafirm trade amounted to $190 billion. Moreover, contrary to the popular impression that U.S. multinationals are responsible for the U.S. trade deficit, their global intrafirm trade balance was a positive $14 billion.

4. IMPLICATIONS FOR EMPIRICAL ANALYSIS: TRADE-FDI LINKS

Modern FDI theory spans many different modeling approaches, but the "eclectic theory" provides a general framework for categorizing the factors that affect a firm's decision to invest abroad. Other theories in turn suggest specific lists of "ownership," "internalization," and "location" advantages.

The principal connections between FDI and trade analyzed in the literature run from FDI to trade. The Kojima and product life-cycle models, for example, suggest specific signs for the impact of FDI on trade, depending on the investment's characteristics. More generally, however, the sign of the investment-trade relationship is not clear (Petri, 1992; Aitken, Hanson, and Harrison, 1994). Be that as it may, the time structure of most models of the investment-trade relationship suggests that changes in FDI at a particular time cause changes in trade at a later time. Evidence that FDI causes trade would support the trade-oriented theories of Kojima, Vernon, and others.

As we argue in Petri and Plummer (1996), at the same time that FDI causes trade, there are also reasons to expect trade to cause FDI. Exports from a country that is contemplating FDI may help to develop the market for its products in a prospective FDI host country by building market acceptance and reputation. At the very least, prior exports will reduce the investor's uncertainty in undertaking FDI. Prior trade may also reduce the investor's transaction costs by financing the acquisition of information about the host country's market that is also necessary for undertaking an investment.

---

[8] Data for this paragraph and the next were taken from Department of Commerce, *Survey of Current Business*, 1990 (Benchmark Survey).

Based on these arguments, Petri and Plummer (1996) and some empirical contributors to this volume use international trade explicitly (and successfully) as an explanatory variable for subsequent FDI flows. To be sure, the significant coefficient of the trade variable in FDI equations also incorporates the contributions of omitted variables that affect FDI and are closely proxied by trade. For example, the attractiveness of a host country's markets to a particular investor should be ideally represented by a variable that captures the host's potential demand for the investor's particular varieties. To the extent that this also affects the investor's prior export's missing measure of the market's interest in the investor's product, the trade variable will be simply a proxy for some common and omitted determinant of both FDI and trade. Similarly, certain transaction costs between the investing and host economies (which presumably negatively affect investment) may affect trade as well as FDI, and in the absence of an explicit measure of these costs, the trade variable will serve as a proxy for them.[9]

While the causal and proxy reasons cannot be fully separated in this research, Petri and Plummer (1996) and other studies do find evidence that a vigorous bilateral trade flow tends to be positively associated with a subsequent bilateral FDI flow. Coupled with findings of a positive empirical effect of trade on investment, these interactions suggest a type of "hysteresis" (an idea associated with the trade literature of the 1980s) in which trade flows help to pave the way for later investment flows and vice versa. Thus an intense trading relationship may help to set the stage for more investment and then still more trade in the future.

5. CONCLUSIONS

Firms are increasingly conscious of investment opportunities abroad, and transaction costs associated with international activities appear to be declining, from transportation and communications costs to cultural differences. In this context, many firms are developing new global corporate strategies that place increasing reliance on international direct investment flows. Although in the

---

[9] Many, but not all, transaction costs between economies affect both investment and trade linkages. Costs shared by both types of linkages include, for example, the investments needed to overcome cultural differences. Transport costs, however, may more directly affect trade than investment, as discussed in the empirical sections of this study.

past FDI was thought to be a substitute for exports, this does not appear to be the case with actual FDI; trade is increasing rapidly alongside FDI, and intrafirm trade in particular is comprising an increasing share of international trade.

Reflecting the complexity and variety of actual FDI flows, the analytical literature on FDI has shifted decisively toward explanations based on imperfect markets and a broad range of explanatory factors. The dominant paradigm (Dunning's "eclectic" approach) encompasses numerous specific explanations that highlight various dimensions of factor endowments and of market structure.

While there has been progress in identifying a wide range of FDI determinants in the analytical literature, much remains to be done on the empirical side. In particular, the empirical links between FDI and trade, FDI and technology transfer, and, more generally, FDI and economic development need to be established more firmly. Some of the chapters cited in this survey, as well as several chapters in this volume, constitute an effort to address this gap.

REFERENCES

Aitken, Brian, Gordon H. Hanson, and Ann E. Harrison (1994), "Agglomeration Economies, Foreign Investment, and Export Behavior," mimeo, International Monetary Fund, July.

Brainard, S. Lael (1993a), "A Simple Theory of Multinational Corporations and Trade with a Trade-Off between Proximity and Concentration," NBER Working Paper No. 4269, February.

(1993b), "An Empirical Assessment of the Factor Proportions Explanation of Multinational Sales," NBER Working Paper No. 4583, December.

(1997), "An Empirical Assessment of the Proximity-Concentration Tradeoff between Multinational Sales and Trade," *American Economic Review*, 87 (September): 520–544.

Brezis, Elise S., Paul R. Krugman, and Daniel Tsiddon (1993), "Leapfrogging in International Competition: A Theory of Cycles in National Technological Leadership," *American Economic Review*, 83 (December): 1211–1219.

Buckley, Peter J., and Mark Casson (1976), *The Future of the Multinational Enterprise*, London: Macmillan.

Coase, Ronald H. (1937), "The Nature of the Firm," *Economica*, 4: 386–405.

Dunning, John H. (1985), *Multinational Enterprises, Economic Structure and International Competitiveness*, New York: John Wiley.

Helpman, Elhanan (1984), "A Simple Theory of International Trade with Multinational Corporations," *Journal of Political Economy*, 92: 451–472.

Horstmann, Ignatius, and James Markusen (1992), "Endogenous Market Structure in International Trade," *Journal of International Economics*, 32: 109–129.

Hymer, S. H. (1976), "The International Operations of National Firms: A Study of Direct Foreign Investment," Ph.D. dissertation, Massachusetts Institute of Technology.

James, William E., Seiji Naya, and Gerald Meier (1989), *Asian Economic Development*, Madison: University of Wisconsin Press.

Kojima, Kiyoshi (1973), "A Macroeconomic Approach to Foreign Direct Investment," *Hitotsubashi Journal of Economics*, 14: 1–21.

Lipsey, Robert E. (1993), "Foreign Direct Investment in the United States: Changes over Three Decades," in K. Froot, ed., *Foreign Direct Investment*, Chicago: University of Chicago Press and NBER.

Lizondo, J. Saul (1991), "Foreign Direct Investment," in International Monetary Fund, *Determinants and Systemic Consequences of International Capital Flows*, Washington, DC: International Monetary Fund.

Naya, Seiji, Kernial S. Sandhu, Michael G. Plummer, and Narongchai Akrasanee (1990), *ASEAN–U.S. Initiative*, Singapore: Institute of Southeast Asian Studies.

Petri, Peter A. (1992), "Platforms in the Pacific: Trade Effects of Direct Investment in Thailand," *Journal of Asian Economics*, 3: 173–196.

Petri, Peter A., and Michael G. Plummer (1996), "The Determinants of U.S. Direct Investment Abroad: Evidence of Trade-Investment Linkages," Brandeis University, GSIEF Working Paper, July.

Plummer, Michael G., and Manuel Montes (1994), "Direct Foreign Investment in China: An Introduction," in S. LaCroix, M. G. Plummer, and K. Lee, eds., *Emerging Patterns of East Asian Investment in China*, New York: ME Sharpe.

Ramstetter, Eric D., ed. (1991), *Direct Foreign Investment in the Asia-Pacific Region*, Boulder: Westview Press.

Ramstetter, Eric D. (1992), *Foreign Direct Investment and Exports of Manufactures from Developing Economies. Part I: Economic Policies*, mimeo prepared for the UNCTAD Secretariat.

(1993), *Foreign Direct Investment in the Asia–Pacific Region*, a monograph prepared for UNCTAD.

Ramstetter, Eric D., and Michael G. Plummer (1991), "Motives and Policies Affecting Direct Foreign Investment in ASEAN," *Asian Economic Journal*, 5: 175–197.

Vernon, Raymond (1966), "International Investment and International Trade in the Product Cycle," *Quarterly Journal of Economics*, 80: 190–207.

(1993), "Where Are the Multinationals Headed?" in K. A. Froot, ed.,

Foreign Direct Investment, Chicago: University of Chicago Press and NBER.

Comment

Jeffrey H. Bergstrand

Peter Petri and Michael Plummer have compiled a balanced and insightful survey article on the theoretical and empirical determinants of foreign direct investment (FDI). First, the authors offer a succinct organized review of the predominant competing theories of FDI and of the theoretical relationship between FDI and international trade. Regarding theoretical determinants of FDI, the authors note (though ineffectively at the subsection's conclusion) that Dunning summarizes the likely critical elements that FDI source firms should possess: an ownership advantage, an internalization advantage, and a locational advantage. The authors cite recent important works in the theory of multinationals that shed light on theoretical determinants of FDI, such as Helpman (1984) and Brainard (1993a,b, 1997), which provide conceptually sharp discussions of the important factors underlying multinational firm behavior.

Although overall quite thorough in their survey, the authors did omit discussing an important recent paper by Markusen and Venables (1995). Markusen and Venables present a two-country analytical model in which each country has one national firm and one multinational firm. National firms are distinguished (from multinationals) by producing all output in the base country, facing only one set of fixed plant costs and one set of fixed firm (i.e., headquarters) costs. Multinationals face fixed firm costs at home but fixed plant costs at home and abroad (the latter representing FDI). The foreign plant produces solely for the local market. Markusen and Venables show that, in equilibrium, multinational firms are more likely to exist when incomes are high, firm-level scale economies are high relative to plant-level scale economies, and transport costs and tariffs are high. For instance, when transport costs are high, the gains from exporting by taking advantage of plant economies of scale are eroded relative to producing and selling output locally (consistent with Brainard's work), and international trade is lower. This theoretical result suggests that international trade should be higher when fewer firms are multinational, in the absence of outsourcing (which is precluded in their model). This theoretical framework provides some justification for several empirical findings by Kawai and Urata in Chapter 8, this volume. Kawai and Urata, using a gravity equation empirical framework, find that international trade and distance are negatively related. FDI and distance are positively related; if FDI is prominent when multinationals exist, and multinationals are more likely to exist when transport costs are high, then distance and FDI should be positively correlated.

The authors here discuss the contribution of recent work by Brainard (1993a,b, 1997) as well. Brainard's papers are important in refining the relationship between theoretical and empirical determinants of multinational firm sales and investment. Using gravity equations, Brainard finds weak support for factor proportions differences to explain affiliate sales of multinational firms but strong support for proximity-concentration factors. She finds that freight factors have a strong dampening effect on trade flows, as typical gravity equation estimations find. However, freight factors have small or insignificant effects on affiliate sales. Furthermore, multinationals' export sales decrease with higher transport costs, but local sales are unaffected or, in some cases, increase. This is consistent with the empirical results of Kawai and Urata in the next chapter.

Empirical work by Petri and Plummer (1996), as well as the subsequent chapters in this volume by Kawai and Urata, Jai-Won Ryou, and Shang-Jin Wei, use the gravity equation as an econometric modeling tool for exploring: (1) the determinants of FDI, and (2) the relationship between trade flows and FDI flows. The gravity equation has been used much less frequently to model (foreign direct) investment flows in contrast to (merchandise) trade flows. The gravity equation's success in modeling trade flows has a long and rich history. General equilibrium models of international trade in Anderson (1979), Helpman and Krugman (1985), and Bergstrand (1985, 1989, 1990), discussed recently in Deardorff (1998), have provided rigorous theoretical rationales for the gravity equation's empirical success. However, a rigorous theoretical framework for using the gravity equation to model (foreign direct) investment flows is lacking at present, as noted in the comment of Kawai and Urata in this volume.

Yet the recent work by Brainard and by Markusen and Venables, already cited, suggests that the gravity equation is likely a useful empirical device for analyzing investment flows; a recent contribution in this dimension is Hufbauer, Lakdawalla, and Malani (1994). General equilibrium theories suggest that multinational firms are more likely to exist (and hence increase investment flows into new plants abroad) when countries are more similar in size. It is straightforward to show that bilateral flows are related multiplicatively to national output levels (as gravity equations represent) in the context of these models when the countries are more equally sized. Also, these recent theoretical models suggest that multinational firms (and hence FDI) are more likely to exist when transport costs are high. This is consistent with the gravity equations of investment flows reported in Kawai and Urata but is inconsistent with those reported in Ryou and in Wei.

Finally, recent anecdotal evidence suggests that multinational FDI flows to quite distant regions and countries (with commensurately high transport costs) are generally for the purpose of localizing production for local sales, tending to impede world trade. Multinational FDI flows to closer foreign countries (with commensurately low transport costs) are generally for shifting intermediate production abroad for later import and final distribution at home (i.e., outsourcing), tending to augment (intrafirm) international trade. Clearly, more research is warranted to establish more clearly the theoretical and empirical linkages between international trade, multinational sales, and foreign direct investment.

REFERENCES

Anderson, James E. (1979), "A Theoretical Foundation for the Gravity Equation," *American Economic Review*, 69 (March): 106–116.

Bergstrand, Jeffrey H. (1985), "The Gravity Equation in International Trade: Some Microeconomic Foundations and Empirical Evidence," *Review of Economics and Statistics*, 67: 474–481.

(1989), "The Generalized Gravity Equation, Monopolistic Competition, and the Factor-Proportions Theory in International Trade," *Review of Economics and Statistics*, 71: 143–153.

(1990), "The Heckscher-Ohlin-Samuelson Model, the Linder Hypothesis, and the Determinants of Bilateral Intra-Industry International Trade," *Economic Journal*, 100: 1216–1229.

Brainard, S. Lael (1993a), "A Simple Theory of Multinational Corporations and Trade with a Trade-Off between Proximity and Concentration," NBER Working Paper No. 4269, February.

(1993b), "An Empirical Assessment of the Factor Proportions Explanation of Multinational Sales," NBER Working Paper No. 4583, December.

(1997), "An Empirical Assessment of the Proximity-Concentration Tradeoff between Multinational Sales and Trade," *American Economic Review*, 87: 520–544.

Deardorff, Alan (1998), "Determinants of Bilateral Trade: Does Gravity Work in a Neoclassical World?" in Jeffrey A. Frankel, ed., *The Regionalization of the World Economy*, Chicago: University of Chicago Press.

Helpman, Elhanan (1984), "A Simple Theory of International Trade with Multinational Corporations," *Journal of Political Economy*, 92: 451–472.

Helpman, Elhanan, and Paul Krugman (1985), *Market Structure and Foreign Trade*, Cambridge, MA: MIT Press.

Hufbauer, Gary, Darius Lakdawalla, and Anup Malani (1994), "Determinants of Direct Foreign Investment and Its Connection to Trade," United Nations Conference on Trade and Development (UNCTAD), *UNCTAD Review*, New York: United Nations.

Markusen, James R., and Anthony J. Venables (1995), "Multinational Firms and the New Trade Theory, NBER Working Paper No. 5036, February.

Petri, Peter A., and Michael G. Plummer (1996), "The Determinants of U.S. Direct Investment Abroad: Evidence of Trade-Investment Linkages," Brandeis University, GSIEF Working Paper, July.

CHAPTER 8

Are Trade and Direct Investment Substitutes or Complements? An Empirical Analysis of Japanese Manufacturing Industries

Masahiro Kawai and Shujiro Urata

1. INTRODUCTION

Interdependence among countries has increased substantially since the end of World War II. The main force behind this growing interdependence is international trade. Indeed, it is the rapid expansion in world trade, resulting largely from liberalization of manufacturing trade, that has led to substantial growth of the world economy. In recent years, however, foreign direct investment (FDI) has become a major contributor to deepening interdependence among countries. Between 1980 and 1996, world FDI grew at an annual average rate of 12.6 percent, significantly higher than the corresponding growth rate of 6.5 percent for world trade (both in nominal terms).[1]

Rapid FDI expansion has given rise to an important and interesting question regarding the relationship between FDI and international trade. Does international trade promote or discourage FDI? Does FDI facilitate or restrict international trade? These questions concern whether FDI and trade are complements or substitutes (i.e., whether they exert positive or negative influences on each other).

Theoretically, FDI and trade can be either complements or substitutes. Within the framework of the Heckscher-Ohlin (H-O)

An earlier version of this chapter was presented at the International Conference on Economic Development and Cooperation in the Pacific Basin, held in Berkeley, California, on June 30–July 1, 1995. The authors thank Hiro Lee, Julia Lowell, David Roland-Holst, other conference participants, and anonymous referees for their helpful comments and discussions. Urata acknowledges research support from the Japan Foundation's Center for Global Partnership. David Leheny provided editorial assistance.

[1] International Monetary Fund, *Balance of Payments Statistics Yearbook*, various issues, and *International Financial Statistics Yearbook*, various issues.

model, Mundell (1957) showed that FDI and trade are perfect substitutes; in other words, trade reduces incentives for FDI and vice
versa. In contrast, by relaxing the assumptions used in the H-O
model, Markusen (1983) obtained a case where FDI and trade can
be complements. Specifically, he demonstrated that FDI expands
trade when trade is induced by non–H-O factors, such as differences
in technologies between trading partners. A crucial determinant of
this relationship is whether FDI is undertaken in an export industry or import-competing industry in the host country. FDI undertaken in an export industry tends to expand trade, while FDI
undertaken in an import-competing industry tends to reduce trade.
As for the impact of trade on FDI, non–H-O models that take into
account dynamic changes in trade and production structures, such
as the product cycle model, give rise to a causal relationship where
trade promotes FDI. Given the theoretical possibility of the two con-
trasting relations between FDI and trade, the question of which
type of relationship actually exists is an empirical issue.

Rapid economic growth in developing countries of East Asia in
recent years that has been accompanied by rapid FDI and trade
expansion appears to lend support to the argument that FDI and
trade are complements. Indeed, a number of empirical studies have
shown the presence of a strong nexus between FDI and trade and
the contribution of this nexus to rapid economic growth in East
Asia.[2] Both internal and external factors in the East Asian countries have contributed to the creation of the FDI-trade nexus.
Important internal factors include the liberalization policies concerning manufacturing trade and inward FDI adopted by these
countries, as these policies not only attract export-oriented FDI but
also promote manufacturing exports from these countries. As for
external factors, substantial realignments of the currencies in East
Asia, such as a sharp appreciation of the Japanese yen in the
1985–88 period and the subsequent appreciation of the Korean won
and the New Taiwan dollar, have encouraged outflows of FDI from
Japan, Korea, and Taiwan to other developing East Asian countries,
particularly in export-oriented manufacturing industries.

Given the importance of sectoral differences in the scale and performance of FDI flows, one problem of the past studies is their
exclusive focus on the overall relationship between FDI and trade

---

[2] See, for example, Kawai (1994b) and Petri (1995).

at the aggregated level. Such an approach, though useful, masks variations in the FDI–trade interaction at the sectoral level. The purpose of this chapter is to investigate the relationship between Japan's outward FDI and its trade in eight manufacturing industries by explicitly taking into consideration its FDI destinations and trading partners. The choice of Japan is due to the availability of data and Japan's importance in FDI and trade in East Asia.

The chapter is structured as follows. Section 2 reviews recent trends in Japanese outward FDI, paying special attention to its geographical and industrial composition and its role in East Asia. Sections 3 and 4, respectively, discuss the motives behind Japanese FDI and the patterns of sales and procurement by overseas affiliates of Japanese firms, both of which have important influences on the interaction between Japan's FDI and trade flows. Section 5 undertakes an econometric examination of such interactions by using a gravity model. Section 6 concludes the chapter.

2. RECENT TRENDS IN JAPAN'S FOREIGN DIRECT INVESTMENT

2.1. Overall Review

Japan's FDI increased very rapidly and underwent major changes in its regional and sectoral composition in the latter half of the 1980s (Figures 8.1 and 8.2).[3] The scale of FDI during the four-year period of 1986–89 was unprecedented, far exceeding the total FDI from all previous years combined. The FDI/GDP ratio rose from 0.4 percent in 1980 to 2.4 percent in 1989. The FDI boom during this period coincided with the beginning of a series of structural adjustments not only in Japan but also in other parts of East Asia. Equally as dramatic as the size of the boom was the pace at which the outflows declined after reaching a peak in 1989; the FDI/GDP ratio went down to a meager 0.3 percent in 1993.

Japan's FDI in the 1980s was directed largely to North America and Europe, mainly in services and manufacturing. These two developed regions together absorbed two-thirds of Japan's FDI outflows. Although a smaller share of Japan's FDI went to East Asia in the 1980s, investments in manufacturing were relatively active.

---

[3] This section draws on Kawai (1994b).

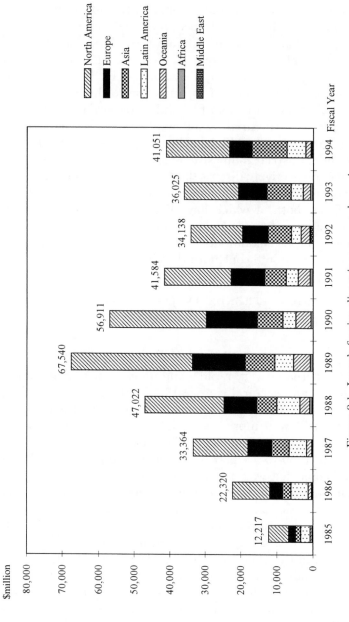

Figure 8.1. Japan's foreign direct investment, by region.

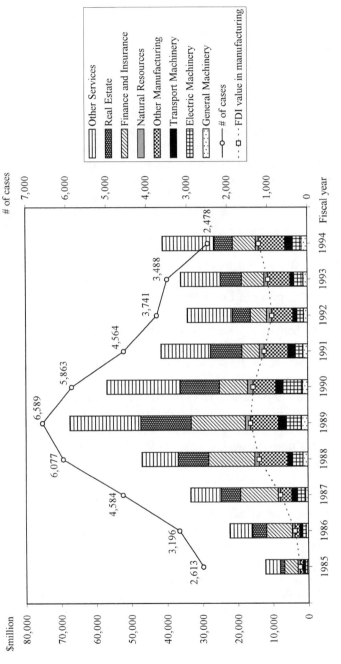

Figure 8.2. Japan's foreign direct investment, by industry and sector.

Changes have occurred in the patterns of Japan's FDI in the 1990s, however. First, Japan's direct investment in East Asia has started to rise, resulting in an increase in the region's share in Japan's total FDI. Second, manufacturing firms have become increasingly active in FDI, particularly in East Asia.

Several factors might be attributable to the changes in the volume and the regional and sectoral composition of Japanese FDI in the latter half of the 1980s. First, the globalization of business activities that started in the early 1980s, made possible by a rise in Japanese firms' managerial and technological capabilities, was a natural underlying factor behind the surge of Japanese FDI. The rapid and sharp appreciation of the Japanese yen was apparently the most important macroeconomic factor leading to the expansion of FDI in the second half of the 1980s as well as during the 1992–95 period.

The sharp appreciation of the yen stimulated Japanese FDI in two ways. One was the dramatic "relative price" effect. The yen appreciated by 37 percent between 1985 and 1988 on a real, effective basis using the International Monetary Fund (IMF)'s index of relative normalized unit labor costs. These relative price effects substantially reduced Japan's international price competitiveness. To cope with the rise in domestic costs relative to other countries, Japanese firms in the tradeable sector had three choices. First, they could reallocate their productive resources (capital, labor, R&D stocks, and managerial resources) away from the tradeable sector to the nontradeable sector. Second, they could upgrade their technology and productivity within the tradeable sector and increase the proportion of high value-added products. The third choice was that Japanese firms could move their production base from the home market to foreign countries where production costs were lower. These were precisely the industrial structural adjustments that the Japanese economy underwent in the latter half of the 1980s, and the process resumed in the first half of the 1990s in the face of renewed yen appreciation.

Another way in which yen appreciation had a positive impact on Japanese FDI outflows was the "liquidity" or "wealth" effect. To the extent that yen appreciation made Japanese firms relatively more "wealthy" in the sense of increased collateral and liquidity, it enabled them to finance outward FDI relatively more cheaply than their foreign competitors. In addition, the Bank of Japan injected liquidity into the economy in the second half of the 1980s, pushing up the prices of stock shares and land. Such an increase in liquidity and the subsequent asset-price inflation also had a positive impact on Japan's FDI outflows.[4] Indeed, the prices of Japanese stock shares rose by 80 percent (Nikkei Stock Index) between 1987 and 1989, contributing to a surge in Japanese investment outflows. However, the stock index declined by almost 40 percent between 1989 and 1990, exerting a detrimental influence on Japan's FDI outflows in the first few years of the 1990s.

The second important factor underlying the recent changes in the regional and sectoral composition of Japan's FDI was trade friction with, and protectionist sentiment in, industrial host countries such as the United States and European countries. Trade friction between Japan and the United States goes back to the 1960s and has spread from textiles, electrical appliances (e.g., color television sets and audio-video equipment), steel, and automobiles to high-technology products such as machine tools and semiconductors in the past three decades. The Japanese industries faced with friction with the United States have tried to adopt voluntary export restraints (VERs) and/or to invest directly in the United States. The textile, color television, and steel industries chose to establish VERs, the electrical appliance industry chose to make direct investments in the United States, and the automobile industry did both. Japanese firms that have shifted their production base to developing East Asia have been able to avoid direct trade conflicts while exporting their products from the host country to the U.S. market.[5]

The third factor affecting the sectoral composition of Japan's FDI is that the need for financial and other supporting services rose as Japanese subsidiaries expanded their business activities in the host countries. In addition, FDI in the real estate industry increased due to sharp increases in land prices in Japan during the so-called "bubble economy" period in the second half of the 1980s.

[4] Kawai (1994a) shows that Japan's exchange rate appreciation and inflation in shares and stock prices, relative to those of the other industrialized countries, had a significant effect on FDI outflows in the 1980s.

[5] See Kawai and Urata (1996) for empirical evidence of such triangular trade patterns.

2.2. Japan's FDI in the Developing East Asian Economies

Since the 1980s, Japan's direct investment in East Asia has primarily been aimed at the manufacturing and service sectors. A distinct characteristic of Japanese FDI in Asia is the relatively large share of manufacturing in comparison with other regions. Major factors behind Japan's manufacturing FDI in East Asia include the region's robust economic growth, low unit labor costs, liberalization and pro-FDI policies, and the yen appreciation.

Since the mid-1980s, geographical distribution of Japan's FDI within Asia has changed significantly, from the newly industrializing economies (NIEs) of Korea, Taiwan, Hong Kong, and Singapore to the Association of Southeast Asian Nations (ASEAN),[6] then to China and other Asian economies in transition. The Asian NIEs attracted FDI until the late 1980s through FDI promotion policies. In particular, policymakers in Korea, Taiwan, and Singapore promoted inward FDI in their pursuit of high-tech industrialization. These countries enjoyed high growth rates, to a large extent induced by the simultaneous expansion of trade and inward FDI.

However, Japan's FDI in the Asian NIEs reached a peak in the late 1980s just as overall Japanese FDI also peaked. The Asian NIEs started to lose some of their cost advantages due to rapid wage increases and currency appreciation. In addition, they graduated from the U.S. Generalized System of Preferences (GSP) status in 1989, thereby further reducing their attractiveness as host countries for FDI. Firms in Japan and other industrialized economies therefore started to explore other East Asian countries such as ASEAN as hosts for investment. Labor-intensive manufacturing firms in the NIEs also began to shift their operations to ASEAN and other Asian countries.

Japanese FDI in the ASEAN-4 (Malaysia, Thailand, Indonesia, and the Philippines) used to be mainly in the resource-intensive sectors, a reflection of the relative abundance of natural resources in the region. This type of investment, however, has not increased significantly in recent years largely due to the stagnation of resource prices. Instead, investment in manufacturing industries

---

[6] This observation applies to new FDI. A lack of data precludes one from obtaining accurate statistics, but there are signs showing that Japan's FDI undertaken with reinvested earnings has grown in the ASEAN countries. See, for example, Okamoto and Urata (1994) for the case of Malaysia.

has been prompted by appreciation of the yen since 1985, as well as appreciation of the NIEs' currencies against ASEAN's. In particular, FDI flows from Japan and the NIEs to ASEAN countries increased sharply in the late 1980s although the trend varied greatly across source countries. In addition, the ASEAN countries' shift from inward-oriented to outward-oriented strategies and their unilateral liberalization of trade and inward FDI flows in manufacturing industries have been important factors in attracting FDI to ASEAN. Such regime changes have been prompted by the earlier success of outward-oriented policies in the NIEs.

FDI inflows into China have also grown quickly since the late 1980s, resulting from China's gradual but persistent economic reforms, open-door liberalization policy, and the political and social stability of the country despite the Tiananmen Square incident in 1989. As of 1995, China was the largest recipient of Japanese FDI in Asia. The coastal area of China has attracted capital not only from Japan, Hong Kong, and Taiwan but also from the ASEAN countries and has been enjoying the most rapid economic growth in the whole of East Asia. Capital inflows have been the vehicle of economic transformation of China, dynamically changing its trade patterns and industrial structure. The strong interaction between FDI and trade has contributed to the rapid change. As a result of the emergence in some ASEAN countries of serious obstacles to business operations such as shortage of developed infrastructure and skilled manpower, the relative attractiveness of China as a host to FDI has increased. In recent years, Japan's outward FDI in other Asian countries such as Vietnam and India, though still small in scale, has begun to rise.

2.3. Japan's Manufacturing FDI in East Asia

Japanese manufacturing FDI in East Asia is characterized by a steady rise with relatively small fluctuations compared to overall Japanese FDI in East Asia. It increased more than sevenfold in eight years, from US$0.5 billion in 1985 to US$3.7 billion in 1993. The rate of increase in Japanese manufacturing FDI in East Asia during the period was greater than the rate of increase in Japan's manufacturing FDI in the world, and the share of East Asia rose from 19.6 percent in 1985 to 32.9 percent in 1993. The share of manufacturing in overall Japanese FDI in East Asia also rose from

32 to 55 percent over the 1985–93 period. The geographical shift in the importance of Japanese manufacturing FDI away from the NIEs to ASEAN and then to China is pronounced.

Sectoral composition of Japanese manufacturing FDI in East Asia has changed notably since the latter half of the 1980s (Table 8.1). The most remarkable development is the sharp expansion of Japanese FDI in the electric machinery (including electronics) sector. Until the mid-1980s, Japanese FDI in electric machinery in East Asia was relatively small compared with other sectors. In the Asian NIEs, Japanese FDI in chemical products, general machinery, and transport machinery was respectively greater than that in electric machinery; in ASEAN, Japanese FDI in transport machinery, iron and steel, and textiles was larger than that in electric machinery. However, since the mid-1980s, electric machinery has become the sector with the most active FDI. In China, Japanese FDI also became the largest in electric machinery between the mid-1980s and the early 1990s. It is interesting to observe that the largest recipient of Japanese FDI in electric machinery changed from the NIEs in 1986–88 to ASEAN in 1989–93 (figures not shown in the table), which was closely followed by China.

The relative importance of Japanese manufacturing FDI in sectors other than electric machinery differs across countries in East Asia. Based on the cumulative FDI over 1986–93, chemicals and food had a large share of Japanese FDI in the Asian NIEs, while chemicals and primary metals (ferrous and nonferrous metals) had a large share in ASEAN. In addition to these sectors, machinery and transport machinery also recorded large shares in both the Asian NIEs and ASEAN. The fact that a sizable amount of Japanese FDI was directed to material-producing sectors in East Asia, such as chemicals and primary metals, may be explained by the increased demand for materials due to rapid industrialization not only in the host countries but also in East Asia as a whole.

3. MOTIVES BEHIND JAPANESE FOREIGN
DIRECT INVESTMENT

A number of factors promoting recent Japanese FDI were noted in the previous section. This section examines the motives behind Japanese FDI in more detail, because these motives influence the relationship between FDI and trade patterns, which is our main concern in this chapter.

Several questionnaire surveys on the motives of Japanese firms for undertaking FDI are conducted on a regular basis. The most comprehensive is a survey conducted by the Ministry of International Trade and Industry (MITI).[7] Table 8.2 summarizes the results of the MITI survey on the motives for Japanese FDI in manufacturing in Asia, North America, and Europe. One common motive behind Japanese FDI in the three regions is the importance of local sales. Expansion of local sales is a particularly important motive for Japanese FDI in North America and Europe. Indeed, as many as 80 percent of the respondents indicated local sales as one of their motives for undertaking FDI in these regions. Obviously, high purchasing power of local population is one factor explaining the importance of local sales as a motive behind Japanese FDI in these developed regions. In addition, the survey results reveal that some Japanese firms set up plants for local sales to avoid trade friction. Japanese FDI undertaken with such a motive would reduce Japanese exports by replacing them with local production.

The share of respondents indicating that local sales is an important motive was significantly lower for Japanese FDI in Asia compared to that in North America and Europe, at around 60 percent. By contrast, the export motive captured a relatively large share among the Japanese firms undertaking FDI in Asia. Approximately one out of four firms responded that exporting to the third countries (i.e., countries other than Japan) was one of their motives, while one out of five firms indicated that exporting to Japan was one of their motives.[8] One would therefore expect that Japanese FDI in East Asia tends to stimulate exports from host countries to Japan. The large number of respondents identifying the use of local

---

[7] The MITI conducts a comprehensive survey of overseas activities of Japanese firms every three years. The results of the survey are published under the title of *Kaigai Toshi Tokei Soran [Comprehensive Survey of Overseas Activities of Japanese Firms]*. In the 1992 survey, a questionnaire was sent to 3,378 Japanese multinationals, 1,594 of which responded. The respondents covered the activities of 7,108 overseas affiliates. The Export-Import Bank of Japan also conducts a questionnaire survey asking a number of questions, including motives, every year, but its coverage is significantly smaller.

[8] Although the share of firms expressing export as a motive for undertaking FDI in Europe is quite large, the export for most of these cases may be classified as de facto local sales. This is because the European Union may be considered as a single market.

Table 8.1. *Japanese Foreign Direct Investment in Manufacturing in East Asia ($US million)*

A. 1983–1985 (cumulative)

Host country	Food	Textiles	Wood & paper	Chem. prod.	Primary metals	General mach.	Electric mach.	Transp. mach.	Other manuf.	Manuf. total
NIEs	27.9	11.0	3.4	240.5	28.6	169.3	117.2	126.5	90.1	814.5
Hong Kong	9.7	3.1	0.3	3.5	...	1.8	8.4	...	4.8	31.6
Korea	6.4	4.7	0.6	9.5	4.2	12.7	27.2	26.8	13.3	105.4
Singapore	10.2	0.8	0.7	207.6	11.4	134.5	44.7	4.1	20.7	434.7
Taiwan	1.6	2.4	1.8	19.9	13.0	20.3	36.9	95.6	51.3	242.8
ASEAN-4	37.3	165.8	23.5	56.0	175.5	40.2	66.2	179.1	55.6	799.2
Indonesia	4.0	117.9	15.4	28.5	75.4	3.4	11.3	57.2	22.0	335.1
Malaysia	3.3	16.9	5.7	6.4	88.1	3.2	30.5	82.5	21.6	258.2
Philippines	11.3	...	0.1	6.3	6.7	0.3	2.2	34.5	2.2	63.6
Thailand	18.7	31.0	2.3	14.8	5.3	33.3	22.2	4.9	9.8	142.3
China	14.4	2.4	1.5	5.7	4.4	3.2	4.2	0.6	7.8	44.2
East Asia total	79.6	179.2	28.4	302.2	208.5	212.7	187.6	306.2	153.5	1,657.9

Table 8.1 (continued)

B. 1986–1993 (cumulative)

Host country	Food	Textiles	Wood & paper	Chem. prod.	Primary metals	General mach.	Electric mach.	Transp. mach.	Other manuf.	Manuf. total
NIEs	727.2	258.3	62.4	927.8	564.2	593.5	1,675.9	518.4	865.1	6,192.8
Hong Kong	83.6	50.1	3.3	37.2	61.8	145.6	321.9	46.4	191.6	941.5
Korea	83.4	45.1	8.5	208.9	88.1	141.8	374.0	276.1	140.3	1,366.2
Singapore	465.7	131.0	31.7	449.1	93.2	145.6	480.9	9.6	202.8	2,009.6
Taiwan	94.5	32.1	18.9	232.6	321.1	160.5	499.1	186.3	330.4	1,875.5
ASEAN-4	381.9	594.2	382.0	2,142.1	1,211.4	953.4	3,000.7	863.6	1,535.6	11,064.9
Indonesia	83.4	279.4	244.3	1,473.7	302.4	46.9	204.3	289.3	161.5	3,085.2
Malaysia	25.4	26.3	84.9	300.3	297.0	249.2	1,351.6	143.1	896.6	3,374.4
Philippines	39.2	14.7	7.7	61.3	125.0	25.2	327.2	170.1	101.4	871.8
Thailand	233.9	273.8	45.1	306.8	487.0	632.1	1,117.6	261.1	376.1	3,733.5
China	160.6	474.7	55.1	167.7	159.7	417.0	895.9	132.1	535.7	2,998.5
East Asia total	1,269.7	1,327.2	499.5	3,237.6	1,935.3	1,963.9	5,572.5	1,514.1	2,936.4	20,256.2

Source: Ministry of Finance, International Finance Bureau Annual Report, various issues.

Table 8.2. *Motives behind Japanese Foreign Direct Investment in Manufacturing in Various Regions of the World: 1992*

Industry	World					Asia				
	Local sales	Exports to third countries	Exports to Japan	Use of local labor	To avoid trade friction	Local sales	Exports to third countries	Exports to Japan	Use of local labor	To avoid trade friction
Manufacturing total	69.6	22.3	14.6	43.6	8.6	62.4	25.5	21.1	65.0	2.0
Food	50.0	22.5	26.1	29.6	2.8	53.2	30.6	27.4	48.4	0.0
Textiles	55.6	31.6	31.0	69.6	0.6	50.8	32.3	37.9	80.6	0.0
Wood and pulp	33.3	2.8	33.3	33.3	8.3	20.0	6.7	33.3	46.7	0.0
Chemical products	75.8	18.9	10.1	29.0	7.3	77.7	20.2	12.4	44.6	1.6
Iron and steel	84.6	9.9	4.4	41.8	4.4	82.7	13.5	5.8	59.6	0.0
Nonmetallic prod.	77.2	16.3	15.2	46.7	10.9	82.6	23.9	17.4	76.1	0.0
General machinery	73.6	20.1	4.2	39.3	8.8	64.4	26.4	9.2	64.4	3.4
Electric machinery	71.0	25.2	13.8	43.6	9.0	59.6	28.2	20.6	70.6	1.8
Transport mach.	74.1	15.2	12.6	41.7	18.4	68.8	15.0	18.8	65.6	8.8
Precision inst.	66.7	29.3	14.7	32.0	10.7	45.5	27.3	27.3	60.6	3.0
Coal and petro. prod.	50.0	12.5	25.0	25.0	0.0	50.0	0.0	25.0	50.0	0.0
Other manufac.	67.5	27.1	17.1	55.6	6.3	55.2	31.2	26.8	69.2	0.4

Table 8.2 (continued)

Industry	North America					Europe				
	Local sales	Exports to third countries	Exports to Japan	Use of local labor	To avoid trade friction	Local sales	Exports to third countries	Exports to Japan	Use of local labor	To avoid trade friction
Manufacturing total	78.8	12.0	10.4	14.4	15.7	80.9	31.4	2.1	21.4	13.0
Food	53.2	10.6	25.5	10.6	0.0	58.3	16.7	8.3	8.3	0.0
Textiles	100.0	20.0	0.0	20.0	10.0	63.6	54.5	0.0	18.2	0.0
Wood and pulp	53.8	0.0	30.8	15.4	7.7	66.7	0.0	0.0	33.3	33.3
Chemical products	78.6	8.3	9.5	10.7	7.1	75.4	31.6	1.8	7.0	3.5
Iron and steel	90.0	6.7	0.0	16.7	13.3	100.0	0.0	0.0	0.0	0.0
Nonmetallic prod.	81.3	3.1	9.4	9.4	12.5	80.0	60.0	0.0	20.0	20.0
General machinery	76.4	9.7	1.4	23.6	33.3	78.7	21.3	1.6	21.3	23.0
Electric machinery	77.2	14.8	11.1	8.0	15.4	89.7	34.2	3.2	14.8	16.8
Transport mach.	86.5	11.7	11.7	14.4	27.9	62.2	28.9	0.0	17.8	26.7
Precision inst.	87.0	34.8	8.7	17.4	13.0	80.0	26.7	0.0	0.0	0.0
Coal and petro. prod.	50.0	0.0	0.0	0.0	0.0	...			...	
Other manufac.	82.2	13.1	10.3	22.4	9.3	86.5	35.1	1.4	55.4	1.4

Note: The figures indicate the percentage share of the firms indicating the motive in total number of surveyed firms.
Source: Ministry of International Trade and Industry, *Kaigai Toshi Tokei Soran [Comprehensive Statistics on Japanese Foreign Direct Investment]*, No. 5, 1994.

labor as their motive for FDI in East Asia suggests that Japanese firms shift their production base to East Asia in order to produce labor-intensive products for exports. Japan has long lost a comparative advantage in labor-intensive products, and Japanese firms are increasingly utilizing abundant labor in developing Asian countries. Japanese FDI in textiles may be a typical example reflecting such an FDI strategy on the part of Japanese firms.

A large number of Japanese machinery manufacturers noted the use of local labor as a motive for FDI. Although the machinery sector is capital intensive, this behavior may be explained by the Japanese firms' strategy of breaking up the production process into several subprocesses and locating labor-intensive subprocesses in labor-abundant countries. Such an arrangement gives rise to a production system under which an international division of labor is pursued within a firm, leading to the emergence of interprocess, intrafirm, and intraindustry trade.[9]

We have already noted that export expansion is an important motive for Japanese FDI in East Asia. Expansion of export-oriented FDI by Japanese firms has taken place largely in response to the trade liberalization policies implemented by a number of East Asian countries in recent years.[10] Differences in the motives for Japanese FDI in different regions are reflected in the trade patterns of foreign affiliates, which are analyzed in the next section.

4. TRADE PATTERNS OF JAPANESE AFFILIATES IN HOST COUNTRIES

To find the basic relationship between Japan's FDI and trade, we now examine trade patterns of Japanese affiliates in host countries. We conduct our analysis at the sectoral level and by the geographical location of affiliates. As before, special attention is focused on the FDI-trade relationship involving Japan and East Asia. We begin by examining the procurement patterns of foreign affiliates and then turn to their sales patterns.

---

[9] See Urata (1993) for empirical evidence.

[10] For a concise discussion on the recent experiences of trade and FDI liberalization in several Asian countries, see, for example, Institute of Developing Economies (1994).

4.1. Procurement and Import Patterns

Beginning with the sources of procurement of intermediate goods by foreign affiliates of Japanese firms, one finds approximately 40 percent of total procurement coming from Japan for all the foreign affiliates (Table 8.3). The degree of reliance on Japan for the supply of intermediate goods is slightly lower for the affiliates in Asia than for those in North America or in Europe. One reason why Asian affiliates depend less on Japan for the supply of intermediate goods appears to be related to their relatively long history.[11] Procurement networks are relatively well developed, making it unnecessary for affiliates in Asia to purchase the intermediate goods from Japan.

The patterns of procurement of intermediate goods by foreign affiliates of Japanese firms differ substantially among sectors. The four machinery sectors (general machinery, electric machinery, transport machinery, and precision instruments) rely heavily on Japan for the supply of intermediates. A main reason for this is underdevelopment of local procurement networks for high-quality parts in the host countries.

Production of machinery requires a large number of parts and components, and the competitiveness of machinery products crucially depends upon the quality of parts. Furthermore, it is often the case that production of certain machinery requires parts specifically made for those products. Machinery producers have adopted a type of product development called "design-in," whereby new products and new parts are developed simultaneously. The adoption of design-in reflects the importance of ensuring the quality and specificity of parts for manufacturing products. These characteristics of machinery production lead to a closer relationship between parts suppliers and assemblers or producers of finished products. In many cases, the parent firms become major suppliers of parts to their foreign affiliates because of the limited availability of the required parts in local markets.

In addition to the required characteristics of parts such as

---

[11] These assertions are supported by the following observations: The percentage share of affiliates established before 1980 in total number of affiliates in Asia as of 1992 was 35.8 percent, significantly higher than the corresponding shares for the affiliates in Europe and North America, respectively, at 28.9 and 24.3 percent (MITI, *Kaigai Toshi Tokei Soran*, 1994).

Table 8.3. *Procurement and Sales of Foreign Affiliates of Japanese Firms: 1992 (percent of total procurement or sales)*

A. Procurement

Industry	World			Asia			North America			Europe		
	Local proc.	Imp. from Japan	Imp. from third count.	Local proc.	Imp. from Japan	Imp. from third count.	Local proc.	Imp. from Japan	Imp. from third count.	Local proc.	Imp. from Japan	Imp. from third count.
Manufac. total	46.5	40.9	12.6	48.5	37.9	13.6	51.5	41.7	6.8	28.8	44.6	26.6
Food	84.8	6.1	9.1	72.0	4.5	23.5	86.1	9.2	4.7	99.7	0.1	0.2
Textiles	44.4	20.8	34.8	40.7	22.4	36.9	81.7	18.3	0.0	11.1	27.0	61.9
Wood and pulp	89.1	7.8	3.1	83.7	13.2	3.1	93.0	5.9	1.1	58.8	23.1	18.1
Chemical prod.	64.9	26.2	8.9	71.4	16.9	11.7	70.3	28.1	1.6	41.8	46.0	12.2
Iron and steel	75.5	16.4	8.1	29.0	47.3	23.7	99.4	0.6	0.0	...	...	...
Nonmetallic prod.	67.0	9.9	23.0	64.8	9.2	26.0	73.8	12.8	13.4	69.0	19.1	11.9
General mach.	43.4	47.6	9.0	49.0	47.8	3.2	48.6	44.1	7.3	32.1	52.3	15.6
Electric mach.	26.6	53.8	19.6	36.6	46.7	16.7	25.0	65.6	9.4	15.6	50.3	34.1
Transport mach.	55.1	39.3	5.6	52.9	43.8	3.3	57.3	36.3	6.4	45.0	41.8	13.2
Precision inst.	22.7	58.3	19.0	34.2	60.2	5.6	28.8	67.1	4.1	9.4	51.7	38.9
Petroleum prod.	86.8	10.3	2.9	92.6	3.8	3.6	63.6	36.4	0.0	...	...	...
Other manufac.	61.8	24.2	14.0	58.6	27.5	13.9	64.1	30.3	5.6	63.7	11.2	25.1

Table 8.3 *(continued)*

B. Sales

Industry	World			Asia			North America			Europe		
	Local proc.	Imp. from Japan	Imp. from third count.	Local proc.	Imp. from Japan	Imp. from third count.	Local proc.	Imp. from Japan	Imp. from third count.	Local proc.	Imp. from Japan	Imp. from third count.
Manufac. total	76.7	6.3	17.0	66.1	15.8	18.1	91.9	2.8	5.3	55.7	1.2	43.1
Food	63.7	20.8	15.5	46.0	26.5	27.4	78.7	18.5	2.8	84.2	14.8	1.0
Textiles	58.5	11.3	30.2	56.1	14.2	29.7	99.0	1.0	0.0	53.4	3.0	43.6
Wood and pulp	47.7	32.5	19.8	50.2	47.2	2.7	49.0	33.9	17.1	72.2	0.0	27.8
Chemical prod.	64.5	4.9	30.6	64.7	4.9	30.4	80.1	5.4	14.5	45.3	1.4	53.3
Iron and steel	95.8	0.8	3.4	85.5	2.1	12.4	98.0	0.6	1.4	100.0	0.0	0.0
Nonmetallic prod.	67.7	18.1	14.2	63.3	21.4	15.3	89.4	5.1	5.5	27.3	3.1	69.6
General mach.	72.3	4.2	23.5	53.0	23.6	23.4	86.1	0.8	13.0	57.2	0.5	42.4
Electric mach.	60.6	9.3	30.1	45.7	27.2	27.1	89.2	2.6	8.1	45.0	1.2	53.8
Transport mach.	94.1	1.4	4.5	92.6	1.7	5.7	96.4	1.1	2.5	82.3	0.5	17.2
Precision inst.	71.4	21.3	7.3	36.9	51.8	11.3	94.7	3.6	1.6	92.6	1.1	6.3
Petroleum prod.	58.1	0.8	41.1	55.9	0.0	44.1	68.9	7.1	24.0	0.0	0.0	0.0
Other manufac.	80.7	4.4	14.9	78.6	9.4	12.0	94.8	2.8	2.5	61.4	0.9	37.7

Source: Ministry of International Trade and industry, *Kaigai Toshi Tokei Soran [Comprehensive Statistics on Japanese Foreign Direct Investment]*, No. 5, 1994.

quality and specificity, timing of parts delivery is important for machinery firms to produce products competitively. This is because the cost associated with maintaining inventories can be minimized by reducing the amount of inventories held at production plants, which in turn is achieved by synchronizing the timing of delivery and use of parts. In order to establish such arrangements efficiently, parent firms become major suppliers of parts to their foreign affiliates.

So far, to explain the high intrafirm trade ratios for the machinery sectors, we have focused on factors related to production, that is, the requirement of a large number of parts and components for the production of machinery. One can also identify another characteristic of machinery, the need for after-sales services such as repair and maintenance, that also tends to promote a closer relationship between affiliates and parent firms in the procurement of parts. This is because provision of such services may require parts supplied by the parent firms.

High dependency on Japan for the supply of intermediate goods in the machinery sectors is observed for the affiliates in all three regions. As for the affiliates in Asia, the iron and steel industry also exhibits high dependency on Japan. This may reflect the fact that heavy industries, which supply materials to the iron and steel industry, have not been developed in Asia. In contrast to the high dependency on Japan for the supply of intermediate goods in machinery and iron and steel, the dependency is low in coal and petroleum products, food, nonmetallic minerals, and wood and pulp, because natural resources used for the production of these products are abundant in Asia.

4.2. Sales and Export Patterns

Turning to the sales patterns of foreign affiliates of Japanese firms, one finds that on average 6.3 percent of their sales are exported to Japan. However, the average share hides wide variations in the shares of exports to Japan in total sales among the affiliates in different regions and sectors. The percentage share of exports in total sales is quite high for the affiliates in Asia, registering 15.8 percent, while the corresponding shares are significantly lower for the affiliates in North America and Europe, respectively registering 2.8 and

1.2 percent. These observations are consistent with the aforementioned findings on the motives of Japanese FDI in different regions.

One observes wide variations in the share of exports in total sales across sectors. Among the affiliates of Japanese firms, wood and pulp, precision instruments, food, and nonmetallic products exhibit high export shares; the corresponding shares are significantly smaller for iron and steel, coal and petroleum products, and transport machinery. Several factors leading to high export shares are examined in detail later. One important reason for the low export shares in iron and steel and transport machinery is that these sectors receive little incentive to export because they are given import protection.

For the affiliates in Asia, the shares of exports to Japan in total sales are particularly high for precision instruments and wood and pulp; approximately 50 percent of their sales are exported to Japan. These two sectors are followed by electric machinery, food, general machinery, and nonmetallic products, each showing approximately 25 percent of their sales being exported to Japan. By contrast, the shares of exports to Japan in total sales are very limited for transport machinery, iron and steel, and chemical products.

High shares of exports to Japan observed for wood and pulp, as well as food, reflect the strategy of Japanese firms to develop and import these natural resource-based products in East Asia, which are in short supply in Japan. High export shares to Japan for machinery sectors excluding transport machinery are largely attributable to the global strategies of Japanese firms in these sectors. Specifically, two types of strategies may have led to such an outcome. One is product differentiation, and the other is interprocess specialization. Under the product differentiation strategy, firms assign the production of low-technology or labor-intensive products to their Asian affiliates, while technology-intensive products are assigned to plants based in Japan. Products manufactured under such an arrangement are traded to serve the respective markets; low-tech products manufactured in Asia are exported to Japan, while high-tech products manufactured in Japan are exported to Asia.

Under the interprocess specialization strategy, Japanese firms seek to minimize production cost by dividing the entire production process into a number of subprocesses and by locating each subprocess in a country where that particular subprocess may be performed most efficiently, or at least cost. For example, the production of television sets takes place in the following manner: TV tubes and integrated circuits are produced at a parent firm in Japan and shipped to the subsidiary in Asia. There, television sets are assembled using the imported components, and some of the final products are exported back to Japan. One should note that not only final products but also some intermediate goods are exported to the parent firms in Japan. Such procurement practices, called "international sourcing," by parent firms in Japan has been increasing in recent years as the technological capabilities of their Asian affiliates have improved. The international production arrangement formed under this strategy may be described as interprocess specialization, and the international trading pattern that emerges as a result may be described as interprocess, intrafirm, intraindustry trade. As with product differentiation strategy, the assignment of production processes is determined mainly by the technological capabilities and factor proportions of the countries in the arrangement.

These two types of production strategy pursued by Japanese firms lead to the situation where relatively large proportions of general machinery, electric machinery, and precision instruments are exported by Asian affiliates to Japan. It should be added that an earlier observation of high reliance on Japan for parts supply in the machinery sectors could be explained by the interprocess, intrafirm, international strategy adopted by Japanese firms.

An examination of the patterns of procurement and sales of foreign affiliates of Japanese firms in this section indicates the presence of a strong, positive relationship between Japanese FDI and trade. Japanese FDI in East Asia tends to stimulate Japanese export significantly, and this positive effect appears similar regardless of destinations of FDI and export. Among manufacturing sectors, the effect is particularly strong in machinery and in iron and steel. Japanese FDI also stimulates Japanese imports, particularly in the case of East Asia, though this positive effect appears small in comparison to the impact of Japanese FDI on Japanese exports. The effect of Japanese FDI on Japanese imports is relatively strong for wood and pulp, precision instruments, and food in all countries, and for nonmetallic products, general machinery, and electric machinery in Asia.

5. ECONOMETRIC ANALYSIS OF INTERACTIONS BETWEEN JAPAN'S FDI AND TRADE

5.1. The Gravity Model

This section examines econometrically the extent of interactions between Japan's bilateral FDI outflows and trade for eight manufacturing sectors. The findings in the previous sections suggest the presence of different types of such interactions across different sectors. The empirical analysis in this section is an attempt to test the presence of FDI-trade interactions by extending the "gravity model" of bilateral trade flows.

The standard gravity model of international trade relates bilateral trade flows to the levels of economic activity in the exporting and importing countries and to the distance between them.[12] We extend this framework to examine how Japan's FDI and trade flows are interrelated. In particular, we ask whether Japan's FDI and trade are complements or substitutes. If FDI and trade affect each other positively and exhibit "two-way" interactions, they are clearly complements, and if FDI and trade affect each other negatively, they are clearly substitutes. To examine this, we run two types of regression equations separately, one for Japan's bilateral trade, and the other for Japan's bilateral FDI outflows, by including the size of FDI in the first equation and the volume of trade in the second equation as explanatory variables.[13]

An advantage of using the gravity model is its empirical success in explaining bilateral trade flows. Although the gravity model is often criticized for the lack of solid theoretical foundations, several studies have shown that theoretical support exists for the model.

---

[12] See Drysdale and Garnaut (1982) and Deardorff (1998) for a survey of the gravity approach. Frankel (1993), Frankel and Wei (1993), Eaton and Ho (1993), and Eaton and Tamura (1994) recently applied this framework to issues of regional trade arrangements and the determinants of trade flows. In addition, Eaton and his co-authors estimated the FDI flow equation using the gravity model and examined the correlation between the residuals in the trade and FDI equations. Kawai (1994b) examined the FDI-trade interactions more directly than Eaton and his co-authors did, using aggregated data for Japan's trade and FDI outflows. This chapter extends Kawai's approach and tests the relationship by using disaggregated manufacturing data.

[13] This chapter focuses on the role of Japanese FDI outflows and does not analyze the role of FDI inflows. This is because the amount of FDI inflows to Japan has been small, and until very recently, the Ministry of Finance has not published detailed country cum industry breakdown data for inflows.

Anderson (1979) demonstrated that gravity equations can be derived from the properties of expenditure systems under the assumptions of similarities in preferences for traded goods, in trade tax structures, and in transport structures across countries. Deardorff (1998) demonstrated that the use of gravity equations could be justified by standard trade theories such as the Heckscher-Ohlin model. He suspected, however, that gravity equations could not be used to test any one model because they are designed to cover a large class of trade models. In light of these observations, our estimates should be interpreted with some caution.

5.2. Trade Equations

The first regression equation we examine is that for trade. The dependent variable in the trade equation is *TRADE* (exports, imports, or exports plus imports), in log form, between Japan and its trading partner in a given year. We have a maximum sample of forty-eight countries over the 1980–92 period for eight manufacturing sectors, that is, food, textiles, wood and pulp, chemical products, primary metals, general machinery, electric machinery, and transport equipment (see the Appendix Table). The two most important explanatory variables are, first, the economic sizes of Japan and the trading partner (*GNP* expressed in U.S. dollars) and, second, the geographical distance between Tokyo and the capital or major city of each trading partner (*DISTANCE* expressed in kilometers).[14] Other explanatory variables used are per capita income (*GNP/POP*), two regional dummy variables (*APEC* and *EAEC*), and, most importantly, the FDI outflow variable (*FDIFLOW*(-1)).

The basic gravity equation to be estimated is

$$\log TRADE_{ij} = \alpha_0 + \alpha_1 \left(\log GDP_i + \log GDP_j \right)$$

$$+ \alpha_2 \left(\log \frac{GDP_i}{POP_i} + \log \frac{GDP_j}{POP_j} \right) + \alpha_3 DISTANCE_{ij}$$

$$+ \alpha_4 APEC_i + \alpha_5 EAEC_i + \alpha_6 FDIFLOW_{ij} \left(-1 \right) + u_{ij}$$

(8.1)

[14] This is the essence of the "gravity model," named for the analogy with the law of gravitational attraction between masses. The *DISTANCE* variable is taken from Gary L. Fizpatrick and Marilyn J. Modlin (1986), *Direct-Line Distances: International Edition*, London: Scarecrow Press.

Here, a subscript j refers to Japan, and i refers to an individual trading partner ($i = 1, 2, \ldots$, n). The regional dummy variable *APEC* is expected to capture how much of Japan's active trade with APEC members (Asian NIEs, ASEAN-4, China, Australia, New Zealand, United States, Canada, Mexico, and Chile) may be attributable to a special regional effect. The regional dummy variable *EAEC* (Asian NIEs, ASEAN-4, and China) is included to examine if and to what extent Japan's trade is influenced by a special regional factor associated with East Asia. The FDI variable included on the right-hand side of the equation is the last period's outflow of Japan's FDI in trade partner i. The FDI used is a variable for the last period, rather than the current period, to ensure that it is exogenous with respect to the *TRADE* variable.[15]

The ordinary least squares (OLS) regression results are reported in Tables 8.4a–8.4c. These tables respectively summarize the results when the dependent variable *TRADE* is represented by exports, imports, and the sum of exports and imports. The results largely confirm earlier findings in the literature: *GNP* and *GNP/POP* have positive and statistically significant effects on trade, and *DISTANCE* has a negative and statistically significant impact on trade, in almost all manufacturing sectors. Exceptions are found in some of the sectors, however. Specifically, *GNP/POP* has negative and significant influence on imports of wood and pulp and on exports of primary metals, and *DISTANCE* has a positive and significant impact on imports of primary metals.

The positive and statistically significant coefficients on *GNP/POP* in textiles, chemical products, general machinery, electric machinery, and transport equipment (Tables 8.4a and 8.4b) suggest that Japan's trade in these products is of an intraindustry type. This is because intraindustry trade tends to take place between countries with similar levels of income and that Japan's per capita GNP is one of the highest in the world. This interpretation is also sup-

---

[15] It should also be noted that *TRADE* is a calendar year variable ending in December of the current year while *FDIFLOW* is a fiscal year variable ending in March of the following year. The *TRADE* variable is obtained from the AIDXT (Ajiken Indicators for Development Extended Trade), which is the Institute of Developing Economies' trade data retrieval system, built upon the United Nation's (UN) trade statistics by incorporating the information on UN nonmember economies such as Taiwan. The *FDIFLOW* variable is from the Ministry of Finance's unpublished data. *GNP* and *POP* variables are taken from the World Bank, *World Tables*, International Monetary Fund, *International Financial Statistics*, and Asian Development Bank, *Key Indicators of Developing Asian and Pacific Countries*.

Table 8.4a. *Gravity Model of Japan's Bilateral Exports (Pooled Sample for 1980–92)*

	Food	Textiles	Wood & pulp	Chemical products
Constant	9.465**	15.385**	−1.092	4.128**
	(2.830)	(1.500)	(1.193)	(1.086)
log GNP_i + log GNP_j	0.014	0.331**	0.436**	0.544**
	(0.062)	(0.037)	(0.029)	(0.030)
(log GNP_i/POP_i + log GNP_j/POP_j)	0.636**	0.124**	0.282**	0.055**
	(0.084)	(0.036)	(0.041)	(0.027)
log $DISTANCE_{ij}$	−1.582**	−1.772**	−0.701**	−0.951**
	(0.259)	(0.119)	(0.103)	(0.088)
APEC	0.809**	0.913**	1.420**	0.448**
	(0.289)	(0.121)	(0.122)	(0.094)
EAEC	0.190	−0.436**	0.695**	0.772**
	(0.458)	(0.218)	(0.181)	(0.162)
log $FDIFLOW(-1)$	0.167**	0.039**	−0.021*	0.064**
	(0.031)	(0.013)	(0.012)	(0.010)
Adjusted R^2	0.455	0.703	0.804	0.803
Sum of Squared Errors	2080.3	411.6	192.0	262.1
No. of Observations	482	486	347	512

Note: The dependent variable is log *EXPORT*, where *EXPORT* is Japan's exports to its trading partner.
Numbers in parentheses are the estimated standard errors of the coefficients.
* significant at the 10 percent level.
** significant at the 5 percent level.

ported by the positive and statistically significant coefficients on *FDIFLOW*, as is discussed later, in both the export and import equations for these products, which indicate the possibility of intraindustry, interprocess division of labor and of "reverse" imports. In addition, machinery products are often claimed to be subject to product differentiation, which tends to induce intraindustry trade.

In contrast, the finding that the coefficient on *GNP/POP* for exports of primary metals is negative and statistically significant (Table 8.4a) suggests that Japan's export of metal products is

Table 8.4a *(continued)*

	Primary metals	General machinery	Electric machinery	Transport equipment
Constant	8.862** (1.868)	6.428** (1.448)	−1.185 (1.072)	−1.873 (1.895)
log GNP_i + log GNP_j	0.535** (0.043)	0.404** (0.031)	0.470** (0.028)	0.447** (0.050)
(log GNP_i/POP_i + log GNP_j/POP_j)	−0.284** (0.045)	0.083** (0.030)	0.304** (0.025)	0.344** (0.047)
log $DISTANCE_{ij}$	−0.772** (0.154)	−0.729** (0.103)	−0.487** (0.080)	−0.407** (0.152)
APEC	1.559** (0.157)	0.539** (0.095)	0.472** (0.083)	1.163** (0.155)
EAEC	0.380 (0.268)	0.036 (0.187)	0.689** (0.188)	−0.187 (0.259)
log $FDIFLOW(-1)$	0.019 (0.014)	0.085** (0.011)	0.058** (0.009)	0.004 (0.014)
Adjusted R^2	0.632	0.721	0.820	0.499
Sum of Squared Errors	670.6	234.2	188.5	636.4
No. of Observations	508	451	482	486

driven by differences in per-capita incomes, or relative factor endowments (particularly capital/labor ratios), and is not of an intraindustry type. Japan tends to export primary metals to relatively poor, labor-abundant countries, reflecting differences in comparative advantage. The general observation that product differentiation in primary metals is not particularly extensive also supports the view that intraindustry trade is not very active in these products.

An unexpected positive coefficient on *DISTANCE* in the import equation for primary metals may reflect the crucial importance of the presence of natural resources in the trading-partner countries, such as iron ore and other minerals necessary for the production of these products. These resource-rich countries may well be located far from Japan, meaning that the *DISTANCE* variable has a positive effect on Japan's imports of primary metals. This finding,

Table 8.4b. *Gravity Model of Japan's Bilateral Imports (Pooled Sample for 1980–92)*

	Food	Textiles	Wood & pulp	Chemical products
Constant	4.084** (1.638)	9.012** (2.753)	−6.223** (2.451)	−6.304 (3.804)
log GNP_i + log GNP_j	0.610** (0.036)	1.015** (0.068)	0.887** (0.059)	0.325** (0.107)
(log GNP_i/POP_i + log GNP_j/POP_j)	0.003 (0.049)	0.148** (0.066)	−0.010 (0.066)	0.782** (0.094)
log $DISTANCE_{ij}$	−1.059** (0.150)	−3.126** (0.219)	−0.869** (0.212)	−0.752** (0.310)
APEC	1.994** (0.167)	−1.227** (0.221)	2.667** (0.250)	0.954** (0.328)
EAEC	−0.912** (0.265)	0.478 (0.400)	−1.500** (0.371)	0.184 (0.568)
log $FDIFLOW(-1)$	0.035** (0.018)	0.055** (0.023)	0.112** (0.024)	0.180** (0.035)
Adjusted R^2	0.684	0.684	0.677	0.421
Sum of Squared Errors	696.9	1385.5	809.5	3214.8
No. of Observations	482	486	347	512

Note: The dependent variable is log *IMPORT*, where *IMPORT* is Japan's imports from its trading partner.
Numbers in parentheses are the estimated standard errors of the coefficients.
* significant at the 10 percent level.
** significant at the 5 percent level.

combined with the statistically insignificant coefficient on *GNP/POP* in the import equation, further supports the view that these products are not subject to intraindustry trade.

Both *APEC* and *EAEC* dummies have positive coefficients in most cases, indicating that special regional factors positively affect Japan's bilateral trade. Thus the presence of a regional bias in Japan's trade appears to be confirmed.

The estimated coefficients on *FDIFLOW*(-1) in the equations for the sum of exports and imports are positive in all the manufacturing sectors and statistically significant in seven out of eight

Table 8.4b *(continued)*

	Primary metals	General machinery	Electric machinery	Transport equipment
Constant	−30.535**	−23.134**	−10.276**	−35.176**
	(4.725)	(5.076)	(3.876)	(4.137)
log GNP_i + log GNP_j	0.733**	0.683**	0.562**	1.305**
	(0.109)	(0.108)	(0.103)	(0.109)
(log GNP_i/POP_i + log GNP_j/POP_j)	0.094	0.998**	1.068**	1.088**
	(0.114)	(0.106)	(0.091)	(0.102)
log $DISTANCE_{ij}$	1.980**	−0.642*	−2.016**	−1.447**
	(0.390)	(0.362)	(0.289)	(0.331)
APEC	2.933**	0.203	0.617**	0.536
	(0.396)	(0.333)	(0.300)	(0.339)
EAEC	2.172**	1.487**	1.181**	1.434**
	(0.677)	(0.657)	(0.533)	(0.564)
log $FDIFLOW(-1)$	0.088**	0.258**	0.328**	0.144**
	(0.036)	(0.037)	(0.033)	(0.030)
Adjusted R^2	0.379	0.561	0.725	0.650
Sum of Squared Errors	4290.4	2879.7	2463.3	3033.2
No. of Observations	508	451	482	486

sectors (see Table 8.4c), indicating that Japan's FDI tends to promote its overall trade. However, the results on the export and import equations reveal more detailed information about the effects of FDI on trade than the result on the gross trade equation alone.

Focusing on the export equation, the coefficients on FDI are positive and statistically significant for food, textiles, chemical products, general machinery, and electric machinery. Although the coefficients are positive in primary metals and transport equipment, they are not statistically significant. For wood and pulp, however, the coefficient on FDI is negative and statistically significant. These results indicate the presence of a complementary relationship between Japan's FDI and its exports in all manufacturing sectors with the exception of wood and pulp, which has a substitutability relationship. The complementary relation for machinery

Table 8.4c. *Gravity Model of Japan's Bilateral Exports plus Imports (Pooled Sample for 1980–92)*

	Food	Textiles	Wood & pulp	Chemical products
Constant	7.940**	13.958**	−1.147	3.490**
	(1.423)	(1.307)	(1.149)	(1.293)
log GNP_i + log GNP_j	0.476**	0.518**	0.511**	0.446**
	(0.031)	(0.032)	(0.028)	(0.036)
(log GNP_i/POP_i + log GNP_j/POP_j)	0.045	0.075**	0.153**	0.266**
	(0.042)	(0.031)	(0.039)	(0.032)
log $DISTANCE_{ij}$	−1.157**	−1.958**	−0.541**	−0.928**
	(0.130)	(0.104)	(0.100)	(0.105)
APEC	1.795**	0.157	1.981**	0.282**
	(0.145)	(0.105)	(0.117)	(0.112)
EAEC	−0.902**	−0.104	−0.461**	0.457**
	(0.230)	(0.190)	(0.174)	(0.193)
log $FDIFLOW(-1)$	0.051**	0.050**	0.064**	0.092**
	(0.016)	(0.011)	(0.011)	(0.012)
Adjusted R^2	0.704	0.789	0.828	0.740
Sum of Squared Errors	525.80	312.1	177.9	371.5
No. of Observations	482	486	347	512

Note: The dependent variable is log $(EXPORT + IMPORT)$, where $EXPORT + IMPORT$ is the sum of Japan's exports and imports.
Numbers in parentheses are the estimated standard errors of the coefficients.
* significant at the 10 percent level.
** significant at the 5 percent level.

is consistent with our earlier findings from the procurement patterns of foreign affiliates of Japanese firms. The machinery sectors' high dependency on Japan for the supply of intermediate products can be inferred from the positive and statistically significant coefficients on FDI in Japan's export equations for general machinery and electric machinery.[16] The substitutability result for wood and

---

[16] The complementarity relationship for food, however, is not necessarily consistent with the low procurement dependency on Japan (Table 8.3).

Table 8.4c *(continued)*

	Primary metals	General machinery	Electric machinery	Transport equipment
Constant	4.675**	4.404**	−0.924	−3.024
	(1.640)	(1.407)	(1.069)	(1.881)
log GNP_i + log GNP_j	0.464**	0.431**	0.469**	0.487**
	(0.038)	(0.030)	(0.028)	(0.050)
(log GNP_i/POP_i + log GNP_j/POP_j)	−0.305**	0.116**	0.325**	0.355**
	(0.039)	(0.029)	(0.025)	(0.047)
log $DISTANCE_{ij}$	0.006	−0.633**	−0.550**	−0.412**
	(0.135)	(0.100)	(0.080)	(0.151)
APEC	1.583**	0.443**	0.457**	1.090**
	(0.138)	(0.092)	(0.083)	(0.154)
EAEC	0.418*	0.216	0.691**	−0.126
	(0.235)	(0.182)	(0.147)	(0.257)
log $FDIFLOW$(−1)	0.048**	0.086**	0.062**	0.003
	(0.013)	(0.010)	(0.009)	(0.013)
Adjusted R^2	0.603	0.740	0.830	0.522
Sum of Squared Errors	517.0	221.4	187.4	627.2
No. of Observations	508	451	482	486

pulp is also consistent with the earlier finding of the low procurement dependency on Japan for these products.

Turning to the effect of Japan's FDI on its imports, one observes that the coefficients on FDI are positive and statistically significant in all manufacturing sectors. These results indicate that Japan's FDI promotes "reverse" imports of final goods in some sectors and imports of intermediate goods in other sectors. The observed strong relationship between Japan's FDI and its reverse imports in general machinery and electric machinery, reflected in large coefficients on *FDIFLOW*(-1), is consistent with the earlier observation that an interprocess division of labor is undertaken by Japanese firms in these sectors. To be more specific, Japanese machinery firms tend to export parts and components and import finished products that are manufactured in their foreign subsidiaries. This type of interprocess division of labor may have become more extensive since the second half of the 1980s because Japan now imports more intermediate goods for the production and exports of higher value-added parts and components.

The effects of Japan's FDI on the sectoral trade balances (exports minus imports) can be obtained from the estimated coefficients on FDI in the export and import equations (see Tables 8.4a and 8.4b). The estimated coefficients on exports are smaller than those on imports in all sectors with the exception of food. Thus FDI tends to worsen trade balances in all manufacturing sectors except food.[17]

5.3. FDI Outflow Equations

Next, we estimated the FDI outflow equation. The explanatory variables are similar to those used in the trade equation with the exception that the *TRADE* variable is included instead of the FDI variable:

$$\log FDIFLOW_{ij} = \beta_0 + \beta_1\left(\log GDP_i + \log GDP_j\right)$$
$$+ \beta_2\left(\log\frac{GDP_i}{POP_i} + \log\frac{GDP_j}{POP_j}\right) + \beta_3 DISTANCE_{ij}$$
$$+ \beta_4 APEC_i + \beta_5 EAEC_i + \beta_6 TRADE_{ij}\left(-1\right) + v_{ij}$$

$$(8.2)$$

The dependent variable (*FDIFLOW*) is Japan's FDI outflow to country i in the current year, and *TRADE*(-1) on the right-hand side of the equation is Japan's bilateral trade with country i in the last period. For *TRADE*, three alternative measures are used: Japan's exports to country i (*EXPORT*), its imports from country i (*IMPORT*), and the sum of exports and imports (*EXPORT* + *IMPORT*). The FDI equation is undoubtedly very simple, but it

---

[17] Although not reported in this chapter, we also run the regression on the natural log of the export/import ratio using the gravity variables and FDI as explanatory variables. The results confirmed that the coefficients on FDI are negative and statistically significant in wood and pulp, chemical products, general machinery, electric machinery, and transport equipment, while the coefficient on FDI is positive and statistically significant in food.

allows us to test some of the central elements of the "gravity" approach.

The regression results for FDI using *EXPORT*, *IMPORT*, and *EXPORT* + *IMPORT* as explanatory variables are summarized in Tables 8.5a–8.5c, respectively. The estimated coefficient on *GNP* is positive and statistically significant in all manufacturing sectors except wood and pulp (see Tables 8.5b and 8.5c), suggesting that the economic or market size of the host country is an important element for promoting Japan's FDI. This result confirms our earlier observation that local market sales is an important motive behind Japan's FDI in manufacturing sectors with the possible exception of wood and pulp, in which exporting rather than local sales is a more important motive. The signs of the coefficients on *GNP/POP* are different across sectors. The coefficients are negative, although not always statistically significant, in textiles, wood and pulp, chemical products, electric machinery, and transport equipment, suggesting that Japan's FDI in these sectors tends to be undertaken in low per-capita income countries. By contrast, the coefficients on *GNP/POP* are positive, although not always statistically significant, in food and general machinery, indicating that Japan's FDI in these sectors is undertaken in high per-capita income countries.[18]

The coefficient on *DISTANCE* is always positive and statistically significant in at least five sectors out of eight, implying that Japan's FDI may have been motivated to overcome natural impediments to trade measured by *DISTANCE*. A similar result has been obtained in the case of aggregate FDI equations for Japan (Kawai, 1994b), although such a tendency does not seem to be observed persistently in countries other than Japan.[19]

The coefficient on the *EAEC* dummy is always positive and, in six out of eight cases, statistically significant, while the *APEC* dummy is positive and statistically significant in only four cases.

---

[18] The coefficients on *GNP/POP* are statistically insignificant in primary metals and textiles, no matter which *TRADE* variable (exports, imports, or exports plus imports) is used as an explanatory variable.

[19] On the other hand, this result may reflect the fact that we have omitted most of the African countries, which are far away from Japan, from our sample due to the very small size (mostly zero) of Japan's FDI outflows in, and trade with, these countries.

Table 8.5a. *Gravity Model of Japan's Bilateral FDI Outflows by Using Exports as an Explanatory Variable (Pooled Sample for 1980–92)*

	Food	Textiles	Wood & pulp	Chemical products
Constant	−24.385**	−53.288**	−13.475**	−45.003**
	(3.945)	(5.315)	(5.508)	(4.440)
log GNP_i + log GNP_j	0.681**	1.163**	0.762**	0.883**
	(0.084)	(0.130)	(0.170)	(0.167)
(log GNP_i/POP_i + log GNP_j/POP_j)	0.152	−0.103	−0.053	−0.093
	(0.129)	(0.127)	(0.199)	(0.118)
log $DISTANCE_{ij}$	0.429	2.399**	0.216	1.625**
	(0.387)	(0.490)	(0.514)	(0.422)
APEC	2.608**	−0.489	5.277**	0.318
	(0.406)	(0.449)	(0.613)	(0.422)
EAEC	2.093**	6.692**	0.759	4.626**
	(0.654)	(0.709)	(0.855)	(0.702)
log $EXPORT(-1)$	0.341**	0.558**	−0.679**	1.137**
	(0.063)	(0.157)	(0.245)	(0.190)
Adjusted R^2	0.493	0.416	0.284	0.523
Sum of Squared Errors	4370.1	5071.7	4183.3	5050.9
No. of Observations	482	486	347	512

Note: The dependent variable is log *FDIFLOW*.
Numbers in parentheses are the estimated standard errors of the coefficients.
* significant at the 10 percent level.
** significant at the 5 percent level.

Controlling for distance, Japanese FDI appears to be strongly biased toward EAEC countries.

The most important coefficient is that on *TRADE* (-1), which captures the effect of trade on FDI outflows. It is positive and statistically significant in all manufacturing sectors when imports are used as an explanatory variable (Table 8.5b). When exports are used instead, the coefficient on this variable becomes negative and statistically significant in the wood and pulp industry. When the sum of exports and imports is used as an explanatory variable, the coefficient on *TRADE* (-1) becomes positive and statistically sig-

Table 8.5a *(continued)*

	Primary metals	General machinery	Electric machinery	Transport equipment
Constant	−45.442** (5.469)	−64.063** (5.379)	−49.423** (4.735)	−35.064** (6.154)
log GNP_i + log GNP_j	1.064** (0.144)	0.767** (0.147)	0.979** (0.167)	1.675** (0.165)
(log GNP_i/POP_i + log GNP_j/POP_j)	0.011 (0.142)	0.491** (0.123)	−0.010 (0.139)	−0.750** (0.165)
log $DISTANCE_{ij}$	2.166** (0.470)	2.211** (0.434)	1.444** (0.398)	0.764 (0.517)
APEC	2.875** (0.509)	−0.247 (0.405)	0.453 (0.419)	2.881** (0.540)
EAEC	5.309** (0.786)	5.845** (0.725)	4.782** (0.702)	1.318 (0.877)
log $EXPORT(-1)$	0.054 (0.137)	1.530** (0.186)	1.245** (0.209)	0.128 (0.147)
Adjusted R^2	0.425	0.566	0.560	0.302
Sum of Squared Errors	6225.1	3954.2	4548.2	7405.4
No. of Observations	508	451	482	486

nificant in all sectors except transport equipment. These findings suggest that larger bilateral trade flows, defined by imports or the sum of exports and imports, would induce greater FDI outflows from Japan. However, the negative coefficient on *EXPORT* in the FDI equation for wood and pulp again confirms the substitutability relationship between exports and FDI in this sector. In other words, Japan does not invest much in countries to which it ships large volumes of exports.

6. CONCLUDING REMARKS

This chapter has revealed wide variations in the relationship between Japan's FDI and trade across different manufacturing sectors, which are masked by the previous studies examining the relationship between FDI and trade at the aggregated level. Strong

Table 8.5b. *Gravity Model of Japan's Bilateral FDI Outflows by Using Imports as an Explanatory Variable (Pooled Sample for 1980–92)*

	Food	Textiles	Wood & pulp	Chemical products
Constant	−23.592**	−47.183**	−9.925**	−39.384**
	(4.053)	(4.910)	(5.490)	(4.555)
log GNP_i + log GNP_j	0.534**	1.121**	0.014	1.446**
	(0.118)	(0.149)	(0.170)	(0.123)
(log GNP_i/POP_i	0.408**	−0.078	−0.219**	−0.260**
+ log GNP_j/POP_j)	(0.123)	(0.127)	(0.187)	(0.127)
log $DISTANCE_{ij}$	0.208	2.177**	1.156**	0.785**
	(0.406)	(0.491)	(0.485)	(0.395)
APEC	2.460**	0.337	2.832**	0.671
	(0.485)	(0.439)	(0.632)	(0.419)
EAEC	2.539**	6.365**	1.116	5.555**
	(0.678)	(0.715)	(0.850)	(0.683)
log $IMPORT(-1)$	0.280**	0.232**	0.492**	0.260**
	(0.127)	(0.086)	(0.117)	(0.056)
Adjusted R^2	0.467	0.410	0.304	0.510
Sum of Squared Errors	4590.4	5126.0	4064.8	5191.4
No. of Observations	482	486	347	512

Note: The dependent variable is log *FDIFLOW*.
Numbers in parentheses are the estimated standard errors of the coefficients.
* significant at the 10 percent level.
** significant at the 5 percent level.

positive two-way interactions between Japan's trade (whether measured by exports, imports, or the sum of the two) and FDI are found in food, textiles, chemical products, general machinery, and electric machinery. In particular, strong two-way interactions, or complementary relations, are found to exist for these sectors between exports and FDI. For primary metals and transport machinery, the result is inconclusive because a two-way interaction between trade and FDI is not always statistically significant. For wood and pulp, a positive two-way interaction is found only between imports and

Table 8.5b *(continued)*

	Primary metals	General machinery	Electric machinery	Transport equipment
Constant	−40.652**	−47.830**	−38.337**	−21.237**
	(5.659)	(5.858)	(4.611)	(6.615)
log GNP_i + log GNP_j	0.994**	1.196**	1.064**	1.222**
	(0.130)	(0.125)	(0.126)	(0.179)
(log GNP_i/POP_i + log GNP_j/POP_j)	−0.019	0.233	−0.295**	−1.068**
	(0.136)	(0.140)	(0.131)	(0.170)
log $DISTANCE_{ij}$	1.848**	1.429**	1.828**	1.134**
	(0.474)	(0.430)	(0.373)	(0.508)
APEC	2.570**	0564	0.556	2.710**
	(0.489)	(0.398)	(0.381)	(0.501)
EAEC	4.994**	5.654**	4.273**	0.736
	(0.794)	(0.749)	(0.648)	(0.862)
log $IMPORT(-1)$	0.123**	0.365**	0.558**	0.339**
	(0.053)	(0.053)	(0.053)	(0.067)
Adjusted R^2	0.431	0.548	0.617	0.336
Sum of Squared Errors	6162.0	4122.0	3961.4	7045.1
No. of Observations	508	451	482	486

FDI, while the interaction between exports and FDI is negative and statistically significant. In other words, exports and FDI in wood and pulp exhibit a strong substitutability relationship. Analyzing data on sales and procurement by foreign affiliates of Japanese firms and judging from the estimated coefficients on per-capita GNP in the trade equations, intraindustry trade is active in textiles, chemical products, general machinery, electric machinery, and transport equipment. It has been shown that in a number of sectors Japan's trade with the APEC member countries is significantly larger than nonmember countries (controlling for distance and other characteristics), and its FDI outflow to the EAEC economies is significantly larger than non-EAEC economies.

Table 8.5c. *Gravity Model of Japan's Bilateral FDI Outflows by Using Exports plus Imports as an Explanatory Variable (Pooled Sample for 1980–92)*

	Food	Textiles	Wood & pulp	Chemical products
Constant	−26.067**	−55.614**	−12.138**	−42.683**
	(4.111)	(5.241)	(5.409)	(4.410)
log GNP_i + log GNP_j	0.458**	0.894**	−0.126	1.030**
	(0.111)	(0.153)	(0.183)	(0.147)
(log GNP_i/POP_i + log GNP_j/POP_j)	0.383**	−0.101	−0.375**	−0.302**
	(0.122)	(0.125)	(0.189)	(0.123)
log $DISTANCE_{ij}$	0.484	3.021**	1.363**	1.447**
	(0.413)	(0.523)	(0.492)	(0.407)
APEC	2.089**	−0.130	1.901**	0.571
	(0.484)	(0.421)	(0.742)	(0.411)
EAEC	2.702**	6.425**	0.951	4.909**
	(0.673)	(0.701)	(0.836)	(0.685)
log [$EXPORT(-1)$ + $IMPORT(-1)$]	0.496**	0.842**	1.114**	0.980**
	(0.139)	(0.177)	(0.241)	(0.155)
Adjusted R^2	0.476	0.428	0.311	0.527
Sum of Squared Errors	4515.8	4969.0	4025.2	5010.9
No. of Observations	482	486	347	512

Note: The dependent variable is log *FDIFLOW*. *EXPORT*(−1) + *IMPORT*(−1) is the sum of exports and imports in the previous year.
Numbers in parentheses are the estimated standard errors of the coefficients.
* significant at the 10 percent level.
** significant at the 5 percent level.

The two-way interactions between Japan's FDI and trade reflect the deepening interdependence of Japan's economic activities with those of the rest of the world, and particularly with the APEC and EAEC economies. Since the economies of East Asia are projected to grow at relatively rapid rates into the twenty-first century, Japan's involvement in the region through FDI and trade is bound to rise. Indeed, both Japan and East Asia are likely to benefit from such interactions, as they appear to complement each other in their

Table 8.5c *(continued)*

	Primary metals	General machinery	Electric machinery	Transport equipment
Constant	−46.111**	−60.896**	−49.236**	−34.924**
	(5.338)	(5.364)	(4.712)	(6.163)
log GNP_i + log GNP_j	0.880**	0.688**	0.939**	1.671**
	(0.146)	(0.153)	(0.167)	(0.167)
(log GNP_i/POP_i + log GNP_j/POP_j)	0.121	0.429**	−0.059	−0.751**
	(0.143)	(0.125)	(0.141)	(0.165)
log $DISTANCE_{ij}$	2.084**	2.108**	1.546**	0.764
	(0.457)	(0.430)	(0.399)	(0.517)
APEC	2.258**	−0.116	0.433	2.891**
	(0.526)	(0.430)	(0.416)	(0.537)
EAEC	5.068**	5.547**	4.700**	1.310
	(0.785)	(0.730)	(0.700)	(0.876)
log [EXPORT(−1) + IMPORT(−1)]	0.417**	1.590**	1.306**	0.128
	(0.155)	(0.190)	(0.207)	(0.148)
Adjusted R^2	0.433	0.568	0.564	0.302
Sum of Squared Errors	6137.8	3939.1	4510.1	7405.7
No. of Observations	508	451	482	486

economic activities. Specifically, Japan can provide not only financial resources, production technologies, and managerial resources but also a large market for final consumer goods. At the same time, East Asia can offer high-quality labor and a growing market for capital and intermediate goods.

This chapter has found the presence of a strong trade-FDI nexus in disaggregated Japanese manufacturing sectors. To increase our understanding of the relationship between trade and FDI, an investigation of the behavior of multinational firms is warranted. The examination of firm-level micro data would be of critical importance in such a study.

REFERENCES

Anderson, James E. (1979), "A Theoretical Foundation for the Gravity Equation," *American Economic Review*, 69: 106–116.

Deardorff, Alan V. (1984), "Testing Trade Theories and Predicting Trade Flows," in R. W. Jones and P. B. Kenen, eds., *Handbook of International Economics*, Vol. 1, Amsterdam: North-Holland.

——— (1998), "Determinants of Bilateral Trade: Does Gravity Work in a Neoclassical World?" in Jeffrey A. Frankel, ed., *The Regionalization of the World Economy*, Chicago: University of Chicago Press.

Drysdale, Peter, and Ross Garnaut (1982), "Trade Intensities and the Analysis of Bilateral Trade Flows in a Many-Country World: A Survey," *Hitotsubashi Journal of Economics*, 22: 62–84.

Eaton, Jonathan, and Corrinne Ho (1993), "Trade and Investment in the North America–Pacific Region: Does NAFTA Matter?" *Asian Economic Dynamism and New Asia–Pacific Economic Order: Post–Cold War U.S.–Japan Economic Relations and New Regionalism*, The Proceedings of Kyushu University International Symposium 1993, Kitakyushu: Kyushu University.

Eaton, Jonathan, and Akiko Tamura (1994), "Bilateralism and Regionalism in Japanese and U.S. Trade and Direct Foreign Investment Patterns," *Journal of the Japanese and International Economies*, 8: 478–510.

Frankel, Jeffrey A. (1993), "Is Japan Creating a Yen Bloc in East Asia and the Pacific?" in J. A. Frankel and M. Kahler, eds., *Regionalism and Rivalry: Japan and the United States in Pacific Asia*, Chicago: University of Chicago Press and NBER.

Frankel, Jeffrey A., and Shang-Jin Wei (1993), "Trade Blocs and Currency Blocs," NBER Working Paper No. 4335, April.

Institute of Developing Economies (1994), *The Developing Economies, Special Issue: Trade Liberalization and Productivity Growth in Asia*, Vol. 32, No. 4, December.

Kawai, Masahiro (1994a), "Accumulation of Net External Assets in Japan," in R. Sato, R. M. Levich, and R. V. Ramachandran, eds., *Japan, Europe, and International Financial Markets: Analytical and Empirical Perspectives*, Cambridge: Cambridge University Press.

——— (1994b), "Interactions of Japan's Trade and Investment: A Special Emphasis on East Asia," Discussion Paper Series No. F-39, Institute of Social Science, University of Tokyo, October.

Kawai, Masahiro, and Shujiro Urata (1996), "Trade Imbalances and Japanese Foreign Direct Investment: Bilateral and Triangular Issues," Discussion Paper Series No. F-52, Institute of Social Science, University of Tokyo, May.

Markusen, James R. (1983), "Factor Movements and Commodity Trade as Complements," *Journal of International Economics*, 14: 341–356.

Mundell, Robert A. (1957), "International Trade and Factor Mobility," *American Economic Review*, 47: 321–335.

Okamoto, Yumiko, and Shujiro Urata (1994), "Japan's Foreign Direct Investment in Malaysia in the 1990s," paper presented at the Third Annual Conference on Japan, "Revitalization of Japan's Economy: Implications for Malaysia," Kuala Lumpur, April.

Petri, Peter A. (1995), "The Interdependence of Trade and Investment in the Pacific," in E. K. Y. Chen and P. Drysdale, eds., *Corporate Links and Foreign Direct Investment in Asia and the Pacific*, NSW Australia: Harper Educational Publishers.

Urata, Shujiro (1993), "Japanese Foreign Direct Investment and Its Effect on Foreign Trade in Asia," in T. Ito and A. O. Krueger, eds., *Trade and Protectionism*, Chicago: University of Chicago Press and NBER.

APPENDIX

Appendix Table. *The Sample Countries and Period used for Regression Analysis*

	Food	Textiles	Wood & pulp	Chemical products	Primary metals	General machinery	Electric machinery	Transport equipment
United States	1980–92	1980–92	1980–92	1980–92	1980–92	1980–92	1980–92	1980–92
Canada	1980–92	1980–92	1980–92	1980–92	1980–92	1980–92	1980–92	1980–92
Australia	1980–92	1980–92	1980–92	1980–92	1980–92	1980–92	1980–92	1980–92
New Zealand	1980–92	1980–92	1980–92	1980–92	1980–92	1980–92	1980–92	1980–92
Austria	1980–92	1980–92	1980–92	···	1980–92	···	···	···
Belgium–Luxembourg	1980–92	1980–92	···	1980–92	1980–92	1980–92	1980–92	1980–92
France	1980–92	1980–92	1980–92	1980–92	1980–92	1980–92	1980–92	1980–92
Germany	1980–92	1980–92	1980–92	1980–92	1980–92	1980–92	1980–92	1980–92
Ireland	1980–92	1980–92	···	1980–92	1980–92	1980–92	1980–92	1980–92
Italy	1980–92	1980–92	1980–92	1980–92	1980–92	1980–92	1980–92	1980–92
Netherlands	1980–92	1980–92	1980–92	1980–92	1980–92	1980–92	1980–92	1980–92
Norway	1980–92	···	···	1980–92	1980–92	1980–92	1980–92	1980–92
Spain	1980–92	1980–92	1980–92	1980–92	1980–92	1980–92	···	1980–92
Switzerland	···	1980–92	···	1980–92	···	1980–92	1980–92	1980–92
England	1980–92	1980–92	1980–92	1980–92	1980–92	1980–92	1980–92	1980–92
Nigeria	1980–92	1980–92	···	1980–92	1980–92	1980–92	1980–92	1980–92
Zaire	···	···	···	···	1980–89	···	···	···
Zambia	···	···	···	···	1980–91	···	···	···
Bangladesh	···	1984–92	···	1980–92	1980–92	···	1984–92	···
China	1980–92	1980–92	1980–92	1980–92	1980–92	1980–92	1980–92	1980–92
Fiji	1984–92	···	···	···	···	···	···	···
Hong Kong	1980–92	1980–92	1980–92	1980–92	···	1980–92	1980–92	···
India	1980–92	1980–92	···	1980–92	1980–92	1980–92	1980–92	1980–92
Indonesia	1980–92	1980–92	1980–92	1980–92	1980–92	1980–92	1980–92	1980–92
Korea	1980–92	1980–92	1980–92	1980–92	1980–92	1980–92	1980–92	1980–92
Malaysia	1980–92	1980–92	1980–92	1980–92	1980–92	1980–92	1980–92	1980–92

Pakistan	...	1980–92	...	1980–92	...	...	1980–92	1980–92
Papua New Guinea	1980–92	...	1980–92	...	...	...	...	...
Philippines	1980–92	1980–92	1980–92	1980–92	1980–92	1980–92	1980–92	1980–92
Singapore	1980–92	1980–92	1980–92	1980–92	1980–92	1980–92	1980–92	1980–92
Sri Lanka	1984–92	1984–92	1984–92	1980–92	1984–92	...	1984–92	1984–92
Thailand	1980–92	1980–92	1980–92	1980–92	1980–92	1980–92	1980–92	1980–92
Vanuatu	1980–92	...	...	...	...	...	...	...
Taiwan	1980–92	1980–92	1980–92	1980–92	1980–92	1980–92	1980–92	1980–92
Greece	...	1984–92	...	1984–92	1980–92	...	...	1980–92
Hungary	...	...	...	1980–92	...	1980–92	...	1980–92
Portugal	1980–92	1980–92	1980–92	1980–92	1980–92	1980–92	1980–92	1980–92
Turkey	1980–92	...	...	...	1980–92	...	1980–92	1980–92
Iran	...	1980–92	...	1980–92	1980–92	1980–92	1980–92	1980–92
Saudi Arabia	...	...	1980–92	1980–92	...	1980–92	1980–92	1980–92
Argentina	1980–92	1980–92	1980–92	1980–92	1980–92	1980–92	1980–92	1980–92
Brazil	1980–92	1980–92	1980–92	1980–92	1980–92	1980–92	1980–92	1980–92
Chile	1980–92	1980–92	1980–92	1980–92	1980–92	1980–92	1980–92	1980–92
Colombia	1984–92	1984–92	...	1984–92	1984–92	1984–92	1984–92	1980–92
Mexico	1980–92	1980–92	...	1980–92	1980–92	1980–92	1980–92	1984–92
Panama	1980–92	...	1980–92	...	1980–92	1980–92	...	1980–92
Peru	1980–92	1980–92	...	1980–92	1980–92	...	1980–92	1980–92
Venezuela	1980–92	1980–92	...	1980–92	1980–92	1980–92	1980–92	1980–92
Total number of observations	482	486	347	512	508	451	482	486

Comment

Julia Lowell

This chapter has made a significant contribution to the examination of the relationship between trade and foreign direct investment (FDI) by using bilateral, industry-level data as opposed to aggregate data. I especially liked the way that Masahiro Kawai and Shujiro Urata used descriptive statistics to suggest which of the theories of FDI, with their different implications for the relationship between FDI and trade, seem most plausible for particular manufacturing sectors. The survey data on Japanese motives for FDI, and the sales and procurement data for Japanese affiliates abroad, is particularly illustrative.

However, I have two suggestions on how to refine and extend the chapter. First, the chapter would be much improved if the authors were to specify more clearly their alternative hypotheses about the relationship between trade and FDI. Central to this step is the definition of trade: Whereas FDI is unambiguously defined to be Japanese investment flows into the destination country, Japanese trade with the destination country is variously defined in terms of Japanese exports, imports, or exports plus imports. The theoretical relationships between FDI and these various trade measures may differ substantially.

My second suggestion, which follows directly from the first, is to respecify the empirical model in order to test the alternative hypotheses directly. It is not at all clear that a gravity model is the optimal approach for looking at relationships between FDI and trade when specific alternative hypotheses can be derived. A more theoretically grounded model might also provide greater guidance to the choice of estimation procedure, thus avoiding some of the problems associated with applying ordinary least squares (OLS) to a pooled time-series panel of data.

ALTERNATIVE HYPOTHESES

One way to specify alternative hypotheses is to determine the factors that contribute to a firm's choice whether to export from home production facilities or establish a production base in the foreign target market. Table 8.6 suggests four generic cases that correspond to four alternative hypotheses about the relationship

Table 8.6. *Alternative Hypotheses for Firm's Export/Investment Decision*

Case	Motive	Hypothesis	Data
1	Factor cost advantage in home (destination) country.	Trade and investment are substitutes.	Source country FDI industry *i*; source country exports (imports), industry *i*.
2	Factor cost advantage in home country for some processes.	Trade and investment are complements *by stage of processing*.	Source country FDI, industry *i*, *process k*; source country exports, industry *i*, *process l*.
3	Factor cost advantage at destination country, but initial high FDI transaction costs. (FDI has learning curve.)	Trade and investment are complements *over time*.	Source country FDI, industry *i*, *time t*; source country exports, industry *i*, *time t–1*.
4	Factor cost advantage in home country but protected market in destination country.	Trade and investment are substitutes; destination country production not sold abroad.	Source country FDI, industry *i*; source country exports and imports, industry *i*.

between within-industry (and even within-firm) FDI and trade. Although three of the four cases are testable given the data used in the chapter, Case 2 requires further breakdowns in the data that may not be available.

The industry-level trends in Japanese FDI described by Kawai and Urata through descriptive statistics and survey responses may also be categorized using these four cases. For example, yen appreciation during the late 1980s suggests that Case 1 may have been increasingly relevant over the period, while growing trade friction favors Case 4. The changing geographic distribution of FDI also points to the relevance of Case 1. The survey results on the composition of investment and procurement patterns for certain industries provide evidence for Cases 2 and 3.

EMPIRICAL MODEL

Within the context of the model presented, there are at least two troubling features of the OLS estimation procedure used by Kawai and Urata. First, the income (*GDP*) and per-capita income

(*GDP/POP*) variables are likely to follow nonstationary time-series processes. As a result, the parameter estimates that are derived in the chapter may be unstable. An initial step toward solving this problem might be to look at a cross-section of data for different years and report those estimates. Second, it is also likely that there exists significant cross-country heterogeneity bias in the data. Certainly the finding of positive and significant parameter values for the regional dummies *EAEC* and *APEC* indicate a degree of heterogeneity in intercepts; heterogeneity in slopes is also likely. One economically interesting approach to this problem would be to test for differences across countries grouped according to information provided by the survey data.

A more general critique concerns the empirical model itself, which falls within the class of gravity models. As argued by Kawai and Urata, these models are useful in that they do a pretty good job of explaining statistical variations in bilateral trade flows. Most recently, they have been used to determine the extent to which patterns of trade between countries can be explained by the economic size and simple geographic proximity of the partners (e.g., Frankel, Stein, and Wei, 1995). However, the gravity model is not an obvious choice when specific alternative hypotheses about the relationship between FDI and trade can be derived. In extensions to this research, therefore, the authors should consider empirical specifications where the explanatory variables are derived from economic theory.

REFERENCE

Frankel, Jeffrey, Ernesto Stein, and Shang-Jin Wei (1995), "Trading Blocs and the Americas: The Natural, the Unnatural, and the Supernatural, *Journal of Development Economics* 47: 61–95.

## CHAPTER 9

Korea's Outward Foreign Direct Investment and the Division of Labor in the Asia–Pacific

Jai-Won Ryou

1. INTRODUCTION

Foreign direct investment (FDI) has emerged as an engine of growth for the world economy and has drastically changed the structure of division of labor in both developed and developing countries. Korea is no exception to this general trend. Since the mid-1980s, Korea's outward FDI has surged, and Korea has emerged as a major investor in Asian developing countries. The progress of globalization and industrial restructuring of the Korean economy is likely to result in continued growth of FDI.

FDI is an important channel in reinforcing the process of market-driven integration in global as well as regional economies because it purports to bring mutual benefits to both host and source countries. The host country can gain benefits including employment creation, transfer of technology, and management know-how. For the source country, or multinational corporations, FDI provides an excellent opportunity to maximize firm-specific advantages by lowering production costs and gaining improved access to new markets.

FDI does not always result in positive economic effects, however, as there are mixed views on the effects of Korea's outward FDI. On the one hand, outward FDI is perceived to contribute to the promotion of industrial restructuring and exports through trade between parent firms and their affiliates. On the other hand, it is presumed to replace domestic investment and exports, thereby accelerating "deindustrialization." The proponents of the latter view argue that outward FDI should be closely regulated to minimize the negative impact on the domestic economy.

The author thanks Chung H. Lee, David Roland-Holst, and particularly Hiro Lee for helpful comments. The author is responsible for any remaining errors.

In order to provide useful policy recommendations, as well as to secure international cooperation on investment policies, a detailed empirical analysis is required. However, there have been few systematic efforts to quantify the effects of FDI on trade and industrial adjustment in Korea. Reflecting the fact that outward FDI from Korea is still in its infant stage, some of the previous studies (e.g., Lee and Lee, 1991; Lee and Plummer, 1992) have focused on the motives or determinants of investment, while some other studies (e.g., Ryou, Kim, and Min, 1992) have relied on survey data to sketch the economic impact of FDI. Only recently has the interaction between trade and FDI come to receive due attention (Kim, 1994).

The purposes of this chapter are to analyze the effects of Korea's outward FDI on trade patterns in the Asian Pacific region and to assess its implications for the regional division of labor. We attempt to answer the following questions: How can one characterize and evaluate Korea's regional trade and FDI patterns in the global context? How strong is the correlation between the growing importance of Asian developing countries as Korea's trading partners and the recent increases in Korea's FDI in these countries? What is the interaction between Korea's FDI and trade in manufacturing industries, and what does it imply for industrial adjustment at national and regional levels?

Korea's outward FDI has undoubtedly affected the international trade between Korea and its major trading partners, and the interaction between trade and FDI is not a unique phenomenon to any specific country. It has been an important topic for discussion for economists, entrepreneurs, and policymakers. Many of the previous studies based on the experiences of advanced countries generally conclude that outward FDI is positively related to exports, implying complementarity between the two (e.g., Lipsey and Weiss, 1981; Blomstrom, Lipsey, and Kulchycky, 1988). Recent studies on Japan's FDI in East Asia also confirm a positive relationship between trade and FDI (Kawai, 1994; Kawai and Urata, Chapter 8, this volume). However, a strong substitutability is also found between FDI and exports, as shown in U.S. FDI in Latin America (Graham, 1994). The complementarity between FDI and exports could also be explained by the heightening of protective barriers in the major export market (Wakasugi, 1994).

Our results support a complementary relationship between

Korea's FDI and trade. Outward FDI promotes exports to the host country, as well as imports from the host country. The nature of correlation between trade and FDI differs across industries. For some manufacturing industries, there appears to be a reverse causation from exports to FDI. However, the deindustrialization phenomenon has proven to be overestimated.

This chapter is organized as follows. Section 2 provides an overview of recent trends in Korea's outward FDI and regional economic ties. In Section 3, Korea's trade and FDI are analyzed in the framework of a generalized gravity model, and the interaction between Korea's outward FDI and trade is examined. In Section 4, outward FDI and trade in the manufacturing sector are closely scrutinized, and the question of industrial adjustment is addressed. Section 5 summarizes the major findings and draws final conclusions.

2. KOREA'S OUTWARD FDI AND TRADE IN THE ASIA–PACIFIC

2.1. Overview of Korea's Outward FDI

Korea's outward FDI began in 1968 with investment in Indonesia for forestry development. However, the government generally discouraged outward FDI because it was thought to aggravate the domestic capital shortage under the chronic balance of payments deficits. It was only in the mid-1980s that the liberalization of government regulations on outward FDI took place, as the current account deficit turned to a surplus. In the past decade, Korea's outward FDI continued to rise rapidly, responding to changes in the internal as well as external investment climates: soaring wages and land prices at home, and deepening regionalism and protectionism abroad.

As shown in Table 9.1, the total number of approved cases of outward FDI increased from 74 to 1,949 cases during the 1986–94 period, and its total value increased from $365 million to $3.7 billion. The realized values of outward investment also continued to grow, with the annual amount surpassing $1.0 billion in 1991 and $2.0 billion in 1994. The total value of Korea's existing investments abroad rose from $645 million in 1986 to $7.6 billion in 1994.

Despite the rapid increase, the size of Korea's FDI is still very

Table 9.1. *Trends in Korea's Outward Foreign Direct Investment*

	Approvals		Actual investments		Withdrawals[b]		Total existing investments	
Year	No.[a]	Amount[a]	No.	Amount	No.	Amount	No.	Amount
1986	74	364.9	52	183.9	19	22.7	476	645.1
1987	110	371.1	92	410.5	32	89.6	536	966.0
1988	253	479.3	176	223.8	32	59.7	680	1,130.1
1989	368	943.3	269	569.6	23	177.2	926	1,522.5
1990	517	1,624.8	339	959.3	22	146.1	1,243	2,335.7
1991	539	1,605.6	453	1,125.4	23	88.1	1,673	3,372.9
1992	632	1,210.0	500	1,255.0	35	121.4	2,138	4,506.6
1993	1,050	1,888.5	682	1,317.7	66	246.0	2,754	5,578.0
1994	1,949	3,722.7	1476	2,346.7	68	275.8	4,161	7,648.8

[a] The numbers in cases and the amount in millions of current US dollars.
[b] Include liquidation.
Source: Bank of Korea, *Outward Foreign Investment Statistics Yearbook*, 1995.

small. In 1994, the ratio of outward FDI flow to GNP was only 0.6 percent, while the ratio of the accumulated stock of outward FDI to GNP was 2.0 percent. Although these ratios are much smaller than those of Japan or Taiwan, Korea's outward FDI is likely to continue to grow rapidly with the implementation of trade and investment liberalization policies, particularly by the Asia Pacific Economic Cooperation (APEC) member countries.

The recent increase in the number of cases of outward FDI is dominated by small-scale investments. The average value of each investment amounted to $2.0 million in 1994. Up until 1994, investments valued at less than $1.0 million constituted 72.8 percent of the total number of investment but accounted for only 11.9 percent of the total value. In contrast, large-scale investments of more than $10.0 million accounted for only 3.1 percent of the total number of cases but 55.9 percent of the total value.

With regard to the share of FDI by industry, the manufacturing sector has been the most active. As shown in Table 9.2, the manufacturing sector held 54.8 percent of total existing investments in 1994, while its share of outward FDI flows in 1994 set a record at 65.0 percent. Among nonmanufacturing sectors, resource-related

Table 9.2. Korea's Outward FDI by Industry (percent)

Industry	Actual investments							Total existing investments in 1994[a]
	1986	1988	1990	1991	1992	1993	1994	
Forestry and fishery	2.3	6.1	2.9	1.3	2.2	0.9	0.4	2.4 (3.4)
Mining	44.3	29.3	16.4	11.0	12.0	11.0	4.8	8.9 (1.2)
Manufacturing	40.0	36.6	51.0	53.2	51.9	40.7	65.0	54.8 (63.7)
Construction	1.0	2.8	0.5	1.1	0.0	1.5	2.7	1.8 (2.3)
Transportation	0.0	2.8	0.5	1.1	0.8	0.5	0.5	0.5 (1.6)
Trade	7.9	19.1	22.9	20.7	24.2	31.1	20.8	22.9 (19.4)
Real estate	1.6	3.3	0.4	0.9	2.9	4.7	0.5	2.0 (0.7)
Other sectors[b]	2.9	2.6	5.7	11.0	6.0	10.0	5.3	6.7 (7.7)
All sectors	100.0	100.0	100.0	100.0	100.0	100.0	100.0	100.0 (100)
Amount (US$ million)	183.9	223.8	959.3	1125.4	1255.1	1317.4	2346.7	7648.8(4,161)

[a] The shares of the number of cases are given in parentheses.
[b] Agriculture and unspecified service sectors (except banking and insurance).
Source: Same as Table 9.1.

Table 9.3. *Korea's Outward FDI in Manufacturing (percent)*[a]

Industry	1988	1989	1990	1991	1992	1993	1994
Food processing	2.4	2.7	6.4	5.6	5.4	4.9	4.0
Textiles and apparel[b]	10.3	17.0	13.7	13.1	13.7	13.8	13.0
Footwear and leather			4.8	4.0	4.0	4.7	5.0
Wood and furniture	3.1	1.8	2.5	3.9	4.1	3.9	2.8
Pulp and paper	2.3	2.9	1.6	2.0	2.2	2.4	2.1
Chemicals	7.9	10.0	13.3	11.6	11.6	11.4	9.7
Nonmetallic minerals	8.0	6.7	3.8	6.0	5.2	5.2	5.5
Basic metals	41.0	29.3	23.3	16.1	17.5	14.9	11.1
Machinery and equipment[c]	3.5	26.2	27.2	32.5	29.3	30.1	38.8
Other manufacturing	1.5	3.4	3.2	5.2	6.9	8.9	8.0
All Manufacturing	100.0	100.0	100.0	100.0	100.0	100.0	100.0
Amount (US$ million)	389.9	531.0	1,061.2	1,648.2	2,273.7	2,749.0	4,191.1

[a] These shares are based upon the total existing investments at the end of the year. Data are available from 1988.
[b] The figures for 1988 and 1989 include footwear and leather.
[c] Include fabricated metal products.
Source: Same as Table 9.1.

investment in the forestry, fishery, and mining sectors has been stagnant, while investment in the service sector has also shown steady growth due to increases in investment in the trade sector.

The recent increase in FDI in the manufacturing sector is largely concentrated in labor-intensive industries such as textiles, garments, footwear, and electric and electronic appliances.[1] Table 9.3 shows that the machinery and equipment sector, which includes household electric and electronic products, accounted for the largest share in the manufacturing sector in 1994 with 35.2 percent of total investment. In contrast, the share of investment held by capital-intensive industries is relatively small. The chemical and basic metal industries accounted for 9.7 percent and 11.1 percent of total investment in 1994, respectively. Investment in heavy industries is closely linked with a favorable investment environment provided by the host countries, indicative of the development policy objectives of those countries.

[1] In spite of rapid changes in trade and FDI environment, Korea's FDI until the late 1980s bore a close similarity to the early investment patterns of Japan in its industrial composition and regional distribution (Hamada, 1972).

2.2. Korea's Regional Trade and FDI Patterns

Since the mid-1980s, Korea's intraregional trade in the Asian Pacific has undergone a drastic change: growing interdependence as reflected in the growing total trade volume, and growing competition with other developing countries in the major export markets. Intraregional trade within the Asian Pacific region has dominated Korea's external trade. Exports to and imports from APEC countries have been about 70 percent of Korea's total exports and imports in recent years (Table 9.4). The breakdown of intraregional trade by country reveals Korea's heavy reliance on the United States and Japan, as is the case with most Asian developing countries. In 1990, for example, the United States and Japan accounted for 29.9 percent and 26.6 percent of Korea's total exports, while imports from these two countries accounted for 26.7 percent and 26.6 percent of Korea's total imports.

Since 1990, Korea's reliance on the United States and Japanese export markets has shown a declining trend, whereas the dominance of Japan and the United States as suppliers of imported goods has not changed significantly. Between 1990 and 1993, Korea's export shares to the United States and Japan fell from 29.9 percent and 26.6 percent to 21.7 percent and 19.4 percent, respectively. This change reflects the increasing competition between Korea and other Asian developing countries, such as members of the Association of Southeast Asian Nations (ASEAN) and China. Partly because of increasing similarity in export structures among Asian developing countries, Korea's international competitiveness in the labor-intensive market has suffered.

Korea's trade with Asian developing countries has been growing much more rapidly than that with the United States and Japan. Imports from the Asian developing countries are no longer negligible: 8.2 percent from ASEAN and 4.7 percent from China in 1993. Also in 1993, 11.2 percent of Korea's exports were shipped to ASEAN countries, while 14.4 percent were exported to China and Hong Kong. These market shares are quite large, considering the fact that European countries accounted for 12.0 percent of Korea's exports in the same year.

Korea's outward FDI has also evolved in recent years. Until the early 1990s, Korea actively invested in the ASEAN countries. However, after the diplomatic normalization, China emerged as a

Table 9.4. Regional Distribution of Korea's Trade and FDI (percent)

	Exports			Imports			Outward FDI			Inward FDI		
	1987	1990	1993	1987	1990	1993	1987	1990	1993	1987	1990	1993
East Asia	29.8	36.8	46.1	46.9	37.3	40.8	33.0	30.0	40.4	49.3	31.6	28.5
Japan	17.8	26.6	19.4	33.3	26.6	23.7	0.3	1.1	4.4	46.7	29.4	27.4
China	0.0	0.0	6.4	0.0	0.0	4.7	0.0	1.6	20.6	0.0	0.0	0.0
Hong Kong	4.8	6.2	8.0	0.8	1.0	1.1	4.7	5.8	7.7	0.6	0.4	2.4
Taiwan	1.2	1.9	2.7	1.9	2.1	1.7	0.0	0.2	0.1	0.2	0.5	0.2
ASEAN	4.2	7.8	11.2	6.5	6.9	8.2	31.9	23.0	10.5	2.3	1.8	0.9
Indonesia	0.5	1.7	2.5	2.0	2.3	3.1	31.5	16.5	4.5	0.0	0.0	0.0
Malaysia	0.6	1.1	1.7	2.6	2.3	2.3	0.2	1.7	1.8	0.0	0.0	0.0
Philippines	0.5	0.8	1.1	0.3	0.4	0.4	0.1	3.2	1.0	0.0	0.0	0.0
Singapore	2.0	2.8	3.7	1.1	1.3	1.8	0.1	0.3	0.3	2.3	1.7	0.9
Thailand	0.6	1.5	2.1	0.5	0.7	0.6	0.0	1.4	2.8	0.0	0.0	0.0
NAFTA countries	42.2	33.4	24.6	24.1	26.7	23.5	44.6	47.4	29.7	24.3	40.5	32.8
United States	38.9	29.9	21.7	21.4	24.3	21.3	42.2	34.5	28.8	24.0	40.0	32.6
APEC total	71.9	70.3	68.3	71.1	68.2	68.5	78.4	75.5	70.3	73.6	72.2	61.5
Europe	14.1	13.9	12.0	11.3	12.1	12.3	1.6	4.4	13.0	14.1	22.2	28.3
Rest of the world	14.0	15.8	19.7	17.6	19.7	19.2	20.0	20.1	16.7	12.3	5.6	10.2
Total	100.0	100.0	100.0	100.0	100.0	100.0	100.0	100.0	100.0	100.0	100.0	100.0
Amount (US$ billion)	47,303	65,027	83,535	41,026	69,858	84,338	397	1,022	1,318	1,063	803	1,044

Sources:
International Monetary Fund, Direction of Trade Statistics Yearbook, 1994.
Ministry of Finance, The Current Status of Inward Direct Foreign Investment, various issues.
Bank of Korea, Outward Foreign Investment Statistics, various issues.

strong competitor to ASEAN. As shown in Table 9.4, China's share in Korea's total outward FDI jumped from 1.6 percent in 1990 to 20.6 percent in 1993, while ASEAN's share declined from 23.0 to 10.5 percent during the same period. Korean firms have been looking for new investment opportunities not only in China but also in other Asian developing countries. For example, Bangladesh, India, Pakistan, Sri Lanka, and Vietnam have been emerging as viable destination countries.

In contrast with outward investment, inward investment comes mainly from advanced countries. In 1993, the United States, Japan, and European countries, respectively, accounted for 32.6 percent, 27.4 percent, and 28.3 percent of direct investment in Korea. This draws a quite different picture from 1987, when 46.7 percent of foreign investment in Korea was undertaken by Japanese firms.

2.3. Motivations for Outward FDI and Trade Linkages

The growing importance of Asian developing countries as Korea's trading partners is a positive sign for the complementary division of labor in this region. It may be reasonable to assume that the increase in Korea's FDI in these countries is closely linked to the recent establishment of regional trade ties.

Table 9.5 summarizes motivation for Korea's FDI by region. The major motivation behind Korean firms' decisions to invest in developing countries is the abundance of low-wage workers in the host country. The selection of a particular country is greatly affected by its labor condition. Also important are the advantages of exporting to third-country markets. On the other hand, Korea's investment in developed countries serves other purposes: gathering information, penetrating into the host country's market, and gaining access to advanced technologies (Ryou, Kim, and Min, 1992).[2]

Regional differences in industrial distribution of investment confirm the diverse motivations. Investment in the manufacturing

---

[2] Korean firms have shown a dominant preference for independent management, with a desire to place foreign affiliates under their complete control. Although investment with 100 percent ownership continues to decrease, it still constituted 51 percent of the total number of cases in 1994. In terms of investment amount, it accounted for 59 percent of total investments. Investment with more than 50 percent ownership accounted for 81 percent of total cases and 85 percent of total value in 1994.

Table 9.5. *Motivation for Korea's FDI by Region*

	ASEAN	China	South Asia	US	Mexico	Latin America	EU	Oceania
Cheap labor	4.8	4.7	4.9	0.6	4.7	4.7	1.6	2.1
Trade barriers	1.0	0.4	1.7	1.3	1.7	0.9	4.5	1.6
Raw materials	1.1	1.7	0.6	2.8	0.7	0.3	1.9	0.6
Natural resources	0.5	0.6	0.5	1.8	0.3	0.1	0.9	0.7
Market access	1.5	2.0	0.9	3.5	0.3	1.1	4.5	2.1
High technology	0.2	0.3	0.2	3.3	0.0	0.1	2.5	0.6
Information gathering	2.0	2.5	1.3	3.7	1.3	1.4	4.0	2.0
Third country market	2.6	2.5	2.7	2.1	3.3	2.7	4.1	2.1
Number of samples	93	44	11	12	3	27	8	7

The scale is from zero to five, with zero representing the minimum and five the maximum degree of importance.
Source: Korea Institute for International Economic Policy (KIEP), 1992.

sector is most active in Asia, accounting for 54.5 percent of Korea's total existing investments in that sector as of 1994. In particular, investment in Asia is concentrated in labor-intensive industries such as textiles, apparel, and footwear. In contrast, in North America, which holds 27.5 percent of Korea's total investment in the manufacturing sector, basic metals and household electric goods account for the largest share. Interestingly, the share of the service sector, such as finance, insurance, and wholesale and retail trade, is very high for advanced countries: 39.7 percent for North America and 41.7 percent for Europe in 1994.[3]

These different patterns in foreign investment transform the nature of trade. The 1992 survey conducted by the Korea Institute for International Economic Policy (KIEP) shows that Korean affiliates in the developing countries export more than 80 percent of their products, most of which go to third-country markets such as the United States and the EU. Meanwhile, those in the developed countries export less than 50 percent of goods produced in host countries.

The majority of Korean affiliates in the developing countries maintain strong ties to their parent firms. Most Korean affiliates

---

[3] Korea's outward FDI by region and industry is available from the author upon request.

import new or second-hand production facilities from Korea. They also procure a large portion of raw and intermediate materials from Korea. The amount of raw materials purchased in the local market, though continuously increasing, still constitutes only a small portion of total raw materials purchased. A recent survey of Korean firms investing in China shows that the amount of local purchase accounts for about 33 percent, while imports from Korea equal about 57 percent (Korea Trade Association, 1995).

3. INTERACTION BETWEEN KOREA'S TRADE AND OUTWARD FDI

3.1. The Analytical Framework

Now let us consider if there exists a relationship between the growing importance of APEC countries as Korea's trading partner and the recipient of Korea's outward FDI. The framework for our analysis is based on a generalized gravity model that incorporates the Heckscher-Ohlin type factor-intensity explanation of international trade (e.g., Leamer, 1974; Eaton and Tamura, 1994, 1996). The basic logic behind this approach is that the intensity of bilateral trade between two trading partners is susceptible not only to their market sizes and the distance between the two countries but also to differences in the relative factor endowments.

Gravity models have been used extensively in the empirical trade literature (e.g., Eaton and Tamura, 1994, 1996; Frankel and Wei, 1993; Kawai, 1994; Kawai and Urata, Chapter 8, this volume). While gravity equations for describing trade flows have been derived under a large class of models (Deardorff, 1998), those for explaining direct investment have not been theoretically derived and thus could be subject to some criticisms. In addition, the question of how to model FDI for empirical analysis is controversial (Brainard, 1993, 1997).[4] On the one hand, if FDI aims primarily at utilizing production factors (e.g., labor) at lower cost, then it could be explained by differences in relative factor endowments. On the

---

[4] See Chapter 7, this volume, by Petri and Plummer for the literature review of Brainard (1993, 1997) and other studies on multinational corporations and foreign direct investment.

other hand, if FDI is motivated by trade barriers or access to the local markets, then it is instead affected by such factors as the host country's market size and transportation costs. The extended gravity model is flexible enough to embrace these alternative views on FDI. Of course, this kind of eclectic model is based on the premise that FDI, a major form of international capital flows, originates from the same determinants as those of international trade. Hence, this perspective may be too broad to explain the strategic behavior of multinational corporations.

A general form of the gravity model for trade and FDI incorporating measures of factor endowments may be expressed as follows:

$$Z_i = f\left(Y_i, DIS_i, YPC_i, DEN_i, HC_i, APEC_i\right) \qquad (9.1)$$

where dependent variable Z_i may be one of the following four variables: Korea's exports to country i, imports from country i, outward FDI to country i, or inward FDI from country i. Y_i is country i's GDP, DIS_i is the distance between Korea and its trading partner i, YPC_i is per-capita income of country i, DEN_i is the relative factor intensity of land (land–population ratio), and HC_i is the relative factor intensity for human capital. $APEC_i$ is a regional dummy variable that takes the value of one if trading partner i is an APEC member and zero otherwise.

It is assumed that the model can be expressed in a log-linear form as:

$$\log Z_i = \beta_0 + \beta_1 \log Y_i + \beta_2 \log DIS_i + \beta_3 \log YPC_i$$
$$+ \beta_4 \log DEN_i + \beta_5 \log HC_i + \beta_6 \log APEC_i + u_i \qquad (9.2)$$

where u_i is the disturbance unexplained by the model.

One problem in equation (9.2) is that some observations of Z_i, particularly for those of an FDI variable, may have zero values, causing $\log Z_i$ to be undefined. If observations with zero values of Z_i are excluded, the estimation results would be biased. The problem becomes more serious if the observable range for the dependent variable is restricted. One way of correcting this problem is to assume that trade or FDI is observable only if its value is greater than a cut-off point, a:

$$Z_i = Z_i^* \text{ if } Z_i^* > a$$
$$Z_i = a \text{ otherwise} \qquad (9.3)$$

To deal with the problem of censored data, the model is re-specified as follows:

$$\log\left(Z_i + a_0\right) = \beta_0 + \beta_1 \log Y_i + \beta_2 \log DIS_i + \beta_3 \log YPC_i$$
$$+ \beta_4 \log DEN_i + \beta_5 \log HC_i + \beta_6 \log APEC_i + v_i$$
$$\equiv X_i'\beta + v_i$$

(9.4)

where $X_i' = (1, \log Y_i, \log DIS_i, \log YPC_i, \log DEN_i, \log HC_i, APEC_i)$, and we assume that $v_i \sim N(0, \sigma^2)$. Equation (9.4) is a special case of the Tobit model. A constant (a_0) is added to the dependent variable to accommodate for the cut-off point not being zero. The value for a_0 may not be arbitrarily selected but is estimated using the maximum likelihood method. The log-likelihood function is[5]

$$\log L\left(Z, X'; \beta, a_0\right) = \left\{-\log\left(Z_i + a_0\right) - \frac{1}{2}\left(\log 2\pi + \log \sigma^2\right)\right.$$
$$\left. - \frac{1}{2\sigma^2}\left[\log\left(Z_i + a_0\right) - X'\beta\right]^2\right\}$$

(9.5)

The maximum likelihood estimates of a_0 and β maximize $\log L$ $(Z, X'; \beta, a_0)$.

3.2. Estimation of Trade and FDI Equations

The sample of the variables just summarized is composed of 124 observations corresponding to each of Korea's trading partners and covers years 1987, 1990, and 1993. Data for each dependent or independent variable would be self-explanatory except for human capital (HC). As a proxy for HC, the ratio of students enrolled in postsecondary educational institutions to the total population is used (United Nations, *Statistical Yearbook* 1988/89).[6]

Table 9.6 presents the maximum likelihood estimation results for the generalized gravity model as specified in equation (9.4)

[5] See Eaton and Tamura (1994, 1996) for the derivation.
[6] The ratio of enrollment in secondary educational institutions seems to be inappropriate in our case as a proxy for human capital. Secondary education is well established in most countries so that the ratio of students enrolled in secondary educational institutions does not show much difference among countries.

Table 9.6. *Trade and Investment Equations, 1993 (maximum likelihood, Tobit estimates)*

Dependent variable: log $(Z + a_0)$, Z = exports, imports, outward FDI, or inward FDI.

Variable	Exports	Imports	Outward FDI	Inward FDI
a_0	0.06	0.23	0.45	0.60
	(0.34)	(1.88)	(2.41)	(2.02)
Constant	7.27	1.13	2.62	−7.52
	(8.18)	(4.19)	(3.33)	(−3.03)
log DIS	−0.58	−0.80	−0.66	−1.02
	(−6.22)	(−5.90)	(−9.90)	(−3.38)
log Y	0.72	0.90	0.56	0.82
	(13.25)	(9.86)	(8.17)	(5.32)
log YPC	−0.40	−0.14	−0.35	0.90
	(−6.13)	(−1.28)	(−2.41)	(2.78)
log HC	0.62	0.37	0.70	1.01
	(7.15)	(2.24)	(2.80)	(1.93)
log DEN	−0.24	0.21	−0.06	−0.31
	(−6.68)	(1.97)	(−0.53)	(−1.54)
$APEC$	0.73	1.05	1.59	−1.24
	(2.04)	(1.97)	(2.54)	(−1.52)
Log-likelihood	−567.3	−537.6	−164.1	−77.4
# Observations	124	124	124	124
Number of X=0	0	11	71	103

Numbers in parentheses are the ratios of estimated coefficients to Eicker-White standard errors.

Sources:

(a) Exports and imports: IMF, *Direction of Trade Statistics Yearbook*, various issues.

(b) Outward FDI: Bank of Korea, *Outward Foreign Investment Statistics Yearbook*,1995.

(c) Inward FDI: Ministry of Finance, *The Current Status of Inward Direct Foreign Investment*, 1995.

(d) DIS: Defense Mapping Agency, *Distance between Ports*, 1991.

(e) Y, YPC: IMF, *International Financial Statistics*, various issues.

(f) HC, DEN: United Nations, *Statistical Yearbook*, 1988/89.

applied to Korea's trade and outward FDI in 1993. The results suggest that Korea's trade and outward FDI can be explained reasonably well. As expected, the coefficient on the market size (GDP) of Korea's trading partners is positive and significant for both trade and direct investment. The coefficient on distance between Korea and trading partners is negative and statistically significant in all four equations. While the negative and statistically significant coefficients on distance are expected in trade equations, those are not expected in FDI equations because of low transaction costs.[7] The result for outward FDI suggests that Korea's outward FDI is still at an early stage and thus directed toward more familiar Asia–Pacific countries rather than toward countries of Europe, Africa, or Latin America.

The coefficients of per-capita income are negative except for the case of inward FDI. Per-capita income may be interpreted as reflecting capital–labor ratio, in light of the fact that variables for the density of land and human capital are included in the equations. However, it is difficult to interpret a negative sign on per-capita income because it may suggest that Korea's trade is more active with developing countries.[8] Instead, the results may imply that Korea's trade as well as outward FDI is inclined toward countries larger in population. If the market size in equation (9.4) is represented by population instead of national income, the coefficient of per-capita income becomes positive.

Korea's trade and outward FDI appear to increase as trading partners become more abundant in human capital. The effect of the land–population ratio is mixed, however. Korea exports more to countries with higher population densities but imports more from countries with relatively large territories.

The overall poor performance of the model in the case of inward FDI partly reflects the fact that more foreign investment is accounted for by a relatively small number of countries. In 1993, only 21 out of 124 trading partners invested in Korea, causing a relatively low overall explanatory power for the inward FDI equation.

Let us now turn to the problem of ongoing effects of regional integration on Korea's trade and outward FDI. Korea shows strong regional ties as manifested in the statistically significant positive sign on the regional dummy variable (APEC) with the exception of inward FDI.[9] A comparison of values predicted from estimation

---

[7] Kawai and Urata (Chapter 8, this volume) find that the coefficients on distance are positive and significant for FDI equations in several manufacturing industries.
[8] The estimation results of 1987 and 1990 are quite different, showing positive but insignificant values for per-capita income variable.
[9] Since I am focusing my discussion on Korea's outward FDI and trade, the results on inward FDI are not reported in the remainder of the chapter.

Table 9.7. *Korea's Trade and FDI Bias toward the APEC Countries*

	Exports			Imports			Outward FDI		
	1987	1990	1993	1987	1990	1993	1987	1990	1993
America									
United States	2.7	2.6	0.8	1.5	1.0	0.0	5.0	3.0	2.2
Canada	1.4	1.5	0.5	0.1	−0.4	−0.7	3.1	2.8	−0.3
Mexico	−0.1	1.1	0.2	0.5	0.2	−1.2	0.6	−0.9	0.3
Chile	1.0	1.0	1.2	1.9	2.0	2.1	1.7	0.0	0.8
East Asia									
Japan	−0.2	−0.1	−2.0	−0.7	−0.8	−2.3	−1.0	−2.3	−2.5
China	−5.2	−5.8	−0.4	−5.6	−6.9	−0.9	−0.2	−0.4	1.8
Hong Kong	1.4	1.6	1.2	1.0	1.5	1.1	2.4	0.2	1.5
Taiwan	0.4	1.0	0.5	1.2	1.7	0.3	0.1	−0.1	−1.5
ASEAN									
Indonesia	0.5	1.6	0.5	1.9	2.3	1.4	6.9	3.1	2.2
Malaysia	0.8	1.4	1.1	2.2	2.3	1.5	2.2	1.5	1.9
Philippines	−0.5	−0.1	−1.9	−0.9	−0.2	−2.6	1.2	0.3	−0.9
Singapore	1.5	1.8	1.7	2.5	3.1	3.0	1.6	0.8	0.9
Thailand	0.4	1.2	0.3	0.3	0.8	0.0	1.1	0.6	1.7
Oceania									
Australia	0.8	1.2	0.8	0.5	0.4	0.2	2.5	0.9	1.5
New Zealand	−0.2	−0.2	−0.6	−0.2	0.5	0.7	0.6	−0.7	−1.2
P. New Guinea	0.5	0.1	0.4	3.1	2.6	3.2	2.8	2.3	2.2

The above numbers denote residuals derived from the maximum likelihood estimation of equation (9.4) without the regional dummy variable.
Sources: See Table 9.6.

and the actual values of dependent variables confirms a regional bias toward the Asia–Pacific in Korea's trade and outward FDI.[10] Korea's trade and FDI ties with APEC countries are stronger than predicted by the model, as indicated by positive residuals from the estimation of equation (9.4) (Table 9.7). This phenomenon is particularly apparent with North American and ASEAN countries.

Korea maintains strong economic relationships with the United States, but the linkage has been weakened. This is confirmed by the decreasing size of residuals for the export, import, and outward FDI regression equations. Despite the close ties between Korea and

---

[10] It does not intend to draw any normative implications for regional cooperation. It only tries to review changing patterns of Korea's trade and FDI. Note that the regional dummy (APEC) is not included in this exercise.

Japan, the linkage is not as strong as one might expect. Korea's poor performance in exports and outward investment suggests the existence of trade and investment barriers, particularly informal ones, in the Japanese market. The same may apply to the Korean market with respect to Japanese exports. Meanwhile, what is noteworthy is China's emergence as a major trading partner of Korea. Given the geographical proximity and the potential of the Chinese economy, the interdependence with China is likely to accelerate.

For most APEC countries, there is a close correlation between the trade residuals and the FDI residuals. Chile, Hong Kong, and the ASEAN countries with the exception of the Philippines are good examples. This correlation implies that FDI in Asia or North America is closely related to rapid expansion of exports and imports.

3.3. Empirical Assessment of Trade–FDI Interaction

The interaction between trade (exports and imports) and outward FDI appears to exist from the results in the preceding section. However, the relationship between them is not clear theoretically. For example, it is not determinable whether or not FDI will promote trade. From the viewpoint of the factor endowments theory of trade, the relationship between FDI and exports is not clear because it would depend on whether or not FDI reinforces differences in factor endowments (Helpman, 1984). From the management standpoint, FDI may promote exports through cost reduction, supply of intermediate goods, or improvement of the producer's market image, unless the market size is fixed. Thus a more rigorous analysis is in order.

First, let us consider the correlation matrix of residuals from estimation of equation (9.4). Any significant correlation of residuals can be interpreted as implying that interaction among variables concerned is stronger than explainable by the variables included in the model. Panel A of Table 9.8 shows that interactions among residuals of estimation based on the annual data are all positively related, but the correlation is not very strong, except between exports and imports, and to some extent between trade (both exports and imports) and outward FDI. Interestingly, the correlation between trade and outward FDI is considerably higher in 1987 and 1990 than in 1993.

Table 9.8. *Correlations Structure of Residuals*

A. Regression of the annual data

	EX–93	IM–93	OFDI–93	EX–90	IM–90	OFDI–90	EX–87	IM–87	OFDI–87
EX–93	1.00								
IM–93	0.57	1.00							
OFDI–93	0.10	0.08	1.00						
EX–90	0.46	0.43	0.08	1.00					
IM–90	0.34	0.53	0.24	0.75	1.00				
OFDI–90	0.11	0.12	0.69	0.27	0.36	1.00			
EX–87	0.43	0.37	0.05	0.83	0.68	0.22	1.00		
IM–87	0.29	0.51	0.31	0.70	0.92	0.40	0.65	1.00	
OFDI–87	0.11	0.10	0.71	0.27	0.40	0.76	0.30	0.45	1.00

B. Regression of the pooled data

	All countries	APEC countries	Non-APEC countries	Developed countries	Developing countries
EX–IM	0.68	0.64	0.65	0.53	0.69
EX–OFDI	0.24	0.64	0.22	0.11	0.23
IM–OFDI	0.27	0.53	0.29	0.17	0.28

Based on estimation of equation (9.4).

When the sample is divided into subgroups, the correlation among variables becomes more apparent. As shown in panel B of Table 9.8, residuals based on the pooled data reveal that interaction between trade and outward FDI are very strong for the APEC countries. If developing and developed countries are compared, the interaction between trade and FDI is a little stronger in the case of developing countries.

This correlation structure summarizes a general picture of interaction among trade and outward FDI but provides no information about causality among them. For example, it is possible that the interaction may be caused by a common factor affecting both trade and FDI that is not included in the model.

In order to analyze outward FDI's effect on trade, or vice versa, one possibility is to use outward FDI (*OFDI*) or trade (*T*: exports or imports) as an explanatory variable and to test the hypothesis that its coefficient equals zero:

$$
\log\left(T_i + a_0\right) = \beta_0 + \beta_1 \log Y_i + \beta_2 \log DIS_i + \beta_3 \log YPC_i
$$
$$
+ \beta_4 \log DEN_i + \beta_5 \log HC_i + \beta_6 \log APEC_i
$$
$$
+ \beta_7 \log\left(OFDI_i - t\right) + \varepsilon_i \tag{9.6}
$$

$$
\log\left(OFDI_i + a_0\right) = \beta_0 + \beta_1 \log Y_i + \beta_2 \log DIS_i + \beta_3 \log YPC_i
$$
$$
+ \beta_4 \log DEN_i + \beta_5 \log HC_i + \beta_6 \log APEC_i
$$
$$
+ \beta_7 \log\left(T_i - t\right) + \eta_i
$$

$$
\tag{9.7}
$$

It should be noted that the simultaneity of *OFDI* and *T* makes the use of current values for these variables inappropriate. Furthermore, the simultaneous equation system comprising the foregoing equations is latent with an identification problem. If lagged dependent variables are used instead, we can mitigate the seriousness of these problems and still sustain consistency with our previous discussion.[11]

---

[11] The maximum likelihood estimates of current endogenous variables are positive and statistically significant. But both the two-stage least squares estimation and the maximum likelihood estimation using instrumental variables show that they are negative and insignificant.

Table 9.9. *Interactions between Korea's Exports and Outward FDI, Pooled Data (maximum likelihood, Tobit estimates)*

A. Dependent variable: log (Exports + a_0)

Variable	All countries	APEC countries	Non-APEC countries	Developed countries	Developing countries
a_0	2.07	0.70	1.62	0.34	1.52
	(5.05)	(2.92)	(4.76)	(0.79)	(4.21)
Constant	7.52	1.06	9.66	6.56	10.01
	(80.16)	(5.32)	(39.76)	(11.27)	(103.71)
log *DIS*	−0.61	0.25	−0.92	−0.55	−0.87
	(−37.59)	(4.30)	(−89.99)	(−6.56)	(−43.23)
log *Y*	0.44	0.07	0.48	0.72	0.39
	(10.50)	(0.94)	(10.54)	(15.09)	(7.49)
log *YPC*	−0.12	0.62	−0.15	−0.35	−0.16
	(−2.64)	(7.83)	(−2.37)	(−3.12)	(−4.09)
log *HC*	0.50	0.24	0.49	0.68	0.50
	(6.35)	(1.08)	(7.01)	(4.27)	(6.12)
log *DEN*	−0.20	−0.44	−0.15	−0.24	−0.15
	(−8.74)	(−16.31)	(−4.63)	(−3.63)	(−5.47)
log $OFDI_{-3}$	0.50	0.54	0.62	−0.08	0.56
	(5.73)	(4.19)	(4.58)	(−.95)	(4.61)
Log-likelihood	−1148.6	−243.5	−900.4	−185.4	−857.6
# Observations	248	32	216	44	204

Numbers in parentheses are the ratios of estimated coefficients to Eicker-White standard errors.
Sources: See Table 9.6.

Table 9.9 reports information of the interaction between exports and outward FDI derived from the maximum likelihood estimation of equations (9.6) and (9.7). Because of lack of observations in consecutive years, two separate data sets covering 1990 and 1993 are pooled together, and the outward FDI or trade variable added as an explanatory variable takes a three-year lagged value.

The positive and significant coefficient on the outward FDI variable in the export equation (panel A) suggests that an increase in direct investment would increase exports to the host country. The export promotion effect of FDI differs between developed and

Table 9.9 *(continued)*

B. Dependent variable: log $(OFDI + a_0)$

Variable	All countries	APEC countries	Non-APEC countries	Developed countries	Developing countries
a_0	0.93	0.75	0.73	0.13	1.26
	(3.96)	(1.38)	(2.68)	(1.89)	(3.77)
Constant	5.82	−0.48	7.25	−5.61	10.45
	(17.61)	(−0.25)	(10.39)	(−6.36)	(22.17)
log DIS	−0.97	−0.13	−0.99	−0.07	−1.38
	(−9.63)	(−0.60)	(−10.75)	(−0.33)	(−21.22)
log Y	0.44	0.66	0.39	2.37	0.28
	(8.92)	(4.14)	(9.30)	(39.70)	(9.41)
log YPC	−0.36	−0.86	−0.32	−2.83	−0.21
	(−4.19)	(−5.15)	(−4.16)	(−12.22)	(−2.71)
log HC	0.61	−0.19	0.82	1.81	0.67
	(5.01)	(−0.64)	(4.06)	(3.91)	(4.44)
log DEN	0.07	0.11	−0.09	0.48	0.09
	(0.90)	(1.10)	(−0.80)	(14.69)	(1.03)
log $EXPORTS_{-3}$	0.13	0.43	0.05	−0.48	0.04
	(1.72)	(2.49)	(0.54)	(−2.49)	(0.51)
Log-likelihood	−330.6	−106.3	−213.6	−48.4	−225.5
# Observations	248	32	216	44	204

developing countries when the sample is divided into the two groups, however. Direct investment in developed countries does not help increase exports, whereas direct investment in developing countries promotes exports. This finding is consistent with the motivations for Korea's FDI in developing countries and the procurement behavior of Korean affiliates (see section 2.3).

Similarly to export promotion, outward FDI affects Korea's imports from the host country. Although the results are not reported here, the coefficient on the lagged value of outward FDI turned out to be statistically significant, except for the case of developed countries. However, an increase in imports does not promote direct investment as the coefficients on imports were insignificant in all cases.

A comparison of the results reported in the two panels of Table 9.9 suggests that the causality from exports to outward FDI is generally weaker than that from outward FDI to exports. Only the case of APEC countries reveals a strong investment promotion effect of exports (panel B). The case of developed countries shows a negative and significant coefficient on the lagged export variable, suggesting that investment may be used as an instrument to circumvent trade barriers in developed countries.

In sum, Korea's outward FDI and exports generally have a mutually complementary relationship. Korea's outward FDI promotes exports both globally and regionally. In contrast, the effect of exports on outward FDI is significant only for APEC countries. Outward FDI in the Asia–Pacific countries also promotes imports. Meanwhile, trade promotion effects of outward FDI are not significant in the case of developed countries, reflecting differences in motivations for FDI.

4. KOREA'S OUTWARD FDI AND INDUSTRIAL ADJUSTMENT

4.1. Trade Promotion of Outward FDI in Korean Manufacturing

In this section, we continue to investigate the interaction between FDI and trade with a focus on four manufacturing sectors with relatively large shares of Korea's outward FDI: textiles and apparel, footwear and leather, chemicals, and machinery and equipment. One characteristic of these industries is the seemingly insignificant correlation between FDI and exports. This is also the case between FDI and imports with the exception of the textiles and apparel industry. One notable reason for this insignificant relationship between outward FDI and trade stems from the fact that Korea targets third countries instead of the host country as its major export markets. This can be traced further to the division of labor among Korea, Japan, and the United States: Korea's dependence on Japan for its imports of capital goods and intermediate goods, and the reliance on the United States for Korea's exports of manufactured products.

The footwear industry is a typical example of Korea's regional trade and FDI patterns. APEC member countries invited 93.7

percent of Korea's total outward FDI in this industry in 1993, with China and ASEAN countries accounting for more than 80 percent. Exports to these countries amounted to less than 20 percent, however. In contrast, the chemical industry provides a different picture to the traditional division of labor of Korea. For example, China's share accounted for 10.3 percent of Korea's total outward FDI and 10.5 percent of Korea's exports in 1993. Exports to ASEAN are rapidly increasing, reflecting growth in the domestic markets in these countries.

The interaction between trade and FDI in the manufacturing sectors is analyzed using the same method as in the previous section. For each manufacturing industry, a formal test based on estimation of equations (9.6) and (9.7) is adopted. Table 9.10 reports the maximum likelihood estimation results for both export and import equations. The results show vast differences across industry on the trade promotion effect of outward FDI.[12]

The textiles and apparel as well as footwear and leather industries are the most notable examples of export-oriented industries that are losing competitiveness. In these industries, outward FDI promotes exports to the host country. This finding is consistent with the firm-level survey results indicating that the foreign affiliates of Korean firms import intermediate goods from their parent firms. The export promotion effect of outward FDI is not clear with the chemical and machinery and equipment industries.

In general, the import promotion effect of FDI is insignificant. This finding reflects that reexports to Korea by foreign affiliates are not sizable, even though these industries are export-oriented. The outward FDI in the chemical industry shows a positive and significant effect on imports. It may be explained by a difference in

---

[12] The correlation structure of residuals from estimation of equation (9.4) is as follows:

	EX93-OFDI93	IM93-OFDI93	EX93-OFDI90	IM93-OFDI90	EX90-OFDI90	IM90-OFDI90	EX90-OFDI93	IM90-OFDI93
Textiles and apparel	0.21	0.27	0.18	0.29	0.07	0.37	0.11	0.34
Footwear and leather	0.33	0.40	0.20	0.36	0.25	0.68	0.31	0.62
Chemicals	0.08	0.58	0.06	0.55	0.08	0.70	0.07	0.66
Machinery and equip.	0.06	0.48	0.02	0.41	0.10	0.63	0.16	0.64

Note that the 1987 data on outward FDI in the manufacturing industries are not available.

Table 9.10 *Trade and FDI in Korea's Manufacturing Sectors, 1993 (maximum likelihood, Tobit estimates)*

Dependent Variable: log $(T + a_0)$, T = exports or imports

Variable	Textiles and apparel		Footwear and leather	
	Exports	Imports	Exports	Imports
a_0	10.33	1.49	2.75	1.70
	(4.66)	(6.36)	(5.31)	(6.99)
Constant	8.66	10.86	2.88	6.67
	(30.82)	(41.38)	(12.33)	(14.49)
log DIS	−0.54	−1.50	−0.44	−1.76
	(16.50)	(40.16)	(−18.42)	(−24.82)
log Y	0.86	1.74	1.36	1.93
	(10.59)	(16.38)	(16.72)	(11.33)
log YPC	−0.47	−0.56	−0.54	−0.74
	(−9.93)	(−24.07)	(−11.28)	(−12.05)
log HC	0.59	0.53	0.73	0.74
	(5.12)	(2.01)	(3.76)	(2.02)
log DEN	0.04	−0.82	−0.28	−0.23
	(1.32)	(−14.92)	(−13.80)	(−6.46)
$APEC$	0.14	−1.06	0.52	−1.08
	(0.24)	(−1.42)	(0.61)	(−1.46)
log $OFDIK_{-3}$[a]	0.19	0.12	0.21	−0.11
	(3.50)	(1.83)	(1.81)	(−1.09)
Log-likelihood	−1214.8	−703.9	−870.9	−567.5
# Observations	124	124	124	124
Number of X=0	5	43	27	59

[a] Outward DFI stock ($OFDIK$) is used because the flow data are not available.
Sources: See Table 9.6.

market orientation and, more common to that industry, by the product differentiation.[13]

The foregoing results on disparity between export-promotion and import-promotion effects across manufacturing sectors might suggest that Korea still maintains the traditional trade linkages despite the recent increase in outward FDI. However, the growth

[13] The causality from the lagged exports to outward FDI is apparent for the textiles and apparel, and machinery and equipment industries.

Table 9.10 *(continued)*

Variable	Chemicals		Machinery and equipment	
	Exports	Imports	Exports	Imports
a_0	18.02	1.64	23.99	1.77
	(4.81)	(7.08)	(4.88)	(3.60)
Constant	12.32	2.42	11.74	8.36
	(91.62)	(6.06)	(80.72)	(32.60)
log *DIS*	−0.65	−1.34	−0.21	−1.24
	(−26.83)	(−21.22)	(−7.59)	(−29.01)
log *Y*	0.72	1.93	0.89	1.02
	(13.89)	(13.35)	(36.60)	(17.04)
log *YPC*	−0.50	−0.01	−0.73	0.46
	(−21.77)	(−.36)	(−22.70)	(8.79)
log *HC*	0.46	1.16	1.01	1.05
	(4.62)	(2.71)	(11.38)	(3.51)
log *DEN*	−0.14	−0.74	−0.32	−0.73
	(−4.43)	(−10.02)	(−18.03)	(−13.42)
APEC	0.61	−1.73	1.01	0.89
	(1.14)	(−1.56)	(1.73)	(0.90)
log *OFDIK_3*	0.10	0.36	−0.04	0.12
	(1.74)	(4.30)	(−0.59)	(1.31)
Log-likelihood	−1173.9	−760.9	−1346.8	−838.9
# Observations	124	124	124	124
Number of $X=0$	0	58	4	35

of Asian markets is expected to result in a gradual change of this traditional division of labor. A gradual increase in imports of textiles and apparel, as well as of chemicals, can be seen as such a sign. Judging from the experience of Japan, reimports of the labor-intensive goods as well as the capital-intensive goods produced by the standard technology are likely to increase soon (Urata, 1992).

4.2. Outward FDI and Deindustrialization

Now let us consider the so-called deindustrialization phenomenon. On the one hand, it is sometimes argued that outward FDI is detrimental to the domestic economy because it leads to an increase in imports of manufactured goods from overseas affiliates. On the other hand, outward FDI may be considered to reflect an ongoing process of industrial adjustment centering on capital- and technology-intensive industries.

Table 9.11 provides the extent of outward FDI, export specialization, and import penetration in ten manufacturing industries. As shown in the table, outward FDI is still of very minor importance. The ratio of outward FDI stock to the domestic capital stock (tangible fixed assets) shows a rising trend, but in 1993 it was only 1.6 percent for the manufacturing sector as a whole. The most notable cases were labor-intensive industries such as textiles and apparel (2.4 percent), footwear and leather (6.7 percent), and wood and furniture (3.5 percent).[14]

Outward FDI and exports in the manufacturing sector are positively related. The former has been considerable in export-oriented industries such as textiles and apparel, footwear and leather, and machinery and equipment. Except for the wood and furniture industry, outward FDI has been relatively inactive for the inward-looking industries. This disparity might be explained by a fall in international competitiveness of export-oriented industries. The correlation coefficient between changes in the outward FDI ratio and changes in the export-specialization index during 1990–93 was −0.7. This figure suggests that an increase in outward FDI occurred to a large extent in industries experiencing a loss in export competitiveness.

It is interesting to note that the share of imports in total demand for manufactured goods shows a decreasing trend. The import penetration ratio in the manufacturing sector as a whole declined from 26.4 percent in 1987 to 20.3 percent in 1993. This reflects that increases in demand for domestic products were larger than increases in demand for imported products during 1987–93. In other words, despite increasing imports, increases in domestic production aimed at the growing domestic market caused the share of imported goods to shrink. The ratios of outward FDI stock to the domestic capital stock and the import penetration ratios are neg-

---

[14] One might ask if the value of domestic capital stock is overestimated due to Korea's high land prices. The overall picture does not change significantly if we instead compute the ratio of outward FDI flows to the gross fixed capital formation in the manufacturing sector (2.0 percent in 1990).

Table 9.11. *Korea's Outward FDI, Export Specialization and Import Penetration (percent)*

Industry	Outward FDI/Capital Stock[a]		Export Specialization Index[b]			Import Penetration Index[c]		
	1990	1993	1987	1990	1993	1987	1990	1993
Food processing	1.0	1.0	−40.6	−55.3	−59.8	19.5	18.4	15.1
Textile and apparel	1.7	2.4	77.0	73.2	68.1	24.1	23.6	14.4
Footwear and leather	3.4	6.7	73.0	73.1	61.8	25.6	24.7	16.3
Wood and furniture	1.7	3.5	−52.3	−70.6	−85.0	29.9	26.7	26.3
Pulp and paper	0.4	0.8	−49.4	−55.1	−42.5	13.5	13.3	9.3
Chemicals	0.8	0.8	−28.2	−36.8	−17.7	21.5	21.9	19.7
Nonmetallic minerals	0.7	1.2	−28.4	−50.0	−48.1	19.2	19.4	12.5
Basic metals	1.9	2.4	−1.0	−7.3	12.7	25.7	24.1	19.4
Machinery and equip.[d]	0.9	1.4	9.2	1.5	9.2	36.1	29.6	25.0
Other manufacturing	2.0	14.2	60.9	57.9	33.6	21.7	33.1	26.8
All manufacturing	1.2	1.6	14.1	3.8	8.0	26.4	24.5	20.3

[a] Outward FDI/Capital Stock = The amount of total existing foreign investments/the amount of domestic capital stock (tangible fixed assets).
[b] Export Specialization Index = (Exports − Imports)/(Exports + Imports).
[c] Import Penetration Index = Imports/(Production − Exports + Imports).
[d] Include fabricated metal products.

Sources:

(a) Korea Trade Association, *Korea Trade Statistics* (on-line service).
(b) National Statistical Office, *Report on Mining and Manufacturing Survey* (1987, 1990).
(c) National Statistical Office, *Report on Industrial Census* (1993).

atively correlated, but the value of the correlation is statistically insignificant.

The current increase in Korea's outward FDI in manufacturing sectors, particularly in Asia, is "trade-oriented" so that it should contribute to industrial restructuring in the region.[15] The recent increase in outward FDI can be seen as a result, rather than a cause, of the changing patterns of international division of labor. However, the impact of outward FDI on domestic industrial adjustment is far from significant, although not negligible, for most manufacturing industries.

5. SUMMARY AND CONCLUSIONS

Korea's outward foreign direct investment has increased dramatically since the mid-1980s. The total value of Korea's existing investments rose from $0.65 billion in 1986 to $7.6 billion in 1994. Manufacturing industries, particularly those that are losing international competitiveness, constitute a large component of this rapid increase in FDI. Typical examples are labor-intensive industries, such as textiles, garments, footwear, and electric and electronic appliances. Another component of the rapid increase in FDI is a significant increase in small-scale investments of less than $1.0 million.

This chapter has provided several interesting findings as summarized in the following paragraphs.

(1) Korea's outward FDI is primarily concentrated in the Asian Pacific region. Asia and North America accounted for 41.9 and 35.3 percent of the value of total existing investments at the end of 1994, respectively. In contrast, Europe accounted for only 12.8 percent of total existing investments in 1994. To some extent, these regional differences reflect the motives behind Korea's outward FDI: to utilize cheap labor in manufacturing export goods in developing countries, and to gain market access by circumventing trade barriers in industrialized countries.

(2) Korea's FDI and trade in the Asian Pacific is most prominent with Asian developing countries, while Korea's traditional reliance on Japan and the United States has lessened. However, the division

---

[15] This type of relationship has been suggested by Kojima (1973, 1975).

of labor in the region is not easy to characterize. For instance, Korea's economic ties with Asian developing countries have shown a considerable change, as bilateral economic transactions with China have rapidly increased. Since the normalization of diplomatic relationship in 1992 between China and Korea, China has competed with ASEAN to host Korea's outward FDI. By 1994, China had become the largest recipient of Korea's FDI. Still, Korea's FDI in China is dominated by small-scale investment aimed at exploiting low-wage labor.

(3) The maximum likelihood estimates of the generalized gravity model suggest that Korea's trade and FDI are positively affected by the trading partner's market size and negatively by the distance between Korea and its partner. Population also turns out to be an important determinant of Korea's trade and FDI patterns, whereas its trade and FDI have a tendency to lean toward countries with abundant human capital.

(4) Korea's trade and FDI show a clear propensity toward a regionalization in the Asia–Pacific. This phenomenon is particularly evident with North American and ASEAN countries, and more recently with China. While Korea maintains strong economic ties with Japan, its relatively low levels of exports and outward investment to Japan might suggest extensive trade and investment barriers there. Korea also has significant trade and investment barriers. In this sense, a concerted effort for liberalization is needed to gain more fully from growth and increasing interdependence of the Pacific Rim economies.

(5) Korea's outward FDI is shown to promote exports to the host country, as well as imports from that country. Whereas exports generally promote outward FDI, imports do not. Thus there appears to be a mutually expansionary linkage between outward FDI and exports, particularly for the APEC countries. Of course, the significance of this linkage differs depending on the motivations for FDI. Dividing the sample into developing and developed countries reveals that Korea's outward FDI toward developing countries promotes exports to the host countries as well as imports from them. In contrast, direct investment in developed countries has no clear effect on exports to and imports from those countries.

(6) The interaction between FDI and trade in manufacturing differs across industry. Although outward FDI has a tendency to promote exports to the host country in industries that are losing

international competitiveness, such as textiles and apparel, this tendency is not observed in the machinery and equipment industry. The import promotion effect of FDI is generally insignificant, except in the chemical industry.

(7) Despite increases in reimports from Korean affiliates abroad, the so-called deindustrialization phenomenon is exaggerated. The ratio of foreign direct investment to domestic investment is very small, averaging only 1.6 percent in manufacturing industries in 1993. Moreover, the share of imports in demand for manufactured goods has decreased in recent years.

The policy implications of this study are simple and clear: A liberal trade environment should be nurtured, and FDI should be further facilitated to promote ongoing industrial adjustment in the Asian Pacific. Given the complementary relationship between trade and FDI, both trade and investment should be liberalized to help the Asia–Pacific region realize fully its growth potential. In this sense, more systematic efforts are imperative to guarantee multilateral liberalization of regulations on FDI. Considering the growing importance of FDI in regional economic integration in the Asia–Pacific region, a binding investment code incorporating the right of establishment and national treatment is much needed. Policymakers must be reminded that the level of FDI is the most critical barometer of the investment environment. In this era of globalization, it is no longer meaningful to distinguish between domestic and foreign firms.

REFERENCES

Blomstrom, M., Lipsey, R. E., and Kulchycky, K. (1988), "U.S. and Swedish Direct Investment and Exports," in R. Baldwin, ed., *Trade Policy Issues and Empirical Analysis*, Chicago: University of Chicago Press and NBER.

Brainard, S. L. (1993), An Empirical Assessment of the Factor Proportions Explanation of Multinational Sales, NBER Working Paper No. 4583.

——— (1997), "An Empirical Assessment of the Proximity-Concentration Tradeoff between Multinational Sales and Trade," *American Economic Review*, 87: 520–544.

Deardorff, Alan V. (1998), "Determinants of Bilateral Trade: Does Gravity Work in a Neoclassical World?" in Jeffrey A. Frankel, ed., *The Regionalization of the World Economy*, Chicago: University of Chicago Press.

Eaton, Jonathan, and Akiko Tamura (1994), "Bilateralism and Regionalism in Japanese and U.S. Trade and Direct Foreign Investment Patterns," *Journal of the Japanese and International Economies*, 8: 478–510.

(1996), "Japanese and U.S. Exports and Investment as Conduits of Growth," in T. Ito and A. O. Krueger, eds., *Financial Deregulation and Integration in East Asia*, Chicago: University of Chicago Press and NBER.

Frankel, Jeffrey A., and Shang-Jin Wei (1993), "Trade Blocs and Currency Blocs," NBER Working Paper No. 4335.

Graham, E. M. (1994), "US Direct Investment Abroad and US Exports in the Manufacturing Sector: Some Empirical Results Based on Cross Sectional Analysis," mimeo, Washington, D.C.: Institute for International Economics.

Hamada, Koichi (1972), "Japanese Investment Abroad," in Peter Drysdale, ed., *Direct Foreign Investment in Asia and the Pacific*, Toronto: University of Toronto.

Helpman, Elhanan (1984), "A Simple Theory of International Trade with Multinational Corporations," *Journal of Political Economy*, 92: 451–471.

Kawai, Masahiro (1994), "Interactions of Japan's Trade and Investment: A Special Emphasis of East Asia," Discussion Paper Series No.F-39, Institute of Social Science, Tokyo: University of Tokyo.

Kim, Jundong (1994), "Exports and Outward FDI in the Era of Globalization," Seoul: Korea Institute for International Economic Policy (in Korean).

Kojima, Kiyoshi (1973), "A Macroeconomic Approach to Foreign Direct Investment," *Hitotsubashi Journal of Economics*, 14: 1–21.

(1975), "International Trade and Foreign Investment: Substitutes or Complements," *Hitotsubashi Journal of Economics*, 16: 1–12.

Korea Trade Association (1995), *Current Status and Performance of Korean Firms Invested in China*, Seoul: Korea Trade Association (in Korean).

Leamer, Edward E. (1974), "The Commodity Composition of International Trade in Manufactures: An Empirical Analysis," *Oxford Economic Papers*, 26: 350–374.

Lee, Chung H., and Keun Lee (1991), "A Transition Economy and Outward Direct Foreign Investment," paper presented at the APO-EWC Seminar on the Role of Foreign Investment in Development, Seoul, September 16–20.

Lee, Keun, and Michael G. Plummer (1992), "Competitive Advantages, Two-Way Foreign Investment, and Capital Accumulation in Korea," *Asian Economic Journal*, 6: 93–113.

Lipsey, Robert E., and Merle Y. Weiss (1981), "Foreign Production and Exports in Manufacturing Industries," *Review of Economics and Statistics*, 63: 488–494.

Ryou, Jai-Won, Sijoong Kim, and Chung-Ki Min (1992), "The Current

Status of Korea's Outward Foreign Direct Investment and Policy Issues," Policy Report 92-07, Seoul: Korea Institute for International Economic Policy (in Korean).

Urata, Shujiro (1992), "Changing Patterns of Direct Investment and the Implications for Trade and Development," mimeo, Tokyo: Waseda University.

Wakasugi, Ryuhei (1994), "Is Japanese Foreign Direct Investment a Substitute for International Trade?" *Japan and the World Economy*, 6: 45–62.

Comment

Chung H. Lee

Many of the issues relating to the trade-investment nexus are still very controversial, and this informative and well-crafted chapter by Jai-Won Ryou is an attempt to address some of these issues in the context of South Korea (henceforth Korea). Specifically, it raises the following three questions: (1) What is the linkage between Korea's trade with developing Asia on the one hand and Korea's FDI in the region on the other? (2) How does Korea's outward FDI affect both the exports to and imports from the host country? (3) What is the interaction between FDI and trade in manufacturing industries and its implications for Korea's industrial adjustment? In answering these questions, the author utilizes a generalized gravity model and derives some interesting empirical results. I basically concur with the overall conclusions of the chapter and its sound policy recommendations. However, a gravity model of the type used in this chapter does not appear to provide satisfactory answers to the foregoing questions.

The model specifies bilateral trade or FDI between Korea and another country as a function of GDP, per-capita income, land–population ratio, and human capital of the latter (and Korea's FDI in that country in the case of trade), as well as the distance between the two countries. Relations between FDI and trade are not, however, so simple and straightforward as to be captured adequately in such a model. The motives for FDI can vary from industry to industry and from country to country, and its effect on trade can be, therefore, that of either complementarity or substitution.

As the author himself points out, Korea's outward FDI can be roughly divided into two groups – one group of FDI has gone to developing Asia, and the other to North America and the European Union (EU). The first group of investment is basically from some of the labor-intensive industries in which Korea has been losing its comparative advantage, and the motivating factor is to maintain price competitiveness in the export markets. In other words, Korean investment in developing Asia has been carried out by and large to create export platforms for markets in North America and EU. The effect of this FDI on bilateral trade is thus limited to Korea's export of capital and intermediate goods to the host countries with a resulting bilateral complementary relationship between outward FDI and exports.

Korean FDI in North America and EU, which is largely in manufacturing and trading, is for the purpose of securing the host country markets either by manufacturing locally or by importing from Korea or Korean subsidiaries in developing Asia. In the case of investment in manufacturing facilities, there will be strong substitutability between Korea's outward FDI and its exports. In the case of investment in trading, however, there may be some complementary relationship between the two because FDI in trading will facilitate exports from Korean affiliates in developing Asia as well as directly from Korea. The point of the discussion is that, given the different motivations for and, consequently, the different effects of FDI, a gravity model such as the one utilized in this chapter seems to add very little to what one could learn by careful investigation of statistical and survey data, as the author has done in the first half of the chapter.

A short comment on the effect of outward FDI on deindustrialization seems to be warranted. Given the small size of Korea's outward FDI, hardly anyone would expect it to bring about deindustrialization of the entire manufacturing sector. If, however, one is to ask whether Korea's outward FDI has had the effect of gutting some specific manufacturing industries, it is a different matter. As Ryou concludes, its effect on certain labor-intensive industries has been far from negligible. But for Korea, which is still in the process of becoming a mature industrialized economy, losing these industries does not mean that deindustrialization is taking place. It is more likely that Korea is shifting into capital- and technology-intensive manufacturing industries. In that case, the effect of outward FDI on the economic structure of Korea is far from that of deindustrialization of the entire manufacturing sector and rather that of facilitating structural adjustments in accordance with changing comparative advantage.

Finally, what has happened in Korea in recent years with regard to its FDI and trade pattern is very similar to what Japan went through during the 1970s. To those who are acquainted with some of the Japanese writings on FDI and on what is called the "boomerang effect," the issues raised in this chapter are all too familiar. A study comparing Japan and Korea may thus shed light on the relationship between FDI and trade as well as between FDI and structural changes in a "catching-up" economy.

## CHAPTER 10

China's Absorption of Foreign Direct Investment

Shang-Jin Wei

1. INTRODUCTION

In 1978, when the economic reform just started, China was a country without any foreign direct investment (FDI). Now, with almost 40 billion U.S. dollars of inflow in 1995 alone and $135 billion cumulatively since the start of the reform, it carries the distinction of being the largest developing-country host to direct international investment and the second largest host in the world.

Is China a black hole for international direct investment? Will it attract more investment at as rapid a rate as it has in the last five years? Many developing countries in Asia and elsewhere are concerned that FDI flows to China might displace investment going to their countries.

Contrary to the perception that China may have attracted too much FDI, a number of observations suggest that China may be an *underachiever* as a host to FDI. On the one hand, over 50 percent of FDI going to China, in terms of both annual flows and the cumulative stock, comes from overseas China, particularly from Hong Kong and Taiwan. On the other hand, over 80 percent of FDI originates from OECD countries, principally from the United States, Japan, Great Britain, France, and Germany. Thus China may not have attracted enough direct investment from these source countries relative to some international norm. Indeed, using data on FDI distribution in 1990, my earlier study (Wei, 1996) finds that, relative to gross national product and other economic and geographic characteristics, China is an underperformer as a host

I would like to thank K. C. Fung, Hiro Lee, David Roland-Holst, and other participants of the International Conference on Economic Development and Cooperation in the Pacific Basin for helpful comments; Chen Huaxuen, Esther Drill, Greg Dorchak, and especially Jungshik Kim for excellent research assistance; and Esther Drill for efficient editorial assistance. I alone am responsible for any errors that remain.

country for investment originated from the United States and major European source countries.

The current chapter extends Wei (1996) in two dimensions. First, the issue of whether China is still an underachiever is reexamined using a more recent data set. Given the rapid growth of inward FDI, this underachievement could be a past phenomenon.[1] Second, the FDI equation is respecified by including a number of additional indicators of a host country, such as its wage level and degree of corruption. Section 2 provides an overview of foreign invested firms in China. In section 3, I attempt to put China's hosting of FDI in an international perspective. Using data on outward investment from fourteen OECD source countries, a "normal" amount of FDI inflow is estimated as a function of the host country's economic characteristics. China's actual receipt of investment from these countries is then compared with the model prediction. Section 4 concludes the chapter.

2. GENERAL FEATURES OF FOREIGN INVESTMENT IN CHINA

Up to 1991, foreign capital going into China largely took the form of loans. In 1991, the size of FDI was slightly above 60 percent of that of loans. But the relative sizes of the two were reversed in 1992. In 1993, the total amount of realized foreign direct investment reached US$27.5 billion, more than twice that of the loans (US$11.2 billion) (Table 10.1).

Two types of data on direct investment are typically reported in Chinese statistics: contractual value and realized amount. A contractual value reflects the amount of investment that foreign investors plan or intend to invest in China (over a period of time) at the time the investment application is approved by the Chinese government. The actual investment is not bound by this "contractual" amount and is typically much smaller. Indeed, the reported "contractual" amount may even inflate the planned or intended investment because local government officials may have an incentive to announce (or to lure foreign investors to agree on) a large number. For all practical purposes, only the realized amount or

---

[1] Ideally, we would like to use more recent information than 1992, but that appears to be the most current year for which a consistent cross-country data set is available.

Table 10.1. *Realized Foreign Capital Inflows to China, 1990–93 (millions of US dollars)*

	1990	1991	1992	1993
Total	10289	11554	19202	38960
External Loans	6535	6888	7911	11189
Loans from foreign governments	2524	1810	2566	3041
Loans from international financial institutions	1066	1365	1306	2268
Export credit	898	1162	989	1221
Commercial bank loans	2044	2443	1778	3271
Bonds and equity shares issued abroad	3	108	1271	1388
Foreign Direct Investment	3487	4366	11007	27515
Joint ventures	1886	2299	6115	15348
Contractual joint ventures	674	764	2122	5238
Wholly-owned foreign firms	683	1135	2520	6506
Joint exploration	244	169	250	424
Other Foreign Investment	268	300	284	256
International leasing	30	7	45	46
Compensation trade	159	208	172	89
Export processing/assembly	79	85	67	120

Source: China Ministry of Foreign Economic Relations and Trade, *Almanac of China's Foreign Economic Relations and Trade*, 1991/92, 1992/93, and 1993/94.

what is sometimes called "actual utilization" is economically meaningful. All of the following data on foreign investment reflect realized values unless noted otherwise.

As Table 10.2 indicates, FDI inflows to China have grown exponentially. During 1979–81, the average annual inflow of foreign direct investment (excluding "compensation trade" and export processing) was less than US$0.25 billion (Kueh, 1992, table 2b). The total amount of realized foreign direct investment in China in 1991 was already US$4.37 billion. The realized foreign capital in 1992 and 1993 reached US$19.2 billion and $39.0 billion, respectively. The realized foreign direct investment in these two years was US$11 billion and $28 billion, respectively, with a growth rate of 145 percent. By the end of 1993, the total number of registered foreign invested/managed firms reached 167,500, of which 83,100

334   SHANG-JIN WEI

Table 10.2. *Realized Foreign Direct Investment in China, 1983–95 (billions of US dollars)*

	China	All developing countries
1983	0.64	16.29
1984	1.26	16.13
1985	1.66	12.25
1986	1.88	13.24
1987	2.31	18.33
1988	3.19	25.33
1989	3.39	31.13
1990	3.49	28.65
1991	4.37	
1992	11.01	
1993	27.52	
1994	33.77	
1995	37.50	

Sources:
(1) Data for 1983–90 are from Amirahmadi and Wu (1994), Table 2. The original source that the authors attribute to is IMF's *Balance of Payment Statistics Yearbook* (1990 and 1991).
(2) Data for 1991 are from China State Statistical Bureau (1994), those for 1992–94 are from China State Statistical Bureau (1995), and the data for 1995 are an estimate from *China Country Commercial Guide* by the American Embassy in China (1996).

(or 49.6 percent of the total) were newly established in 1993 (China State Statistics Bureau, 1994). In that year, China was the largest host country of FDI in the world. In both 1994 and 1995, China received somewhere in the neighborhood of $40 billion and was the second largest recipient of FDI after the United States.

Foreign direct investment takes one of the following four forms: equity joint ventures, contractual joint ventures, wholly owned foreign firms, and joint exploration (mainly in offshore oil explorations). The values of the four forms during 1990–93 are reported in Table 10.1. In terms of percentage shares of total value in 1993, joint ventures and wholly owned foreign firms accounted for the lion's share of the FDI (55.8 percent), up from 26.0 percent in 1990. The wholly owned foreign firm is the fastest growing form of FDI in recent years. In 1993, it had grown 850 percent times over the 1990 value.

The spatial distribution of the foreign invested firms within China has some discernible regularity. They tend to locate in regions with preferential policies such as special economic zones, close to Hong Kong and Taiwan, and with good-quality labor force and good infrastructure (Cheng and Zhao, 1995).

Does foreign direct investment contribute significantly to China's growth and reforms? Some recent evidence suggests that it does. Using a unique data set covering 434 cities over the 1988–90 period, Wei (1996) finds that cities with higher foreign investment at the beginning of the sample period tend to grow faster in the subsequent years. This is true even after one controls for differential factor growth and human capital distribution. Furthermore, once one controls for the contribution of the FDI and exports, the so-called special economic zones do not seem special at all relative to other Chinese cities. Hence, their spectacular growth appears largely attributable to their spectacular attraction of foreign firms.

3. CHINA'S ABSORPTION OF FDI IN AN INTERNATIONAL PERSPECTIVE

This section discusses FDI in China from an international perspective. To accomplish this, I first estimate a gravity-type model to establish a "norm" for inward investment from major source countries, and then compare whether China is an underachiever or overachiever as a host country to FDIs from these countries.[2]

Worldwide foreign direct investment has more than doubled in nominal terms between 1975 and 1985, and quadrupled between 1980 and 1990, to reach a record high of US$200 billion in 1989 and US$234 billion in 1990 (United Nations, 1992, 1993). To keep our discussion about FDI in China in perspective, we note that FDI is largely a North–North phenomenon. An overwhelming proportion of FDIs goes into developed countries. The developed countries accounted for 97 percent of all FDI outflows in the 1980s, reaching $226 billion in 1990. In terms of FDI inflows, the devel-

[2] The discussion in this section is largely based on Wei (1996).

oped countries accounted for 83 percent in the 1985–1990 period (United Nations, 1993).

Of the FDI that does go into developing countries, the Asia–Pacific's share has been increasing over time, from about 30 percent in 1980 to over 50 percent by 1989. In 1989, for example, of the approximately $30 billion FDI that went into the developing world, about $17 billion went into the Asia–Pacific region. Between 1980–82 and 1986–88, FDI had increased by a factor of 3 in newly industrializing economies in the region and ASEAN countries, and by a factor of 13 in China (United Nations, 1992). The rapid increase in the case of China certainly reflects its original low base.

The distribution of FDI in terms of major source countries for 1990–91 is summarized in Table 10.3. In 1991, Hong Kong is the dominant supplier of foreign direct investment. Of the total US$4.4 billion direct foreign investment, Hong Kong contributed $2.4 billion, or about 55 percent. This is a typical pattern. Hong Kong's share in total direct investment in China has been above 50 percent for every single year except one since the beginning of the open-door policy in 1979. One should note, however, that part of the reported Hong Kong investment is actually Taiwan investment in disguise (to avoid political inconvenience with its home government). Another (small) part of the reported Hong Kong investment is really mainland capital in disguise (to take advantage of preferential treatment accorded to foreign capital by the mainland).

Japan is the second largest source country. With an investment of US$532.5 million in 1991, it accounted for 12.2 percent of the total. The next two major suppliers are the United States and Germany, accounting for 7.4 percent and 3.7 percent, respectively. It is worth noting that other East Asian economies, particularly those with a large Chinese diaspora, such as Macao, Singapore, Thailand, and Indonesia, have also supplied a significant amount of direct investment to China.

The primitive and imperfect legal regime in China is one important reason for the lopsided distribution of the supply of foreign direct investment. On the one hand, investors from the United States and other large source countries of multinational corporations are wary about the security and stability of their investment in China. On the other hand, for the overseas Chinese (particularly those residing in Hong Kong), the cultural and linguistic link

Table 10.3. *Source Country Distribution of Foreign Direct Investment in China (flow data, millions of US dollars)*

Country	1990	1991	1992	1993
World	3487	4366	11292	27771
Hong Kong	1880	2405	7706	17445
Taiwan	. . .	. . .	1053	3139
Japan	503	533	748	1361
USA	456	323	519	2068
Germany	64	161	91	62
Macao	33	82	203	588
Singapore	50	58	126	492
Britain	13	35	39	221
Italy	4	28	27	100
Thailand	7	20	84	234
Australia	25	15	35	110
Switzerland	1	12	29	47
Canada	8	11	59	137
France	21	10	47	141
Bermuda	. . .	8	1	19
Netherlands	16	7	28	84
Norway	2	6	5	1
Philippines	2	6	17	123
Panama	7	4	8	15
Ireland	. . .	3	1	2
Indonesia	1	2	20	66
Malaysia	1	2	25	91
Kuwait	. . .	. . .	7	84
Russia	. . .	. . .	16	42

Sources:
(1) China Ministry of Foreign Economic Relations and Trade, *Almanac of China's Foreign Economic Relations and Trade*, 1991/92, 1992/93, and 1993/94.
(2) China State Statistical Bureau, *Statistical Yearbook of China 1994*.

helps to reduce information and contractual costs. To contribute to the skewed source-country distribution, some regions in China offer explicit or implicit preferential policies to overseas Chinese whose ancestry was from those regions.

There is another distinct characteristic about investment from overseas Chinese that may be worth noting. The average size of investment from an overseas Chinese investor is much smaller than that from nonethnic Chinese. One explanation is simply that overseas Chinese tend to have small- or medium-size firms (either because of cultural reasons or because the industries they typically operate in have small optimal scales). The other explanation, which I find at least as plausible as the first one, is a transaction cost story associated with China's primitive legal system. Other things equal, the imperfect legal protection implies a high transaction cost for firms in China, because learning ill-defined customs and vague operating rules is costly. Overseas Chinese can largely circumvent this problem due to linguistic and culture advantage or personnel connection. Hence, nonethnic Chinese investors may perceive a higher transaction cost than do overseas Chinese. If this transaction cost is fixed irrespective of the size of investments, then small projects may not yield adequate returns to overcome this cost and are unlikely to be implemented. The minimum amount of investment for nonethnic Chinese is thus larger than for overseas Chinese.

3.1. Toward an Empirical Model of FDI Distribution

A norm for bilateral investment is notoriously difficult to establish because FDI is likely influenced by a long list of factors, many of which are difficult to measure or observe. We consider a reduced form specification for bilateral investment (flow or stock). Let I_{ij} be the direct investment from country i to country j. We have

$$I_{ij} = f\left(X_i, Y_j, Z_{ij}\right) \tag{10.1}$$

I explain the three categories of determinants in turn. X_i is a vector of variables that influence the measured size of the overall magnitude of outward investment from country i. It includes legal restrictions on or incentives for capital outflow, including country i's corporate tax schedule and the treatment of foreign affiliates' tax payments to host countries' governments. The key feature of variables in this vector is that they are common to all outward investments of country i, irrespective of destinations.[3] Our X vector should include an indicator for the deviation of country i's measurement method from the "normal" definition of FDI in the

---

[3] In our sample, most countries' outward direct investment is realized investment, but some such as Japan report only government approval data.

sample. Our statistical specification in the later part of the chapter allows us to be less specific about this vector.

Y_j is a vector of variables related to the overall attractiveness of country j to FDI. I classify the factors into two subcategories. The first group includes macroeconomic characteristics of the host country, such as the size of the host country (measured by GDP), the level of development, and the wage rate. The second subcategory includes all restrictions on and incentives for inward foreign investment. One important restriction that is included in the equation is the extent of corruption and bureaucracy.[4] In addition, many countries grant tax holidays or reduced taxes for foreign firms' profits, providing incentives for source countries to locate their direct investment to these countries.[5]

Z_{ij} is a vector of variables that are specific to the host and source-country pair and that influence the incentives or disincentives for investment going from country i to country j. Here, two measures are adopted. The first is the "greater circle distance" between the host and source countries. The second is a dummy variable to indicate whether the source and host share a common language.

To implement the FDI function, I assume a linear specification of the following form:

$$\log FDI_{ij} = \alpha_i + \beta_1 \log GDP_j + \beta_2 \log DIS_i + \beta_3 \log\left(\frac{GDP_j}{Pop_j}\right)$$
$$+ \beta_3 \log Wage_j + \beta_4 OECD \cdot \log Wage_j + \beta_5 Corruption_j$$
$$+ \beta_6 \log Distance_{ij} + \beta_7 \log Language_{ij} + u_{ij}$$

(10.2)

3.2. Data

The basic data set for this part of the chapter is outward FDIs from fourteen major OECD source countries in 1990 and 1992. GDP in domestic currency is taken from the International Monetary Fund's

---

[4] The source is Paolo Mauro (1995). Because corruption and bureaucracy indices are highly correlated, I construct a single indicator that is equal to the equally weighted average of the two.

[5] However, I do not have tax data for this study.

International Financial Statistics. The exchange rates for 1990 and 1992 (annual averages) are used to compute GDP in U.S. dollars. Data on population are obtained from the World Bank's *World Development Report.* I have also made use of the wage rate from the International Labour Organisation (ILO)'s *Yearbook of Labour Statistics.*

The five largest source countries of direct investment over the period 1987–92 are Japan, United Kingdom, United States, France, and Germany (United Nations, 1992). Their annual average outflows of investment during the period are 36.5, 30.5, 23.9, 19.5, and 17.1 billions of U.S. dollars, respectively. The total investment outflow from the five accounted for about 70.5 percent of all outward investment of the developed countries.

3.3. Basic Results

Table 10.4 reports the basic regression results. The first column is the result of a fixed-effects regression assuming source-country specific intercepts, using the 1990 and 1992 panel data. The coefficient on the GDP variable is positive and significant as expected. A 1 percent increase in the size of a host country is associated with a 0.55 percent increase in FDI. A 1 percent increase in per-capita GDP is associated with a 0.08 percent larger FDI flow, but the estimate is not significant. Furthermore, geography matters: A 1 percent increase in distance is associated with a 0.4 percent reduction in FDI. This confirms our casual impression that outward foreign investment is highly regionalized. Investment is, to some extent, a neighborhood event.

A popular hypothesis for why FDI goes to developing countries is that capital searches for cheap labor. To test this, I include a measure of average hourly wage rate (in U.S. dollars) in the regression. I find it useful to distinguish between developed and developing country hosts, so I also include an OECD dummy and an interactive term between the OECD dummy and logarithm of the wage rate. As it turns out, for developing countries, a 1 percent reduction in the wage rate helps to attract 1.7 percent more FDI. But the labor cost effect by and large becomes irrelevant when it comes to FDI from one developed country to another.[6]

---

[6] This is reflected in the observation that the sum of the coefficients on the wage term and wage/OECD interaction term is not significantly different from zero.

Table 10.4. *Inward FDI Equation (dependent variable: log FDI$_{ij}$)*

	1990–92 Panel	1992 Stock
log GDP$_j$	0.55**	0.76**
	(0.08)	(0.10)
log GDPPC$_j$	0.08	−0.70
	(0.31)	(0.36)
log Distance$_{ij}$	−0.44**	−0.67**
	(0.10)	(0.13)
OECD Dummy	1.15*	0.23
	(0.57)	(0.74)
1992 Dummy	1.03**	
	(0.20)	
log Wage$_j$	−1.72**	−1.17**
	(0.37)	(0.45)
(OECD Dummy)(log Wage$_j$)	1.08**	0.87*
	(0.28)	(0.36)
Linguistics	1.91**	1.52**
	(0.27)	(0.34)
Corruption and red tape[a]	−0.45**	−0.54**
	(0.09)	(0.11)
Number of observations	497	217
Standard error of regression	2.14	1.77
R^2	0.62	0.65
Adjusted R^2	0.61	0.63

Note: Standard errors are in parentheses. Source-country dummies are in the regression but not reported here.
[a] Corruption and red tape indices are defined on a 0–10 scale, with 0 being least corrupt and 10 most corrupt.
*Significant at the 5 percent level.
**Significant at the 1 percent level.

The result on the measure of corruption and bureaucracy is as expected. The more corrupt and/or bureaucratic the host country is, the less FDI it is expected to receive. The estimate for the linguistic dummy shows that sharing a common language or colonial tie helps to promote FDI in a quantitatively significant way: Inward FDI is almost 200 percent higher than otherwise.

A competing specification for panel data set is what is called the "random-effects model." In such a model, the source-country specific intercept is assumed to be a random draw from a common distribution that is uncorrelated with the error term of the regression (Hsiao, 1986). The five source countries are not drawn randomly from the pool of all source countries, but they are instead chosen deliberately because they are the largest source countries. Thus the fixed-effects model is the appropriate model to use.[7]

In the second column, I use only the FDI stock data in 1992. The coefficients on GDP, distance, the wage rate, linguistics, and corruption and red tape are of the expected sign and statistically significant. The values of these coefficients are broadly similar to those obtained from the regression with the 1990–92 data. It is worth pointing out that, in spite of a less rigorous microeconomic foundation of the specification, the adjusted R^2 of over 0.6 is reasonably large for cross-country regressions.

3.4. China and Other Asian Economies' Reception of Foreign Investment Relative to the International "Norm"

The statistical model in the last section has effectively established a norm of inward foreign investment as a function of a host country's size, level of development, wage, degree of corruption, linguistic tie, and geographic location. It can then be investigated whether China and other host countries have attracted more or less foreign capital compared with the empirical norm.

Using the model that uses the 1992 FDI stock (the second column of Table 10.4), I examine the difference between actual foreign investment and the model predictions for China, India, and the four Asian newly industrialized economies (NIEs). The basic economic characteristics of the six economies are summarized in Table 10.5. The computed differences of inward investment relative to the norm are reported in Table 10.6.

Despite the fact that China was one of the largest developing host countries of FDI by the end of the 1980s, it might not have hosted enough FDI relative to the norm after one adjusts its volume of FDI by its size and other characteristics. In terms of the FDI stock in 1992, the results suggest that China had not attracted large investment from the major source countries (the United

---

[7] The random-effects model is also performed as a robustness check of our fixed-effects model. For our data set, the random-effects specification produced very similar estimates to the fixed-effects model.

Table 10.5. *Country Indicators*

	GDP ($ million)		GDP per capita ($)		Wage ($/hour)		Corruption	Red Tape
	1990	1992	1990	1992	1990	1992		
China	387,428	482,963	345	407	0.22	0.25	10*	8*
Hong Kong	69,999	92,000	12,069	15,333	2.88	3.53	2	0.25
India	299,853	271,908	362	312	0.36	NA	4.25	6.75
Korea	253,658	304,911	5,928	6,984	5.01	6.14	4.75	3.5
Taiwan	158,999	210,999	7,813	10,143	NA	NA	3.25	2.75
Singapore	36,500	48,547	12,167	17,215	4.62	6.21	0	0

Note: Corruption and red tape indicators are taken from Mauro (1995). I redefine his measure so that 0 means least corrupt and 10 most corrupt.

* denotes author's own estimates.

Sources:

(1) International Monetary Fund, *International Financial Statistics*.

(2) International Labour Organisation, *Yearbook of Labour Statistics*.

(3) World Bank, *World Development Report*, 1992, 1994.

Table 10.6 *Actual–Predicted FDI (1992 stock)*

Source country	Host country					
	China	Hong Kong	India	Korea	Singapore	Taiwan
UK	...	1.489	...	...	2.429	...
Germany	-2.492	1.476	...	1.074	2.312	...
Japan	...	-2.878	1.719	2.312	-1.141	-0.398
USA	-3.435	0.893	...	1.839	1.383	...

Note: Based on the second column of Table 10.4.

States, Germany, France, and the United Kingdom).[8] For example, it received 91.7 and 96.8 percent less investment from Germany and the United States than it could have based on its economic characteristics.[9] The Japanese investment in China will probably grow fast. Two surveys of Japanese firms conducted by Japan's Export–Import Bank in 1992 and 1993 reported China as the most promising destination of Japanese FDI in the medium term (Kinoshita, 1994).

Part of the reason for the Chinese underachievement is its late entry to the game. The open-door policy was only a decade old in 1990. The more important reason for the underachievement is the imperfect legal protection that China still offers to foreign investors. Fortunately, overseas Chinese appear less concerned about the imperfect legal environment and have marched into the country in large numbers. The investment from overseas Chinese perhaps makes up much of lost shares from other major source countries in the world.

We should note that the GDP and per-capita GDP variables might have substantially underestimated China's true size and level of development. After adjusting for purchasing power, the World Bank and IMF found that China's per-capita GDP was likely to be on the order of US$2,000 rather than $300, as reported in Table 10.5. A more conservative measure by Lardy (1994) puts the estimate at $1,000. This would still increase the magnitude of

---

[8] An empty entry means that the recorded actual investment is zero. FDI data used in the regressions come from the United Nations, which records many bilateral FDI flows/stocks as zero.

[9] $\exp(-2.492) - 1 = -0.917$, and $\exp(-3.435) - 1 = -0.968$.

China's GDP and per-capita GDP by a factor of 1.7 relative to the exchange-rate-based measure. If PPP-adjusted values were used in estimating the FDI model, one would expect even greater under-achievement by China in attracting FDI from the major source countries.

India has many similarities with China, in terms of its size, level of development, and history of policy toward FDI. In terms of stock of FDI, India has hosted too little FDI from the major source countries except from Japan and possibly from Britain. (Being a former colony of Britain helps in this case.) India is catching up fast, particularly with FDI from the United States.[10]

The four Asian NIEs are all well known to be very open in terms of their trade policies, but their policies toward foreign direct investment have differed markedly in the past. On the one extreme, Singapore and Hong Kong are very open to foreign investment. Both have hosted substantially more stock of FDI than an average economy in the world with similar economic and geographic characteristics. On the other extreme, up to 1990, Korea and Taiwan were much more cautious toward foreign-invested firms in their territories. Both hosted less than average direct investment from the United States, Germany, France, and the United Kingdom (Wei, 1996). The results based on the updated data suggest that Hong Kong and Singapore continue to be very open, whereas Korea and Taiwan appear to have caught up fast in the 1990s: Their inward FDI stock positions are more normal now than in 1990.

To summarize, in contrast to its reception of vast investment from overseas Chinese, China so far has not attracted enough direct investment from U.S. and European source countries. However, this is not drastically different from the earlier situations in Korea and Taiwan, although the latter two are catching up fast.

3.5. China and Hong Kong as One Unit

It is sometimes remarked that Hong Kong and China should be treated as one economic unit for many economic purposes. This is so, not only because Hong Kong has reverted back to China's rule, but the two economies have increasingly been closely interlinked in terms of trade and investment. Moreover, some of the foreign

---

[10] See Reddy (1994) for a more detailed discussion.

direct investments in Hong Kong are in fact intended for mainland China.

China by itself is an underachiever as a host of FDI, while Hong Kong is an overachiever. Thus a reasonable question to ask is whether the two collectively have attracted enough FDI. To examine this, a model-predicted value for a united China–Hong Kong region is compared with their actual reception of FDI. For the purpose of the thought experiment, the united region's GDP is defined as the sum of GDP of China and Hong Kong. Per-capita GDP, the wage rate, and corruption are population-weighted averages of the two regions' corresponding numbers. I take China's distances from the source countries as those for the united region. Not surprisingly, the resulting numbers are somewhere between those for China and Hong Kong. As it turns out, because Hong Kong is an outlier as an extremely open economy toward foreign investment, its above-average absorption of FDI compensates partially for the relatively insufficient absorption of FDI by China. This observation is consistent with the notion of an economically integrated Hong Kong and South China economy. It is also consistent with the hypothesis that part of the FDI from Hong Kong to China is FDI from the OECD source countries in disguise.

4. CONCLUDING REMARKS

Foreign investment in China comes disproportionately from overseas Chinese, particularly those residing in Hong Kong. An empirical norm of inward FDI is established as a function of the host country's size, development level, wage level, corruption, linguistic tie, and geographic location. Relative to an "average" host country, China appears to host too little foreign investment from the major source countries (the United States, Germany, France, Japan, and the United Kingdom). By contrast, Hong Kong (as well as Singapore) is a spectacular overachiever. If one is willing to consider China and Hong Kong as one economic unit, their position of inward FDI is much closer to the international norm.

REFERENCES

Amirahmadi, Hooshang, and Weiping Wu (1994), "Foreign Direct Investment in Developing Countries," *Journal of Developing Areas*, 28: 167–190.

Cheng, Leonard K., and Haiying Zhao (1995), "Geographical Patterns of Foreign Direct Investment in China: Location, Factor Endowments, and Policy Incentives," paper presented at the American Economic Association Meetings, Washington, DC, January 6–8.

China Ministry of Foreign Economic Relations and Trade (1992, 1993, 1994), *Almanac of China's Foreign Economic Relations and Trade*, 1991/1992, 1992/93, 1993/1994, Beijing: Ministry of Foreign Economic Relations and Trade.

China State Statistics Bureau (1994), "Statistical Report on National Economy and Social Development in 1993," *People's Daily* (overseas edition), March 2.

China State Statistical Bureau (1995), *Statistical Yearbook of China 1995*, Beijing: State Statistics Bureau.

Hsiao, Cheng (1986), *Analysis of Panel Data*, Econometrics Society Monograph No. 11, Cambridge: Cambridge University Press.

Kinoshita, Toshihiko (1994), "Japan's Foreign Direct Investment in East and Southeast Asia: The Current Situation and the Prospect for the Future," report, Research Institute for International Investment and Development, Export–Import Bank of Japan, Tokyo.

Kueh, Y. Y. (1992), "Foreign Investment and Economic Change in China," *China Quarterly*, 131: 637–690.

Lardy, Nicholas R. (1994), *China in the World Economy*, Washington, DC: Institute for International Economics.

Mauro, Paolo (1995), "Corruption and Growth," *Quarterly Journal of Economics*, 110: 681–712.

Reddy, J. Mahender (1994), "United States Investment in India," paper presented at the Sixth Biennial Conference on U.S.–Asia Economic Relations, sponsored by American Committee on Asian Economic Studies and Asia Pacific Center of Brandeis University, Brandeis University, June 16–18.

United Nations (1992), *World Investment Directory 1992*, Vol. 1, *Asia and the Pacific*, New York: United Nations.

——— (1993), *World Investment Directory 1992*, Vol. 3, *Developed Countries*, New York: United Nations.

Wei, Shang-Jin (1996), "Foreign Direct Investment in China: Source and Consequences," in T. Ito and A. O. Krueger, eds., *Financial Deregulation and Integration in East Asia*, Chicago: University of Chicago Press and NBER.

World Bank (1992), *World Development Report 1992: Development and the Environment*, New York: Oxford University Press.

World Bank (1994), *China: Foreign Trade Reform*, Washington, DC: World Bank.

Comment

K. C. Fung

This chapter by Shang-Jin Wei is extremely informative and provides a good mixture of institutions and empirical analysis. There are four comments I would like to make. The first is on the central result of the chapter: China is an underachiever in attracting FDI from the United States, Germany, and other major source countries. This result may be surprising at first, but it does make a lot of sense. Multinational firms faced with the decision as to which country to invest in would naturally compare expected returns and risks among various investment opportunities. China may pose a particular difficulty because of the lack of well-defined property rights and the existence of political risks. From a microeconomic standpoint, higher risks and lower expected returns may already explain why some of the major source countries are not investing as much in China compared with the norm based on various economic characteristics. It would have been useful if the author had included an experiment that would compare investing in China with investing in other economies in transition where property rights are not well defined and there are substantial risks. This result can also explain why overseas Chinese such as those from Hong Kong and Taiwan seem to be investing a disproportionate amount in China (Fung, 1997a,b). In the absence of enforceable contracts, other informal instruments such as linguistic ties, familial connections, and geographical proximity (which allows quicker acquisition of information) can serve both as a way to estimate risks and as a means to increase the likelihood of getting self-enforcing agreements.

This comment leads directly to my second point, which is on the model. As already discussed, looking at the determinants of investments, we have to look at risks, information, and expected returns. The model in this chapter, while interesting, is too broad to be connected with the empirical analysis and, more importantly, its interpretations. A better approach might be to derive an equation based upon the maximization of investors' expected returns and use it both in the regression and in the analysis. Alternatively, the author could conveniently use models of multinationals, as recently surveyed by Krugman (1995). These recent approaches try to model the decision to engage in FDI by looking at the tradeoff between losses in scale economies associated with multiplant production and gains from reductions in transport costs.

The third point is related to the relationship between investment and growth in China. Whereas it is fully justifiable to presume that FDI leads to higher growth, it is also reasonable to assume that growth induces larger inflows of FDI. Indeed, FDI can be attracted to areas where outputs and local demands are growing (e.g., Cheng, 1995). This argument implies that FDI is not an exogenous variable but instead should be treated as endogenous. My hunch is that the results would not change significantly even when one takes the endogeneity into account, although I have no empirical proof on this point. But perhaps in future work, the author should deal with this issue more directly.

The fourth and last point deals with the data. When one is conducting empirical research using Chinese data, it would be useful to discuss in greater detail the sources and quality of the data, as well as methods used to construct additional data. Chinese data on trade and investment are often perceived as not very reliable. Indeed, even U.S. data involving Chinese trade are inaccurate (Fung and Lau, 1996). Thus an acknowledgment of this potential problem would be helpful to readers. In addition, some of the data used in the chapter are not quite up to date. For example, the most recent *Almanac of China's Foreign Economic Relations and Trade* used in the paper is 1993/1994, but the most recent data available are actually 1996/1997. Thus data presented in some of the tables can be updated.

REFERENCES

Cheng, L. (1995), "Foreign Direct Investment in China," Working Paper, Hong Kong University of Science and Technology.

Fung, K. C. (1997a), "Accounting for Chinese Trade: Some National and Regional Considerations," in R. Baldwin, R. Lipsey, and J. D. Richardson, eds., *Geography and Ownership in Economic Accounting*, Chicago: University of Chicago Press and NBER.

(1997b), *Trade and Investment: Mainland China, Hong Kong and Taiwan*, Hong Kong Centre for Economic Research Monograph, Hong Kong: City University of Hong Kong Press.

Fung, K. C., and Lawrence J. Lau (1996), "The China-United States Bilateral Trade Balance: How Big Is It Really?" Occasional Paper, Asia/Pacific Research Center, Stanford University.

Krugman, Paul R. (1995), "Increasing Returns, Imperfect Competition and the Positive Theory of International Trade," in G. M. Grossman and K. Rogoff, eds., *Handbook of International Economics*, Volume 3, Amsterdam: North-Holland.

## CHAPTER 11

The Impact of Foreign Investment in Indonesia: Historical Trends and Simulation Analysis

Iwan J. Azis

1. INTRODUCTION

Foreign investment in Indonesia is best understood in a historical and geographical context. The phenomena of "export-orientation" and "import-substitution," the resulting dual economy, the assimilation of "capitalism," utilization of the country's comparative advantage (natural resource base), protection measures such as import quotas, and concerns over income distribution and regional disparities all have definite historical antecedents in this country.

Having gone through a colonial rule for three centuries, it is not unusual for a country like Indonesia to experience some distrust toward external influence, including foreign capital and investment. This perception prevailed after independence in 1945, although it was muted considerably when the New Order government came to power in 1966. Residual suspicion continued among certain groups of society until the late 1970s, but today's opponents of foreign capital are confined to two types. The first is a small group of vested domestic interests seeking to protect markets rather than foster xenophobia. A second group, more recent and politically active, consists of pressure groups concerned with the social and welfare (distributional) impact of foreign investment. These social interest groups were a significant impediment to the dramatic policy changes of the mid-1980s.

The objectives of this chapter are twofold: to delineate the historical context for modern Indonesian foreign investment policy,

The author wishes to acknowledge comments from anonymous readers. Thanks are also due to Irma Adelman for her suggestions on interpreting the results of model simulation. The views expressed in the chapter, however, remain the author's.

and to elucidate the impacts of foreign investment on the country's overall welfare and its distribution between household groups and across regions. The chapter is organized as follows. The next section is devoted to a survey of Indonesia's historical experience with foreign capital and investment, from the 1500s up to the late 1970s. This overview will reveal how a number of phenomena and policy conventions regarding foreign investment in the past have carried over to modern Indonesia. This is followed by discussion of the new, more open, investment policy initiatives of the 1980s, which continue to prevail today. Section 3 follows with the foreign investment impact analysis. The first component of this analysis uses a social accounting matrix (SAM) and multiplier methods to assess the static interregional impacts (welfare distribution between regions) of foreign investment. This is followed by a more flexible, general equilibrium analysis of foreign investment impacts on household income distribution, with special reference to the rural–urban dichotomy.

2. HISTORICAL OVERVIEW

2.1. From the Portuguese to the Dutch

Recorded history of foreign investment in Indonesia dates back to the 1500s, when the Portuguese came to the region.[1] In that period, the center of trade had moved from Java, ruled by Kertanegara during the thirteenth century, further north to Malacca, an area established by refugees from Indonesia who may have escaped from the Kingdom of Majapahit (1294–1478). For some time, Malacca was the site of "markets" where products from China, India, and Indonesia were exchanged. Foreign "investors" (e.g., the Portuguese) understood that peace (stability) was important for doing business in a foreign land. This may explain some of the Portuguese' early emphasis on peacekeeping. When word of abundant spices in eastern Indonesia reached the West, an expedition was sent to the Maluku islands, including Ternate, Tidore, Ambon, Banda, and Halmahera. As it turned out, this was a lucrative venture.

---

[1] Actually, some records indicate that Marco Polo reached the shore of Sumatra in the early 1200s, but only as a visitor.

The Dutch arrived in the mid-1590s, and their merchants became the first organized private foreign investors doing business in Indonesia. The term "foreign investment," however, was not comparable with what we know today, in the sense that the capital was not invested in Indonesia or intended to develop the Indonesian economy. Rather, some money was invested to establish a trading company (*Compagnie van Verre*, 1594–98) that sponsored a voyage that finally landed in Sunda Kelapa, the early name of Jakarta. Although at the beginning the company suffered a series of losses (financial and human), this marked the opening of a new trade route to Indonesia, setting the precedent for many subsequent investments and missions that would follow.

In 1602, a United East-Indies Company (or VOC, *Verenegigde Oost-Indie Compagnie*) was formed. The VOC was given a dual authority, as a monopolistic commercial organization and as a bearer of sovereign power. Such a mix between merchants and government in the international field indicated a suffusion of public and private foreign interest that was characteristic of the colonial period.[2] Like the Portuguese, the Dutch were interested in securing peace to foster success in their investments. One area reflecting such interest was the control over many local laws.

As far as investment policy is concerned, during the VOC period (ending in 1799) there was a swing of the pendulum from strong and weak regulation. The strong regulation period was characterized by explicit controls over spice contracts, including who had rights as buyers, quantities, and prices. During the period of weak regulation, smuggling activities became widespread, adding to already substantial losses suffered by the VOC. This prompted the Dutch government's decision in 1799 not to renew the VOC's charter. Under Napoleon Bonaparte's rule, one of his marshals (Daendels), became the governor-general of Indonesia, and new investment rules were implemented to avoid the VOC's past mistakes. Among others, one rule maintained that investment in Indonesia should avoid the use of rice lands. This statute was only indirectly humanitarian, recognizing that these lands were needed by the people to fulfill their biological needs and thereby secure the profitability of foreign ventures. Furthermore, Europeans or

---

[2] See Charles Himawan, "The Foreign Investment Process in Indonesia," Gunung Agung-Singapore MCMLXXX, 1980, p. 99.

Chinese were allowed to buy or lease wastelands, marking the beginning of foreign private land ownership.

Investment policy under the Portuguese, Dutch, and French had one primary objective in common: to secure a large supply of spices for export to Europe. All were successful, albeit in different degrees, in production (supply) but less so in marketing (exports). This was especially true during the Daendels period, when the British Navy frequently blockaded spice shipment.

Under British rule (1811–16), an additional objective of investment policy arose: market expansion for British textile products.[3] The concept proposed by Sir Thomas Stamford Raffles, who became the lieutenant governor of Java, seemed eminently logical: Raise Indonesian living standards to promote their purchasing power for British textiles. As promising as it sounded, however, the outcomes were otherwise. The approach taken was to hand over lands to the village headmen, who in turn would let cultivators use the lands but subject to a certain tax (Land Tax Law). Raffles preferred the village headmen to the regents because the latter were considered pro-Dutch. When the system was changed to one of direct rent payment to the British government in Jakarta, many land taxpayers used an intermediary channel, mostly the Chinese. This was partly due to the fact that this group could provide credit (albeit with a high interest rate) along with the risk of dispossession if the loan were unpaid. Hence, these middlemen benefited from the new tax law. The village headmen and some regents also gained from the system by skillfully rendering their services and authority to get money. The peasants were ultimately the victims, as poverty increased and production of agricultural goods declined.

Free participation by foreigners in the utilization (read: exploitation) of land and labor did not come until 1870, when the returning Dutch government enacted what might be considered the first investment law, the Agrarian Law. This statute represented a dramatic change in the Dutch attitudes toward Indonesia, seeing Indonesia as a land of opportunity for Dutch private investors. With this statute also came something more like Western "capitalist" values. For example, private capitalists were now allowed to lease

---

[3] A shift in British textile exports from the costlier and heavier cloths to the lighter and cheaper fabrics, which has been evident since the mid-1700s, was a widespread phenomenon during that time. See John (1969).

lands from individual peasants (collective agreements were no longer required) when they saw potential profits from operating the land. Unsurprisingly, production of many agricultural goods went up, as did exports.[4] However, equally unsurprising was the emergence of Boeke's type of dual economy. Social relationships became dominated largely, if not solely, by economic considerations, and the living conditions of many Indonesians deteriorated sharply. It was this period that the Dutch referred to when they finally conceded the "unethical" character of their rule in Indonesia.

A reform was then proposed (upon Queen Wilhelmina's order), introducing income taxation; the land tax system was improved; and a trade tax was imposed on income generated from resources other than land. Having found extreme abuses of labor in the past, some improvements were made. In addition, credits were given to raise living standards of the poor.

Foreign investments (mostly Dutch) kept expanding, and by the beginning of the twentieth century, British investment, especially in tea plantations, had grown very rapidly. Other foreign investors found it profitable to work in forestry and mining sectors. The Swiss, German, and British invested a considerable amount in the tobacco sector. Exports were still bound mainly for Holland, and agricultural products predominated. In the manufacturing sector, a restrictive strategy was implemented. Indonesian capitalists were confined to small-scale industries, thereby protecting imported manufactured goods from Holland. Extensive infrastructural investments (e.g., ports, roads, and bridges) were also made to secure Dutch economic interests, many of which are still in use.

A new market for Indonesian products (i.e., the United States) emerged after the end of World War I. As foreign demand not only increased but also diversified to nonagricultural products such as cement, cooking oil, beer, and paper, it soon became apparent that skilled labor was very scarce in the country. The good news coming from this trend was new emphasis on training and education in Indonesia. On the negative side, most export revenues went to private investors and those who held power, with very little left for farmers. It should also be noted that, comparatively speaking, the

---

[4] Detailed analysis on production and export performance during the period can be found in Creutzberg (1975).

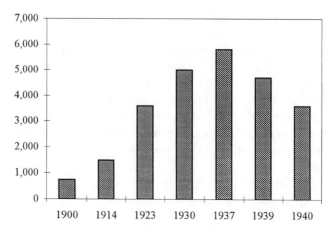

Figure 11.1. Estimates of foreign investment in Indonesia, 1900–40
(million guilders).

Dutch were much less concerned with the colony's educational
progress than, for example, were the British in India.

Despite the investment and export boom after the end of World
War I (see Figure 11.1), in general the government failed to utilize
its windfall revenues to enhance the welfare of the majority of
Indonesians. Poverty worsened when the Great Depression of 1929
prompted increased protectionism by a number of Indonesia's
trading partners, including the country's own colonial government.
Exports declined sharply, from 1,488 million guilders in 1929 to 505
million guilders in 1935, and employment was drastically reduced
(Wertheim, 1956). During this difficult period, the Japanese were
alone in achieving significant Indonesian market penetration. The
largest market share of Japanese goods in Indonesia was in low-
priced, low-quality cotton textiles and apparel. The penetration of
this product was so strong that the colonial government felt it necessary to limit these Japanese imports by implementing a quota
system. This was one of several factors that prompted anger, and
a subsequent military attack (1942), on the part of the Japanese.

The quota system was exceptional in a generally laissez-faire
Indonesian policy regime. Instead, in order to reduce overall
import dependence, the manufacturing sector was for the first time
opened to capitalists, both foreign and Indonesian. As evident from
Figure 11.1, this induced rising foreign investment during 1930–37,

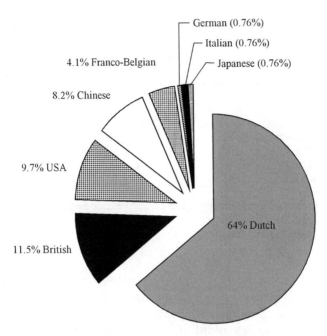

Figure 11.2. Distribution of foreign investment in Indonesia, 1939. (Source: G. Gonggrijp, *Schets eener Economische Geschiedenis van Indonesie*, Haarlem, Bohn, 1957, p. 167.)

although it declined again toward the end of the decade. The Crisis Import Ordinance, enacted in 1933, removed some restrictions on establishing plants and at the same time provided limited protection against import competition (Hill, 1988). By 1939, the Dutch, British, and Americans were the top three investors (Figure 11.2). The major Dutch investments were in petroleum, cement, and sugar. The British followed more or less the same pattern, with considerable emphasis on export activities.[5] Other estimates made by H. G. Callis (1942) indicate that, at the outbreak of World War II, foreign investors in Indonesia were ranked in the following order: Dutch (63 percent), British (14 percent), overseas Chinese (11 percent), and American (7 percent).

Compared with British investment in India, the Dutch foreign

---

[5] This "export-oriented" environment, however, did not alter the composition of the main beneficiaries of such activity (i.e., the investors and the colonial power). Virtually no spillover effects were created.

Table 11.1. *Foreign Investment in Colonial India and Indonesia (percentage)*

Sector	British Investment in India, 1938	Dutch Investment in Indonesia, 1940
Sugar, rubber, and other agriculture	16	45
Mining	18	19
Transport and public utilities	24	14
Manufacturing	15	2
Agricultural banks	n.a.	10
Managing agencies	16	n.a.
Miscellaneous	12	10

n.a. = not available
Sources: Tomlinson (1985) and Callis (1942), processed from Hill (1988)

investment in Indonesia was much less diversified, focused almost exclusively on primary processing industries. As Table 11.1 reveals, the disparity of manufacturing share in investment between these two cases was over sevenfold. It was the Americans, not the Dutch, who pioneered development of Indonesia's manufacturing sector. Besides U.S. interests in the petroleum extraction, General Motors built the first motor-vehicle assembling plants in Indonesia. Goodyear was the first to build a tire plant in the country in Bogor, West Java, and the Union Carbide and Carbon Company was the first to manufacture dry batteries in Indonesia. U.S. companies were also active in production of many smaller manufactured goods.

When the Japanese occupation began in 1942, the first "nationalization" took place, in which all assets and properties owned by Europeans and Chinese were confiscated.[6] This seriously interrupted the integration of the Indonesian economy with the rest of the world, a process that began in earnest after the Great Depression. Like the British, the Japanese maintained rice land for rice for its original crop, but to feed their own soldiers rather than Indonesians. Like the Dutch, the Japanese repatriated most of the surplus generated from activities in Indonesia to their home

---

[6] The Japanese still used and kept Western labor, whose expertise in various activities was useful to their operations.

country. During the Japanese period, such practices were even more extreme. Practically nothing was left for the Indonesians.

2.2. Post independence

With the bombing of Hiroshima and Nagasaki, dramatic changes were initiated. Indonesia declared independence in August 1945, but Allied troops soon landed near Jakarta, creating a series of long and exhausting conflicts. With respect to integrating the economy with the outside world and the role of foreign investment, there were sharply opposing views among Indonesians during that time. One group, led by Sjahrir, looked favorably on foreign capital. The opposing group, led by the communist Tan Malaka, was opposed to capitalism generally and foreign capital in particular. Fortunately, the dispute was resolved without outside intervention, with an eventual inclination toward welcoming foreign investment. This failed to boost inflows of foreign investment significantly, however, because at this time many countries were preoccupied with efforts to rehabilitate their economies, and the Indonesians were engaged in their war of independence.

It was not until 1950 that an investment-related law was enacted, based on the "Hague Treaty." This treaty was considered by foreign investors as a protective umbrella for their continued operation in Indonesia. Many aspects of this law would look familiar to students of contemporary Indonesian investment law. For example, while there was legal recognition of foreign rights to invest in plantation, mining, industrial, and trading sectors, this statute also enunciated elements of public interest and obligations for foreign investors to facilitate Indonesian equity participation. This attempt at balanced protection of economic rights had very limited success, and eventually a parliamentary motion was floated to annul the Hague Treaty with the objective to eliminate foreign private capital. While this motion was unsuccessful, it marked the inception of the process of "Indonesianization."

The establishment of *Benteng Group*, an economic interest group consisting of indigenous Indonesians (in contrast to Indonesian-born non-indigenes, the majority of whom were Chinese), was meant to counter the dominance of foreign capital power by granting exclusive rights to import certain products. This certainly facilitated the quest for Indonesian profits, but, as often happened to countries in the early stages of development, corruption and nepotism became widespread. Meanwhile, a general antipathy toward foreign capital grew pervasive, and public opinion increasingly associated foreign capital with foreign imperialism. The political and ideological climate during those days clearly favored socialism, albeit of a non-Marxist variety, and a large number of the government's policies still reflected a perceived need to struggle against imperialistic and capitalistic forces in the quest for an egalitarian state.

This period of confusion lasted through six different cabinets, negating any substantive efforts to achieve economic development and welfare enhancement. Under the consensus-based impetus of nationalism, however, the process of Indonesianization continued. The prescribed "solution" to preservation of the Indonesian national interest was to expel foreign agents by abolition of the Hague Treaty and make scapegoats of the Chinese merchant class. Antiforeign sentiment extended from foreign investment to foreign aid. These events were concentrated in 1956, and the Five-year Development Plan (1956–61) was devised as a nationalist alternative to the status quo.[7] It soon became apparent that this plan was completely futile. To make matters worse, a series of rebellions occurred in various regions outside Java (North Sumatra, Central Sumatra, South Sulawesi, and North Sulawesi). Among the important motives behind the act was dissatisfaction with central government allocation schemes for regional export revenues.

Meanwhile, the process of Indonesianization continued, inducing significant divestment. Only after a military decree in 1957 did this trend toward property confiscation, mostly from Dutch enterprises, abate. Despite persistent feelings of distrust toward foreign investment, in 1958 a new foreign investment law was introduced, reaffirming the government's commitment to make the economy open to foreign investment.[8] Actual investment trends contradicted these intentions, however. Foreign direct investment was negligible during the first half of the 1960s (see Figure 11.3). Balance-of-payment statistics even show negative values in these accounts for a number of years. The primary culprit was the government's deci-

---

[7] Interestingly enough, the preparation of the plan, under the "second cabinet" of Ali Sastroamidjojo, was made with the help of some U.S. experts.

[8] There were also fears of further revolts by regions outside Java if foreign investment tended to exacerbate the interregional gap of development.

sion to nationalize all assets confiscated from the Dutch, the beginning of the process of *nationalization*. Major nationalized assets other than those of the Dutch belonged to Malaysian and British enterprises (in 1963), followed by those of American firms (in 1965).

Meanwhile, the economy was in disarray, with runaway inflation peaking at almost 600 percent, and with flat or declining nominal per-capita income. Microeconomic distortions were pervasive, as was corruption. These conditions fostered political tension and resurgence of the Indonesian Communist Party (the strongest outside the Communist bloc). A coup attempt, later known as *Gestapu*, took place on September 30, 1965, failed, and brought the new government to power.

2.3. New Order Government

Given the chaos that prevailed during the last years of the old regime, a major overhaul in the economy was necessary, first and foremost in the area of financial policy. Having identified monetization of the budget deficit as the major impetus for the country's extremely high inflation, the new government implemented more rigorous fiscal discipline.[9] Such a bold change was initiated by a group of economists, primarily graduates from the Faculty of Economics, University of Indonesia, who later became known as the "economic technocrats." Since most of them, including their leader, Widjojo Nitisastro, were educated at the University of California, Berkeley, they were later known as the "Berkeley Mafia."

Since the beginning, the New Order government recognized the existence of a link between foreign investment and foreign aid, and the importance of both to the economic recovery. This recognition is implicit in the 1967 law on foreign investment, but it should be noted that overall the 1967 law was not at all liberal. In some ways, this approach was typical of developing countries' attempts to embrace the concept of using foreign capital in a two-gap model sense. The government hoped to bridge domestic investment-savings imbalances with external finance, while at the same time reaping the benefits of technology and international marketing linkages (see Chapter 1, this volume).

[9] For further discussions of this subject, see Azis (1994a) and Woo et al. (1994).

Given the past experience, the level of development, and the political climate at that time, the size of the country, and its cultural heterogeneity of the people, the cautious approach of the 1967 law was not surprising. In light of these considerations, it was emphasized there that the role of foreign investment was to "supplement" domestic investment, and a dominant role for the former was not admissible. There were also provisions requiring national participation, thereby limiting both short- and long-term foreign participation. As nonspecific as it was, the 1967 law was actually not more restrictive than its predecessors. On the contrary, the 1967 law marked the beginning of the open-door policy of the new government.[10] It would be naive to assume that the provisions of the law were intended as immutable in the face of changing economic. As shown from evidence in the 1980s, the law was indeed adaptable.

In 1969, the foreign exchange control system was abolished, making the rupiah fully convertible at market rates. Capital transfers were legalized and facilitated, with no questions asked by tax authorities regarding the origin of funds. Efforts to attract foreign capital were also made on the fiscal front. A set of tax incentives and duty exemptions were introduced. Another critical incentive was the provision of legal protection to foreign investment.

Foreign capital recorded under direct investment in the capital account began to turn positive and markedly increased (see again Figure 11.3) after persistent outflows for a number of years. It was only then that one could begin looking at the real factors responsible for Indonesia's comparative advantages. Typically, natural resources and low-cost labor were the two major sources. Despite a mandate stated in the constitution that government must control the resources and economic activities considered important to the livelihood of society at large, there was in practice only weak ideological aversion to foreign investment.

In the 1970s, when a strong import substitution strategy was implemented, the size of the domestic market became an important consideration. To counter relatively low domestic purchasing

---

[10] On the ownership issue, there was no mention of the share that foreign investors could hold at the time the investment was established.

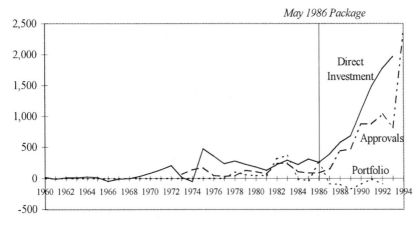

Figure 11.3. Foreign investment in Indonesia: direct investment and portfolio investment ($ million) and approvals ($10 million), 1960–94. (Source: Capital Investment Coordination Board [BKPM]; IMF, *International Financial Statistics.*)

power, most requests by foreign investors for protection from competing imports were granted. Statistics indicate that it was during this period that Japanese investment (mostly in consumer goods) began to pour in. Interestingly enough, it was only later that similar concessions were granted to domestic investors. Nevertheless, this gave impetus to a genuine process of industrialization in the country.

When the first oil boom came in 1973–74, the government was able to provide massive subsidized investment credits, mostly via the state-owned development bank (BAPINDO). The pendulum later swung back to more restrictive policies toward foreign investment. As shown in Figure 11.3, the values of foreign investment nosed down. The jump in 1975 was primarily due to new oil investments by foreign firms who perceived potential profits from a quadrupling of oil prices. But the domestic industrial class, both Chinese and indigenous, also emerged during this "easy-credit" period. Some were involved in joint ventures with foreign investors. In retrospect, this was the period where policy toward foreign investment was considered restrictive, largely because all new foreign investments were expected to be in the form of joint ventures. Along with a strong import substitution strategy, the prevailing trade regime imposed a heavy anti-export bias. Through the newly formed Board of Investment (BKPM), investment licensing began to expand.

At the same time, negative sentiment against foreign investment – especially but not exclusively that of the Japanese – was escalating and culminated in January 1974, with a riot during the visit of Prime Minister Tanaka. Since then, the pendulum of attitudes toward foreign investment clearly has swung toward a more restrictive environment for foreign interests. This began with reductions of tax incentives, followed by a strong divestment condition, stipulating that Indonesian equity in joint ventures should reach 51 percent after a fixed period of time. Perhaps the most controversial policy was the reinstatement of the so-called "negative list," indicating the number and types of sectors closed to foreign investment.[11]

Between the period of restrictive foreign investment and the time of economic reform in the mid-1980s, there were series of mixed signals regarding attitudes and policies. At times, when foreign investment approvals declined from $1.8 billion in 1975 to $0.45 billion in 1976 following the Pertamina crisis, and then continued to drop (see Figure 11.3), efforts were made to revive foreign investment. The BKPM issued a priority list (DSP) in the hope that investment approvals could be made more transparent, specifying those areas and sectors that the government was trying to promote. Unfortunately, DSP was full of ambiguity and unclear criteria, but at least the government's attitude had shifted in favor of more foreign investment.[12]

A second oil crisis came in 1979. With abundant financial resources, the government was once again less than enthusiastic about relaxing investment regulations. On the contrary, new restrictions were imposed, among other things with respect to the Indonesian equity in joint ventures (the minimum for local equity was 20 percent). Both direct investment and the approval values consequently declined until 1981 (see Figure 11.3).

---

[11] This "negative list" was far more restrictive than the "negative list" reinstated in 1989.

[12] For example, the question of whether a sector is permanently or temporarily closed was not well described; similarly, no clear description can be found for product definitions. Then there were also a number of exceptions made but, again, with unclear explanations. The criterion of "employment creation," for example, was difficult to define when no benchmark number was set.

2.4. Foreign Investment during the Period of Deregulation and Liberalization

When a major external shock hit the Indonesian economy in the early 1980s, the pendulum of economic policy swung back to the direction of more liberalization. The shock of the 1980s was largely propelled by the worldwide recession of 1982–83 and a plunge in oil prices from almost $30 per barrel in 1985 to less than $10 in August 1986. Given the fact that petroleum royalties generated around 60–70 percent of government and export revenues, these events dramatically affected the economy.

A major reform was urgently needed, and a stabilization and structural adjustment (SSA) program was begun. The stabilization component was reflected in the continued enforcement of the balanced budget policy. With a sharp drop in oil revenues, this implied a considerable budget cut. A number of large industrial projects were postponed, and civil service salaries were frozen for three consecutive years. On the revenue front, a major tax reform was introduced in 1984. A new income tax law was promulgated, extending coverage and collection rates. Perhaps the most significant component of the tax reform was the introduction of the value-added tax (VAT) in 1985. The VAT was levied at a rate of 10 percent in manufacturing and construction sectors, and also on fuel oils. On luxury goods sold in domestic markets there was an additional tax of 10–20 percent. Today, the VAT and the income tax are the largest sources of government revenue after petroleum royalties.

In the monetary side, a major reform was instituted in June 1983. Aimed at dismantling the old system of monetary control, a more indirect approach, based on reserve money management with open market operations, was initiated. A new monetary instrument was introduced, a central bank certificate known as *Sertifikat Bank Indonesia* (SBI), along with its counterpart promissory note known as *Surat Berharga Pasar Uang* (SBPU). With this new instrument, the central bank sought greater control of reserves by reclaiming its share of net foreign assets (NFA) and, when needed, creating debt instruments.

More important for the analysis of foreign investment was the Indonesian exchange rate policy. Two major devaluations were implemented, one in March 1983 (28 percent) and the other in 1986 (31 percent). This was an integral part of the SSA program, as was another component – phasing out of both tariff and non-tariff import barriers.

The first trade and investment policy package was introduced in May 1986. This allowed foreign ownership up to 95 percent (from 80 percent), as long as it was export-oriented (exporting at least 85 percent of output) or required large capital commitments (above $10 million). There was no divestment requirement in these cases. For non–export-oriented firms, the phase-down requirements were 20 percent in five years and 51 percent within 10 years.[13] Firms operating in export-oriented activities could also distribute their own products locally, and some retail trade was opened for foreign firms. The opening of a Japanese department store "SOGO" marked the beginning of a new era in this area. In the same package, an export credit scheme was initiated for joint ventures to participate. Unsurprisingly, figures for direct investment and approved foreign investment started to rise sharply, as clearly shown in Figure 11.3.

Another important development related to the May 1986 package was the establishment of a government agency, called P4BM, and later renamed BAPEKSTA, to administer the duty-free and drawback measures. It is no exaggeration to say that the early operations of this agency were to a large extent responsible for the success of the dramatic (yet relatively smooth) shift from import substitution to export orientation. Clearly, this was the period in which export-oriented strategy prevailed in the policy debate. It also explains why most investments, domestic and foreign, favored the export-oriented sector.

As shown in Table 11.2, the share of export-oriented domestic investment went up from 52.5 percent to 65.5 percent between 1986 and 1987, with revenue of foreign exchange reaching around $3.9 billion annually. The rate of increase in foreign investment was even more dramatic (from 38 percent to 52.9 percent).[14] The number of foreign investment projects also jumped from fifty to seventy during the same period. It appears that such a jump was only the beginning of a longer trend. As indicated in the table, by the end of the decade, around 70 percent of private investment,

---

[13] Actually, non–export-oriented investments can enjoy the same benefits provided they are located in the least developed regions of eastern Indonesia, or employ high technology, or require large capital (above $10 million).

[14] For further discussions on the shift, see Azis (1989).

Table 11.2. *Export-Oriented Investment Post "May 1986 Package"*

	1986	1987	1988	1989	1990
Domestic Investment					
Number of new projects	316	565	845	863	1329
Export-oriented projects	166	370	594	623	937
(percentage from total)	(52.5)	(65.5)	(70.3)	(72.2)	(70.5)
Expected annual exports					
($ million)	1,778.1	3,943.1	5,545.5		
Foreign Investment					
Number of new projects	50	70	145	294	432
Export-oriented projects	19	37	105	231	311
(percentage from total)	(38.0)	(52.9)	(72.4)	(78.6)	(72.0)
Expected annual exports					
($ million)	243.3	507.0	1,069.4		

Source: Capital Investment Coordination Board (BKPM).

both foreign and domestic, was export oriented. Hence, improvement of investment climate and the adoption of an export-oriented strategy had boosted foreign investment flows in the export-oriented sector. These are all the "pull factors," and, to balance the story, it is equally important to consider the role of "push factors."

The substantial appreciation of Japanese yen, later followed by similar trends in the Korean won and Taiwanese dollar, had led to the rapid increase in investments (industrial relocation) from these countries. After May 1986, the Korean and Taiwanese investments were particularly dominant. This trend was detected by the government, although in this regard Indonesia was often considered the last to react among the Association of Southeast Asian Nations (ASEAN) countries. Table 11.3a indicates that by 1988, Korea and Taiwan dominated the new foreign investments in Indonesia, with 17.2 percent and 10.3 percent, respectively.

Notice that during the same period there was an absolute decline in the new investment from Japan, from $0.5 to $0.2 billion (Table 11.3b), largely because competition to attract Japanese capital to other ASEAN countries was mounting. Unfortunately, Indonesia was not so favorably regarded by Japanese investors at that time. A Japanese survey organization (*Keizei Doyukai*) indicated in 1987 that in various respects the investment climates in Indonesia and

Table 11.3a. *Approved Foreign Investment by Country of Origin, 1987–94 (number of projects and percentage)*

	1987 (share)	1988 (share)	1989 (share)	1990 (share)	1991 (share)	1992 (share)	1993 (share)	1994 (share)
Japan	18 (13.8)	24 (16.6)	63 (21.4)	76 (17.6)	82 (21.8)	51 (16.7)	54 (16.4)	79 (16.1)
Asian NIEs	19 (14.6)	65 (44.8)	149 (50.7)	249 (57.6)	183 (48.7)	134 (43.9)	124 (37.7)	233 (47.5)
Korea	5 (3.8)	25 (17.2)	64 (21.8)	86 (19.9)	54 (14.4)	28 (9.2)	22 (6.7)	36 (7.3)
Taiwan	3 (2.3)	15 (10.3)	50 (17.0)	94 (21.8)	58 (15.4)	23 (7.5)	21 (6.4)	55 (11.2)
Hong Kong	10 (7.7)	12 (8.3)	16 (5.4)	35 (8.1)	26 (6.9)	40 (13.1)	24 (7.3)	39 (7.9)
Singapore	1 (0.8)	13 (9.0)	19 (6.5)	34 (7.9)	45 (12.0)	43 (14.1)	57 (17.3)	103 (21.0)
USA	8 (6.2)	6 (4.1)	14 (4.8)	16 (3.7)	8 (2.1)	15 (4.9)	18 (5.5)	20 (4.1)
Others	85 (65.4)	50 (34.5)	68 (23.1)	91 (21.1)	103 (27.4)	105 (34.4)	133 (40.4)	159 (32.4)
Total	130 (100.0)	145 (100.0)	294 (100.0)	432 (100.0)	376 (100.0)	305 (100.0)	329 (100.0)	491 (100.0)

Source: Capital Investment Coordination Board (BKPM).

Table 11.3b. *Approved Foreign Investment by Country of Origin, 1987–94 (US$ million and percentage)*

	1987 (share)	1988 (share)	1989 (share)	1990 (share)	1991 (share)	1992 (share)	1993 (share)	1994 (share)
Japan	532 (36.5)	247 (5.6)	769 (16.3)	2,241 (25.6)	929 (10.6)	1,511 (14.6)	836 (10.3)	1616 (6.2)
Asian NIEs	172 (11.8)	1,584 (35.9)	1,197 (25.4)	2,599 (29.7)	1,983 (22.6)	2,668 (25.8)	2,637 (32.4)	12,089 (46.3)
Korea	23 (1.6)	200 (4.5)	466 (9.9)	723 (8.3)	301 (3.4)	618 (6.0)	661 (8.1)	1,852 (7.1)
Taiwan	7.9 (0.5)	910 (20.6)	158 (3.4)	618 (7.1)	1,057 (12.0)	563 (5.5)	131 (1.6)	2,496 (9.5)
Hong Kong	135 (9.3)	240 (5.4)	407 (8.6)	993 (11.4)	278 (3.2)	1,021 (9.9)	384 (4.7)	6,055 (23.2)
Singapore	6 (0.4)	240 (5.4)	166 (3.5)	265 (3.0)	346 (3.9)	465 (4.5)	1,460 (17.9)	1,686 (6.5)
USA	73 (5.0)	672 (15.2)	348 (7.4)	154 (1.8)	276 (3.1)	923 (8.9)	445 (5.5)	988 (3.8)
Others	681 (46.7)	1,905 (43.2)	2,405 (51.0)	3,758 (42.9)	5,590 (63.7)	5223 (50.6)	4,227 (51.9)	11,444 (43.8)
Total	1,457 (100.0)	4,408 (100.0)	4,719 (100.0)	8,751 (100.0)	8,778 (100.0)	10,323 (100.0)	8,144 (100.0)	26,136 (100.0)

Source: Capital Investment Coordination Board (BKPM).

the Philippines were perceived by many businessmen as relatively unfavorable compared to other ASEAN countries.[15]

While it was still dominant in value terms, the investment from Asian Newly Industrialized Economies (ANIEs, consisting of Korea, Taiwan, Hong Kong, and Singapore) also declined in 1989. Again, competition from other ASEAN countries was a factor, and by this time, new competition was arising from China. In fact, statistics indicate that during 1986–90 the annual FDI flows to China had increased more than triple, reaching $2.9 billion, compared to the flows in 1981–85. The increase was much smaller in Indonesia, from $0.24 to $0.6 billion. Realizing the urgency of securing continued foreign investment flows, the chairman of the BKPM stated in 1989 that the country would put priority on attracting new investments from Japan and the four ANIEs. In 1990, total approved investments (including expansions) almost doubled, reaching $8.8 billion, more than half of this from Japan and ANIEs. Among the ANIEs, the largest number of new projects in that year was from Taiwan, while Hong Kong was first in terms of total value.[16]

The push factors originated not only from the currency appreciation. In 1986, the Korean government set up two important agencies: the Promotion Agency for Small-Scale Companies, and foreign investment consulting centers for firms planning to invest in Southeast Asian countries. The establishment of the Korean Export–Import Bank in 1987 was another important development. Strong push factors were also discernible in Taiwan during this period. Abolition of foreign exchange controls in August 1986 induced outflows of Taiwanese investment to various countries, including Indonesia. Prior to that, the foreign exchange controls prevented Taiwanese investors from investing openly in other countries (Thee, 1992). In addition to these developments, the number of trade and investment missions sent by Taiwan and Korea to Southeast Asian countries increased considerably during this period.

One can discern in Tables 11.3a and 11.3b a dramatic increase in investment from Singapore, from $6 million in 1987 to $265

---

[15] The report was presented at the 13th ASEAN-Japanese Businessmen Meeting in Kyoto, March 1987.
[16] The U.S. investment in Indonesia persistently declined from $0.67 billion in 1988 to $0.35 and $0.15 billion in 1989 and 1990, respectively.

million in 1990. At one point in 1993, Singapore even outpaced Japan and the other ANIEs. In this respect, the newly developed "Growth Triangle" – involving Johor (Malaysia), Singapore, and Batam Island in Riau (Indonesia) – played a major role. The basic concept of the Triangle was "to link three areas with different factor endowments and different comparative advantages to form a larger region with greater potential for economic growth."[17] It is easy to understand why Singapore, having severely limited land endowments, first initiated and later enthusiastically promoted the Triangle. On the contrary, there were more challenges (distribution and substitution problems) from Malaysia and Indonesia.

Although originally designated as a logistics and operational base for oil and gas industries, Batam became a bonded area or duty-free zone in 1978 and was destined to become a high-tech center. Since Batam has an almost independent status, policies on foreign investment were, in practice, independently designed.[18]

After the May 1986 package, there were two policy changes considered important to the development of foreign investment in Indonesia. The first was the December 1987 package, the second the replacement of DSP with a negative list (sixty-four sectors were listed), indicating that any sector not on the list was open for foreign investment. On the other hand, a wide variety of objectives that the government wished to achieve were reflected in the December 1987 package. These responded to pressures to open up the economy further in order to compete with neighboring countries. In addition, they responded to at least three critical conditions arising from the domestic environment at that time: the need to (1) expand the capital market, (2) earn maximum foreign exchange in the face of mounting debt-service levels, and (3) safeguard against undue income inequality, both between income groups and between regions.

The 1987 package clearly stated that Indonesian ownership in a foreign investment establishment should be reduced from 75

[17] L. T. Yuan (1991, p. 3).
[18] In October 1989, a new policy was announced, in which 100 percent foreign ownership was allowed in the zone, and only 5 percent should be divested within five years (compare this with 51 percent divestment requirement in the rest of Indonesia with in fifteen years). But it was the 1989 policy that started generating positive and tangible responses in Batam. In the policy package, private companies, both foreign and domestic, are allowed to set up industrial estates. At any rate, the rise of Singaporean investments in Indonesia since 1986 was largely due to investments in Batam.

percent to 51 percent to merit so-called national treatment. To boost the capital market, this percentage was lowered to 45 percent if 20 percent of this was sold in the capital market. The minimum requirement of 5 percent Indonesian ownership for export-oriented investment from the May 1986 package was reemphasized, this time with no further obligation to phase down. The 5 percent minimum requirement also applied to those with only 65 percent export requirement (not 85 percent), as long as they were located in one of the provinces in eastern Indonesia, but after ten years and fifteen years, phase-down requirements ought to be met (20 percent and 51 percent, respectively). The concern with income disparity was reflected in the new DSP list, which kept small-scale industries closed to foreign investment.

Other important signs of relaxed restrictions were apparent in the package. For example, foreign investors were allowed to diversify up to 30 percent of their existing capacity with no requirement for a new license. A more precise guideline was provided through the use of International Standard Industrial Classification (ISIC). To help the domestic investors secure additional funds and acquire foreign investment status, foreign investors could reinvest their profits in new or existing domestic companies. As indicated in Table 11.3b, the approved foreign investment jumped dramatically following the 1987 package, from $1.5 to $4.4 billion in 1988, and continued to rise until 1992.

In general, the climate for foreign investors in Indonesia was fairly conducive from the second half of the 1980s until the early 1990s. Most observers and business communities perceived that the country had even entered the process of total liberalization. No serious debates were engaged on the dominance of foreigners in property ownership. Then came the episode of "deregulation fatigue." Practically no major packages were announced during this period, except for the regular policy measures usually announced prior to the consultative meeting of IGGI (intergovernmental group on Indonesia, later renamed consultative group on Indonesia, or CGI). One of the important reasons behind such a trend was the strong growth of the economy, close to 7 percent, during Repelita V (1989–93). Even when foreign investment approval declined by more than 20 percent in 1993 (i.e., from $10.3 to $8.1 billion), the overall growth rate was still around 6.5 percent. A consistent pattern seemed to be appearing, whereby substantial deregulation was implemented when economic growth was weak and less ambitious reforms were pursued when the economy was strong.

To most observers, a foreign investment–related package announced in October 1993, known as Pakto 1993, was perceived as a mix of liberalization and new restrictions or even "take backs" of previous liberalization (FIAS, 1994).[19] The only major step in the package was perhaps the transfer of authority to issue investment licenses to second-level regional government authority (Dati II). The package also stipulated that the National Land Agency (BPN) at Dati II level would be the only office in charge of land entitlement, and land reservation permits were abolished. As discussed in Pangestu and Azis (1994), this apparent decentralization measure was actually more of a gimmick. The fact that most matters are delegated to two central offices that operate in the region (i.e., BPN and BKPMD) reflects rather further application of the *deconcentration* (not decentralization) principle. The two offices would serve as the extended arms of the central agencies.

Linking the trend of the regional foreign investment distribution with the October 1993 package is not entirely justified. As shown in Table 11.4, there was indeed a rather significant change in the distribution from 1993 to 1994, in which the percentage approvals in Java declined from 81 percent to 58 percent, the most drastic of which was in West Java. On the other hand, most approvals increased outside Java, although the largest increase was still in the western part of the country (i.e., Sumatra). In the past few years, the government has expressed concern about the increasing economic gap between eastern and western Indonesia. The 1993–94 trend clearly offered nothing to ameliorate such concerns. Furthermore, looking at the trend in prior years, a drop in Java's share along with a significant increase in Sumatra's share also occurred in 1991–92 (Table 11.4), irrespective of new policies. It is therefore doubtful that the October 1993 package caused the decline in Java's share in 1994; at most, perhaps the "image of decentralization" affected the psychology of investors. Pakto 1983

---

[19] Actually, there was another package announced in 1992, an important item of which was the allowance of 100 percent foreign ownership, albeit only in certain sectors. Otherwise, the tone of the package was similar to the previous ones, except that another locational condition (in the bonded zone) was added to the list of those entitled for the minimum phase-down requirement.

was not really intended to enhance regional autonomy, much less to promote decentralization. Rather, it was designed mainly to streamline investment procedures. Such a move was considered necessary from a macroeconomic perspective, given a slowdown in investment activities, particularly foreign investment, in 1993.

It was not until June 1994 that the government announced a major package. While the economy remained strong, with an estimated growth rate of 7.3 percent or 7.1 percent (depending on the base year being used), competition from the neighboring countries (e.g., China and Vietnam) had increased. Even countries in South Asia (e.g., India and Bangladesh) began to show their competitive muscle. Another major impetus came from the planned Asia Pacific Economic Cooperation (APEC) meeting scheduled for the same year in Bogor, Indonesia. Having held the chairmanship of the APEC throughout the meeting, the Indonesian position toward trade and investment liberalization was quite progressive and even considered daring by some. It was so far-reaching that some member countries were surprised by it. Until today, however, the Indonesian government's actions have been far from the tenor of that November 1994 meeting. Progress has been slow, and the "brave" Indonesian policymakers have not shown correspondingly "brave" proposals in various discussions prior to the upcoming APEC meeting in Osaka.

One of the restrictions most complained about by foreign investors since the inception of the 1967 law on foreign investment has been the duration of investment licenses, only up to thirty years. Over the years, this point has been contested without success. Many investors suggest that the government remove the provision from the law. The primary reason behind the restriction was an implicit interpretation of the famous Article 33 of the Constitution that stipulates that economic activities affecting the livelihood of many people should be controlled by the government. In the June 1994 package, the restriction was, for the first time in almost three decades, softened by the insertion of the term "will be automatically renewed, as long as there are perceived positive benefits to the economy and to national development."[20]

---

[20] Somewhat unrelated to the package, preparation of a new plan was also under way to extend the rental period of land use for investment in Batam from thirty years to eighty years.

Table 11.4. *Approved Foreign Investment in Indonesia by Regions in the 1990s (US$ million and percentage)*

	1990	(share)	1991	(share)	1992	(share)	1993	(share)	1994	(share)
JAVA	6,135	(70.1)	7,187	(81.9)	6,002	(58.1)	6,566	(80.6)	15,173	(58.1)
Greater Jakarta	1,594	(18.2)	4,217	(48.0)	1,131	(11.0)	1,669	(20.5)	1,858	(7.1)
West Java	3,450	(39.4)	2,376	(27.1)	4,498	(43.6)	2,508	(30.8)	5,207	(19.9)
Central Java	111	(1.3)	131	(1.5)	43	(0.4)	50	(0.6)	1,832	(7.0)
Yogyakarta	7	(0.1)	37	(0.4)	48	(0.5)	56	(0.7)	0	(0.0)
East Java	973	(11.1)	426	(4.9)	282	(2.7)	2,283	(28.0)	6,276	(24.0)
SUMATRA	1,170	(13.4)	995	(11.3)	2,452	(23.8)	1,368	(16.8)	7,105	(27.2)
Aceh	192	(2.2)	0	(0.0)	0	(0.0)	529	(6.5)	2,638	(10.1)
North Sumatra	627	(7.2)	36	(0.4)	658	(6.4)	78	(1.0)	225	(0.9)
West Sumatra	2	(0.0)	0	(0.0)	3	(0.0)	66	(0.8)	98	(0.4)
Riau	247	(2.8)	951	(10.8)	1,734	(16.8)	609	(7.5)	3,966	(15.2)
Jambi	0	(0.0)	0	(0.0)	0	(0.0)	0	(0.0)	39	(0.2)
Bengkulu	0	(0.0)	0	(0.0)	0	(0.0)	34	(0.4)	9	(0.0)
Lampung	58	(0.7)	3	(0.0)	51	(0.5)	52	(0.6)	47	(0.2)
South Sumatra	44	(0.5)	5	(0.1)	6	(0.1)	0	(0.0)	83	(0.3)

KALIMANTAN	701	(8.0)	24	(0.3)	441	(4.3)	13	(0.2)	2,059	(7.9)
West Kalimantan	7	(0.1)	13	(0.1)	0	(0.0)	2	(0.0)	8	(0.0)
East Kalimantan	561	(6.4)	4	(0.0)	74	(0.7)	1	(0.0)	101	(0.4)
Central Kalimantan	11	(0.1)	3	(0.0)	6	(0.1)	0	(0.0)	0	(0.0)
South Kalimantan	123	(1.4)	5	(0.1)	361	(3.5)	10	(0.1)	1,951	(7.5)
SULAWESI	131	(1.5)	13	(0.1)	91	(0.9)	40	(0.5)	1,448	(5.5)
North Sulawesi	8	(0.1)	7	(0.1)	26	(0.2)	32	(0.4)	41	(0.2)
Central Sulawesi	1	(0.0)	2	(0.0)	2	(0.0)	0	(0.0)	6	(0.0)
Southeast Sulawesi	0	(0.0)	2	(0.0)	61	(0.6)	0	(0.0)	6	(0.0)
South Sulawesi	121	(1.4)	2	(0.0)	3	(0.0)	8	(0.1)	1,395	(5.3)
OTHERS	615	(7.0)	559	(6.4)	1,336	(12.9)	157	(1.9)	351	(1.3)
Bali, NTT, NTB	613	(7.0)	557	(6.3)	521	(5.0)	52	(0.6)	39	(0.1)
Maluku, Irja, E. Timor	2	(0.0)	3	(0.0)	815	(7.9)	105	(1.3)	312	(1.2)
TOTAL	8,751	(100.0)	8,778	(100.0)	10,323	(100.0)	8,144	(100.0)	26,136	(100.0)

Source: Capital Investment Coordination Board (BKPM).

Another major step taken with this package was the opening up of nine sensitive sectors, but only through joint ventures. The following nine were previously closed to foreign investment (again, due to Article 33): telecommunications, generation and production of electricity, drinking water, automatic generation plant, mass media, ports, railways, shipping, and air transport.

These were the most dramatic changes made in the package. In addition, a number of the phase-down requirements were further relaxed (basically, the decision is now left to the shareholders): the ownership requirement, the initial capital requirement, and the location requirement. It is not clear whether the more than three-fold surge of foreign investment approvals in 1994, from $8.1 to $26.1 billion, was entirely caused by the package; perhaps only some of the investment hike, especially in manufacturing investment (see Table 11.5), could be attributed to the package.

The latest deregulation package was announced on May 23, 1995. Again, it came just before the upcoming CGI meeting, although the government denied that there was any connection between the two. In addition to reduction of import tariffs, the most important of which were for the automotive sector and the traditionally protected maize products, measures to reduce non-tariff barriers, more particularly import licensing, were also announced. In the area of investment, import tariffs were exempted for those who planned to restructure a business by using at least 30 percent of initial investment funds. The issuance of investment permits was further simplified. But perhaps the most significant move in the investment area was changes made in the negative list. Sectors removed from the list range from palm oil to rattan, cigarettes, and disposable gas lighters to the automotive and aviation maintenance sectors.

On the other hand, surprisingly, telecommunication, railway, port development, and electricity production, transmission, and distribution were added to the list.[21] In addition, some sectors were absolutely closed to new investments. Another interesting component of this package was the announcement of a tariff phase-out

---

[21] Recall that many of these categories were opened in the June 1994 package. Furthermore, these are the highly needed infrastructure, the provision of which (supply and prices) is increasingly more critical in the coming years.

Table 11.5. *Approved Foreign Investment by Sector in Indonesia in the 1990s (US$ million and percentage)*

	1990	(share)	1991	(share)	1992	(share)	1993	(share)	1994	(share)
Agriculture	168	(1.9)	14	(0.2)	66	(0.6)	138	(1.7)	690	(2.6)
Forestry	2	(0.0)	1	(0.0)	138	(1.3)	0	(0.0)	0	(0.0)
Fisheries	20	(0.2)	11	(0.1)	28	(0.3)	22	(0.3)	40	(0.2)
Mining	116	(1.3)	0	(0.0)	2,312	(22.4)	0	(0.0)	0	(0.0)
Manufacturing	5,668	(64.8)	3,970	(45.2)	5,670	(54.9)	3,423	(42.0)	20,647	(79.0)
Elect., gas, and water	0	(0.0)	0	(0.0)	0	(0.0)	2,276	(27.9)	2,766	(10.6)
Construction	77	(0.9)	26	(0.3)	41	(0.4)	97	(1.2)	91	(0.3)
Trade, restr., and hotel	864	(9.9)	402	(45.8)	919	(8.9)	1,088	(13.4)	433	(1.7)
Transport and comm.	803	(9.2)	167	(1.9)	14	(0.1)	85	(1.0)	145	(0.6)
Finance and real estate	894	(10.2)	403	(4.6)	716	(6.9)	598	(7.3)	1143	(4.4)
Services	140	(1.6)	167	(1.9)	420	(4.1)	418	(5.1)	180	(0.7)
Total	8,751	(100.0)	8,778	(100.0)	10,323	(100.0)	8,144	(100.0)	26,136	(100.0)

Source: Capital Investment Coordination Board (BKPM).

plan. For example, in the automotive sector, the tariff for the sedan category was reduced from 175 percent to 125 percent, and it was also stipulated that this rate would be reduced to 40 percent by the year 2003. Such a definite time schedule for tariff reduction was, as far as the author can recall, a first for an Indonesian government deregulation package. It is very likely that this move was prompted by the ASEAN Free Trade Area (AFTA) proposal announced in Chiang Mai, Thailand. To wit, under the "normal track," scheme tariffs are to be lowered to a threshold of 20 percent by 1998 and 5 percent in 2003 (five years earlier than the original plan).[22] A further threat of competition from China and neighboring countries could have been an important factor.

Data on approved foreign investment show that another boom occurred in 1995. Recorded approvals went up strongly, although the number of unrealized investments was also reported to be increasing. Looking at the data more carefully, a large portion of the increase was due to one large petrochemical investment. It is therefore not surprising that this fact, along with a major riot that took place in July 27, 1996, has produced a drop in both approvals and realization for 1996.

In a society experiencing increased economic openness, greater political freedom and democratization are usually also in demand. The July 27 riot reflects such a demand, and partly resonates dissatisfaction with the distributional impact of the country's robust economic growth over the last ten years or so. While the trend of opening up the economy further, including promotion of foreign investment, is likely to continue regardless of who leads the country in the post-Suharto period, reducing disparities in economic welfare between regions and between income groups will remain an important policy agenda. The historical experience described in the preceding sections supports this conjecture. Improving such a safety net generally has little to do with foreign investment, but this activity can induce negative distributional effects, which are legitimate concerns for policymakers. With this motivation, we embark on the following impact analysis.

---

[22] The "fast track" scheme was 5 percent duty by the year 2000. Those commodities outside the two schemes are subject to tariff reductions on a gradual basis between 1995 and 2000.

3. IMPACT ANALYSIS

3.1. A Multiplier Analysis of Interregional Disparities

As indicated earlier, issues of regional distribution and income distribution in a country as large and as diverse as Indonesia are at least as critical as macroeconomic issues. It is obvious from Table 11.4 that foreign investment is unequally distributed across regions, with Java and Sumatra (western part of Indonesia) the average largest recipients; taking some 80 percent to 90 percent of total foreign investment in the country. Many studies, among others Hill (1989), Azis (1992, 1994b), and Kim, Knaap, and Azis (1992), have shown that the distribution of gross regional domestic product (GRDP) has been more or less similar to investment distribution. However, Azis (1992) showed that, while foreign investment in the postreform period tends to further concentrate in Java and the western part of the country, the regional distribution of GRDP was less skewed.[23]

It is difficult to trace and specify quantitatively the link between foreign investment and the overall economy of a region. Intersectoral transactions do help to elucidate this problem, however, and for this reason we implement a multiplier analysis using an Interregional Social Accounting Matrix (IRSAM).

The Social Accounting Matrix (SAM) is a data system linking production accounts, institutions, and factors of production. Receipts of sectors or institutions are listed across a row, and its expenditures are listed down in column. The defining characteristic of SAM is that it captures the circular interdependence in the economic system.[24] In a SAM framework, any sectoral production shock will generate value-added effects, from which, along with possible transfers among different institutions, different institutional and household incomes are influenced. This income in turn affects consumption (and saving) patterns, feeding back to output, employment, and more value-added effects. All these linkages correspond to an implicit multiplier, capturing direct and indirect

---

[23] Indicated by increased entropy from a 1.35–1.42 range to 1.65–1.88. See Azis (1992).
[24] For an elaboration of SAM methodology, see Pyatt (1988). Further extensions of SAM, using decomposition methods known as structural path analysis, can be found in Defourny and Thorbecke (1984).

Table 11.6a. *Baseline Condition: Eastern versus Western Indonesia*

	Household Incomes (Rp. billion)	Wages (Rp. billion)	Capital Incomes (Rp. billion)	GDRP (Rp. billion)	Per-capita HH Incomes (Rp. 000)
Java	100,454	62,677	52,462	115,140	911
West (Incl. G. Jakarta)	46,469	30,619	28,984	59,604	1,313
Central Java	22,180	14,295	10,141	24,436	778
East Java	31,805	17,762	13,337	31,100	902
Sumatra	32,142	19,162	29,062	48,224	883
Western Indonesia	132,596	81,839	81,524	163,363	904
Kalimantan	9,770	6,219	11,395	17,615	1,073
Sulawesi	8,780	4,763	3,562	8,325	702
Others	9,680	5,366	5,087	10,453	891
Eastern Indonesia	28,230	16,348	20,044	36,392	869
Indonesia	160,826	98,187	101,569	199,755	897
Share of Total					(Indonesia=100)
Java	62.46	63.83	51.65	57.64	101.48
Western Indonesia	82.45	83.35	80.27	81.78	100.70
Eastern Indonesia	17.55	16.65	19.73	18.22	96.85

Source: Based on IRSAM 1990.

effects. Hence, the impact of, say, increased foreign investment on sectoral production will be transmitted through SAM multipliers ultimately to generate household income distribution. When separate accounts for different subnational regions are available, the resulting effects on both intraregional and interregional distribution, measured in terms of income or production (reflected through GRDP), can also be obtained. This comprehensiveness, consistency, and ability to measure the direct and indirect effects makes SAM useful for an impact analysis.

The present analysis focuses on two particular issues: interregional and intraregional disparities. Table 11.6a, which depicts the baseline condition of interregional income distribution in 1990, is compared with the results of simulating IRSAM 1990 for increased foreign investment, especially in the export-oriented sector (see again the analysis of Table 11.2), which is concentrated, but not exclusively, in Java (based on Table 11.4). This should reflect a typical pattern of foreign investment distribution in Indonesia. The resulting comparison is made in Table 11.6b.

Table 11.6b. *Simulation of Increased Foreign Investment in Export-Oriented Sector (Mostly in Java: Eastern versus Western Indonesia [baseline = 1])*

	Household Incomes	Wages	Capital Incomes	GDRP
Java	1.26	1.26	1.32	1.29
West (incl. G. Jakarta)	1.28	1.29	1.33	1.31
Central Java	1.26	1.24	1.32	1.28
East Java	1.24	1.24	1.29	1.26
Sumatra	1.23	1.20	1.27	1.24
Western Indonesia	1.25	1.25	1.30	1.27
Kalimantan	1.26	1.22	1.32	1.28
Sulawesi	1.22	1.19	1.23	1.21
Others	1.23	1.20	1.25	1.22
Eastern Indonesia	1.24	1.20	1.28	1.25
Indonesia	1.25	1.24	1.30	1.27
Share of Total				
Java	63.00	65.00	52.50	58.51
Western Indonesia	82.64	83.87	80.44	82.09
Eastern Indonesia	17.36	16.13	19.56	17.91

Source: Simulation Results of IRSAM 1990.

It is clear from Table 11.6b that the results tend to favor the western regions, whose GRDP increases by 27 percent compared to 25 percent for the eastern regions. Of the GRDP components, the wage disparity is most noticeable, increasing 25 percent in the west but only 20 percent in the eastern islands. Looking at distribution within each category, it appears that the massive inflows of foreign investment in the Greater Jakarta and West Java areas (refer again to Table 11.4) tend to exacerbate regional wage disparities. By all accounts, the wage increase in these areas is the largest (close to 30 percent) among all regions in Indonesia. A similar pattern appears to the capital income. It is interesting to note, however, that Kalimantan's surge of capital income resulting from the increased foreign investment is comparable with that of Java (around 32 percent), although Greater Jakarta and West Java still have the highest increase.

Unfortunately, with the present tool of analysis, no migration can be assumed to take place. With such limitation, Tables 11.6a and 11.6b suggest that the pattern of increased foreign investment will result in a worsening income distribution between regions in eastern Indonesia, in which the high-income Kalimantan will grow faster (32 percent) than the low-income Sulawesi (23 percent).[25] Hence, with a pattern of increased foreign investment typical of recent trends in Indonesia (i.e., toward export sectors and concentrated in Java and Sumatra), the multiplier analysis shows that interregional disparities – be they within the eastern region, within the western region, or within Java – are likely to get worse.

What about disparities between income groups? The lack of data on household distribution in each region did not permit such analysis. However, data on household distribution are available for a two-region (Java and non-Java) classification. The following analysis is based on such a setting.

First of all, as shown in the third column of Table 11.7b, the conclusion regarding interregional disparity remains unchanged (i.e., the high-income Java will likely gain greater benefits than the lower-income regions outside Java), even in percentage terms. The GDP ratio between the two will increase from 78.9 percent to 80.5 percent. As expected, much of the change originates in the manufacturing sector.[26] In both Java and non-Java, urban–rural disparity also tends to get wider. Although no changes are apparent in total household income (i.e., Table 11.7a of the baseline and Table 11.7b of the increased foreign investment scenario produced the same ratio between Java and non-Java [162.29 percent]), interesting results are observed in the distribution between household groups. For example, growth of the low-income nonfarm sector outside Java seems to be higher than income growth of the same household category in Java. This suggests that the trend of interregional disparity can be analyzed neither in general terms nor by using a single variable only (often, mistakenly, GRDP), because different household groups may experience different trends of income.

The two tables also reveal that the disparity in the rural nonfarm category will likely decline, reflected in a reduced ratio between income of the rich and that of the poor, from 2.16 to 2.13 in Java, and from 1.84 to 0.37 outside Java. A similar change, albeit smaller,

---

[25] Notice from the last column of Table 11.6 that of all regions included in the IRSAM, Sulawesi has the lowest per-capita household income.

[26] A more convincing conclusion of this type can be derived if a more detailed sectoral classification is made, particularly one that separates the manufacturing from the mining sector.

is estimated to occur in the distribution between farm and nonfarm incomes. By setting the income of the poorest group (agricultural employees) to unity, one can see that, within the farm sector, the relative position of the poorest will likely improve compared to agricultural non-employees. Unfortunately, no further classification within the latter group is available, preventing us from making conclusions regarding income distribution between the poor (owning land of less than 0.5 hectare) and the rich (having greater than 1.0 hectare of land).

In the nonfarm category, income distribution in the rural sector improves slightly, especially outside Java, where the relative position of the rich declines from 5.05 in the baseline to 4.42 in the foreign investment scenario. A similar trend is also predicted in the non-Java urban sector, where the relative position of the urban high-income group will decline from 4.73 to 4.37. On the contrary, in both rural and urban sectors, the relative position of the low-income group is estimated to rise.

In sum, the IRSAM multipliers have shown that the impact of increased foreign investment in export sectors, especially when concentrated in Java, will generate an improved relative income distribution within regions (reducing intraregional disparity) but worsening income distribution between regions (increasing interregional disparity). Income inequality between Java and non-Java, or between eastern and western Indonesia, is likely to get worse. A better interregional disparity may be reachable if new foreign investments are more uniformly spread over regions outside Java or in the eastern part of Indonesia. Such a dispersal of foreign investment is unlikely at this stage of development, however, and thus growing interregional disparity seems inevitable.

4. INCOME DISTRIBUTION WITH A CGE MODEL

The IRSAM approach suffers from a number of drawbacks common to multiplier analysis, including implicit fixed prices, and the assumption of underutilized capacity (supply will respond automatically and without price adjustment to any demand shock). A price-endogenous model that imposes supply constraints would remove such drawbacks. For the purpose of this study, a computable general equilibrium (CGE) model is used with a specification of foreign capital flows (FCAP), one component of which is foreign

Table 11.7a. *Baseline Condition: Java versus Non-Java*

	Java	Non-Java	Indonesia		Ratio of Java to Non-Java
Household Income Ratio				**Household Income**	
Farm/Total HH	0.36	0.50	0.41	Farm HH	1.62
Nonfarm: High-income HH/				Nonfarm HH	2.09
low-income HH	2.16	1.84	2.05	High income	2.20
Urban HH/Rural HH	0.72	0.35	0.56	Low income	1.88
				Urban HH	2.59
				Rural HH	1.28
Relative Income	(Agric. Employees = 1.00)				
Farm Employees	1.00	1.00	1.00	Farm Employees	1.95
Farm Nonemployees	8.29	14.51	10.40	Farm Nonemployees	1.11
Rural Low-income	1.73	1.98	1.82	Rural Low-income	1.70
Rural High-income	3.78	5.05	4.21	Rural High-income	1.46
Urban Low-income	3.39	3.31	3.36	Urban Low-income	2.00
Urban High-income	7.30	4.73	6.43	Urban High-income	3.00
GRDP Composition (%)					
GRDP	100.00	100.00	100.00	GRDP	0.79
Agriculture and Food	23.74	19.01	21.10	Agriculture and Food	0.99
Manufac. and Mining	51.86	45.20	48.14	Manufac. and Mining	0.91
Trade, Transp. and Services	17.39	24.19	21.19	Trade, Transp. and Services	0.57
Other Services	7.01	11.60	9.58	Other Services	0.48

Source: Based on IRSAM 1990.

Table 11.7b. Simulation of Increased Foreign Investment in Export-Oriented Sector (Mostly in Java): Distribution between Java and Non-Java)

	Java	Non-Java	Indonesia		Ratio of Java to Non-Java
Household Income Ratio				Household Income	
Farm/Total	0.35	0.50	0.40	Farm HH	1.62
Nonfarm: High-income/				Nonfarm HH	1.15
low-income	2.13	1.64	1.96	High income	2.13
Urban/Rural	0.75	0.37	0.59	Low income	2.33
				Urban HH	1.80
				Rural HH	2.60
					1.28
Relative Income	(Agric. Employees = 1.00)				
Farm Employees	1.00	1.00	1.00	Farm Employees	1.82
Farm Nonemployees	7.91	13.16	9.77	Farm Nonemployees	1.10
Rural Low-income	1.75	2.00	1.84	Rural Low-income	1.59
Rural High-income	3.79	4.42	4.01	Rural High-income	1.56
Urban Low-income	3.52	3.32	3.45	Urban Low-income	1.93
Urban High-income	7.46	4.37	6.37	Urban High-income	3.11
GRDP Composition (%)					
GRDP	100.00	100.00	100.00	GRDP	0.81
Agriculture and Food	20.15	16.54	18.15	Agriculture and Food	0.98
Manufac. and Mining	60.03	51.47	55.29	Manufac. and Mining	0.94
Trade, Transp. and Services	14.14	21.65	18.30	Trade, Transp. and Services	0.53
Other Services	5.68	10.34	8.26	Other Services	0.44

Source: Simulation Results of IRSAM 1990.

investment. The basic model follows that of Azis (1996a, 1996b, 1997), and the equations related to foreign investment and capital flows are described in the following paragraphs.

The openness of the Indonesian economy suggests that the exchange rate must be specified to account for influences on the prices of intermediate inputs and capital, as well as tariffs and other revenues. However, that is only part of the story, because the exchange rate will also influence capital account balances by altering foreign capital flows. In such a setting, capital flows other than official flows can be modeled as:

$$FCAP = \sigma_0 + deg \cdot \sigma_1 \left(r - rf - RISK - \left(dEXR - 1 \right) \right) \quad (11.1)$$

where EXR denotes the exchange rate, r and rf are the domestic and foreign interest rate, respectively, and $RISK$ is the risk premium. This equation basically specifies that capital flows will respond to three major factors: interest rate differential, risk premium, and the expected change in the exchange rate. Parameter "deg" reflects the intensity of controls that the government exerts on capital flows; its value ranges from 0 (totally closed to international capital flows) to 1 (complete capital account liberalization). In this respect, σ_0 may be defined as the autonomous volume of capital flows.[27]

The risk premium is modeled as determined by a debt-service ratio:

$$RISK = \alpha_0 + \alpha_1 \left[\left(\sum_{br} AMORT_{br} + \sum_{br} INT_{br} \right) \Big/ \sum_i E_i \cdot pwe_i \right] \quad (11.2)$$

where $AMORT$ and INT are amortization and interest payments, respectively, E denotes exports, and pwe is world price of exports. The specification of, and the parameters in, the foregoing two equations are based on results obtained from an econometric study over the period 1980–90.

In a consistent multiperiod simulation, $FCAP$ will affect the size of the capital stock, and it will then change the composition of relative factor prices, leading to changes across the labor market.[28] But $FCAP$ is only one of the sources of capital augmentation,

---

[27] This specification is close to what is known as "stock specification for international capital flows." See Khan and Zahler (1989).

[28] The basic data of sectoral capital stock and investment by sector of destination are taken from Keuning (1988) and Keuning (1991), similar to that used by Lewis (1991).

another being domestic investment. In this regard, the model makes a detour from "Walrasian general equilibrium" modeling in that the domestic private investment ($DOMINV$) is determined via an equation taken from an independent econometric study:[29]

$$DOMINV_i = \lambda_i \cdot VA_i^{\lambda 1i}\left(1 + \lambda\right)^{\lambda 2} \qquad (11.3)$$

From such a specification, movement in the exchange rate (crawling depreciation or one-shot devaluation) can bring about two opposing forces in the foreign capital account. On one side, it can reduce inflows because of increased expectation of the change in the exchange rate. On the other hand, it can augment flows via increased exports or reduced risk premia.

For the purpose of the present analysis, foreign investment ($FORINV$) is taken as policy variable. The impact of this on income distribution is not direct, going rather through the dynamics of the capital account in flows of private and public borrowing, amortization, and changes in foreign reserves (DFR), and the net exports as reflected in the deficit on current account (DCA):

$$BORROW_{Private} = FCAP - \sum_i FORINV_i - BORROW_{Public} \qquad (11.4)$$

$$DFR = \sum_{br} AMORT_{br} - BORROW_{br} - \sum_i FORINV_i - DCA \qquad (11.5)$$

Total private investment is therefore:

$$\sum_i PINV_i = \sum_i \left(FORINV_i \cdot EXR + DOMINV_i\right) \qquad (11.6)$$

The combined private and government investment, after adjustment for inventory changes, reflects changes in capital stock. In turn, these changes will determine the new ($t + 1$) capital stock:

$$K_{i(t+1)} = \left(1.0 - DEPR_i\right)K_i + dK_i \qquad (11.7)$$

where $DEPR$ is depreciation rate, and K denotes the capital stock. In turn, the production function is affected by such changes. It is through this transmission mechanism that household income will eventually be determined. The present analysis makes use of this channel to determine the repercussions of increased foreign invest-

---

[29] See Shafik and Chhibber (1988). The quoted study only estimated aggregate investment; further improvement for sectoral investment is shown in Thorbecke et al. (1992).

ment in the export-oriented sector upon household income distribution.

By altering the size and the sectoral composition of foreign investment, one could trace the impact of those changes on a number of endogenous variables. In the following analysis, these variables are classified into two groups: macroeconomic variables and income distribution variables – the latter basically consist of direct information on incomes of different household categories. Unlike the household classification in the earlier multiplier analysis, the one used in the CGE model is more disaggregated – there are eight household categories, eight factors of production, and thirty sectors. For more detailed explanations on the model, see Azis (1996b, 1997).

The second column of Table 11.8 shows the simulation results based on (estimated) actual increases and sectoral composition of foreign investment inflows in 1990. The lower part of Table 11.8 lists the per-household incomes of different household groups, with their values in the benchmark year normalized to unity. Under this scenario, most macroeconomic variables show the expected changes (e.g., increased prices, larger current account deficit, and greater values of GDP). The resulting income distribution, however, would be difficult to anticipate on the basis of intuition alone.

The difference between simulation 1 and 2 in Table 11.8 is in the sectoral emphasis of foreign investment. By keeping the total investment constant, a greater emphasis on agricultural investment is represented in simulation 2. This scenario appears to generate greater labor demand and GDP growth. These rather surprising results stem from the fact that in Indonesia there is a strong positive feedback between agricultural investment and private consumption. Furthermore, foreign investment in the agricultural sector will require fewer imports of capital goods and intermediate inputs than its counterpart in industry. Hence, with greater consumption and less imports, GDP gains are greater. Exports in simulation 2 are also less because of a lower rate of depreciation than in simulation 1, and this also leads to greater country risk. Lower exports are also due to the fact that most agricultural products are for domestic consumption (direct consumption and intermediate use).

It should be noted that greater GDP in simulation 2 does not imply a proportionally greater increase of household income. As indicated in Table 11.8, income growth for practically all household categories is less under simulation 2. The most meaningful explanation for this finding is that, taking indirect effects into account, export-oriented industries are more income generating than domestic market sectors. When we compare the incomes of the poorest and the richest, it appears that income distribution under simulation 2 is slightly more unequal than under simulation 1. Hence, export-oriented investment is not only more income generating but also more disparity improving. For the perspective of urban–rural income distribution, the export-oriented scenario also gives better results, albeit only slightly. Notice that even for the total agricultural household, income growth is higher under the scenario of export-oriented foreign investment (32.7 percent compared to 32.4 percent).

Perhaps it is more realistic to compare simulations 3 and 4, in which the total amount of foreign investment is not kept constant but is increased by some 25 percent. The additional investment under simulation 3 is assumed to occur in the export-oriented manufacturing sector, whereas in simulation 4 the new investments are in the agricultural sector. The resulting pattern of change in macroeconomic variables is more or less the same as in the preceding comparison. Again, despite the lower exports and lower total investment, the pro-agricultural scenario produces greater GDP mainly because the private consumption (the largest component of GDP) will grow faster.

On the income-distribution front, results show that the more export-oriented scenario will again generate greater incomes for all household categories, produce a slightly better urban–rural income distribution, and induce greater income growth for agricultural households as an aggregate. However, when looking at the numbers more carefully, one can see that the magnitudes are different from the previous comparison. For example, the gap between the income growth of agricultural households in the two scenarios is less (32.7 percent versus 32.6 percent) than the gap in the previous case (32.7 percent compared to 32.4 percent). A similar pattern holds for the urban–rural distribution. Interestingly enough, in the present comparison, a much less clear conclusion can be obtained with respect to disparities between the poorest and the richest group.

Table 11.8. *Results of CGE Model Simulation on Foreign Investment*

A. Macroeconomic Variables

	Benchmark 1985	Simulated 1990	Simulation 1	Simulation 2	Simulation 3	Simulation 4
Real GDP (Rp. billion)	97,848	102,333	102,312	102,379	102,304	102,341
Price Index	1.000	1.161	1.161	1.159	1.162	1.160
Exchange Rates (Rp./US$)	1,120	1,832	1,839	1,817	1,842	1,830
Interest Rates (percent)	18.00	22.64	22.66	22.59	24.39	24.34
Current Account (US$ billion)	-3.173	-3.355	-3.355	-3.355	-3.356	-3.356
Country Risk	0.0200	0.0182	0.0182	0.0183	0.0182	0.0182
Foreign Capital (US$ billion)	0.987	0.255	0.255	0.255	0.256	0.256
Foreign Investments (US$ billion)	0.299	3.046	3.046	3.046	3.807	3.807
GDP Components (Rp. billion)						
Real Private Consumption	61,086	59,488	59,431	59,630	59,405	59,510
Real Government Consumption	11,442	14,401	14,401	14,401	14,401	14,401
Real Investments	2,487	27,611	27,625	27,576	27,635	27,607
Real Exports	21,102	25,620	25,654	25,542	25,669	25,609
Real Imports	20,655	25,427	25,465	25,338	25,483	25,415
Labor Demand (000)	65,951	58,700	58,665	58,786	58,650	58,718
Rural	47,814	43,760	43,737	43,818	43,726	43,769
Urban	18,137	14,940	14,928	14,968	14,923	14,944

Table 11.8 (continued)

B. Income Disparity Variables

	Benchmark 1985	Simulated 1990	Simulation 1	Simulation 2	Simulation 3	Simulation 4
(Per-Household Income: 1985 = 1.000)						
RURAL	1.000	1.550	1.282	1.280	1.282	1.281
Agriculture	1.000	1.326	1.327	1.324	1.327	1.326
Agricultural Workers	1.000	1.260	1.260	1.258	1.260	1.259
Farm Small	1.000	1.308	1.308	1.306	1.309	1.308
Farm Medium	1.000	1.339	1.340	1.338	1.341	1.339
Farm Large	1.000	1.367	1.368	1.365	1.368	1.367
Rural Low-income	1.000	1.198	1.199	1.198	1.199	1.198
Rural High-income	1.000	1.223	1.224	1.222	1.224	1.223
URBAN	1.000	1.272	1.272	1.271	1.272	1.272
Urban Low-income	1.000	1.270	1.270	1.270	1.270	1.270
Urban High-income	1.000	1.266	1.267	1.266	1.267	1.266

Simulated 1990: based on estimated actual distribution of foreign investment.
Simulations 1 to 3: foreign investment sectoral reallocation with the same total.
In Simulation 1, foreign investment in nonmanufacturing sector is decreased by 50 percent and added to the export-oriented manufacturing sector.
In Simulation 2, foreign investment in export-oriented manufacturing sector is decreased by 50 percent and added to the agricultural sector.
Simulations 3 and 4: total foreign investment is increased by 25 percent:
In Simulation 3, the increase is added to the export-oriented manufacturing sector.
In Simulation 5, the increase is added to the agriculture sector.

At any rate, what these simulation exercises have shown is that the structures of foreign investment and production are inter-related with income distribution via the usual triangular cycle through production, factors, and households. From this analysis, it can be stated that, in general, increased foreign investment in the export-oriented manufacturing sector will generate a relatively better income distribution between household groups (intra-regional distribution).

5. CONCLUSION

This chapter was inspired by the principle that contemporary trends in developing-country foreign investment are best viewed from an historical perspective. In the Indonesian case, many of the concepts and terminology found in today's discussion, such as export orientation, import substitution, and rural–urban gap in the dual-economy sense, were well understood centuries ago and trace their origins at least as far back as colonial times. Furthermore, the use of import quotas, regional dissatisfaction with the excessive centralization, worsening welfare and distribution as a result of the (colonial) government's investment policy, and the important role of investment laws, are some of the many economic phenomena of the past that have maintained their relevance in present times.

Indonesia has a long history of foreign investment and official policies regulating it. During the colonial period – the Portuguese (1500s), the Dutch (mid-1590s to mid-1790s), and the French-Dutch (early 1800s) – the objectives of investment policy were similar (i.e., to secure a large supply of spices for export to Europe). This was export-oriented investment of a different nature, but many of its structural features would be familiar today. During a short period of British rule (1811–16), an import substitution strat-egy was added to the objectives, mainly to facilitate imports of British textile products. To achieve this, an unsuccessful attempt was made to improve Indonesian living standards, thereby to raise the purchasing power of the population.

Prior to World War II, foreign investments by the Dutch, British, American, and local Chinese were most prominent, but it was the Americans who really began the country's industrialization process. General Motors, Goodyear, and Union Carbide were among the earliest companies investing in the manufacturing sector, at times when others were still focused on primary export products such as mining and agriculture. After independence, there was a period when the political and ideological climate favored socialism, albeit of a non-Marxist variety. Antipathy to foreign capital, especially from the West, was fostered at this time by the idea of struggle against imperialistic and capitalistic forces. There were also periods where a number of regions expressed openly their dissatisfaction (regional separatism) with Javanese dominance in the central government. This was aggravated by arrangements mandating the transfer of regional export revenues to the central government. These doubts persist to the present and have impelled the government to reduce income disparities between regions.

Immediately after the new government came to power, a new foreign investment law was enacted (1967), recognizing a link between investment and foreign aid and the importance of both to economic development. But given past experience and the political climate at that time, the role of foreign investment was stipulated as only a "supplement" to domestic investment (in a two-gap model sense), implying that it should in no way become dominant. Soon after the promulgation of the law, the foreign exchange controls, an important obstacle to attract foreign investment, were abolished. However, during the import-substitution period of the 1970s, no significant incentives were offered to foreign investors; on the contrary, investment regulations expanded. Consequently, flows of foreign investment stagnated.

It was not until a major external shock, including the plunge in oil prices, hit the economy in the early 1980s that the pendulum swung back to the direction of more liberalization. The first "pull" came from a deregulation package in May 1986. But the push factor was also prominent. Asian currency realignment (e.g., yen, Taiwanese dollar, Korean won) and policy changes in a number of ANIEs prompted a large influx of investments from these countries. The establishment of the Growth Triangle, linking Singapore, Johor, and Batam island, also contributed to the rise of foreign investment. In parallel with the government's outward-oriented strategy, the majority of these investments were export oriented.

Since then, the government has made a series of policy changes aimed at attracting more foreign investment. These changes are concentrated in the following areas: tariff reduction, divestment, ownership requirements, and reduction of sectoral restrictions. Increased competition, primarily from China, India, and neighboring ASEAN countries, also became an important factor that prompted these policy changes. International pressures (e.g., the formation of AFTA, the non-binding principles within APEC, and the completion of the GATT round in the early 1990s) also played a significant role.

Looking ahead, one of the most critical determinants in the country's economic prospects and future investment is the political succession.[30] The question most frequently raised is "How will economic policies in general, regarding foreign investment in particular, be shaped, given the nontransparency of the succession issue?" In a society opening to the global economy, greater political freedom and democratization are usually in demand, and Indonesia is no exception. The July 27, 1996, riot reflects this demographic transition, and it partly resonates dissatisfaction with the distributional effects of the country's robust economic growth during the last decade or so. Two alternatives can be envisioned: The government can respond by gradually relaxing some restrictions, or it can resist evolution in the political system. Should the latter approach prevail, one might expect "compensatory" or mitigating economic policies (i.e., the government will reinforce its effort to maintain high economic growth). Either way, the trend of economic opening, including more extensive foreign investment, appears likely to continue regardless of how the political transition is managed.

It should be emphasized that external policy or domestic leadership issues aside, increasing inequality between and within regions in Indonesia poses a challenge to economic sustainability and political stability. Providing for and strengthening the social safety net is therefore a priority, albeit often obscured by the more simplistic goal of high economic growth. While this has less to do with foreign investment, it is in the country's best interest to avoid or mitigate any adverse distributional consequences of foreign investment activity. This notion, combined with the fact that equity

---

[30] Because of President Suharto's age, another presidential term for him is likely to be a binding natural limitation. Yet at this moment, the problem of succession is still not transparent.

issues have always been prominent in the country's development policy debate, motivated the analysis of the impact of foreign investment on intraregional and interregional distribution. Multiplier analysis and CGE model simulation have been used to provide the distributional assessments. In both cases, the impacts are traced through an interdependent system that links production, factor employment, and household incomes.

The results show that intraregional income distribution will not deteriorate with increased foreign investment, but the interregional distribution (including the rural–urban gap) will. They also indicate that export-oriented investment is not only more income generating but also more beneficial in terms of reducing intraregional disparities. To the extent that improving interregional distribution has become an important goal, such results were achievable only under a counterfactual scenario where foreign investments are more spread over regions outside Java, especially in the eastern part of Indonesia. Unfortunately, such a distribution would not be expected to occur spontaneously at this stage of the country's development.

Finally, it must be emphasized that the quantitative impacts generated from the simulation are not very large, suggesting that the eventual outcomes on relative incomes are due less to foreign investment than to other factors that might be influenced by economic and social policy.

REFERENCES

Azis, I. J. (1989), "Economic Development and Recent Adjustment in Resource-Rich Countries," in T. Fukuchi and M. Kagami, eds., *Perspectives on the Pacific Basin Economy: A Comparison of Asia and Latin America*, Tokyo: Asian Club Foundation and Institute of Developing Economies.

(1992), "Regional Balance and the National Development Strategy," in S. Sediono and K. Igusa, eds., *Regional Development and Industrialization of Indonesia*, Tokyo: Institute of Developing Economies.

(1994a), "Indonesia," in J. Williamson, ed., *The Political Economy of Policy Reform*, Washington, DC: Institute for International Economics.

(1994), "Notas sobre desarrollo regional y descentralizacion en Indonesia," *Planeacion and Desarrollo*, Vol. 25, Santafe de Bogota, D.C., Colombia: Departamento Nacional de Planeacion.

(1996a), "Exchange Rate, Capital Flows and Reform Sequencing in Indonesia: Policy Trend and CGE Model Application," paper presented at the Workshop on Macroeconomic Policies and Exchange Rate Management, USAID and International Center for Economic Growth, Washington DC, September.

(1996b), "CGE Modeling for Developing Countries," in S. Ichimura and F. G. Adams, *The East Asian Development Pattern Forecasts to the Year 2010*, Kitakyushu: International Center for the Study of East Asian Development.

(1997), "Impacts of Economic Reform on Rural–Urban Welfare: A General Equilibrium Framework," *Review of Urban and Regional Development Studies*, Vol. 10, No. 1 (January).

Callis, H. G. (1942), *Foreign Capital in Southeast Asia*, New York: Institute of Pacific Relations.

Creutzberg, P. (1975), *Changing Economy in Indonesia*, Vol. 1: *Indonesia's Export Crops 1860–1940*, The Hague: Martinus Nijhoff.

Defourny, J., and Thorbecke, E. (1984), "Structural Path Analysis and Multiplier Decomposition with a Social Accounting Matrix Framework," *The Economic Journal*, 94: 111–136.

FIAS (1994), *Indonesia: Enhancing the Foreign Direct Investment Environment in Indonesia to Sustain Future Growth*, Washington DC: International Finance Corporation and the World Bank.

Hill, H. (1988), *Foreign Investment and Industrialization in Indonesia*, Oxford-New York: Oxford University Press.

(1989), *Unity and Diversity: Regional Economic Development in Indonesia Since 1970*, Oxford: Oxford University Press.

John, A. H. (1969), "Aspects of English Economic Growth in the First Half of the Eighteenth Century," in W. E. Minchinton, ed., *The Growth of English Overseas Trade*, London: Methuen & Co.

Keuning, S. (1988), "An Estimate of the Fixed Capital Stock by Industry and Type of Capital Good in Indonesia," Working Paper Series No. 4, Statistical Analysis Capability Programme, April.

(1991), "Allocation and Composition of Fixed Capital Stock in Indonesia: An Indirect Estimate Using Incremental Capital Value Added Ratios," *Bulletin of Indonesian Economic Studies*, Vol. 27.

Khan, M. S., and Zahler, R., (1989), *Macroeconomic Effects of Changes in Barriers to Trade and Capital Flows: A Simulation Analysis*, Washington DC: IMF.

Kim, J. T., Knaap, G., and Azis, I. J., eds. (1992), *Spatial Development in Indonesia: Review and Prospects*, London: Avebury.

Lewis, J. (1991), "A Computable General Equilibrium Model of Indonesia," Development Discussion Paper No. 378, Boston: Harvard Institute for International Development, July.

Pangestu, M., and Azis, I. J., (1994), "Survey of Recent Development," *Bulletin of Indonesian Economic Studies*, Vol. 30, No. 2 (August).

Pyatt, G. (1988), "A SAM Approach to Modeling," *Journal of Policy Modeling*, 10: 327–352.

Shafik, N., and Chhibber, A. (1988), *Investment and Savings in Indonesia*, Washington DC: World Bank.

Thee, K. W. (1992), "The Investment Surge from the Asian Newly-Industrialising Countries into Indonesia," *Asian Economic Journal*, Vol. 6 (November).

Thorbecke, E., et al. (1992), *Adjustment and Equity in Indonesia*, Paris: OECD Development Centre.

Tomlinson, B. R. (1985), "Foreign Investment in India and Indonesia, 1920–1960," paper presented to Project on the Comparative Study of India and Indonesia, New Delhi, January.

Wertheim, W. (1956), *Indonesian Society in Transition*, The Hague: van Hoeve.

Woo, W. T., Glassburner, B., and Nasution, A., (1994), *Macroeconomic Policies, Crises, and Long Term Growth in Indonesia, 1965–1990*, Washington DC: World Bank.

Yuan, L. T. (1991), *Growth Triangle*, Singapore: Institute of Southeast Asian Studies and Institute of Policy Studies.

Comment

William E. James

Investment, non-oil exports, and economic growth have all accelerated impressively as Indonesia has moved toward a more open and market-oriented economy. Indonesia has been regarded as one of the more successful developing countries and has a particularly enviable record in poverty alleviation. In recent years, however, the issue of how a more open and liberal economic system affects the distribution of income and wealth, both among households and across regions, has become of increased concern. In this context, Professor Asiz has made a valuable contribution with the analysis in this chapter.

Within the space allowed, I focus my comments on the second and third sections of his chapter. I highly recommend the first section, however, for the excellent summary it provides of the history of foreign investment in Indonesia. Of particular interest are the historical patterns of FDI flows and his narrative of the vicissitudes of Indonesian policy toward foreign capital.

Foreign direct investment is a major focus of interest. In this context, I would join a number of other commentators in warning that data problems abound. FDI approvals data are notoriously inaccurate, and even realized FDI figures are usually presented as unadjusted values, in historical prices, and (in the case of BKPM and Bank Indonesia) include both domestic and foreign equity. And although IMF balance-of-payments data on FDI flows also suffer from shortcomings, they at least are reasonably consistent over time and across countries.

Professor Asiz notes that even after passage of the Foreign Investment Law of 1967, there were continuing "mixed signals" concerning Indonesia's position regarding foreign investment having the upper hand in policy circles. Policies toward foreign trade were simultaneously shifted away from the inward-looking import substitution regime to an outward-looking export promotion strategy. More liberal treatment of foreign investors was accompanied by adoption of a GATT-consistent duty drawback scheme and a shift from heavily protectionist quantitative restrictions to a more open tariff-based trading system. This helped encourage investors to move into export-oriented manufacturing activities, as is demonstrated by the increasing weight of export-oriented projects in the BKPM data on investment approvals. Further deregulation came in the form of adoption of a "Negative List" of sectors where FDI was restricted or closed in 1987. Moreover, the list had been pared from sixty-four sectors to only nineteen by May 1995.

Professor Asiz points out that a period of "deregulation fatigue" set in between 1992 and 1994, and there were even some "take backs" on previous reforms in the area of FDI. However, from the standpoint of trade policy, the period of fatigue was even longer, from 1991 to 1995. As numerous papers at a recent conference on Deregulation in Indonesia (hosted by the Association of Indonesian Economists and the World Bank) demonstrated, there was no reduction in the simple or import-weighted average tariff between 1991 and 1995. The increasing competitiveness within the region and globally, however, provided some motivation to overcome such reform fatigue, at least in the area of FDI.

A major difficulty facing foreign investors in Indonesia was divestiture regulations that force foreign owners to turn over controlling shares of equity to local interests within a relatively short time period. The deregulation package of June 1994 essentially eliminated the divestiture requirement and placed Indonesia among the most liberal countries in the region in terms of foreign investment regimes.

In addition to competition for FDI, there is also a perception of mounting competition by a host of new export-oriented economies like China, Sri Lanka, India, and the Philippines in the areas of natural resource–based and labor-intensive manufactures. These pressures, along with Indonesia's commitment to the Uruguay Round agreement, the ASEAN Free Trade Area (AFTA), and the APEC initiatives begun in Bogor, may also have helped to bring about the tariff reform of May 23, 1995. This deregulation package not only reduced a substantial number of tariffs; it also set a precedent by committing Indonesia to a time-bound schedule of tariff cuts that will result in all tariffs being 10 percent or less by the year 2003. Indeed, as Professor Azis notes, this reform will mean that the overwhelming majority of Indonesian tariffs will be either 0 or 5 percent by that year. Such a preannounced schedule of trade liberalization may not effect the amount of investment as much as its allocation among sectors.

In the third section of the chapter, Professor Azis presents results from two different analytical approaches in order to estimate the effect of that foreign investment on the regional and household distribution of income in Indonesia. He first applied a multiplier analysis that indicates that foreign investment worsens the regional distribution of GDP between Java (where it is already concentrated) and non-Java. The multiplier analysis also results in greater regional wage disparity. However, regional GDP and wages within a region may not be accurate guides for assessing the impact of foreign investment on income distribution between households in Java and elsewhere in Indonesia. The model does not take account, for example, of significant labor mobility and seasonal migration that occurs as laborers from outside Java take up employment in Java. The disparity implied by the location of production is greater than would be found in household budget and consumption surveys. Labor mobility allows households outside Java to take advantage of opportunities for employment, particularly in West Java. Investment that facilitates mobility of factors of production could complement foreign investment, reducing regional income disparities as measured by household income and consumption. The multiplier analysis also finds that foreign direct investment reduces inequality within a region's households, perhaps because investments are made in relatively labor-intensive activities.

A CGE model is used to derive a second set of results in a more rigorous framework of analysis. Space considerations don't permit detailed comments on the model used, but I would like to discuss a key equation of the model (1) on the specification of capital inflows.

$$FCAP = \sigma_0 + deg \cdot \sigma_1 \cdot \left(r - rf - RISK - \left(dEXR - 1 \right) \right) \quad (1)$$

Basically, foreign capital is modeled as a response to three major variables:

1. the difference between domestic and foreign interest rates,
2. a country risk premium, and
3. The expected change in the exchange rate.

It would be helpful to the reader if the proxies and data used in constructing the equations of the model were spelled out more explicitly. A constant term that represents autonomous investment is also included. The expected signs of the first two variables are clearly positive and negative, respectively. However, the expected sign of the exchange rate variable is ambiguous. Devaluation, while increasing the profitability of investment in tradeables (+), also raises the cost of imported capital equipment and intermediate inputs (−). Hence, the sign of the third variable could be either positive or negative, depending on the properties of the investment projects. In reality, a stable real exchange rate (where depreciation just offsets the difference between domestic and foreign inflation, or better yet, where the inflation gap is eliminated) would probably have a positive effect on foreign investment inflows, other things being equal.

Depreciation of the exchange rate to promote export competitiveness (exchange rate protectionism) has arguably been used in Indonesia. The effects of such a policy on the amount of foreign investment may be ambiguous, but the effect on the composition of foreign investment might be substantial. In particular, the growth of FDI in export-oriented production could partially be explained by such a policy. However, to the extent that exporters are dependent on imported inputs and equipment, such a policy may not be successful unless augmented by schemes to permit duty-free access to imported equipment and duty drawback on other imported materials. Some discussion of these points could compensate for omissions in the model itself.

Professor Azis undertakes four simulations and examines the impact of each on income distribution at the regional and household levels. Two simulations assume constant total foreign investment but reallocate the investment between agriculture and manufacturing. The other two involve an exercise of increasing foreign investment by 25 percent in manufacturing and then in agriculture (holding the other sectors' investment constant in each case). The results seem to be small in magnitude, though it is encouraging to see that investment in (export-oriented) manufacturing has a positive impact on household income distribution.

Overall, Professor Azis is to be congratulated for providing a stimulating and creative chapter that illustrates both the potential and limitations of the techniques applied in seeking answers to very significant and politically important issues regarding the impact of foreign capital on income distribution.

## PART V

Trade, Resources, and the Environment

CHAPTER 12

Economic Development
and the Environment in China

Wang Huijiong and Li Shantong

1. INTRODUCTION

China has achieved rapid economic growth since initiating economic reforms and opening to the outside world in the late 1970s, and it has emerged as an indispensable component of the "East Asian Miracle." It is worth emphasizing, however, that China has been committed to industrial growth and technology development since the 1950s. Industrialization has been a primary objective of development strategy since the establishment of the People's Republic of China (PRC), despite occasional debate about the best means to achieve this objective. Four decades of effort to industrialize the country have resulted in pervasive changes in economic structure. The shares of total value-added attributable to the primary, secondary, and tertiary sectors has shifted from 52, 22, and 26 percent in 1952 to 21, 48, and 31 percent in 1995.

This rapid industrialization has inevitably affected the environment. In the latest decades of a much longer period of industrialization, the international community has gained deeper understanding of linkages between economic development and the environment. Although China is a latecomer in this process, it can benefit from many precedents and experiences originating elsewhere.

There are many environmental issues in China, but the most prominent one today is the use of coal, the country's major energy resource. Burning this fuel with current technologies emits CO_2 – the greenhouse gas most important in quantity, thereby contributing to climate change – and SO_2, the primary constituent in acid rain. Because of the importance of global warming and acid rain

We thank David Roland-Holst and other conference participants for helpful suggestions.

405

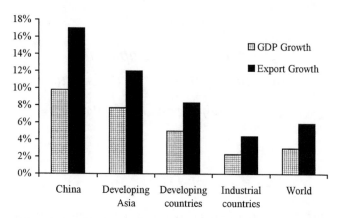

Figure 12.1. A decade of growth, 1985–94. (Source: International Monetary Fund, *World Economic Outlook*, October 1994.)

to China and the world, this chapter focuses on links between the economy and these two environmental issues, with emphasis on energy-related CO_2 and SO_2 emissions. Other environmental problems will be surveyed more generally.

In section 2 of this chapter, we provide and overview economic growth patterns and the structure of energy demand and supply in China. This provides a basis for discussion in section 3 of industrialization and its impact on the environment. Since these issues have arisen relatively recently in China, evidence is still limited, but section 3 still provides some general inferences about development–environment linkages. Section 4 surveys long-term and short-term policy options for the Chinese government in dealing with environmental problems and economic growth. Section 5 examines Chinese environmental issues from an international perspective, and section 6 closes with concluding remarks.

2. ECONOMIC GROWTH AND ENERGY CONSUMPTION

2.1. China's Economic Growth from an International Perspective

China has experienced remarkable economic growth in recent years, with the external sector acting as the primary engine of

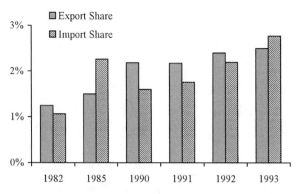

Figure 12.2. China's share in world trade. (Source: International Monetary Fund, *Direction of Trade Statistics*.)

growth and opening this vast country to the outside world. The growth rate of GDP averaged 9.3 percent during 1980–90 and 12.0 percent during 1990–95. These high economic growth rates are even more remarkable when compared to the relatively slow growth experienced by industrial economies during the same period. China has also become the leading growth economy in developing Asia, taking a place at the center of the celebrated "East Asian Miracle." It is also worth noting that the country's rapid economic growth has been accompanied by pervasive structural change. Total valued-added shares for primary, secondary, and tertiary sectors had shifted from 30, 49, and 21 percent in 1980 to 27, 42, and 31 percent in 1990, and to 21, 48, and 31 percent by 1995. Figures 12.1 and 12.2 compare economic growth rates and trade shares for China and the rest of the world.

2.2. Pattern of Economic Growth and Energy Consumption

2.2.1. Measurement of Economic Growth
To better understand links between economic growth and energy supply and demand patterns, a brief description on the features of the Chinese System of National Accounts (SNA) is warranted. Prior to its economic reforms, China used a framework of national accounts modeled on the Soviet system of the 1950s, but this system differs in significant ways from SNA. As one growth indi-

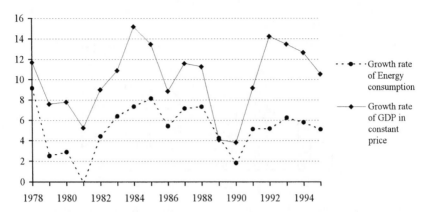

Figure 12.3. Growth rate of energy use and GDP.
(Source: *Statistical Yearbook of China*.)

cator in the Chinese statistical system since the 1950s, national income, measured from the production side, represents value-added to a country's material wealth by the five "material production sectors."[1] Deductions from gross output of each sector are made for depreciation and other intermediate inputs to arrive at value-added; the figures for each sector are then aggregated to obtain national income produced (or "Net Material Product," NMP). China's Bureau of Statistics has used two basic adjustments – depreciation and nonmaterial services not covered by the original framework – to arrive at the value of GDP. Official values of GDP are available since 1978, with the value of GDP generally 19–23 percent higher than national income.

2.2.2. GDP and Energy Consumption Growth

Energy is the lifeblood of an industrial economy, and in a rapidly industrializing country like China, national economic growth is closely related to the growth of energy consumption and production. Figure 12.3 plots the growth rates of energy consumption and GDP from 1978 to 1995, over which period their correlation coefficient is 0.6683.

[1] The sectors are agriculture, industry, construction, transport communications, and commerce.

Table 12.1. *Income and Energy Use in Different Planning Periods*

Year	National Income (billion yuan)	Energy Production (MTCE)	Energy Consumption (MTCE)	Energy Consumption/ National Income (MTCE/ billion yuan)
1952	58.9	51.92	54.11[a]	0.9187
1957	90.8	98.61	96.44	1.0621
1962	92.4	171.85	165.40	1.7900
1965	138.7	188.24	189.01	1.3627
1970	192.6	309.90	292.91	1.5208
1975	250.3	487.54	454.25	1.8148
1980	368.8	637.35	602.75	1.6344
1985	702.0	855.46	766.82	1.0923
1990	1442.9	1039.22	987.03	0.6841

[a] 1953 figure. Since an energy consumption figure for 1952 is not available in national statistics, the statistics of 1953 are used.
Source: *China's Energy Statistical Almanac 1991.*

2.3. Growth of the Economy and the Energy Sector

Although its per-capita energy use is low, China's aggregate economic growth is associated with relatively intensive energy consumption. The energy intensity of Chinese GDP was 2.43 KCE[2] per U.S. dollar in 1993, compared to an average of 0.38 for six developed countries of the Group of Seven industrialized countries. Table 12.1 provides national income and energy production and consumption for selected years. Energy consumption per unit of national income increased steadily from 0.92 in 1953, peaking at 1.81 in 1975 and falling to 0.68 in 1990. This transition is largely the result of structural change in the economy and resultant shifts in patterns of specialization and resource intensity, particularly with respect to energy consumption.

For several decades, China's strategy for industrialization was modeled on that of the former Soviet Union. This was charac-

[2] KCE, Kilogram of Standard Coal Equivalent, which is coal with 7,000 kilocalorics per kilogram of coal.

Table 12.2. *Change of Value and Structure of National Income*

Year	Growth Rate of Energy Production (%)	Growth Rate of Energy Consumption (%)	Growth Rate of National Income (%)	Elasticity of Energy Production	Elasticity of Energy Consumption
1953	6.59		14.00	0.47	
1957	19.64	9.59	4.50	4.37	2.13
1962	−19.03	−18.88	−6.50	2.93	2.90
1965	9.24	13.61	17.00	0.54	0.80
1970	34.13	28.86	23.30	1.46	1.24
1975	17.12	13.24	8.30	2.06	1.60
1980	−1.28	2.88	6.40		0.45
1985	9.88	8.15	13.50	0.73	0.60
1990	2.25	1.15	4.80	0.47	0.23

Source: China's Energy Statistical Almanac 1991.

terized mainly by an accelerated buildup of heavy industries and large-scale production with capital-intensive and modern technical processes. In both countries, this pattern of industrialization proved to be less successful in raising living standards than one that targeted light industries first and then moved to heavy industries as the newly industrialized economies (NIEs) have done. Nevertheless, this pattern of development established an extensive foundation of industry and technology in China. From the second five-year plan to the fifth five-year plan (1976–1980), development of heavy industries was the dominant priority, despite the fact that Chairman Mao once assigned the opposite priorities for sectoral development in industrialization (agriculture, light industry, and heavy industry). This is a major reason for high energy intensity of consumption in the Pre-Reform Era. This trend has moderated since the launch of economic reform in late 1978, as the ratio of light to heavy industries increased from 0.89 in 1980 to 0.97 in 1990.

It can also be seen from Tables 12.1 and 12.2 that before 1980 the growth rate of energy demand increased rapidly in comparison with the growth rate of the national economy. This is mainly due to the process of industrialization and the priority given to heavy industry before the 1980s. In 1953, the growth rate of national income (NI) is much higher than the growth rate of energy supply,

Table 12.3. *Average Annual Growth Rate of Energy Production and Consumption across Different Planning Periods*

	Average Annual Growth Rate during Different Planning Periods[a]						
	First 5– Second 5	Second 5– Adjustment	Adjustmt.– Third 5	Third 5– Fourth 5	Fourth 5– Fifth 5	Fifth 5– Sixth 5	Sixth 5– Seventh 5
Production (%)	25.5	–9.1	7.8	12.8	7.9	4.1	5.7
Consumption (%)	24.0	–8.4	8.5	12.5	7.1	3.9	6.4

[a] First 5 means the first five–year planning period, Second 5 the second five–year planning period, etc.
Source: Statistical Yearbook of China.

because China was predominantly an agrarian society before 1952. It can be seen that the elasticity of energy consumption was as low as 0.23 in 1990, due to structural change in the economy as well as improvements in efficiency of energy utilization.

3. PATTERNS OF GROWTH IN ENERGY SUPPLY AND DEMAND

3.1. Historical Energy Supply and Demand

Energy demand in China has in the past been met through domestic resources and production. Table 12.3 shows the average annual growth rate of energy production and consumption between different planning periods (i.e., comparing five-year intervals beginning about 1950). These trends will facilitate understanding of more detailed patterns of economic growth and energy consumption, discussed in the following subsection.

3.2. Structure of Energy Production and Consumption of Energy

The data in Figure 12.4 summarize the structure of consumption for different energy resources. These figures clearly reveal the dominant role that coal plays in consumption, although a declining trend in the share of coal since the 1960s is discernible. The latter effect is largely due to the discovery of petroleum in the

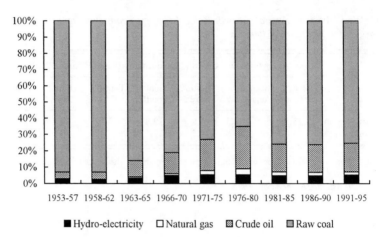

1953-57 1958-62 1963-65 1966-70 1971-75 1976-80 1981-85 1986-90 1991-95

■ Hydro-electricity   □ Natural gas   ▨ Crude oil   ▧ Raw coal

Figure 12.4. Structure of primary energy consumption. (Sources: *China's Energy Statistics Almanac 1991*; *Statistical Yearbook of China 1995*.)

Northeastern provinces (Hebei, Henan, Hubei) and a large gas field in Sichuan province. Hence, there were increasing shares of petroleum and natural gas in domestic energy production and consumption from the 1960s to the 1970s. The production of petroleum became sluggish in the 1980s, however, with a growth rate of only 3.5 percent from 1981 to 1990, and the share of coal in total energy production and consumption in China increased slightly during that period. Figure 12.4 also illustrates the low share of hydroelectricity energy of consumption in China, only 5.1 percent of consumption in 1990. Apparently, the country is seriously under-utilizing the rich potential of its water resources. The development of electric power in China is interesting in comparison with other countries such as Japan, Norway, Switzerland, France, the U.S.A., and Canada. Those countries generally give hydro-energy resources higher exploration priority then thermal plants. In China, however, most of the hydroelectric potential is located in relatively under-developed regions (especially the mountainous southwest), far from large cities and commercial centers. In addition, institutional and technical challenges to hydroelectric capacity development are formidable.

It can be seen from Figure 12.4 that a conspicuous feature of Chinese energy consumption is the high share of coal in total

Table 12.4. *Energy Source Shares of Country Energy Production, 1989 (percent)*

Country	Coal	Oil	Natural Gas	Hydro-electricity	Nuclear Electricity	Total
			Comparison of Energy Sources			
China	74	19	2	5	0	100
India	60	23	6	11	1	100
Japan	8	1	2	26	63	100
USA	33	27	27	5	10	100
USSR	19	36	39	4	3	100
Rest of World	. . .	. . .	. . .	. . .	. . .	. . .
World Total	27	38	21	7	6	100

Source: Lawrence Berkeley Laboratory (1992), *China Energy Databook*, Berkeley: University of California, Berkeley.

energy use – over 90 percent during the first two five-year periods; it remains around 73 percent by 1986–90. This is extremely high compared to other countries. Even in India, where coal is also a major energy source, it accounted for only 60 percent of total primary energy use in 1980. The unique features of energy source shares are apparent in Table 12.4, which gives international comparisons of energy source shares around the 1990s. Although this table cannot provide completely up-to-date information because China has commissioned nuclear power plants in the decade of the 1990s, it does capture the general picture.

4. INDUSTRIALIZATION AND THE ENVIRONMENT

4.1. *Energy Consumption and Environmental Pollution*

The development of modern society is characterized by the close relationship between economic growth and energy consumption, and of course there are also certain linkages between energy consumption and environmental pollution. Figure 12.5 depicts Chinese energy consumption and (pretreatment) atmospheric and water pollution. The correlation coefficients between energy consumption and (pretreatment) atmospheric and water pollution are

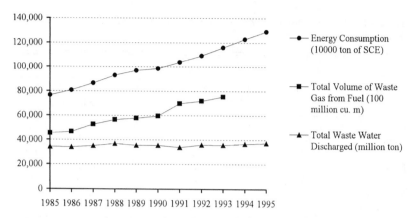

Figure 12.5. Energy consumption and pollution of atmosphere and water.
(Source: *Statistical Yearbook of China*.)

0.97 and 0.41, respectively, indicating a close relationship between pollution and energy consumption.

4.2. Chinese Environment Protection and Trends in Environment Quality

4.2.1. Environment Protection in China: A Retrospective

China focused its attention on industrialization in the early 1950s, but because of its relative isolation, the history of environmental protection is only about two decades old. Chinese environmental protection was initiated only in the early 1970s (whereas the Clean Air Act was established in 1956 in some developed countries), "Limits to Growth" was published in 1972, and the Stockholm Declaration was negotiated in 1972. China participated in the Stockholm Conference and soon afterward (1973) launched its first national conference on environmental protection. The period 1973–83 was the real inception of environmental protection in China. In the first national conference on this subject, China for the first time began to recognize its environmental problems, which were already relatively serious. After this conference, a temporary environmental protection policy group and office were set up. A limited amount of work on environmental protection was done, and an environmental administration team was trained at this time.

The period 1983–89 marked an important transition in Chinese environmental management. The country began to realize that it could not simply relive the "pollute first, clean up afterward" cycle adopted by the developed countries during their early industrialization. In the second national conference, the leadership of party and government affirmed that "Environmental protection is one of the basic national policies." Since then, Chinese environmental management has been strengthened, and the legal basis and regulations for environmental protection have been gradually established. Finally, a new period of environmental protection has transpired from 1989 to the present. Targeted policies of environmental protection have been implemented since 1994, when they were legitimated in an official document, "China: Agenda Towards the 21st Century," approved by the State Council of PRC.

4.2.2. Trends in Environmental Quality
There have been significant steps to improve Chinese environmental quality in recent years, and these come from several sources. The scope of the present exposition allows for only an overview of this subject. A more in-depth examination of these issues is currently being undertaken in China by several departments, including the Development Research Center at the State Council.

Examination of data in Table 12.5 reveals that China's energy consumption per unit of GDP decreased during the 1978–93 period. The resulting gain in energy efficiency over the fifteen-year period is 48.3 percent. This improvement is likely to have resulted from changing economic structure and more efficient energy utilization, but it is difficult to separate these two factors.

There have been noticeable improvements in environmental protection measures in the past decade.[3] For example, in 1986, 57 percent of all fuel gas was treated, and 50.7 percent of treated industrial wastewater met water quality standards. By 1993, these two figures had increased to 68.8 percent and 75.4 percent, respectively. They reflect both more extensive monitoring and

---

[3] At the national level, the National Bureau of Environmental Protection of China publishes an official report every year giving assessments of environmental quality. The government also published "Technical Guidelines on Environmental Impact Assessment" (HJ/T2-93) in 1993, which consists of three parts: general, atmospheric environment, and underground water environment.

Table 12.5. *Energy Consumption per 10,000 Yuan of GDP*

Year	Energy Consumption (10,000 ton of SCE)	GDP in billions of 1978 Yuan	Energy Consump. per 10,000 Yuan of GDP
1978	57,144	362.4	15.8
1979	58,588	390.0	15.0
1980	60,275	420.4	14.3
1981	59,447	442.5	13.4
1982	62,067	482.4	12.9
1983	66,040	534.9	12.3
1984	70,904	616.1	11.5
1985	76,685	699.1	11.0
1986	80,850	761.1	10.6
1987	86,632	849.1	10.2
1988	92,997	944.8	9.8
1989	96,934	983.2	9.9
1990	98,703	1,020.9	9.7
1991	103,783	1,114.8	9.3
1992	109,170	1,273.5	8.6
1993	115,993	1,445.3	8.0
1994	122,737	1,628.3	7.5
1995	129,000	1,800.1	7.2

Source: *Statistical Yearbook of China 1996*.

greater levels of average conformity with environmental quality standards.

Two atmospheric pollutants, SO_2 and particulates, are of special concern to Chinese environmental experts and are coming under intensified official scrutiny. Although more favorable aggregate trends in environmental quality have now been established, several special categories remain relatively hazardous. We discuss them in more detail in the following sections.

4.3. Statistics on Atmospheric Pollution

Complete statistics and data on atmospheric pollution are not available before 1986. The following paragraphs summarize the available statistics on essential components of atmospheric pollution. It should be emphasized that the pollution statistics may be biased on the lower side, because official monitoring and statistics are confined to state-owned enterprises. Township and village

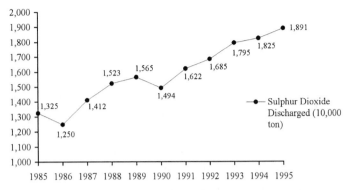

Figure 12.6. Discharge of SO$_2$, 1985–95.
(Source: *Statistical Yearbook of China*, 1986–96 issues.)

enterprises contribute about 30 percent to total value-added in industry, yet their pollution from them is not included in the national accounts for pollution. It is estimated that a factor of 1.3–1.4 should be applied to correct the following data for atmospheric and water pollution.

4.3.1. Statistics for SO$_2$

Discharge of SO$_2$ is mainly due to combustion of fossil fuels, especially soft coal. Therefore, those sectors that have a higher share in coal consumption are also the sectors with higher share of SO$_2$ discharge. Figure 12.9 shows that the electricity sector, nonmetallic mineral processing, chemical engineering, and metallurgy each represent more than 10 percent of all SO$_2$ discharges, while the electricity sector has a share as high as 46.1 percent.

4.3.2. Statistics for Particulates

The data on industrial soot refer to the soot discharged into the atmosphere after the process of gas treatment. This includes the suspended particulate matter (SPM) produced in combustion processes and in various industrial processes. Several sectors contribute the majority share; for example, in 1991, the electricity sector, the chemical sector, and the nonmetallic mineral processing sector contributed 29.6 percent, 6.1 percent, and 32 percent shares of the total discharge, respectively. The electricity sector had

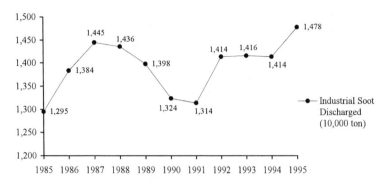

Figure 12.7. Discharge of industrial soot, 1985–95. (Source: *Statistical Yearbook of China*.)

a high share of soot produced in combustion, and the nonmetallic mineral processing sector (mainly cement) had a high share of soot produced in a manufacturing process.

It is also interesting to note the shape of the graph (the clip from 1988–90 is a result of the economic austerity program in this period) and also improvements due to environmental protection measures. Industrial soot in 1995 is 102.3 percent that of 1987, the previous peak.

4.3.3. Statistics for CO_2

CO_2 is the most important greenhouse gas (GHG), representing about 55 percent of all GHG emissions and 75 percent of energy-related GHG emissions. It is widely believed that the rising atmospheric concentration of GHG could result in a change in the global as well as regional climate, entailing severely detrimental economic and ecological effects. China has not estimated its CO_2 emissions in the past, although early estimates of climate change due to CO_2 concentration had been done in developed countries. Several international organizations and groups of scholars such as the OECD, the International Panel on Climate Change (IPCC), the International Institute for Applied Systems Analysis (IIASA), and the World Bank have estimated CO_2 emissions in China and other countries/regions. At the moment, a Chinese research institution is carrying out research to estimate a proper coefficient to be applied to the combustion of coal, petroleum, and natural gas to derive induced CO_2 emissions. One value of CO_2 emissions, calculated by the Energy Research Institute of China, is 564 million tons of carbon equivalents based upon statistics for consumption of fossil fuels; another figure, from IPCC, is 630 million tons. There are many studies that project CO_2 emissions by region to the year 2050. For example, OECD (1995) and Coppel and Lee (1996) estimate that China's CO_2 emissions will increase by 2.5 percent per year, from 600 million tons of carbon in 1990 to 3.1 billion tons in 2050, in the baseline scenario of the OECD's GREEN model. Therefore, the serious challenge of growth of CO_2 must be recognized if proper policies are to be adopted. Still, greenhouse gases are a relatively new field of research. In addition to CO_2, greenhouse gases include methane (CH_4), nitrous oxide (N_2O), and chlorofluorocarbons (CFCs), but according to recent information from IPCC, fully fluorinated compounds (FFCs) remain in the atmosphere longer and trap more heat per molecule emitted than almost any other gas. It has been suggested by the World Resources Institute (WRI) that "the international community should not allow FFC emissions or new uses to grow unchecked." The effects of those greenhouse gases will be examined in a separate study.

4.3.4. Acid Rain–pH Concentration

Although a large number of monitoring stations for acid rain have been established, detailed official information and academic research for China are still unavailable in this important area. The formation of acid rain is a very complicated process, requiring a lot of coordinated studies on climate, soil characteristics, and pollutants. Much work of this kind is already extant for Western countries, but it will require years of determined effort for China to catch up. For example, a research team organized by the World Resources Institute and the Energy and Resource Group at the University of California at Berkeley worked for more than eighteen months on research for "The American West's Acid Rain Test." In the Netherlands, the study of emission reduction objectives for acidifying substances included NH_3, NO_2, SO_2, and volatile organic compounds (VOC). By contrast, at present one can find only an index of SO_2 in China's official statistics. This succinctly but persuasively clarifies the difficulty in explaining the causes of acid rain in China. In any event, SO_2 is the main contributor to acid rain. Cities with more than 1.5 percent share of national total SO_2

discharged are listed in Appendix Table A12.2. Appendix figure A12.1 provides a map of China with cities with high frequency of acid rain.

It is claimed in the National Report on Environment in 1993 that acid rain is restricted in certain local areas where, based upon statistics for seventy-three cities, the range of annual average pH value of precipitation is 3.94–7.63. In this group, 49.3 percent of the cities had an annual average pH below 5.6. The frequency of acid rain in Ganzhou, Changsha, Nanchong, Yibin, Huaihua, Chongqing, Wuzhou, Nanchang, Luzhou, Hangzhou, Hengyan, and Guiling was higher than 70 percent. "An Outline on Comprehensive Prevention and Abatement of Acid Rain" was drafted by China's National Bureau of Environmental Protection in 1993, and research and policy development in this area is very active.

4.4. Statistics for Water Pollution

Organic compounds dominate China's water pollution. Heavy metal pollutants had once been under better control in the seventh five-year planning period, but the situation has worsened in recent years. Pollution of the water system is described separately later.

4.4.1. Rivers

China has seven major river systems, and nearly one-half of them are polluted. The quality of 86 percent of the urban river section is below official standards. For example, an evaluation of a 200-km section of the Huai River revealed that 78.8 percent of this stretch of river is below standard for drinking water, 79.7 percent of the river section is not adapted to the standard of water for fisheries, and 32 percent of the river section is not adapted to irrigation use. Many regions of the Huai River have rates of cancer incidence more than twenty to thirty times the normal rate of incidence. Based upon incomplete statistics of twenty-nine rivers in fifteen provinces and municipalities, there are around 2,800 km of river where fish populations are negligible.

4.4.2. Lakes

The lakes of China are generally polluted, especially with heavy metal contaminants that are among the most serious waterborne

Table 12.6. *State of Pollution of City Rivers Monitored by the State*

Pollutant	Statistics of number Monitored City	Statistics of number Monitored River	No. of rivers with sampling exceeding the standard	No. of river sector with rate of exceeding standard>50%	No. of river section with annual average value exceeding the standard
pH	98	131	47	4	4
Suspension solids	95	126	89	35	49
Total hardness	93	126	39	23	25
Dissolved oxygen	96	129	79	37	31
Index of manganic acid salt	97	129	90	59	64
BOD	97	130	83	51	59
Ammonia nitrogen	98	131	78	44	42
Nitrite	98	131	70	15	24
Nitrate	96	128	0	0	0
Volatile phenol	96	128	77	32	46
Total cyanide	96	128	9	1	1
Total arsenic	96	128	21	101	3
Total mercury	89	119	49	24	29
Chrome 6 valence	97	130	13	0	0
Total lead	92	124	28	7	8
Total cadmium	91	123	29	8	9
Petroleum	83	108	94	73	84

Source: China Environmental Yearbook 1995.

pollutants. Dian Lake, for example, is the largest source of drinking water for Kunming municipality (over 2 million people) in Yunnan province. It provides 54 percent of the total water supply to this city, but due to the discharge of industrial waste water and sewage by households surrounding the lake, it is seriously polluted by heavy metals and remains well below the minimum official standard for drinking water.

The state of pollution in urban rivers monitored by the state is summarized in Table 12.6, which shows that the number of rivers with toxic metals exceeding standards is quite high. Generally, rivers in the northern part of China have more excessive annual values exceeding the standard than do rivers in southern China. This may be due to the fact that rivers in the southern part of China, coming mainly off the Himalayan plateau, have larger annual flows than those of northern China.

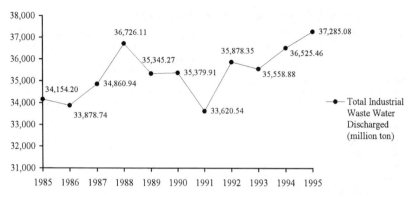

Figure 12.8. Discharge of industrial waste water, 1985–95. (Source: *Statistical Yearbook of China*, 1986–96 issues.)

4.4.3. Water Quality

One leading environmental issue for China is the quality of its water resources. Total annual average surface water in China is around 2,638 billion m^3, ranking sixth in the world. But per-capita water resources measure $2,500\,m^3$, less than one-fourth of the average per-capita water resources for the world. Moreover, water resources per-hectare land of water resource measure only $87.9\,m^3$, which is about one-half the world average. Therefore, China is classified as one of thirteen countries experiencing water shortage. The spatial distribution of the water resources is also quite uneven, rich in the southwest and poorer in the northwest. This shortage of water must inevitably affect production in industry and agriculture, as well as public health generally.

Figure 12.8 shows the trend in discharges of industrial waste water from 1985–1995. It can be seen from Table 12.7 that the sectors with the highest share of total waste water discharge are chemical engineering (30.5 percent), metallurgy and processing (16.0 percent), paper making (9.7 percent), electricity (9.7 percent), and agro-food (8.7 percent). The shape of the graph after 1988 captures effects of the austerity program on economy, as well as improvements in waste-water discharge due to more rigorous enforcement of environmental standards. This explains the lower value of discharge of waste water in 1993 than in 1988, although GDP in 1993 is 1.51 times that of 1988.

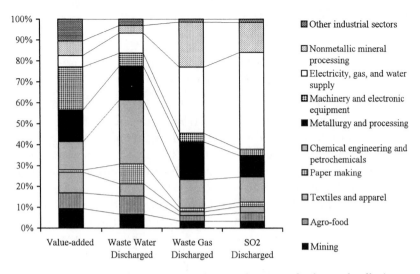

Figure 12.9. Structure comparison of sectoral output of value and pollution.
(Source: *Statistical Yearbook of China 1994.*)

Table 12.7. *Comparison of Sectoral Output of Value and Pollution*

Industrial Sector	Value-added (Share of Industrial Output)		Waste Water discharged (Share of total W.W.)		Waster Gas Discharged (Share of total W.G.)		SO₂ Discharged (Share of total SO₂)	
	100 million yuan	%	10,000 ton	%	100 million cum.	%	ton	%
Mining	1,202.85	9.4	148,675	6.7	3,518	3.4	463,653	3.4
Agro-food	960.7	7.5	192,716	8.7	2,832	2.8	561,452	4.1
Textile and apparel	1,276.09	9.9	129,410	5.8	1,800	1.8	401,307	3.0
Paper making	151.06	1.2	215,810	9.7	1,731	1.7	280,770	2.1
Chemical engineering and petrochemicals	1,738.19	13.5	676,528	30.5	13,912	13.6	1,610,667	11.9
Metallurgy and processing	1,944.33	15.1	355,736	16.0	18,574	18.1	1,410,585	10.4
Machinery and electronic equip.	2,632.46	20.5	136,747	6.2	4,220	4.1	410,779	3.0
Electricity, gas, and water supply	691.11	5.4	265,675	9.7	32,264	31.5	6,283,378	46.1
Nonmetallic mineral processing	897.82	7.0	82,807	3.7	22,107	21.5	1,941,594	14.4
Other industrial sectors	1,348	10.5	69,099	3.0	1,570	1.5	197,400	1.6
Total	12,842.6	100	2,273,203	100	102,528	100	13,561,585	100

Source: Statistical Yearbook of China 1994.

4.5. Effect of Industrial Structure on the Environment:
An Initial Exploration

Different sectors of economic activity have different impacts on the environment. For example, the electricity, gas, and water sector has a lower share in value-added of total industrial output but very high shares of total discharge for waste gas and SO_2. Likewise, industrial activities are generally more pollution-intensive (even with modern technologies) than services, a fact that highlights one of the central environmental dilemmas facing developing countries. As they make the transition from agrarian to industrial society, they pass through a structural bottleneck that concentrates their output, employment, and value-added into activities that are more pollution-intensive at any level of technological advancement. This can foster an impression of environmental irresponsibility, even though the pollution intensity of their GDP is inevitably higher than more advanced countries because of differing economic structure. Indeed, the worlds' most modern societies are no longer really industrial economies. Obtaining up to 75 percent of their GDP from tertiary activities, they have relegated industry to the marginal status that agriculture attained there after World War II.

For the Chinese case, a detailed sectoral analysis is given in the appendix. Figure 12.9 and Table 12.7 also provide a comprehensive picture.

5. GOVERNMENT POLICIES
FOR ENVIRONMENTAL PROTECTION

Government environment policies at the national level are best discussed from two perspectives: (1) long-term policies, and (2) short- and medium-term policies.

5.1. Long-term Environmental Policy at the National Level –
"China: Agenda towards 21st Century"

Following the Earth Summit in Rio de Janeiro in 1992, the Environmental Protection Committee of the State Council prepared a White Cover Report entitled "China: Agenda towards 21st Century." This policy document dealt with population, the environment, and development. The project was led by the State

Box 12.1. *Abstracts from Chapter 13 of "China: Agenda towards 21st Century"*

Sustainable Energy Production and Consumption

Introduction

13.1 – 13.4 ...

13.5   Four programs are set up in this chapter:
    A. Comprehensive energy planning and management;
    B. Improvement of energy efficiency and energy saving;
    C. To push forward pollutantless coal-mining technology and clean coal technology;
    D. Development and utilization of new energy and renewable energy resources.

Program

A. Comprehensive Energy Planning and Management

Basis for Action
13.6 – 13.8 ...

13.9.   Before the end of this century, the strategy and public policy for the development of China's energy and environment are to place emphasis both on development and saving, as well as to improve the composition of energy and its location. The development of the energy sector should be based upon coal, be centered around electricity, and strive to develop hydroelectric power fully, petroleum and natural gas actively, nuclear energy properly, and new and renewable energy sources appropriately, based upon local conditions. To reduce environmental pollution, energy needs to be utilized more efficiently through scientific and technological progress.

Target
13.10 – 13.12 ...

Action
13.13 – 13.20 Essential action in these articles is to increase the share of electricity in the energy sector, develop nuclear energy both through domestic effort and joint ventures, extend rural electrification, and promote energy-saving cookers, biogas, and new and renewable energy resources.

Box 12.1 *(continued)*

13.23 (International cooperation) Proceed with extensive international cooperation and exchange; learn the experience of international advanced comprehensive planning, management measures, and policy instruments adapted to Chinese concrete conditions; import and transfer advanced technology and process from abroad through various channels to upgrade the domestic technological level of energy production and utilization; obtain access to international grant and financial resources through bilateral and multilateral means to strengthen the construction of Chinese energy industry; promote academic exchange and training of personnel.

B. Improvement of Energy Efficiency and Energy Saving

Basis of Action 13.24–13.27

Target   13.28–13.29

Action   13.30–13.37

C. To Push Forward Pollutantless Coal Mining Technology and Clean Coal Technology

Basis of Action
13.41 ... To develop pollutantless coal mining technology and clean coal technology; to control the discharge of greenhouse gases such as CH_4 and CO_2 ...

Target 13.42

Action
13.43–13.51 The efficiency of utilization of conversion of energy, to lower the production cost, increase the share of new energy resource in energy supply structure.

13.56 The hydropower capacity should reach more than 80,000 M.W. before the year 2000; utilization of solar energy should reach 2–3 million TCE, energy from wind power should reach 200 M.W., capacity of utilization of geothermal power should reach more than 800,000 TCE to raise the efficiency of utilization of biomass; the method of utilization will be transformed gradually mainly to biogas production and clean liquid.

Planning Commission (SPC) and the State Science and Technology Commission (SSTC), with the participation of fifty-two line ministries and 300 experts. The final draft was completed and approved by the State Council on May 25, 1994. It is claimed to represent a national policy for sustainable development over a long term.

Sustainable development is an integrated approach of basic policy measures and instruments of social, economic, and ecological systems. The concept and approach of this document are illustrated in Box 12.1, with targets and action on "Sustainable Energy Production and Consumption." A more detailed discussion of policy response to environmental issues related to this document is provided in subsequent sections.

5.2. Short- and Medium-term Policy Responses

Four areas of medium- and short-term energy policy response to environmental issues are worthy of special emphasis.

5.2.1. Price Distortions in the Energy Sector

There are significant and extensive price distortions in various types of energy, but reform of the price system is beginning to reduce these disparities. The government has tried to correct price distortions with a gradual approach, and we can only summarize its main features here.

China's reliance on coal as a major source of energy and its effects on the environment were clearly recognized in the National Report:

> As coal will continue to be China's primary source of energy for a considerable period of time, in the absence of major breakthroughs in combustion technology and in coal conversion, atmospheric pollution and acid rains are likely to worsen.

The government's policy on price reform generally is to liberalize prices gradually. Table 12.8 summarizes the historical record of energy sector price reform.

This gradual approach seeks to achieve convergence between the market price and planned price. Now that the government has liberalized the coal price and adjusted crude oil prices in the direction of international market prices, more than 10 percent of crude

Table 12.8. *Plan and Market Prices for Selected Energy Sectors, 1985-91 (yuan per ton)*

	1985		1988		1991	
	Coal	Crude oil	Coal	Crude oil	Coal	Crude oil
Planned price (a)	26.4	100	61		83	204
Nonplan price (b)	77.4	545	148		141	580
(b)−(a)	51.0	445	87		58	376
(b)/(a)	2.93	5.45	2.43		1.70	2.84

Sources: Tian Yuan and Qiao Gang (1991), *China's Price Research*; *China Price 1992* (February).

oil is traded below the planned price. In the case of electricity, too many planned prices are currently being implemented without a coherent, unifying rule. A new power plant, built through joint venture or with imported equipment, might be allowed to sell its electricity at a higher price to cover actual production cost, while the existing power plants have to sell their electricity at a lower, planned price. Much remains to be done to achieve significant price reform in the energy sector.

5.2.2. Development of New Coal Technologies and Nonfossil Fuel Energy

These issues have been emphasized in the long-term strategy section of the "Agenda towards 21st Century" document (see 13.9 of Box 12.1). These are high priorities, targeted by the SSTC for research on clean coal technology in particular. Emphasis in this area is hardly surprising, given the country's vast endowments of coal and the adverse environmental consequences of exploiting it with existing technologies. Among the many technical areas addressed in this study are technologies of ash and sulfur removal, preparation of coal slurry, fluidized bed combustion technology, coal gasification, and combined cycle generation technology. Coal-based, fuel-cell, and MHD-generation technology will also be studied and developed over the long term.

The Ministry of Electricity is also committed to increase significantly the shares of hydropower among China's energy sources. There are some practical engineering problems, but exceptionally rich hydropower energy resources are located in the southwest (e.g., Yunnan province and Tibet). They are far from the load center, however, and the key issue will be balancing high transmission costs against the environmental costs of local generation with imported fossil fuels.

5.2.3. Improvement in Energy Efficiency

China is a country with very high energy intensity – 1.69 tons of coal equivalent per 1,000 US$ GDP in 1990 against a world average of only 0.43. A recent study shows that if PPP is used to measure GDP, China's energy may be around two times the world average.[4] In any case, there is great potential for improvement in Chinese energy efficiency, and this will translate into improved environmental quality. It is recognized in 13.9 of Box 12.1 that "to reduce environmental pollution, energy needs to be utilized more efficiently through scientific and technological progress." It is also a guiding priority of energy development strategy to the year 2000 that emphasis should be placed on both energy resource development and energy conservation. The SSTC has identified several areas of energy-saving technology in the guidelines for Science and Technology development from 1990–2020. These include the following:

- utilization of waste heat and heat pumps
- energy-saving techniques for industrial boilers
- energy-saving technology for auxiliary equipment in power plants, such as fans and pumps
- energy-saving techniques in petroleum and petrochemical enterprises
- energy saving for household electrical appliances
- co-generation of heat and electricity
- improvement of various types of manufacturing processes and establishment of an energy-management information system

All these approaches are relevant to the future of Chinese energy policy and practices.

---

[4] These PPP calculations are from independent sources and are not officially recognized by China.

5.2.4. International Cooperation
In a modern society and in the context of economic globalization, mankind increasingly shares its common biosphere. Developed countries are leading in the effort at pollution abatement because of their accumulated knowledge, wealth, economic structure, and institutional coherence. The United Nation's Framework Convention on Climate Change (FCCC) recognizes the potential gains from international cooperation and endorses principles that share the benefits and encourage universal implementation of GHG abatement policies. OECD (1995) and Coppel and Lee (1996) suggest that "joint implementation" (i.e., the implementation of policies and measures jointly by developed and developing countries to curtail GHG emissions) could improve welfare in both regions while meeting the CO_2 abatement targets. Therefore, active policies to promote international cooperation are very important for the protection of the environment. China is fully aware of this, as can be seen in item 13.23 of Box 12.1, where international cooperation is emphasized.

5.3. Environmental Institutions, Monitoring,
Management Policies, and Major Issues

5.3.1. Environmental Administration
Since 1973, the State Council had established an environmental administration directly under its control; later on, a separate line ministry was established as the Ministry of Urban and Rural Construction and Environmental Protection; and finally a National Bureau of Environmental Protection was established. Corresponding organizations exist at the provincial and municipality levels. There are fifteen official responsibilities of the organizations of environmental protection:

1. Organize and prepare programs and plans for environmental protection;
2. Organize and prepare guidelines and policies of environmental protection;
3. Draft laws and regulations of environmental protection;
4. Set up environmental standards;
5. Supervise environmental protection work of various departments and regions;

6. Approve, supervise, and monitor the implementation of "Three Simultaneities";[5]
7. Promote more advanced management and treatment technology;
8. Environmental supervision, survey, and evaluation;
9. Plan Nature Preservation Zones;
10. Organize management of the marine environment;
11. Supervise and manage poisonous chemical materials;
12. Organize and develop research in environmental science;
13. Organize and develop environmental education;
14. Organize the activities of environmental propaganda;
15. Guide and coordinate environmental protection activities in various line ministries, various regions, and various units.

5.3.2. Monitoring and Supervision System

Monitoring and supervision systems were established at the national, provincial, municipal, and country levels, even at the village and township levels in favorable circumstances; environmental monitoring stations were also established. Currently, there are around 2,200 environmental monitoring stations with a total staff of around thirty-five thousand. Various resource administrative ministries, such as agriculture and forestry, and various industrial health and military departments have also established sectoral environmental monitoring and supervision institutions. Based upon the "Law of Environmental Protection of the PRC," the National Bureau of Environmental Protection has established the National Environmental Monitoring Network in concert with various line ministries of the State Council. The National Environmental Monitoring Network is shown schematically in Figure 12.10.

5.3.3. Guidelines and Policies of Environmental Management

The six principal official guidelines for environmental management are:

1. The major guideline for environmental protection is set up in Article 4 of the "Law of Environmental Protection of the PRC."

---

[5] The Chinese term "Three Simultaneities" means that whenever there is any kind of new project, environmental protection should be simultaneously implemented with (1) the design, (2) construction, and (3) operation of the project.

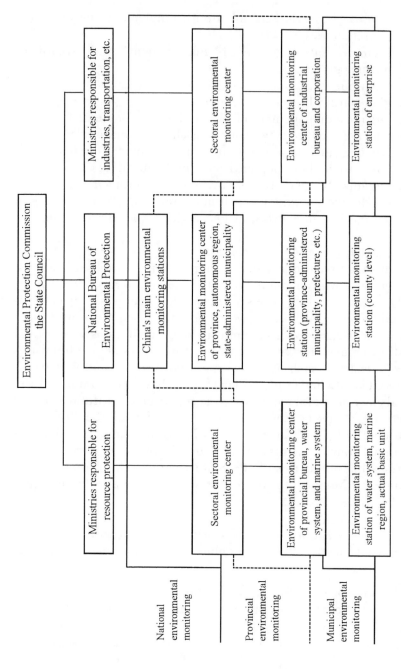

Figure 12.10. National environmental monitoring network.

It is stated in eight sentences each with four words (environmental protection with Chinese characteristics):

- overall planning
- reasonable location
- comprehensive utilization
- transform detrimental into useful
- rely upon the masses
- everybody takes action
- to protect the environment
- to benefit the people

2. Environmental policy for industrial location (includes relevant
   urban environmental policies).
3. Energy-related environmental policy (includes relevant urban
   and rural environmental policy, industrial and transportation
   energy policy).
4. Water-related environmental policy, particularly in the context
   of regional water distribution.
5. Natural environment protection policy.
6. Promote techno-economic policy congenial to environmental
   protection (which includes encouragement of comprehensive
   utilization, control of industrial pollution through technological
   rehabilitation of enterprises, pollutant discharge fees for
   discharge in excess of standards, promote the polluter pays
   principle).

5.3.4. Major Issues

Although the state has exercised considerable effort to catch up by
establishment of institutions, environmental problems in China
remain serious, as is evident from the data on air and water pollution. The major issues in this area are:

1. Environmental protection has not become an integrated
   part of the national economic and social development plan.
   For example, in the investment planning for fixed assets,
   there is no separate item for the investment of environmental
   protection.
2. Insufficient financial inputs for environmental protection; generally, the financial input for environmental protection represents less than 1 percent of GDP; there is no treatment of
   SO_2 discharges; a fair part of urban sewage from households,

and industrial waste and rubbish, are often discharged without treatment.

3. Environmental laws and regulations have not been implemented seriously.
4. Environmental institutions lack enough authority or personnel to implement their functions properly.
5. Backwardness in science and technology would hinder any serious attempt to improve the environmental quality.
6. Greater public awareness is needed of environmental issues at all levels.

5.4. The Environmental Issue of the Agricultural Sector

The agricultural sector has an essential position in the Chinese economy because it accounts for 20.9 percent of GDP and 52.9 percent of the economically active population (1995). In 1993, the cultivated land of China was 9.8 percent of the surface area of the whole country, and the country has one of the world's lowest ratios of arable land per capita. Therefore, appropriate use of land resources, as well as more informed environmental policy toward the agricultural sector, should be high priorities in China. Several specific aspects of this are now summarized.

5.4.1. The Preservation of Arable Land Resources
Rapid rural industrialization in China (i.e., development of town and village enterprises, or TVEs) has made important contributions to economic growth and rural prosperity of the Chinese population generally, but it has also had a negative effect by competing for limited land resources. This fact has come to the attention of the state, and the central government has put priority emphasis on development of the agricultural sector. Hence, strict records are now kept, and supervision is maintained on sublets of state-owned land and transfers between regions.

5.4.2. Detrimental Effects of Pesticide and Chemical Fertilizer Use
It is estimated that the area of annual pesticide utilization in China is 15 billion "hectare times" (i.e., the same hectare may be sprayed more than once and is counted each time), and the annual fertilizer use is around 29.3 million tons. The effective rate of utiliza-

tion is only 30 percent, however, which is around one-half of the advanced agricultural area abroad. The other 70 percent is either volatized into the atmosphere or flows through the soil, lakes, or rivers, leading to the major cause of the excessive nitrate content in drinking water.

5.4.3. Environmental Impact of Town and Village Enterprise Development
The development of TVEs in China has its positive contribution to the national economy and the living standard of the rural household, but its negative impact on the environment is also serious. This situation is exacerbated by the low technological level of production processes in TVEs and insufficient local monitoring capacity by environmental protection institutions. For example, TVEs will consume three tons of coal for one ton of coke, and SO_2 discharged by TVEs is around 15.1 percent of total discharge in 1990, under incomplete monitoring conditions. It is projected that the industrial waste water discharged by TVEs may reach 6.15 billion tons by the year 2000, with an average annual growth rate of 6.6 percent during 1990–2000. COP discharges may reach 1.84 million tons, with an average annual growth rate of 2.3 percent during 1990–2000. All these issues must receive enough attention to better secure sustainable economic growth. Recently, the state has taken decisive action to close down some TVEs with serious pollution problems.

6. CHINESE ECONOMIC GROWTH AND ENVIRONMENT FROM AN INTERNATIONAL PERSPECTIVE

6.1. International Comparison of Economic Activity and Environmental Loading

China has enjoyed very rapid and unprecedented economic growth for more than a decade. To put its environmental experience during this period in context, it is useful to compare economic activity and environmental loading across several countries. This provides a reference for projecting future environmental impact on China as it continues its growth and economic development.

Table 12.9. *International Comparison of Economic Activity and Environmental Loading (1992)*

Indicator	China	Japan	USA	OECD Europe
Area (1000 km^2)	9,597	378	9,809	4,490
Population (millions)	1,162	124	255	439
Population density (person/km^2)	121	328	26	98
GNP (1987 prices, billions of US$)	491	2,988	4,924	5,767
GNP/capita (US$)	423	24,094	19,311	13,141
Energy consumption (million tons of oil equivalent)	710	451	1,984	1,439
Energy consumption (ton/capita)	0.61	3.64	7.78	3.28
Energy consumption (ton/km^2)	7.4	119.3	20.2	32.0
Energy consumption (ton, oil equivalent/GNP in millions of US$)	1,445	151	403	250
CO_2 discharged (million tons of carbon equivalent)	733	349	1,581	1,071
Carbon (ton/capita)	0.63	2.81	6.20	2.44
Carbon (ton/km^2)	7.6	92.3	16.1	23.9
Carbon (ton/GNP in millions of US$)	1,493	117	321	186

Source: Imura, Hidefumi, and Takeshi Katsuhara (1996), *Environmental Problem of China*, 2nd Edition, Tokyo: Toyo Keizai Sinposha.

6.2. Response and Experience of Neighboring Countries to China's Environmental Issues

Japan is one of China's most prominent neighbors and trading partners, and its perspective on Chinese environmental issues exemplifies the regional experience of China's more industrialized neighbors. We use Japan as an example in the following discussion.

6.2.1. Urban Economic Development and Environmental Issues

China has a high share of secondary or industrial activity in GDP, more than 56 percent in 1993. Most Chinese cities are industrial cities, as was the case with Japan in the 1960s. Industrial restructuring, modernization of equipment and relocation of industry, promotion of equipment renewal, and investment on key projects for improvement of production equipment and environment are as likely to be part of modernization in China as they were in Japan. Moreover, technological differences between the two countries create the basis for a collaborative approach to China's technological renovation.

6.2.2. The Pressing Necessity to Deal with the Issues of Urban Environmental Infrastructure

It is correctly noted by outside observers that high economic growth of China will induce serious shortages in urban environmental infrastructure, such as sewage disposal. Our center has recently been involved in a UNDP project entitled "Sustainable Development of the Yellow River Delta," which could represent a pilot project for studying sustainable development of the nation in the future. This study found that sewage disposal and treatment are very serious problems that must receive attention in China's future urban planning. This experience may also be relevant to new industrial economies in east and southeast Asia. The high economic growth of the "East Asian Miracle" may have a dark side if infrastructural needs are not correctly anticipated.

6.2.3. Lifestyle of the Urban Population

Much of the impetus for economic modernization, particularly on the demand side, has historically been modeled on Western consumption patterns. In populous Asia, one issue where this tendency is likely to have very serious environmental ramifications is in the transportation sector. Private car ownership and use patterns need to be balanced properly with public transportation from the point of energy consumption and environmental issues.

6.3. China's Energy-Environmental Issues from the Japanese Perspective

China's energy and environmental issues have raised major concerns in neighboring countries such as Japan and South Korea. The Research Institute of the Ministry of International Trade and Industry (MITI) has implemented joint research programs on energy and the environment. We abstract from this report to conclude this part of the chapter.

Observations of air pollutant emission in the two countries show that their extent of air pollutant generation, removal, and emission depends largely on the difference in their industrial structures and final demand structures, which are indications of their economic states of development, as well as the differences between their technical coefficients for energy emission factors and outputs. The tasks for conserving the environment on the global level must of necessity be set at levels which can be achieved by a variety of countries at different development stages, without hampering the attainment of their targets for economic development. If not, this will likely pose a hurdle to the making of any international accords regarding such issue.

7. CONCLUSION

7.1. China's Awareness of Its Responsibility in Global Environmental Issues

Compared with other countries at similar income levels, China has made significant gains in recognition of environmental policy challenges, capacity development for environmental monitoring, and more rigorous control of environmental damage arising from economic activity. China is a latecomer to industrialization as well as in environmental science, technology, and management, but it is making serious efforts to catch up. In the process of industrialization, China has achieved high economic growth rates since the late 1970s. China participated in the United Nation's Conference on Human Environment in Stockholm in 1972, enunciated environmental protection as a basic national policy in 1983, and participated in the Earth Summit in Rio de Janeiro in 1992. An extensive program of environmental policies is being carried out by a variety of different line ministries, in coordination with regional and local governments.

7.2. The Role of Energy

Energy plays a dominant role in economic growth and Chinese environmental issues. This chapter has surveyed the links between energy supply and demand and economic growth, including a quantitative assessment of their environmental impacts. Although data of this kind are still limited in China, the analysis presented here clearly illustrates the importance of anticipating energy-related environmental damage as this arises from continued industrialization. Macro and micro policies toward energy development and utilization have been examined in some detail in this chapter.

7.3. Sustainable Development and Policy Challenge

The general recognition of global environmental issues is of recent origin. Caldwell points out in 1984, for example, that "at the beginning of the twentieth century, neither environment as an integrative ecological concept nor the biosphere as the planetary life-support system was an object of public concern." But sustainable development had been accepted worldwide by the late 1980s, especially after the Earth Summit in 1992. Achieving sustainable development requires the effort of one generation even for developed countries. This can be illustrated from the quotation from an official document of one developed country that "It is understood that this will not be possible within a generation in all cases. This

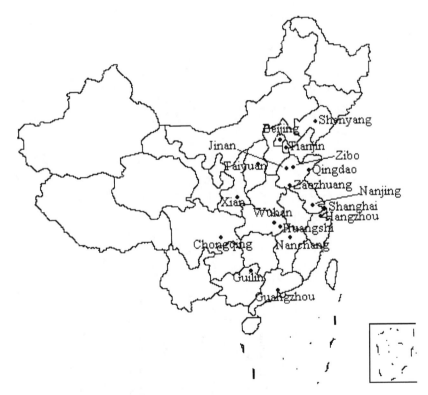

Figure A.12.1. Chinese cities with high frequency of acid rain.

APPENDIX

Table A12.1. GDP, Energy Consumption, and Pollution, 1985–95

	1985	1986	1987	1988	1989	1990	1991	1992	1993	1994	1995
GDP (100 million yuan)	8,964	10,202	11,963	14,928	16,909	18,548	21,618	26,638	34,634	46,622	58,261
Total energy consumption (10,000 ton of SCE)	76,682	80,850	86,632	92,997	96,934	98,703	103,783	109,170	115,993	122,737	129,000
Atmospheric pollution:											
Total volume of waste gas from fuel (100 million m^3)	45,373	46,467	52,624	56,417	57,613	59,478	69,941	72,028	75,401	N.A.	N.A.
Waste gas emission (100 million m^3)	73,970	69,679	77,275	82,380	83,065	85,380	101,416	104,787	109,604	113,630	123,407
Sulphur dioxide discharged (10,000 ton)	1,325	1,250	1,412	1,523	1,565	1,494	1,622	1,685	1,795	1,825	1,891
Soot discharged (10,000 ton)	1,295	1,384	1,445	1,436	1,398	1,324	1,314	1,414	1,416	1,414	1,478
Industrial dust discharged (10,000 ton)	1,305	1,075	1,004	1,125	840	781	579	576	617	583	639
Industrial dust retrieved (10,000 ton)	1,431	1,644	1,603	1,861	1,786	1,987	2,161	2,451	2,641	2,629	2,895
Water pollution (million ton)											
Total waste water discharged	34,154	33,879	34,861	36,726	35,345	353,780	33,621	35,878	35,559	36,526	37,285
Industrial waste water discharged	25,740	26,024	26,375	26,839	25,209	24,869	23,567	23,385	21,949	21,551	22,189
Industrial waste water treated	5,682	6,321	6,784	7,234	7,539	8,024	15,589	17,568	17,934	19,845	21,566
Industrial waste water untreated	20,058	19,703	19,591	19,605	17,670	16,845	7,977	5,817	4,015	N.A.	N.A.
Reaching industrial discharge standards	9,870	11,059	12,072	12,389	12,033	12,461	11,820	12,362	12,049	11,970	12,287
Reaching industrial discharge standards after treatment	3,197	3,470	4,042	4,157	4,348	4,639	4,233	4,449	4,503	4,756	4,814

Source: Statistical Yearbook of China, various issues.

Table A12.2. SO_2 Discharged in Waste Gas of Selected Cities (unit: thousand ton)

City	Sum of 5–6th Plan	1981	1982	1983	1984	1985	Sum of 7–8th Plan	1986	1987	1988	1989	1990
Beijing	1,410	263	260	277	300	310	1,657	323	321	321	344	346
Tianjin	1,050	187	193	213	271	186	1,235	256	267	251	241	220
Taiyuan	726	142	138	144	132	170	841	175	171	173	166	157
Shengyang	783	133	139	156	167	188	731	147	140	131	155	158
Shanghai	1,391	233	223	267	324	344	2,000	355	434	405	391	415
Nanjing	694	146	133	138	148	129	742	141	131	150	150	170
Hangzhou	323	59	63	65	66	70	474	93	92	98	98	93
Nanchang	284	45	55	54	71	59	288	60	57	56	60	55
Jinan	725	106	130	115	178	196	1,054	196	208	229	211	210
Zibo	718	168	134	150	130	136	1,248	163	243	273	287	282
Zaozhuang	609	113	129	105	133	129	544	126	110	113	98	99
Qingdao	921	146	180	190	199	206	1,406	278	261	284	279	304
Wuhan	703	144	133	128	141	157	644	120	127	130	132	135
Huangshi	508	112	86	118	109	83	432	80	87	101	78	86
Guangzhou	478	117	98	84	89	90	537	95	92	99	119	132
Guilin	176	64	24	25	30	33	156	38	30	29	31	27
Chongqing	632	115	120	126	132	139	3,610	682	746	762	711	709
Xian	708	164	146	125	130	143	923	195	194	196	196	143
Total	12,839	2,457	2,384	2,480	2,750	2,768	18,522	3,523	3,711	3,801	3,747	3,741

is because the consequences of man–environmental problems may only become manifest after several decades and because some problems can only take longer to solve." Recognizing the nature and scope of the problem takes time, and so does the technological innovation needed to solve it economically. A recent study by WRI points out that industrialized countries are struggling to curtail their greenhouse gas emissions to 1990 levels by the year 2000, but lifetime commitment points to curbing emissions of fully fluorinated compounds (FFC) – a family of little-known but extremely potent and long-lived greenhouse gases – as a cost-effective way toward this goal.

Although sustainable development is now a recognized and accepted priority worldwide, a nation faces many challenges to achieve it. It requires joint effort by politicians, sociologists, economists, scientists and engineers, and the private sector. China has committed itself to face these challenges with developed countries, working together to achieve a better environment for all future generations.

REFERENCES

China State Statistical Bureau (1991), *China: Energy Statistics Almanac 1991*, Beijing: China Statistical Publishing House.

China State Statistical Bureau (1986–96), *Statistical Yearbook of China*, 1986, . . . , 1996, Beijing: China Statistical Publishing House.

Coppel, Jonathan, and Hiro Lee (1996), "The Framework Convention and Climate Change Policy in Asia," in R. Mendelsohn and D. Shaw, eds., *The Economics of Pollution Control in the Asia Pacific*, Brookfield, Vermont: Edward Elgar.

Imura, Hidefumi, and Takeshi Katsuhara (1996), *Environmental Problem of China*, 2nd Edition, Tokyo: Toyo Keizai Sinposha.

Lawrence Berkeley Laboratory (1992), *China Energy Databook*, Document LBL-32B22 UC-350, Berkeley: University of California, Berkeley.

OECD (1995), *Global Warning: Economic Dimensions and Policy Responses*, Paris: OECD.

Comment

Mark Poffenberger

First, I compliment the authors on producing such a useful summary of the energy situation in China. Looking into the future, there are few issues that will have as much environmental impact, within a nation or globally, as China's energy policies and pro-grams. This is due to a number of factors. First, China is the world's largest user of coal; per-capita use is low and likely to grow rapidly in the future. Coal, as an energy source, creates many environ-mental problems due to gas emissions and water requirements. With an economic growth rate currently over 8 percent per annum, industrial demands for coal-based energy will continue to expand rapidly. As the authors point out, China's industry is heavily energy intensive, using about seven times as much coal to produce a dollar of GDP as the average G-7 economy.

Although China does possess immense hydroelectric potential, analysts still project that coal will continue to be the primary com-ponent of power generation. It will also be a major source of energy for domestic consumers. Household coal consumption doubled between 1979 and 1984, and this trend is likely to continue. To meet these demands in recent years, over 80,000 small coal mines were opened throughout the country, creating immense regulatory chal-lenges for this industry.

The problems of water pollution associated with coal use within the energy sector are very significant in China. In the northeast particularly, where water resources are already reaching scarcity levels, water availability for power generation becomes a critical problem. At least one hundred kilos of water are required for each kilowatt hour generated by coal. In Chansi Province, for example, where a third of the nation's high-quality coal is located, plans to establish a power plant generating 20 to 24 gigawatts would require 12 billion tons of water for cooling alone. Currently, the province's entire water requirement for industrial, agricultural, and domes-tic use is only 7 billion tons.

The development of the coal-driven energy sector also has significant ramifications for land resources. By the end of the 1980s, coal mining activities and ash disposal areas occupied over 100,000 hectares of land, with another 60,000 being added during the 1990's. Perhaps even more serious is the impact of emissions of air quality. SO_2 gases already contribute significantly to acid rain, which threatens agricultural and forested areas in southeastern China in particular. The health implications of deteriorating air quality in highly populated urban environments would seem to justify careful monitoring.

The authors, as well as other China energy specialists, predict that the nation will continue to consume increasing quantities of coal to meet its growing power needs, and the environmental and social costs will be enormous if cleaner practices are not adopted. With a vast and growing population and limited water, farm, and forest resources, China needs to be especially conservation minded to improve its living standards sustainably. A number of strategies should be considered by policymakers to minimize the impact of coal use in the energy sector on the natural resource base and society.

The efficiency of coal use in China is low compared to other countries. Energy conservation is approximately 30 percent of total energy input into service-generating power, versus 60 percent in Japan. This in part reflects management by state enterprises that have little incentive to boost performance. Commercial rates are set for state enterprises and often have no relation to production costs or demand conditions. As a consequence, many government-run coal and gas operations are running at a constant loss. If cleaner, more efficient industries are to evolve, new policies will need to be developed to provide energy enterprises with economic incentives to adopt improved technologies and strengthen operation and maintenance systems.

Experience from the United States with command and control environmental regulations has been mixed, and there are many indications that this approach may not be effective within the Chinese context. The lack of advocacy groups or judicial mechanisms to monitor and prosecute polluters effectively will undermine the efficacy of environmental controls. Even in the United States, confrontational systems to leverage change and achieve compliance with environmental regulations have not worked well. The question is, "What type of incentives can be created that will encourage the Asian energy sector to move toward better technologies?" It is argued by economists that, given the high rates of growth in the Asia region, there is a window of opportunity to replace technology from the 1950s. Economic incentives that reward energy enterprises for restructuring now could be extremely strategic in establishing clean technology and longer-term competitiveness in the Chinese economy.

The authors have noted that the Chinese government has subscribed to international environmental conventions, and is setting ambitious targets to deal with gas emission problems, but operational mechanisms need to be established that strongly encourage managers of enterprises to make the huge investments needed in new technologies. In looking at the environmental problems facing the countries of the former Soviet Union, it is clear that postponing these investments is ill advised. The cost of "end-of-pipe" clean-up approaches is far higher, in terms of both direct costs and externalities, than making a timely transition toward a cleaner energy sector.

CHAPTER 13

Outward Orientation and the Environment in the Pacific Basin: Coordinated Trade and Environmental Policy Reform in Mexico

John Beghin, David Roland-Holst, and
Dominique van der Mensbrugghe

1. INTRODUCTION

Economic growth and integration in the Pacific region have been remarkable, both in Asia and, less conspicuously, in Latin America (Mexico, Chile, and Costa Rica). At the same time, economic prosperity resulting from rapid growth has inspired doubts about its cost in terms of pollution and environmental degradation. As incomes rise rapidly, demand for a better environment and pollution abatement will inevitably increase. This chapter analyzes the interface between growth, world market integration, and the environment in Mexico. In particular, we examine how tradeoffs between growth and environmental objectives take place and can be minimized by using policies that coordinate taxes on pollution emissions with outward-oriented trade strategies.

In recent years, a resurgence of interest in trade and environment linkages has occurred in the context of multilateral agreements such as the Uruguay Round of the GATT/WTO and the

This study was part of the OECD Development Centre research programme on Sustainable Development: Environment, Resource Use, Technology, and Trade. We thank Maurizio Bussolo and Sébastien Dessus for excellent research assistance. The views expressed in this chapter are those of the authors and should not be attributed to their affiliated institutions.

NAFTA. Most of this new debate has been rhetorical rather than empirical. Recently, however, several rigorous essays have appeared that attempt to quantify the linkages between trade, growth, and the environment, especially in the context of economywide models of domestic pollution (for example, Grossman and Krueger, 1992; Lee and Roland-Holst, 1997) and transboundary or multilateral pollution (for example, Perroni and Wigle, 1994; Whalley, 1991). These essays show that fears of extensive environmental degradation brought about by free trade are not generally substantiated by available evidence. Most essays find little interface between transboundary pollution and free trade. The link between trade and pollution appears to arise primarily from the expansion of aggregate output rather than new patterns of international specialization. Surely, this type of real output and income growth is the primary intention of most outward-oriented trade reforms. To mitigate the adverse environmental effects of economic growth is a problem facing all countries, but this is no justification for protectionism.

This being said, there is some evidence of environmental asymmetry in existing trade patterns. For example, Lee and Roland-Holst (1997) detect a kind of implicit domestic pollution abatement in trade between Japan and Indonesia. Japan imports goods that are pollution-intensive (in their production phase) from Indonesia. Moreover, it appears that Indonesia specializes in production activities that release substantial effluents, and implicitly exports pollution services to the rest of the world, especially to industrialized countries, with these goods. To a significant extent, the observed patterns of specialization and their environmental consequences are inevitable results of differing stages of economic development. Most of the OECD countries, for example, now derive over two-thirds of their GDP and employment from relatively low pollution service activities. Indeed, in the so-called "industrialized countries," industry has been relegated to the minority status occupied by agriculture.

Despite these evolutionary differences, it is still reasonable to inquire about a link between greater outward orientation (or globalization generally), patterns of North–South specialization, and domestic environmental damage. We investigate this question in the context of Mexico and its NAFTA partners, and our conclusion is generally negative. Whereas the regional accord would stimulate aggregate Mexican growth, our evidence indicates that the pattern of domestic production would actually be induced to shift toward greener activities.

Another interesting issue, raised both in the political debate and in recent economic analysis, is the coordination of trade and environment policy. NAFTA, for example, has an explicit environmental side agreement. The Uruguay Round recognized environmental standards and identified situations as legitimate domestic policies with multilateral implications. Despite this, however, the GATT/WTO strongly discourages the use of trade barriers for environmental purposes. Economic theory concurs with this view (Beghin et al., 1997; Copeland, 1994; Lloyd, 1992). Summarized as "free trade and protected environment," this means abolition of impediments to international trade, but with significant regulation in place to control the environmental impact of expanded activities (Runge, 1994). In this chapter, we provide empirical evidence supporting the coordinated approach of combining outward orientation and environmental protection with effluent taxes or permits. The cost of environmental intervention is minimized under free trade because major distortions have been removed (i.e., effluent taxes do not have second-round effects on trade distortions and vice versa).

In addition, specialization permits abatement by importing cheaply as a substitute for polluting domestic production. Our results suggest that the right combination of policy reforms can mitigate both expansion of trade-induced pollution and the real contractionary effects of environmental policy. Thus it appears that more liberal and outward-oriented trade policy can coexist with policy interventions to protect the domestic environment.

A last important and perhaps most original aspect of the present approach relates to modeling of effluents and abatement. Most economywide studies of trade and environment linkages rely on effluent intensities associated with output in fixed proportion. Such an approach does not allow for substitution between nonpolluting factors (labor and capital) and polluting intermediate consumption, such as chemicals or energy. The characterization of pollution in our analysis links pollution emissions to the use of polluting intermediate inputs, rather than being directly held in fixed proportion to output levels. This approach permits substitution away from energy and aggregate intermediates to reduce the effluent intensity of output.

Although we maintain the assumption of fixed proportions between intermediate inputs (Leontief intermediate demand), we allow for substantial substitution away from aggregate intermediate consumption by use of more or less capital, labor, and/or energy. Furthermore, the adjustment process is embedded in a dynamic framework to take account of exogenous components of factor supply and productivity growth over the twenty-year period 1990 to 2010. This is coupled with a vintage capital specification that permits investment-driven evolution toward cleaner technologies. Thus the capital stock grows and allows for further substitution away from energy and polluting intermediate consumption. Another advantage of the input-based approach to effluent estimates is the ability to develop estimates for nonmanufacturing sectors, using information on their inputs. This is a major improvement compared with the standard, output-based measures, estimates for which exist only in manufacturing sectors (see Hettige et al., 1995).

The input-based approach to effluent modeling is the first attempt to capture a "technical" effect in abatement – in other words, a reduction of pollution achieved by changing the input and factor mix to produce the same good (Copeland and Taylor, 1994). Previous essays permitted abatement only via a reduction of aggregate activity (a scale effect) or changes in the nature of activities undertaken in the economy (a composition effect). The present approach captures all these effects.

We use a sequence of three stages to present our analysis. First, pollution abatement policies are considered alone, and their effects on growth, sectoral allocation, and trade are evaluated. The next step is to consider trade liberalization alone. Trade distortions in place before the NAFTA and Uruguay Round accords are removed progressively over time, and results calibrate the expansionary effects of trade liberalization and its environmental implications. In a third and last scenario, we combine trade and environmental policies and show how they interact.

We find that the growth-environment tradeoffs in Mexico would not be unduly detrimental to the economy. The only stubborn pollutant group in this context is bio-accumulative toxic substances released in water, which has high opportunity cost in terms of the economic contraction induced by tax-based mitigation instruments. Apart from this relatively small group, economic growth with coordinated trade liberalization and pollution taxes is sustainable in the sense that pollution emissions can be mitigated significantly over time. As Grossman and Krueger (1992) found in a related context, our results indicate that trade expansion alone occasions significant environmental damage in only a few sectors (e.g., energy). In the case of Mexico, we find no evidence to support the view that Mexico would specialize in dirty industrial activities. On the contrary, labor-intensive specialization under free trade translates into less pollution-intensive aggregate output. Increasing outward orientation by Mexico induces a combination of contraction and expansion of polluting activities whose aggregate net is almost neutral to the environment in terms of the average pollution intensity of GDP.

If environmental taxes or permits were introduced in Mexico, industries would abate using different policies. In the case of pollution taxes, the technological effect dominates in many sectors except for the dirtiest ones, where substitution away from pollution-intensive intermediates is difficult. The composition effect is dominant in this latter case, as these sectors are forced to contract under emission taxation. At the same time, trade liberalization facilitates imports as a substitute for dirty domestic output without penalizing consumption. Hence, under combined reforms, the composition effect often is dominant because it represents the cheaper abatement method for the economy.

The next section reviews some important facts on the Mexican integration in regional and global trade. In section 3, we present the model used in our simulations. The simulation scenarios are discussed in section 4, followed in section 5 by the results themselves. Section 6 is devoted to concluding remarks.

2. MEXICO'S INTEGRATION IN THE REGIONAL AND WORLD ECONOMY

Since 1985, Mexico has been following structural adjustment reforms that have reversed its inward orientation, leading in this decade to a progressively more open economy. The policy reforms arose primarily in response to the 1982 debt crisis and Mexico's desire to join the trading community of the GATT/WTO. Many historical import substitution policies were incompatible with the GATT/WTO membership and had to be dropped. Both the Uruguay Round agreement and Mexico's membership in NAFTA substantially advanced this transformation toward an open economy, more integrated regionally in the Pacific Basin and globally. Foreign and repatriated domestic capital played a significant role in facilitating this transformation.

Despite import substitution policies prevailing in the 1960s, Mexico started a liberal economic zone program at this time, better known as Maquiladoras, that allowed foreign investors to set up plants and assembly lines in Mexico, for reexport, at advantageous terms. Other forms of foreign direct investment were permitted to produce goods destined to the domestic markets (Peres Nunez, 1990). Abstracting from the 1982 crisis, the Maquiladoras program has been very successful, with a major presence by U.S., E.U., and Asian manufacturers (Peres Nunez, 1990; Chen and Drysdale, 1995; Agosin, 1995). Asian investment has been substantial and visible in automobiles (e.g., Nissan plants) and electronics (e.g., Sony). Foreign investment in Mexico has been further stimulated by the new outward orientation and integration of the Mexican economy, both of which tend to decrease investor uncertainty linked to government behavior. This integration of the "two sides" of the Pacific Basin is often neglected in the economic analysis of the Pacific Basin, focusing as it does on U.S. and intra-Asian trade.

Under the NAFTA, the distinction between the foreign investment in the Maquiladoras and the rest of the country will be phased out early in the next century. The Maquiladoras have also attracted scrutiny from environmental groups because of the environmental degradation that came with the expansion of concentrated economic activity in these free zones. In some instances, this attention has led to misguided criticism of free trade for lacking environmental stewardship (Runge, 1994; Johnstone, 1995).

In addition to removal of border measures, Mexico has undertaken extensive domestic policy reform. Domestic distortions are being removed progressively, and state interventions in production and marketing of various goods have been dramatically reduced. Privatization of the formerly large state sector has been under way and is a continuing part of the structural adjustment policy initiated in the early 1980s (World Bank, 1994, pp. 3–6).

3. THE TEQUILA MODEL

The _Trade and Environment eQUILibrium Analysis_ (TEQUILA) model has been adapted from a prototype computable general equilibrium (CGE) model developed at the OECD Development Centre for its sustainable development research program. Here we describe only the salient features of the model, which are fully documented in Beghin, Dessus, Roland-Holst, and van der Mensbrugghe (1996). The original aspect of this modeling effort resides in its environmental component, which is a departure from the existing literature. Our description devotes special attention to this unique aspect of the TEQUILA model.

The model is recursive dynamic in the sense that each period is solved as a static equilibrium problem, given an allocation of savings and expenditure on current consumption. Savings increase the pool of investment, and the capital stock grows over time. The model is multisectoral and details ninety-four independent production activities. Production is based on constant returns to scale technology and is modeled by a series of nested CES functions. Final output is derived from a combination of non-energy intermediate inputs, a composite bundle of energy, and value-added (labor and capital). Non-energy intermediate inputs are assumed to be used in fixed proportions with respect to total non-energy intermediate demand. The energy-value-added bundle is decomposed into a labor aggregate on the one hand, and a capital-energy bundle on the other. Labor demand is further decomposed into eight occupational categories.

The capital-energy bundle is disaggregated into capital demand and demand for an energy aggregate. Finally, the energy bundle is decomposed into different base fuel components. One of the key advantages of this type of production structure is that emissions are attributable to intermediate consumption rather than final output. Substitution possibilities exist between value-added, energy, and non-energy intermediate goods, allowing for decreased pollution associated with production if pollution taxes are put in place.

In the case of pure Leontief technology (no substitution) or fixed output-based effluent measures, abatement of pollution can be achieved only by output reductions. The transformation from output- to input-based pollution effluent is based on the methodology of Dessus, Roland-Holst, and van der Mensbrugghe (1994), who derived econometric estimates of these input-based effluent intensities by matching data from a social accounting matrix dis-aggregated at the 4-digit ISIC level to the corresponding IPPS pollution database of Wheeler and colleagues at the World Bank (Hettige et al., 1995). These input-based measures are then deflated to 1990 prices and converted to Mexican pesos. Emissions are modeled as being generated by both the final consumption and the intermediate use of polluting goods. In certain sectors, there is an autonomous component of emission that is directly linked to the level of output – this due to unusually high effluent intensities. Our approach provides conservative estimates of substitution possibilities to abate pollution for two reasons. First, we assume conservative values for the elasticities of substitution between labor, capital, and energy. Second, the Leontief assumption maintained within the intermediate-consumption aggregate is unduly pessimistic, since it precludes substitution within the various types of goods entering intermediate consumption and understates the true substitution possibilities.

Excise taxes per unit effluent are used to achieve pollution mitigation. These taxes are measured as unit of currency per unit of emission and are tacked onto the producer price of the polluting commodity. Pollution itself is characterized by a vector of thirteen types of emissions, broadly grouped into chemical toxics, bio-accumulative metals, air pollution, and water pollution. Chemical toxics and bio-accumulative emissions are expressed for three media (air, water, and soil). There are then the following effluents: toxic pollutants in air, water, and land (TOXAIR, TOXWAT, TOXSOL); bio-accumulative toxic metals in air, water, and soil (BIOAIR, BIOWAT, BIOSOL); air pollutants such as SO_2, NO_2, CO, volatile organic compounds (VOCs), and total suspended particulates (PART); and, finally, water pollution as measured by biological oxygen demand (BOD) and total suspended solids (TSS).[1]

The estimated effluents reveal some useful stylized facts about pollution in Mexico. A few sectors are responsible for most of the pollution emissions. These are the energy sectors, petrochemical, minerals and their transformation, and cement; agriculture is a

---

[1] See Hettige et al. (1995) for a detailed description of these effluent and their health effects.

major contributor to toxic water pollution. Many emission types are correlated (the same sectors are often intensive in several effluents), and there is relatively little substitution across discharge media (water, air, and land), so limited analytical and administrative resources could profitably be focused on a subset of effluents and industries. Based on these stylized facts, a simple yet powerful policy implication emerges: namely, the possibility of implementing a limited number of pollutant taxes on a limited number of industries, achieving major economywide environmental gains.

Another key feature of the model is the vintage structure of capital. The model assumes a putty/semi-putty production technology. It is normally assumed that substitution possibilities for existing old capital are smaller than the substitution possibilities of new capital coming from the new investment pool, implying that acceleration of investment would allow producers more flexibility in reacting to emission taxes.[2]

The calibration of the model is based on a detailed social accounting matrix for Mexico, with ten labor categories and twenty households (ten urban and ten rural categories). The bulk of labor and capital income is distributed to the different households, and it is therefore possible to assess the distributional impacts of changes in both trade and environmental policies. Households are utility-maximizers, and their preferences are consistent with the extended linear expenditure system (ELES).

Labor is assumed to be perfectly mobile across sectors, while capital is only partially mobile, reflecting differences in the transferability of capital equipment across sectors. Both wages and capital returns are determined by economywide equilibrium conditions. However, the labor supply curve is differentiated by labor type, and full employment conditions are assumed, that is, labor markets equilibrate.

Trade is modeled assuming that goods are differentiated with respect to region of origin and destination. On the import side, we account for the heterogeneity of imports and domestic goods with the CES specification attributed to Armington. Symmetrically, we use a CET specification for domestic output, where domestic producers are assumed to differentiate between the domestic and export markets. We further assume that Mexico is a small country

---

[2] Capital includes land and machinery.

facing constant world prices. Import price distortions are expressed as ad-valorem tariffs, as is consistent with the outward orientation of the Mexican economy following its structural adjustment starting in the mid-1980s to join GATT/WTO.

The model includes three closure rules governing the government budget, saving/investment, and trade balance. The government budget surplus/deficit is set fixed in real terms. Normally, some tax rate is endogenous to achieve this budget balance. If the household income tax rate is endogenous, this closure rule can generate significant impacts on the distribution of income. The second closure rule makes domestic investment savings-driven. Changes in saving levels – household, government, or foreign – will have a direct impact on the investment level. The final closure rule holds that the trade balance is fixed in terms of foreign currency. The impact of this closure rule is that trade liberalization typically leads to a real depreciation, as increasing import demand must be matched by rising exports at constant world prices.

There are three essential dynamic components in the prototype model. The first is capital and labor accumulation. Labor supply is assumed to grow exogenously, while the capital stock evolves with investment activity. The second element is productivity growth. There are efficiency factors for capital, labor (by each occupation), and energy. The efficiency factors are normally exogenous, but the capital efficiency factor is imputed in the benchmark simulation to achieve a specified trajectory of real GDP growth. The third element is a vintage capital assumption. The composition of the capital stock, which will determine the degree of flexibility in production, is influenced by the time path of total and sectoral investment allocation. Older existing capital can be moved from one sector to another but at some cost of transformation.

4. SIMULATION SCENARIOS

Three basic sets of scenarios are considered: environmental taxes, trade opening, and coordination of the two. These scenarios are in reference to a twenty-year (1990–2010) base trend called business-as-usual (BAU). The latter determines the reference growth and pollution trajectory in absence of environmental, trade, or other policy reforms. The first policy reform scenario looks at the impact of piecemeal environmental policies, elucidating the extent of the growth–environment tradeoff in Mexico and how international trade influences it. Specifically, the policy calls for phasing in a 25 percent emission reduction with respect to reference trends for one type of effluent at a time. The phasing entails sequential reductions of 10 percent in 1995, 15 percent in 2000, 20 percent in 2005, and 25 percent in 2010.

The second scenario considers a piecemeal unilateral trade liberalization, along with a modest increase in export prices to mimic terms-of-trade effects that would follow from NAFTA and increased access to North American markets. Trade distortions are expressed as ad valorem tariffs that are eliminated progressively from their reference levels (1989): 90 percent of original tariffs in 1995, 60 percent in 2000, 30 percent in 2005, and no tariff in 2010. Terms-of-trade effects are assumed to be similarly progressive, increasing observed world prices by 2 percent in 1995, 4 percent in 2000, 7 percent in 2005, and 10 percent in 2010.

The objective of this second set of reform scenarios is to see how the environment is affected by an outward-oriented strategy and to reveal induced changes in sectoral composition of production and trade. The latter is of special interest because it might reveal evidence of specialization in dirty production, with an implicit transfer of environmental services to countries buying Mexican exports or, conversely, of dirty domestic industries contracting under world market discipline. Economywide models are ideally suited to elucidate the reallocation of resources across sectors.

The third set of simulations examines coordinated trade and environmental reforms. Here, the objective is to see how free trade and environment policies combine their impacts on efficiency and the environment. This coordinated type of reform is supported by economic theory, because targeted environmental policies minimize the dead-weight loss of intervention, and the absence of trade distortions precludes negative feedback from environmental taxes to efficiency via an exacerbation of trade distortions.

5. RESULTS

We present the results in four tables (two tables for the single reforms and two tables for the coordinated ones). First, results on pollution changes, sectoral allocation, and aggregate variables are presented in Table 13.1 for the individual abatement taxes and for trade liberalization. Table 13.2 presents the decomposition of

Table 13.1. Aggregate and Sectoral Results of Individual Abatement and Trade Liberalization (all figures are percentage changes with respect to base trends in 2010)

| | Aggregate abatement of 25 percent by type of emission | | | | | | | | | | | | | Trade Liberaliz. |
	TOXAIR 1	TOXSOL 2	TOXWAT 3	BIOAIR 4	BIOSOL 5	BIOWAT 6	SO_2 7	NO_2 8	CO 9	PART 10	VOC 11	TSS 12	BOD 13	14
Aggregates														
Toxic Index	-19.41	-23.37	-16.19	-5.99	-6.07	-5.49	-2.92	-2.92	-10.42	-3.02	-15.70	-.08	-12.26	2.50
Bio-accum Index	-31.07	-23.20	-.98	-24.57	-24.72	-9.10	-.35	-.34	-2.25	-1.00	-3.31	-.41	-1.03	3.87
SO_2-NO_2-CO Index	-12.67	-15.06	-20.25	-2.85	-1.38	-7.49	-14.68	-14.79	-16.18	-16.44	-17.46	-1.30	-5.49	4.84
Real GDP	-1.12	-1.31	-.56	-.66	-.60	-4.39	-.29	-.29	-.42	-.39	-.73	-.04	-.56	3.22
Labor Supply	-.15	-.24	-.42	-.13	-.11	-2.23	-.01	-.01	-.03	-.05	-.15	-.01	-.24	.16
Capital Stock	-1.31	-1.52	-.68	-.83	-.74	-5.76	-.33	-.32	-.46	-.46	-.79	-.06	-.67	4.25
Total Exports	-2.55	-2.79	-2.04	-1.11	-1.00	-4.20	-1.22	-1.25	-.78	-1.32	-.97	-.05	-1.46	21.95
Total Imports	-1.03	-1.01	-1.04	-.47	-.40	-3.36	-1.03	-1.06	.01	-1.09	.45	-.02	-.65	31.86
Sectoral Output														
Agriculture	-.47	-1.30	-4.61	.24	.25	-2.37	-.12	-.11	-.33	-.15	-1.33	.00	-2.14	-2.44
Mining	-23.35	-27.37	-20.49	-8.94	-7.99	-10.45	-5.77	-5.61	-5.12	-6.87	-5.18	-1.14	-20.26	12.80
Food Processing	.13	-.28	-1.95	.20	.22	-1.99	-.05	-.06	-.01	-.07	-.81	.00	-1.09	2.02
Textiles	-1.69	-3.83	-1.01	.48	.46	-1.29	.10	.12	-3.61	.11	-6.06	.02	-.55	.37
Wood and Paper	-1.26	-1.29	-1.98	-.43	-.38	-4.49	-.30	-.25	-1.22	-.47	-4.21	-.02	-.96	-.01
Petroleum	-16.28	-22.38	-28.43	.59	.32	-3.03	-19.72	-19.82	-20.04	-19.33	-27.70	.17	-9.33	1.90
Chemicals	-10.88	-15.83	-7.39	-1.00	-1.03	-2.94	-.41	-.42	-13.46	-.43	-21.76	-.03	-4.52	-.09
Processed Minerals	-9.43	-9.54	-1.19	-9.51	-8.90	-13.32	-.81	-1.01	-.53	-1.71	-.13	-.51	-2.27	2.63
Other Manufac.	-3.62	.23	4.55	-5.13	-4.64	-2.35	.58	.55	1.31	.15	1.63	-.27	3.58	14.94
Services	-.09	-.17	.17	-.26	-.23	-5.66	-.30	-.28	.01	-.36	-.06	-.01	.04	4.03

Table 13.2. Composition of Pollution Adjustments (Level changes in thousands of metric tons)

| | Aggregate abatement of 25 percent by type of emission | | | | | | | | | | | | | Trade Liberaliz. |
| | TOXAIR | TOXSOL | TOXWAT | BIOAIR | BIOSOL | BIOWAT | SO₂ | NO₂ | CO | PART | VOC | TSS | BOD | |
	1	2	3	4	5	6	7	8	9	10	11	12	13	14
TOXAIR														
Composition	-.13	-.11	-.04	-.07	-.07	.00	-.01	-.01	-.04	-.01	-.06	.00	-.03	-.01
Technical	-.03	-.03	-.02	-.01	-.01	.00	-.01	-.01	-.01	-.01	-.02	.00	-.01	.01
Scale	-.02	-.02	-.01	-.01	-.01	-.03	.00	.00	-.01	-.01	-.02	.00	-.01	.03
TOXSOL														
Composition	-.36	-.46	-.29	-.09	-.10	-.03	-.04	-.04	-.24	-.04	-.38	.00	-.21	-.07
Technical	-.10	-.13	-.07	-.03	-.03	.00	.00	.00	-.06	.00	-.10	.00	-.07	.02
Scale	-.07	-.08	-.04	-.04	-.03	-.14	-.02	-.02	-.04	-.02	-.06	.00	-.03	.11
TOXWAT														
Composition	-.03	-.05	-.07	.01	.01	.00	-.01	-.01	-.02	-.01	-.03	.00	-.05	-.03
Technical	-.03	-.03	-.07	.00	.00	.00	-.03	-.03	-.02	-.03	-.02	.00	-.03	.01
Scale	-.02	-.02	-.01	-.01	-.01	-.03	.00	.00	-.01	.00	-.01	.00	-.01	.02
BIOAIR (x1000)														
Composition	-1.10	-.80	.10	-.90	-.90	-.30	.00	.00	-.10	.00	.00	.00	.00	.00
Technical	-.30	-.20	.00	-.30	-.20	-.20	.00	.00	-.20	-.10	-.10	-.10	.00	.00
Scale	-.10	-.10	-.10	-.10	-.10	-.20	.00	.00	-.10	.00	-.10	.00	-.10	.20
BIOSOL (x100)														
Composition	-4.16	-2.79	.18	-3.25	-3.27	-.67	.04	.04	-.12	-.04	-.10	-.05	.09	-.10
Technical	-.81	-.63	-.10	-.59	-.61	-.03	.00	.00	-.04	.01	-.14	.00	-.09	.10
Scale	-.39	-.45	-.25	-.21	-.19	-.81	-.10	-.10	-.22	-.13	-.36	-.01	-.17	.64
BIOWAT														
Composition	.00	.00	.00	.00	.00	.00	.00	.00	.00	.00	.00	.00	.00	.00
Technical	.00	.00	.00	.00	.00	.00	.00	.00	.00	.00	.00	.00	.00	.00
Scale	.00	.00	.00	.00	.00	.00	.00	.00	.00	.00	.00	.00	.00	.00

SO₂														
Composition	-.01	-.01	-.03	.00	.00	-.02	-.03	-.03	-.01	-.03	-.01	.00	-.01	.00
Technical	-.03	-.02	-.11	.00	.00	.00	-.10	-.10	-.03	-.10	-.03	.00	-.01	.02
Scale	-.01	-.01	-.01	-.01	-.01	-.02	.00	.00	-.01	.00	-.01	.00	.00	.02
NO₂ (×100)														
Composition	-.33	-.51	-1.74	.18	.16	-.86	-1.71	-1.73	-.44	-1.74	-.58	.02	-.53	.00
Technical	-1.84	-1.34	-6.59	.00	-.07	-.08	-5.97	-6.03	-1.72	-5.93	-1.56	.05	-.67	.01
Scale	-.71	-.82	-.46	-.37	-.34	-1.46	-.19	-.19	-.39	-.23	-.66	-.02	-.30	.01
CO (×100)														
Composition	-.09	-.14	-.07	-.01	-.01	.00	-.01	-.01	-.13	-.02	-.18	-.01	-.04	-.03
Technical	-.03	-.03	-.02	-.03	.00	-.03	-.01	-.01	-.07	-.03	-.04	-.02	-.01	.01
Scale	-.02	-.02	-.01	-.01	-.01	-.04	-.01	-.01	-.01	-.01	-.02	.00	-.01	.03
PART (×1000)														
Composition	-1.40	-1.80	-4.40	-.80	-.20	-4.70	-4.90	-4.80	-2.00	-5.70	-1.10	-.50	-1.50	.00
Technical	-5.50	-3.50	-17.90	-2.10	-.20	-3.10	-16.30	-16.40	-8.40	-18.30	-4.20	-1.60	-1.60	.00
Scale	-2.20	-2.60	-1.40	-1.20	-1.10	-4.60	-.60	-.60	-1.20	-.70	-2.10	-.10	-.90	.00
VOC (×100)														
Composition	-5.46	-8.34	-4.65	.12	.02	.75	-.92	-.94	-7.42	-.83	-12.08	.05	-2.43	-.02
Technical	-1.49	-2.30	-1.14	-.18	-.19	-.05	.00	-.01	-1.73	.00	-2.72	.00	-.81	.01
Scale	-1.52	-1.76	-.99	-.80	-.73	-3.15	-.40	-.40	-.84	-.49	-1.42	-.05	-.65	.02
TSS														
Composition	-1.68	-1.95	-1.04	-.94	-.63	-.79	-.23	-.23	-1.60	-.59	-1.52	-.28	-.70	-.37
Technical	-.66	-.53	-.71	-.74	-.09	-.93	-.40	-.41	-1.52	-1.07	-.48	-.52	-.28	.15
Scale	-.39	-.45	-.25	-.20	-.19	-.80	-.10	-.10	-.21	-.13	-.36	-.01	-.16	.63
BOD (×100)														
Composition	-1.14	-2.09	-2.65	.24	.21	-.28	-.27	-.26	-.55	-.23	-1.00	.02	-2.30	.00
Technical	-.55	-.82	-.71	-.06	-.06	-.02	.00	.00	-.24	.00	-.39	.00	-.81	.00
Scale	-.38	-.44	-.25	-.20	-.18	-.79	-.10	-.10	-.21	-.12	-.36	-.01	-.16	.01

pollution abatement for the same scenarios. All results refer to deviations from the BAU scenario and are expressed in percent. Tables 13.3 and 13.4 provide similar information for the coordinated policies.

Effluent taxes inducing 25 percent reduction in individual effluent categories lead to relative reductions of real GDP (row 4 of Table 13.1). In light of the extent of pollution reduction, however, these negative growth effects are surprisingly small, ranging from $-.29$ percent (NO_2 reduction) to -4.4 percent (BIOWAT reduction). The three toxic pollutant indices (TOXAIR, TOXWAT, and TOXSOL) are highly correlated. A few industries are responsible for most of the pollution emissions and typically discharge several types of pollutants simultaneously; the composition effect induced by a tax on a specific pollutant decreases other emissions because of low substitution between discharge media and high correlation between different types of emissions by medium.

The decomposition of pollution abatement is presented in Table 13.2. It reveals that the composition effect is dominant in the most polluting industries, such as petroleum refining or cement. By contrast, the technological effect, measured by the decrease in pollution intensity per unit of output, is dominant for many sectors in which it is relatively inexpensive to abate pollution by substituting away from polluting inputs without reducing output. Scale effects are the least important source of abatement with taxes. Hence, the tradeoff between environment and economic growth does not appear to be acute in Mexico, because only a small GDP reduction is associated with major abatement of emission for several pollution groups.

Unilateral trade liberalization and better terms-of-trade induce a 3.2 percent rise in real GDP, but also an increase in all major pollutants by about the same proportion (from 2.5 to 4.8 percent). In the absence of policies that alter the relative costs of polluting activities, the scale effect is thus dominant for all pollutants and most sectors. There appears to be a positive abatement effect via a changing composition of output toward cleaner goods. However, dirty activities expand in a few sectors (e.g., energy sectors like oil, gas, and electricity). Examples of win–win cases are the staple agricultural activities that are responsible for toxic water pollution and the fertilizer industry, which also contracts under free trade.

Table 13.3. Aggregate and Sectoral Results of Individual Abatement Combined with Trade Liberalization (all figures are percentage changes with respect to base trends in 2010)

	Aggregate abatement of 25 percent by type of emission												
	TOXAIR 1	TOXSOL 2	TOXWAT 3	BIOAIR 4	BIOSOL 5	BIOWAT 6	SO_2 7	NO_2 8	CO 9	PART 10	VOC 11	TSS 12	BOD 13
Aggregates													
Toxic Index	-19.69	-23.10	-14.78	-3.98	-4.10	-3.64	-1.37	-1.37	-8.50	-1.42	-13.99	2.43	-10.87
Bio-accum Index	-31.10	-20.98	3.99	-24.66	-24.69	-6.35	3.63	3.65	1.67	2.72	.83	3.35	3.84
SO_2-NO_2-CO Index	-9.91	-11.71	-17.24	1.89	3.35	-3.52	-14.47	-14.65	-12.29	-16.36	-13.93	3.51	-1.29
Real GDP	2.02	1.89	2.65	2.54	2.61	-1.67	2.85	2.85	2.81	2.74	2.50	3.18	2.63
Labor Supply	.06	-.03	-.41	.05	.07	-2.31	.15	.16	.14	.11	.01	.15	-.08
Capital Stock	2.85	2.71	3.54	3.39	3.49	-2.21	3.83	3.84	3.80	3.68	3.45	4.19	3.56
Total Exports	19.26	19.38	20.40	20.73	20.89	16.90	20.31	20.27	21.45	20.19	21.40	21.89	20.70
Total Imports	30.67	31.01	31.28	31.22	31.35	27.29	30.31	30.27	32.13	30.23	32.75	31.83	31.42
Sectoral Output													
Agriculture	-2.71	-3.53	-7.23	-2.08	-2.07	-5.08	-2.58	-2.57	-2.70	-2.61	-3.69	-2.43	-4.57
Mining	-16.31	-22.76	-15.12	6.31	6.95	.71	4.13	4.42	8.34	3.33	8.29	11.77	-15.74
Food Processing	2.55	2.17	.41	2.36	2.36	-.23	1.98	1.96	2.10	1.96	1.33	2.03	1.13
Textiles	-1.36	-3.44	-.52	1.00	.97	-.92	.53	.56	-3.30	.56	-5.89	.40	-.06
Wood and Paper	-1.02	-.79	-1.63	-.41	-.36	-4.80	-.34	-.28	-1.12	-.55	-4.23	-.03	-.67
Petroleum	-16.97	-22.73	-28.88	3.13	2.75	-1.24	-23.58	-23.72	-19.29	-22.82	-27.60	2.14	-9.07
Chemicals	-12.74	-17.31	-7.74	-1.25	-1.30	-3.16	-.53	-.55	-14.74	-.53	-23.61	-.11	-4.87
Processed Minerals	-8.00	-7.22	2.45	-8.87	-8.08	-12.28	1.73	1.40	2.31	.49	3.06	1.98	1.22
Other Manufac.	12.69	18.72	23.34	8.20	8.97	12.66	16.32	16.25	17.50	15.59	18.26	14.56	21.93
Services	4.04	3.99	4.27	3.77	3.81	-2.35	3.63	3.65	4.02	3.56	3.95	4.02	4.15

Table 13.4. Composition of Pollution Adjustments, Combined with Trade Liberalization (Level changes in thousands of metric tons)

	Aggregate abatement of 25 percent by type of emission												
	TOXAIR 1	TOXSOL 2	TOXWAT 3	BIOAIR 4	BIOSOL 5	BIOWAT 6	SO₂ 7	NO₂ 8	CO 9	PART 10	VOC 11	TSS 12	BOD 13
TOXAIR													
Composition	-.15	-.13	-.05	-.08	-.09	-.02	-.02	-.02	-.05	-.02	-.07	-.01	-.04
Technical	-.03	-.02	-.01	-.01	-.01	.00	.00	.00	-.01	.00	-.01	.00	-.01
Scale	.01	.01	.02	.02	.02	-.01	.02	.02	.02	.02	.01	.03	.02
TOXSOL													
Composition	-.48	-.58	-.38	-.17	-.17	-.10	-.12	-.12	-.32	-.12	-.46	-.07	-.31
Technical	-.08	-.11	-.05	-.01	-.01	.02	.02	.02	-.04	.02	-.08	.02	-.05
Scale	.04	.03	.07	.07	.07	-.05	.09	.09	.07	.08	.05	.11	.09
TOXWAT													
Composition	-.06	-.08	-.11	-.02	-.02	-.03	-.04	-.04	-.05	-.04	-.06	-.03	-.08
Technical	-.02	-.02	-.06	.01	.01	.01	-.03	-.03	-.01	-.03	-.01	.01	-.02
Scale	.01	.01	.02	.02	.02	-.01	.02	.02	.02	.02	.01	.02	.02
BIOAIR (x1000)													
Composition	-1.30	-.80	.10	-1.10	-1.10	-.30	.00	.00	-.10	-.10	.00	-.10	.00
Technical	-.20	-.20	.00	-.30	-.20	-.20	.00	.00	-.20	-.10	.00	-.10	.00
Scale	.10	.10	.10	.10	.10	-.10	.20	.20	.10	.10	.10	.20	.20
BIOSOL (x100)													
Composition	-4.70	-3.04	.24	-3.82	-3.83	-.82	-.01	-.01	-.21	-.13	-.15	-.16	.14
Technical	-.75	-.54	.00	-.52	-.54	.05	.09	.09	.06	.11	-.04	.10	.01
Scale	.23	.20	.41	.41	.43	-.27	.51	.51	.43	.48	.28	.62	.49
BIOWAT													
Composition	.00	.00	.00	.00	.00	.00	.00	.00	.00	.00	.00	.00	.00
Technical	.00	.00	.00	.00	.00	.00	.00	.00	.00	.00	.00	.00	.00
Scale	.00	.00	.00	.00	.00	.00	.00	.00	.00	.00	.00	.00	.00

SO_2													
Composition	-.01	-.01	-.03	.01	.00	-.02	-.04	-.04	-.01	-.04	-.01	.00	-.01
Technical	-.02	.00	-.10	.02	.02	.02	-.10	-.11	-.01	-.10	-.01	.02	.01
Scale	.01	.01	.01	.01	.01	-.01	.01	.01	.01	.01	.01	.02	.01
NO_2 (x100)													
Composition	-.29	-.50	-1.75	.37	.34	-.84	-2.06	-2.09	-.36	-2.07	-.52	.15	-.52
Technical	-.95	-.29	-5.90	1.18	1.10	1.08	-6.42	-6.51	-.60	-6.31	-.45	1.22	.39
Scale	.41	.36	.75	.74	.78	-.48	.92	.92	.78	.87	.51	1.12	.89
CO (x100)													
Composition	-.14	-.18	-.11	-.04	-.04	-.03	-.05	-.05	-.17	-.06	-.22	-.04	-.07
Technical	-.02	-.03	-.02	-.02	.01	-.03	.00	.00	-.06	-.03	-.03	-.01	.00
Scale	.01	.01	.02	.02	.02	-.01	.03	.03	.02	.03	.01	.03	.03
$PART$ (x1000)													
Composition	-1.50	-2.00	-4.60	-.60	-.10	-5.10	-6.00	-6.00	-1.90	-6.90	-1.10	-.30	-1.60
Technical	-3.10	-.60	-16.00	1.00	2.90	-.20	-17.60	-17.80	-5.20	-19.80	-1.20	1.50	1.20
Scale	1.30	1.10	2.30	2.30	2.40	-1.50	2.90	2.90	2.40	2.70	1.60	3.50	2.80
VOC (x100)													
Composition	-8.35	-11.06	-6.93	-1.88	-2.00	-1.20	-3.15	-3.17	-9.89	-3.02	-14.74	-1.95	-4.71
Technical	-1.08	-1.81	-.63	.32	.31	.45	.51	.51	-1.19	.52	-2.19	.52	-.31
Scale	.88	.77	1.61	1.59	1.67	-1.03	1.98	1.98	1.67	1.87	1.09	2.42	1.92
TSS													
Composition	-2.28	-2.50	-1.46	-1.37	-1.07	-1.22	-.67	-.66	-1.99	-1.07	-1.95	-.65	-1.14
Technical	-.55	-.39	-.58	-.60	.05	-.84	-.36	-.37	-1.31	-1.12	-.33	-.38	-.12
Scale	.22	.20	.41	.41	.43	-.26	.51	.50	.43	.48	.28	.62	.49
BOD (x100)													
Composition	-1.69	-2.77	-3.26	.15	.10	-.64	-.70	-.68	-.84	-.62	-1.28	-.27	-2.99
Technical	-.46	-.71	-.60	.04	.04	.09	.10	.10	-.12	.10	-.27	.11	-.69
Scale	.22	.19	.40	.40	.42	-.26	.50	.00	.00	.00	.27	.61	.48

The results on decomposition show that little noticeable technology effect occurs in the absence of incentives to shift the input mix to achieve abatement, but they show that emissions exhibit a reduction of intensity via a composition effect. The division of labor induced by free trade is slightly cleaner than the one prevailing before the reform. This is an important result, showing that Mexico will not turn into a pollution haven in terms of domestic investment flowing into dirty activities.

An important aspect of the incidence of these reforms is the social costs and benefits of pollution reduction and the preservation of environmental assets. At the present time, we have made no attempt to incorporate this kind of valuation in the model, but it should be borne in mind that the abatement levels achieved are one to two orders of magnitude larger than the combined direct and indirect economic costs in percentage terms.

To see the possible effects of coordinated reforms, we have reproduced analogous results (Tables 13.3 and 13.4) for trade liberalization combined with each of the individual abatement policies. The main advantage of coordinated reforms is to combine efficiency gains from free trade with distortions implemented to achieve second-best environmental objectives. Real economic growth (real GDP in Table 13.3) is positive for all but one environmental tax (BIOWAT). Food processing, services, and manufacturing other than chemicals and metals expand with the coordinated policy reforms.

The abatement multiplier effects vary little compared to their values under the first scenario. Aggregate trade expands by about 20 percent for exports and 30 percent for imports, quite comparable to the expansion induced by trade liberalization alone. One could reasonably conclude from this that domestic environmental policies in this country are relatively "transparent" with respect to the real and dynamic gains from trade. In other words, the effects of trade and environment policies generally are decomposable and, based on comparison of Tables 13.1 and 13.3, nearly additive.

However, an examination of the decomposition of pollution abatement reveals a very different pattern from what occurred in response to environmental reform alone. As shown in Table 13.4, the composition effect is significantly larger in the joint reform. Enhanced trading possibilities induced a stronger substitution of imports for dirty domestic output and a specialization in cleaner goods that can be exported. Furthermore, compared to the single environmental reform, the scale effect contributes positively to effluents. This is the generic effect of growth, which is offset primarily by the changing composition and, to a lesser but significant extent, by cleaner technology (input mix) in production.

We can summarize the effects of outward orientation as follows. Free trade induces an aggregate pro-growth scale effect detrimental to the environment and a composition-substitution effect that mitigates environmental degradation. In addition, free trade has a secondary effect on the technology component. Imports are cheaper and cleaner from a domestic perspective, and this hinders the former incentives to decrease emission intensities that may have existed in effective protection of output. Abatement may have been subsidized in some industries because cleaner inputs may have been cheaper to producers prior to the trade reform. Trade liberalization provides international price discipline for pollution abatement achieved by modifying the input mix in domestic production. This latter beneficial aspect of free trade has not been emphasized in previous studies.

6. CONCLUSIONS

We presented simulation results relating international trade, growth, and pollution in Mexico using a CGE model that incorporates pollution in production and consumption. This unique approach allowed us to separate and identify abatement by scale, composition, and technology sources. We uncovered diverse abatement possibilities specific to sectors, reflecting the ease or difficulty in substituting away from polluting inputs. Free movement of goods offers the possibility to abate by importing pollution-intensive goods at the least cost, without incurring further misallocation of resources due to trade distortions in abatement activities.

In the Mexican case, we found no evidence of specialization into dirty activities arising from trade liberalization. Pollution increases at about the same rate as aggregate output, but the new division of labor is actually slightly cleaner than the prereform one, due to the realization of comparative advantage for Mexico in labor-intensive activities. Trade orientation appears to have little influence on pollution emitted, except through the expansion of output.

In terms of environmental reform, the introduction of effluent taxes decreases pollution in intermediate and final use at a low cost in terms of forgone aggregate income. We do not explicitly model the benefits of having less pollution emitted, although decreased pollution translates into reduced mortality and morbidity and should have a positive value to private agents. Because we do not have information on ambient concentration and health impacts, we could not estimate the welfare gains associated with reduced emissions (see Espinosa and Smith, 1995, for such estimation). It is likely that these gains exceed the "cost" of abatement (i.e., forgone GDP). The modest GDP loss induced by the taxes is an encouraging result.

As mentioned in the context of model specification, many effluents are complements with respect to emission taxes, and we found that a tax on any major emission category had a broad impact on several emission types. This result has very practical implications for policy design and implementation. It would be appropriate to target a subset of sectors and pollutants that produce the major emissions. This will reduce the number of policy instruments, achieving significant abatement with lower administrative costs.

REFERENCES

Agosin, M. R., ed. (1995), *Foreign Direct Investment in Latin America*. Inter-American Development Bank, distributed by Johns Hopkins University Press, Baltimore.

Anderson, K., and R. Blackhurst, eds. (1992), *The Greening of World Trade Issues*, Ann Arbor: University of Michigan Press.

Beghin, J., S. Dessus, D. Roland-Holst, and D. van der Mensbrugghe (1996), "Prototype CGE Model for the Trade and the Environment Programme," *OECD Development Centre Technical Papers* No. 116, Paris.

Beghin, J., D. Roland-Holst, and D. van der Mensbrugghe (1994), "A Survey of the Trade and Environment Nexus: Global Dimensions," *OECD Economic Studies*, 23: 167–192.

—— (1997), "Trade and Pollution Linkages: Piecemeal Reform and Optimal Intervention," *Canadian Journal of Economics* 30: 442–455.

Chen, E. K. Y., and P. Drysdale, eds. (1995), *Corporate Links and Foreign Direct Investment in Asia and the Pacific*, Pimble, Australia: HarperCollins.

Copeland, B. R. (1994), "International and the Environment: Policy Reform in a Polluted Small Open Economy," *Journal of Environmental Economics and Management*, 20: 44–65.

Copeland, B. R., and S. M. Taylor (1994), "North-South Trade and the Environment," *Quarterly Journal of Economics*, 109: 755–787.

Dessus, S., D. Roland-Holst, and D. van der Mensbrugghe (1994), "Input-Based Pollution Estimates for Environmental Assessment in Developing Countries," *OECD Development Centre Technical Papers* No. 101, Paris, October.

Espinosa, J. A., and V. K. Smith (1995), "Measuring the Environmental Consequences of Trade Policy: a Nonmarket CGE Analysis," *American Journal of Agricultural Economics*, 77: 772–777.

Grossman, G. M., and A. B. Krueger (1992), "Environmental Impacts of a NAFTA," CEPR Discussion Paper series No. 644, London, April.

Hettige, H., P. Martin, M. Singh, and D. Wheeler (1995), "The Industrial Pollution Projection System," *World Bank Policy Research Working Paper* No. 1431, Washington, DC: World Bank.

Johnstone, N. (1995), "International Trade, Transfrontier Pollution, and Environmental Cooperation: A Case Study of the Mexican-American Border Region," *Natural Resource Journal*, 35: 33–62.

Lee, H., and D. Roland-Holst (1997), "Trade and the Environment," in J. F. Francois and K. A. Reinert, eds., *Applied Methods for Trade Policy Analysis: A Handbook*, Cambridge: Cambridge University Press.

Lloyd, P. J. (1992), "The Problem of Optimal Environmental Policy Choice," in K. Anderson, and R. Blackhurst, eds., *The Greening of World Trade Issues*, Ann Arbor: University of Michigan Press.

Peres Nunez, W. (1990), *Foreign Direct Investment and Industrial Development in Mexico*. Development Centre Studies. Paris: OECD.

Perroni, C., and R. Wigle (1994), "International Trade and Environmental Quality: How Important Are the Linkages?" *Canadian Journal of Economics*, 27: 551–567.

Runge, C. F. (1994), *Freer Trade, Protected Environment. Balancing Trade Liberalization and Environmental Success*, New York: Council on Foreign Relations Press.

Whalley, J. (1991), "The Interface between Environmental and Trade Policies," *The Economic Journal*, 101: 180–189.

World Bank (1994), "Mexico: Agricultural Sector Memorandum," Report No. 13425ME, Natural Resources and Rural Poverty Division, Washington, DC: World Bank.

Comment

David Zilberman and Linda Fernandez

This is a good chapter. It addresses a relevant and important question, and it is creative methodologically. It develops new data and comes up with results that seem very reasonable even though they may be based on some unreasonable assumptions.

The chapter takes a general equilibrium approach to addressing the issues of development, trade, economic growth, and the environment, and it confirms in an economywide context some empirical findings that are based on more detailed industry studies. Specifically, the chapter finds that significant environmental objectives can be achieved without debilitating losses to the economy; policies combining trade liberalization with incentives for improvement in environmental quality can enhance the objectives of both economic development and environmental quality improvement.

Two detailed micro studies that confirm this chapter's findings are: (1) Khanna's (1995) dissertation, which shows that one can reduce carbon dioxide emissions and increase energy efficiency in India by reducing energy subsidies and slashing tariffs on imported coal; (2) studies on water management (see Boggess et al., 1993) showing that introduction of water trading drastically reduces the costs of improving water and environmental quality, and there are cases where the introduction of efficient water pricing improves both output and environmental quality. These micro studies, as well as this chapter by Beghin et al., suggest that one should not separate policies that pursue environmental quality and reforms that improve market efficiency but rather combine them.

Another important empirical finding of the chapter is that environmental policies are not distributed equally across the economy. Rather, there are some hot spots that are responsible for more significant environmental damage. Each medium (air, water, and soil) has its own trouble spots, but there is much heterogeneity among industries when it comes to environmental degradation, and policy design must recognize this fact.

Micro-level studies (see, e.g., Zilberman et al., 1991, in the context of pesticides) recognize this point and further recognize that there is significant variability within polluting industries. Therefore, policies that ban certain practices across-the-board, or treat all producers in a polluting industry equally, can lead to gross inefficiency. Instead, efficient policies (pollution taxes, transferable permits) that discriminate among producers and attain environmental quality improvements at least cost are preferable. One of the reasons that environmental regulations are perceived to be so costly is the use of inefficient instruments, especially command and control. The results of this chapter confirm that achieving environmental objectives is not that costly when efficient policies are used.

Micro-level studies suggest that responses to reduced resource availability or tougher environmental regulations include:

1. Shifting industrial composition toward less pollution-intensive industries
2. Adoption and innovation of new, cleaner (resource efficient) technologies
3. Reduction in the scale of production.

A recent study on the response of California agriculture to reductions in water due to the recent drought suggests that one-third of the response reflected shifting composition of production activities (away from water-intensive crops), one-third reflected adoption of more efficient (water-saving) technologies, and one-third reflected a reduction in scale (see Zilberman et al., 1995). This chapter also considers three similar responses to policy changes – namely, a composition effect, a technology effect, and a scale effect. However, technology is not considered explicitly in the authors' approach, and innovation is largely ignored. The chapter suggests that much of the response to environmental policy will be through the composition effect. However, the technology effect may represent the impact of new technology adoption in the stylized world presented in this chapter. The chapter's overemphasis on the role of the composition effect relative to the technology effect results from its stringent assumptions regarding technology. In particular, it is assumed that capital is rigid but allows easy substitution between intermediate inputs, energy, and labor inputs.

We applaud the authors for assuming capital rigidity, but it must be remembered that there can also be a lot of rigidity in labor markets. If stricter environmental regulations in China reduce production in the mining and petroleum sectors, workers cannot be expected to switch painlessly to the electronics or apparel sectors. So reducing the cost of adjustment for labor may contribute to the overestimation of composition effects. Further, sometimes there are very few substitution possibilities between energy and intermediate inputs in the production of final goods. Underestimating these rigidities would again lead to overestimation of compositional adjustments. Thus the authors' underemphasis on innovation and adoption, along with overestimation of substitutability and flexibility in production, may lead to overestimation of the importance of the composition effect and underestimation of the role of technology in response to policy change.

Although the chapter uses effluent coefficients for intermediate polluting inputs, these are derived from U.S. data (Hettige et al., 1995). The authors merely convert these coefficients to pesos via an exchange rate (Dessus et al., 1994). This conversion cannot take account of important differences in technology, resource intensity, and input composition that exist between sectors in the two countries.

The optimistic view of freer trade assumes that environmental policy will be improved through increased imports of higher-quality inputs, especially raw materials and fuels. But here the perspective on environmental quality is partial. Increased imports of coal will improve environmental quality in the importing country but may actually increase global pollution of some materials through extra transportation. Thus one has to recognize the difference between national environmental quality and global environmental quality. This distinction is not made in many studies, but it is an important flaw in partial analysis.

The chapter takes the objective of environmental quality as exogenous and does not recognize environmental improvements as elements in preferences of policymakers. A more complete analysis would recognize that environmental quality affects individual utility and that, generally, it is a luxury good. As the economic situation in a country improves, people demand more environmental amenities, and thus environmental quality can become endogenous to the model.

REFERENCES

Boggess, William, Ronald Lacewell, and David Zilberman (1993), "Economics of Water Use in Agriculture," in Gerald A. Carlson, David Zilberman, and John A. Miranowski, eds., *Agriculture and Environmental Resource Economics*, New York: Oxford University Press.

Dessus, S., D. Roland-Holst, and D. van der Mensbrugghe (1994), "Input-Based Pollution Estimates for Environmental Assessment in Developing Countries," *OECD Development Centre Technical Papers* No. 101, Paris, October.

Hettige, H., P. Martin, M. Singh, and D. Wheeler (1995), "The Industrial Pollution Projection System," *World Bank Policy Research Working Paper* No. 1431, Washington, DC: World Bank.

Khanna, Madhu (1995), "Technology Adoption and Abatement of Greenhouse Gases: The Thermal Power Sector in India," Ph.D. Dissertation, Department of Agricultural and Resource Economics, University of California, Berkeley.

Zilberman, David, Ariel Dinar, Neal MacDougall, Madhu Khanna, Cheryl Brown, and Federico Castillo (1995), "Individual and Institutional Responses to the Drought: The Case of California Agriculture," Working Paper, Department of Agricultural and Resource Economics, University of California, Berkeley.

Zilberman, David, Andrew Schmitz, Gary Casterline, Erik Lichtenberg, and Jerome B. Siebert (1991), "The Economics of Pesticide Use and Regulation," *Science*, Vol. 253 (August 2): 518–522.

Index

473